Teddy Kennedy is our last living link to the Kennedys of Camelot, the Kennedys of myth. . . . I do not believe that anyone else in American public life has been forced, for so long, to live with the burdens that have been imposed upon him, both by his family and by a nation so captivated by the myth.

—Joe McGinniss, "Author's Note," *The Last Brother*

Acclaim for the Searing *New York Times* Bestseller by Joe McGinniss

THE LAST BROTHER

THE RISE AND FALL OF TEDDY KENNEDY

"Controversy rages around this book . . . the sad story of Teddy Kennedy, neglected by his parents, overshadowed by his older brothers, who grew up to drive too fast, drink too much, and through carelessness and arrogance, destroy his own bright promise."

—*Cosmopolitan*

"Harsh but oddly compassionate . . . It's all told with verve. . . ."

—*Kirkus Reviews*

"*THE LAST BROTHER* hits home. It makes the reader stop and think, because McGinniss obviously knows what he's talking about, writes so clearly and links together so many pertinent facts. Like a lawyer building a complicated case, McGinniss presents circumstantial evidence that will win over more than a few reader-jurors."

—*Buffalo News*

For orders... individual consumers, can place orders, please write to Mail Order Department, Paramount Publishing, 200 Old Tappan Road, Old Tappan, NJ 07675.

Books by Joe McGinniss

The Last Brother
Cruel Doubt
Blind Faith
Fatal Vision
Going to Extremes
Heroes
The Dream Team
The Selling of the President

Joe McGinniss

THE LAST BROTHER

POCKET **STAR** BOOKS

New York   London   Toronto   Sydney   Tokyo   Singapore

"The Gang That Sang 'Heart of My Heart' " by Ben Ryan, Copyright © 1926 (Renewed 1954) c/o EMI Robbins Catalog Inc. World print rights controlled and administered by CPP/Belwin, Inc., Miami, FL. International copyright secured. All rights reserved.

The lines from "Diving into the Wreck" are reprinted from *The Fact of a Doorframe, Poems Selected and New, 1950–1984*, by Adrienne Rich, by permission of the author and W. W. Norton & Company, Inc. Copyright © 1984 by Adrienne Rich. Copyright © 1975, 1978 by W. W. Norton & Company, Inc. Copyright © 1981 by Adrienne Rich.

A Pocket Star Book published by
POCKET BOOKS, a division of Simon & Schuster Inc.
1230 Avenue of the Americas, New York, NY 10020

ISBN: 0-671-89452-8

First Pocket Books printing August 1994

10 9 8 7 6 5 4 3 2 1

POCKET STAR BOOKS and colophon are registered trademarks of Simon & Schuster Inc.

Cover art by Marvin Mattelson, based on photos by Archive Photos and Burt Glinn/Magnum

Printed in the U.S.A.

THIS BOOK IS DEDICATED
TO ALAN WILLIAMS,
EDITOR, MENTOR AND
DEAR, DEAR FRIEND.

Contents

Contents

I came to explore the wreck. . . .
I came to see the damage that was done. . . .
the wreck and not the story of the wreck
the thing itself and not the myth
the drowned face always staring
toward the sun . . .

—Adrienne Rich,
"Diving into the Wreck"

Introduction

T

EDDY KENNEDY WAS RIDING A TRAIN THE FIRST TIME I met him. It was June 8, 1968. The train was carrying the body of his brother Bobby from New York to Washington. At some point during that long, doleful journey, Teddy walked through each of the crowded cars, shaking hands, thanking the mourners for being there. Stunned and somber, he softly exchanged a word or two or a silent nod with those he knew, then moved on.

Impressions linger: the sense that what might have been the last heroic era our nation would know in my lifetime had just ended; the awareness that for millions of the most luckless and helpless among us the single spark that might have ignited hope and sustained faith had been extinguished; the recognition that for the hundreds aboard that train who'd known Bobby Kennedy far better than I had, the pain, grief and despair would not fade for many years—the feeling of loss, perhaps never.

But there seemed also almost an unspoken understanding—as each of us aboard that creaking, swaying funeral train shook Teddy's hand and offered grim condolences—that he would now, in his turn, pick up the torch; would somehow, as Bobby had tried to do, breathe new life into the myth, would now become a legendary figure, like his brothers.

That, at the very least, he'd become President. Which is not how it turned out, not at all.

We must start with Jack, however briefly, because without Jack there would have been no myth. Without Jack, the lives of many, but of Teddy in particular, would have taken a different course.

One night in New Haven, in the fall of 1960, I caught a fleeting glimpse of Jack. I was a freshman at Holy Cross College in Worcester, Massachusetts, and had gone to New Haven to visit a friend at Yale. A crowd of thousands lined the streets in bitter cold on the last Saturday night before the election as Jack sped by in the backseat of an open convertible, waving and grinning, en route to an outdoor speech on the town green.

I didn't hear the speech and I never saw Jack again, except on television.

In the spring of 1962, more than a year into Jack's term, after the Bay of Pigs but before the Cuban missile crisis, it was announced that his youngest brother, Teddy, would run for Jack's former United States Senate seat from Massachusetts. I recall some distant grumbling about the Kennedys trying to establish an American royal family, but at overwhelmingly Irish Catholic Holy Cross this sentiment was muted.

No one I knew seemed to care much what happened to Teddy. Jack was the glamorous figure. Jack was the first Catholic President. Jack was the man with the wit, the charm, the beautiful wife; the public figure who first defined for so many of us who'd passed through adolescence under the Eisenhower administration the concept of style. Teddy was just the kid brother.

I was still at Holy Cross on Friday afternoon, November 22, 1963, when a friend came into my dormitory room to say he'd just heard on his car radio that President Kennedy had been shot. Then and for the next seventy-two hours, I felt the same shock, disbelief, horror, sadness and admiration for the magnificent Kennedy family experienced by almost everyone in America.

INTRODUCTION

Teddy seemed a very small part of the terrible, beautiful, wrenching pageant that unfolded during those days. My only recollection of him was from the morning of the funeral when he marched, hatless, up Pennsylvania Avenue next to Jacqueline and Bobby.

Four years later, in the fall of 1967, I met Bobby. I was then a columnist for the *Philadelphia Inquirer*, soon to travel to Vietnam, and he, who had begun to speak out so fervently against the war there, had agreed to talk to me before I left.

I remember the following: The afternoon was bright and cold. He wore a blue shirt with the sleeves rolled up. He had big teeth. Behind his desk, there were cartons containing copies of his new book, *To Seek a Newer World*.

I remember how small he seemed physically: hard but small. And how ill at ease he was, talking privately to someone he did not know. In time, I recognized this for what it was—shyness—because it was a trait that I myself possessed, perhaps the only thing I can say I had in common with Bobby Kennedy.

We talked—he talked, mostly—for forty-five minutes. He spoke haltingly, his voice often trailing off, his sentences often grammatically incomplete. To be honest, I was so overwhelmed to be in his presence that I recall little that he told me about Vietnam. Soon enough, I would see for myself.

But I remember his asking me to have my office send him copies of the columns I wrote from Vietnam. I thought this was a nice gesture, a courtesy he did not have to bother to extend me, and I was pleased. It never occurred to me that he would actually read anything I wrote from Vietnam, for I was by no means an influential journalist and the *Inquirer*, in those days, was not a paper widely respected or read outside Philadelphia.

As I left, he wished me luck and, thinking briefly perhaps of what he knew of guns and bullets, said, "If you get up near, ah, areas where there's trouble, ah, be careful." I told him I would. He said, "I wouldn't want to hear that anything had happened."

There was an awkward moment of silence. I knew I should thank him and leave but I wanted to linger for just another minute.

Finally, he reached behind his desk and took one of the books out of a carton. "Here," he said, "why don't I give you this." And he inscribed it: "For Joe McGinniss —with best wishes for the future—and if you find the answer, please let me know."

I saw him again in April. By then he was running for President. It was the day after Lyndon Johnson had announced that he would not run for reelection. Bobby was scheduled to campaign in Philadelphia and some of its blue-collar suburbs that night. I'd flown to New York in the afternoon, having arranged with his office to fly back to Philadelphia with him that evening.

We spoke briefly in a private lounge before boarding the flight. He said, "That sounded like quite a trip you had through the Delta." I was surprised. Upon my return from Vietnam I'd received a short note thanking me for having sent him what I'd written, but it had seemed almost a form letter, of the sort that was mailed out daily to thousands of constituents and well-wishers. Now it appeared he'd actually read the columns. I was twenty-four. He was Bobby Kennedy, running for President, just like Jack. After that, it would have been hard for me to dislike him.

That night, I found myself standing amid a mob of people on a street corner in lower Delaware County, outside Philadelphia, a heavily Republican area where in 1968 there was also considerable support for the segregationist George Wallace.

The open limousine in which Bobby and his wife, Ethel, were riding turned the corner. Suddenly, there were the sirens of fire engines, the glare of spotlights, and thousands of young people, hysterical and mindless, screaming ecstatically, as if he were one of the Beatles. These were hero-hungry kids. They cared nothing for issues. They wanted only to touch and see and scream, and to feel close to something they knew was special.

They poured into the street, past police lines. His car

was forced to a halt. The kids swarmed everywhere, mobbing the car, reaching toward him, bumping, tugging, screaming.

He was standing on the trunk of the car, swaying as it inched forward through the crowd. A bodyguard named Bill Barry—who, many years later, would answer the door in Palm Beach and tell local police that Teddy was not at home—had an arm clamped around Bobby's waist, a safety belt to prevent the crowd from seizing and devouring him.

I was up close to the car and I guess I was taller than most of the kids. At least, Bobby spotted me and gestured.

"Come up here," he said. "Come up in the car." And he reached out and pulled me with his hand, and the police and Secret Service, once they were convinced he was pulling and not being pulled, parted briefly to let the new passenger aboard.

Bobby was grinning and shaking his head to show that he thought it was crazy, but a mob like that puts an edge on the man who leads it: an artificial, temporary edge, like two martinis, but while it is there it lifts you beyond yourself and feeds you, and, fed by it, Bobby leaned again into the crowd as his wife leaned out the other way, and the mad clutching and grasping went on. The kids flung themselves at him and he rode them as a surfer rides a wave.

Later, as the car sped up and finally outdistanced them, Bobby sat down in the backseat. His face seemed alive and bright with both delight and disbelief.

The night was cold and he slipped into an overcoat. He shook his head again and grinned. "They tell me, 'Talk about the issues,' " he said. " 'Talk about the issues.' Those kids really care about the issues." And Bobby did an imitation of a frenzied crowd cheering, to show that the issues could get nowhere in that atmosphere. There would be other crowds, other occasions on which he could and would talk about the very real and significant issues that had impelled him to enter this race. But this mindless hysteria was a part of it too, and I was grateful to him for letting me have a sense of what it was like to be the object of all its uncontrolled emotion.

A few minutes later, the car got to a shopping center where he was scheduled to make a speech. I had to go back to the paper and write my column for the morning. I never saw him again.

In early June, the phone rang. I don't know what time it was. Three-thirty, quarter to four in the morning. It was my mother.

"Bobby Kennedy's been shot."

I was sleepy. I had just gone to bed after watching him make jokes with Roger Mudd after winning the California primary. I think the first thing I asked her was where.

I thought she said in the leg.

"In the leg?"

"In the head."

I was on the next flight from Philadelphia to Los Angeles.

A large and somber crowd was keeping vigil outside the hospital. Now that I was there, I didn't know what to do next. Then I saw Jimmy Breslin, the New York columnist who had been extraordinarily generous and helpful to me all my professional life. Breslin knew everybody, of course, while I knew no one there except Bobby himself.

Bobby was on the fifth floor of the Good Samaritan Hospital. The corridor outside the intensive care room was filled with staff and friends, all those people who had tied their lives to his.

They waited with enormous self-control and dignity. Nobody argued or cursed. Nobody cried. They knew he was going to die but they waited with sorrow and composure. It was 5:00 P.M. and already people were whispering about only a couple of hours more, and in various rooms up and down the hall members of the famous, efficient Kennedy staff went to work, planning their second funeral in five years.

"He was so happy last night," a man who'd been with him was saying. "He heard early that he was going to do all right and he kept walking up to people and saying, 'Later, we'll go over to the Factory for a drink. And tell so-and-so. I want him there. Tell him to be sure he comes with us. I'll chase that Humphrey all over the country,' he kept saying. 'He won't be able to get away. I'll make him take a stand.' "

There was a television set in room 533, where I was. The news came on at 6:00 P.M. and a Los Angeles announcer said, "In case you may not have seen it Tuesday night, we are now going to show you exactly what happened at the Ambassador Hotel." Then Bobby walked into the picture with Ethel at his side, and he was grinning.

One by one, without saying anything, the Kennedy people got up and left room 533. But nobody turned off the television, and Bobby's jubilant voice followed them down the hall.

"Probably another couple of hours" was all anyone would say. But it was almost midnight before Bobby's three oldest children came down the hall and went into the intensive care ward. Half an hour later, Jacqueline, who had been in the ward, at Bobby's bedside with Ethel, came out and asked softly, "Where is room five-four-three?"

It was at the far end of the hall—the room that had been set aside for her—and two staff men took her to it. Then everyone started to sag a bit and people began drifting into the hospital rooms with empty beds. In the hall, Robert Kennedy, Jr., who was fourteen, walked by, crying.

At ten minutes before two, I was sitting in a chair in room 533, fighting off sleep, when Pierre Salinger stepped in. George Plimpton lay on one of the beds, his wife sitting in a chair beside him.

Salinger tapped Plimpton on the leg and simply nodded. Then he looked at the other bed.

"Who's over there?"

"Jerry."

Jerry Bruno, the advance man, was sleeping with his face toward the wall. He also had been advance man for Jack's trip to Dallas in November of 1963.

INTRODUCTION

Salinger walked over and shook Jerry Bruno gently by the shoulder.

"It's over," he said.

Then someone turned on the television. Downstairs, outside the hospital, Bobby's press secretary, Frank Mankiewicz, was making the announcement that Robert Francis Kennedy had died at 1:44 A.M., on June 6, 1968, at the age of forty-two.

A week after shaking his hand on the train, I saw Teddy on television. He was sitting on a lawn chair in front of the Hyannis Port house where he'd spent so many of the summers of his youth, and thanking the American people for the tremendous outpouring of sympathy that had helped the family—or what was left of it —through the dark and tragic time of Bobby's death.

He was flanked by his aged but defiant mother and by his mute and paralyzed father, who'd suffered a stroke in 1961, and in the service of whose dreams his three older brothers had died.

Looking directly into the camera, Teddy said, "Each of us will have to decide in a private way, in our own hearts, in our own consciences, what we will do in the course of this summer and future summers."

That summer, he could barely lead his own life. Any thought of his leading the country was out of the question.

Yet the demands were already being made. Even before he left the Los Angeles hospital where Bobby had died, Teddy had been confronted by Allard Lowenstein, the antiwar and civil rights activist who'd tried so hard, the year before, to persuade Bobby to mount a campaign against Lyndon Johnson and the Vietnam War.

Lowenstein, who himself would later fall victim to an assassin's bullet, had shouted, somewhat gracelessly, "You've got to take the leadership! Now that Bobby's gone, you're all we've got!"

That was what it had come down to for Teddy and that was the way it would always be, not just for that summer but for as many years into the future as he could see. Joe Junior was gone, Jack was gone, now Bobby was, too, and Teddy, however inadequate he might be, however unqualified he secretly knew himself to be, was the only Kennedy we had left.

It was Teddy's turn now. Only he could fulfill his father's dream, the dream that had created the mythic landscape that came to be known as Camelot, even as it had destroyed, one by one, those Kennedys who'd sought to rule it.

"You're all we've got." At thirty-six, Teddy faced the prospect of confronting those words and that sentiment for the rest of his life.

It would not be enough, by any means, to be merely "a" Kennedy anymore; to live out his own life, whatever that might have become. He was being told that he was now "the" Kennedy. The nation which had first been seduced by the myth had since grown addicted, and now demanded that Teddy live not only his own life but also, simultaneously, the unlived portions of the lives of his three older brothers.

Where one Kennedy stopped, the next began. This message had been indelibly imprinted on the sons years before. Each must, in his turn, do his father's bidding. But Teddy, that summer, could not. When the supporters of Bobby and of Eugene McCarthy were pummeled by mobs of enraged policemen in the streets of Chicago, Teddy was not to be found. He was gone. Out of the picture. Off the train.

At Christmas, I received a large picture of Bobby, signed "With Christmas wishes" by Ethel. The only time I'd met her had been in the backseat of the car during the motorcade outside Philadelphia. I put the picture in a silver frame.

The following summer, the body of a young woman was found in Teddy's car, at the bottom of a pond. He said he'd accidentally driven off a bridge.

Until the young woman's body was found, it had been widely assumed—and knowing nothing about him except what I read in the popular press, I certainly shared in the assumption—that Teddy would run for the Presidency, and undoubtedly win, in 1972. He did not run. For some time afterwards, all talk of a Kennedy Restoration stopped. Richard Nixon, whom Jack had beaten in 1960 —and whom, many felt, Teddy could have beaten in 1968 —won reelection.

Early in 1974, as part of a broader book project, I found myself needing to talk to Teddy. I did not yet know how difficult it was for him to talk about abstract concepts, or about himself. I did not realize the degree to which he shunned introspection.

After considerable wrangling with his press secretary, and only through the intervention of mutual friends, it was agreed that I could travel with (or near) Teddy as he made two separate three-day swings through Massachusetts, something he did every year during the Senate recess. The days and nights would be filled with public appearances. No assurance was given that I'd have the chance—or that he'd have the inclination—to talk about the subject that most interested me: how he managed to go on being Teddy when he had to be Jack and Bobby as well.

He had just turned forty-one. He was younger than Jack had been when elected President, younger than Bobby had been when he was killed. But there was about Teddy that winter the unmistakable air of someone already past his prime. He seemed jittery and guarded, moving forward—at an impossibly frenetic pace—only because he so greatly feared what truths he might have to contemplate if he stopped.

He made at least a dozen speeches a day. He would start at breakfast, sometimes before, and continue late into the night—being seen, heard, touched, being experienced. Renewing the legend at its roots. Despite the discovery, in 1969, of the young woman's body in his car at the bottom of the pond, he remained, in Massachusetts at least, a figure who created ripples of excitement wherever he went. Four years later, he was, however flawed, the last link we had to our idealized, glorified images of Jack and Bobby. He was the last Kennedy.

He kept moving, always moving: Quincy, Weymouth,

Hingham, New Bedford, Fall River, Framingham, Worcester, Palmer, Springfield, Holyoke, Lowell, Lawrence, Everett, Tewksbury, Peabody, Malden, Waltham. For six days, he caromed around the state like a pinball.

It was a campaign atmosphere without a campaign. Before and after each appearance there was a great milling and rushing of aides. Instructions were shouted, doors were slammed, cars were shifted frantically into reverse, U-turns were made on busy streets, speed limits were exceeded, traffic lights, bad weather, hunger pangs were ignored.

It did not seem to matter that there was no opponent, no genuine purpose to it all. This was the way Jack had done it and this was the way Bobby had done it and this was the way Teddy was going to do it. There would not be any slippage. The torch had to be carried and the torch had to be carried fast.

On four of the six days he was accompanied by his nephew Joe, Robert Kennedy's oldest son. On the sixth day, he was accompanied also by Caroline, daughter of Jack, and by Courtney, daughter of Robert. For one day he was joined by a son of brother-in-law Sargent Shriver, and, on the final evening, by Kathleen, daughter of Robert, and her husband.

And, each day, he also seemed to be accompanied by members of his family who were not present.

He went to the cafeteria of the Sacred Heart School in North Quincy. It was a low-ceilinged building, smoky and hot, and jammed with the adoring women of the parish. He talked about his older son, who'd just lost a leg to cancer. After the amputation, he said, his son had received a football from the New England Patriots, a basketball from the Celtics, a baseball from the Red Sox and a hockey stick from the Boston Bruins. And he'd said, "I know I have to learn sports again, Daddy, but do I have to learn them all at once?" Teddy told this anecdote at least six times every day.

He went to Holyoke High School. The band played. Female students jumped and shrieked. He was given a Holyoke High School varsity letter sweater for his son who'd lost the leg to cancer. He told the anecdote about the sports equipment, in response.

Outside, snow was falling heavily. Other schools, and many offices, were shutting down. The roads were becoming impassable. It did not matter. The show must go on.

He went to the Springfield Young Democrats Club that night. The hall was crowded, smoky and hot. He arrived at 8:30, an hour late. There was frenzied cheering and loud Irish music. Consumption of alcohol on the premises was not forbidden.

Teddy said to the crowd, "This is the biggest gathering of young Democrats I've been to since last Saturday, when I had dinner at Ethel's house." A huge picture of Bobby hung overhead. The mayor of Springfield gave a speech about Bobby. "None of us will ever forget . . . seems like only yesterday . . . touch football on the lawn . . . dedicated himself to youthful ideals . . . man of deep compassion . . . none of us can ever forget . . . wished to seek a newer world . . . dreamed things that never were and said, why not. . . ."

Then the mayor spoke about the spirit of the Kennedy brothers: "The spirit of the Kennedy brothers emanates . . . The spirit of the Kennedy brothers is a source of inspiration . . ."

Teddy was presented with a painting of Bobby. It had been done by a local artist who was almost totally paralyzed; who had, the mayor said, "only the use of a couple of fingers on one hand." He'd labored for months on the painting because Bobby had been such an inspiration to him.

Teddy took the picture, looked at it, expressionless, and passed it to an aide, who would later put it in the trunk of a car.

He went to Saint Mary's High School in Westfield. The introduction was made by a Father O'Connor, who spoke of "two beautiful women, Mrs. Rose Kennedy and Mrs. Joan Kennedy." Then Father O'Connor told a story about how once he had sat on a dais with Joan Kennedy at a time when "that beautiful woman was very, very, very much expecting." He recalled having been "very impressed by the very beautiful and radiant Mrs. Joan Kennedy.'' Then, taking note of the fact that Teddy had arrived an hour late, Father O'Connor concluded: "I don't know what Senator Kennedy has going for him except a very wonderful mother and a very beautiful wife.''

He went to the New Bedford High School auditorium. A song was sung in his honor. It was "Abraham, Martin and John," which had to do with the assassinations of Abraham Lincoln, Martin Luther King and John and Robert Kennedy.

He went to the office of a newspaper publisher. On the wall was a copy of the front page from November 22, 1963: "PRES. KENNEDY IS DEAD . . .''

He went into a reception office at a high school. There was one book on a table. *John F. Kennedy: Words to Remember. With an Introductory Note by Robert F. Kennedy.*

He went to Fall River for ceremonies marking the induction into a nautical museum of the destroyer *Joseph P. Kennedy*, named for the first of his brothers to die.

He went to a New Bedford supermarket to discuss high prices with shoppers. He was approached by an old man. "Now don't you do like your brother and—like your two brothers did. We need you alive.''

I approached him one night after dinner. I said, "Senator, I know you've been busy for these three days and we haven't had much chance to talk, but I hope that when you come back next week we will.''

"It's hard to tell," he said. "I keep a pretty full schedule up here.''

"Well, I'll see you next week, anyway.''

"You think you can stand another three days?" he asked.

"Oh, sure. This is interesting.''

There seemed a sudden flash of curiosity. "It is?" he said.

"Well, at least as much for me as it is for you.''

He just laughed.

* * *

INTRODUCTION

The second week was an almost exact replica of the first. He kept a full schedule. We did not get a chance to talk. It was obvious he did not want to talk. But I kept after his press secretary and finally it was arranged for me to see him for half an hour in his Senate office in Washington, as, some years before, I had seen Bobby.

But the press secretary warned me: "It makes him uncomfortable as hell to have people come in and want to talk about the Kennedy mystique or the myth of the Kennedys or the Kennedys as heroes, that sort of thing. That's just something he doesn't like to deal with. I've seen it happen so many times in the past: Things are going fine, he's very loose and relaxed, and then somebody brings up the Kennedy legend stuff, or asks him something about Camelot or carrying the torch, and he freezes. He absolutely freezes. His eyes glaze over and that muscle on the right side of his face starts to twitch and then it's all over, buddy. He pulls back into his shell and you've had it."

I saw him at noon. He looked heavy and tired. His wife, the beautiful and radiant Joan, had been hospitalized for alcoholism. His son had a leg cut off because of cancer. Mary Jo Kopechne had died at Chappaquiddick. His three brothers were dead, two of them murdered. His own back had been broken in a plane crash. And now he was expected to run for President.

He said he still did not understand what I wanted. I said I was writing a book and that I wanted to put him in the book. I said I wanted to spend some time with him and get to know him.

He nodded. Everybody wanted something. I was perspiring. I wished that we were having this conversation over a drink instead of on little chairs in the corner of his office. I wished that it were 1967 and that I was talking to Bobby instead of to him. Probably almost everyone he dealt with every day wished that they were talking to Jack or to Bobby instead of to him. That was a big part of what I wanted to write about.

"Tell me about the book," he said.

"Well, it's sort of a book about the hero in America

and what's happened to him and why we don't seem to have heroes anymore the way we used to.''

He looked at me intently and said nothing.

"I mean, well, you know, it's sort of going to be like a book about my search for the vanished American hero.''

He continued to stare silently at me. His face looked awfully puffy. It occurred to me that he might be badly hung over.

"Of course," I said, "I realize that this isn't a subject we can really talk about at great length, because I know how . . . well, how it's just, ah, kind of hard to talk about.'' I smiled. He did not.

"But you see, it seems to me that this kind of book— and now I'm not trying to make you uncomfortable—but that there really would have to be something about the Kennedys and, I mean, about yourself in particular in this kind of book.''

He was still staring. Waiting. His eyes seemed hooded. His face was absolutely expressionless.

"You know," I went on, perspiring even more heavily now, "everybody says we don't have heroes anymore, but, on the other hand, there is this special sort of feeling about the Kennedys. About, you know, the whole Kennedy thing. That's why I'd like to spend a little time with you.''

There seemed so much of him that had been buried for the sake of the legend. What was it costing him, and how aware was he of the cost? Which of his illusions had survived? How tightly did he cling to them? What would happen if he let go? I wanted to know what it was like down there where he lived his inner life. "The thing itself and not the myth.''

"Look," I said, somewhat desperately now, "five years ago, everybody thought your brother Bobby was a hero. Including me. I spent a little time with him that spring. I wrote about him. In fact, I was up in the hospital when he died. And now, see, there's all that feeling floating around out there loose and you seem to be the only one it can focus on.''

INTRODUCTION

He was still staring. But not, it seemed, quite so intently. In fact, his eyes now seemed glazed. He remained silent. And then a muscle on the right side of his face began to twitch.

The meeting ended. I did not see him again for almost fifteen years.

What was your life anyway but the tiny black spot of what you've done against the infinite white of possibility?

—Robert Boswell, *Mystery Ride*

What was your life anyway but the tiny black spot of what you've done against the infinite white of possibility?

— Robert Boswell, *Mystery Ride*

Part One

Part One

1

IT WAS NOVEMBER 22, 1963. TEDDY LOOKED UP AT THE clock again. Not yet 1:30. God. How long had he been here? What time had this session begun?

There were days, friends would say later, especially Fridays—or Monday mornings—when he would be sitting there wondering for the thousandth time if he hadn't made a mistake, after all. If he shouldn't have followed his first instinct, which had been to move west after the 1960 campaign and settle there, making whatever he could of himself on his own.

Instead, he'd followed the path his father had laid out for him, one that led first back to Massachusetts and then here, to Washington, where he'd been since January. He was Edward Moore Kennedy, the junior senator from Massachusetts—very junior at age thirty-one—but perceived primarily as Teddy, the President's kid brother, the one nobody, including himself it often seemed, took seriously.

One-thirty. Who was talking now? One of those old Republicans. What was his name? Prouty—the estimable Winston Prouty of Vermont—speaking to a nearly empty chamber.

Teddy might not even have been quite sure what ob-

3

scure piece of legislation Prouty was talking about. Not that it mattered. What mattered to Teddy on Friday afternoons was the clock, which, as so often proved the case as he sat in the Senate chamber, stubbornly seemed to refuse to move forward.

Only 1:35. Prouty still going. Teddy glanced down at the gobbledygook printed on the page in front of him— the piece of legislation under discussion. S. 2265. A bill to amend the Library Service Act in order to increase the amount of federal aid given to libraries, especially to public school libraries in urban areas.

Even if he hadn't been paying close attention, Teddy could have assumed that Prouty was speaking against it, because Prouty was a Republican who didn't want to spend money on anything and because there weren't any urban areas in Vermont anyway, and, for all Teddy knew, not even any libraries either. Most of what Teddy knew about Vermont was that it was the place you went skiing when you didn't have time to get to Colorado or Switzerland.

And there was no reason for Teddy to pay attention. His staff would tell him how to vote on this bill: presumably, yes. Anything that had to do with federal aid to the cities, the vote was yes. That much he'd learned in his first year.

Just before Prouty had begun, Wayne Morse of Oregon had ranted on about how "school after school across the country does not have a library," and had urged immediate passage of the bill. That was when, it appeared, that Teddy had tuned out. Schools should have libraries. Simple as that. Not a big issue like civil rights, like the nuclear test ban treaty, like getting the funding to put a man on the moon before the Russians.

Those were issues Teddy found himself caring about, at least intermittently. They were important. It was useful and necessary to have debate on issues such as those.

But libraries in schools? It may never have occurred to him that schools didn't have libraries. Certainly all the schools he had gone to—and there had been ten of them, most of them boarding schools, before he was fourteen— had had libraries.

4

Undoubtedly, that Friday afternoon, Teddy would have liked simply to get up and walk out. Claude Hooton was already in town from Houston for the weekend. Claude had been one of his closest friends at Harvard. For sheer hell-raising there was no better companion than Claude. There were no better weekends in Washington than those on which Claude Hooton came to town.

He was here this weekend to help Teddy and Joan celebrate their fifth wedding anniversary. The actual date was not for another week—November 29—but by then Teddy and Joan would be in the middle of the Thanksgiving weekend at Hyannis Port and their anniversary would be swallowed up by all the other, more important, family activity.

He glanced again at the clock. Not quite 1:40. If only, right now, this very minute, he could just scoop up all the papers on his desk, stuff them into the briefcase by his feet, and get up and walk out of the Senate, leaving Prouty right there in midsentence, and go home and take a shower and hook up with Claude and go out for a few drinks.

But he couldn't leave. At this precise moment, Teddy was not just a member of the United States Senate, he was serving as its presiding officer. This was not quite the honor it seemed. The Constitution required that the presiding officer's chair be occupied either by the Vice President or by an elected member before any official business could be conducted.

That meant somebody always had to sit in the chair. It was a chore all senators dreaded because no matter how boring the debate, you could not doze off or sneak out. When one member finished his prattle, another would stand and take his place, asking to be recognized. It was the duty of whoever was sitting in the chair to acknowledge the request.

He gazed up toward the almost empty gallery. He guessed there were not more than fifty spectators in attendance. A federal school library funding debate was not enough to pack the house on a Friday afternoon in November.

Only eight members of the Senate were present. In

addition to Prouty and himself, there were Morse; Jennings Randolph of West Virginia, a real drone; Everett Dirksen, whose antics always gave Teddy a kick, even if they so often irritated Jack; Spessard Holland of Florida, whom he didn't know well—Florida's other senator, George Smathers, was the old family friend and nighttime companion of Jack's; Mike Mansfield of Montana, a fine and decent man and the new majority leader, who'd replaced Lyndon Johnson after the election and who'd already taught Teddy so much about the inner, arcane workings of the Senate; and Harrison Williams of New Jersey, who'd always struck Teddy as a nice guy too, if a bit of a lush, but who would one day get caught with his hand so deep in the till that he'd wind up in federal prison.

Teddy could never say Jack hadn't warned him about the boredom. When their father first made it clear that Teddy would be going to the Senate, Jack had taken him aside and repeated something he'd often told Teddy before: the nights were wonderful, filled with all the women a man could want; but the days—those endless, dreary, repetitive Senate days—those were the swamps through which Teddy, like Jack before him, would have to slog before he could get to the nights.

Having to listen to Winston Prouty, on a Friday afternoon the week before Thanksgiving, preaching about the evils of using taxpayers' money for library books, was about as deep in the morass as Teddy had yet found himself.

But this was time that could be used to sign letters. And, as always, he had plenty of letters to sign. He opened a correspondence folder prepared by his staff and began to scrawl his signature at the bottom of page after page.

Suddenly, he looked up from his folder and down at the Senate floor. The time was 1:42. There was some sort of disturbance. The press liaison fellow had just come running onto the floor. This was highly out of order. No one, ever, under any circumstances, came running onto the Senate floor.

6

Teddy glared down with a look of disapproval. But his annoyance at the breach of decorum was quickly replaced by curiosity. Something very unusual was happening. The press fellow was running from member to member, whispering something to each, then dashing on.

Ev Dirksen slumped in his seat, looking as if he'd just been kicked in the groin. Spessard Holland's mouth gaped open even wider than usual. There seemed an expression of genuine horror on his face.

Then Teddy saw the press fellow staring up at him and standing, for a moment, as if paralyzed.

Riedel, that was his name. Richard Riedel—now running toward him. And Mike Mansfield was rushing toward him too.

Riedel scrambled up the dais. The poor fellow looked to be in pain. He must have been almost sixty years old. Maybe he was having a heart attack. Maybe Teddy, as presiding officer, should summon a doctor.

But then, just as Mansfield reached his side, Riedel spoke. Shouted, in fact.

"The most terrible thing has happened! It's terrible! Terrible!"

Teddy was still holding in his right hand the pen he'd been using to sign his correspondence.

"What is it?" Teddy asked. His first thought, he later told friends, was that it was Dad. Dad had finally succumbed to the effects of the stroke he'd suffered two years earlier.

But Riedel was in such distress, and Mike Mansfield, too, that Teddy knew it had to be worse. But what could be worse—a nuclear war?

"Your brother," Riedel said. Then he paused, as if grasping that thus far he'd imparted very little information. It occurred to him, in that instant, that as awful as it was, he'd have to say more because, for one thing, Teddy had two brothers.

"Your brother, the President," Riedel exclaimed. "He's been shot!"

* * *

Those present would later recall that it was as if a veil fell across Teddy's eyes. A veil that, in the opinion of many, would never lift.

"How do you know?" he asked tonelessly.

"It's on the ticker," Riedel said, referring to the wire service news ticker that brought constant reports from the outside world to the hermetically sealed Senate press office.

"Just came in on the ticker," Riedel repeated.

Teddy began to gather his papers. He didn't scoop them, he didn't sweep them into his briefcase, he gathered them in as orderly a fashion as possible, considering that his hands were shaking so badly, and he placed them in his briefcase as neatly as he could. He did not want his secretarial staff to have to retype all the letters he'd just signed.

Riedel now had a hand on Teddy's shoulder. Teddy didn't like this. He did not like to be touched by people he scarcely knew.

"Maybe you can take a jet to Texas," Riedel said.

What the hell was he talking about—a jet to Texas. Teddy looked to Mike Mansfield, who stood silently, tears streaming down his long, weathered face.

"Is there anything I can do?" Riedel persisted.

"No," Teddy said. "No."

Mansfield said nothing. He just cried.

Teddy didn't know where he should go, but he knew he needed to leave the rostrum, needed to get away from this press officer, needed to find out what was happening.

2

Once down from the rostrum, Teddy walked as quickly as possible—even at this moment his sense of senatorial decorum would not permit him to run—toward the lobby, toward wherever these tickers were, these tickers that had spewed forth this incomprehensible message that Teddy knew had to be garbled somehow, had to be wrong.

Riedel still had his hand on Teddy's shoulder. He was still repeating himself. "I'm really very sorry," he was saying. "I'm so sorry, Senator. I hope it's not serious."

Teddy pulled open the heavy, leather-covered door that led from the Senate chamber to the private lobby behind the rostrum. He was growing irritated with this fellow. If the man had nothing more useful to say than that he was sorry and that he hoped it wasn't serious and that maybe Teddy should take a jet to Texas, then he'd be better off just keeping quiet.

Teddy did not say any of this. By nature, he was a courteous man in public situations. And already he could sense that this was a very public as well as a very private situation.

It was only much later that he would come to realize that Riedel's words and actions were the first manifesta-

9

tions of a phenomenon he would encounter innumerable times in the hours, days and weeks ahead: what had happened to Jack had caused a veil to drop, not only over his eyes but over the eyes and heart of the nation. Complete strangers experienced a degree of shock, horror and sorrow every bit as intense as that felt by Teddy himself.

What had happened in Dallas that afternoon—and he did not yet have any idea what it was—would prove to be something from which not only he but the nation would never fully recover.

That public grief could be as powerful as its private counterpart was something unique in Teddy's experience. Long afterwards, friends said, he'd find it difficult to comprehend certain words and actions of others—staff members, friends, total strangers—until he reminded himself that in many essential ways their loss seemed to them as great as his own did to him.

Where were these tickers? He had to see these tickers.

But when he got to them he saw only a swarm of people, all chattering, buzzing, straining to look over one another's shoulders as the Teletype machines continued to spit out their inchoate and incomplete bits of information.

"Too crowded," Teddy mumbled.

For him, of course, at that moment, the mob around the Teletype machines would have parted as had the Red Sea for Moses. But again, Teddy's instinctive courtesy took control. He did not want to shove his way to the front of the line.

Besides, he wanted privacy. He wanted to go someplace where he could be alone for a moment while he tried to reach Bobby on the telephone.

All his life, at the bad times, it had been Bobby to whom he'd reached out. And almost always, Bobby had been there for him. Bobby was his greatest source of strength, of solace. And always, in every circumstance, of utterly clear thinking and common sense.

Bobby was the brother closest to him in age, being only seven years older, while Jack was fifteen. And Bobby—gruff outward appearance, cold arrogance and a certain spiteful streak notwithstanding—was the family member most able to empathize with the suffering or discomfort of others.

He was, perhaps, the only one with that ability. The only one whose spirit had proven strong enough to withstand their parents' efforts to strip away from the children or to crush within them all capacity to feel emotion, in order that they might be better able to compete.

At the start of World War II, Teddy had been abruptly sent home from London, where his father was serving as United States ambassador to England. Throughout the ensuing decade of loneliness and isolation during which his preoccupied parents had shuttled him back and forth among all those boarding schools, it had been Bobby who'd been there for him.

It had been Bobby who would come from Milton Academy, or, later, from Harvard, to visit him, when his mother and father seemed too busy, or too indifferent to his fate.

At a time when Teddy was so overweight, so academically deficient, so socially inept that he would try to make a joke of it, signing his letters to his family "Fat Ted"— during these miserable years, with Joe Junior dead and Jack already occupied with adult pursuits, Bobby had been the one member of the family who had refused to give up on Teddy, who showed him that love, affection and tenderness were not given only as rewards to those who had achieved perfection.

"Bobby was the one who used to call me up to see how I was getting along," Teddy would recall years later. "On the two or three weekends I was able to get off from the boarding school outside Boston, he'd spend the weekend with me. I'll never forget how we used to go to the big, empty house at Cape Cod—just the two of us, rattling around alone. But Bobby was in charge, taking care of me, and always making sure I had something to do."

Now it was Bobby who would again be in charge, who would make sure, first, that Teddy knew what was happening, and second, that he would know what to do.

But how to reach Bobby? Outside the Senate chamber now, Teddy no longer felt constrained from running. And so he ran the few steps to the private office maintained by the Vice President for those times when he presided personally over the Senate.

This was a room not much used by Lyndon Johnson. More often, it served as a private meeting place for members who wished to conduct background discussions with members of the press. At the moment Teddy entered, it was empty.

He picked up a telephone. He had to reach Bobby. Only Bobby would know what was happening. Only Bobby could tell him what to do.

He tried to dial Bobby's office at the Justice Department, but the telephone seemed to be dead. No dial tone, no buzz, no way even to reach one of the remarkably patient and efficient congressional telephone operators.

He put the phone down momentarily, picked it up and this time heard a dial tone. He dialed Bobby's number. First, 187, the internal code for the Justice Department, then Bobby's personal extension, 2001.

A busy signal. This was hopeless. He had at least shaken off the irritating press officer, but now he was standing alone in a Senate office, unable to make contact with the outside world.

He burst out of the private office, leaving its useless telephone behind, and ran blindly down a flight of stairs, past a guard station and out into the drab gray afternoon, surprisingly warm for late November.

For a moment, Teddy was totally disoriented. He'd been in such a hurry—but such a hurry to get where?— that he wasn't even sure which exit he'd used to leave the Capitol.

Another senator's young legislative assistant—Teddy never did get the fellow's name—was driving by, listening to the bulletins from Dallas coming over the car radio.

As soon as he saw Teddy, he jammed on his brakes. There was no one, other than the President himself, who could have been a more unlikely sight, standing alone and befuddled on the sidewalk between the Capitol and the Senate Office Building, at this precise moment in history.

The young aide said, "Senator? Would you like a ride to your office?"

Teddy gazed at the car, at the driver. A ride. His office. Yes, of course, get to his office. There, he had a hundred phones. From there, he could reach Bobby right away. From there, he could begin directing his staff, though he did not yet know precisely the nature of the event to which he'd be directing them to respond.

Wordlessly, he climbed into the car. The radio was on, but to Teddy it seemed just a buzz. Like the tickers in the Senate, the car radio was something that might transmit useful information to others, but for Teddy, as he would later recall, Bobby had seemed the only reliable source.

The ride lasted only half a block. He had been that close to his office all along.

Then he saw Claude Hooton standing on the sidewalk, waiting for him, having sensed that it was to his office that Teddy would go first. But what did Claude know? Did he know what had happened to Jack?

People were crying. In the distance, and from inside the Senate Office Building, radios and televisions blared.

Jack, the President, had been shot. It must have seemed to Teddy—though this was not something he much wanted to talk about in later years—that he'd been shoved suddenly across an invisible barrier, into a land he'd never seen before, a land he'd never known existed.

At least Claude was with him. Good old Claude. But Claude, who always had so much to say, who was so quick with a joke that Teddy would often start to laugh just at the sight of him, knowing how much jollity lay ahead—Claude appeared to be crying, or to have been crying very recently.

And for once, Claude had nothing to say. He simply reached out and took Teddy by the arm.

3

INSIDE TEDDY'S OFFICE, EVERYONE SEEMED TO HAVE his or her own radio, his or her own TV. Why did the members of his staff have so many radios? Why did they bring them to work? Was this what they did all day, listen to the radio, instead of doing their jobs?

On the other hand, maybe there weren't so many radios. Maybe there were only one or two. Maybe it just sounded to Teddy, at that moment, as if hundreds of radios filled the rooms of his office suite, all blaring the same terrible news that the President had been shot. Just that the President had been shot and nothing more.

He had to talk to Bobby right away.

But even in his office, the phones did not work. He picked up one after another. All were dead. Yet the phones seemed to be ringing constantly. Incoming calls were being received but outgoing calls could not be made.

Martin Agronsky of NBC was on line three. Would Teddy be flying to Dallas? He didn't know. How was he supposed to know? He didn't even yet know what had happened.

Accompanied only by Claude, Teddy retreated inside his private office and closed the door. He was simply going to sit here, behind his desk, very calmly using his telephone, until he was able to reach Bobby. He didn't care if it took all afternoon. He had to talk to Bobby before he could do anything else.

Claude sat quietly in a corner. In all the years he'd known Claude, through all the experiences they'd shared —many of which had been good times, but not all—he'd never known that Claude could look so sad.

Even Teddy's own phone line was dead. He picked up the receiver, pushed button after button, put it down. Picked it up again, hit the buttons again, one after another.

Finally, on some line, he reached an operator. He told her who he was, and that he had to reach the Attorney General right away. He told her to try Bobby's office at the Justice Department. She asked him to hold.

In a moment, she was back on the line. She told him Bobby was not at the Justice Department, he was at the White House. That didn't make sense. But Teddy said, "Put me through to him right away."

The operator explained that she could not. Bobby was on a private line to Dallas and had left word he was not to be interrupted by anyone, for any purpose.

Teddy said yes, but this was his brother. This was the President's brother, too. He needed to talk to the Attorney General right away.

The operator was as sympathetic and understanding as she could be. She explained that Teddy, being in the legislative branch and not the executive branch, did not have an executive branch telephone extension in his office and that thus there was no way to splice him into Bobby's call.

This was getting hopelessly confusing. And frustrating. Under the best of circumstances, Teddy was far from the most patient of men. Patient men, no matter what their names, no matter who their brothers or fathers might be, did not become United States senators at age thirty.

Teddy slammed down the receiver. What was this bullshit? Executive branch? Improper extension? Jesus Christ, Bobby was right there, in the White House, on the goddamned telephone talking to somebody, and there was no way for Teddy to get through? What a mess. When Jack got back from Texas, Teddy would really have to speak to him about these communications problems.

Then a wave of true alarm washed over the wall of Teddy's shock. In a moment of painful clarity, he realized that during however much time had passed since the press officer had first approached him on the dais, he still had not acquired a single piece of useful information.

Jack had been shot. That was all he knew. He opened the door to his outer office. Somebody said—or did he just think this?—that it was possible a coup d'état was under way. That a military takeover of the United States government might be occurring.

The notion was preposterous. It had happened in South Vietnam three weeks before, but this was the United States, not South Vietnam. Still, both Jack and Bobby had alluded on occasion to their awareness of how infuriated some elements within the military were at what they considered Jack's weakness in the Cuban crises, his pledge never to invade the island, his failure to go to war over the Berlin Wall, his halfhearted response to Communist aggression in Vietnam, his endorsement of a treaty that would prohibit the further testing of nuclear weapons, except underground. And J. Edgar Hoover, Teddy knew, was furious with both Jack and Bobby for their refusal to stamp out the civil rights movement.

In recent weeks, both Jack and Bobby had been unusually tense. Teddy had been aware of that. He'd thought that maybe over Thanksgiving they'd all have a chance to sit down together and chat. It was only a year until the 1964 election. Right-wing support for Republican Barry Goldwater was growing. Jack's popularity rating had slipped, in October, to its lowest point since his election.

But a coup? An armed military takeover that involved the shooting of the President? It did not seem even remotely plausible, yet why could he not complete a phone call? Something very strange—something quite frightening, really—was going on, and Teddy, as yet, did not have a clue as to its nature or dimension.

What about his wife? What about Joan? Suppose there was some sort of insurrection under way. They might try to kill all members of the Kennedy family. Bobby, Ethel, Teddy himself. Even poor Joan, who still had trouble keeping straight the branches of government in which her husband and brothers-in-law served. Maybe even his children: his three-year-old daughter and his two-year-old son.

"Get my car," he told an aide. He was suddenly obsessed with the idea of driving home and making sure Joan and the children were all right. From home, he could try Bobby again. He couldn't have any less success on his home phone than he'd had either at the Capitol or in his office.

"My car," he repeated. "Right away."

But his car wasn't in its parking place in the Senate garage. Teddy was told a staff member had taken it out earlier in the day to run errands and had not yet returned.

He didn't like the sound of this. Not at all. Neither did Claude. And neither did Milt Gwirtzman, a staff member who had once worked for Jack and who'd been sent over to Teddy's office in January, essentially to make sure he didn't screw up and somehow embarrass the President.

Some newspaper reporters, in analyzing Teddy's staff, had referred to Gwirtzman as "Teddy's own Sorensen." That was a laugh. Ted Sorensen was Jack's speech writer. When America listened to its President, when the world listened to the vibrant young American leader, it was the charismatically handsome Jack they saw, and it was the unmistakable timbre and cadence of Jack's voice they heard, but the words that they found so inspiring were Ted Sorensen's.

What was funny about calling Milt Gwirtzman Teddy's Sorensen was that until only a few weeks ago, Teddy had been under strict instructions from his brothers to publish nothing, to make no speeches of substance, to not even grant interviews to journalists from outside Massachusetts.

Until quite recently, it had seemed that one of Jack and Bobby's highest priorities had been rendering Teddy

17

silent and invisible. There would not be "too many Kennedys" if the third of them was never heard from or seen.

So Milt Gwirtzman, another Harvard man who was a fine speech writer, and one whose loyalty to the Kennedys was absolute, had spent most of his year on Teddy's staff using none of his talents to their fullest. He was, in fact, Teddy's anti-Sorensen: the aide whose primary job it was not to nurture and craft through use of language an image for the officeholder but, through vigilant insistence that no language at all be used in Teddy's behalf, to prevent the formation of any image whatsoever.

Teddy's turn for image would come later, it was explained. The 1960s were to be Jack's years of glory.

But Milt Gwirtzman owned a Mercedes. And he'd not permitted any junior staff member to take it to run errands. It was here, it was ready, so Claude, Milt and Teddy ran to it and sped away from the Senate Office Building, racing toward Teddy's home in Georgetown.

On his way out the door, Teddy had grabbed a small transistor radio from a secretary. He sat in the front seat, the tiny instrument pressed to his ear, as if what he heard through it would somehow be more authoritative, more authentic, than any information received on a regular car radio—even if the car was a Mercedes.

Claude sat in the back, stunned into silence, near tears. He knew he should be helping Teddy, but he didn't know how. So he buried his face in his hands and hoped that Jack was alive, that Jackie was all right, and that Milt would make it to Teddy's house without getting them all killed in an accident.

There was construction going on outside the State Department. It was a useless goddamned organization anyway, in Teddy's opinion, and to be caught in a construction delay right there seemed somehow more than he should have been expected to tolerate.

He was almost at the point of jumping from the car, so frustrated was he by the delay, when through the static of the transistor, he heard a faint voice saying that a report had just been received that the President was still alive.

Alive! Well, that was something. How long ago had he been shot? No one knew. But if he was still alive, at this moment, then possibly the injuries were not so serious after all. Nobody knew, that was the thing. There had been a garbled report of a head wound, of the presidential limousine speeding toward a nearby hospital.

The would-be assassin or assassins were still at large. But Jack was alive. That was what mattered. If he was alive, Teddy was sure he'd be all right.

From the back, Claude moaned, "My God, my God, the President shot—and in my state."

Teddy did not even turn around.

Even with the construction delay, the trip from the office to Teddy's town house took less than fifteen minutes. Before Milt could turn off the engine, Teddy was out the front door and sprinting up the steps. He called for his wife. He called again. There was no answer.

Then a maid appeared. The children were fine, the maid said, and Mrs. Kennedy had gone out to get her hair done.

Her hair done! Jack had been shot in Dallas and Joan was out getting her hair done? Then Teddy realized that Joan could not possibly have heard the news from Dallas. Otherwise, she would never have gone out. In fact, she still probably had no idea there was anything wrong. And Teddy himself still didn't know how wrong things were.

Joan was getting her hair done because it was the night they were going to have their anniversary dinner. That's why Claude was here. But wait—all of that was happening in that other world, the one that looked so much like this one but the one from which Teddy had been so rudely yanked an hour earlier, the one to which he might never return.

"I'll get her," Milt said, once he learned the address of the beauty parlor.

Teddy let him go. He'd come home to be sure Joan was all right. She wasn't home. He wasn't sure. But let Milt deal with her. Teddy remained obsessed by the need to contact Bobby.

* * *

19

But none of the phones in Teddy's house worked. He and Claude went from room to room, picking up receiver after receiver. The lines were dead. They were cut off from all communication with the outside world, still not knowing how Jack was, what had happened to him, what Bobby was doing at the White House, whether or not there might be a coup under way after all.

If there was, Teddy realized, whoever was behind it could send men bursting through the town house door at any moment to gun him down. But if Jack was alive, as the radio had said, then there couldn't really be a coup.

He paced his living room floor, waiting for Milt to get back with Joan. He would ask Milt what to do. Milt had a cool head. Milt was experienced. Just as Milt had known to leave the office in his Mercedes, Milt would know what to do next.

Milt and Joan were back at the house within minutes.

"The phones are gone," Teddy told them. "All of them."

Joan immediately suspected the worst. There was a coup. Or if not a coup, something bad. "There must be some national reason," she said.

It took Teddy a moment to realize that this remark didn't make sense. But then, little that he'd said had made sense either. It became overwhelmingly important that before another moment passed, he somehow get to a working telephone and reach Bobby.

This was the distillation of every nightmarish experience he'd ever had within his family. He'd come along too late. He was the last of them, always on the outside, looking in. When Jack won his crucial victory in the West Virginia primary, Teddy had been in Montana, unable to reach Bobby, at West Virginia headquarters, on the phone.

And the night Jack was elected President, Teddy had been the only family member not present at the Hyannis Port compound. He was still en route back from the West, where he'd been given charge of thirteen states. Ten of them, including vital California, had been lost.

And so, instead of being there to share the moment of

triumph, he'd been a continent away, forced to send a telegram of apology that he hoped, in the full flush of victory, his father and brothers might think amusing.

"Can I come home," he had wired, "if I promise to win the western states in 1964?"

No one in Hyannis Port was amused. Jack had been elected, but no thanks to Teddy. Thanks to deals his father had made. Deals his father would rather not have made, might not have had to make if Teddy had done a better job in the West. Deals in which Teddy had no part. Deals of which Teddy had known nothing.

And now, at what might be a moment of not just family but national crisis, it was happening again. He was stuck incommunicado in Georgetown with one of Jack's former assistants, his slaphappy friend Claude from Harvard, and his wife with her freshly done hair.

Milt said that he would stay with Joan. He suggested that Teddy and Claude go outside and split up, heading in opposite directions. That each of them knock on every door until one of them found a working phone. Then, whoever found one first should put through a call to the White House and make it clear that Teddy had to speak to Bobby right away.

"If you get something," Teddy said to Claude as they went their separate ways down Georgetown's Twenty-eighth Street, "let me know."

4

It WAS NOW 3:00 P.M. FOR ALMOST NINETY MINUTES, anyone in America who had been listening consistently to a radio or television broadcast knew more about what had happened in Dallas than did Teddy.

Increasingly frantic as the afternoon light began to fade from the gray November sky, Teddy was charging back and forth along the 1600 block of Georgetown's Twenty-eighth Street, looking for a phone that would work.

It seemed inconceivable that an hour and a half after the death of the President of the United States had been announced to the American people, his youngest brother thought he was still alive, but in the chaos of the afternoon, and because of his insistence on talking to Bobby and only to Bobby, Teddy had inadvertently put himself in the position of being one of the last people in the country to hear the news.

Claude Hooton had soon realized that the idea of their setting out in opposite directions lacked a certain logic, for if Claude was first to find a phone that worked he wouldn't know what to do with it. Even if he was put through to the White House, even if he did get Bobby on the line, what would he say? "Hold the phone while I run out and try to find your brother"?

So Claude had reversed direction and had caught up with Teddy. Together, the two friends continued their frenzied quest for what, between the hours of 2:00 and 4:00 P.M. that day, seemed to be the rarest commodity in Washington: a working telephone.

Teddy was not the only person in the nation's capital that afternoon to fear that the shooting of the President and the sudden breakdown of the telephone system were somehow linked—that an armed coup d'état was under way.

Tom Wells, the Secret Service agent assigned to protect Jack's five-year-old daughter, Caroline, whenever she ventured forth from the White House, was thinking exactly the same thing.

Just after 1:30 P.M.—after Jack had already died, but before the news was broadcast—Caroline had crossed the White House driveway and had climbed into the backseat of a station wagon driven by the mother of a school friend. For the first time in her life, the President's daughter was going to sleep over at a friend's house on a Friday night.

Even then, of course, she was technically no longer the President's daughter, but neither she nor the friend's mother driving the station wagon nor Agent Wells yet knew that.

The mother, driving along Washington's Rock Creek Parkway, had turned on the car radio. Instead of the music she'd expected to hear on WGMS, she caught a portion of a news bulletin.

". . . shot in the head, and his wife, Jackie . . ."

Instinctively, she turned off the radio and looked quickly at Caroline in the rearview mirror. The little girl seemed not to have heard. The mother then looked behind her at Agent Wells, who she knew was following, as he always followed Caroline, in a Secret Service car.

Wells had his car radio tuned to a different station. They were just passing the National Zoo when his program was interrupted by a bulletin that said, "We have an unconfirmed report of a shooting in the area of the presidential motorcade in Dallas."

Ahead of him, the mother driving Caroline headed toward Chevy Chase Circle. Now, on his car radio, Wells heard that there were unconfirmed reports that members of the presidential party, and possibly even the President himself, had been shot.

The two cars proceeded for another half mile before the station wagon in which Caroline was riding stopped for a red light. Immediately, Wells jumped from his car and ran to the driver's door.

"What should I do?" she asked.

"Nobody knows whether or not it's serious," he said. "Keep going. But turn off your radio."

"I already did," she said.

Using the microphone inside his sedan, Wells radioed to Secret Service headquarters for instructions. On his AM radio, he was now hearing from Dallas how police had apparently chased two gunmen up "a knoll" in the vicinity of the shooting.

United Press International had been so quick to communicate details of the assassination that Wells, listening on his car radio, knew more than agents at Washington headquarters, who were unable for the moment to contact their colleagues in Dallas.

Wells was a relatively junior agent, assigned to the presidential detail only one year earlier, but he felt he had to make a decision.

He radioed Washington headquarters again. "I feel the danger has grown," he said. "We don't know whether this is an isolated thing, or a plot or a coup. If it's a coup, Washington is sure to be a part of it." He feared for Caroline's safety. "They might be trying to kill the whole family," he said. He told headquarters that in the absence of instructions to the contrary, he would stop the car in which Caroline was riding, transfer her to his own sedan, and rush her back to the White House.

The mother in the station wagon resisted at first, arguing that no one knew Caroline was with her and that therefore she'd be safer at their house than in the White House, which, if an armed coup was under way, was sure to be a target, sooner or later. Besides, she did not want to see Caroline upset by a sudden change of plans.

But Wells insisted. He stuck his head inside the station wagon and said, "Caroline, you have to go back to your house. You better bring your overnight bag with you. Maybe you can go out again a little later."

"I don't want to go," she said, sinking down in her seat.

Wells didn't want to be impatient with the child, but this was the greatest crisis of his professional life, perhaps the greatest crisis in the nation's history, and his sole responsibility was to be sure that Caroline Kennedy was not harmed.

"We don't have any choice," he said, perhaps more brusquely than he'd intended. "Something has come up. Miss Shaw will probably tell you." Maude Shaw was the White House nanny, who supervised care of both Caroline and her younger brother, John.

"I know what it's about," Caroline said.

Wells did not know how to respond.

Hugging her teddy bear and choking back tears, Caroline climbed out of the station wagon and into the front seat of Wells's car.

After they'd driven for a quarter mile in silence, Caroline spoke.

"Why do we have to go home?" she asked.

Wells pondered what sort of answer to give. But before he could say anything, she said, "Never mind. I know."

He didn't know how much she knew, or how much she should know. But he sensed it was not his place to tell her anything. It was his place, and his duty, simply to return her to the presumed security of the White House and then await further instructions.

"Mommy has changed her plans," Wells finally said. "She'll probably be coming back tonight. She wanted you and John to be home."

He realized he had said only "Mommy." He had said nothing about Daddy. But Caroline never asked.

The car was silent. Wells realized that by taking charge of Caroline, he'd cut himself off from any further news. With the little girl sitting next to him he didn't dare turn on his car radio.

He had her back to the White House by 2:15. Maude

Shaw was waiting for her there. Like everyone else, the nanny was in a state of confusion and massive shock.

Her fixation was on transportation. Knowing that the President was dead, she said to a Secret Service agent, "Oh dear. I don't know how to drive. What will I do without White House cars?"

The agent did not think the time was yet right for him to remind her that she'd have to do not only without the cars but without the White House itself. Lyndon Johnson would soon be moving in.

The breakdown of the telephone system throughout Washington was not the result of any conspiracy, but was caused simply by a technology not equipped to handle the unprecedented demands made upon it.

Throughout the city, and at the Pentagon across the river in Virginia, all callers were experiencing the same frustration as Teddy. They simply could not get a line. There were no dial tones. There were no operators. Nothing worked. No one seemed to know what was broken, or why, or when it might be fixed.

But in many government offices as well as private homes, the shooting of the President coupled with the sudden failure of the telephone system in the nation's capital carried a highly sinister implication.

As William Manchester has written, "Between 2 and 4 P.M. in Washington it required no great leap of imagination to picture the country crawling with sinister figures industriously sabotaging communications. What set this aspect of the crisis apart was its immunity to rank; all flashing lights looked alike to switchboard operators, and automated exchanges could not distinguish between the phone of an exasperated Senator and one in the hands of a child. Completing a call required luck and persistence, and the list of the luckless included a number of men and women who were accustomed to very quick service."

Dwight Eisenhower's wife was unable to reach him by phone. Jacqueline Kennedy's mother was unable to reach her daughter. Supreme Court justices, congressmen, White House aides, members of the Joint Chiefs of

Staff—they all faced the same problem as Teddy: finding a telephone that worked.

The Secret Service in Washington could not communicate directly with its agents in Dallas. Because the President had planned to spend only three hours in the city, technicians from the Signal Corps had installed no special direct lines. Even Bobby was able to keep abreast of developments only through an indirect link that went through a temporary switchboard installed on the seventh floor of a hotel in Fort Worth.

Finally, the Chesapeake and Potomac phone system just broke down entirely from the overload of simultaneous calls.

Ringing the doorbells of town house after town house, Teddy and Claude had finally found one whose owner was home, was willing to come to the door, recognized Teddy and was willing to let him try to use her telephone.

There was a dial tone. It was now almost 3:30 P.M. but Teddy had suddenly gotten lucky. He reached the White House, only to be told that Bobby had already left for his home.

Unwilling to put the phone down, afraid that he'd never get a dial tone again, Teddy asked a White House operator to put his call through to Hickory Hill.

Bobby himself answered on the first ring. As soon as he heard Teddy's voice, before Teddy could even ask a question, Bobby said simply, "He's dead."

There were a hundred questions, a thousand questions, that Teddy needed to ask Bobby all at once. But Bobby did not just then have time for questions, not even from his younger brother.

He said quickly, "You'd better call your mother and our sisters." Then he hung up.

Later, it would seem strange that Bobby had said "*your* mother"; not "our mother," or "Mom." His choice of pronoun implied much about the distance that had formed between Bobby and his mother over the years. But, later, so many other things would come to seem even stranger.

27

Teddy did not want to call his mother in Hyannis Port. He dreaded the thought of talking to her at this moment. For one thing, he still didn't know what to say.

"He's dead." That was all Bobby had told him.

His mother would have a thousand questions, as Teddy did, and he'd be able to provide her with few if any answers.

But Bobby had told him to do it. He had no choice. He put down the phone, paused a moment, then picked up the receiver to dial Hyannis Port. But now this phone in this town house was as dead as all the others he had tried.

Teddy and Claude ran out the door and down the steps and back to Teddy's own home. There, Milt Gwirtzman told him, the phones were still out. But both Milt and Joan had been watching television. They too now knew that Jack was dead.

"What about my house?" Milt suggested. "Maybe we'll have better luck there."

Claude said that he would stay with Joan and the children. Teddy and Milt ran to the Mercedes and sped to the Gwirtzman home, eight blocks away. But there too the phones were dead.

For a moment Teddy did not know what to do, where to turn, whom to talk to. Then, in desperation, he focused on what had been, after all, the center of power, the holy grail for which the family had quested.

"Let's go to the White House," Teddy said.

The two men did not speak to each other during the ride. They'd heard the news—the worst news possible—from separate sources and neither found himself able or willing to risk comment.

Approaching the White House, Milt saw that a huge crowd had gathered on Pennsylvania Avenue, cutting off direct access to the building.

"Go to the east gate," Teddy said. This was a private entrance, used primarily by staff and by diplomatic visitors who wished to avoid the scrutiny of the press.

Milt turned the Mercedes onto East Executive Avenue and pulled up to the gate. The guard there recognized Teddy immediately and waved them through. As Milt brought the car to a stop on the gravel driveway outside the east entrance, Teddy jumped from it and raced up the steps.

But the door was locked. He pulled at it, to no avail. He pounded on it.

As Milt ran up the steps to join him, Teddy finally succumbed to his mounting frustration and building grief and, pounding the door with both fists and tugging the handle as hard as he could, he shouted, "Doesn't ANY-THING work?"

At that moment, he seemed close to tears, possibly even to nervous collapse.

But Milt, standing alongside, calmly tried an adjacent door, which was unlocked. Together, the two men entered the White House.

Teddy at first did not know which way to go. He did not know, really, why he had come here, whom he wanted to see.

Well, he wanted to see Jack, of course, sitting at his Oval Office desk and grinning mischievously as he greeted his youngest brother with some sort of lewd remark.

But Jack wasn't there. Jack would never be there again. Jack was in Texas. Jack was dead.

Teddy walked aimlessly down the central east-west corridor of the White House. At an open door, he saw one of Jack's personal physicians, Janet Travell.

"Do you want a sedative?" she asked. She had a bag right there on her desk, ready to administer an injection or dispense a pill.

"No," Teddy said. "What I really need is a working telephone."

She suggested that he use her examination room as an office. Her phone was as likely as any other in the building to be operative. He used the private White House line that went not through the civilian telephone system but through the army's Signal Corps. In this way, he was connected to his parents' house in Hyannis Port, and to his mother.

Their conversation was brief. She told him she'd already heard the news. Just that. She'd heard the news. She already knew that Jack was dead. There was nothing to be done about it. She was going out for a walk on the beach.

Teddy asked if his father, largely bedridden since his stroke two years earlier but still fully alert mentally, had yet been told.

His mother said no, she didn't think so, and she didn't think either that telling him would be a good idea. The news might prove too much for him to bear. In any event, she did not intend to tell him.

Rose had been married to Joe Kennedy for almost half a century, and for almost every one of those years she'd been aware that he cared nothing for her and that she cared nothing for him.

Their marriage had been largely a business enterprise. Children were the product they manufactured and brought to market. Now that the children were grown— now that they'd been packaged and sold to America— the two Kennedy parents had absolutely nothing to say to each other.

When Joe suffered his stroke, Rose had let him lie in bed for hours while she'd played golf. Only upon her return from the golf course had she permitted medical help to be summoned.

As her husband was rushed to the hospital, paralyzed and sinking into coma—his condition, in all likelihood, far worse than it would have been if he'd received treatment sooner—Rose had said there was nothing further she could do.

Instead of going to the hospital to be with him, she'd taken her regular afternoon swim.

Teddy hung up. Somebody would have to tell his father. Maybe Ann Gargan, the niece who cared for him. Or maybe one of the paid nurses, like Rita Dallas. Or maybe Joey Gargan could drive down from Boston. Or maybe the Cardinal. Cardinal Cushing, his father's old friend. Or maybe it should be a doctor.

To Teddy, for the moment, the question of who should

tell his father that Jack was dead seemed simply one more insoluble problem in a world suddenly filled with them.

It seemed another matter, among so many, about which he would have to ask Bobby's advice.

Teddy soon learned from White House aides and military advisors that no coup was in progress. Jack had been assassinated. Lyndon Johnson had already been sworn in as President and, along with Jacqueline, was flying back to Washington in the plane that carried Jack's body.

He didn't know who had shot Jack, or why. He didn't know anything that had happened in Dallas. For the moment, that did not concern him. Jack was dead. That was the single, overwhelming fact whose enormity filled his mind and heart, leaving no room for concentration on or even curiosity about anything else.

He did know he'd better not take any sort of sedative. He felt muddled enough as it was and he was sure that in the hours ahead some dreadfully unpleasant public tasks would be thrust upon him, and that for the sake of the family's image—and because it was the way both his father and Jack would have wanted it—he would have to carry them out with dignity and efficiency.

Bobby had said, "Call your mother and our sisters." He had just begun to think about the sisters—Eunice, Pat and Jean, where were they, did they know, how could he reach them?—when a presidential military aide stepped into the office he was using and told him his sisters had been informed and they were safe.

Moments later, Eunice arrived at the White House. She was married to Sargent Shriver, director of the Peace Corps and a very decent fellow. Eunice was the oldest of Teddy's living sisters, except for Rosemary, who'd suffered from emotional disturbances and whom their father had had lobotomized, and who, ever since, had been hidden from both public and family view in an institution in Wisconsin, unable to speak or to feed herself or even to think.

Eunice was not only the oldest but the most domineering of the sisters. Their father had once said of her, "If she'd been born with a set of balls she's the one who would have been President." She was tough, no doubt about it, often high-strung, but among the sisters clearly the one most like their father.

Teddy was glad to see her. Though they were not particularly close on a personal level—separated by more than ten years of age, by quite different personalities and by very different kinds of experience growing up within the family—Eunice was the closest Teddy could come to Bobby right now; the closest to having with him a person who would know exactly the right thing to do and how to do it.

She seemed amazed that he'd had only one brief telephone conversation with Bobby. What good was he doing anyone, just sitting in the office of the White House physician? She told him to give her the phone. She said they had to talk to Bobby again immediately. They had to plan; they had to coordinate.

She was right, of course, and this was what Teddy had been planning to do, just as soon as he could force himself to focus. But once Eunice arrived it actually happened. She reached Bobby within minutes and, with Teddy also on the line, the three of them had a longer conversation.

Little emotion was expressed. Kennedys did not express emotion openly, not even to one another, especially at times of emergency. Emergency required action, which was something with which emotion interfered. Emergency required logistical planning, which was something at which both Bobby and Eunice were expert.

It was determined that Teddy and Eunice would fly to Hyannis Port aboard a private plane. Their father undoubtedly knew by now that Jack was dead. He'd need at least some of the children there to console him, and possibly medical attention, which they knew from past experience Rose would be reluctant to provide. And even their mother, as stoic as she might appear, would benefit from their presence in the house.

Besides, they'd have to bring her back to Washington, Bobby said. Rose would have to attend the funeral and burial even if their father could not.

* * *

The historian James MacGregor Burns had been wrong when he described Jack, years earlier, as the sort of man at whose funeral no strangers would cry. More tears would be simultaneously shed by strangers watching this funeral and burial—which would be televised to every corner of the globe—than ever before in history.

Instinctively, without even having to discuss it—for this sort of knowledge had been both bred into their genes and imparted to them by word and example by both their parents since the earliest years of their lives—each of the surviving Kennedys knew that the process of mythmaking would begin in earnest within hours and that they must do nothing to impede it. This was what they owed their father, what they owed each other and, most of all, what they owed Jack.

Bobby said he would stay in Washington to oversee all national and international logistics. He would be at Andrews Air Force Base to greet the plane that would be carrying both Jacqueline and the body of Jack. He would attend the autopsy that would be performed at the Bethesda Naval Hospital. Jack's aides had so quickly rushed the body out of the Dallas hospital where death had been pronounced—in violation of Texas law, about which none of them could possibly have cared less at that moment—that no autopsy had yet been done.

Yet for purposes of history, an exact description of the wounds would have to be recorded. Bobby already knew that in time there were going to be many questions raised about the circumstances surrounding Jack's death, and he, more than anyone, knew the vital importance of controlling the nature of the answers provided.

So he would stay in Washington. From there, he would manage the autopsy, the lying-in-state, the funeral and the burial—the combination of which would be, in a sense, Jack's last campaign.

Later, Teddy would tell friends that even in those early hours he had been worried about Bobby. He'd never heard his brother sound quite so lifeless, so empty, so drained of spirit. Teddy himself was virtually numb with shock and grief, but there seemed an added dimension to Bobby's despair. It was as if Bobby was suffering even more acutely than the rest of them; it seemed that to his grief there was added an element of something not entirely unlike fear. Or could it have been, for some reason, guilt?

Teddy was informed that the private aircraft was ready for the flight to Massachusetts. He called home to tell Joan to stay there; that he and Eunice were going to Hyannis Port and they'd be bringing his mother back with them. That she should stay in touch with Bobby, who would tell her what to do.

It apparently did not occur to Teddy to bring his wife to Hyannis Port with him. They did not have that kind of relationship. Besides, Joan performed poorly in times of crisis.

The thing to do with Joan was to keep her out of sight, to keep her locked inside the Georgetown house with her two young children. Joan was not close enough to the center of this tragedy to be part of the public spectacle of grief and mourning. The next hours were to belong to Bobby and—most of all—to Jacqueline, whose grace and courage in Dallas were already being inflated to legendary proportions by media trained to portray the Kennedys as glamorous, romantic and heroic—media now so stunned by the enormity of what had occurred that afternoon that no description of exemplary behavior, no words of praise or glorification were considered excessive, just as no words of condemnation for the presumed assassin—now identified as one Lee Harvey Oswald, a pro-Castro activist who'd once lived in the Soviet Union—were too harsh.

About to rush from the White House to Andrews Air Force Base for the flight to Hyannis Port, Teddy suddenly realized that Jack's two children were upstairs.

He didn't know if they knew.

He could not leave without going up to see them, without trying to comfort them however he could if they did know, or—if they'd not yet been told—at least inquiring as to what arrangements had been made for informing them.

In the hours that had elapsed since the press aide had first approached him in the Senate, Teddy had been so frantic about so much, driven nearly mad with frustration by his inability for so long to find a working telephone, that he'd scarcely considered that in addition to whatever other ramifications the murder of Jack would have internationally, nationally and within the family—and he knew that they would be enormous and that the reverberations would be felt for years—the assassination had deprived five-year-old Caroline and John-John, who was to turn three the following Monday, of their father.

Teddy ran up to the family's private quarters to see them. He hadn't known Caroline had been about to spend her first night at a friend's house. He hadn't known about the tense transfer of the little girl from the station wagon to the Secret Service sedan.

But he saw as soon as he arrived in the upstairs nursery that while she undoubtedly sensed that something was seriously awry, she did not yet know the whole story. She did not yet know that her daddy was dead and that her mother, even then, was flying back to Washington wearing a dress still stained with his blood and with flecks of tissue from his brain.

And John-John knew nothing at all. Except that Uncle Teddy was suddenly here in the middle of the afternoon, which was not at all part of the usual routine, and Uncle Teddy looked very pale and worried.

Luella Hennessey, who'd been his own governess when he was John-John's age, who'd taken him and Bobby on walks in London, who'd cared for him—who'd raised him, really, while his mother spent so many months away from home during the first six years of his life—had come to the White House upon hearing the news. She had anticipated that Maude Shaw, nanny to Caroline and John-John, might need assistance.

Upon seeing her, Teddy was struck by a new wave of sadness. He so associated her with his own early childhood. Now he was no longer a child. She was no longer a young woman. But she and he suddenly found themselves together, for the first time in many months, even years—together here in the White House, with Jack's children. And Jack was dead. He would never see Jack again.

Teddy found being in the children's presence an almost unbearable agony. "He was so overwhelmed," Luella Hennessey would later recall, "so shocked he could barely speak."

He walked toward his old governess and said only, "Lulu, it's nice to have you here." Then he kissed her, which was highly out of character. The act made Miss Hennessey even more clearly aware of how acute was Teddy's distress.

"His face was so white and so drawn," she said. "I got the feeling that if he said any more he would break down and cry."

But maybe he would have to say more. Maybe it was his role to tell the children. Bobby and Eunice and he had not discussed that. But he was here with them now, and even though all televisions and radios were off, and the nurses were doing their best to keep the children distracted and occupied, surely they would have to be told.

Jacqueline, however, would be back within hours. She was their mother. It was for her, really—not for him—to tell the children of their father's death.

No, this was not Teddy's business. This was not Teddy's place. If he were to blurt out something now, simply in order to ease his own pain, she might never forgive him. Undoubtedly, even now, flying east, she was trying to compose the words she'd use to tell them; was trying to think of the best ways to make them understand, of any means at all by which she might be able to soothe and console them.

So Teddy hugged the children quickly and left the room. He had to get away from them fast. Another minute in their presence and he might have broken down completely. As a lonely and frightened five-year-old, he'd been able to bury his head in Luella's lap and have her stroke his back and rub his neck and assure him that everything would be all right.

But he was too big for that now. He was grown up. He was a senator. He was a Kennedy. Until about three hours earlier, he had been the brother of the President and had looked forward to at least five more years of that special status, before emerging as a likely occupant of the White House himself.

Now it was gone—in a quick burst of gunfire in an unfamiliar city two thousand miles away. And Jack was gone too. And nothing would be all right ever again, not for any of them. Not for these warm and loving children, not for their mother, not for his only living brother, not for himself, and not for his own mother and father, whom he now had to fly to Hyannis Port to see.

He said little to Eunice during the flight. A late-November darkness had fallen by the time the small plane landed at Otis Air Force Base on Cape Cod. Teddy gazed out the window. So many times before—and usually they'd been happy times—he'd come to the Cape, anticipating a festive occasion at the big wooden house overlooking the water.

To be a part of this, to be near it himself, he and Joan had bought their own Hyannis Port home, less than a mile up a private road from the houses owned by Jack and by Bobby, and from the big house at which he'd spent so many summers and holidays.

It was here, on the Cape, that the Kennedys most resembled the close-knit, mutually supportive family that America imagined them to be. It was here that the reality of their complex and emotionally attenuated lives came closest to matching the image of them that their father had so painstakingly crafted and purveyed, at such staggering expense.

As the plane rolled to a halt, Teddy saw banks of bright lights. Television. Of course. He should have expected television. The assassination of Jack was a national event —a worldwide event. Every word spoken, every action taken, every new detail of the life of any living family member, would now take on monumental significance.

In addition to all else that it was, the assassination of Jack, with its aftermath, would become the ultimate media event in American history. The scene here, at the air base, was a small one, soon to be dwarfed by the grand and somber spectacle of the dead President's body being unloaded from Air Force One upon its return to Washington, but Teddy's family scenes had always been the small ones. He'd grown used to that, had come to accept it as his fate, even to welcome it in a way, because he was freed from so many of the more intense pressures that Jack and Bobby had always faced.

Teddy stepped slowly out of the plane, onto the steps and into a raw Cape Cod evening. He didn't know what he should say to the press. He didn't see how he could stand up to a barrage of shouted questions, a clamor for fresh detail, especially when he had none to provide.

But he quickly found he didn't have to. Out of the throng of newsmen, one stepped forward, as if designated, and instead of asking him a question, made a statement.

"Senator," he said, "we apologize for being here at this time of tragedy."

Teddy had been prepared for sympathy, for deference, and he'd certainly not expected any insensitivity from the press, but this outright apology for their obviously necessary presence took him by surprise.

He nodded in the direction of the man who'd spoken. Lights shone, cameras whirred, flashbulbs popped, but the sense of regret that this had to be done at all was almost as sharp as the chill wind that began to blow across the airfield.

"I understand, gentlemen. I understand," Teddy said, and nodded courteously.

And that was it. No one asked a single question. They stepped aside, even the photographers, to let him and Eunice pass. No one tried to follow. Teddy and his sister climbed into a waiting limousine for the short drive to Hyannis Port.

5

TEDDY'S MOTHER, ROSE, WAS WAITING IN THE LIVING room. With her was his cousin Joey Gargan, who had sped down from Boston upon hearing the news. Except for Bobby, there was probably no one in the world who'd been as close to Teddy for as long as Joey Gargan.

Joey's mother and Teddy's mother were sisters. Joey's father had been a brilliant attorney in Washington, in the early stages of a career that promised to be stellar even by Kennedy family standards, when he suddenly died of a heart attack. A few years later, when Joey was eleven, his mother had died too.

From that point forward, Joey had been practically a member of the Kennedy family. They'd brought him to live in the big house at Hyannis Port. This had been the idea of Teddy's father, who thought that Joey, two years older than his plump and ineffectual youngest son, might be able to teach Teddy a few things about being a boy in the Kennedy mold.

Basic things: how to sail a boat, how to climb a tree, things like that. The family had always employed a staff of professional instructors to develop the children's athletic skills, and both father and mother had instilled in them a fierce need to win at all times, at any cost; but

Teddy, being so much younger, had missed out on a lot of the intramural scrambling that had toughened his brothers.

His father thought Joey Gargan, a rugged and fearless little fellow, would be a good example for Teddy. The arrangement was fraught with the potential for tension and mutual distaste, but Teddy and Joey had become fast friends from the first and had remained so for years.

Joey had gone on to law school, too, and had a practice, but his central role in life, as had been ordained when the Kennedys permitted him to join the family, was to serve their interests. For several years, this service had consisted primarily of being a companion to Teddy. More recently, as Jack's career had advanced and as Bobby had moved alongside to serve him, it had taken the form of whatever sort of campaign work and low-level political coordination was required at any given time.

Joey had not turned out to be a genius, but he was a handy fellow to have around: a good companion socially and an able assistant, whose energy, discretion and loyalty proved more important than judgment, insight or other intellectual attributes. Joey could be given all sorts of disagreeable chores and would perform them rapidly and efficiently and without complaint. Service to the Kennedys had become his true vocation.

As always, Teddy was glad to see him. With just his mother and Eunice in the house—and his father upstairs —the atmosphere might have been unbearably grim. Not that Joey was going to get their minds off their woes, but with him, at least, Teddy could permit himself some small display of feeling. With Joey, as with almost no one else, Teddy could occasionally lower the Kennedy mask and simply be his own fallible self.

Rose seemed impatient. She said she'd been waiting to go for a walk on the beach but had wanted to be at the house to greet Teddy and Eunice. For Rose, at all times, it was important to observe social conventions.

But Teddy said, wait a minute. Before anybody went for a walk, what about Dad? Who was upstairs with him now? Who had told him about Jack? How had he taken it? How was he?

Rose explained that Teddy's father had not yet been told. She had not wanted to tell him and she didn't think he should hear it from a servant or learn about it from television.

She thought, in fact, that Teddy, as the oldest son now present in the house, should be the one to tell him Jack was dead. That the dream which had sustained the old man for decades, the dream he'd converted to reality by spending tens of millions of dollars in both legal and illegal ways—this dream of seeing his oldest son as President, the dream whose fruition had been his life's work—had suddenly turned to ashes and to dust.

Yes, Rose said, it would be fitting for Teddy to be the one to tell his father. But first, why didn't they all take a walk on the beach? She'd been kept waiting quite long enough.

Whatever warmth had lingered into the November afternoon in Washington had long since been driven from Hyannis Port by high winds. Having changed from his suit into a heavy woolen sweater and woolen pants, Teddy joined his mother and Eunice and Joey Gargan for the walk.

To Teddy this hardly seemed the time for a walk on the beach. Aside from being cold and windy, it was dark. Also, away from the house they would not be reachable by telephone, by Bobby or Jean or Pat or Joan or Ethel, or any of a hundred other people who might be trying to call them at any moment.

Rose, however, would not be deterred. And Teddy was still too stunned by the news that his father had not been told of Jack's death to offer more than a perfunctory objection. Besides, he'd learned many times, over many years, that when his mother made up her mind to do something, she did it; and if she'd made up her mind that you were going to do it with her, you did it too.

But what a strange, almost surreal experience. With the wind at almost gale force, big hulking Teddy, frail Eunice, little birdlike Rose and faithful, chunky Joey

Gargan striding briskly along the darkened beach—to
Rose a brisk walk was the only kind of walk worth taking
—even as the mute, disabled founder of the dynasty lay
in his bed of pain and ignorance and even as Jack's body
was arriving back in the capital he'd left as President only
the day before.

"Joey," Rose said, over the wind.

"Yes, Aunt Rose."

"You should read more."

"Excuse me, Aunt Rose?"

"You should read more, Joey. You don't read enough
books."

For the moment, no one made any response. Teddy
could not understand why his mother was talking about
books. Or why she was addressing her remarks to her
nephew.

"Didn't you hear me, Joey?" The wind was blowing
hard and Rose's voice did not carry well. Teddy was
flapping his arms back and forth in a futile effort to stay
warm.

"Yes, Aunt Rose, I heard you," Joey said. "And I
will. I'll read more books." Joey didn't know what else
to say, but he already saw that to say nothing had been a
mistake.

"Read about Marlborough," Rose said.

"Yes, Aunt Rose." To Joey, Marlboro was a cigarette.

"And read Fox."

Joey had no idea who Fox was. He looked at Teddy,
who merely shrugged.

"And Burke," Rose said. "Edmund Burke."

At last: someone Joey had heard of, though he could
claim no familiarity with the works of the eighteenth-
century British statesman and political thinker.

"Yes, Aunt Rose. Edmund Burke."

"Read them all," Rose said. "They'll improve your
mind. Make you a better person. Like Jack."

So that was it. Like Jack. Marlborough, Fox and
Burke. Among Jack's favorite role models, at least insofar as his mother knew.

At the Squaw Island causeway, which led out to Teddy

and Joan's house, they turned and walked back along the beach in silence.

Inside the house, his face reddened, his hands raw, Teddy poured himself a drink and walked to the grand piano that dominated the living room. He stared at the keyboard in silence.

The problem of his father was much on his mind. The time had come. It could not be put off.

"I guess," Teddy said, "I guess I'll go up and tell him now."

Rose was already talking about the funeral. She wanted someone to contact Cardinal Cushing. It was very important to her that Cardinal Cushing take control of funeral arrangements and that they be handled in a way that was both liturgically correct and as filled with pomp as the Catholic Church would allow.

Both Eunice and Joey Gargan said they'd go upstairs with Teddy. Rose wanted no part of the scene. Her contribution was to suggest that one of the old man's nurses prepare a glass of milk with a heavy sedative, in case he became overly distraught.

Filled with dread, and accompanied by his oldest functional sister and his oldest friend, Teddy entered his father's bedroom, at the east end of the second floor, preparing himself to say the most awful words he would ever have to utter in his life.

The Ambassador was wide awake and cranky. His niece Ann Gargan, Joey's sister, who had taken over much of the responsibility for his care, had not wanted him to hear about the assassination on television, or to witness any of the frightening, poignant scenes being broadcast on every channel. But it was his custom to watch the evening news on television after awakening from his afternoon nap.

She'd been telling him that the television set was broken, but it was obvious he didn't believe her. Nothing in his house was ever broken. He did not permit it. She'd been trying to distract him by playing phonograph records—one of the Wagner operas he'd begun listening to at the time of the death of Joe Junior—but with his one good hand he'd motioned impatiently for her to turn the music off. Then, with his face growing pinker as his irritation mounted and his blood pressure rose, he'd begun to gesture at the television set.

He wanted to watch the evening news.

Taking this all in as he entered the room, Teddy saw no reason to hold off on the sedative. He motioned to the nurse to give his father the glass of milk that contained it.

"Dad," he said, in the most cheerful voice he could muster, "I, ah, I'm on my way to Boston. I have to give a speech. So I thought I'd stop by and say hello."

The old man's eyes darted from Teddy to Eunice to Joey Gargan and back again. He could not speak, he could scarcely move, but his mental acuity had not diminished. He could not communicate his own thoughts or feelings, but he remained able to absorb and to understand almost everything he saw or heard. The stroke had rendered him dumb but not stupid.

Something was wrong.

Now was the time to tell him what it was.

But Teddy could not bring himself to do it.

He looked down at his stricken father in the bed and he realized he was not able, at that moment, to utter the necessary words. What would be the harm, he thought, in letting his father have one last peaceful night?

Why not tell him in the morning? After they'd all had some sleep and more chance to absorb the shock themselves. And maybe, as a matter of fact, it would be a good idea to get one of his father's doctors down from Boston to be present when the news was finally broken. The neurologist, perhaps, in case the shock of hearing that Jack was dead triggered another stroke. And maybe a heart man, too, just in case.

Yes, Teddy could go downstairs and get on the phone and begin to make those arrangements. That would be something useful to do. Then he could mix himself another drink and think a bit longer about just what words he should use the next day. Maybe he'd even consult the doctors about that. It was a family tradition to turn to outside experts for help in specialized matters. And in his whole life Teddy had never been involved in a matter more specialized than telling his ailing father that the son who'd realized his life's ambition had been shot in the head and was dead.

But his father was gesturing, angrily now, toward the television set. There were five people standing in the room: Teddy, Eunice, Joey and Ann Gargan, and the nurse who'd given the old man the milk laced with the sedative.

The old man wanted somebody to turn on the television set. Immediately.

Teddy pretended he only then understood the meaning of his father's gestures.

"Oh, the television. Sure, Dad," he said.

He walked to the set, switched it on with one hand while, bending, he used the other to unplug it. No sound came forth, no picture filled the screen.

Teddy turned back to his father in the bed.

"Doesn't work, Dad. I think it's broken. We'll get somebody to fix it tomorrow."

But as he said this, Teddy was standing in full view of his father, with the unplugged cord still in his hand.

The old man's face turned from pink to red. He gestured even more furiously.

Teddy looked down at the plug in his hand. "Oh," he said, as if it were some strange new scientific object. Then he looked at his father and smiled. And then got down on his knees, his back to his father's bed, and maneuvered the plug toward the socket. At the same time, however, he reached out with his right hand and clumsily, desperately, grabbed at any exposed wires he could find.

He yanked as hard as he could and felt a cluster come loose in his hand. Then he put the plug in the socket. He took a quick look at the rear of the set. He didn't know much about television, but he'd done so much damage with his quick, furious tugs that he was confident the set would not work.

And it didn't. Teddy turned back to his father.

"Still no good, Dad," he said. "We'll fix it in the morning."

The old man glared at him, convinced that something very wrong was happening but knowing that it was beyond his powers to determine what it was until one of his children or nurses was willing to tell him.

The nurse reentered the room, bringing a second glass of milk, this one containing an even more potent sleeping medication.

Old Joe Kennedy eyed it suspiciously. As William Manchester has written, by this point those in the room "had reached a peculiar understanding. Obviously he knew that something momentous had happened; he was waiting to be told what. They knew he knew."

But they'd also decided not to tell him until tomorrow. Before long, he figured that out as well. And must have figured, at the same time, that the sooner he could make tomorrow come, the better. And so, without objection, he took the second glass of milk and drained it.

Rather quickly, the drug took effect and the old man's face sagged to one side, his eyes closing.

Teddy muttered something about not being late for his speech in Boston and left the room.

He knew that nothing would be easier in the morning. But at least the morning was not now.

Downstairs, Rose was impatient. She wanted Teddy to call Cardinal Cushing right away.

The Cardinal took Teddy's call immediately. He'd been expecting to hear from the family. Teddy explained his mother's desire that the Cardinal supervise all details relating to the funeral mass and burial.

The Cardinal said he'd never had any doubt that this was the role he would play. He had, in fact, already begun preparations and consultations with his staff.

The funeral mass, he said, would be in Washington, the nation's capital, because Jack had been a head of state. But the burial would be in Boston, because first, last and always Jack was and would be a Kennedy and Boston was the Kennedys' home.

Not the family cemetery plot in Brookline, the community adjacent to Boston where Jack had been born. The Cardinal explained that Brookline's narrow streets would present a logistical nightmare. The trip to the cemetery would become a traffic jam lasting for hours, causing discomfort and embarrassment for all concerned.

Besides, Jack was too big for Brookline. Yes, he'd been born there, but, as befitted an assassinated President, his grave should be somewhere more grand than a mere family plot.

The Cardinal said he'd decided that a tomb in the center of Boston Common would be most appropriate. There might be a few legal technicalities to be disposed of, but he'd deal with the mayor, with the governor, with whoever had the authority to grant approval.

Teddy said Boston Common sounded fine, but he supposed he should check back with Bobby. The Cardinal said yes, by all means tell Bobby the burial would be at Boston Common and that Cardinal Cushing himself would officiate at the funeral mass in Washington and that the Cardinal would see to it personally that Jack received the sort of funeral and burial to which he was entitled, and that both the family and the nation would remember for years to come.

From watching television downstairs, Teddy knew that Air Force One, bearing the new President, Jack's body and Jacqueline, had landed at Andrews Air Force Base shortly after 6:00 P.M. and that both Jacqueline and Bobby had accompanied the body to the hospital where the autopsy would be performed.

He remained concerned about Caroline and John-John. He didn't want to bother either Bobby or Jacqueline until the ordeal of the autopsy was behind them, but he was sufficiently concerned about the children to call the White House again, hoping to get a status report.

It turned out that the children were no longer there. Nor was anyone else who could give him useful information. Earlier, Ben Bradlee, the *Newsweek* correspondent who had been a friend of Jack's for many years, and who was well known to both Caroline and John-John, had come to the White House with his wife and with Jacqueline's mother, a social acquaintance of theirs. Their intention was to remain with the mother until Jacqueline herself returned.

The friend at whose house Caroline was supposed to spend the night had been brought back to the White House to play with her, but it was Bradlee himself, lying on the floor next to John-John, who kept the boy amused by telling him fictitious adventure stories that starred a three-year-old boy named John.

All the while, Bradlee would later recall, they were awaiting with a mixture of dread and anticipation the return of Air Force One, bearing Jack's body and Jacqueline, from Dallas.

It was evident that despite Caroline's words to the Secret Service agent earlier in the afternoon, neither of the children had any real idea of what had happened.

"I haven't the heart to tell them," their nanny, Maude Shaw, kept whispering. "I can't do it." As terrible as the moment would be, all who occupied the family quarters were yearning for the return of Jacqueline, so she herself could tell her children the news and the rest of them could abandon their painful charade.

Suddenly, from outside came the familiar noise of a helicopter preparing to land on the lawn behind the White House.

Both Caroline and John-John ran to the nearest window. "That's Mommy and Daddy!" they shouted. John-John turned back to Ben Bradlee. He said proudly, "Daddy's here."

Bradlee, struggling to maintain his composure, said that probably wasn't him yet but that "Daddy will be back later."

Then came the sound of a second helicopter, which again sent the children racing toward the windows. "There they are!" the two of them shouted again. "Mommy and Daddy are home."

Bradlee knew this wasn't true. He knew that not even Jacqueline could yet be returning to the White House, because Air Force One had not yet landed at Andrews. But the children's repeated squeals of delight were proving too much for him.

"I'm going to tell them," Bradlee said to his wife.

"You can't," she said. "You don't have the right."

Even as he wrestled with this decision, a third, then a fourth, then a fifth helicopter arrived. No one at the White House had ever heard anything like this onslaught of whirring rotor blades. For just a moment, the old fear swept the room: maybe there was a military coup after all.

No one upstairs in the family quarters knew what was happening. The children kept shouting "There they are!" with the arrival of each new helicopter. But the choppers were departing as well as arriving. Later, Bradlee and the others would learn that the fleet of helicopters had been dispatched to carry high-ranking members of the govern- ment—Supreme Court justices, congressional leaders, undersecretaries in the executive branch—from the White House, where they'd been told to assemble, to Andrews Air Force Base, where they would gather to await the landing of Air Force One, in a gesture of respect both to the fallen President and to his successor.

But even before the plane arrived, a call came from Secret Service headquarters. The agent who was accom- panying Jacqueline had sent a coded message from Air Force One saying that the President's widow wished her children taken to her mother's home in Georgetown be- fore anyone from the traveling party returned to the White House.

The instruction seemed odd, but it came from Clint Hill himself, Mrs. Kennedy's personal bodyguard, and so it had to be obeyed. As it turned out, Hill, not wanting to present the grieving widow with yet another decision, had taken it upon himself to transmit the instruction, feel- ing that in all probability Jacqueline would prefer her children to be in a secluded location, away from the bus- tle and tumult that were sure to engulf the White House later in the evening.

Caroline's friend was sent home, and Caroline and John-John, with overnight bags rapidly repacked, trav- eled from the White House to the home of their grand- mother, accompanied by their nanny and by several Secret Service agents.

The Bradlees, along with Teddy's sister Jean and Jacqueline's mother, left the White House for Bethesda Naval Hospital, which was the first place Jacqueline would go after leaving Air Force One, because it was where her husband's body was being taken.

She arrived, still in her blood-stained clothes, at about 7:00 P.M. Bobby was with her. Immediately, she collapsed into Ben Bradlee's arms.

A phone rang. Bobby took the call.

"They think they've found the man who did it," he reported. "He says he's a Communist."

This news seemed particularly upsetting to Jacqueline, as if it had somehow diminished the importance of Jack's death.

"Oh God," she said. "Some silly little Communist. He didn't even have the satisfaction of being killed for civil rights."

Then her mother suggested that instead of returning to the White House, Jacqueline spend the night with her in Georgetown. She added that that was where the children were.

"Why are they there?" Jacqueline asked.

Her mother explained about the coded instructions from Air Force One. Jacqueline seemed horrified. "I sent no message," she said. "They should be in their own beds. Tell Miss Shaw to bring them back and put them to bed."

But she herself did not yet feel able to speak to them or see them. Her mother reminded her that neither of the children yet knew their father was dead.

The thought of breaking this news to them was something else that Jacqueline felt she could not bear. Too much had happened, in too few hours, and too much still lay ahead.

She told her mother she could not tell them, not yet.

So this terrible chore, after having been understandably shirked by so many, finally fell, as did many other distasteful tasks connected to life in the Kennedy family, to hired help.

Jacqueline's mother called Maude Shaw and said, "Mrs. Kennedy wants you to tell them."

The nanny said she didn't think she would be able to do it.

"You must," Jacqueline's mother said coolly. "There's no one else."

"I can't. I don't have the heart," the nurse said.

"You have to," Jacqueline's mother repeated. "Mrs. Kennedy is too upset." Then she hung up.

During that first bleak Hyannis Port night, after calling his own house only to learn that Joan, unwell, had taken to her bed, unable or unwilling to speak to anyone, and that her sister, who'd flown up from Texas for the fifth-anniversary celebration, was taking care of his children, Teddy brooded mostly over the fact that it would be his grim and unavoidable task to break the news to his father in the morning.

6

Teddy got out of bed early. His mother had told him he had to go to mass. There would be reporters and photographers outside the church—respectful, of course; nonintrusive during this unprecedented moment of familial and national grief, but present nonetheless. It would be desirable for the late President's mother and brother and sister to be seen attending mass at the small white church in Hyannis Port where the late President himself had attended services.

Teddy had been twelve when Joe Junior died in the explosion of his military aircraft over the English Channel during World War II. He vividly remembered the day the family received the news and the long months of his father's silent brooding that had followed. But that day, that event, had not been even remotely as painful as this.

That had been a purely private tragedy. Outside the family and its small circle of friends and somewhat larger circle of business and political allies and enemies, Joe Junior was known to no one. Besides, his death had come at a time when families all over America were receiving those dreaded visits from clergymen and grim-faced military officers.

So Joe Junior's death, while not expected—in fact, the

air of invulnerability he'd had about him was one of his characteristics that Teddy had admired and envied most —had not been a statistical fluke.

But this: this was too much to comprehend. This was not only the most public tragedy in the life of the family, but in the history of twentieth-century America. And this time Teddy would have to be more than a silent spectator. Teddy would have to participate. He'd have to function, as would they all.

This, among many other things, was what being a Kennedy meant. That you kept moving forward, always forward, never weakening, never pausing, never looking back, never permitting a moment of self-pity to distract from the collective need to appear braver, nobler, more heroic than any other family in the world.

He knew there would be enormous outpourings of sympathy and grief, but, as yet, Teddy could not even begin to comprehend how vast and powerful and long-lasting these would be. He was aware, however, that along with the sympathy would go scrutiny. The family's demeanor would be examined for hours on end, for days, by the psychological and emotional X-ray machine that modern television had become.

God forbid if in these moments of supreme stress any of them should be found wanting, should be considered not to have measured up. The nation might understand, might forgive, but the family would not. Thus, in addition to all else that Jack's assassination was, it became, for Teddy, the occasion of the greatest test of his life to date.

The first challenge was not long in coming. Teddy and Eunice went to the eight o'clock mass, joining their mother, who had already attended the mass held at 7:00 A.M. Outside the church, photographers stood back at a respectful distance, some even with heads bowed, all seeming reluctant, for the first time in Teddy's memory, to take a picture of a Kennedy.

But when he got back to the house, he was told his father was already awake, restless, ornery and suspicious. Teddy knew he would have to climb the stairs to the old man's bedroom and tell him that Jack had been killed.

Teddy told everyone to get out of the dining room, to leave him alone. He wanted to have breakfast by himself. Not with his mother, not with Eunice, who was sometimes even harder for him to cope with than was his mother—not even, on this particular morning, with Joey Gargan.

The neurosurgeon from Boston had arrived. His name was Russell Boles, and soon after the December 1961 stroke, he'd taken over supervision of the medical aspects of the old man's case.

Early on, at the insistence of Rose, the family had given up on any true form of rehabilitation. With more effort, with more encouragement, the old man might well have been able to walk more, to learn to speak in a manner that would permit others to understand him, even possibly to learn to write again.

But the truth was—while most of the family considered the stroke to have been a disaster of the first magnitude —Rose had seemed almost relieved to see her husband rendered largely helpless.

As has been reported by his private nurse, Rita Dallas, Rose had been particularly insistent that he not be forced to do any more physical or speech therapy than he wanted, which wasn't much. In those crucial early weeks and months after a stroke, when the greatest rehabilitative strides are possible, Rose had done all in her power to discourage any sustained effort in that direction.

She seemed almost happy to have him helpless in his wheelchair, gazing silently out the window, watching her climb into the backseat of the limousine to be taken out for a round of golf; seemed to feel something approaching delight in watching him sputter and fume as her baggage was assembled in the front hall in preparation for yet another foreign trip that she could make without him.

She'd waited many years for just such a circumstance as this—where he'd never be able to hurt her again—and many of those closest to the family believed that she was in no hurry to see it altered.

He was not entirely bedridden. He was dressed each

day and brought down by elevator to the first floor, where he was fed at the family dining table. He was able to read newspapers and watch television and understand what he was seeing. He even continued to make the occasional business trip, if he considered a particular matter to be so pressing that it required his personal intervention.

Only three weeks earlier, his father had taken a trip to Chicago. Teddy wasn't quite sure what the purpose had been, but of course the family had many business interests, many political allies in Chicago. The city of Chicago, and some of its more prominent residents, had played a large role in Jack's election in 1960. No one, it seemed, had ever sat Teddy down and explained to him the details of that particular operation. As with so many other aspects of family business—serious family business—information was doled out on a need-to-know basis and the consensus among the old man, Jack and Bobby had seemed to be that Teddy needed to know very little.

But the 1964 election was—had been—only a year away. It would not have been an irrational act on the Ambassador's part to travel to Chicago to try to personally smooth over any ruffled feelings, to make whatever preliminary arrangements might need to be made for 1964, or just to make a personal evaluation of the chemistry in Chicago, of which way the wind was blowing, and with what velocity.

He could no longer communicate, but he could receive written or oral communication. If he'd become aware that someone in Chicago might be feeling the need to tell him something personally, he was perfectly capable of traveling to Chicago to listen. Whether or not he was still able to act on the information he received was a question to which the answer was less clear.

But it no longer mattered. There would be a 1964 presidential campaign, but the Kennedys would have no personal interest in the outcome. It would be President Lyndon Johnson running for election, a man they scorned and despised. A man of whom they'd intended to rid themselves, replacing him with a new vice presidential candidate. Now he'd be sitting in Jack's office, sleeping in Jack's bedroom. Directing the affairs of a nation that was only just beginning to realize, on this chill, foggy morning, how deeply Jack, for all his detachment and cynicism, had touched its soul.

"There comes a time," social critic Norman O. Brown had written in 1961, "—I believe we are in such a time—when civilization has to be renewed by the discovery of new mysteries, by the undemocratic but sovereign power of the imagination, by the undemocratic power which makes poets the unacknowledged legislators of mankind, the power which makes all things new. The power which makes things new is magic. What our time needs is mystery: what our time needs is magic."

Jack had provided both, to a degree never before experienced in America. The mysteries would endure, and would deepen, for decades to come. But the magic had been truly transformed in that fraction of a second in Dallas the day before, when the fatal shot struck Jack's head. The magic would now exist only in the hearts and memories of the people to whom, in retrospect, in death, Jack would come to mean so much more than he had in life. The magic would be transformed into the most powerful and pervasive myth ever to grip the American imagination.

In death, Jack would become for the nation what Joe Junior, in death, had become for the family: an icon to be worshiped and revered for the rest of one's days.

As William Manchester would write, "Once a leader becomes a martyr, myth naturally follows. The Kennedy we knew in life vanished forever on November 22. . . . Legends, because they are essentially tribal, override details. What the folk hero was and what he believed are submerged by the demands of those who follow him. In myth, he becomes what they want him to have been, and anyone who belittles this transformation has an imperfect understanding of truth."

Then Manchester would quote Santayana: " 'Love is very penetrating, but penetrates to possibilities rather than to facts.' In love, nations are no less imaginative than individuals. . . . The nub of the matter was that Kennedy had met the emotional needs of his people. . . .

His oratory had electrified a country grown stale and listless.''

But now Teddy had to go upstairs and tell his father that Jack was dead.

He instructed a member of the household staff to call a television repairman. Once his father had been told, the old man would want to watch every detail on television. The doctor said there would be no harm; that in fact it would be less stressful for him to be aware of what was happening—especially to be aware of the depth and power and genuineness of the tributes to Jack's greatness that had already begun to pour forth from individuals all across America and around the world.

But the doctor also said that his own presence in the room when Teddy told his father—the sudden appearance of the neurologist at a time when he was not scheduled to make a regular examination—would needlessly frighten the old man. The doctor said he'd wait outside, in the hall, and would participate only if there seemed to be a medical emergency.

Teddy, however, could not bear to do this alone. Nor would he be permitted to. Rose wanted no part of it. She'd been told, she had borne the shock, she'd maintained her dignity, her composure, her religious faith. How her stricken husband handled it was up to him. Whatever happened, they'd manufacture a suitable story for public consumption. Something that would serve to enhance the myth.

It was Eunice who insisted on being with Teddy when he told his father. Eunice, so driven, so tense, was as openly frantic now as Teddy, on the surface, was controlled.

And she made it clear she didn't trust Teddy to do this right. He'd blundered so badly and so often before. Within the family, he was still so hard to take seriously. And this was one of the most significant moments in family history—too important to be left to Teddy alone.

So Eunice would go upstairs with him. The nurse, Rita Dallas, would be there too. Teddy told the nurse to bring the morning papers with her, because once he'd given his father the bare facts of the tragic story, it would be easier to let the old man read the details in the newspapers—with Rita Dallas turning the pages for him—while waiting for the television repairman to arrive.

It was 10:00 A.M. when they entered Joe Kennedy's room. Teddy could see at once that his father was highly suspicious. He knew. He knew. Nobody had told him, but he knew. He could see it on their faces, he could smell it in the air. And if he were to search the deepest recesses of his badly damaged brain to try to imagine the worst tragedy that could befall him and the family at this moment, he would come directly to the truth: that Jack, his oldest living son, the President, had died.

He might have thought it was an airplane crash. That was, after all, how two of his other children had died. And he knew that Jack had been flying to Dallas. But Teddy would have to tell him it had not been an airplane crash. Teddy would have to tell him that Jack had been murdered.

They gathered at the foot of the bed. Outside, the gray November fog had not yet begun to lift. The old man's eyes darted rapidly from one of them to the other. The nurse was holding the newspapers behind her back.

Teddy found it hard to speak. It had never been easy for him to talk to his father. It was as if whatever he'd say would not be good enough. Teddy had been afraid of disappointing his father all his life—had always known that nothing he could do would ever satisfy the old man's expectations of him; that never, in his father's eyes, would he be the equal of his brothers.

He stood silently, searching for the right words with which to begin. Eunice, her eyes filled with tears, her face rigid, glared at him.

Still, Teddy was unable to speak. At this moment of supreme importance, at this moment at which his true Kennedy-ness was being tested as never before, Teddy seemed unequal to the task.

He wanted to speak. He was going to speak. He just needed one more moment to think of how to begin. And so he stood at the foot of the bed, as mute as his father, his hands clasped behind his back, unable even to look the old man in the eye.

Finally, Eunice could take it no more. She threw herself on the bed and began to shout: "Daddy! Daddy, there's been an accident! But Jack's okay. Jack was in an accident, Daddy." She was screaming and crying all at once, utterly incoherent and out of control, making no sense whatsoever, but her raw hysteria was clearly alarming her father more than anything else that had happened since the previous afternoon.

"Daddy! Oh, Daddy," Eunice went on. "Jack's dead! He's dead but he's in heaven. Oh God, Daddy, Jack's okay, isn't he?"

Sobbing, she slid from the bed and struggled to regain her physical and emotional balance.

There was no turning back now. Teddy saw the horror freeze his father's features. He feared that a fatal stroke was imminent. He stepped in front of Eunice, to the head of the bed, and leaned toward the old man's face.

"There has been a bad accident," he said, as calmly as he could. "The President has been hurt very badly."

No, this was still not good enough. It still sounded like a plane crash and it still sounded as if Jack might have survived.

"As a matter of fact," Teddy said, "he died."

Then he stepped back from the bedside and motioned to the nurse to bring the newspapers forward. Better to let the old man read it for himself. Better to get the television fixed as quickly as possible. Better to get out of that room, out of that house, out of Hyannis Port. No matter what he would have to face in the hours, days and weeks to come, it could not be worse than this.

As Eunice continued to wail, the nurse placed the newspapers on the tray that lay across the old man's bed. The front pages said it more boldly and plainly than either Teddy or Eunice had been able to.

Tears flowed freely down the old man's face. He gazed at the ceiling. His expression, which, since the stroke had paralyzed his facial muscles, had always been slightly unnatural, was now a grotesque mask of agony.

Teddy left the bedroom and summoned the doctor.

From this point forward, the doctor would be in charge. Teddy felt he had to leave as soon as possible. Whatever he would have to face in Washington, however public a role he'd have to play for the sake of the dynasty, for the sake of the family image, for the sake of the myth, it could not be more agonizing than this: to be trapped inside the Hyannis Port house with his mother and father and Eunice, surrounded by lowering, darkening clouds and thick November fog, cut off from the outside world, from life itself.

When he went downstairs to tell his mother that his father now knew, and that he had survived, he found that she was not there. Once again, she'd gone out for a solitary walk.

Teddy was desperate to get back to Washington, but he knew he could not leave without first consulting Bobby. He could do nothing now without first consulting Bobby.

Bobby had taken over. Bobby was now the ruler of the clan. At the instant of Jack's death, Bobby had inherited the cumulative power that had flowed from the father and had been amplified and expanded by the achievements, real and imagined, of the two older sons, now both martyrs to family ambition and to the cause of freedom around the world.

It was Bobby now who must pick up the fallen standard and carry it forward, with Teddy forced to follow even more closely behind. Death had propelled Teddy from the last rank, where all had thought he'd spend his life in the comfort of relative obscurity, to a position uncomfortably close to the front.

His mother had once hoped that Teddy would discover a religious vocation and enter the priesthood, where, eventually, family influence could bring about his elevation to a rank of modest power, perhaps that of bishop.

Now, with Jack dead, he would have to devote his life to the advancement of Bobby's career, just as Bobby had done for Jack. That much was unquestioned. But after Bobby, then what? Teddy was still only thirty-one.

Grossly unqualified, he'd been pushed into the United

States Senate by his father. But what now? What would become of him now, with Jack dead, but with the most potent legend America had ever known already springing to life? What new expectations would he have to face? What even more extraordinary demands would be made upon this really rather ordinary young man whom circumstance and family pressure had placed in a position which, through his own talent and ambition, he would never have come close to attaining and to which, left to his own devices, he would not, in all probability, have even aspired?

7

HE MANAGED TO GET THROUGH TO BOBBY AT THE White House. Chaos was reigning at Hyannis Port. Their mother was plunging outdoors without a word to anyone and disappearing into the fog, talking to the ocean, talking to herself, talking to God. A repairman had fixed Dad's television set and he now knew everything that had happened, everything that was going to happen. A doctor had tried to sedate him but the old man seemed to be growing increasingly agitated. And Eunice was so brittle that the sound of the telephone ringing threatened to split her in two.

Teddy badly wanted to get out of there. He wanted to come back to Washington, to help Bobby do whatever needed to be done. He did not want to remain stranded in this big, drafty house, enshrouded in fog.

Bobby told him to calm down, get a grip on himself. Just because everyone around him was cracking up was no reason why Teddy should too. In fact, the reactions of others made it all the more important for Teddy to keep control not only over himself but over whatever situations might develop at Hyannis Port throughout the day.

He said it would not be a good idea for Teddy to return

to Washington. Things in Washington, too, were very tense, with everyone at the point of total physical exhaustion and so emotionally drained that no one seemed able to think straight.

A question had arisen about the choice of burial site. Soon enough, Bobby would be on the phone to their mother, explaining it all. For now, though, he had his hands full and would appreciate it if Teddy could grapple on his own with whatever difficulties arose in Hyannis Port.

Teddy could go for a walk with Joey Gargan, steer as clear of Eunice as possible and check in later. Besides—as if it mattered—the weather in Washington was terrible. The rain that would soon spread to the Cape had already begun to fall torrentially in the capital.

Bobby sounded exhausted, very worried, and totally preoccupied. Teddy had no wish to add to his burdens. If Bobby said stay, Teddy would stay.

But he did put in a plea for reinforcements. Especially for someone to deal with their mother. Bobby said he'd speak to Father Cavanagh. This was an old family friend who had been president of Notre Dame University. Just that morning, Father Cavanaugh had officiated at a mass in the East Room of the White House, where Jack's flag-draped coffin lay.

Bobby would dispatch him promptly to Hyannis Port to comfort Rose and their father. He wasn't the Pope, or even Cardinal Cushing, but he was sufficiently prestigious to satisfy Rose's need to feel she was getting special treatment from her church.

The other chore Teddy had to take care of was informing the Boston newspapers that the Ambassador had been told of the President's death and had accepted the news with courage and stoicism.

These were the moments in which indelible images were created. It was vital that every aspect of the family's response to the tragedy be presented in just the right light.

This was something Joey Gargan could do, as long as Joey knew exactly what to say. The impression to convey was that Teddy had bravely and steadfastly taken it upon himself to break the tragic news to his father.

If the Kennedy family had one special gift that surpassed all others, it may have been the uncanny ability to disclose just enough details of personal tragedy to inculcate in the public an ever growing sense of awe at the clan's ability to withstand and even to be strengthened by each new travail.

Every tragedy contained within itself the seed of enhanced opportunity. The secret was in knowing how to cultivate this rare and fragile life form. Each new death, if properly managed in terms of public relations, was also, for the survivors, a growth opportunity.

No one in the family could hope to match the Ambassador's skill in this department. On the other hand, the assassination of Jack was an event of such unprecedented tragic magnitude that, even with imperfect handling, legends that would endure for decades could bloom overnight. The soil was ripe. One simply had to keep the basic principles in mind: Kennedys were brave, Kennedys maintained poise and dignity, Kennedys were tough enough to endure the most violent buffetings of fate. They would behave in their grief as they'd been trained to; as Jack would have wanted them to.

"A source close to the family" disclosed to a *Boston Globe* reporter that afternoon that Joe Kennedy had taken the news of Jack's death "remarkably well," that he had displayed "tremendous courage." As had his youngest son, Teddy, who had insisted upon breaking the news to his father personally.

The *Globe* was also able to report that Rose, "the indomitable mother of the fabulous Kennedys . . . bore up with bravery."

Teddy was going so stir-crazy by midafternoon that despite the fact that a driving, bone-chilling rain had started to fall, he left his father's house and walked the nine tenths of a mile up the beach to the causeway that led to his own home.

One can imagine that Teddy might have preferred to take his walk alone, but Eunice insisted on coming with him, lecturing him every step of the way on his new responsibilities, not only during the upcoming weekend of mourning and burial, but in the weeks, months and years that lay ahead.

Among all the sisters, Eunice had for years taken the dimmest view of Teddy. She'd been the least amused by his antics, the quickest to condemn his missteps, the slowest to forgive his transgressions. He did not need her hectoring him now.

Suppose—not that there is any evidence he considered this—he suddenly just veered left, away from his sister, and plunged, fully clothed, into the roiling, frigid waters of Nantucket Bay? Just swam out into the mist until exhausted? Then floated on his back and let the cold waves carry him wherever they might, while the noise of the surf and the wind drowned out the sound of human voices.

But of course he couldn't do that. Instead, he returned to his father's house, where Bobby had told him to stay, and where his father was becoming increasingly hard to control.

While Teddy and Eunice walked on the beach, Joe Kennedy had pulled himself from his bed and had begun a pathetic attempt to dress himself. It soon became evident that he intended to go to Washington. He'd seen enough of Jack's casket on television, enough of Bobby's and Jacqueline's somber but resolute expressions. He wanted to be there, even if in a wheelchair, seated by the side of his fallen son.

It was entirely possible that despite his disabilities, Joe Kennedy, at that moment, had a clearer idea than almost anyone else in America of how unlikely it was that Jack had been assassinated by a crazed, lone, Communist gunman. The old man had been in Chicago only three weeks earlier. He knew that years earlier he'd made promises he hadn't kept. And that quite possibly, Jack had paid for these unkept promises with his life.

Struggling fiercely against the nurses who tried to restrain him, the old man made it clear he expected to be flown to Washington immediately. It was not only the casket of the dead President he had to see, it was Bobby, still alive, still unharmed, but the only person in the family except for himself who knew how deep and murky and treacherous were the waters that flowed beneath them.

The nurses asked what they should do with his father. Get him dressed, he said. Take him out for a ride. Take him to the airport. Let him see that the *Caroline,* their private plane, was not there. Let him see for himself that there was no way for him to fly to Washington. By then the physical and emotional effort should have exhausted him sufficiently to allow them to bring him back, sedate him again and get him to bed.

So in the driving rain, in the gathering darkness of late afternoon, this was done. Ann Gargan drove the old man to the airport and he sat in the back of the car, watching helplessly the takeoffs and landings of commercial planes he knew he could not fly in because of his physical condition.

Eventually, with a gesture no longer defiant but resigned, he signaled his niece to drive him back to the house. Father Cavanagh would be there soon. He could go back to bed. He could drink his milk and sedative. Jack was dead. It was too late. Whatever his errors of judgment, however he'd underestimated the threat his sons had faced, it was too late. Jack was dead. The damage could not be undone.

Teddy, by then, must have been desperate to return to Washington. But Bobby insisted that he remain in Hyannis Port. Bobby wanted Teddy to stay with their mother, and he most definitely did not want their mother arriving in Washington that night.

Enough was already going on in Washington. There was enough acrimony, enough nerves rubbed raw, enough people insisting that they knew better than anyone just the way everything connected with the funeral and burial should be done.

Above all, there was Jacqueline, in dire emotional straits but totally preoccupied with ceremonial details.

She had become obsessed with the idea that the funeral and burial of the husband with whom she'd shared so little intimacy in life should leave an indelible mark upon the collective emotional life of the country. And that her taste and sense of what was fitting should determine the shape, the size and the precise detail of even the smallest filigree.

The assassination of Jack had given her the chance to put her own stamp on American history, and if she insisted on taking full advantage of the opportunity, who was to begrudge her the right?

She wanted a ritual that would make the nation realize that Jack's assassination was every bit as profound a tragedy as the murder of Abraham Lincoln. That was the historic company Jacqueline wanted Jack to be in: not William McKinley, not James Garfield. Abraham Lincoln.

No one in the White House disagreed, but still there were high tensions. Chief among the subjects of dispute was the choice of grave site.

It had never occurred to Jack's Boston-based aides such as Kenny O'Donnell and Larry O'Brien that the President would be buried anywhere but in Massachusetts. They thought Cardinal Cushing had overstated the logistical difficulties of Brookline, and that a burial in Boston Common might seem ostentatious, but even as that question remained under discussion they'd proceeded with plans to have Jack's body shipped—by either rail, air or water—from Washington to Boston.

In a phone call from Hyannis Port, Eunice reported that the family enthusiastically endorsed the idea. "We're all going to be buried around Daddy in Boston," she said. When Bobby, in Washington, agreed, the issue seemed settled.

But no one had consulted Jacqueline. And she was insistent that the burial would be in Arlington National Cemetery. Jack belonged to the nation, to history now, and it would be grossly inappropriate to inter his body in the parochial environs of a family plot in Brookline, or even in the Boston Common.

It was not a matter for discussion, Jacqueline said. The

burial would be at Arlington. The only question was the choice of a site within the federal military cemetery and she'd had Secretary of Defense Robert McNamara over there for hours, looking at possible locations. Forget the plan to transport the President's body from Washington to Boston aboard a crepe-draped naval destroyer. It would not happen. The Bostonians, the political and personal aides whom she'd always held in low regard, could simply go home before the burial if they didn't like it, taking their cigars and spittoons and long-winded, pointless tales of political skulduggery with them. Jacqueline's mind was made up.

In Hyannis Port, both Eunice and Rose were distressed. Rose had always resented what she considered her daughter-in-law's high-handedness, but this was too much. If only Joe were able to speak out. He'd set matters right within minutes.

She looked querulously across the living room at Teddy. Outside, the rain beat down against the windows and shutters of the old wooden house. Teddy could do no more than shrug. This was beyond him. He lacked seniority. Besides, he tended to agree with Jacqueline. Rose turned away in disgust.

Later, Bobby said with deliberate understatement that Jacqueline's insistence upon Arlington "made it rather difficult for me." For he had to deal with Eunice and with his mother on the telephone. But he felt strongly that Jacqueline had the right to make the choice. She had, after all, been First Lady, and he, like Teddy, was not at all convinced her choice was wrong. Jack had been President. He'd become a national figure in life and already was looming even larger in death. Why bury him as if he'd been just a Boston politician who'd gotten lucky?

With Bobby's approval, the issue of Arlington was settled once and for all, but hard feelings abounded in the wake of the decision. So strong were they that Bobby told Teddy it would be disastrous for the Hyannis Port group to come to Washington that night.

Bobby told Teddy, in fact, not to come to Washington until late Sunday afternoon for the Monday funeral.

Bobby wanted to keep Rose away from Jacqueline as long as possible. This meant that Teddy would have to miss the dramatic and emotional transfer of the President's casket from its White House resting place to the Capitol, where it would lie in state through Sunday night, but that could not be helped.

Teddy was the youngest and his role now was to remain with his mother and sister. At the moment, there was no contribution he could make in Washington and a great deal of harm that the premature arrival of Rose or Eunice might inflict.

There were those who believed that Jacqueline detested Rose with as much passion as she'd ever mustered over anything in her life. Her emotional condition was currently so fragile that the presence of an imperious mother-in-law and angry sister-in-law would be, in Bobby's judgment, more than the President's widow could stand.

8

THUS, LIKE ALMOST EVERYONE ELSE IN AMERICA—
and, indeed, in much of the world—Teddy spent most of
Sunday watching television. But it is unlikely that anyone, anywhere, felt more alone, more forsaken, more
dejected and forlorn than did Teddy throughout that unforgettable day.

It had always been his belief that however junior and
sometimes unsatisfactory a member, he was a part of the
Kennedy family. Indeed, this was central to his identity;
not only to the way he lived his life but to the way he
perceived himself.

Now this assumption was contradicted by the undeniable fact that he was in Hyannis Port, no closer to his
living brother or to his dead one than millions of other
Americans; no less dependent upon television to link
him to the dramatic and historic events occurring in
Washington than was any other anonymous citizen of the
country.

Later he would recall that he'd sat, dazed, in front of
the television set, trying insofar as it was possible to
avoid confrontation with his mother or with Eunice. In
the big bedroom above, his father lay in bed, alternately

ordering his own television set turned on and off, as if trying to decide which approach—denial or immersion—might better assuage his own silent agony.

For much of the time, through that seemingly endless Saturday night and into Sunday morning, cameras focused on the East Room of the White House—on the flag-draped coffin in which Jack's body lay. Military honor guard units kept watch over the coffin through the night, changing each thirty minutes with a terrible and silent precision, the faces of the young men so entirely devoid of expression that one imagined how intense must be the hurt each felt internally.

Occasionally, the television coverage would switch from the chilling silence of the White House vigil to actions abroad. Long before Sunday morning came to Hyannis Port, it spread across the European continent and to England, the country which still evoked in Teddy such powerful childhood memories.

He watched in silence as the cameras showed the choir of Westminster Abbey singing "The Battle Hymn of the Republic." He still had clear recollections of Westminster Abbey from the days when his father had been Ambassador, and he and Bobby had lived and played together at the six-story residence at Princes Gate. Having recovered his health temporarily, Jack had come over for the summer that first year, before returning to Harvard. England had made a lasting impression upon him, too.

As a minister delivered a eulogy, the camera showed pew after pew packed with British men and women—aristocrats and commoners alike—weeping unashamedly and uncontrollably.

And, in Hyannis Port, in front of the television set, Teddy wept too.

At some point on Sunday morning, he became aware of two things: the weather was clearing and his father had made it through the night.

He also learned that his wife was in very bad shape. He'd not paid much attention to her Saturday, which was not unusual. He'd not paid much attention to her throughout their married life. In marrying her, he'd done only what had seemed the right thing at the time.

Unlike Jacqueline, however, and unlike Ethel and his mother and his sisters, Joan was not tough. Assisted—supported, really—by her sister, Joan had dragged herself to the White House Saturday morning for the private mass for family and close staff said by Father Cavanagh. But then she had utterly collapsed.

Joan had been taken back to Georgetown and put to bed. And there she'd stayed, throughout the day Saturday and through the night, while her sister took care of the children. Overwhelmed by the horror, terrified by the violence and the possibility that more might spring forth at any moment, cut off from almost any contact with her husband, Joan had simply crumpled.

Under any circumstances, the stresses of life among the Kennedys were more than ordinary people could tolerate. And Joan was, above all, an ordinary person. She was more physically attractive than most women and had some aptitude for playing the piano, but mentally and emotionally she was in no way exceptional, and—being extremely fragile psychologically—in no way suited for the strain of being a Kennedy wife.

And that was under ordinary circumstances. It was no wonder she could not cope with a presidential assassination. Millions of citizens, who'd never met Jack, who'd never seen him except on television, who might not even have voted for him in 1960 or have voted for him in 1964, felt as if they'd suffered a sudden death in their immediate family.

For Joan, it was infinitely worse. It was simply more than she could bear, so she did not bear it. As William Manchester has delicately phrased it, "Senator Kennedy's wife was the only Kennedy mother who spent Saturday at home, and she was unable to see anyone."

But this was Sunday now and Teddy would be flying down with Eunice and Rose and Joey Gargan. The funeral and burial would take place the next day. Joan would simply have to pull herself together. Afterwards—for years afterwards—there would be plenty of time for all of them to collapse. But they owed it to Jack—to his memory, to his myth—to conduct themselves in the manner he would have expected, at least until his coffin was lowered into the ground.

Rose went to the seven o'clock mass and stayed for the eight o'clock, too. Teddy and Eunice joined her for the eight.

Bobby called to say, "Jackie's had another bad night." For the first time, it may have occurred to Teddy that Washington could be worse, not better, than Hyannis Port.

He spent the rest of the morning watching television. Sitting alone in Hyannis Port, the sun now shining, the waves of Nantucket Bay a brilliant blue, he watched as the networks cut back and forth from the White House to the Capitol. Preparations were being completed for the afternoon procession up Pennsylvania Avenue that would carry Jack's casket on a horse-drawn caisson from the White House, which he would never occupy again, to the rotunda of the Capitol, where, after eulogies were delivered by Chief Justice Earl Warren, Senate majority leader Mike Mansfield, and Speaker of the House John McCormack, the body would lie in state.

Then the networks cut to Dallas. Teddy again saw the shriveled, scruffy little Oswald—the assassin—the man who'd shot and killed his brother for reasons that remained, to Teddy, thoroughly obscure.

Oswald was being transferred from one jail to another. He came forward, into the view of the television cameramen, surrounded by Dallas policemen and looking like some sort of failed hillbilly singer who'd spent the night in a drunk tank. It seemed incomprehensible that all by himself, acting on psychotic whim, this man could have put an end to one of the most glorious careers in American political history.

Then there was a commotion on the screen. There was a pop. There was screaming. Teddy couldn't see Oswald anymore. He had a brief glimpse of a fat man wearing a suit and a fedora hat. The fat man was being wrestled to the ground by police. Everyone seemed to be screaming all at once, including the television announcer.

Oswald had been shot! Someone—the fat man in the fedora—had walked right up to the President's assassin in the middle of Dallas police headquarters and had shot him squarely in the stomach.

Teddy jumped from his chair and ran to the bottom of the stairwell. Eunice was upstairs with his father. He didn't know if that TV set was on or off. He didn't know if his father should be seeing this or not. He could scarcely believe he had seen it himself.

"They shot him!" Teddy yelled up the stairs. "They shot Oswald! I think they killed him!"

Then he hurried back to the television. An announcer said Oswald, badly hurt, had been rushed by ambulance to Parkland Hospital, the same one to which Jack had been taken two days earlier.

In Washington, a solemn announcer was saying in a hushed voice that Jacqueline and Robert Kennedy had just entered the East Room of the White House, where, one last time, for just the two of them, the President's coffin would be opened, permitting a final farewell.

This was more than Teddy could bear. Chained to a television set in Hyannis Port while Jackie and Bobby were saying good-bye. Jacqueline placed a letter she'd written the night before inside the coffin. No copy was kept. No one would ever know what her last words to her dead husband had been. The letter would be buried with the body, would lie forever beneath the soil of Arlington.

Bobby gazed briefly at the face of his brother in death. He removed his *PT 109* tie clip. Earlier, he'd cut a lock of his own hair. Now he placed both these objects in the coffin. Then he put his arm around Jacqueline. After a moment of silent prayer, he helped her stand. They turned and left the East Room. The lid of the coffin was closed.

This was not shown on television. Teddy only learned

later of the details of their final viewing of his brother. But the details scarcely mattered. What did matter to Teddy was that they were there and he was here, cut off from the center, out on the fringe, as he had been his whole life.

A quick bulletin from Dallas announced that emergency surgery was being performed on Lee Harvey Oswald.

Teddy gazed silently, disbelievingly, at the screen. The networks were back in Washington now, at the White House. The doors swung open. Jack's casket was carried slowly, almost clumsily, down the steps to the waiting caisson.

Jacqueline, in black dress and veil, followed closely, with Bobby next to her. Then Teddy saw Caroline and John-John come out the door, into the bright midday sun, and start slowly, haltingly, down the steps, each of them taking one of their mother's hands, following the body of their father.

Behind Jacqueline and her children, behind Bobby, whose face so clearly revealed the intensity of his suffering, Jack's closest aides and oldest friends formed ranks. They were all there: O'Donnell, O'Brien, Sorensen, Bundy, Salinger, Powers, Jack's old navy friend Red Fay, Torbert Macdonald, with whom Jack had spent the last weekend of his life.

Everyone was there. Except Teddy, who watched helplessly on television.

And then the terrible, magnificent and unforgettable march began. First, there came the sound of muffled drums. "The broken roll," Manchester has aptly called it. "The dreadful stutter."

It was a sound never to be forgotten by anyone who heard it that day. Years later, recurring in dreams, the sound would awaken powerful men from deep sleep.

But Teddy heard it only on television. As he saw, only on television, the caisson on which Jack's body lay, followed by the nervously prancing riderless horse. And then the ten limousines, filled with members of the Kennedy family. Everyone was there, it seemed, except Teddy.

His exclusion, deemed necessary by Bobby, was not something about which he would ever complain—except maybe, on occasion, late at night, to Joey Gargan, after they'd both had a lot to drink—but being on the outside looking in, at this grandest and most awful moment in family and national history, added a sharp stab of pain to the ache of grief that had been threatening, for almost forty-eight hours, to bring him to his knees and keep him there.

The leaves were off the trees in Washington, the branches bare. The sky was as blue as the waves in Nantucket Bay. The air was cold. Not the bitter cold of Inauguration Day in 1961, but cold.

Eighteen blocks of Pennsylvania Avenue separated the White House from the Capitol. Jack had made the trip to make his first State of the Union address. He'd made it again only weeks later to deliver an unprecedented second State of the Union. And, of course, to deliver similar addresses to Congress in 1962 and 1963.

One of the proudest moments of Teddy's life had come in January when he stood in the Senate chamber with his ninety-nine new colleagues and the more than four hundred members of the House, to applaud the entrance of the President.

Now Jack was making his final trip to the Capitol. There would be no applause, only tears.

The procession lasted for thirty-nine minutes. The caisson reached the east steps of the Capitol. There it paused. All was silent momentarily. Then Teddy heard the firing of the first shot of the twenty-one-gun salute.

The shots were to be fired at five-second intervals. Before the second, the navy band began to play. Throughout the salute, the navy band played "Hail to the Chief." It was the only song Jack really liked, Jacqueline had

76

once said, mocking his cultural limitations. Well, it was a song poor Jack would never hear again.

The wind rose and bare branches swayed as the casket was carried slowly up the Capitol steps.

Just as slowly, the casket was wheeled inside the rotunda as Jacqueline, Caroline and John-John, followed by Bobby, walked behind.

Inside, Mansfield, Warren and McCormack delivered their brief eulogies. It was Mansfield who brought fresh tears to the eyes of many.

He'd written his comments himself, in pencil, and had rewritten the last paragraph a dozen times through the darkness of the long night before.

"There was a father," he said, "with a little boy and a little girl, and the joy of each in the other. And, in a moment, it was no more." He paused.

Closing with a recitation of the unique gifts and talents Jack had brought to the Presidency, Mansfield asked rhetorically, "Will we have now the sense and responsibility to take them?" He paused again.

"I pray to God," he said, his voice now faltering, "that we shall. And, under God, we will!"

Then Teddy watched as Lyndon Johnson—President Lyndon Johnson: good God, it still did not seem possible —stepped to the casket to lay a floral wreath.

The ceremony inside the rotunda had lasted only fourteen minutes. Somehow, it seemed incomplete.

"Can I say good-bye?" Jacqueline whispered to Bobby as Teddy watched on television.

Bobby nodded.

So Jacqueline took Caroline by the hand and said, "We're going to go say good-bye to Daddy, and we're going to kiss him good-bye and tell him how much we love him and how much we'll always miss him."

The two of them, mother and daughter, stepped forward together and knelt at the side of the casket.

Caroline looked at her mother, wondering what she should do.

"You know," Jacqueline said softly. "You just kiss."

And the two of them bent forward to gently brush their lips against the flag. In that same moment, five-year-old

Caroline reached beneath the flag with one hand, and, apparently in one last attempt to get as close to her father as she ever would again, touched the wood of the casket inside which his body lay.

As Teddy, and millions of others, watched on television.

9

FINALLY, LATE THAT AFTERNOON, TEDDY WAS PERMITted to return to Washington. Within forty-eight hours, his brother had gone from being President of the United States to being the contents of a long wooden box draped with an American flag, and Teddy hadn't yet been able to see the box.

But now the moment had come. The funeral would be the next morning. They could no longer keep Rose away. Bobby had called after returning to the White House from the ceremony at the Capitol. Each time Teddy spoke to him, his brother seemed to have aged another five years.

Teddy would have to tread softly, Bobby said. The atmosphere remained very tense. Jacqueline, so obsessed with ceremonial detail, was coming up with a new idea every hour, and brooking no disagreement about any of them.

She had, for example, decided that there should be an eternal flame burning at Jack's grave.

That had been a bad moment, Bobby said. When she first mentioned the eternal flame, everyone in the room had been stunned. Later, Jacqueline herself would recall them as looking "horrified."

Sargent Shriver, head of the Peace Corps and husband

of Teddy's sister Eunice, had stammered something about there already being one at the Tomb of the Unknown Soldier in Arlington, in which case it would seem improper, not to mention grandiose, to have another installed.

But he hadn't been absolutely sure about the Unknown Soldier. He'd said he would have to find out.

"I don't care if there is one," Jacqueline had said. "We're going to have it anyway."

With each passing hour, this frail young widow for whom America was shedding so many tears was acting increasingly like a reigning monarch. She'd wanted Arlington, she got Arlington. She'd wanted a horse-drawn caisson accompanied by a riderless horse, she'd gotten a horse-drawn caisson accompanied by a riderless horse. Now she wanted an eternal flame and there was no doubt that—even if they had to snuff out the one at the Tomb of the Unknown Soldier, or steal it—she would get her eternal flame.

Shriver said, "I want to be sure you're not subjecting yourself to criticism. Some people might think it's a little ostentatious."

"Let them," Jacqueline said.

Shriver quickly ascertained, to his relief, that there was no eternal flame at the Tomb of the Unknown Soldier—that, in fact, the only two eternal flames in the world burned in France and at the site where Abraham Lincoln had delivered the Gettysburg Address.

That made the flame even more of an imperative for Jacqueline. If Lincoln had a flame, Jack would have one too. A hundred years had been required to idealize and mythologize Abraham Lincoln. Jacqueline seemed determined to achieve equal status for Jack within three days.

In every detail, his funeral was to be patterned after Lincoln's. If Lincoln had it, she would not permit Jack to go without it. It was a shame, in a way. If Jack could only have lived to see how Jacqueline was fighting to glorify him and to immortalize him, he might have learned to love her, after all.

* * *

Teddy and his mother and sister and Joey Gargan left Hyannis Port, telling the Ambassador he could watch them on television the next day and that they'd be back in a few days for Thanksgiving.

The old man seemed beyond knowing, beyond caring. How much guilt was buried in his grief—how aware he was of the extent to which he'd been responsible for Jack's fate—no one would ever know.

At 4:20 P.M., as darkness began to fall, Teddy, Rose and Eunice, and Joey Gargan boarded a private plane at Otis Air Force Base for the flight to Washington.

A small contingent of press, expecting this departure, had gathered at the air base. Teddy noticed the same deference, the same respect, the same sense that their very presence was an inexcusable invasion of the family's privacy that the press had shown when he'd arrived Friday night.

But so much had happened in these two days that this time Teddy felt it necessary to make a statement.

So, just before climbing the steps to board the aircraft, he turned to say, "On behalf of my family I want to express appreciation for the outpouring of thoughtfulness and prayers that have come from the American people. This has been a source of tremendous consolation to both my parents and they wanted me to express their great thanks to all of the people who have been so kind in remembering them now."

For the first time in memory, as he finished these brief remarks, Teddy saw newspaper photographers crying.

Upon arriving in Washington, they went directly to the White House. Teddy needed so badly to contribute. He needed so badly to feel that he belonged. But by the time he arrived, all the decisions had been made.

Jacqueline had thought it would be appropriate for Bobby and Teddy to conclude the burial service by reciting quotations from Jack's speeches, at the grave. It would be the last event of the majestic and heartbreaking public spectacle. The words—just like the words to be spoken at the funeral mass—would have to be precisely right.

Ted Sorensen and McGeorge Bundy had been given the task of combing through Jack's speeches—almost all of which had been written by Sorensen anyway—to find the most suitable excerpts.

Then Jacqueline learned that at Lincoln's funeral there had also been readings from Scripture, so she set them to work riffling through pages of the Bible, looking for whatever phrases might equal those spoken over the casket of Lincoln.

By the end, the whole thing became almost grotesque. It was determined that at the grave site Teddy would read three passages from Jack's speeches, while Bobby would read four. Teddy would go first, Bobby last. And Bobby's excerpts were intended to be the ones people would remember. That was only just and proper. He was, after all, the oldest surviving brother and the one to whom the dynastic torch would next be passed.

Jacqueline instructed Sorensen and Bundy to prepare what she called a "ballot," listing all possible selections. Then everyone got to vote for his or her favorite. But of course it was not a true democracy. Jacqueline alone would make the final choice.

As feared, Rose's arrival at the White House increased the level of tension. It was Shriver's task to keep the dead President's mother away from the dead President's widow who so despised her.

But all her life Rose had struggled to be the center of attention. She was not about to give up now. If there was an inappropriate remark to make, she would make it.

"Think of Jackie," she announced to a roomful of family members at a moment when Jacqueline was not present. "She's so young and now she doesn't even have a home!"

Teddy, accompanied by Joey Gargan, removed himself from his mother's presence as soon as he could. He wandered into a meeting where the eternal flame was still being discussed. Logistical problems had presented themselves and the military, in charge of physical details at Arlington, had suggested that the problems might prove insoluble.

Bobby had turned Dick Goodwin loose on them. One of the youngest, brightest and most abrasive of Jack's aides, Goodwin was well equipped to cut quickly and mercilessly through layers of bureaucracy.

He'd already solved the problem and now he was regaling a group of other aides with his story.

An army officer had told him they could not install an eternal flame at Arlington because they didn't know how and because "Europe is the only place they know about them."

"Then fly to Europe," Goodwin said. "It's only six hours. But be back here by tomorrow with a goddamned flame."

Then a military official had asked him just what Mrs. Kennedy meant by "eternal." He said perhaps it could be arranged to have a kerosene pot burn for a few hours, covering the period before, during and after the burial service.

"Eternal," Goodwin had said, "means forever!"

The final objection raised was that some sort of liquid gas or propane would have to be used as fuel and that it might prove too dangerous. Also, it could prove inordinately difficult to light, which would surely be an embarrassment to Mrs. Kennedy, since it was understood that she intended to light it herself.

"Listen," Goodwin said, almost biting his cigar in half. "If you guys can design an atomic bomb, you can put a little flame on the side of a hill and you can make it so Mrs. Kennedy can light it."

Dinner was served at the White House. Joan was still a wreck, still not participating. Forever after, her failure to be a true Kennedy in these days of crisis and tragedy would be considered, even by Teddy, an almost unforgivable sin.

It was obvious that Rose could not dine at the same table, or even in the same room, as Jacqueline. But she also could not be made to dine alone. Teddy had already done his hard time: now it was somebody else's turn. Eventually, Prince Radziwill, husband of Jacqueline's sister, Lee, was assigned the task. He trudged gamely upstairs.

Jacqueline, Bobby and Lee Radziwill ate together in a sitting room. Teddy was not invited to join them. Instead, he ate in the main dining room with a much larger group of in-laws and cousins and a somewhat astonishing variety of guests, including—to many raised eyebrows—the Greek shipping billionaire Aristotle Onassis, on whose yacht Jacqueline had greatly enjoyed herself the previous month during a cruise of the Aegean Sea.

After dinner, fortified by drink and by the presence of Joey Gargan, Teddy knew the time had come for him to visit the Capitol, where Jack's body lay in state.

Throughout the evening, others had gone. Jacqueline and Bobby together, leaving Teddy behind; later, Rose with a larger group; but still not Teddy.

It began to seem to some that even though he knew he had to make this final pilgrimage, he didn't want to. He was the only one among them, it was recalled, who had not yet seen the casket. The only one whose most recent moment in Jack's presence had been at a time when Jack was still alive.

Not until midnight could Teddy, accompanied by Gargan, bring himself to go.

As they approached the Capitol, the dome of which was being kept aglow throughout the night, Teddy was amazed by what he saw. It was cold out, down in the thirties, yet thousands, tens of thousands, hundreds of thousands of American citizens were lined up, five abreast, willing to wait for hours through the frosty night for a chance to say a final, personal farewell to Jack.

For the first time, Teddy began to sense the magnitude to which the myth had grown. He was told that the original plan had been to keep the rotunda open until 9:00 P.M. to permit private citizens to walk silently past the slain President's bier.

But Bobby had quickly seen that the outpouring of grief and the need to express it made that plan unrealistic. By 9:00 P.M., when Bobby had intended that the public viewing would end, there were—by police estimates—a quarter of a million people still in line.

"Veneration is the only explanation for their endurance," Manchester has written. "They knew how brief their time inside would be. They would be permitted a few moments to circle the coffin, to kneel quickly, and to leave flowers with two soldiers; that was all. Yet they would not turn back. By midnight a hundred thousand had passed through and the line behind them was three miles long."

Midnight was when Teddy arrived, driven in a black Mercury sedan. He and Gargan were led to a private elevator. They entered the rotunda from the south. Teddy's presence was immediately noted by the crowd, those finally in from the cold and lined up silently, awaiting their turn to pay their last respects.

The moment he was observed, the line stopped. Ordinary citizens stepped aside to let Teddy and Joey Gargan pass. A soldier unhooked the velvet rope behind which the casket lay, permitting them to kneel at its side.

For Teddy, after two gloomy, isolated days in Hyannis Port, the contrast, as well as the sudden new welling of grief that proximity to the casket brought, proved almost too much.

Joey Gargan was afraid for a moment that Teddy might collapse; that with so many eyes trained upon him, he might fall sobbing to the floor and not be able to get up.

But Teddy fought back the waves of feeling. This was so very, very different from watching a procession on television. This was so very, very final, so very, very real.

He did not stay long. He could not. He got up and turned, and, with Joey Gargan holding his arm, walked back through the silent crowd, his head bowed, tears filling his eyes.

After he departed, the line re-formed, the slow stream of mourners began to flow again. It would continue throughout that still and chilly night until 8:30 Monday morning, when finally the doors had to be closed in order to ready the casket for its journey to the cathedral for the funeral mass.

Teddy would never be able to articulate which had moved and shocked him more: the suddenness of being there, so close to Jack, yet knowing, in a way he had not known from television, that he would forever after be impossibly far away; or the astonishing spectacle of those hundreds of thousands, lined up for miles in the cold.

But it must have occurred to him, even in the midst of his grief and fatigue, that the role of being the youngest brother of the martyred and venerated ex-President might carry with it more complexity and more burdens, if fewer rewards, than had the role of being the Congressman's or the Senator's or the candidate's or the President's kid brother, or of having been known primarily as the Ambassador's youngest son.

Teddy was confident that he would make it through the night and the following day. But he was less sure about the weeks, months and years that would follow. Neither he nor his parents nor his brothers had ever anticipated that he would be expected to acquire a mythic dimension of his own.

Nor could he—or they—foresee how high a price he would pay for the dubious privilege of being forced to pretend that he was someone he was not.

10

ONE OF JOEY GARGAN'S JOBS HAD BEEN TO MAKE SURE that Teddy had the right clothes for the funeral.

But Joey had messed up. He hadn't checked. He'd taken for granted something he should not have: that the set of formal wear he'd acquired for Teddy was complete.

Now, at 9:30 A.M., on as crisp and clear a morning as Washington could offer in the autumn, Teddy stood in an upstairs bedroom of the White House, in his underwear.

He was using language that even Joey had seldom heard him use before. At exactly 10:00 A.M., the entire Kennedy family was to leave the White House and ride to the Capitol in a caravan of limousines for the first public event of the day of Jack's burial. This funeral would involve hundreds of cars, and world leaders from every continent, including Charles de Gaulle, Prince Philip of England, and Haile Selassie, the emperor of Ethiopia.

On this most somber morning the family would ever have to face, the most solemn morning the nation had experienced in this century, on a day when the mourners who would line the six-mile route from the White House to St. Matthew's Cathedral and then to Arlington National Cemetery would number more than one million—

a crowd unprecedented in the history of the nation's capital—Teddy didn't have a pair of pants.

He didn't have the hat or gloves either.

Why hadn't Joey checked? Why hadn't Joey paid attention?

Across the whole world, tens, even hundreds of millions of people would be staring at their television screens, having been told that the Kennedy family would be leaving the White House for the melancholy ride up Pennsylvania Avenue to claim the casket of their fallen leader, and nothing would happen.

No one would appear. The doors to the White House would stay closed. Everyone in the world would wonder why. And the answer would be because Teddy didn't have a pair of pants.

He looked ridiculous in his dress shirt and tie, with his socks pulled up high on his bulky calves and the long coat of his rented morning suit—rented by stupid Joey Gargan!—hanging down below his boxer shorts.

And he felt even worse. If it weren't so awful, it would almost be funny. But on this day nothing was funny.

Finally, Bobby summoned Jack's valet. Jack had a pair of formal pants. They were pressed and hanging in his closet. They were, in fact, the pants Jack had worn on the day of his inauguration.

But Teddy's waistline, even then, was considerably larger than Jack's. Unless the pants were altered radically, there was no way Teddy could wear them.

The valet appeared instantly. He measured Teddy's waist. He disappeared. Within minutes—remarkably few minutes considering the circumstances—he reappeared bearing Jack's inaugural pants, the waist newly and considerably enlarged.

He also had a pair of Jack's gloves into which Teddy was able to squeeze his hands.

But Teddy's large head was far too big for Jack's top hat. There was no way to get it on his head.

Struggling into the pants that his slain brother had worn on the day he became President of the United States—as the minute hand of the large clock on the wall moved toward its highest point—Teddy continued to curse at Joey Gargan.

Screw it, Bobby said. Screw the hat. Someone protested that protocol required top hats. Someone else said the word had already gone forth to the entire diplomatic corps and to the leaders of dozens of nations around the world, all of whom had come to Washington for the funeral: top hats were de rigueur.

Do you want Teddy to be the only person in the parade without a hat? Bobby barked. Christ, Teddy had almost had to ride up Pennsylvania Avenue in his underwear! Screw the hats.

And Bobby picked up the top hat he had intended to wear and threw it angrily into a corner of the room.

And so, ten minutes later, as the bareheaded Kennedy brothers left the White House, with Teddy walking stiffly down the steps, no doubt praying that Jack's pants would not rip, diplomats, heads of state, cabinet members, congressional leaders, other dignitaries and honored friends frantically stuffed top hats on the floors of limousines or handed them to aides, as if the very idea of wearing a top hat to the funeral of the American President had been a preposterous one.

On the ride up Pennsylvania Avenue, Bobby made a change in plans. Instead of waiting in the limousine for the casket to be carried down the Capitol steps by the honor guard, he decided that he and Jacqueline, and this time Teddy, too, should have a last private moment inside.

Not Rose. Not the sisters. Just the three of them. Bobby and Jacqueline and Teddy. In total privacy—no photographers, no television cameras—they would say their final good-byes. All else would be for the nation, for the world, for history. This last visit to Jack's coffin was just for them.

Flanking Jacqueline, the brothers climbed the marble steps to the East Rotunda at 10:40 on the bright, chilly morning. Inside, the three knelt in silence at the coffin for ten minutes, their bowed heads resting softly against the flag. Then, wordlessly, they rose, turned and made their exit.

As the caisson rumbled back down Pennsylvania Avenue toward the White House, they rode in silence.

They left their limousines at the curving gravel driveway. From the White House to the cathedral, they would walk. Inside his formal jacket, Teddy carried the piece of paper with the words of Jack's he would recite at the grave; the words Sorensen and Bundy had chosen for him the day before.

He'd read them over. They were fine. They were not as fine as Bobby's but they were perfectly acceptable. He only hoped he'd be able to read them without crying. It would not be good, crying in public at the end.

As bagpipes began to play, Teddy and Bobby stepped up to either side of Jacqueline. They were to be her escorts for the day. Finally freed from his Hyannis Port cell, Teddy was now a full-fledged member of the ceremonial family.

It was just the two of them now. Just him and Bobby. Joe Junior, Jack, their father, no matter how many more years he might live—they were all part of an irretrievable past. How had it so quickly, so painfully come to this?

Bobby walked on Jacqueline's right side and Teddy on her left. The pants were fine. The valet had done his job well. They would not rip. They actually felt comfortable. This was something Jack would have gotten a laugh out of—Teddy having to wear Jack's pants to Jack's own funeral. For years, Teddy would have taken a ribbing from Jack about that.

But there would be no more ribbing. No more Jack.

As on the day before, when he'd watched on television, Teddy heard the sound of muffled drums. How much darker, how much graver they sounded when one heard them in person. Television had really given Teddy no idea of how things were.

This was a sad and terrible day, but it was also the day of the greatest pageant in which Teddy had ever participated. In that sense, it was like his childhood months in London long ago, when he'd been six years old and bright with the excitement of finding everything around him new and splendid, being in the center of so much pomp and circumstance, finding so much attention lavished upon him by so many obviously important people.

That was when he'd first awakened to just a bit of what it meant to be a Kennedy. He knew more now; some good, some bad. But there was so much more he did not know. So much he had yet to learn, all of it more painful than he could have then imagined.

"We'd better pick it up a little bit," Teddy said in a soft voice to Jacqueline and Bobby. "To keep up with the band."

At the mass, Teddy sat in the front row, next to Bobby, with Jacqueline and her two children. The service was long, highly structured and, to those not familiar with the intricacies of the Roman Catholic liturgy, largely incomprehensible.

The white-haired, raspy-voiced Cardinal Cushing chanted prayer after prayer. He'd been old Joe Kennedy's friend but he'd been close to Jack, too, and over the years Jacqueline had come to like and to respect him; not a reaction she had automatically to clergy.

Cushing had married her and Jack. Cushing had baptized Caroline. And now he himself was slowly dying of cancer, his body already riddled with the disease. And there, right next to her, inside the flag-draped coffin, was Jack, already dead.

Suddenly, it was too much. "There was everything going," she said later, and, at the time, she bent forward, wracked with uncontrollable sobs. Only when it came time for holy communion was she able to stop crying. She was first to the altar rail, followed by Bobby, then by Teddy. Then by Rose.

Almost a quarter of a century before, Teddy had received his first holy communion—from the Pope. Now it was Cardinal Cushing who placed the wafer on his tongue. Returning to the front pew, he sat stolid and immobile, hoping Jacqueline would be able to last.

The remainder of the mass was a blur: words, words

and more words, interspersed with music that did not touch him. But then, at the end, Cushing reawakened the pain.

Circling the casket three times, sprinkling it with incense and holy water, he chanted—that voice as sharp and grating as a stone being scraped across a sidewalk—the Latin verses that traditionally concluded a Catholic funeral service.

Then he stopped. And, standing directly over the coffin, he cried out spontaneously: "May the angels, dear Jack, lead you into paradise. May the martyrs receive you at your coming. May the spirit of God embrace you, and mayest thou, with all those who made the supreme sacrifice of dying for others, receive eternal rest and peace. Amen."

Jacqueline, Bobby and Teddy sat still as statues, stunned and awed by the Cardinal's unexpectedly personal and passionate farewell. "It wasn't just a ceremony anymore," Jacqueline said later. "He was saying goodbye to a man."

Then Cushing himself, clad in all his splendid and colorful vestments, began to cry.

Again, this proved too much for Jacqueline. She trembled, and wept. And then she felt the small hand of Caroline, reaching up to grasp her own.

"You'll be all right, Mummy," Caroline whispered. "Don't cry. I'll take care of you."

Outside, the brightness of the afternoon was almost physically painful. For the last time—at a tempo slower than ever before—"Hail to the Chief" was played for Jack, as his casket was carried down the steps of the cathedral.

With Bobby and Teddy directly behind her, Jacqueline gripped the hands of her children. Recalling that one of little John-John's favorite games had been to play soldiers with his father, she said, "John, you can salute Daddy now and say good-bye."

And he did, on this, his third birthday. Raising his tiny right hand to his brow, he held his arm stiffly as the flag-draped casket that contained his father's body was carried past him and placed, for the last time, on the caisson that would carry it the three miles to the cemetery.

Of all the images that have lingered for thirty years, it is perhaps that one—of little John-John's salute—which still evokes the strongest feelings, the sharpest pain.

Even Bobby, at the time, was forced to look away and to momentarily close his eyes. And Cardinal Cushing, watching from across the street, felt such a sudden and severe burning in his chest that he feared he might be having a heart attack. "Oh God," he said months later, still moved to tears at the memory, "I almost died."

Then Jacqueline and Bobby and Teddy climbed into their limousine. The children were taken to a different car. They'd done enough. They were not going to the cemetery. They would be taken back to the White House, the place they still considered their home.

But their sudden absence—atop all the other stresses of the day—seemed to take a toll on Jacqueline. Sitting with Bobby and Teddy in the backseat, waiting for the slow ride to the cemetery to begin, she started to cry. Again, she did not seem able to stop.

Bobby and Teddy looked across her, at each other. In addition to the sadness each felt, they were made terribly uncomfortable by Jacqueline's torment. And neither of them knew what to do.

Teddy looked at his wristwatch. They'd been sitting in the car for more than ten minutes and still there was no sign that the final procession was even about to begin.

Finally, Bobby said that as bad as it was, it could have been worse.

Jacqueline looked up at him, uncomprehending.

"Teddy," he said, "tell her whose pants you're wearing. And tell her why."

She turned to Teddy, the tears still streaming down her face.

And he found himself once again playing the role that had seemed since childhood to be the one for which he was best suited: court jester.

"It wasn't really my fault," he began. "You can blame the whole thing on Joey Gargan." And then he was off into the story, vividly re-creating the sights and sounds of earlier that morning, as he'd stormed around the upstairs bedroom in his underpants, frantically eyeing the ticking clock.

He stretched the story out as long as he could, until the limousine finally began to move. Jacqueline did not laugh, but at least she was not crying anymore.

On the way to Arlington, both Teddy and Bobby took out the eulogies that had been prepared for them to read at the end of the burial service.

Teddy's began with a brief excerpt from the speech Jack had given in Los Angeles upon accepting the Democratic party's presidential nomination.

"The New Frontier of which I speak," it read, "is not a set of promises—it is a set of challenges. It sums up not what I intend to offer the American people, but what I intend to ask of them."

Then there was a quote from one of his State of the Union addresses:

"Our nation is commissioned by history to be either an observer of freedom's failure or the cause of its success. Our overriding obligation in the months ahead is to fulfill the world's hopes by fulfilling our own faith.

"It is the fate of this generation to live with a struggle we did not start, in a world we did not make. But the pressures of life are not always distributed by choice. And while no nation has ever faced such a challenge, no nation has ever been so ready to seize the burden and the glory of freedom."

And, last, there was a longer quote from his major address to the United Nations:

"However close we sometimes seem to that dark and final abyss, let no man of peace and freedom despair. For he does not stand alone. If we all can persevere, if we can in every land and office look beyond our own shores and ambitions, then surely the age will dawn in which the strong are just and the weak secure and the peace preserved. . . .

"Never have the nations of the world had so much to

lose or so much to gain. Together we shall save the planet or together we shall perish in its flames. Save it we can, and save it we must, and then shall we earn the eternal thanks of mankind and, as peacemakers, the eternal blessing of God.''

That one, Teddy knew, would be the hardest. He was not sure he could make it through to the end of that one without crying.

Bobby looked up from his own sheet of paper and shook his head. He said he was having second thoughts about the readings. Coming at the end of such a long and emotional day, they might have about them the air of anticlimax.

Teddy disagreed. Above all, he wanted to participate. The reading was the one thing he would do by himself, on his own. It would be his sole contribution to the nation's collective memory of this unforgettable day. Hard as it would be, Teddy wanted very much to do it.

It was now almost 3:00 P.M. Already, the late November sun was starting its descent toward the western horizon. The temperature had never climbed out of the thirties. With even a slight breeze, the air felt bitterly cold. But the flat low angle at which the sun shone through the bare branches of the trees around the grave site illuminated the scene with an unforgettable, almost surreal, golden glow.

''The Star-Spangled Banner'' was played. Immediately upon its conclusion, a group of bagpipers began a final, mournful Celtic lament, ''Mist-Covered Mountain.'' The coffin was raised from the caisson for the last time and carried up the small rise to the grave site that Jacqueline had selected.

At the open grave, the coffin was placed gently on the metal rack that would be used to lower it into the ground. Teddy watched it all, having finally been joined by his wife, who had pulled herself together for the funeral and who'd ridden to the cemetery in a different limousine.

Joan was concerned about Teddy. He was clutching in one hand the sheet of paper from which he would read at the end of the service. She wondered if he'd be able to do it.

Suddenly, fifty F-105 jets in a V-shaped formation screamed across the sky. In their wake, appearing silent and huge as a blimp, flying ahead of the sound of its own engine, came Air Force One. The plane that had taken Jack everywhere, including to Dallas alive and from Dallas dead.

Air Force One flew so low over the cemetery that Teddy, gazing upward, felt for a moment as if, were he only to stand on his toes and reach out, he would almost be able to touch it.

The left wing dipped twenty degrees. In three seconds, it was level again. Then came a three-second dip to the right. Then it was gone, heading, like the fighter jets, like the sun, toward the glowing western horizon.

Teddy watched the plane grow smaller and smaller and then vanish, the sight of it replaced by the thunderous roar of its engine, which now boomed across the hillside.

Of the many military units from different branches of the armed forces, Teddy's eyes fell upon a squadron of cadets from the Irish army, who'd been flown over to participate in the graveside service.

For some reason, it was the Irish cadets, more than anything else, that got to Teddy. The sight of these young men, just children really, from the small and distant island from which his own grandparents had come so long ago, never dreaming for a moment that one of their heirs would someday serve as President of the vast and intimidating new land in which they'd chosen to make their home—this was too much for Teddy to bear.

It was as if this squadron of cadets, standing next to the grave into which his brother's body would soon be lowered, the grave in which it would forever lie, not only brought home to Teddy the reality of Jack's death in a more acute, unfiltered way than anything before, but as if they somehow personified—in their youth, their sadness, their pride—all the triumphs and tragedies the Kennedy family had experienced over three generations.

His hands began to tremble. He, too, momentarily had to close his eyes. And in that moment Teddy must have known he could not do it. He must have known he would not be able to read.

The Irish cadets marched to the grave in drill formation. Then, to the rhythm of a cadence softly uttered in the Gaelic language, they made way for the return of Cardinal Cushing.

Again, the aged, ailing prelate abandoned the traditional form and ritual of the graveside prayer. As he'd done at the cathedral, he spoke in English, not in Latin, his hoarse and strident voice cutting through the already wintry air.

"Oh God, through Whose mercy the souls of the faithful find rest, be pleased to bless this grave and the body we bury herein, that of our beloved Jack Kennedy, the thirty-fifth President of the United States, that his soul may rejoice in Thee with all the saints, through Christ the Lord. Amen."

He then recited the few final words from the customary liturgy: "I am the resurrection and the life. He who believeth in Me, although he be dead, shall live. And everyone who liveth and believeth in Me, shall not die forever."

He closed by asking that God grant his faithful servant John eternal rest and perpetual light.

A final twenty-one-gun salute was fired.

The Cardinal sprinkled holy water on the casket.

Taps was about to be played.

The time for the readings had come. The Cardinal looked expectantly toward Bobby and Teddy.

A feeling of panic swept over the President's youngest brother, who was scheduled to read first.

"I don't think I should do it now," he said to Jacqueline. He could not bring himself to say, "I can't."

"No, no, you should," she whispered to him.

But he could not bring himself to step forward.

After a brief but awkward pause, the final military tribute proceeded.

"Firing party—fire three volleys!" a sergeant shouted.

Three loud, distinct cracks of rifle fire were heard.

The bugler, standing on the crest of the hill overlooking

the grave, knew that as soon as the echo from the last volley of fire had faded, he was supposed to play taps.

There would still be time for Teddy to step forward and to read. But he could not.

Taps was played, never more slowly or more hauntingly.

Eight young soldiers, specially trained, quickly and flawlessly removed the American flag from Jack's coffin.

The marine band played the hymn "Eternal Father."

When it was over, the superintendent of Arlington National Cemetery, accompanied by Cardinal Cushing, carried the folded American flag to Jacqueline.

"Mrs. Kennedy," he said softly, so overcome with emotion that he was barely able to speak, "this flag is presented to you in the name of a most mournful nation."

She stood stock-still, not looking at him.

He leaned forward and whispered, "Please accept it."

She had no choice. He placed it in her hands: the bright triangle of red, white and blue.

To all watching—and all were watching—the colors of the flag made a startling contrast to the plain black of the suit she'd worn to the funeral—the same plain black suit she'd worn on January 2, 1960, the day Jack announced his candidacy.

Bobby and Teddy were standing on either side of her. The Cardinal knew they were supposed to step forward and read. He thought that somehow they'd missed their first cue. He was here to be sure they did not miss their last.

The time had come. He approached Teddy to lead him to the grave. Teddy would not look at him. He reached out to take Teddy's arm.

Teddy looked up at Jacqueline, then at Bobby. He shook his head. No. He could not do it. He would not be able to read. He wasn't even able to speak to Cardinal Cushing.

Again, the Cardinal tugged at Teddy's arm.

Then Jacqueline spoke: "No, Your Eminence."

Cushing did not understand.

And Teddy stood, as if stricken both dumb and paralyzed.

One last time, Cushing tried to pull him forward.

"I said no, Your Eminence," Jacqueline repeated.

Finally, the Cardinal understood. He might not know why, but he knew that Teddy would not be reading and that if Teddy didn't, then Bobby would not either.

He briefly hugged Jacqueline and retreated from the family group.

There were four of them then, standing at the grave site. Jacqueline, Bobby, Teddy and now Rose.

An army officer approached, said to Jacqueline, "This is the saddest moment of my life," and handed her the burning taper that she would use to light the eternal flame.

He led her to it; she bent forward and held the taper to an unlit torch that projected upward from the ground, to be fed by propane carried through an underground tube.

At Richard Goodwin's insistence, the army had figured out a way to make an eternal flame that Jacqueline would be able to light.

As the torch ignited and the flame sprang upward into the darkening sky, Jacqueline turned and handed the still-burning taper to Bobby.

He leaned forward and briefly put the end of the taper into the flame. Then he turned and handed the taper to Teddy.

Teddy was still badly flustered. For a moment, it looked as if he would not take the taper from Bobby's hands. Then he did, as if in a trance, and waved it slowly in the direction of the glimmering flame.

Quickly, the army officer who'd given the taper to Jacqueline took it from Teddy's unsteady hand. The eternal flame had been lit. The taper could now be extinguished.

The service was over. The moment for last words from the family, for a final reading from Jack's most inspiring and visionary public utterances, had come and gone.

There was nothing for any of them to do now but return to the limousines and to the White House, where they would form a receiving line and host a reception for the foreign leaders, other dignitaries and family friends.

Also, it was John-John's birthday. Upstairs, there

would be a party for him with ice cream, cake and three candles to blow out.

At the White House, two buffets had been laid in separate rooms. More than two hundred representatives of foreign nations would attend, in addition to at least as many staff, family and friends. The important thing was to have Jacqueline spend as little time as possible with Rose.

Teddy went upstairs as soon as he got to the White House. He was in no mood to greet dignitaries.

A television set was on in an upstairs hallway. Highlights of the day's events were being shown. Despite the lack of graveside readings, there had been no shortage of highlights. Teddy found himself drawn irresistibly to the television, watching what he had just experienced, as in Hyannis Port he'd watched obsessively those events from which he'd been excluded.

Jacqueline approached him. She reminded him that there were hundreds of guests milling about downstairs and that while she went to her room to change her clothes, it might be nice if a member of the family was there to greet them.

Teddy found his sisters, Eunice, Pat and Jean. The four of them went downstairs to mingle. Through an aide, Jacqueline announced that she would receive visitors privately in the upstairs Oval Room, but that there were only four she would so honor: Charles de Gaulle; Eamon de Valera, the president of Ireland; Prince Philip, Duke of Edinburgh and husband of Queen Elizabeth; and Haile Selassie.

Downstairs, Rose had installed herself in a sitting room, where, as the mother of the slain President, she too was expecting to hold a royal court. But it was considered essential that the most renowned, bejeweled and grandly titled of the guests be seen first by Jacqueline, and only later, if at all, by Rose.

After holding her private audiences, Jacqueline did come downstairs, where she and Teddy—but, notably, not Rose—stood at the head of a formal receiving line.

Bobby, plagued by so many doubts, thoughts and fears

of which Teddy as yet had no awareness, was too restless, too troubled to stand that still for that long. Instead, he roamed the White House, from corridor to corridor, floor to floor.

As evening fell, the guests slowly departed. The mood among those remaining began to change. As a cousin of Jacqueline's, John Davis, has written, "It is an Irish custom to hold a lively, boisterous party immediately after the burial of a relative or a friend, during which large amounts of alcohol are consumed."

By early evening, Davis reported, "the past four days, witnessing first the murder of the President, then the murder of his assassin, had been so depressing and so bewildering that everyone was in a mood to forget temporarily what had happened and enjoy what turned out to be an unexpected reunion of family and friends. The nightmare was suspended."

Davis himself had to leave early to catch a flight to Europe. But before doing so he wanted to pay his respects to the President's mother.

He sought her out, approached her and shook her hand. "She surprised me," he wrote later, "by responding in a cool, utterly controlled voice." What surprised him even more—indeed, alarmed him—was what she said.

"Oh, thank you, Mr. Davis, but don't worry. Everything will be all right. You'll see. Now it's Bobby's turn."

Upstairs, in the family quarters, the drinks flowed freely. It was 7:00 P.M., time for John-John's birthday party. The little boy was already in an apparently festive mood. At some level, of course, he had to know that something terrible was wrong—that Daddy had died and gone to heaven—but all day he'd seen soldiers and horses and excitement, more excitement than he'd ever seen before.

He was wearing a paper party hat and marching around the upstairs dining room with a toy rifle in his arms, pretending to be his favorite kind of hero—a soldier.

Then ice cream, cake and presents were brought in and

John-John sat at a small table with his sister, Caroline. For the adults, Bloody Marys seemed to be the drink of choice, the ratio of vodka to mix rising with each.

For the first time in days, Teddy could feel himself starting to relax. The worst was over now. He was at a party for a three-year-old, the kind of event at which he felt very much at home. Where nothing beyond his capacities would be expected. Where his performance would not be scrutinized and criticized.

He had long since taken off the formal coat with its typewritten page of unrecited words still inside. He must have felt a brief pang as the children's nanny lit the birthday candles on the cake. The memory of the eternal flame was very fresh.

But Jacqueline was rising to the occasion, as she'd risen to every one since the first shot was fired in Dallas. This was her son's birthday. This was a party. This was just family and friends. Time to clap hands, time to sing.

It was she, in fact, who first suggested that they all sing some of Jack's favorite songs. Teddy thought this a splendid idea. Especially after consuming a few drinks, he enjoyed singing. It was one thing he thought he did well. And it seemed one of the few totally innocent activities from which he derived genuine pleasure.

At the cemetery, he had not even been able to speak. But here, at John-John's party—with the whole world not watching—he found himself in splendid form.

The first song they sang was "That Old Gang of Mine." Teddy noticed that Bobby had moved to the side of the group, had not joined in.

Then Teddy said he knew a good one. "Heart of My Heart." That was one of Jack's favorites. In fact, he recalled for the group, it was a song the three Kennedy brothers had once sung together in public.

At the very end of Jack's 1958 senatorial campaign— the one in which he'd compiled the most lopsided victory margin in the history of Massachusetts politics—he'd found himself in the Dorchester section of Boston, a working-class neighborhood in which a large portion of the population was of Irish descent.

Jack had campaigned hard that fall. Not in Massachusetts, where he made remarkably few appearances, but around the country, speaking in behalf of other Democratic candidates, building the national base that would serve him so well in 1960.

So that night, in Dorchester, he was hoarse, but in high spirits and tired of hearing himself talk. He proposed, since it was one of those rare campaign events at which Bobby and Teddy were also present, that instead of his giving just another campaign speech—since the crowd was so Irish and so friendly—that the Kennedys treat them to something special.

He said to the crowd that if they clapped long enough and loud enough, he was sure that both his brothers would join him atop the bar of the saloon where this particular campaign event was being held, and would join him in singing one of his favorite songs, "Heart of My Heart."

Teddy was delighted. Bobby was not, but even he was a good sport. Everything was going so well. Everyone was in such a fine mood.

No one bothered to record it on tape, but it might have been the last time—and one of the only times—the three living Kennedy brothers had sung together in public.

"Heart of My Heart." They had belted it out. The crowd had loved it. And now Teddy wanted to sing it again. To bring back memories. To reawaken that memory in particular.

It was more than Bobby could bear. He'd been slipping, bit by bit, throughout the late afternoon and early evening. From the moment he received the first phone call at Hickory Hill on Friday afternoon, he'd been under more pressure than anyone. While Jacqueline was the primary object of the nation's outpouring of sympathy— which Bobby in no way begrudged her—it had been Bobby on whose shoulders ultimate responsibility for so much had lain.

And it was Bobby, too, who knew so much the others didn't. It was Bobby who knew, as the others didn't, that there was almost no possibility that Lee Harvey Oswald had acted alone, out of some twisted, psychotic rage, to assassinate the President.

Bobby and Bobby alone—except for their stricken father—knew the myriad other possibilities. His guilty knowledge would weigh him down for years to come. Already, the burden was taking its toll.

As Teddy launched into "Heart of My Heart," his strong baritone joining the high-pitched tenor of Dave Powers, one of Jack's oldest Boston friends, Bobby turned and walked out the door and down the hall.

He didn't want to sing that song. He didn't want to hear it. He must have been afraid that the memory of that glorious night in Dorchester, just five years earlier, would be more than he could bear.

Teddy sang loudly and well. Ice cream was melting, birthday cake was smeared across the tablecloth, discarded gift wrapping lay on the floor and Teddy had a fresh drink in his hand.

"I love that melody, 'Heart of My Heart,' " he sang.

> *"I love that melody,*
> *'Heart of My Heart,' brings back a memory,*
> *When we were kids*
> *On the corner of the street,*
> *We were rough and ready guys,*
> *But oh, how we could harmonize . . ."*

He and Dave Powers carried it all the way through to the end. By then, Bobby was far away, with enough doors closed behind him so he could no longer hear the melody or words.

> *"Friends were dearer then,*
> *Too bad we had to part.*
> *Now I know a tear would glisten*
> *If once more I could listen*
> *To the gang that sang 'Heart of My Heart.' "*

When it was over, Teddy might have realized it had not been such a good idea after all, singing that song. John-John was making noise again and wanted to march, but the adults all seemed to be staring in different directions, and none of them toward Teddy.

Even Joan, his wife, said maybe it was time for them to go home. He had another drink. But no one sang any more songs. And then he realized Joan was right. He was finished. Jack was dead. Day was done.

But the adults all seemed to be staring in different directions, and none of them toward Teddy.

Even Joan. His wife. said maybe it was time for them
to go home. He had another drink. But no one sang any
more songs. And then he realized Joan was right. He was
finished. Jack was dead. Day was done.

Part Two

"**I**N THE NEXT GENERATION," JOE KENNEDY REmarked to his friend Morton Downey, the singer, soon after the stock market crash of 1929, "the people who run the government will be the biggest people in America."

It was an insight that, while not seeming especially profound in retrospect, would alter the course of many lives, as well as that of American history.

At forty, Kennedy was already a millionaire many times over, having been a bank president, a stock market manipulator, an importer and distributor of illegal shipments of liquor during Prohibition and, in Hollywood, a producer and distributor of low-budget, low-quality highprofit motion pictures. "Melodrama is our meat," he would say in Hollywood, comparing his operation to Woolworth's as opposed to Tiffany's.

He was a trim, fit man with a broad grin, boundless energy, great charm, remarkable intuition, keen intellect, insatiable ambition and absolutely no recognition of a moral dimension to human life.

Soon after his graduation from Harvard, in 1912, Kennedy, the son of a saloonkeeper and small-time ward politician, married Rose Fitzgerald, the daughter of the former mayor of Boston. Successfully dodging the draft in World War I, he began to father children at a rapid rate. Joe Junior was born in 1915, John in 1917, Rosemary in 1918, Kathleen in 1920, Eunice in 1921, Patricia in 1924 and Robert in 1925.

In 1926, attracted by both the glamour and the opportunities for profit in the rapidly expanding motion picture industry, he left his family behind on the east coast and moved into a house on Rodeo Drive in Beverly Hills. He was accompanied by his personal assistant, Edward Moore, who served him in many capacities, including, as biographer Nigel Hamilton has noted, that of "whoremaster," assuring that the flow of women into and out of Joe's bedroom would be both steady and swift.

He stayed in Hollywood for most of the next three years, returning east once in the spring of 1927—to bring to fruition a few more lucrative business ventures and to impregnate Rose for the eighth time (a daughter, Jean, was born in 1928)—and again in the fall, to move his family from Boston, where he'd been snubbed by the upper reaches of the social hierarchy, to a large estate in the exclusive New York City suburb of Bronxville.

Otherwise, Joe Kennedy basked in the Beverly Hills sun, making large sums of money and, with the logistical assistance of Eddie Moore, enjoying a staggering number of sexual encounters with some of the most alluring starlets in Hollywood. He was having such a good time that even when his father died, in May of 1929, he declined to return to Boston for the funeral.

During those years, enchanted by his proximity to many of America's most renowned celebrities and fascinated by the power of the larger-than-life, celluloid image both to distort reality and to manipulate the emotions of a mass audience, Joe Kennedy learned what he would later regard as the greatest lesson of his life, one that he would repeat interminably to his children: "You must remember, it's not what you are that counts but only what people think you are."

It was also during his Hollywood phase that Joe began an affair with the famed actress Gloria Swanson. This would prove to be by far the most intense and flagrant adulterous relationship of his life, lasting more than a year and a half, and ending, in 1929, only when he became convinced that American society was about to undergo cataclysmic upheaval.

For more than a year he'd sensed that dramatic change was coming, that the piper was about to demand payment for the excesses of the Twenties. Even before 1929, he'd moved half his fortune out of stocks. Now, in early fall, he closed out his remaining positions. By October, when the market crashed, Joe had already converted most of his assets to cash and municipal bonds. With the remainder, he doubled his market profits by selling stocks short as prices plunged.

But he feared that the crash and resulting economic depression would lead to social anarchy, perhaps even a Communist upheaval that might put his entire fortune at risk. The intensity of this anxiety carried him into the political camp of Franklin D. Roosevelt, the one man then active in public life who Joe thought might be able to prevent outright rebellion by the masses.

"I was really worried," he said later. "I knew that drastic changes had to be made in our economic system and I felt Roosevelt was the one who could make them. I wanted him in the White House for my own security and I was ready to do anything to help elect him."

Anticipating, as he'd said to Downey, that political leaders would replace the heads of corporations as the most powerful figures in America, Joe also wanted to be sure that he was numbered among them. As family biographer Doris Kearns Goodwin has written, "Just as he had resolved in the 1920s to be at the center of action by becoming a businessman, so now he saw politics as the only means by which he could remain inextricably involved in the dominant passion of his day."

Political life at that time, however, required adherence to a set of social norms somewhat more restrictive than those of Hollywood. Joe's affair with Gloria had already become such public knowledge—at least at the levels at which the bartering for power took place—that he now needed a way to demonstrate that it was behind him, that his commitment to wife and family had been renewed.

Nothing, in his view, would be quite so convincing as

the birth of a ninth child. But Rose was past the point of easy persuasion. For her, sex had never been anything more than a cross to bear, a duty the Church imposed upon a wife. Indeed, part of her tolerance for Joe's infidelity resulted from the fact that the more other women he had and the more frequently he had them, the fewer sexual demands he made upon her.

She had always been emotionally arid, and her years of marriage to Joe had rendered her even more distant and repressed. As he broached to her the idea of a ninth child, however, Rose saw that this might enable her to pry from her husband what she most wanted out of life.

This included even more servants, long stretches of private time during which no demands of any sort were to be made upon her, and—most important—the right to travel alone where she pleased, when she pleased, and to spend as much money as she wanted on herself.

Having given birth to eight children in fourteen years, the last thing the forty-year-old Rose wanted was another. For once in his life, Joe found himself negotiating from a position of weakness. He had no choice but to grant her demands. It was understood that for the duration of the marriage he would be free to have sexual relations with other women, but it was understood also that none of them would take a place of primacy in his life.

In return, Rose could have all the material possessions she'd ever craved, and would be permitted, once and for all, as much freedom as she wanted from the burdens of childcare and domestic life.

All that would be required to formalize the arrangement would be one last pregnancy, one final birth—tangible proof that Joe had restored a sense of order and propriety to his life.

It was under such circumstances that, on February 22, 1932, their ninth child was born.

All Joe insisted on was the right to name the child if it was a boy, which it was. The name he chose was that of his assistant and "whoremaster," Edward Moore.

2

"**W**HEN YOU HAVE OLDER BROTHERS AND SISTERS,"
Teddy's mother said years later, "they're the ones that
seem more important. When the ninth comes along you
have to make more of an effort to tell bedtime stories and
be interested in swimming matches. There were seventeen years between my oldest and my youngest child and
I had been telling bedtime stories for twenty years."

But no more. When Teddy was only two, Rose went to
Paris for an extended look at the newest fashions. Not
even her twentieth wedding anniversary could bring her
home. Instead, she simply cabled greetings to her husband from her four-star hotel.

In the five years that followed Teddy's birth, in fact,
his mother took more than fifteen trips to Europe by herself. Some of these lasted for months. Nor was this a time
when his father spent much time at home. Joe's career
was on its fastest track yet as he spent the early and mid
1930s pursuing political power through affiliation with
Franklin D. Roosevelt.

At the Democratic convention in the summer of 1932,
Joe prevailed upon his friend William Randolph Hearst to
deliver to Roosevelt enough of the California and Texas
delegates he controlled to set in motion the bandwagon

that led to Roosevelt's nomination. He then donated vast sums of money to Roosevelt's campaign and set about raising even more.

In return, he was permitted to accompany Roosevelt on a thirteen-thousand-mile train trip that fall, from east coast to west and back again. He made a sufficiently good impression (and sufficiently large financial contribution) that despite his reputation for unsavory business dealings and rumored connections with organized crime, the newly elected President named him chairman of the Securities and Exchange Commission, a new federal agency whose purpose was to eliminate many of the stock market abuses by which Joe had built much of his fortune.

Again leaving wife and children behind, and again accompanied by Eddie Moore, Joe moved into a vast Maryland mansion named Marwood, overlooking the Potomac River. He was, as Kearns Goodwin has described, "intelligent, high-spirited, gregarious and affable—the kind of person FDR, delighting in hearty souls, loved to have around him." Using Moore as procurer as well as personal secretary, Joe continued his sexual adventuring, but with sufficient discretion so as not to attract unwanted attention.

With Rose in Europe much of the time, the household in which young Teddy found himself growing up—in Bronxville during the school year and in the family's newly acquired oceanfront house at Hyannis Port in the summer—was, to phrase it gently, chaotic.

Among the older children, even the girls, competitive tensions ran high. "I was twenty-four," Eunice would say years later, "before I knew I didn't have to win something every day." That they must enter every competition open to them and win every competition they entered was the closest thing to an ethical lesson Joe Kennedy ever imparted to his children.

On the rare occasions when he was home, he would, for instance, after a severe and humiliating lecture, send a son to bed without dinner as punishment for the infraction of having finished second in a sailboat race. "My husband," Rose said delicately, "liked the boys to win at everything they tried. He did not have much patience with the loser."

But it was not only their father who drove the children. "Mother was equally competitive about everything," Eunice said. The lesson learned by all was that parental abuse could be avoided only by conquest of others, and approval was bestowed only upon the victor, with even that being conditional—its continuance dependent on yet another triumph in whatever competition loomed next.

Nor were the rivalries solely external. Within the family, the battles for supremacy proved just as fierce. As the oldest, strongest and apparently most talented, it was Joe Junior of whom the most was expected. But John, though two years younger, sickly and frail, was not exempted. On those occasions when he would, through wit or guile, best his bigger brother, Joe Junior would often retaliate by punching him so brutally and repeatedly that the even younger Bobby could only scream in horror at the sight.

When Rose was present, in either Bronxville or Hyannis Port, displays of religious piety were required. She herself would attend two masses each morning, taking holy communion at the first, then eating a dry roll to keep up her strength through the second.

Though daily attendance at mass was not required of the children, there were luncheon quizzes on catechism questions, organized dinner discussions on topics Rose would choose in advance, usually either of a religious nature or concerning current events. In addition, there was the nightly ritual of Rose and the children saying the rosary together.

Highly placed Roman Catholic clerics were among her most prized and carefully cultivated social friends and it was essential, always, that her children make a favorable impression on such men.

Both Joe and Rose made it clear that the three oldest children were viewed as the most talented, and thus entitled to more parental attention, even as more demands were made upon them. "Forming a family within a family," Kearns Goodwin has written, "Joe Junior, Jack and Kathleen were the golden trio who shared all the inesti-

mable advantages of being wealthy, good-looking, confident and intelligent." They were, said one family friend,
"the ones the old man thought would write the story of
the next generation."

Care of the younger ones—with the occasional exception of Rosemary, who was displaying symptoms of emotional disturbance and mental retardation—was left
largely to paid retainers. Rose felt that Eunice, Pat and
Jean, as well as Bobby and the youngest, Teddy, would
be able to manage quite nicely, "free from moral and
physical harm," in her words, "so long as they had a
competent, pleasant governess of high moral standards."

With both parents so absent from his life, Teddy
turned, in his earliest years, toward his siblings in the
hope of receiving attention. Most responsive at first
seemed his oldest brother, Joe Junior, who, already enrolled at Harvard before Teddy had even turned two, did
not see the toddler as a threat to his place of primacy.

One friend recalled an early fall visit to Hyannis Port
in 1934. "The minute we got out of the car," he said,
"Teddy came running up, Joe grabbed him and kissed
him like a father would and hoisted him up on his shoulder. They were like father and son."

Teddy's real father, in the meantime, temporarily left
government service in the fall of 1935, having enjoyed a
successful tenure at the Securities and Exchange Commission. His departure, however, was only a prelude to
what he hoped would be a return at an even higher level.
Secretary of the Treasury was what he had in mind.

Toward that end, at the start of Roosevelt's 1936 reelection campaign, Joe secretly offered to pay *New York
Times* columnist Arthur Krock $1,000 a week to ghost-
write a book that Joe would publish that summer under
his own name. The title, *I'm for Roosevelt,* left little
doubt about either Joe's purpose or his point of view.

From his time in Hollywood, Joe had come to believe
that a man's public image was his most valuable possession and that only the foolish or hopelessly naive would
leave its shaping to chance. Thus, while in Washington,
Joe had established the practice of giving lavish, if discreet, gifts to underpaid reporters who wrote articles fa-

vorable to him. This practice was one he would continue for years, much to the advantage not only of himself but of his sons as they, in turn, entered public life.

He created his own public relations firm, whose sole purpose was to imprint in the public mind the perception that Joe Kennedy was a rugged and brilliant self-made man, whose first love was his large and talented family, and who would place duty to country ahead of any desire for private gain.

Roosevelt was reelected in 1936, but by then he'd come to know Joe Kennedy too well to want him as Secretary of the Treasury. Instead, he offered the lesser post of chairman of the United States Maritime Commission. Privately insulted, Joe knew he had no choice but to accept if he hoped to continue with a career in government, and so, early in 1937, again leaving his family behind, he and Eddie Moore returned to Marwood and the lavish lifestyle and sexual freedom he so enjoyed.

It appeared that the pinnacle of his successful image building had been reached when he learned he was to be the subject of the cover story of the September 1937 issue of prestigious *Fortune* magazine, owned by his friend Henry Luce. Leaving nothing to chance, however, he arranged to review the article before publication.

What he saw infuriated him. It was the first accurate assessment of his character and personality ever committed to print. As Kearns Goodwin describes it, the *Fortune* article portrayed him "as a man driven by his own ambitions with little regard for the institutions he touched, a profiteer willing to take money wherever he could find it."

Joe responded immediately with a letter to the magazine's managing editor in which he termed the article's author a "psychopathic case" and suggested that the unflattering portrait was outright "blackmail," the result of Joe's disinclination to arrange the immediate sale of motion picture rights to a book the writer had recently published.

As in the case of Arthur Krock's hidden role as Joe's ghostwriter, there was no public record made of money changing hands, but against all precedent, the magazine agreed to cancel the original article and assign a new writer who would be certain to portray Joe in a far more flattering light.

The level of national prestige that Joe acquired as a result of the favorable cover story that *Fortune* eventually published created a splendid opportunity for President Roosevelt. In December of 1937, gleefully aware that the appointment would place Joe on the other side of the Atlantic Ocean, far from Washington and any opportunities to make mischief there, Roosevelt offered him the ambassadorship to the Court of St. James. Joe, of course, accepted immediately. As the first Irish-American ever appointed ambassador to England, he considered the new post an honor of the highest magnitude.

As it happened, one of the many effects of this unexpected development was that just as he turned six, Teddy, whose very existence was the result of an act of political calculation on his father's part, was transformed virtually overnight into a boy prince.

3

"NINE CHILDREN AND NINE MILLION DOLLARS,"
said the headline in one London newspaper, announcing
Joe's appointment. Having raised manipulation of the
American press to something resembling an art form, Joe
discovered, to his delight, that in England in early 1938,
exaltation of the Kennedys was a spontaneous phenomenon.

"When Rose finally arrived in the middle of March
with Kathleen and the four youngest Kennedys," Kearns
Goodwin has written, "the British reaction was extraordinary. For the weeks preceding their arrival, the London
newspapers had published dozens of pictures and stories
of the Kennedy family, involving their readers in the
Kennedys in a manner usually reserved for accounts of
the royal family. But when Rose and the children actually
reached London, the warmth of their welcome exceeded
all expectations."

One can only imagine the impact upon the chubby,
freckled six-year-old Teddy of suddenly seeing his picture in newspapers every day, of having strangers grin
and wave and cheer whenever he appeared in public,
of moving into a six-story, thirty-six-room mansion that

housed twenty-three servants and an elevator, of hearing his father now addressed as "Your Excellency."

Through the spring of 1938, London was agog over them all, but most especially pudgy little Teddy, in short pants, long socks and camel's hair overcoat, toting his Brownie camera everywhere, taking pictures of the people taking pictures of him, and all the cuter because more often than not he would be holding his camera upside down.

Neither Joe Junior nor Jack was present during these early months. Joe Junior was in the final semester of a successful Harvard career, due to graduate in June; while Jack, who seemed chronically plagued by mysterious stomach and intestinal ailments, had been forced to leave Harvard in late winter and retreat to the family estate in Palm Beach to recuperate.

Of "the golden trio," then, only Kathleen made the original journey. Given her good looks, charm and ebullience, both Joe and Rose recognized that she would be more of an asset to the family image living in the London embassy residence and plunging into the social whirl of the upcoming debutante season than staying behind to pursue higher education in America.

For his sons, Joe Kennedy knew that the best of schooling was a social necessity, but daughters served a primarily ornamental purpose and Kathleen was the most glittering among them by far; too valuable a bauble to leave behind.

So while Eunice, seventeen, Patricia, fourteen, and Jean, ten, were shipped out to convent schools in the British countryside, and Rosemary, with whom there was clearly something not quite right, was consigned to a school for the handicapped, Kathleen basked in the attention of some of the British aristocracy's most eligible young bachelors, attending, as Kearns Goodwin has described, "the lavish balls and dances that were being held nearly every night between April and August in honor of one or another of the coming debutantes."

Eventually, both Kathleen and Rosemary, along with their mother, were formally presented at court at Buckingham Palace. Later, Joe and Rose held a coming-out party for both daughters at the embassy residence. Whatever the nature of Rosemary's condition, it was not so incapacitating as to prevent her from enjoying a formal London debut—an event the parents would hardly have undertaken had they feared even the slightest risk of embarrassment to themselves. It was, however, as expected, Kathleen who became "the star of the 1938 debutante season."

Almost as fortunate were Bobby and Teddy, who were permitted to attend a private day school and actually live in the embassy residence. Bobby, even then taciturn, introverted and withdrawn, seemed largely unfazed by his new celebrity and went quietly about the business of doing what was expected of him academically and what was demanded of him socially, without displaying any great enthusiasm for his newfound station in life.

Teddy, on the contrary, could scarcely contain himself. The day he moved into the residence he commandeered the elevator and ran the servants ragged, shuttling them between cellar and attic, playing a game he called "department store."

"He was always so bubbly and happy," his governess, Luella Hennessey, would later say. "Always wanting to talk." In the evenings, both Bobby and Teddy were permitted a brief private visit with their father, as the Ambassador prepared himself for the upcoming round of social and diplomatic engagements.

Bobby, so intense and serious, would engage in adult-like conversation about the public events of the time, or about what he'd accomplished that day in school. When Teddy's turn came, however, the governess recalled, "the atmosphere in the room would completely change. Teddy was like the sunshine, lighting up everything in sight and keeping his father young. Through the corridors you could hear them laughing as Teddy jumped up and down on his father's bed until he was exhausted."

Though widely separated by age and temperament, Teddy and Bobby, as the only two children living at the residence full-time, formed a bond. Dressed in identical maroon blazers and gray slacks, they were taken to school in a chauffeured limousine. So clearly different, special, even regal, neither formed any close friendships with classmates, and so upon their return in the afternoon, they would play only with each other, often riding their bicycles on the stone terrace that stretched beyond the mansion.

"They were so different," Luella Hennessey recalled, "but always, after London, there seemed to be something very special between Bobby and Ted."

They were not, of course, entirely secluded. Indeed, each was given a scaled-down version of their father's hectic public schedule and expected to perform his social duties in the finest Kennedy tradition.

Teddy, for instance, was sent one day—as befitted a young prince—to assist Sir Julian Huxley, the eminent biologist and educator, in formally cutting the ribbon that would open the new "Pet's Corner" of the famed London Zoo.

And often, both boys were sent to mingle with the next generation of British royalty—meeting, for example, the future Queen Elizabeth at a tea dance. She and her sister, Margaret, let little Teddy help them attach messages and their addresses to helium-filled balloons which were then sent aloft over London in the hope that someone from afar would reply.

For Teddy, London proved to be an endless carnival, with every day providing a new and more thrilling attraction. "He had terrific animal energy," his sister Jean later recalled. "You never had to push Ted—you always had to hold him back." Eunice would say, "I remember him in London as being overweight, terribly good-natured and laughing constantly."

The laughter may have pleased his father, but the excess poundage did not. Both Joe and Rose were obsessed with personal appearance: their own and that of their children. So revolted were they by obesity that they would not even hire servants they considered overweight. Thus, it was no small matter that this youngest child was turning into "a butterball," as his father once described him to the Queen of England.

Still, with the older children coming so close to the perfection demanded of them, and with Joe's own career in such spectacular ascendancy, the question of Teddy's weight was not one to which sustained attention was devoted. He was, after all, the afterthought. The last and the least of them. The one nobody took seriously, the one of whom little was demanded—save learning to grin broadly when a press camera was pointed his way—and of whom nothing of import was expected.

In June, his father returned to America for the dual purpose of witnessing Joe Junior's graduation from Harvard and receiving, from the same institution, a much coveted honorary degree.

Upon his arrival aboard the *Queen Mary,* Joe Kennedy discovered that his assiduous courting of the American press, even from afar, had paid rich dividends. He was being mentioned seriously as a possible 1940 presidential candidate.

An article in the May issue of *Liberty* magazine had first broached the idea, describing Joe's major assets as "brains, personality, driving power and the habit of success." Also mentioned were his "athlete's figure, clean cut head, sandy hair, clear, straight-shooting eyes, flashingly infectious smile and faultless taste in dress."

The idea of Kennedy as President was quickly picked up by newspapers in Boston, New York and Washington. A columnist in the *Washington Times-Herald* reported that among college seniors due to graduate that June, Joe was the "overwhelming" choice for President in 1940— it being bruited about that Roosevelt would not seek a third term.

In *The Washington Post,* a columnist wrote that of all possible contenders, Joe had "the nearest to the Rooseveltian personality," adding that "all the kinetic Kennedys (and especially the beautiful Mrs.) would be a tremendous assest in a campaign." In conclusion, the writer said, "The mental picture of the White House with nine or ten Kennedys galloping about is most beguiling."

Then, of course, there was the always reliable Arthur Krock, who wrote in *The New York Times* that Joe was "the rage of London," that "his counsel was steadily sought by statesmen," that "his influence was manifest and powerful." Yet, Krock said, Joe was so clearheaded as to remain "undazzled by such a taking up socially and officially as no American perhaps has known abroad since Franklin's day."

None of this pleased President Roosevelt, who had every intention of seeking a third term in 1940, though no desire to announce his plans so far in advance. Recognizing that Joe himself was largely responsible for the "Kennedy for President" boomlet, Roosevelt summoned his ambassador to the White House for a brief meeting, at which the atmosphere, according to a close Roosevelt associate, was "frigid."

The next day, Joe suffered a second blow when he learned that, contrary to rumor and his high expectation, he had not been among those chosen to receive honorary degrees at the Harvard commencement. Walt Disney would, and so would the presidents of Yale and Williams, but to Harvard, despite his meteoric rise in public life, Joe Kennedy was apparently still just a pushy Irish Catholic.

So insulted was he that Joe refused even to attend the graduation ceremony at which his firstborn and most favored son received his degree.

Teddy, all the while, remained immersed in his unreal world of privilege, ceremony and celebrity.

At Cap d'Antibes that summer, at a special ceremony at which he was presented with an insignia of rank, he was made an honorary member of the French 9th Battalion of Alpine Chasseurs.

At Cannes, he was given a motorboat ride on the Mediterranean, which turned into more of an adventure than planned when a sudden mist descended and the seas grew unexpectedly rough. Teddy, however, as the press reported, "remained on deck, quite undaunted, leaning excitedly over the rail and shouting, 'Ride 'em cowboy!' every time the boat went up on the crest of a wave." It was further reported that "he performed a feat on water skis. He stood upright on them the first time he tried, which is something hardly anyone can do."

That winter, the *Boston Globe* devoted thousands of words to an account of a family vacation, headlined: "Kennedys' Holiday Period Proved Great Success. They're Back in London Now After Frolicking at St. Moritz."

It was reported that they were all "extremely proud of their brother Joe's success in coming second in the toboggan race on the Cresta Run," despite his never having ridden such a sled before.

"At ten o'clock every morning," the paper reported, "the whole family went up the ski lift, two at a time, and dropping off at suitable stages—the younger children on the beginners' slopes and the others continuing to the top. Rose went up occasionally with Teddy and Jean and did a little gentle skiing, but she generally preferred to stay behind and skate.

"At 12:30 the whole family would come back to the hotel for lunch, after which the elder children returned to the ski slopes. Teddy and Jean stayed behind and went skating with their mother on the lake which was overlooked by their rooms in the Suvretta Hotel, while Bobby would spend the afternoon at ice hockey."

Teddy, it was mentioned, suffered "a wrenched knee, which put him out of action for three days, much to his disgust," but, the story said, "the whole party is now back in London feeling extremely fit."

Back in London, the family were seated in a private box at the Theatre Royal, Drury Lane, for a pantomime performance of *Babes in the Woods*. Afterwards, "they all met the 'dame,' played by G. S. Melvin, in his dressing room, where he entertained them at an informal tea party. During tea, Teddy was unable to stop laughing at Mr. Melvin, who pretended to be the 'dame' again and took him onto his knee."

The highlight of Teddy's stay, however, was to come in March of 1939 when Eugenio Pacelli, a cardinal of the Roman Catholic Church who had stayed at the Kennedy home while visiting the United States two years earlier, was elected as Pope Pius XII.

The entire family, except for Joe Junior, who was in Madrid taking a firsthand look at the Spanish civil war, traveled to Rome for the Pope's coronation on March 12.

Perpetually in a tizzy over matters of pomp and piety, Rose was electrified by the spectacle and by the special status her family now enjoyed at the Vatican. The day after the coronation, the new Pope granted the Kennedys a private audience. He took special delight in young Teddy, whom he recalled from his Bronxville visit as the fat little boy who'd sat on his lap and asked why he was wearing such a big cross around his neck.

As the family left the papal chamber, Teddy, now seven, held his first press conference. Responding to a barrage of questions from Roman reporters, he calmly said, "I wasn't frightened at all." The Pope, he added, "patted my head and told me I was a smart little fellow. And he gave me the first rosary beads from the table, before he gave my sisters any."

Two days later, on March 15, 1939, Teddy Kennedy became the first American citizen ever to receive his first holy communion from a pope.

For his father, however, life had grown less rewarding and more complicated. As ambassador, Joe Kennedy had enthusiastically supported British Prime Minister Neville Chamberlain's policy of appeasement toward Adolf Hitler and Nazi Germany.

Fearing that an outbreak of war would put his personal fortune at risk—and feeling also that Hitler was a dynamic and visionary leader whose conquest of England would be swift and certain if fighting began—Joe had spoken out both publicly and privately against British involvement.

When, at Munich in September of 1938, Chamberlain promised Hitler that the British would do nothing to prevent his planned conquest of Czechoslovakia, Joe Kennedy had been so pleased and relieved that, Rose later recalled, "he kissed me and twirled me around in his arms, repeating over and over again what a great day this was and what a great man Chamberlain was."

Not everyone agreed. Winston Churchill said in Parliament, "We are in the presence of a disaster of the first magnitude. Our brave people should know that we have sustained a defeat without a war, that we have passed an awful milestone in our history . . . This is only the first sip, the first foretaste of a bitter cup which will be proffered to us year by year unless, by a supreme recovery of moral health and marked vigor, we arise again and take our stand for freedom as in the olden time."

But Joe Kennedy was not swayed. In a formal address at the Trafalgar Day dinner of the Navy League on October 19, he pleaded with his audience to recognize the necessity and even desirability of both England's and America's learning to coexist with dictatorships.

The speech did not prove popular. Within hours, telegrams of protest poured into the White House and the State Department. The *New York Post* said in an editorial, "For Mr. Kennedy to propose that the United States make a friend of the man who boasts that he is out to destroy democracy, religion and all the other principles that Americans hold dear . . . that passes understanding."

In November, Hitler began his pogrom against the Jews with the dreadful events of Kristallnacht on November 9, when gangs of Nazis raced through Jewish neighborhoods, looting, raping and murdering. Thousands of Jewish-owned stores and homes were destroyed, more than two hundred synagogues were set afire, thirty-six Jews were killed and twenty thousand arrested.

On that night, as William Shirer wrote, "the Third Reich turned down a dark and savage road from which there was to be no return."

Joe Kennedy, on the other hand, saw it primarily as a public relations problem for Hitler. He'd already privately advised the German ambassador to England that Hitler's anti-Jewish policy was not objectionable; it was only the highly public way in which he was going about it that would cause him problems.

After the savagery of Kristallnacht, Joe felt compelled

to do more, and thus proposed what came to be known, infamously, as "the Kennedy Plan" for resettling European Jews in sparsely populated areas of Africa and South America where they would no longer prove an irritant to the Nazis.

"The problem," he wrote, "seemed to me essentially a simple one. If a reasonably good area for settlement could be made available somewhere in the world, the problem of financing immigration of Jews to that area could be put as a challenge before those persons of Jewish and non-Jewish extraction who felt sufficiently touched in their pocketbooks as well as in spirit to make possible at least some degree of immigration."

He suggested that an initial fund of between $50 and $100 million "would make a significant dent in the problem," enabling the Jews to "have sufficient financial resources to permit them to contribute to the economy of that country [to which they would be shipped] and not as paupers to lower its standard of living."

Joe's friend the publisher Henry Luce thought this an admirable and innovative approach, writing in *Life* magazine that if the plan succeeded, it "would add new luster to a reputation which might well carry Joseph Patrick Kennedy into the White House."

But Luce's was a distinctly minority view. In both England and America, more and more citizens and government officials were finding Joe's pro-Nazi sympathies repugnant. Only a dwindling number of heads of European, British and American corporations, who feared that war would reduce their profitability, continued to share Joe's view that Hitler should be given anything he wanted since, in any event, he was strong enough to take it by force.

James Mooney of General Motors was one. "We ought to make some arrangement with Germany," he said. "There is no reason why we should let our moral indignation over what happens in that country stand in the way."

In April of 1939, Mooney went so far as to travel to Germany to discuss with Hitler the possibility of a massive loan of United States gold reserves which would permit the Nazis to construct the "New Order" that Hitler had promised to bring to Europe.

From Germany Mooney flew to London, where he found Joe Kennedy an enthusiastic supporter of the idea. Kennedy, in fact, agreed to meet Nazi representatives in Paris within days to discuss ways in which the loan could be arranged. When the White House got word of the proposed meeting, however, Joe was denied permission to attend.

Instead, in London on May 9, he hosted a private meeting for leading Nazi economic planners and reported later to his friend Mooney that they had "seen eye to eye on everything."

By midsummer of 1939, Joe had come to view his mission as twofold: to persuade Roosevelt to give the Nazis financial assistance and, in the increasingly likely event that England succumbed to internal pressures and went to war against Hitler, to convince him that the United States under no circumstances should become involved.

On September 1, German forces rolled across the Polish border and conquered that country within twenty-four hours. The following day, faced with overwhelming sentiment in Parliament that England could no longer idly stand by, a reluctant Chamberlain announced that England felt itself compelled to declare war on Germany.

Near hysteria, Joe called Roosevelt to report personally on Chamberlain's speech. "It's the end of the world," he wailed. "It's the end of everything." Some time was required for the President to restore his ambassador to a state of rationality and self-control, though even at the end of the conversation Joe was predicting that this war, which Hitler would so swiftly and convincingly win, would mean a return to "chaos," and "the dark ages," and, worst of all, might very well lead to the sort of worldwide disorder that would put Joe's fortune at risk.

By now, Roosevelt had grown disillusioned with his ambassador to England. Joe's reputation was further tarnished when it was reported that prior to Hitler's invasion of Czechoslovakia Joe had made massive short sales of stock in Czech companies, thus reaping an enormous personal profit from Hitler's aggression.

No longer was he mentioned as a possible 1940 presidential candidate. Instead, for the first time, calls for his resignation as ambassador were heard on the floor of Congress.

In such an atmosphere, in mid-September of 1939—with trenches being dug, piles of sandbags assembled, gas masks distributed and air raid shelters constructed throughout London—did Teddy and his mother and the other younger children flee England.

4

THE PRE-WAR BRONXVILLE TO WHICH TEDDY returned was a tranquil, elegant, almost pastoral community in which the wealth of the residents was presumed if not always lavishly displayed.

Its compact downtown shopping area, composed almost entirely of high-priced specialty shops and gourmet grocery stores, was dominated, at one end, by the stately, cream-colored Gramatan Hotel. Beyond the shopping area, Pondfield Road, tree-lined and curving gracefully, led gradually to that area of the community which contained the grandest estates.

Half a mile from the center of town, near the top of the hill at which Crampton Road intersected Pondfield, Joe Kennedy had purchased a twenty-room red-brick Georgian mansion, surrounded by five acres of exquisitely landscaped and maintained grounds.

In many ways, the tasteful shopping area of Bronxville as well as the surrounding mansions and lush landscapes might as easily have existed in the picturesque Cotswolds of England.

It was hard to believe that midtown Manhattan, with its teeming masses, was only fifteen miles away. It was equally hard to comprehend that much of America was only beginning to emerge from the worst economic depression in the nation's history. In Bronxville, the depression had been only a rumor.

Thus, the Bronxville to which Teddy returned in the fall of 1939 provided an effective layer of insulation against the harsh realities of the outside world.

He liked it. As in London, he was driven to school by chauffeured limousine, but in this case it was to the Lawrence Park Country Day School, where neither his accent nor his status as the Ambassador's son set him quite so far apart from his peers as they had in London.

Joe Junior had entered Harvard Law School and Jack, his health temporarily restored, was again a Harvard undergraduate. Kathleen was attending Finch College in New York City, which was essentially a finishing school for post-debutantes preparing to launch their social careers, but she longed to return to London, where she had fallen in love.

Rosemary had remained behind in England, at her special school for the handicapped; the younger girls had been sent to American boarding schools, and even Bobby, at thirteen, had been shipped to an austere Catholic prep school in Rhode Island.

That left only seven-year-old Teddy underfoot. "I like it better here," he told a reporter from a local paper who asked him if he missed London. "I have more fun." Indeed, heady as had been the London days, the demands of being a young prince, on virtually constant public display, had been not inconsiderable. Especially for Teddy, who, as the chubbiest and youngest, was even then, as his early biographer Burton Hersh has pointed out, developing "a keen and sometimes panic-stricken sense of who he [was], of obligation to family, to people, to life."

In Bronxville, he could enjoy relative anonymity while in no way sacrificing his status as the youngest child of one of the wealthiest and most renowned families in America.

His mother, unfortunately, took rather a different view. Though there was an ample supply of servants to care for him, and though Rose herself maintained a suite at the Plaza Hotel to which she could retreat when the demands of domestic life grew too onerous, she still saw Teddy primarily as an inconvenience.

That she would have the obligation of supervising his upbringing while her husband lived in splendid isolation at the American embassy residence in London had not been part of the deal she had negotiated with Joe before Teddy's birth.

In late November, Joe was summoned to Washington by Franklin Roosevelt for "consultation." Now that actual war had broken out, Joe's pro-Nazi sympathies and isolationist stance had become an embarrassment to the President. Nonetheless, Joe gave a speech in Boston in early December in which he said, "As you love America, don't let anything that comes out of any country in the world make you believe you can make the situation one whit better by getting into war. There is no place in this fight for us."

Then he traveled to Palm Beach for Christmas, where the family joined him and where Rose raised the issue of Teddy. She made it clear to her husband that she did not intend to be encumbered by the presence of a young child in the Bronxville house. At least while Joe remained in England, Teddy would simply have to be sent off to boarding school, as had the others.

The problem was, he would not turn eight until February and there was no obvious place to send him. Bobby's school, Portsmouth Priory, admitted no students below seventh grade.

Nonetheless, Rose insisted and arrangements were made. When you are a close personal friend of the Pope, you can persuade even as rigorous an institution as Portsmouth Priory to bend its regulations. Thus, early in chill 1940 Teddy was shipped to the Rhode Island school, presided over by the authoritarian Benedictine order of Catholic priests. This marked the beginning of some miserable and chaotic years during which, for all his wealth and sense of privilege, he found himself on no firmer footing emotionally than millions of other war refugees.

Before he reached the age of thirteen, Teddy would

attend ten different day and boarding schools as his parents sought to minimize the inconvenience that his presence posed.

Later, he would claim this had not bothered him. In a splendid example of what by then had become classic Kennedy denial, he would say, "I don't think I felt anything particular about it." And then add: "I don't have any complexes, if that's what you mean."

But it was hard to deny the horror of Portsmouth Priory. "He seemed young and immature," a priest from the school later told another early biographer, James MacGregor Burns, "and didn't get along particularly well."

Of course, he was young and immature: at least five years younger than any other boy enrolled at the school. Fat young Teddy, the son of the rich ambassador who liked the Nazis, became an immediate object of ridicule. He was taunted, teased and beaten by packs of older students.

His classroom time was a loss also, because the school had no curriculum suitable for an eight-year-old. Instead, Teddy took courses prepared for seventh-graders and, as he said later, "found myself completely mystified by Latin."

He endured three lonely, miserable, fear-ridden months at Portsmouth Priory, sleeping, he later recalled, "in my own little cubicle." It was a long way from holding a press conference at the Vatican to being shoved in the mud and pummeled by a bunch of teenagers in Rhode Island, and Teddy was never quite sure what he'd done to warrant such harsh punishment.

One particular afternoon lingered long in his memory. An older boy had knocked him to the ground and was on top of him, punching him in the body and face, when thirteen-year-old Bobby walked by.

Teddy cried out to his older brother for help. But Bobby just looked down and said, "You're a Kennedy. Take care of yourself."

Teddy's father, though not subject to physical abuse, fared not much better that spring. Returning to London, he found that his Boston comments about there being no place in the war for America had provoked considerable hostility among the British.

In April, after a series of sudden and unexpected military reverses, Chamberlain was forced to resign as prime minister. He was replaced by the far more aggressive and inspirational Winston Churchill, a man who had open contempt for Joe Kennedy.

Once Churchill came to power, and particularly after he inspired supporters of democracy around the world with his famous "blood, toil, tears and sweat" speech, Joe found himself increasingly reviled as he clung to his isolationist stance.

He remained convinced that history would prove him correct, and sooner rather than later. "There is always some personal satisfaction in being able to say, 'I told you so,' " he wrote to a friend after France fell to the Nazis in June.

Not long afterwards, he wrote to Joe Junior that "the finish may come quickly. I can see nothing but slaughter ahead." He said the British lacked the moral fiber, the toughness—and the military resources—to withstand Hitler. With his public predictions equally dire, animosity toward him grew, both in England and in America.

But if he could not shape the world, or his country, as he wished, Joe remained convinced that he could control the destinies of his sons and that, using them as surrogates, he might still grasp the highest rungs of power.

He made certain that his oldest son had no doubts about the nature of his ambition. It was Joe Junior, now twenty-five and thriving at Harvard Law School—the golden boy grown to manhood—upon whom he focused his energy. "You are now arriving at the point," he wrote in the summer of 1940, "where you have responsibilities to the family."

To the family. At twenty-five, it was not independence that Joe Junior had earned but, instead, a deeper entanglement with his father's desires, a more profound obligation to bring the sort of honor and glory to the Kennedy hat the Ambassador was rapidly forfeiting through his own words and actions.

For Joe Junior, politics would be the path to power. It was Joe's grand design that his son would become, first, governor of Massachusetts and then, as quickly as Joe's money could make it happen, the first Catholic President of the United States.

Jack, the frail second son, now twenty-three, did not seem suited for the rigors of political life. There were, however, other paths to glory and, as a result of his father's manipulations, Jack was already enjoying a flashy, if passing, success.

In order to graduate from Harvard in 1940, Jack had needed to produce a senior thesis. In it, he'd tried to analyze some of the reasons for England's inadequate preparation for the threat Hitler posed.

Jack had not actually written the thesis. Rather, using vast amounts of research material supplied by his father, he'd dictated drafts and sections to a staff of stenographers and secretaries sent to Cambridge from his father's New York business office. Joe had also written a series of long letters to his son expressing his views of the roots of England's weakness and Jack had copied chunks of them, almost word for word, into the text.

Ragged and patchy as it was, Joe felt the thesis could be used to advantage. He rushed a copy to Arthur Krock, the influential *New York Times* columnist, whom he still kept on private retainer. He told Krock to rewrite the thesis, quickly and anonymously, and then to arrange for its publication as a book.

Working frantically through the spring, Krock tried to transform the sloppily assembled undergraduate essay into a manuscript fit for publication.

Joe also persuaded his friend Henry Luce to write a foreword in which he asserted that young Jack's observations were somehow of special relevance to American readers in a presidential election year.

Even after Krock's hurried ministrations the manuscript remained badly flawed. As pressure mounted, Joe gave the task of final rewriting to his personal speech writer, who later recalled, ''I worked on it two weeks, night and day, delivered it at four o'clock in the morning on the day Eddie Moore was to go to New York and take it to the publisher. When I got it, it was a mishmash, ungrammatical. He had sentences without subjects and verbs. It was a very sloppy job, mostly magazine and newspaper clippings stuck together. I edited it, and put in a little peroration at the end.''

Upon its publication in July, Joe arranged for agents of his in the United States to buy enough copies to ensure that *Why England Slept* would appear on national best-seller lists. And so it did briefly, selling a reported forty thousand copies, of which at least half had been purchased by Joe and shipped in unopened cartons to Hyannis Port, where they were stored in the attic and basement of the Kennedy home.

While Jack spent the summer promoting the book in newspaper and radio interviews, his father expressed pleasure at their success. ''You will be surprised,'' the Ambassador wrote to Jack, ''how a book that really makes the grade with high class people stands you in good stead for years to come.''

That summer, Teddy retreated to the relatively safe haven of Hyannis Port. He was still there in September —his mother having been persuaded, more by school administrators than by her anguished son, that Portsmouth Priory was not a place to which he could return—when the German bombing of London began.

Within a few days, Joe wrote Teddy a letter. The father said to his eight-year-old son, ''I don't know whether you would have very much excitement during these raids. I am sure, of course, you wouldn't be scared, but if you heard all these guns firing every night and the bombs bursting you might get a little fidgety. I am sure you would have liked to be with me and seen the fires the German bombers started in London . . . I know you will be glad to hear that all these little English boys your age are standing up to this bombing in great shape. They are all training to be great sports. . . .''

The point seemed clear: If the little English boys could put up with bombs falling on their city every night, the least Teddy could do was to stop whimpering about the minor inconveniences of Portsmouth Priory. The Benedictines, however, had had their fill. At least for the fall term, Rose was forced to permit Teddy to attend the private Riverdale Country School in New York City.

The Nazi air blitz of London lasted for almost two months. Every night, ton after ton of lethal weaponry was dropped upon densely populated sections of the city in an effort to break the will of the British people. Instead, in their fear and anger, Londoners drew closer together, more united, their resolve to battle Hitler to the end now strengthened beyond challenge.

Only Joe Kennedy, it seemed, lacked the personal courage he was so quick to praise in British schoolboys. It was said in London that during the raids Joe was likely to be hiding out in his "funk hole" with "some Paris model," for the absence of Rose had allowed full reflowering of his impulse toward promiscuity.

After the first few nights, however, not even Paris models could keep his fear in check. He began to leave his office in midafternoon to ensure that he'd be safe in the country each night, far from London before the bombs began to fall.

His cowardice became the talk of the city, angering Londoners and causing other Americans great embarrassment. "Jittery Joe," they called him, and would say, behind his back, "Run, rabbit, run."

He tried to joke about it, saying, hey, he had nine kids, he couldn't take chances. But each morning as the smoke slowly cleared and the fires subsided and more bodies of women and children were pulled from the wreckage of civilian dwellings, the people of London had less and less interest in anything Joe Kennedy had to say.

By October, he'd had enough. He was just plain scared and wanted to get out of the country altogether. Informed by Washington that he was being relieved of his post, Joe made a quick round of good-byes, announcing that once he was home he'd make it clear to all America that "Roosevelt and the kikes are taking us into war."

By then British newspapers were referring to him openly as "a coward . . . a defeatist . . . a crook," and "malevolent and pigeon-livered." The news of his departure was the biggest boost of the year for British morale.

Returning to America in late October, Joe brought a British air raid siren with him as a souvenir. For years afterwards, at Hyannis Port, he would use it to summon the family to meals. Having made it his practice to flee London long before the first siren of the night had been sounded during the blitz, this seemed a peculiar memento, but to Joe it was just one more way of having the last laugh.

The day after Roosevelt's reelection, Joe gave a newspaper interview in his suite at the Ritz-Carlton in Boston that wrecked what was left of his public career.

For ninety minutes he spoke freely to a *Boston Globe* reporter and to two correspondents from a St. Louis newspaper, assuming, apparently, that his remarks were off the record, and, in any event, utterly failing to recognize how repugnant his sentiments were to the vast majority of Americans.

"I'd be willing to spend all I've got left to keep us out of the war," he said. "There's no sense in our getting in. We'd just be holding the bag. People call me a pessimist. I say, 'What is there to be gay about?' Democracy is all done. Democracy is finished in England. And it may be here."

He followed this pronouncement with a long, rambling attack upon the King of England (making fun of his stammer), the British cabinet and Eleanor Roosevelt.

He said, "The queen has got more brains than the cabinet." About the President's wife, he said, "She bothered us more on our jobs than all the rest of the people down in Washington together, wanting us to take care of the poor little nobodies who hadn't any influence. She was always sending me a note to have some little Susie Glotz to tea at the embassy."

Publication of these remarks prompted fierce attacks in the American press. Not even his friendships with Henry Luce and William Randolph Hearst, nor whatever private arrangement he had with Arthur Krock, could protect him from public outrage at his comments, or from Franklin and Eleanor Roosevelt's private fury.

The week before Thanksgiving, the President summoned Joe to his home at Hyde Park, New York, to demand an explanation. The morning meeting was brief. The two men had been together less than half an hour when Roosevelt opened his office door and shouted, "I never want to see this son of a bitch again as long as I live! Take his resignation and get him out of here!"

Eleanor reminded her husband that the next train for New York City did not depart until midafternoon.

"I don't give a damn!" the President replied. "Drive him around Hyde Park, give him a sandwich and get him on that train." Eleanor, who loathed Joe even more than her husband did, was only too happy to oblige.

And thus ended Joe Kennedy's career in government. Any dreams of future glory he still clung to would have to be realized by his sons—in particular, by his oldest son, of whom he wrote, "I find myself much more interested in what young Joe is going to do than in what I am going to do with the rest of my life."

It was not a good fall for Teddy, either. Though greatly relieved to be spared a further ordeal at Portsmouth Priory, he accomplished little at Riverdale.

One can only speculate as to whether his immune system might have been weakened by the stress he undoubtedly felt as he became aware that his father, of whom he'd always been so in awe, had fallen into such sudden and total disgrace, but the fact was that Teddy contracted first pneumonia and then, when that was cured, whooping cough.

Indeed, he attended so few classes at Riverdale that when he transferred to a private school in Palm Beach as his parents headed south for the winter, it was quickly noted by a teacher there that Teddy had "no foundation for fourth grade work." This was not surprising, since he seemed never to have actually finished third grade, nor even second, so helter-skelter had his existence become.

Through the winter of 1940 and spring of 1941 Teddy could not have helped but notice the enormous difference in his father's mood and personality. The good humor, the ebullience, the confidence, the salty charm—all these had vanished and the Ambassador (as he still insisted on being called) sat silently by the swimming pool of his Palm Beach residence and brooded about how the "kikes" had driven him from power.

"After England," the governess Luella Hennessey noted, "Mr. Kennedy began to withdraw more and more into himself. He was not as outgoing or as happy as he had been before and the children felt it." Especially, one can imagine, the nine-year-old Teddy, who had the least idea of what was going on, or why.

In the spring, with Rose on a trip to South America, Joe Kennedy decided to sell the Bronxville house, the closest thing to a home Teddy had ever known. From the Ambassador's point of view, it was a sensible decision, for he had vacation homes now both in Florida and on Cape Cod and permanent suites at the Waldorf-Astoria in New York and the Ritz-Carlton in Boston.

To Luella Hennessey, however, the abandonment of the Bronxville house seemed to mark a great "loss of stability" within the family, and, once again, it seemed to have affected Teddy most of all.

Indeed, Kearns Goodwin has written that "it was Teddy who was hurt the most by the loss of a permanent home. . . . He was a cheerful, loving child, but his cheerfulness was in part a protection against the tension of constantly being thrust into new situations and new schools. . . . For any child, this constant transplantation would be hard. For young Teddy, unsure of his intellect and so overweight at the time that his brothers called him 'fatstuff,' it was extremely damaging."

He was the only one of the male children to grow into adolescence after his father's fall from grace, and—it might be noted—to be confronted constantly during his teenage years with examples of his older brothers' greatness.

Doubly burdened, Teddy grew to maturity both in the sadness of his father's twilight and, before long, in the shadows cast by the glow of Joe Junior's and Jack's heroism.

5

T HE HYANNIS PORT SUMMER OF 1941 WAS THE LAST
time the entire Kennedy family would be together.

Teddy would remember it both with nostalgia and as a
time of great confusion, with many powerful crosscur-
rents passing above and beneath him in all directions,
most of them unfathomable to his nine-year-old sensibility.

His father had become a brooding, snappish presence
best avoided. His mother was rapidly growing more ec-
centric. She'd taken to wearing pieces of tape on her face
to prevent wrinkles and pinning notes on her dress to
remind herself of her daily chores (which consisted
mostly of giving new and ever more dictatorial orders to
cowering servants), and she spent more and more hours
apart from the rest of the family, sequestered in a private
gazebo she'd had constructed on the Hyannis Port
grounds—reading, meditating, planning her wardrobe for
the fall, who could tell?

Joe Junior surprised them all with his announcement
that he'd decided to defer his final year at Harvard Law
in order to enlist as a naval air cadet.

The oldest Kennedy son, who had already announced
to many friends his intention of becoming America's first

Catholic President, was thinking ahead. Old enough now to recognize how his father had been permanently tainted by dodging the draft in World War I and how the family reputation had been even more battered by the old man's warmth toward Hitler, Joe Junior sensed that if his future political career was to carry him as high as he wanted to go, he would have to show that he'd acted patriotically in this hour of national crisis.

Some have suggested that his motives ran deeper; that as the oldest son and the one expected to enjoy quick, dramatic success as an adult, he'd been badly stung by Jack's leapfrogging past him with publication of *Why England Slept*. The quickest way for Joe Junior to regain his place of primacy was to enter military service—preferably the most glamorous, highest-risk branch he could find. The Naval Air Service met those criteria.

"I think Jack is not doing anything," he'd written to his father in the spring, "and with your stand on the war, people will wonder what the devil I am doing back at school when everyone else is working for national defense."

But then, not to be outdone, Jack announced that he was enlisting in a naval officers' training course. It had already been acknowledged that the political future belonged to Joe Junior, that it was the oldest son whom the Ambassador was grooming for the White House; but this did not mean that other forms of competition between the two brothers ceased.

At sixteen, even Bobby was now trying to enter the race for first place in his father's affections. "He was the smallest and least articulate of all the boys," a family friend said later, "but he never stopped trying." And Rose added, "While they all knew what was expected of them, Bobby really worked at it."

It was clear to Bobby that his father did not anticipate that he would rise to the heights envisioned for Joe Junior and for Jack, and that therefore the Ambassador did not push Bobby forward so relentlessly, but, as Kearns Goodwin has pointed out, this "mellower attitude had a paradoxical effect . . . making Bobby struggle even more to win his father's attention and respect."

With three older, more talented, more driven brothers already so far ahead of him, the only role remaining for Teddy, or "Fatstuff," was that of family mascot.

"He was my baby," Rose said later, "and I tried to keep him my baby." As did his sisters, who thought him so cuddly and cute. Later, speaking of his sisters, Teddy would say, "It was like having a whole army of mothers around me. While it seemed I could never do anything right with my brothers, I could never do anything wrong so far as my sisters were concerned."

But even with the sisters, there was a note of condescension. Eunice later remarked that "in the touch football games the girls had to be able to cover the boys, too. Covering Bobby wasn't easy. We all wanted to cover Teddy because he was so little and pudgy."

As the youngest member of such a family, Teddy was not finding self-esteem easy to come by. And there can be no denying that—despite their psychological and emotional shortcomings—the Kennedys, at the physical level, were extraordinary: the good looks, the flashing grins, the relentless energy, the almost palpable surge of sexuality among the men, the verve and self-confidence of all the sisters save Rosemary.

"You watched these people go through their lives," said Chuck Spalding, a visitor to Hyannis Port that summer, who later became one of Jack's closer friends, "and just had a feeling that they existed outside the usual laws of nature; that there was no other group so handsome, so engaged. There was endless action—not just football, but sailboats, tennis, and other things; movement. . . . It was a scene of endless competition, people drawing each other out and pushing each other to greater lengths. It was as simple as this: the Kennedys had a feeling of being heightened and it rubbed off on the people who came in contact with them. They were a unit. I remember thinking to myself that there couldn't be another group quite like this one."

It was, however, beneath the flashy surface, a group in considerable flux and no small degree of turmoil. There were the obvious changes that would come with summer's end: the departure of Joe Junior and Jack for military service in a war their father had so bitterly opposed; Kathleen's move to Washington, where her father had obtained for her (through Arthur Krock) a job as a newspaper reporter.

There was also the addition of eleven-year-old Joey Gargan, who became, over time, the most loyal friend Teddy would ever have.

For Teddy, the introduction of this new force into his life—a cousin only two years older whose main task seemed to be to play with him—proved an immediate tonic. For Teddy, Joey Gargan was, as Burton Hersh has commented, "like the kind of imaginary brother infants need so badly they find him beneath their cribs as soon as their parents leave the room. . . . Here was somebody who was family and trustworthy but at the same time did what you wanted and knew enough to keep quiet about it."

There was also a subtraction, which would not come until summer had ended, but which was to prove far more disquieting for them all, especially for Teddy, who had the least ability to understand.

As she'd grown older, Rosemary, who'd been functional enough to make her formal debut alongside Kathleen in London, was said to have grown more intractable.

There are many theories about Rosemary and very few verifiable facts about her fate. Nigel Hamilton, author of the most recent substantial biography of Jack, has written, "Some who witnessed Joseph P. Kennedy's own behavior at home speculated as to whether he might have sexually abused Rosemary."

This theory—which relies on support not from firsthand recollection but from documented accounts of Joe's attempts to sexually molest the dates of his sons and the friends of his daughters when they were overnight guests in his home—postulates that Rosemary had repressed for years the fact of the abuse she'd suffered from her father. Entering adulthood, she suddenly found herself not only able but needing to talk about it. In such a case, Joe's need to silence her quickly and permanently would have been strong, especially if he was planning to send his oldest son to the White House as President.

Kennedy family biographer Doris Kearns Goodwin has heatedly refuted any such notion. Yet the documentation that might resolve the question remains sealed to researchers.

Whatever the circumstances, Rosemary, who had long been a source of shame to these parents so obsessed with their image of a perfect family, suddenly drove her father to precipitate and—in the absence of any evidence to the contrary—unforgivably immoral and self-serving action.

She had written to him once, after he'd visited her at one of her boarding schools: "I would do anything to make you so happy. I hate to disapoint you in anyway. Come to see me very soon. I get lonesome everyday."

But now, whether he'd sexually abused her or not, he apparently felt he could not permit her disabilities to interfere with the political career he was planning for his oldest son. It would be hard enough, even with all his money and influence, to get a Catholic elected President. But a Catholic with a retarded and possibly even schizophrenic sister?

No. For Joe, the equation was apparently all too simple: for the sake of his oldest son, he would have to sacrifice his oldest daughter. It was a business decision, like so many he'd made throughout his life.

So, at the end of that summer of 1941, he made secret arrangements to have her lobotomized. In a prefrontal lobotomy, a sharp pick was plunged into the frontal lobes of the brain, reducing the patient forever after to a passive, almost vegetative state. In that condition, Rosemary could be more easily hidden from public view and thus would prove less of an impediment to Joe Junior's political career.

Rose always claimed later that she had known nothing about the lobotomy. She said that Joe simply informed her one day that he'd decided the time had come to shift Rosemary to an institution, where her physical needs could be better cared for, and that in consultation with Cardinal Cushing, the spiritual leader of Boston's Roman

Catholics, a splendid home for the retarded had been found in Wisconsin and Rosemary had been sent to live there.

The story Rose told was that Joe had said it would be easier for both mother and daughter if Rosemary were permitted to acclimate herself to her new surroundings without the stress that would inevitably arise from a family visit.

Rose also said that for the next twenty years, until Joe's stroke in 1961, she neither saw her oldest daughter nor even knew what had happened to her. That only twenty years later, when Joe could no longer prevent it, did she lay eyes on Rosemary again and learn for the first time that the lobotomy had rendered her unable to speak, unable to hold her head upright, unable ever again to communicate with or even to recognize any member of her family or anyone else.

The story Rose told was that it was out of consideration for her feelings that her husband had never told her the truth. She has added, in telling this story, that it never occurred to her to question him. In some odd way, she seemed to feel that this absolved her from responsibility.

(And Rosemary lives on, somewhere, though neither Teddy nor his sisters will entertain questions about her condition or the circumstances that led to it, and not even the tabloids have ever pressed for details. Rosemary, indeed, may become the last surviving Kennedy of her generation. No one will ever know.)

All that young Teddy knew was that one day Rosemary was there and the next she was gone forever. Even the highly sympathetic Kearns Goodwin has written, "For Rosemary's sisters and brothers, her sudden disappearance must have been met by dozens of questions that were never fully answered, surrounding the incident with the aura of forbidden mystery. . . . Why, after all these years, did she have to be institutionalized now? And why couldn't any of the family see her? And, most ominously, why wouldn't anyone really talk about what was happening?"

For the youngest Kennedy—the overweight, underachieving, insecure Teddy—the sudden vanishing of Rosemary and the eradication of all traces of her must have been a singularly terrifying experience.

Was this what happened to Kennedys who no longer held out the promise of success, Kennedys who became inconvenient? They were banished? They simply disappeared and no one ever spoke of them again?

In the absence of any assurances to the contrary, it might well have begun to seem to the nine-year-old Teddy that this could be the price of failure within the family: to suddenly cease to exist.

6

URING THE NEXT THREE YEARS, EVEN MORE DRA-
matic change swept through the family, re-forming it,
finally, into the shape it would possess as it stepped forward into the realm of American history and, eventually,
myth.

Throughout this period, as his parents concentrated
their energies on the older, "more important" children,
and as they made their seasonal moves from Cape Cod to
Palm Beach and back again, Teddy fluttered along behind.

Late in 1941, assigned to the Office of Naval Intelligence in Washington, Jack began an affair with a Danish
journalist named Inga Arvad, whom the FBI suspected
of being a Nazi spy. Considerable turmoil ensued when
government agents discovered this liaison between the
suspected enemy operative and a naval intelligence officer who was the son of a former ambassador to England
with pro-Nazi sympathies. Electronic surveillance disclosed that Jack was, indeed, sharing with his new lover
information that the government considered confidential.

News of the affair was leaked to gossip columnist Walter Winchell, who printed an item about it in January of
1942. Fearing a major scandal that would destroy Joe

Junior's political career before it even began, Joe immediately contacted FBI director J. Edgar Hoover, with whom he apparently had developed a useful working relationship over the years. The two seem to have made a secret arrangement. In return for Hoover's promise not to bring criminal charges against Jack and to keep the incriminating evidence locked inside a private file, Joe agreed to travel to Hollywood in order to spy on his former friends and business associates, informing the rabidly anti-Communist and anti-Semitic Hoover of any left-wing plotting being undertaken by Jews.

Informed that Jack still faced imminent dishonorable discharge from military service, Joe apparently also reached a separate arrangement with good friend James Forrestal, undersecretary of the navy, which resulted instead in Jack's transfer to a PT (patrol torpedo) boat squadron based in the Solomon Islands of the South Pacific—as far from Inga Arvad as could be.

With his father preoccupied by these machinations and his mother continuing her solitary travels, visiting shrines to the Blessed Virgin in South America, little attention was paid to Teddy, who shuttled between the Palm Beach Private School and Graham Eckes Academy in Florida, and the Fessenden School in the western suburbs of Boston. He continued to founder both academically and emotionally.

In fifth grade, at the end of January 1943, his overall grade average had fallen to 68, barely passing. While his father was proudly pinning gold aviator's wings on Joe Junior's lapel at a Naval Air Service graduation ceremony in Jacksonville, Florida, the most his mother could say of Teddy, in a letter to other family members, was that, serving as an altar boy at mass, he was making less of a fool of himself than in the past. "I did not see him fall down at all the last time," his mother wrote.

Wounded in spirit and garnering little respect, affection or attention either inside or outside the family, Teddy again summered at Hyannis Port in 1943 with Joey Gargan. Joey, at least, did not laugh at him. Joey did not ridicule him. Joey, in fact, seemed the one person in

Teddy's life who was never judgmental, never critical, and who always seemed to enjoy Teddy's company.

Teddy was with Joey early one morning in August when his father rushed back after his daily horseback ride to shout that he'd just heard on the car radio that Jack's PT boat had been sunk in the Pacific, and that while there had been some casualties, Jack himself was alive and well.

The PT boat, a speedy, highly maneuverable, eighty-foot-long plywood vessel powered by three engines and armed with torpedoes, had been one of several such craft sent to intercept Japanese troopships carrying reinforcements to New Guinea.

Somehow, with Jack at the helm and two of its three engines shut down, the boat had been struck broadside by a Japanese destroyer. During all of World War II, Jack's was the only PT boat ever sunk as the result of being rammed by an enemy ship. Indeed, many familiar with the PT's characteristics could never understand how what was essentially an armed speedboat could have been cut in half by the prow of a much larger, much slower destroyer.

Jack never did offer a satisfactory explanation, but apparently he had not seen or heard the destroyer approaching. He neither fired a torpedo nor ordered his two remaining engines started in an attempt to evade.

The PT boat, cut in half, burst into flames. Two of his thirteen-man crew died instantly. Jack and the other survivors clung to the remainder of the hulk through the night. Eventually, towing a wounded crew member behind him, Jack led the others on a four-mile swim to the safety of a small island, from which they were rescued three days later.

"We were kind of ashamed of our performance," a crew member said later. "I had always thought it was a disaster." The skipper of another PT boat said, "Jack was actually in a lot of trouble" over the sinking of his PT, which had been assigned the number 109.

Once again, however, the lesson that it was not who you were (or what you did) that mattered, but only what people could be made to think, was put into practice.

Two wire-service correspondents assigned to the Solomons at the time were told that Ambassador Kennedy's son and his crew were about to be rescued from a deserted island nearby. Sensing a good story within easy reach, the reporters boarded the rescue craft.

Having learned the details of the incident, the newsmen decided that the-daring-rescue-of-the-Ambassador's-son-who'd-performed-heroically-in-battle would get better play than an account of how a careless commander had needlessly lost both his boat and two of his men as the result of negligence, a freak accident, or some combination of the two.

Thus, the story that eventually came out of the South Pacific was featured on the front page of *The New York Times* of August 20, 1943, under the headline "Kennedy's Son Is Hero in Pacific as Destroyer Splits His PT Boat."

The *New York Herald Tribune* account said that Jack had written a "blazing new saga in PT boat annals." In the sense that his boat had caught fire, this was true.

He was shipped out of the Solomons in late fall. Toward the end, said one squadron leader, "Jack got very wild; some of my old guys said he was crazy." He returned home by way of California. In Los Angeles, he was welcomed by Inga Arvad, who, spy or not, was still working as a journalist. She quickly wrote an account of Jack's heroism which the Ambassador arranged to have syndicated in newspapers across the country. This generated enough interest so that Jack himself held a news conference in Los Angeles.

With each retelling, the magnitude of his heroism seemed to grow. By now, the sinking of his boat was the result of the Japanese response to his courageous attack upon the vastly larger destroyer. And by now it was Jack, almost single-handedly, who'd pulled his men from the flaming, sinking wreckage, led them to safety, kept them alive, and then through further acts of bravery and bold imagination had effected their rescue.

In fact, the rescue was the result of their having been spotted by an Australian naval coast watcher named Arthur Reginald Evans, who'd been secreted atop a nearby volcano, scanning the horizon for signs of enemy activity.

All mention of Evans's role was quickly dropped from Jack's account, however, and each time he embellished the tale, he seemed to grow less uncomfortable.

Even in its early versions, the PT boat story generated so much favorable publicity for Jack that it again upset the delicate balance in the relationship between him and his older brother. Just as had the publication of *Why England Slept,* getting his name on the front page of *The New York Times* as a war hero enabled Jack to once again vault past Joe Junior in terms of public, and thus family, esteem.

Joe Junior did not react well to being even temporarily in second place. He was so upset at seeing Jack's name on the front page of the *Times* that for almost a week after the news of the rescue he refused to call Hyannis Port for further details.

Even Rose, in all her self-absorption, recognized what a blow it was to Joe Junior to see his younger brother win such acclaim. "This," she would write of the bitter and lifelong competition between her two oldest sons, "was the first time Jack had won such an advantage by such a clear margin. I daresay it cheered Jack and must have rankled Joe, Jr."

How much it rankled became clearer in early September. Stopping briefly at Hyannis Port on leave before joining a new aerial combat unit in England, Joe Junior was present for his father's fifty-fifth birthday dinner.

During the meal, a guest from Boston proposed a toast: "To Ambassador Joe Kennedy, father of our hero, our own hero, Lieutenant John F. Kennedy of the United States Navy."

Joe Junior sat stiffly and silently in his chair, forced to raise his glass and to smile through clenched teeth. But later that night, in the bedroom he was sharing with another guest, the police commissioner of Boston, the tension overcame him and he started to cry.

It was just not fair, after how hard he'd worked, after all he'd done, after it had been so carefully arranged by his father that he, the natural leader of the next generation, would be the first of the Kennedy children to bask in national attention, that skinny little Jack should wind up being toasted as a hero.

Sitting up in his bed, Joe suddenly shouted into the darkness, "By God, I'll show them!" By the end of the month, he was on his way to England.

Jack's new status as war hero served also to cast into even sharper relief the difference between what a Kennedy was expected to be and what the youngest member of the family was.

By October of 1943, in sixth grade at Fessenden, Teddy was hitting new lows, failing both English and geography, which had always been considered among his better subjects, and compiling an average of only 58.

Later that fall, after a business trip to Boston during which he'd paid a brief visit to Teddy, Joe wrote grumpily to Rose that Teddy "goes off half-cocked when anybody asks any questions and he gives them an answer even though most times it is wrong."

By midwinter—whether at the school's or the family's request was never made clear—Teddy was withdrawn from Fessenden and enrolled once again in the Palm Beach Private School. By now, his failures had sufficiently irked his father that Teddy was told he would be living at home, in the Palm Beach house, rather than boarding. In that way, his father explained, his academic progress could be more closely monitored.

Improvement came swiftly. Permitted to live at home for the first time during a school year since his brief stint at Riverdale, Teddy set out to show his father that hope remained. During the first half of the spring term of 1944, he received B's in English and math and A's in history and writing. He also won his first election: as vice president of the sixth grade.

But, as would prove to be essentially the story of his life, Teddy again found his fate drastically altered by forces over which he had no control.

Kathleen, who had returned to England the year before, announced in April that she'd become engaged to marry a British aristocrat, William Cavendish, the Marquess of Hartington. Moreover, he was heir to the Duke of Devonshire, which meant that upon his father's death Hartington would become one of the wealthiest and most powerful men in England.

He was, however, a Protestant and, as the prospective Duke of Devonshire, was prohibited both by unbending custom and religious edict from fathering a child who would be raised a Catholic. Under the circumstances, Kathleen explained by letter to her parents, she had no choice but, reluctantly, to marry outside the Catholic Church.

As a woman who had turned piety into not merely a vocation but something approaching a profession, Rose was, as she put it, "heartbroken and horrified" by Kathleen's announcement. Immediately, she cabled her daughter that the marriage must not take place. "What a blow," she wrote later, "to the family prestige."

The news was such a blow to Rose that she fell into a state of nervous collapse. Given her condition, Joe decided that Teddy should no longer live at home. In midsemester, he was shipped north again to the more rigorous and demanding Fessenden, shaken by the sudden disruption of the best school year he'd ever enjoyed and traumatized by his mother's condition and her belief that the entire family would be destroyed by Kathleen's sacrilegious act.

Kathleen did, in fact, marry Hartington in a civil ceremony on May 6, 1944. Learning of this, Rose suffered such a severe breakdown that she required hospitalization.

Immediately upon his return to Fessenden, both Teddy's grades and his spirits plunged. His final marks once again put him perilously close to outright failure: 70 in English and math; 65 in spelling, geography and history.

Again, he returned to Hyannis Port in a state bordering on disgrace, his only solace being that he could look forward to two months of Joey Gargan's companionship, and that his mother and father were both so preoccupied by events in the lives of older family members that they would pay him little heed.

His father had not objected to the marriage in the least. Joe, in fact, rather liked the notion that it linked him to the highest rungs of British aristocracy and that his new son-in-law would someday inherit a fortune even greater than his own.

Likewise, Rose's dramatic overreaction left him unruffled. The two of them had been living essentially separate lives for so many years that he was quite beyond being affected by her emotional condition except to the extent that it inconvenienced him.

And Joe did not want to be inconvenienced that spring because, with Jack, he was embarked on a plan that would inflate the *PT 109* incident to legendary proportions. His reasoning was simple and, as usual, correct: the greater the war hero Jack was perceived to be, the more use he could be in the service of Joe Junior's future political career.

Jack, who was rather enjoying all the attention he'd received since returning from the South Pacific, did not object. He himself, in fact, did much to launch the enterprise.

An old girlfriend of his had married a well-bred young journalist named John Hersey, who was then employed at Henry Luce's *Time* magazine. While in New York on leave, Jack went to dinner, the theater and then the Stork Club with Hersey and his wife.

As the evening wore on, Jack's tale of his Solomon Islands adventure—which by now he had refined considerably—came to seem more and more beguiling. So much so that by the end of the night, with Jack's vigorous encouragement, Hersey had decided to write it up for *Life,* which was Luce's weekly photo magazine.

Not even the Ambassador's friendship with Luce, however, nor the fact that Luce himself had written the foreword to *Why England Slept,* could bring about publication of the story. Editors at *Life* argued persuasively that it was much too long and not sufficiently topical for their format.

There was, however, another national magazine, *The*

New Yorker, which had no objection to printing lengthy and nontimely texts. Hersey succeeded in placing the story there. It was published in early June of 1944.

So thoroughly drenched in glory did the Hersey version of the tale leave Jack that even the Ambassador was satisfied. All that was lacking was an audience of appropriate size, for *The New Yorker,* while popular among sophisticated readers, did not enjoy the mass circulation of *Life.*

Quickly, Joe arranged through personal connections to have *Reader's Digest,* the magazine with the largest circulation in the country, reprint a condensed version of Hersey's article. As a result of the *Digest* publication, millions of readers across America learned that Lieutenant John F. Kennedy, the Ambassador's son, was one of the great American heroes of World War II.

The family's worst shock of 1944—indeed, in many ways the seminal event in Kennedy history—occurred that August, when, early on a Sunday afternoon, two Catholic priests came to the Hyannis Port house to inform Joe that his oldest son had been killed while flying his final combat mission of the war.

In England that spring, Joe Junior had been in even worse emotional condition than his mother. The memory of the awful night when he'd been forced, in his father's presence, to toast the heroism of his younger brother had not faded.

His own combat performance had actually been far more exemplary than Jack's but he'd received credit for it neither publicly nor within the family. After completing his original tour—which consisted of thirty combat missions—he had even volunteered for further duty.

As squadron leader, in fact, he had offered not only his own additional services but those of his crew, not all of whom were pleased at having their lives placed at continuing risk in order that Joe Junior might satisfy some obscure psychological need.

Even though it was Joe Junior, during this extra tour, who flew in combat during the D-Day invasion of June 6, it was Jack who was celebrated as the warrior in the pages of *The New Yorker* and *Reader's Digest*.

And even though it was Joe Junior who was supposed to return home and run for governor of Massachusetts, it seemed to him that Jack had now surpassed him in his father's eyes.

In reality, this hadn't happened. The Ambassador felt, as he had all along, that the difference between his two older sons was the difference between the potential for true greatness and the ability to make the most of lucky breaks. It was still Joe Junior whose role it would be to bring the family all the honor and power the Ambassador himself had failed to deliver. It was still the advancement of Joe Junior's career in politics to which the Ambassador intended to devote the rest of his life, and as much of his fortune as was required. It was still Joe Junior who was his father's favorite son.

But in the hurly-burly of wartime England, Joe Junior lost sight of his father's true feelings. As his extended tour of duty drew to a close, Joe Junior found himself less eager to return to America than desperate to demonstrate his valor in some way that Jack could never equal.

He had already packed for the long flight home when he heard rumors of a new secret and hazardous mission for which experienced pilots would be needed.

For six weeks, since soon after D-Day, the Germans had been pounding the heart of London with barrage after barrage of V-1 bombs, launched from hidden sites along the French coast. Having so stoically endured intensive aerial attack at the start of the war, and feeling that with the success of the D-Day invasion the tide of battle had irrevocably turned, Londoners were now reacting in panic to the unexpected and destructive assault of these unmanned "buzz bombs."

The pace of the V-1 attacks quickened throughout July, a month in which almost twenty-five hundred residents of London were killed by the bombs and more than seven thousand injured. British morale, which had carried the nation farther and for longer than many—including most especially former U.S. ambassador Joseph P. Kennedy

—would have expected, was now collapsing under the merciless battering.

The Germans were launching the V-1s from reinforced concrete bunkers that had withstood all conventional bombing attacks. Desperate measures now seemed called for and a desperate solution was proposed. The United States Army suggested that the insides be scooped out of the largest conventional bomber available and the plane packed with more high explosive than had ever before been carried by an aircraft.

Such a plane would be, in effect, the largest, deadliest guided missile ever built, if only a way could be found to guide it. American scientists and engineers developed a remote control system that showed promise. All that was needed, they felt, was for a pilot to get the mammoth exploding boxcar into the air, point it in the general direction of the French coast, and then bail out by parachute. The remote control system would take over from there, guiding the mighty weapon toward the bunkers that housed the V-1s.

For a pilot, the danger of such a mission was unprecedented. This made it the answer to Joe Junior's most fervent prayers. Single-handedly, he could save all of London from Nazi attack and would become, in the process, the greatest American hero of the war. And there would be nothing that Jack—now hospitalized in Boston following surgery on injured spinal discs—could do to match him. Joe volunteered immediately.

"I am going to do something different for the next three weeks," he wrote to his father, explaining he would not be coming home as expected. "It is secret and I am not allowed to say what it is, but it isn't dangerous, so don't worry."

But by now the Ambassador was already looking past the war, toward Joe Junior's political career. All he wanted was to get his oldest and finest son home safely so together they could begin to plot his first political campaign.

"I can quite understand how you feel about staying there," Joe wrote in early August, "but don't force your luck." With the end of the war to which he'd been so steadfastly opposed now in sight, there was no sense taking any chances. The postwar future was too bright and, for Joe Junior in particular, too filled with the promise of rich reward.

But Joe Junior didn't see it that way. All he could see was that in this family for whom finishing first meant everything, he had now been relegated to second place. There was no way he would return to America and enter public life as the brother of war hero Jack Kennedy.

And so, on August 12, 1944, despite having been warned that the electronic firing system was not working properly, thereby creating a grave risk of premature detonation, he climbed into the pilot's seat of a PB4Y loaded with ten tons of the most powerful non-nuclear explosive material in the world.

He was sitting inside what was at that point the biggest bomb man had ever built. Even loading the explosives onto the plane was considered so dangerous that the army would not permit Caucasian soldiers to do it and instead used members of a Negro battalion.

Just before walking to the plane, Joe Junior had called a friend in England. "I'm about to go into my act," he said. Then he paused. "If I don't come back, tell my dad, despite our differences, that I love him very much." About his mother, he said nothing.

The explosion, less than half an hour later—caused by premature ignition of the firing system—was not surpassed in intensity until the first test of the atomic bomb. In the town over which Joe was flying at the moment of the explosion, fifty-nine buildings were damaged by the force of the blast. No piece of his body was ever found.

As it turned out, the mission was futile and misguided in the first place. The concrete bunkers that Joe's plane was supposed to blow up had been evacuated by the Germans months before; the V-1s were actually coming from different sites. Even a successful strike would have accomplished nothing, would not have spared London a moment's further terror. Joe's death came not in heroic combat but in a pointless accident caused by malfunctioning equipment about which he'd been warned.

In future years, the family would expend large quantities of money and vast stores of energy in an attempt to persuade the American public that just the opposite was true. That, as an official letter provided by the navy stated: "Through Joe's courage and devotion to what he thought was right, a great many lives were saved."

To pretend that such was the case became a matter of considerable importance to the family. There were, after all, questions of prestige involved.

In any event, Joe Junior had accomplished his personal mission. For him, the race was over and he had done what his father had always wanted: he'd finished first.

7

YEARS LATER, AN AIDE WOULD SAY OF TEDDY, "HIS brothers threw him in the water and in the air and dared him to jump off high places and he seemed not to mind. He laughed, and, laughing, made them laugh. Humor. It was what he did. It was his place in the family to make everyone laugh."

But now, with Joe Junior dead—less than a month later, Kathleen's aristocratic Protestant husband was also killed in the war—there was no time or place for laughter. Teddy's father spent the remainder of the Hyannis Port summer secluded in his bedroom behind a locked door, trying to drown out his grief and broken dreams with the sound of the operas of Richard Wagner.

In September, Teddy returned to Fessenden. Soon afterwards, his father decamped for Palm Beach, seeming to no longer care about anyone or anything. The death of his oldest son had irreparably ruptured Joe Kennedy's sense of cosmic order, plunging him into both despair and psychological chaos.

By exploding into unrecoverable fragments high above the surface of the earth, Joe Junior became, in his father's eyes, not so much a dead son as a newborn god. In death, he became instantly immortal. Through physical dismemberment, he became the psychic embodiment of what forever after would be considered the Kennedy ideal.

Though it was Jack who had achieved the greater fame in early life, Joe Junior, by dying in the fashion he did, regained his place of primacy within the family.

Moreover, because there was no risk that he might someday disappoint, his victory was permanent. For the rest of their lives, whatever the other Kennedy sons might accomplish, it would be deemed the merest shadow of what Joe Junior would have been able to do had he lived.

His death, then, locked the family hierarchy permanently into place. All the rest of them would be viewed by the Ambassador as, at best, poor substitutes for the real Kennedy son, the one who, by dying, had assured that he would live perpetually in his father's mind as the ideal to which none of the others could measure up.

Farthest from that ideal, of course, was Teddy.

The notion that Teddy, now twelve and on the verge of adolescence, might be experiencing some degree of inner turmoil as a result of three traumatic events in quick succession—the mysterious banishment of Rosemary, the self-inflicted banishment of Kathleen, and, worst, the sudden death of his oldest brother, who'd been more of a father figure to him than anyone else—did not cause the members of his family, with one exception, to pay him special attention.

Consumed by their own combinations of guilt, grief, anger and ambition, and by the need to move forward, always forward, so as not to fall into the trap of brooding about the past, Teddy's parents, his sisters and his brother Jack all went their separate ways, fending for themselves emotionally and assuming that the others could do the same.

Only Bobby, now nineteen and enrolled at Harvard, seemed to recognize that Teddy might need emotional support. Only Bobby came to Fessenden to see him during that bleak and frightening fall of 1944.

With Bobby alone taking note, Teddy turned in another poor academic performance, finishing the fall term with an average of only 72. He also, for the first time, showed signs of behavioral problems, committing enough disciplinary infractions to be hit with a wooden paddle. Later, he would say he had not minded because "a nice old man" had done the paddling.

It was Jack's idea, that fall, that each of the children should write a personal recollection of Joe Junior, the compilation to be given to their father at Christmas.

Eunice told Teddy that he should write about how "wonderful and strong and calm" their oldest brother had been.

"But he wasn't calm," Teddy protested. "One day he threw me in the ocean."

And then, somewhat perversely, he made his sole contribution to the collection:

I recall the day the year before we went to England. It was in the summer and I asked Joe if I could race with him. He agreed to this so we started down to the pier about five minutes before the race. We had our sails up just as the gun went for the start. This was the first race I had ever been in. We were going along very nicely until suddenly he told me to pull in the jib. I had know Idea what he was talking about. He repeated the command again in a little louder tone, meanwhile we were slowly getting further and further away from the other boats. Joe suddenly leaped up and grabbed the jib. I was a little scared but suddenly he zeized me by the pants and through me into the cold water. I was scared to death practualy. I then heard a splash and I felt his hand grab my shirt and he lifted me back into the boat. We continued the race and came in second. On the way home from the pier he told me to be quiet about what happened in that afternoon . . .

Once more departing from Fessenden in late fall—and again it is unclear whether this was a matter of family or institutional choice—Teddy returned to the more hospitable climate of the Palm Beach Private School, where, for the remainder of the school year, he turned in his best performance yet. His grades, while not outstanding, were adequate and he showed further signs of social and athletic blossoming: being elected seventh-grade president and named captain of the basketball team.

A later examination of school records by James MacGregor Burns disclosed the comment that Teddy, that year, "got along well with all students and participated in all the functions available to him."

Finally, it appeared that Teddy might be finding his own identity; that he might be discovering a self with which he could learn to live.

In the fall of 1945, however, for reasons that have remained obscure, Teddy was sent to his grimmest boarding school yet. It was a dark, forbidding fortress of discipline and spirituality called Cranwell, located in the wintry westernmost region of Massachusetts and governed by unsmiling Jesuit priests.

Though he was still just thirteen, Cranwell became the tenth different school he'd attended and became also a nightmarish reprise of his months at Portsmouth Priory.

Even Teddy himself, in a rare moment of candor about personal feelings, would admit years later that his time at Cranwell had not been happy. "Maybe it was too distant," he said. "Too remote. I suppose I was lonesome."

Cranwell was located in Berkshire County, almost 150 miles from Boston, which meant that not even Bobby could easily drop by for visits. And, true to form, neither his mother nor his father visited the school. For Rose, such an act simply lay outside the realm of her functioning. Even when the "more important" children, Joe Junior and Jack, were at Choate, in Connecticut, an easy limousine ride from either New York or Boston, not once had she visited the campus, although during their prep school years she did make seventeen trips to Europe.

As for Teddy's father, once again he had more important tasks at hand. First, last and always, Joe Kennedy was a speculator. Even at his moment of darkest sorrow, in the summer of 1944, as he sat behind his locked bedroom door with the cries of Wagnerian heroes resounding through the Hyannis Port house, some canny and calculating aspect of him could see the faint glimmer of possibilities not yet foreclosed.

The stock market had taught him that there was no loss from which one could not recover with sufficient nerve and ample reserves of capital. Even grief-stricken, Joe still had his nerve. And as reserve capital he had a second son.

Thus, in April of 1946, he had Jack announce his candidacy for Congress. He would run for the seat in the Eleventh Congressional District once occupied by former Boston mayor, and convicted felon, James Curley.

There was no incumbent, but to outsiders Jack's victory seemed far from assured. There were nine other candidates in the race for the Democratic nomination, including the popular mayor of Cambridge.

But outsiders did not understand how much money the Ambassador was prepared to spend, or how hard Jack would be willing to campaign. He quickly learned what chords played best and struck them forcefully and repeatedly. *PT 109* proved to be a special favorite. As the campaign progressed, he continued to embellish the tale.

"It's getting better all the time," Jack said to a friend. "Now I've got a Jew and a nigger in the story and with me being a Catholic, that's great."

In the campaign's closing days, Jack's father paid to have a hundred thousand copies of the *Reader's Digest* condensation of the John Hersey article distributed to voters in the district.

Then, spending wildly to assure victory by a margin that would attract national attention, Joe announced the formation of the Joseph P. Kennedy Jr. Foundation to honor the memory of his oldest son and, in the foundation's name, pledged more than $600,000 to Boston's Catholic archdiocese—the largest contribution the Boston church had ever received from a single family. Jack, naturally, was photographed handing the check to Cardinal Cushing only days before the election.

Also, sensing that a smashing triumph was close at hand, the Ambassador used his money and influence in publishing circles to have *Look* magazine print a story about Jack so extravagantly flattering that it might as well have been (and, indeed, might have been) written by Joe's own public relations men.

Calling Jack "a fighting conservative," the article said, "He has guts and brains, a war career, an intelligence and a personality which should satisfy the most exacting constituency. His Navy record is a source of envy . . . most important, Kennedy has the looks and Irish personality which often combine in Massachusetts politics to sell a candidate to the voters. . . . Jack Kennedy, if he goes to Congress, won't be in anybody's pocket. . . . He doesn't hesitate now and he won't hesitate in Congress to say what he thinks."

But it was not enough that Jack receive massive amounts of favorable publicity. Joe also saw to it that his leading opponent, the mayor of Cambridge, received little. Calling William Randolph Hearst in California, Joe reminded that newspaper baron of how he had extended a large loan to help sustain Hearst's journalistic empire during a lean time a decade earlier. Joe then said he wanted Hearst's Boston paper, the *Herald,* which was widely read by voters in the district, not only to cover Jack's campaign avidly but to ignore the activities of the Cambridge mayor.

And so it came to pass that the man expected to be Jack's most potent foe could not so much as get his name in the *Herald*—not once—during the closing weeks of the campaign. The Hearst paper would not even publish his paid advertisements.

Jack won, beating the beleaguered mayor of Cambridge by a margin of almost two to one. The Ambassador had expected no less. "With what I'm spending," he said privately, "I could elect my chauffeur."

Arthur Krock and Henry Luce snapped to attention at once. "Kennedy Makes Political Bow," said a front-page headline in *The New York Times,* which did not normally give such prominent display to the goings-on in Massachusetts' Eleventh Congressional District.

Time described the young victor as "grave, earnest, and teetotaling," and also informed its readers that the "boyish-looking bachelor of 29" had "worked hard to prove he was no snob."

Gravely and earnestly, Jack celebrated his win with a six-week vacation that took him first to New York—and, once again, to Inga Arvad—and then to Hollywood, where he grew thoroughly enchanted by the world of celebrity. He wondered aloud to a friend whether he might indeed possess—or, at least, be able to project— the same sort of charismatic appeal as a Gary Cooper, a Spencer Tracy, a Clark Gable. "We'd spend hours talking about it," the friend reported.

Long, long ago, when he'd first encountered the larger-than-life world of Hollywood, Jack's father had instinctively recognized that there was untapped potential in this new medium. He had sensed that there were fortunes to be made and immense power to be gained through the use of film for the mass manipulation of emotion.

Now, a generation later, Joe had refined the concept considerably. He recognized that it could forever transform the American political process, making his oldest son—now Jack—not only President but an international celebrity on a scale not yet imagined by lesser men.

"I'm going to sell Jack like soap flakes," his father bragged. He would, of course, employ the medium of print, which (despite his one disastrous interview given to the *Boston Globe* six years earlier at the Ritz-Carlton) he'd learned to manipulate as effortlessly as he tied his own shoes. But for even greater effect—reaching even larger audiences at even deeper emotional levels—he would use the visual imagery whose power he'd first encountered in Hollywood in the 1920s.

The age of television was about to dawn in America and Joe Kennedy intended to use it in ways that would transform Jack into a national figure far more charismatic than any mere movie actor, crooner or sports celebrity.

And Jack was just shrewd enough to sense that his father was on to something big.

8

On a lesser scale, the fall of 1946 marked a significant turning point for Teddy, too. Not only was he now the son of an ex-ambassador and the younger brother of two war heroes, one of whom was soon to be a congressman, but that September he entered Milton Academy, the prep school from which Bobby had graduated. He would be permitted to remain for four uninterrupted years.

At Milton, founded in 1798, located ten miles south of Boston and boasting an outstanding academic and athletic reputation, as well as a faculty whose members took a deep personal interest in the welfare of their students, Teddy felt, for the first time since the house in Bronxville had been sold, that he'd found a home.

"It's not whether you're better than anybody else that's important," the school said in a publication expressing its educational philosophy. "It's whether or not you tried." For Teddy, such a point of view was revolutionary and exposure to it perhaps the best thing that had yet happened to him in life.

It was at Milton that his personality bloomed; that he grew at least somewhat self-reliant; that he came to recognize that while he would never be a true intellectual—

for the realm of abstract ideas was not one in which he found himself comfortable—he could accomplish enough academically so as to be able to proceed with a life that would be an embarrassment neither to his family nor to himself.

The school was, he later told MacGregor Burns, "a secure and friendly place," which in itself was a marked contrast to any other environment Teddy had known. He also said his years there were "the first time I learned anything."

Not that it came easily. "He was a very good-humored fun sort of kid," one Milton teacher said later, "but he was not a good student. He had been to so many schools before he got here, and one simply can't do that with younger people." Even with extensive and intensive private tutoring, his Milton grades were a steady stream of B's and C's and he graduated in the bottom half of his class.

His cheerful nature and stubborn willingness to make whatever effort was needed to accomplish the task at hand did, however, make a favorable impression on classmates, teachers and athletic coaches.

Having interviewed many of them, MacGregor Burns reported that "his Milton mentors all thoroughly liked Ted Kennedy [but] not one of them apparently saw any leadership qualities in him." This would not have been surprising, for his family role had clearly been that of follower. Leadership had been for the older generation, now represented solely by Jack.

"He was a pragmatist," the Milton headmaster at the time later recalled. "He wanted to do what worked. Sitting in a chair and mulling over philosophy was not his favorite indoor sport. Life for him was to act."

Contact sports provided a suitable forum. Abandoning basketball for the more visceral physical engagement of football, he became, according to one coach, an "absolutely fearless" member of the Milton varsity team. No longer "Fat Teddy," he grew to over six feet in height and much of the fat turned to muscle. Though never speedy or agile, he was fierce. "He would have tackled an express train to New York if you'd asked," one coach recalled.

Part of this was undoubtedly the genetically inherited Kennedy zest for combat. Another aspect may well have had to do with his having had to repress, for so many years, the anger he must have felt as a result of parental neglect, of being treated, within the family, like nothing so much as a piece of excess baggage; as an afterthought —which, of course, he had been.

At Milton, the headmaster said, "contact sports brought out all the fighting Irish in him." Later, in less structured environments, his tendency toward quick anger and his inappropriate and sometimes uncontrolled physical expression of it would come to seem a less positive characteristic.

It was also at Milton that Teddy displayed and developed his first exceptional talent: public speaking. He joined the debating society, which at Milton was an extracurricular activity taken quite as seriously as varsity athletics. To the surprise of many, this generally cheerful but intellectually unstimulated youngest Kennedy proved a formidable debater.

Perhaps all those years at the dinner table listening to his older brothers discuss with his father the issues of the day had given him a sense that he, too, could articulate a view of the larger world into which he was growing. In any event, his debating coach praised him lavishly, as "thoroughly prepared, an accurate thinker, and especially good at rebuttal. He was poised and well informed, especially on questions of public affairs. He always knew what he was talking about."

A personal highlight came during his senior year when the Milton debating squad, of which he was a key member, defeated Harvard's freshman team.

Yet even though he was affable, approachable and often exuberant, Teddy—unlike Jack and Bobby— formed no close or lasting friendships in prep school. In part, one suspects this was the result of the toll taken by the chaotic, disjointed years that had preceded Milton. While mustering the surface affability necessary for survival in a new and unpredictable setting, Teddy had, throughout his childhood, also developed a guardedness; a tendency, which would only grow stronger over the years, to keep a certain emotional distance even from those closest to him.

But there was also another factor at work: his sense of entitlement. He may have been the last and the least within the family, but it was still a family he had been taught to consider as first and foremost in the land. He was a Kennedy, and he made it very clear to classmates that this set him somewhat apart and above; that if he formed friendships with them, it would be on his terms and subject to cancellation without notice or obvious cause. This sense of privilege was another personality trait that would only grow stronger through the years.

To be a Kennedy was, in fact, to be different. If the demands made upon one were greater, so also should be the rewards. Kennedys were wealthier, more glamorous, more driven, while at the same time more insouciant than normal people. They were members of a special clan; a breed apart; especially favored, it seemed for many years, by the gods.

So even at Milton, Teddy developed this larger-than-life persona, this sense of expectation that his wishes would be granted, his desires satisfied, his whims acted upon by those around him who sought his favor.

This was not a particularly appealing trait, but it was one he shared with every other member of his family, save the unfortunate Rosemary. Kennedys genuinely believed that they were better than anyone else, and therefore entitled to more, even when cold, hard fact suggested otherwise. This "Kennedy-ness" was an element of Teddy's nature that would lead him, eventually, to both fame and disaster.

His senior yearbook referred to him as "Smiling Ed" and "the Politician," noting the habit he'd developed of standing in front of the mirror in his dorm room, attempting in private to perfect the smile with which he would, in time, go forth to greet the common man.

* * *

Summers, of course, were still spent at Hyannis Port, where the family ties were renewed and strengthened. His father was focused now almost exclusively on the advancement of Jack's career, and his mother, even when physically present, was off in a dream world of religiosity all her own. But his sisters remained quick to point out to Teddy his imperfections, and Bobby, down from Harvard, still seemed to feel that bringing out the potential that lurked within his younger brother was one of his chief missions in life.

"Bob, quite frankly," Joey Gargan later recalled, "was interested in having us participate. He taught us sailing, for instance, and he wanted Teddy to do well. He worked very hard. He sailed to win and he taught us everything he knew. He'd take the time, he created that kind of atmosphere, he was always able to get Ted to make the extra effort."

So, for Teddy, summer vacation was not a break from the rigors of the academic year but rather the opposite: a time when his Kennedy-ness would be renewed, his competitive edge sharpened; when he'd be reminded all over again that for a Kennedy it was not enough to enter the race; it was essential to win.

One weekend in May of 1947, when he was fifteen, he traveled to Hyannis Port to help celebrate Jack's thirtieth birthday. All the brothers and sisters had gathered, joined by several of Jack's political operatives. A large lunch was served.

At the end, the Ambassador proposed a toast to Jack, the glamorous young congressman so obviously destined for greater things; so obviously fated to bring his father's dreams of glory to fruition.

One after another, around the table, Jack's family and friends toasted him and his successes, both past and future. Then, at the end, it was Teddy's turn.

"Would you like to make a toast?" his father asked.

Teddy got to his feet slowly and somberly, the trademark grin nowhere in evidence.

"Yes," he said, "I would like to drink a toast to our brother who is not here."

Stunned into silence by this violation of the family taboo against speaking openly of past tragedy in private, those gathered around the table sipped from their glasses and Teddy, even more somberly, took his seat.

"I remember," said one who was there, "it took several minutes before any of them could really say anything."

Less than a year later, death struck again. Kathleen, then twenty-eight, was killed in a plane crash in France. She'd been with the new Protestant aristocrat she planned to marry, despite her mother's objections, which were even more furious than in the case of Hartington, because Kathleen's new beau, in addition to being Protestant, was divorced.

Rose had already informed Kathleen that if this second marriage outside the Catholic Church took place, she would never again speak to her daughter, nor mention her name within the family, nor permit her name to be spoken by any other family member in her presence. As had Rosemary, for quite different reasons, Kathleen would cease to exist as a Kennedy.

Even that had not been sufficient to deter her. So now she had met the fate she deserved. God was good. God was just. In His honor, and in order not to defile her own holiness, Rose refused to attend her daughter's funeral, which was held in England. Nor would she allow any of the other children to attend.

Thus, only the Ambassador, who had already been in Europe—preparing, in fact, to meet with Kathleen in Paris in order to make one final attempt to dissuade her from going ahead with the marriage —was present as the body of the second of his children to die violently was lowered into the ground. In England, a country in which his name was still reviled.

"I can still see the stricken face of old Joe Kennedy," an acquaintance remarked long afterwards, "as he stood alone, unloved and despised, behind the coffin of his eldest daughter."

* * *

That summer, Teddy remarked to Joey Gargan in an unusually open moment of private conversation that it struck him as somewhat ominous that even though he himself was only sixteen, three of his eight brothers and sisters had already vanished from his life: Rosemary having disappeared and Joe Junior and Kathleen having died in plane crashes.

Bobby graduated from Harvard that spring but, having not done well enough academically to gain entrance to the Harvard Law School, instead pursued a law degree at the University of Virginia.

That fall, despite little campaigning, Jack, who was still stricken repeatedly by disabling illnesses, still grieving deeply over the death of Kathleen, and filled with thoughts of his own mortality, was reelected to Congress by an overwhelming margin.

In the summer of 1950, Bobby, with one year of law school remaining, married a wealthy young woman from Greenwich, Connecticut, named Ethel Skakel. She had been a classmate of his sister Jean's at the Manhattanville College of the Sacred Heart, in Purchase, New York, a school that, in time, Teddy too would come to know.

First, however, he would come to know Harvard, to which he was admitted as a freshman in September 1950.

9

TEDDY WAS EIGHTEEN THEN, AND HOWEVER MUCH he'd struggled at Milton to make himself count for something, he could not help but harbor the secret fear that nothing he would do in his life—good or bad—could ever count for much within his family. Too much had already transpired. Emotional exhaustion had set in. There were too many ghosts in the Hyannis Port hallways, too many memories of both triumph and death.

Only three of the children—Joe Junior, Kathleen and Jack—had ever commanded his parents' full attention. And two of them were already dead. Excepting only Jack's potential political success, no achievement or transgression of the survivors could ever resonate as loudly as deeds already done.

Teddy thus looked forward to his Harvard years as being primarily ones of social enjoyment and to his role within the family as continuing to be mostly that of court jester. It was the role he'd played since childhood, the only one he knew: the kid brother whose major talent was the ability to make the others laugh.

The one aspect of his life that transcended this rather limited view of himself and his obligations was football. When he entered Harvard, Teddy stood six feet, two inches tall and weighed two hundred pounds. Neither sickly Jack nor skinny Bobby had been able to excel on the football field. Teddy, while certainly not of Big Ten caliber, appeared to have the potential and the determination to succeed at least at the Ivy League level. By so doing, he knew, he could still win the grudging measure of respect from his father he so coveted.

From the start at Harvard, he gravitated toward those most like himself: the freshmen whose interest in athletics, especially football, and in the pursuit of women, laughter and adventure exceeded their intellectual curiosity.

"We were typical jocks," Teddy's lifelong friend Claude Hooton would recall. "Which at Harvard meant that you were identified as stupid. But that didn't matter. The war was over. It was a happy, happy time."

Like his brothers and father before him, Teddy displayed more than a casual interest in obtaining sexual gratification. MacGregor Burns has reported that "he won a small reputation as a date who would take out a girl, make clear his expectations, and either happily realize them or accept defeat with as much surprise and curiosity as disappointment." In later years, he would encounter "defeat" less frequently and would also be less graceful in his acceptance of it.

At Harvard, he neither sought nor seemed capable of developing any deeper level of romantic relationship with a woman. "There was never anyone special," a friend said later. "He never went out too many times with the same girl." For Teddy, as for his father, Joe Junior and Jack, the thrill, such as it was, appeared to be in the conquest. Once that was accomplished, it was time to move on. The names didn't matter, only the numbers. Like all else for the Kennedys, sex was viewed primarily as a ceaseless competition.

By spring, he'd already established himself as a sufficiently promising varsity football prospect to be assigned Winthrop House as his future college residence. "Winthrop," a Harvard yearbook of the time observed, "had ivy and a view of the river, but its courtyards too often resembled the fifty-yard line at Soldier's Field."

If not "Animal House," it was clearly Harvard's jock house, often referred to, in fact, as "the House of the Mesomorphs." Looking ahead to sophomore year, Teddy could see that it was where he belonged, where he wanted to be, where his friends—almost all of them also prospective varsity football players—would be going: a place where the beer and the laughter flowed freely, and for whose residents a football victory over Princeton, never mind Yale, carried with it more significance than graduation summa cum laude.

Having drifted aimlessly through his academic year, however, Teddy found himself, in the spring of 1951, faced with a potentially serious problem.

As it had been at Milton, Spanish was the course that gave Teddy the most difficulty at Harvard. For the others, he would muddle through with C's, he thought, but as the final examination in freshman Spanish approached, he felt in danger of failing both the test and the course, which would render him ineligible for varsity football in the fall, an intolerable prospect.

He chose to deal with the situation pragmatically, as he'd been taught to do, by word and example, all his life. Knowing he could not pass the examination himself, he arranged to have a friend, much more proficient in the language, take it for him, signing Teddy's name to the booklet.

As it happened, however, the graduate student assigned as proctor for the Spanish examination that day was personally acquainted with the student whom Teddy had recruited as his stand-in. When the stand-in, who did exceedingly well on the test, handed in the booklet, the proctor saw that he'd signed it "Edward M. Kennedy."

Within hours, the dean's office had been informed and both Teddy and his accomplice had been expelled from Harvard for cheating.

Before heading to Hyannis Port to break the news to his father, Teddy visited the headmaster of Milton Academy to report what had happened.

Oddly, he seemed to express no remorse. "His first

reaction,'' the headmaster said later, "was simply horror that he'd been caught.''

His father's first reaction, as might have been expected, was to become apoplectic. The stupidity of it! Not the cheating itself—for if he hadn't cheated throughout his business career, Joe would never have amassed the fortune he had—but getting caught! Kennedys did not get caught. Among the family's Ten Commandments, that ranked right next to: Kennedys always finished first.

The reasons for Joe's anger, however, went deeper, and had less to do with Teddy himself than with the plans he'd been laying for the next step forward in Jack's political career.

There had been a time, in the summer of 1947 and for months thereafter, when it seemed that Jack might not have a career. While vacationing in London, he fell sicker than ever before in his life and was rushed to a hospital, where, for the first time, he was diagnosed as suffering from Addison's disease, a disorder caused by malfunction of the adrenal glands.

Once viewed as eventually fatal, Addison's had recently become controllable through daily doses of an adrenal hormone extract, but it remained a severely debilitating condition from which full recovery was impossible. Its most frequent side effect was that it so weakened the body's immune system that the patient was prone to chronic and severe infection.

In late 1949, however, it was discovered that cortisone had a remarkable effect upon those afflicted with Addison's disease. Not only did regular injection of the drug (which soon could be taken orally as well) relieve the symptom of chronic fatigue and eliminate the susceptibility to infection, it put the user in a near-euphoric state.

Thus, after years of battling weakness and lassitude, Jack found himself surging with an energy he'd never before felt. The combination of this daily high and the assurance that the cortisone would protect him from the disease's potentially lethal complications led both him and his father to intensify their focus on his political future.

Maybe he could live out his brother's destiny, after all. Indeed, by spring of 1951, with the Ambassador having decided that Jack should move up from the House to the Senate the following year—taking a seat away from Henry Cabot Lodge—Jack was dashing around the state every weekend, drawing larger and more responsive audiences at every stop, displaying, for the first time, the star quality he'd studied in Hollywood and had always hoped to project.

Suddenly, Teddy's stupidity threatened to undermine the whole embryonic enterprise. Beating Lodge in 1952 would be hard enough under the best of circumstances, especially when the inevitable attacks upon the Kennedy family's unsavory background commenced, but a fresh episode—''Candidate's Brother Expelled from Harvard for Cheating''—could have disastrous repercussions.

For once, Teddy had succeeded in capturing his father's undivided attention, but it was not at all in the manner he had hoped. Nor was his father's response what he expected.

The Ambassador had always been able to put in the fix, to buy any of them out of whatever trouble they were in, and to do the same for himself. Now, Teddy felt, it was his turn. He didn't see why his father couldn't simply pick up the phone, or perhaps make a discreet trip to Cambridge by limousine, and after the usual quiet talks in secluded rooms, come back with the news that all would be well but that Teddy should be more careful in the future.

Jack, for heaven's sake, had become known as a best-selling author when he hadn't even written the book. And when he'd gotten his boat sunk and two of his men killed through his own inattentiveness, he'd wound up portrayed as a hero. Joe Junior was revered as a fallen hero too, despite having gotten killed on what was basically a fool's errand.

But Teddy—as was so often the case—failed to grasp the relevant dynamic. This wasn't about him. This—like virtually every other piece of family business now—was about Jack and Jack's career. There were times when chips were called in, when those for whom favors had been done long ago were told that the time had come for squaring the account.

Joe Kennedy, however, was not going to use up that sort of capital just to bail Teddy out of trouble. He needed to hold it in reserve for the higher-stakes games that lay ahead. If Teddy had been dumb enough to get caught, then it was time he learned a lesson, so that the next time, and the next time, and all the times after that, he'd know enough not to get caught.

If Harvard had thrown him out, he'd stay out, at least until Jack was safely elected to the Senate. The more Joe thought about it, in fact, the more he decided that maybe it was all for the best—assuming his money and influence could keep the incident hushed up.

Teddy had been both reckless and stupid, and, for the eighteen months during which Jack would be campaigning for the Senate, there was nothing to be gained by having a reckless and stupid younger brother lurching around Boston out of control.

So Joe went to work the way he had when the FBI caught Jack with Inga Arvad. Calls were made, meetings were held, certain disbursements of funds were arranged. The purpose of these machinations was not, however, to arrange Teddy's immediate readmittance but only to assure the viability of the cover story the family would put out.

The story would be that, ennobled by the example of his older brothers' military heroism, Teddy had found that he could not in good conscience remain a privileged and pampered college student at a time when other Americans his age were fighting and dying for their country in Korea. So Teddy had taken a voluntary leave of absence from Harvard in order to join the United States Army.

Joe, however, had no intention of letting Teddy get anywhere near the war in Korea. Nor did Teddy object. As MacGregor Burns has pointed out, "One of the most surprising facts of his early life is that he had no wish—and felt no compulsion—to prove himself in battle."

Instead, Teddy was inducted at Fort Dix, New Jersey,

sent to Fort Gordon, Georgia, for basic training, and then shipped to Paris, where his father had arranged for his assignment to a military police honor guard detachment which had the wholly ceremonial task of standing watch over the NATO headquarters office located there.

On the day of his departure from Hyannis Port, his sisters assembled to bid him farewell.

"Bye, Bye, baby," they sang. "Remember you're our baby, when the girls give you the eye."

10

HONORABLY DISCHARGED FROM MILITARY SERVICE with the rank of private first class, Teddy was readmitted to Harvard in the fall of 1953.

Records of exactly what means his father might have used to bring this about remain sealed inside the vaults of the Kennedy Library, but, viewed against the money spent and the influence used to assure Jack's victory over Henry Cabot Lodge in the Senate race the previous fall, any actions taken in Teddy's behalf would have seemed minor by comparison.

Now twenty-one and aglow with new levels of energy and self-assurance, Teddy took up residence in Winthrop House and, as planned, played varsity football.

He was, upon his return, "a different guy," Claude Hooton said. Not exactly a social snob, perhaps, but the sense of privilege, of entitlement, of how special it was to be a Kennedy, seemed to have grown, and to have widened the distance between him and those classmates whom he had treated more as equals when a freshman. As Hersh has described it, there was "a certain subtle stiffening and self-awareness" to the Teddy who returned to Harvard from his two years of military service in Paris.

To be sure, there were new reasons for self-awareness.

Jack's highly publicized defeat of Cabot Lodge the previous fall had made him one of the most charismatic young political stars in America, and, that fall, he married a glamorous socialite.

Joe Kennedy knew that if Jack was to achieve further political advancement, marriage to the right sort of woman would be necessary. She would have to be well-bred, good-looking, Catholic, able to bear children and willing to put up with both the public and the private life that Jack intended to lead. Jacqueline Bouvier, while only twenty-four, seemed to meet all the requirements.

She'd been raised in privileged enclaves of Southampton, Long Island, and Newport, Rhode Island, and educated at Vassar and the Sorbonne.

Their wedding, held in Newport in September, proved a tumultuous event. Part of the crowd of three thousand that had assembled outside the church in hopes of glimpsing the glamorous couple broke through police lines and swarmed toward the bride. Newspapers in Boston, New York and Washington treated the ceremony as the social event of the year, perhaps the decade. It was everything Joe Kennedy had wished, and it could not have failed to make Teddy realize, even more clearly than before, that this family enterprise he was a part of—however junior his status—was achieving a magnitude seldom before witnessed in America.

In other ways, however, Teddy had changed not at all. He still had little interest in academics. One Harvard professor, Arthur N. Holcombe—the only man to have taught not only Teddy and his three older brothers but his father as well—recalled that Teddy's work "was always satisfactory, and I have no doubt that he could have graduated with high distinction if he had wanted to devote more time to his studies."

The point was, he did not. He wanted to devote time to football, to sex, and to general carousing.

"He was thinking about athletic activities and about social activities," Holcombe said. "I think academic activities came out third. He did just what was necessary for him to remain in good standing. I say, frankly, I didn't think he was in the same class with his older brothers.''

Harvard did not engage him any more during his last three years there than it had during his freshman year —perhaps even less so, given that Boston now seemed stiflingly provincial to a rich young man from an influential family who'd just spent two years in Paris.

He continued to associate mostly with other football players, a fairly rowdy and freewheeling group, looked down upon by Harvard's more intellectually oriented majority. He'd occasionally amuse himself by driving golf balls across the Charles River or, more often, by trying to herd various young women into his bedroom. If he could not measure up to his brothers mentally, he seemed determined to prove himself at least their equal in every physical way.

For Teddy, only two things about a woman mattered: her looks and her willingness to allow him to have sex with her. If the second was not quickly displayed, then even the first did not matter, but he did innovate, among his friends, an alphabetical grading system by which prospective or recent dates were rated on a scale from A to E.

Chosen for membership in both Hasty Pudding and the Pi Eta fraternity, Teddy was quick to display an antic side to his personality. His initiation into Pi Eta required him, among other things, to travel to Boston penniless and bring back a full-time prostitute. Within ninety minutes, he had succeeded, apparently persuading her that while he had no cash on his person, he and his classmates would guarantee to make her trip to Cambridge worthwhile.

He drank, but no more than most of his friends. Other than his name, his good looks and his easy social charm (which he employed ever more selectively), Teddy was best remembered by his Harvard classmates for three characteristics: his willingness to involve himself in bizarre escapades, his financial stinginess and his explosive temper.

Characteristic of the escapades was what later became known as the Great Cairo Caper, in which Teddy made a substantial wager with a friend, promising to pay if the friend would fly to Cairo, Egypt, at Teddy's expense, and somehow get himself back to Harvard on his own.

In retrospect, this does not seem a bet that was made while all participants were fully free from the influence of alcohol, but once they were into it, neither Teddy nor the friend wanted to be first to back down. Teddy purchased the one-way plane ticket. The friend, inventing a story about a dying uncle in Egypt, obtained all necessary inoculations from the Harvard infirmary and had a passport hastily issued. Carrying only a paper bag with toothbrush, change of underwear and a camera that would be used to photograph him in Cairo, proving he had truly been there, the friend flew from Logan Airport in Boston to Idlewild in New York, where he was to board the flight to Egypt.

Only at the last moment did Teddy panic, saying he could visualize his father's reaction upon seeing the headline: "Sen. Kennedy's Brother Sends Roommate to Africa."

From Harvard, Teddy paged the friend at Idlewild and begged him to return, offering to pay off in full. Since Teddy had a reputation for being notoriously slow to pay for anything, the friend accepted his offer of surrender and flew not to Cairo but back to Boston, claiming total victory in the war of nerves.

Far more typical of Teddy's handling of money was an incident when, after a football game in Princeton, he invited eight teammates and their dates to join him for dinner at an expensive French restaurant in New York. It was assumed by all that this was his treat. Yet when the check was presented, Teddy added up the cost of each individual meal and insisted on immediate payment from all involved.

As for the temper, there were a number of incidents that tended to indicate that a certain amount of repressed hostility had built up in this youngest and supposedly most affable of the Kennedy boys.

In one rugby match, he got into three separate and

vicious fistfights with opposing players and finally had to be ejected from the game. The referee later said that never before in thirty years had he had to order a player from the field for such loss of control.

"I've thought a lot about that game since," the official said years later. "Rugby is a character-building sport. Players learn how to conduct themselves on the field with the idea that they will learn how to conduct themselves in life. Knocks are given and taken, but you must play by the rules. When a player loses control of himself three times in a single afternoon, to my mind, that is a sign that, in a crisis, the man is not capable of thinking clearly and acting rationally. Such a man will panic under pressure."

Another display of violent temper came one summer vacation when Teddy and a friend, while sailing off the coast of Maine, were rowing a dinghy ashore to buy supplies. A passenger aboard a large yacht that was anchored nearby began to heckle them, suggesting that they row a little faster.

Teddy, according to his friend, "spun the dinghy around so fast I almost fell out of it. The next thing I knew, he was on the yacht and the man was being thrown overboard and all the women were screaming and running below to hide in their cabins."

Then, one by one, Teddy threw the other men on the yacht overboard. "In no time," said his friend, "all of the men—there were about eight of them—were in the water. I never saw anything like it."

Still, within the family, it was his high spirits and determination to be the life of every party that people most associated with Teddy during his college years.

The actor Peter Lawford, who married Teddy's sister Patricia in 1954, recalled that at family gatherings, "when Teddy arrived, it was just like the sun coming out. He was the shining light." In particular, Lawford remembered one New Year's Eve in Palm Beach when they all found themselves at an especially boring party at the home of a hostess who'd filled a display room with monumentally expensive china birds.

"At the stroke of midnight," Teddy said, "I'm going to stand on my head in the bird room."

And, as Lawford recalled, he did. "Always afterward," Lawford said, "we'd say to one another, 'Hey, do you remember the night Teddy stood on his head in the bird room?' "

He would have worse nights in Palm Beach.

It was during his Harvard years, and after his return from the army, that Teddy first began to feel stifled by the Hyannis Port summer routine. He felt urges to explore, to seek new experience, and most important—while still fully appreciating every advantage offered by his surname—a desire to see what he might be able to accomplish on his own, in circumstances where he was not viewed primarily as the ex-ambassador's son and the glamorous senator's youngest brother.

He spent one summer working as a forest ranger in California's Sequoia and King's Canyon national parks. During another he served as a crewman on a Los Angeles–to–Honolulu yacht race. And during one winter vacation he traveled to Acapulco, where he taught water skiing.

Remaining murky was the spot of trouble he encountered in Louisiana en route back, when an encounter with police and a disagreement over, at the very least, the validity of the registration for his car led him to stop over in the New Orleans jail.

But one other aspect of Teddy's Harvard career seems worthy of mention. His induction into the army as an enlisted man exposed him firsthand, in a way none of his naval officer brothers had experienced, to the fact that many people, especially blacks, came from severely disadvantaged backgrounds, and that so much of what he had taken for granted all his life was utterly foreign to them and, moreover, forever unattainable by them.

Upon his return, he quietly began to set aside some time each week to travel to a section of Boston's predominantly black and Puerto Rican South End in order to work as a basketball coach with underprivileged youths.

* * *

Unquestionably, however, from Teddy's point of view, the greatest moment of his Harvard career—in fact, of his life to that point—came in a snowstorm on November 19, 1955, before more than fifty thousand spectators at the Yale Bowl, including his father, when he caught a pass on the Yale six-yard line and carried the ball into the end zone for a touchdown, the only one Harvard scored in a 21–7 defeat.

II

SOME BIOGRAPHERS HAVE WRITTEN THAT AFTER HIS return from the army, Teddy's academic performance improved so dramatically that he graduated from Harvard with honors. Such was not the case.

Like Bobby before him, in fact, he was rejected by the Harvard Law School because of his mediocre grades. To Teddy this seemed, briefly, to offer an opportunity. All his life he'd followed his brothers everywhere. His failure to gain admission to Harvard Law opened a door to new and wider horizons.

Increasingly, even as he gradually began to win acceptance as a legitimate member of it, Teddy had felt vaguely oppressed by his family. The constant pressure to meet ever-rising expectations, the relentless scrutiny and criticism by parents and siblings, the incessant reminders—especially now that Jack was becoming a national figure of significant proportions—that everything one did, good or bad, was magnified in importance simply because one bore the family name: all this had begun to take a toll on Teddy, inciting within him the desire to get away, go someplace new, put some distance between his emerging self and the strains imposed by his heritage.

He had greatly enjoyed the time he'd spent in the West

during college summer vacations; California particularly. Also, Jack, who'd briefly audited a course or two there while in transition between the more focused phases of his life, had spoken highly of Stanford University.

It offered a reputation for academic excellence combined with good weather, an abundance of attractive women, proximity to San Francisco (with Los Angeles within easy striking distance) and three thousand miles of mountain and plain as a buffer between Teddy and the inflexible demands of being a Kennedy.

His father would not hear of it. Teddy was simply too wild, too untrustworthy to be turned loose in California, in a school and community where, if trouble struck, the Ambassador might not have the access and influence necessary to contain it.

No, if Teddy could not go on to Harvard Law, he would follow Bobby to the law school at the University of Virginia. Teddy might yearn for the new freedoms promised by the West, but his father had other priorities. Already, he was preparing Jack for a run at the Presidency in 1960. All he wanted from Teddy, for the moment, was the assurance that his youngest son would attract no negative publicity. Joe Kennedy said he'd feel much more comfortable with Teddy in Virginia than in California. So it was the University of Virginia law school that Teddy entered in the fall of 1956.

Even this was not accomplished without controversy. The university still abided by an honor code that required each incoming student to sign a pledge stating, "On my honor, I have neither given nor received aid" on term papers or examinations.

The records forwarded from Harvard in conjunction with Teddy's application clearly made it impossible for him to sign such a document. And the rule regarding the honor code was quite clear, or seemed to be: no one who did not sign the honor pledge would be admitted to any school within the university.

Once again, however, Teddy benefited from the special privilege that the Kennedy name—and the Ambassador's money and influence—could provide. Over the heated opposition of many faculty members and alumni, an exception was made in Teddy's case and admission was granted, following a secret and sharply divided faculty vote.

For Joe Kennedy, who had been buying votes for Jack in congressional and senatorial elections since 1946, tipping the scales in Teddy's favor by making discreet financial arrangements with certain influential professors and administrators—honor code or no honor code—would not have been out of character. Certainly, for Jack in 1956 he accomplished far more.

In the fall of 1954, and again in February of 1955, Jack's deteriorating spinal discs required surgery. The Ambassador had decided that the weeks of convalescence should be used to further the young senator's reputation as a man of letters. It was time, he decided, for Jack to "write" another book.

The Ambassador had been musing over possible subjects. After consulting with a number of academics, he concluded that the book should focus on United States senators who'd been forced to make controversial decisions about issues of historic importance, often at political cost to themselves. Jack himself thought this a fine idea.

In order that the book have the geographical and political balance necessary to attract a national audience, of the eight senators finally selected for inclusion, three were from the South, three from the Midwest, and two were Republicans. But in order that no one miss the point that Jack himself might someday be worthy of inclusion in such a volume, the remaining two were to be from Massachusetts.

Much of the research was done by a former history professor of Jacqueline's named Jules Davids and by Jack's recently hired speech writer, Ted Sorensen, who quickly found himself immersed in the project to the exclusion of almost every other professional chore.

Davids wrote drafts of what would become the book's first four chapters, after which Sorensen, working up to twelve hours a day for six months, did the rest of the writing. By midsummer, Sorensen, a facile writer whose natural prose style enabled Jack to develop the sort of stirring, invigorating political rhetoric he so much admired in others, had finished the book.

Called *Profiles in Courage,* it was published in January of 1956. "It is refreshing," said a front-page review in *The New York Times Book Review,* accompanied by a picture of Jack, "to have a first-rate politician write a thoughtful and persuasive book about political integrity." With the Ambassador personally financing a publicity campaign, the book almost immediately became a best-seller.

Building on this triumph, Teddy's father made his boldest move yet: an attempt to win for Jack the vice presidential nomination at the 1956 Democratic convention.

Many accounts have suggested that the Ambassador actually opposed such a bid, that Jack launched it on his own and that his father, vacationing on the Riviera, was both stunned and furious when he learned of it.

Such a version, however, while serving to make Jack appear refreshingly independent of his father, is contradicted by all else that is known of the father-son relationship, both before then and after. In public life, Jack almost always did exactly what his father wanted him to do—from accepting Lyndon Johnson as his running mate in 1960, to appointing Bobby as attorney general, to attempting to oust Fidel Castro from Cuba.

Joe recognized that the Democratic presidential nominee, Adlai Stevenson, who'd already been trounced by Dwight D. Eisenhower in 1952, had little chance of winning election. But he also perceived that even if Stevenson were to lose again, Jack's status as number-two man on the ticket and the national exposure he'd receive, especially on television, would vault him past the more senior members of his party and establish him as the early favorite for the far more valuable 1960 presidential nomination. And, should Stevenson somehow win, Jack would be only the proverbial heartbeat from the Presidency.

Aware that Stevenson was not planning to choose a running mate prior to the August convention, the Ambassador set about building such a powerful groundswell of support for Jack that Stevenson would have no choice but to accede to the delegates' clamor for the glamorous young senator from Massachusetts.

Working with some of his old Hollywood cronies, Joe arranged for Jack to narrate the film about the history of the Democratic party that would be shown on the convention's opening day.

The Ambassador was already aware of how powerfully Jack projected on television and was confident he could do the same on film. Also, he'd known for thirty years that celluloid images engaged the imagination and roused the spirit far more passionately than did the flawed individuals behind them.

He felt that the narration could elevate Jack from the status of rising political star to that of instant Hollywood celebrity—but one who could be found right there on the convention floor and who was available to bestow his dazzling aura on what would otherwise be a drab and lifeless ticket.

Joe himself, of course, would have to stay away. His own image had never recovered from the damage he'd inflicted upon it during World War II. Still widely perceived as conniving, greedy and spineless, Joe could not have it thought that he was trying to manipulate Jack's career. It was vital that the young senator be seen as the fresh, unfettered voice of a new generation.

In public, from this point forward, Joe could no longer be seen anywhere near Jack. In reality, of course, he would do what he had always done: run the show. It was Jack on center stage, but the Ambassador was still directing every scene, and the higher the stakes got, the more tightly he exercised control.

The convention was held in Chicago. Joe made sure he was in the south of France well before it—and that *The New York Times* gave prominent display to a photograph showing him there. But he stayed in almost constant telephone contact, speaking frequently to Jack, to James Landis—a former Harvard law professor who had become a trusted aide and whom he'd sent to Chicago as his surrogate—and to various other Chicago acquaintances who could be expected to make their wishes known in unambiguous fashion to the appropriate people at the appropriate time.

The opening day film, so skillfully narrated by Jack, electrified the eleven thousand delegates. It achieved every bit of the impact the Ambassador had hoped for. Jack's personality, said the film's producer, "just came right out. It jumped at you on the screen." *The New York Times* referred to Jack as "a photogenic movie star," and, as the Ambassador had expected, he became an idol overnight, not only in Chicago but among Democratic viewers everywhere.

What the Ambassador had not expected was that despite this outpouring of enthusiasm—magnified even further when Jack gave a spirited nominating speech for Stevenson—the presidential candidate remained unswayed.

Stevenson said he would make no choice of running mate, instead leaving it for the delegates to decide by open ballot the next day. In France, the Ambassador seethed over what he considered Stevenson's timidity and lack of vision. In Chicago, with his brother Bobby acting as his chief aide, Jack began a frantic, twelve-hour quest for delegate votes.

But the Ambassador was not an idle spectator. A series of phone calls to Chicago led to a sudden endorsement of Jack's candidacy by that city's powerful mayor, Richard Daley. And, after a call from the Ambassador, James Landis quickly tracked down the highly influential Speaker of the House, Sam Rayburn of Texas, and won from him a pledge of neutrality at the least.

Jack got enough votes—304—to forestall a first-ballot victory by the preconvention favorite, Senator Estes Kefauver of Tennessee. Then, on the second ballot, Rayburn's protégé, Senate majority leader Lyndon Johnson, astonished many when he rose to say, "Texas proudly casts its vote for the fighting sailor who wears the scars of battle." (As Landis had spoken to Rayburn, Joe had been in telephone contact with Johnson, reminding him that the Kennedy fortune could be put to many uses.)

The second-ballot surge carried Jack to a 618–551 lead over Kefauver and brought him within 34 votes of the nomination. But that was as close as he got. As the third ballot began, the emotional fervor began to subside and delegates started to think more seriously about the implications of having a young and untested Catholic on the ticket.

Jack quickly saw that southern delegations were swinging back to Kefauver and that the fight was lost. Wanting to jump before he was pushed, he raced from his hotel suite, where he'd been watching on television, to the convention floor.

The balloting was suspended to allow him to take the podium. After receiving the longest and loudest ovation of the convention, Jack gracefully and cheerfully moved that Kefauver's nomination be made unanimous by acclamation.

Kefauver might have won the nomination, but it was Jack who had made the indelible impression. His dramatic—and seemingly spontaneous—bid had thrilled millions of television viewers, and the elegance with which he'd accepted the first loss of his political career left them eager to see more of this dynamic new leader with the captivating smile.

Thus, the apparent failure was actually the most significant victory of his life. It was, wrote his biographer James MacGregor Burns, "the moment when he passed through a kind of political sound barrier to register on the nation's memory. In this moment of triumphant defeat, his campaign for the presidency was born."

Within hours, leaving behind Jacqueline, eight months pregnant, he flew to the Riviera, where his friend Florida senator George Smathers, along with Teddy, had arranged to reward him with a little pleasure cruise on the Mediterranean.

The trip was to last for a week. Teddy, given much responsibility for logistics, had seen to it that the boat was well stocked with comely and pliant young women who understood the purpose for which they'd been invited.

Jacqueline had pleaded with Jack not to take this trip. She'd already suffered one miscarriage and, at twenty-eight, was frightened by the prospect of giving birth. Within days of Jack's arrival on the Riviera, in fact, she began to hemorrhage. She was rushed to a hospital by ambulance, losing blood fast. An emergency cesarean section was performed but the baby, a girl, had already died.

Frantic calls were made to the Ambassador, who relayed word to Jack, Smathers and Teddy on their yacht. But Jack said he'd earned this vacation and he was not going to cut it short. Among the women aboard was a particularly voluptuous blonde nicknamed "Pooh," with whom Jack was especially delighted. Only when he tired of her, he said, would he go home.

While the Ambassador publicly claimed to be unable to establish radio contact with the yacht, and Jack and Pooh cavorted off the coast of Elba, Jacqueline lost so much blood that doctors began to fear for her life. Her condition was listed as critical and, as the body of her stillborn baby was disposed of, a priest was summoned to her bedside.

Still Jack refused to go home. For three days, Smathers in person and his father by radiophone tried to make him understand that his entire political career might be at stake.

Already, *The Washington Post* had printed a sympathetic story under the headline "Senator Kennedy on Mediterranean Trip Unaware His Wife Has Lost Baby." On two continents, the Ambassador's cover-up squad was spreading disinformation as fast as it could, but there was no certainty that the false story would hold. How hard could it be, after all, for the Kennedy family to locate a yacht on which two of its members were sailing?

As kid brother, Teddy did not feel it his place to offer Jack either moral or political advice, but Smathers had no such compunctions. He said he would not permit his good friend to destroy the career that had taken him so far in only ten years.

"I told him I was going to get him back there even if I had to carry him," the Florida senator later said.

The yacht docked at Genoa. The girls were dispersed. The Ambassador announced from Cap d'Antibes that after three days of constant effort, communication with Jack had finally been established and, heartsick, he was rushing home to comfort his weakened and grieving wife.

From this incident, as from so many others in 1956, Teddy learned a number of lessons.

First, as his father had been teaching by example for years, wives were to be used for political advantage but only in the most extreme circumstances should they be permitted to interrupt the pursuit of pleasure.

Second, Kennedys could get away with anything. No matter how big a mess any of them might make, their father would always find a way to fix it.

Third, as his father had so often said, and as Teddy discovered when he returned and saw how the Mediterranean incident had created a new wave of sympathy for the courageous young senator and his glamorous and heartbroken wife—who you were in reality placed no limits upon how you could trick the public into perceiving you.

The public actually wanted to be tricked. It really was the simplified, glorified celluloid or televised image to which the public wanted to pledge allegiance. No matter if that was just a mask. The public was happier with fairy tales than truth. And together, Teddy's father and Jack were in the process of concocting the grandest fairy tale ever told in the twentieth century. All Teddy would have to do for the next few years was not garble the few inconsequential lines he'd be given.

12

THE UNIVERSITY OF VIRGINIA WAS LOCATED IN THE
small, quiet and picturesque city of Charlottesville. After
the Mediterranean rambunctiousness of August, the sudden tranquillity proved a shock to Teddy's overstimu-
lated nervous system, but it was one from which he soon
recovered.

Together with John Tunney of California, son of the
former world heavyweight boxing champion and later a
colleague of Teddy's in the Senate, he rented a three-
bedroom brick house on the outskirts of town.

Teddy was not seeking a Spartan existence. The house
was set well back from the road, reached by a long driveway lined with neatly trimmed flowering bushes. Tall
pine trees dominated the large front yard and, from a
screened porch in the rear, one had a quite lovely view
of valleys rolling and dipping into the distance for miles,
until finally they blended with the haze-dimmed silhou-
ettes of the Blue Ridge Mountains.

Soon, Teddy began to enjoy the same sort of social life
he had at Harvard, one in which women were discarded
almost as quickly as they were acquired and it seemed to
be not how the game was played that counted but only
the score, which, in Teddy's case, mounted rapidly.

Tunney was already rather involved with a blonde who lived in Holland and he would think nothing of flying from Washington to Amsterdam for a long weekend, leaving Teddy to organize his own parties at the house.

This he did with frequency and gusto, though also with enough discretion so as not to attract any unwanted publicity. In Europe the preceding summer, he had, in the rather elegant phrasing of biographer Burton Hersh, "savored, with an unusual fullness, the boon of wealth and early young manhood."

Now, however, with Jack widely viewed as the most glamorous and fastest-rising star in American politics, his father had made it extremely clear to Teddy that any actions of his which caused the family public embarrassment would be considered unforgivable.

It was at Thanksgiving that year, as they gathered at the Hyannis Port table, that the Ambassador formally announced to them that Jack would run for President in 1960.

By Christmas, in Palm Beach, he was able to inform them that he'd just concluded a negotiation with Lyndon Johnson whereby, in return for certain unspecified considerations, Johnson would appoint Jack, over several more senior colleagues, to a seat on the prestigious Foreign Relations Committee.

Such committee service would be an important credential to have in 1960 when older rivals for the nomination would presumably try to suggest that Jack was too young and inexperienced to be President.

But it was also over the Christmas holiday that Bobby made a dinner table announcement that darkened the Ambassador's mood.

After his own graduation from law school, Bobby, with his father's assistance, had begun a Washington career as an assistant to family friend Senator Joseph McCarthy of Wisconsin, during those years in which McCarthy recklessly and fruitlessly searched for Communists in high government posts.

Now, Bobby said, Arkansas senator John McClellan

was forming a new Select Committee on Improper Activities in the Labor or Management Field, and he'd been offered the high-profile job of chief counsel.

Within weeks, Bobby said proudly, they'd begin hearings aimed at unseating Teamsters Union president Dave Beck and vice president Jimmy Hoffa, a particularly evil and dangerous man.

The Ambassador was not pleased. In fact, he ordered Bobby to drop the whole idea immediately, telling him how dangerous it could prove, both on a personal level and to Jack's presidential aspirations.

Bobby refused, provoking a dinner table clash that his sister Jean later described as "the worst we ever witnessed."

Joe Kennedy's ties to the organization that would soon become familiar to Americans as the Mafia were both long-standing and complex. He had formed certain alliances over the years, not only during Prohibition but later in Florida, where he'd been part owner of the Hialeah racetrack, and even more so in Chicago, where he'd made major real estate investments after World War II.

The existence of these alliances was not something Joe publicized, but he was acutely aware that they might prove vital to Jack's chances of winning the Presidency in 1960. The last thing he wanted was Bobby antagonizing people whose help he might need. A Senate investigation of labor racketeering would shine unwelcome light into dark corners, many of whose inhabitants Joe knew all too well.

Yet Joe felt constricted from sharing the reasons for his fierce opposition to this new turn in Bobby's career. He had always operated on the assumption that while his children might suspect the worst about him, they could feign ignorance as long as they were shielded from irrefutable fact. Thus, he could tell Bobby only that it might prove too dangerous, but not why; only that there might be unwanted risks involved, not what they were.

But these arguments only made Bobby more determined. For the first time, his zeal could be matched with a cause worthy of it. These would not be the false trails and trumped-up charges of the McCarthy subcommittee: the labor investigations would unmask the face of the real evil that was sapping America's strength.

Bobby also had a more personal reason. Now thirty-one and knowing that in 1960 he'd again have to put his career on hold in order to work full-time on Jack's campaign, he felt he needed at least one opportunity to prove—both to his father and to himself—that he could accomplish something significant on his own.

An effective performance as chief counsel to a Senate subcommittee that conducted televised interrogations of some of America's most vicious, notorious gangsters would make Bobby, too, a national figure. By building a reputation that was independent of his brother's he would demonstrate that, like Jack, he was truly worthy of the Kennedy name.

Bobby would not back down. As Teddy looked on with what others later recalled as a mixture of awe and fear, for the first time in Kennedy family history one of the sons openly defied the father.

It was an act that would prove to have consequences more dire and far-reaching than any of those seated at the 1956 Kennedy Christmas dinner table could have imagined.

Teddy returned to Charlottesville, where he enjoyed basking in Jack's reflected glory but where, on his own, he was building a reputation primarily for academic mediocrity—the steady stream of C's continued—and for outbursts of what MacGregor Burns has referred to as "volcanic physical energy."

At parties, which he both hosted and attended with increasing frequency, he was the center of attention, and not only because of his imposing size, startling good looks and ever more renowned family name.

Already, as a Senate aide would later note, he possessed "a charismatic charm, quick wit and . . . self-assurance." The force of his personality, which within the family was considered so insubstantial, struck outsiders as being, the aide wrote, "like a black hole—once

you were sucked in, there was little way out, so
was its gravity."

Naturally gregarious in social situations, Teddy also
was finding that the consumption of alcohol—something
that had always been strongly discouraged if not forbidden outright within his home—unleashed in him new levels of spontaneity and joviality, as well as sudden and
seldom checked impulses to act in ways he might not
have, had he not so quickly allowed one drink to lead to
the next.

His roommate, Tunney, put it simply. Teddy, he said,
"turns into quite a different person when he isn't working." Increasingly, the concept of "not working" came
to be associated, in Teddy's mind and in his life, with the
concepts of drinking and of obtaining sexual gratification
from as many women as possible in quick succession.

The sex was his way of proving to himself that he did,
after all, measure up to his father and his older brothers.
The alcohol provided him with the first real escape he'd
ever found from the pressures of being who he was, and
from the parallel stress induced by his sense that all too
soon much more than he could readily provide would be
demanded of him.

The gap between the ever more glorified image of Jack
and Teddy's shaky sense of self widened even further in
March when, after extensive lobbying on the part of Arthur Krock, Jack was awarded the 1957 Pulitzer Prize in
biography for *Profiles in Courage*.

Again, the lessons were not lost on Teddy. First, nothing lay beyond his father's power to arrange. Second, the
way you got ahead in life was by taking credit for things
you did not do, then making sure that no one learned the
truth.

Such lessons, however, could prove painful to any
young man who retained even a trace of honor or integrity. Thus, it was perhaps not surprising that in Charlottesville Teddy developed a stomach ulcer that required
medical treatment.

* * *

Meanwhile, throughout the spring and summer, with a verve he sometimes found hard to keep in check, Bobby was publicly hounding Jimmy Hoffa on national television. Hoffa was the Teamsters official who had first affiliated himself with organized crime in the 1940s, using Mafia musclemen to help expand his control over the labor movement in Detroit. In return, Hoffa had given mob leaders access to the Teamsters' enormous pension fund, which they'd used to finance the construction of casino hotels in Havana and Las Vegas.

By late summer, Bobby's cold-blooded, penetrating questions had made Hoffa look foolish and deceitful, while Bobby came across to a national television audience as both brilliant and courageous. His performance sparked such admiration that in October, when the Russians launched the satellite with which they beat America into space, even Lyndon Johnson said an investigation into the Soviet triumph would succeed only "if it had someone like young Kennedy handling it."

"Am very pleased with myself," Bobby wrote in a private journal, and his success did much to improve his personality. "He was much more pleasant to be around," said family friend LeMoyne Billings, "because he hadn't this terrible feeling that he wasn't contributing."

Now it was only Teddy who felt that way.

13

IN THE FALL OF 1957, AFTER A SUMMER SPENT CAROUS-
ing in Europe with John Tunney, Teddy found himself
faced with yet another family obligation.

The Ambassador had donated a considerable amount
of money toward the construction of a new physical education building on the campus of Manhattanville College
in Purchase, New York, the school for well-bred Catholic
girls from which Eunice and Jean, as well as Bobby's
wife, Ethel, had graduated.

In return, the school had agreed to name the building
after the Kennedys. This involved a dedication at which
a family member would speak. With both Jack and Bobby
occupied with more serious pursuits, Teddy was called
up from Charlottesville for the occasion.

Stunningly handsome in a light gray suit and dark, narrow necktie, with a single shock of his sandy hair falling
casually across his broad forehead, Teddy made a few
gracious, innocuous remarks and then, in the company of
his parents and sisters Jean and Eunice, repaired to a
reception.

Manhattanville maintained a rigid code of rules, one of
which was mandatory attendance at certain events, such
as the dedication of new buildings and subsequent recep-

tions. Both nuns and designated students made careful attendance checks during these events. Failure to appear would automatically result in demerits, too many of which could bring one's career at Manhattanville to an untimely halt.

One of the few students willing to risk demerits that afternoon was the blond and beautiful Joan Bennett, a debutante and former model who was the daughter of a wealthy Republican advertising executive. Having attended a football game the previous day, she felt it more important to complete an English paper due the next morning, and so, late that afternoon, she was sitting in her dormitory room, wearing a bathrobe and typing, when her roommate, Margot Murray, rushed in to say that her absence had already been noted, but perhaps if she hurried to the reception, she could claim to have attended the entire ceremony and thus avoid any demerits.

"So," she said many years later, "I got out of my old bathrobe, jumped into something appropriate and ran over. The next thing I remember, I was standing with Margot, and Jean, Ted's sister, came up to me and said, 'Oh, aren't you Joan Bennett?' And I said yes. And she said, 'Remember, we met last August.' I had met her at Ethel Kennedy's brother's house in Greenwich. So Jean and I got to talking and she said, 'Hey, you go to Manhattanville. I went here, too. What class are you?' I told her I was getting out in '58 and we got into a very girl-to-girl conversation, talking about the old nuns and what courses I was taking and how's old Manhattanville now.

"And then she said, 'You live in Bronxville, don't you?' And I said yes and she said, 'Oh, we used to live in Bronxville, too. Where do you live?' Well, I figured out that she used to live about three and a half blocks from where I lived! So, you can see, there were a lot of, 'Gosh, small worlds!'

"But I didn't know she was one of the Kennedys. I had never even heard of the Kennedys. I'd never even heard of them! I took no interest in current events. My lowest grade in college was current events. I didn't know what was going on in the real world.

"Anyway, Jean said she'd like me to meet her little brother and I expected somebody about knee high, but she introduced Ted to my friend Margot and me. The great fun thing is that Margot, who roomed with me for four years, knew a lot of Ted's friends, and so the two of them started talking, 'Do you know who, and this and that?' I mean, it really was kind of a small world. So they picked up the conversation and I knew a lot of these people, too, because Margot had a summer home in Southampton and I used to visit her there.

"Anyway, Ted was in a rush to get back to Charlottesville and there was only one flight he could get out of La Guardia, so Margot, who had a car on campus, said she'd drive him to the airport. So the three of us went and it was kind of fun, the excitement of rushing.

"Ted got back to Charlottesville and that night, or the next night, he phoned me to chat. Didn't ask me out on a date at all. Just phoned to visit. As a matter of fact, there were several phone calls just to say 'Hi,' and 'How are you?' and this and that. Then a couple of weeks before Thanksgiving vacation, he said, 'I'm going to be in New York for a couple of days over the holidays. Could I see you then?' We had a luncheon date in New York and then he drove me back to Bronxville. That was our first date."

In the presence of Joan Bennett, Teddy might have been fully controlled, but back in Charlottesville that winter and early spring, friends began to note a disturbing new tendency toward behavior that was not merely reckless but truly self-destructive.

Though not licensed, or even fully trained, he began to pilot a single-engine airplane. Given that both Joe Junior and Kathleen had died in air crashes, this seemed a bizarre form of recreation.

He showed no more care for himself or for others when driving an automobile. This led, in March of 1958, to his most serious misadventure since the dismissal from Harvard.

"Cadillac Eddie," as he was known in law school, had taken to driving his car—which was actually an Oldsmobile convertible—at high speed through the streets of his university town. The more tension-easing drinks he imbibed on a particular night, the higher would be the rate of speed and the less likely he'd be to let such distractions as red lights slow his passage.

Eventually, his driving technique attracted the attention of law enforcement authorities. A county deputy sheriff named Thomas Whitten was on patrol at the university end of Charlottesville one night in mid-March, when he saw the raggedy Oldsmobile tear through a busy intersection at an estimated ninety miles per hour.

Whitten gave chase but the Oldsmobile, swerving in and out of a series of side streets at speeds high enough to suggest that it was driven by a Hollywood stuntman, eluded him. He finally caught up with it in what turned out to be Teddy's driveway, but by the time Whitten got to the car, the driver had disappeared.

The following Saturday night, Whitten saw the same car race through the same intersection at even higher speed, its driver either unaware of or ignoring a red light. Anticipating that the car would head for the same destination as it had the first time, Whitten was able to stay closer to it, though the Oldsmobile's driver only increased his speed when Whitten turned on his siren and flashing lights.

Whitten chased the Oldsmobile for more than a mile along the curving roads of suburban Charlottesville before it slowed, turned suddenly and jerked to a halt in the driveway. This time, Whitten was next to the car before the driver could escape.

Shining his flashlight into the darkened Oldsmobile, however, Whitten saw no one. He stepped forward and opened the driver's-side door. He pointed his light at the floor of the car, where, curled up beneath the steering wheel, "weak as a cat," as Whitten would say later, was a clearly terrified Teddy Kennedy.

This being in the days before Breathalyzers, no blood alcohol level was recorded, but from Teddy's point of view it was already a bad enough scene: there was the speeding, the failure to stop at a red light, the high-speed chase, the refusal to stop when signaled to, the escape on foot the first night, the hiding beneath the steering wheel the second, plus the fact that he had been driving without a license.

Recklessly and heedlessly, he had endangered his own life and the lives of others. He'd tried first to flee, then to hide. His behavior had been both alarming and pathetic. Worst of all, he'd been caught.

His father moved quickly to contain the damage. Arrangements were made with local court officials to keep the arrest report secret. The police were persuaded to release no details to the local press. A preliminary hearing on the charges, first scheduled for March 28, was quietly postponed for three months.

In the interim, the Ambassador began to shore up such public reputation as Teddy had. In April, a slot was found for him on ABC's *College News Conference* television program, during which he and others questioned the Soviet Union's ambassador to the United States. After the program, Teddy solemnly told reporters that he'd found the ambassador "not as direct in his answers as he might have been."

Then, on May 1, a Kennedy spokesman in Boston announced that Teddy had been appointed manager of Jack's 1958 reelection campaign. The news that this youngest brother, while still a student in law school, would direct the campaign of the most electrifying political figure in America—a campaign widely seen as a springboard to a 1960 presidential bid—received far more press attention than the brief item about Teddy's arrest six weeks earlier, which the Ambassador, not by happenstance, had released to the wire services the same day.

Once again, an apparent setback had reinforced a valuable lesson: damage control can more than offset the damage done.

Teddy, despite his title, would have no control over any aspect of the campaign. The Ambassador would be in full charge, as he'd been since 1946. With the hearings requiring Bobby's presence in Washington, Jack's political aides Kenny O'Donnell and Larry O'Brien would supervise day-to-day chores, assisted by Jean's husband, Steve Smith, who'd been learning to administer the family's financial affairs out of the Ambassador's Park Avenue office in New York.

But Teddy could at least be sent out campaigning for fourteen or sixteen hours a day, which would likely keep him out of trouble for the summer. The hapless opponent was a man named Vincent Celeste, and the goal was to have Jack pile up the most lopsided margin in Massachusetts history, thereby sending a clear message to the national party that in Kennedy they had a winner.

There was no question but that Teddy enjoyed his new role. At twenty-six, for the first time, in however small a way, he was actually doing something useful for the family. And the work was not at all unpleasant.

Based in what the *Globe* described as "the most plush political headquarters Boston has ever seen," and "customarily surrounded by a flock of young beauties," Teddy played the role of kid brother to the hilt.

"He really loved the pace of campaigning," an aide recalled. "You'd go to one fire station in Springfield and then he had to go to all the others. So you'd have fourteen hours of visiting fire stations that day. I remember once we got stalled in a traffic jam and he jumped out and started going from car to car shaking hands and attaching bumper stickers to every car they'd let him. He loved campaigning. You couldn't hold him down."

For the first time, except for football, Teddy had found a constructive activity for which he had both enthusiasm and aptitude. And it was all done in behalf of Jack, the brother he idolized and the one whose accomplishments he wanted so much to emulate.

Eventually, he had to leave the campaign and return to Charlottesville for his final year of law school—not something a traditional campaign manager would have done—but the title had been a useful fiction and the experience had given Teddy's self-esteem a needed boost.

Jack won by more than 850,000 votes, capturing 73.6 percent of those cast. His margin of victory was not only the biggest in Massachusetts history but the largest enjoyed by any candidate in the country that year. And he'd done it while spending fewer than twenty days in Massachusetts during the entire campaign (although the Ambassador spent at least $1.5 million on the race).

Jack had been out across the country, campaigning for other Democratic candidates, burnishing his national image, piling up a stack of favors upon which he could draw in 1960. Teddy had actually made more appearances around the state than had Jack and it was hard for him not to feel that at least a small part of the huge margin was due to his effort.

But then the strangest thing happened. Teddy suddenly married Joan Bennett. As late as mid-August, the *Boston Traveler* had called him "possibly the most 'eligible' bachelor in Massachusetts," and said his good looks "may explain why so many girls volunteer for work at Kennedy headquarters."

Only a month later, there was a small announcement of his engagement to Manhattanville College graduate Joan Bennett, of Bronxville.

And only two months after that, while Teddy was in his final year of law school, they were married in a ceremony oddly low-key by Kennedy standards.

Jack's wedding to Jacqueline had been the most lavish that Newport had seen in thirty years. When Bobby and Ethel had married in Greenwich, more than fifteen hundred had attended the reception.

By contrast, on the frigid final Saturday of November 1958, when Teddy wed Joan, only 158 people were invited, and that included all members of the Kennedy family. New York's Cardinal Spellman, who officiated at the ceremony, declined to attend the reception, citing "pressing church business." Given his long-standing closeness to the Ambassador, this action verged on the personally insulting.

After only a three-day honeymoon, Teddy returned to his law school classes and Joan moved to Charlottesville.

The whole rushed and almost hushed manner in which such a significant event in Teddy's life took place led to some speculation that perhaps a pregnancy had precipitated the marriage.

Given the impulsive, careless behavior he so often displayed in other aspects of his life, such an occurrence would not have been impossible.

It is true that no child was born the following year, but also true that if Joan had miscarried (and she later had at least three miscarriages, as well as three children), it would not have been a development the Ambassador would have publicized.

It had been understood, of course, that, like his brothers, Teddy would someday need an attractive, energetic, Catholic wife, and Joan Bennett seemed an acceptable choice. Still, no one who knew Teddy had expected him to get married yet. And the truth was that Joan, while perfectly nice, and undeniably blond and beautiful, seemed to many who met her neither forceful, independent nor durable enough to survive in the emotional jungle that was the Kennedy family.

And Teddy was as unready to be a husband as he'd been to serve as manager of Jack's campaign. The unfortunate Miss Bennett simply had no idea. "She was blue-eyed, blond and beautiful, and she thought that's what Ted wanted," a friend said later, regretfully.

He graduated from law school the following spring, failing one course and acquiring two more citations for speeding and reckless driving along the way. In most of his courses he received grades of C or lower, and his senior paper, "Problems Raised by the Application of Anti-Trust Policy in Foreign Affairs and the Method to Their Solution," received a grade equivalent to D + and a comment from the instructor that it was: "Disappointing. Some bad linguistic slips, too."

No one suggested that he publish it as a book, and Arthur Krock didn't even read it, much less rewrite it. His one significant accomplishment occurred in April, when he and John Tunney won the law school's annual moot court competition. But even that achievement seemed no more than a metaphor for his life to date.

While Bobby was battling mobsters on national television and Jack was preparing to run for President, Teddy, with his brand-new ulcer and his brand-new wife, was still in moot court.

14

OCCASIONALLY, DURING THE SPRING OF 1959, FRIENDS would ask Teddy what he intended to do with his life. When he was in a mood to answer such a question seriously, his responses were consistent in only one way: he spoke of moving west, away from the family base, to someplace where he could establish his own identity, practice law, maybe use a portion of his trust fund to buy a small newspaper and eventually—though this was quite speculative and far down the road—perhaps even run for the legislature in some state such as Wyoming or Colorado or Arizona.

Even though he had gotten great satisfaction from his active role in Jack's campaign, the one thing about which he seemed clear was that he wanted to build a life of his own, with Joan, as far removed as possible from the centers of power his father and brothers had established in the East.

What it came down to was this: Teddy, or at least a part of him, wanted to live someplace where he would not always and only be looked upon as Joe Kennedy's son and as the kid brother of Jack and Bobby. Someplace where, in fact, he might not even be referred to as "Teddy."

His father, however, had other ideas. Already the Ambassador had succeeded in placing in the *Saturday Evening Post* an adoring article entitled "The Amazing Kennedys." The story described Jack as the "clean-cut, smiling American boy; trustworthy, loyal, brave, clean and reverent, boldly facing up to the challenges of the Atomic Age," and even predicted great things for Teddy, whom it called "the biggest and best looking . . . with the outgoing affability of an Irish cop."

The magazine said, "Fervent admirers of the Kennedys"—a phrase that could be read as a euphemistic reference to Joe himself—"confidently look forward to the day when Jack will be in the White House, Bobby will serve as Attorney General, and Teddy will be the senator from Massachusetts."

Having returned from a belated six-week honeymoon in South America, where he insisted that the distinctly unathletic Joan learn how to ski ("The Andes were better than Vermont," she said later. "At least there weren't so many trees to crash into"), Teddy was told by his father that he would, indeed, be going west that fall, but in Jack's behalf rather than his own.

Although he was now seventy-one, the Ambassador retained complete charge of all details pertaining to the presidential race he was planning for Jack in 1960.

It had occurred to him that the exuberant campaigning style Teddy had displayed in Massachusetts the previous fall could prove a minor asset if judiciously employed.

Having surveyed the national political landscape, the Ambassador had concluded that, in terms of Jack's candidacy, the least significant area of the country was the Rocky Mountain section of the West. Also, in those underpopulated states such as Colorado, Wyoming and Montana, prospective delegates were so widely scattered across such vast areas that to pursue them personally would be an inefficient use of the candidate's time.

But Teddy could be sent to the mountain states, where even if he fell squarely on his oversized face, damage to Jack would be minimal. And so, leaving Joan behind in Boston in the fall of 1959, and filled with hope and eagerness and brimming with energy, Teddy set out for the West.

Even while unofficially scouting the terrain in Jack's behalf—a formal announcement of the presidential candidacy would not be forthcoming until after the new year had begun—he would be on his own, as an adult, to a greater degree than ever before.

It did not take him long to blunder. One night in early October, Teddy, who was described by *Time* magazine as "serving as a sort of general evangelist for his brother," found himself in a student lounge at the University of Denver. In the midst of a heavy early-season snowstorm, only fifteen people had turned out to hear him speak. Unbeknownst to Teddy, who thought he was addressing only members of the university's Young Democrats Club, one of the audience was a reporter for the *Rocky Mountain News*.

Jack, he said, was waging an "all or nothing" campaign for the presidential nomination and under no circumstances would consider the vice presidency. However true this may have been, it was an articulation of the very position Jack had assiduously avoided taking in public, fearing that some would consider it arrogant.

Then, asked his opinion of Jack's potential 1960 opponents, Teddy breezily dismissed them all. Stuart Symington of Missouri, he said, was "not in a position of particular leadership." Hubert Humphrey of Minnesota was "not a significant threat." He described the twice-defeated but still venerated Adlai Stevenson as "ineffectual," and said the Democrats would be "foolish" to nominate him again.

When the remarks were published the next day, a chagrined Teddy attempted a denial, which, when proven false, only compounded the error. *Time* wound up belittling him as "the sorcerer's overeager apprentice."

It was an inauspicious national debut. Like an unsuitable ambassador, Teddy was promptly summoned home.

Late in October, the Ambassador convened a grand summit meeting in Hyannis Port at which Jack's 1960 strategies were laid out in detail. Approximately fifteen people gathered in the living room of Bobby's house at the Kennedy compound on a clear but frosty New England autumn morning. Of these, about half were considered significant.

They were Bobby himself, brother-in-law Steve Smith, Ted Sorensen, Jack's aides Kenny O'Donnell and Larry O'Brien, Pierre Salinger, an assistant to Bobby who would become campaign press secretary, the pollster Louis Harris and John Bailey, the veteran Connecticut politician who would serve as link between this new machine and the leaders of the old one it intended to supplant.

What was perhaps most remarkable about the group was the youth of its members. Other than Bailey, who was in his fifties, the oldest member of this first tier was O'Brien, who, at forty-two, was the same age as Jack himself.

Harris was thirty-eight, O'Donnell thirty-five, Salinger thirty-four, Bobby thirty-three, and Sorensen and Smith only thirty-one—just four years older than Teddy. The gap between Teddy and even the youngest of the others, however, must have seemed to him enormous and unbridgeable.

These were tense, restless, impatient men; young men of bold vision and unbounded imagination but also possessing rigorous self-discipline. They performed their tasks with diligence and alacrity and, like Jack, were not in the habit of finishing anywhere other than first.

Some, like Salinger and O'Brien, conveyed a surface cordiality, while others—most notably O'Donnell, Sorensen, Smith and Bobby himself—operated best behind a wall of curtness and irritability. But even the most glacial of them were, like Jack, almost afire with the need to get to the top immediately. With no visible display of emotion they would cut to shreds anyone they suspected of standing in their way.

It is hard to imagine that, sitting in their midst, Teddy could have failed to realize that these men, including his own brothers and his father, would never take him entirely seriously, would never have full confidence in him, would never treat him as an equal.

It was not just his youth and lack of experience that set him apart. It was that at his core Teddy was simply not as heartless, as driven, as single-minded. There was a large part of him that yearned to consider life a dance, not a journey. But the only music these men heard was the sound of their own internal drummers, driving them onward, ever onward, in lockstep, spurring them to heights to which Teddy—however much he wished to be respected by his father and his brothers—did not aspire.

Also making a deep impression on Teddy were the calmness and quiet confidence displayed by men only a few years his senior as they discussed in detail and with precision the means by which Jack would become the next President of the United States. Even then, as Sorensen was later to say, without inflection, "We knew how it would turn out."

To Teddy, such knowledge must have seemed unattainable. It was as if they were not just of a different generation but of a more evolved species, possessing a brilliance and an utter nervelessness that he knew—however much he might try to pretend otherwise—would always be beyond him.

In Washington, on January 2, 1960, Jack formally announced his candidacy, thus launching the decade that would encompass both the real beginning and the end—in an unalterable and almost unendurable way—also the end of Teddy's doomed attempt to take his place alongside his brothers in the mythic realm his father had created for them.

15

ONCE AGAIN, TEDDY'S ASSIGNMENT WAS THE WEST, and for a while he had great fun there. He quickly discovered that many doors opened to the kid brother of presidential candidate Jack Kennedy and that a surprising number of them led to bedrooms.

His sister Pat's husband, Peter Lawford, was a close friend of Frank Sinatra's. Of all the show business celebrities in America, Sinatra was the one Jack seemed to admire most. There was a studied indifference about Sinatra's manner, a casual cockiness with the hint of an underlying cruelty, an intimation not only that was he a tough guy himself but that much tougher guys would come running if he called.

Sinatra enjoyed knowing that the most glamorous and exciting political figure America had seen in decades idolized him. It seemed a relationship worth cultivating, and it did not take Sinatra long to recognize that the best way to do so was to keep Jack well supplied with women. As Lawford later described it, "I was Frank's pimp and Frank was Jack's."

In early February 1960, in the lounge of the Sands Hotel in Las Vegas—with Teddy present and his eyes practically popping out of his head—Sinatra introduced

Jack to a seductive ex-bedmate of his named Judith Campbell.

For both Jack and Teddy it was lust at first sight. The most remarkable thing about Campbell was how little she looked like what she was. Though dark-haired, she seemed a classically wholesome California girl. Open, trusting and utterly without guile, she had a freckled face that only added to the aura of innocence that made her presence in Sinatra's company both so incongruous and so provocative.

She had, however, been around enough show business and Mafia types, in Las Vegas and elsewhere, to know that you didn't get where you wanted to go by trifling with the kid brother when the big man himself was eyeing you.

With Teddy trailing feverishly along, Jack and Campbell had dinner in the hotel's Garden Room restaurant and then moved to the Copa Room for the floor show. By the end of the evening, Sinatra knew he had made a useful match.

Teddy was so smitten that he tried to persuade Campbell to leave Jack and fly back with him to Colorado on his chartered plane. When rebuffed, he became, as she delicately said later, "childishly temperamental."

For months afterwards, when in bed with Campbell, Jack would refer to that first night, saying such things as, "Boy, if Teddy only knew, he'd be eating his heart out." It seemed to Campbell that "he got a big kick out of the fact that he had succeeded where Teddy had failed."

Teddy returned east briefly in late February in order to be present when Joan gave birth to their first child, a daughter named Kara. But already it was becoming apparent to Joan that Teddy's energies and enthusiasms were primarily directed not toward her and their new baby but toward his brother's presidential campaign.

Desperate not to be totally excluded from his life, she gamely tried her own hand at campaigning, making appearances in such states as Wisconsin and West Virginia. But it quickly became apparent to her, to Teddy and to her sisters-in-law, who patronized her mercilessly, that the political life did not come easily to her.

She returned home to care for her baby, and for the rest of the year had very little contact with her husband. Perhaps the proper role and required duties of a Kennedy wife had not been explained to her in advance, but during 1960 Joan learned the hard way: by living the life.

In March, Teddy was dispatched to Wisconsin, where Jack faced an important early April primary against the liberal Hubert Humphrey.

As a Protestant from the neighboring state of Minnesota, Humphrey saw Wisconsin as a choice location for his first encounter with the Catholic from distant Massachusetts. The Ambassador gave the order that no expense or effort was to be spared. A defeat in Wisconsin would be devastating for Jack, and even a narrow victory would dull the aura of invincibility that seemed—aside from his father's limitless fortune—his greatest asset.

The entire Kennedy family campaigned in Wisconsin for week after frigid week. The terrain was bleak, the voters phlegmatic and inscrutable. But the Ambassador kept dumping dollars into the state and Kennedys galore swarmed across the frozen farmland, grinning, waving, shaking every hand in sight.

Later, all agreed that for the first time in his life, Teddy had stolen the show.

He had arrived one afternoon at a ski jump competition near Madison to make a speech in Jack's behalf. Somewhat jokingly, the meet's director said that if he expected the spectators to listen to anything he had to say, he'd first have to prove his mettle by going off the jump himself.

Teddy was an experienced recreational skier, but the difference between that level of the sport and racing, hunched over, with no poles for support, down a chute from the top of a 180-foot jump and then soaring off into the middle distance has been compared to moving from the diving board of a backyard swimming pool to the cliffs of Acapulco.

Nervously, but not wanting to give offense, he said he would at least go to the top of the jump and watch how the competitors did it for a while. But after only three of the jumpers had slipped from view over the edge of the chute—as far as Teddy knew, never to be seen alive again—he heard, with mounting horror, the public address announcer tell the crowd, "Now at the top of the jump is Ted Kennedy, brother of Senator John F. Kennedy. Maybe if we give him a round of applause he will make his first jump."

Teddy would later say that never before in his life had he felt such sheer physical terror. "I wanted to get off the jump," he said. "Even go down the side. But if I did, I was afraid my brother would hear of it. And if he heard of it, I knew I would be back in Washington licking stamps and addressing envelopes for the rest of the campaign."

Kennedys did not chicken out. It was as simple as that. Teddy, the most suspect among them, was required once again, in highly public fashion, to prove himself worthy of the family name.

Fastening skis at the top of the chute, he looked down, then out at the crowd which, from this height, appeared as clusters of brightly colored ants. Then he simply leaned forward and dipped the tips of the long, narrow jumping skis over the edge of the chute. Gravity and fate took over from there.

He stayed upright on the skis down the length of the chute, then hurtled through the air with absolutely no control over either his posture or his direction. Arms waving and skis flapping, he managed to stay largely upright before hitting the snow, skis first, and crashing into a clump of startled spectators.

The speech itself was anticlimactic, as, for that matter, was the rest of Teddy's stay in Wisconsin. The important thing was, at the moment of truth, he had behaved in the way Jack and his father would have expected, and he came away with admiring newspaper and newsmagazine coverage besides.

* * *

In the election, on April 5, Jack himself finished upright, though none too steady on his political feet. Despite the Ambassador's millions, the flawless organization, the family's weeks of personal campaigning and his own supposedly irresistible appeal, Jack polled only 56 percent of the vote against poor, chattery Humphrey, and even that margin came entirely from heavily Catholic districts of the state. The wary Lutherans had not been impressed.

"What does it mean?" asked one of his sisters in his suite in Milwaukee's Pfister Hotel on election night.

"It means," Jack said, both bitterly and wearily, "that we have to do it all over again."

The next battleground would be West Virginia. There, both Jack and his father knew, he'd need extra help and they both knew where he could get it: from Chicago.

In March, having just introduced Judy Campbell to the man he assured her would be the next President, Frank Sinatra had said he wanted her to meet another friend of his, a man named Sam.

Sam's last name was Giancana. He'd been a close friend of Sinatra's for years. He was one of the two or three most powerful Mafia chieftains in the world and a violent, sociopathic killer. Chicago police estimated that as of March 1960, Giancana had either personally committed or ordered the murders of more than two hundred people.

Once Sinatra explained that Judith Campbell was quickly becoming the favorite mistress of the probable Democratic candidate for President, Sam too seemed to develop a strong romantic interest in her.

Joe Kennedy, as a result of his Chicago business dealings, had been aware of Sam Giancana for years. It would not have been out of character for the Ambassador, alarmed by the close vote in Wisconsin, to seek the assistance of Giancana and his associates, not only for the West Virginia primary but in the larger campaign that lay beyond. Frank Sinatra, as a friend of his son-in-law Peter Lawford and now as a friend of Jack's, would be a perfect intermediary.

At the time, Giancana was not well disposed toward the Kennedys. Bobby had interrogated him on national television during the McClellan Committee hearings and once, after Giancana laughed in response to a question, had said, "I thought only little girls giggled, Mr. Giancana." Sam had not reached the position he now occupied by letting such public insults go unanswered.

But now a new opportunity seemed to be presenting itself. In 1959, Fidel Castro had led a revolution that toppled the badly corrupted government of Cuba. Then he'd shut down all the casinos and even thrown such high-level mob figures as Santos Trafficante in jail.

Cuba had meant billions—not millions, not tens or hundreds of millions, but billions—of dollars of profit for the Mafia. All that had vanished overnight, and as long as Castro remained in power it would not reappear.

Perhaps the thought occurred to Sam that in return for mob assistance in the campaign, the new President would see to it that Castro was removed. And perhaps he recognized that having Judith Campbell shuttling back and forth between his own bed and that of the next President would provide added insurance that prompt action against Castro would be forthcoming. For surely America's first Catholic President would not want it publicly known that for months he'd been sharing a mistress with the boss of the Chicago mob.

In any event, quite likely at his father's behest and certainly with his approval, Jack asked Judith Campbell to arrange a meeting between him and Giancana, saying, "I think I may need his help in the campaign."

Their first meeting took place in Chicago on April 12. It was not an event reported by the press assigned to the Kennedy campaign. The precise nature of the commitments Jack made to Giancana at that meeting were not recorded for posterity; or, if they were, such records have thus far been shielded from public view. But FBI wiretaps later revealed that after this encounter the Mafia began to funnel large sums of money into West Virginia —money that was used to bribe local sheriffs and other election officials. The message that accompanied the gifts was that their recipients were to produce a large vote for Kennedy "by any means possible."

Jack beat Humphrey in West Virginia by a decisive three-to-two margin, achieving what *The New York Times* called "a smashing upset." Humphrey was finished now, having no money left to continue his campaign and having been badly beaten in a liberal and heavily Protestant state he'd expected to win.

The knockout blow Jack had failed to deliver in Wisconsin had been struck in West Virginia—with a little help from Sam and his friends.

Teddy was shipped west again. Through May and June he worked the Rocky Mountain states, living an active bachelor's life, having occasional, increasingly strained telephone conversations with his wife and performing any reckless stunt he was asked to.

At a rodeo in Miles City, Montana, he climbed aboard a bucking bronco and hung on for five and a half seconds before being thrown to the dirt. This earned him the response he most craved: a long-distance call from Jack, laughingly telling him that he'd just arranged with the state party chairman in Wyoming to have a sharpshooter there shoot a cigarette out of Teddy's mouth.

Meanwhile, with the Los Angeles convention fast approaching, the Ambassador was taking care of more serious business. He apparently made an arrangement with J. Edgar Hoover whereby, in return for Hoover's promise of continued silence about Jack's wartime affair with Inga Arvad—as well as many other, more recent indiscretions—he would see to it that Jack's first act as President was to announce that Hoover would continue as FBI director.

Then, en route to the convention, he paused at the Cal-Neva Lodge in Lake Tahoe, a well-known Mafia resort partly owned by Frank Sinatra and Sam Giancana. An FBI report noted that during his stay, the Ambassador "was visited by many gangsters with gambling interests."

It would not have been surprising if the removal from

power of Fidel Castro and the reopening of Cuba to those gambling interests were among the subjects discussed.

Arriving in Los Angeles, the Ambassador quickly discovered that whatever arrangements he'd made in the past with Lyndon Johnson were no longer satisfactory. Apparently seeking an even better deal, Johnson had launched a series of bitter personal attacks upon both Jack and his father.

"I haven't had anything given to me," Johnson told a group of delegates from the state of Washington, deriding Jack for being so wealthy that he'd never had to work for anything. Johnson also said, in sneering reference to the Ambassador, "I never thought Hitler was right."

The attacks gained momentum. Johnson described to the press in great detail how Joe had called him, begging him to grant Jack a seat on the Foreign Relations Committee. He said Jack had been an ineffectual and indolent senator, so frequently missing roll call votes that his colleagues openly joked about his unexplained absences.

He called Jack "a scrawny little fellow with rickets," and added—to the Kennedys' horror, because this had never been so much as hinted at publicly—that Jack was suffering from a secret and obscure disease that could prove fatal.

He also said that if Jack was elected, it would really be the Ambassador who ran the country, so the Democrats might just as well go ahead and nominate the old man himself, instead of playing charades. He added that if Jack was elected, his father would have Bobby appointed secretary of labor, and it would be not only the Teamsters but all unions that would suffer.

The attacks continued until the Ambassador finally contacted Johnson to determine the price of a truce. It was high indeed. The Texan wanted to be Jack's running mate.

Joe Kennedy knew that both Jack and Bobby would be revolted by the prospect, but after due consideration—taking into account not only the further damage Johnson could inflict upon Jack prior to the nomination but the certainty that if Johnson was on the ticket, he could de-

liver Texas's twenty-four electoral votes in November—
Joe seems to have agreed.

With that, the attacks ceased and Jack's nomination
was assured.

Through an alphabetical and arithmetical quirk, the
first-ballot voting provided Teddy with one of the most
rewarding moments of his life.

Even before the balloting began, Teddy said later, "we
knew where we stood to within a vote and a half. We also
knew that it was going to be Wyoming."

Wyoming lay not only near the end of the alphabet (the
order of voting left only the Virgin Islands, the Canal
Zone, Puerto Rico and Washington, D.C., to follow it)
but in the heart of what had been designated as Teddy's
territory. He'd made seven trips to the state in the weeks
leading up to the convention and had grown particularly
friendly with Tracy McCracken, the head of the Wyoming delegation.

"We had ten of the fifteen delegates for sure," Teddy
said, "and before the balloting started I went to Tracy
and said, 'Tell me, if it comes down to where Wyoming
can make the difference, would you be willing to commit
all fifteen in your delegation?' 'Are you dreaming?' he
said. 'You've got to be. Because it's hard for me to
believe our last five delegates are going to make that
much difference. If it comes down to that, though, I
will.' "

When the time came for Wyoming to vote, Jack was
still eleven short of the majority he needed, with no guarantee of any to come from the offshore territories or from
the District of Columbia. But there stood Teddy, in the
midst of the Wyoming delegation, one beefy arm clasped
firmly around the shoulders of Tracy McCracken. Teddy
was there to make sure McCracken honored the pledge
of unanimous support he'd made so lightly earlier in the
day.

Before McCracken spoke a word into the microphone,
Jack knew he had the nomination won. He could tell,
looking at the television screen, from the enormous, exul-

tant grin on Teddy's face. In his whole life, he'd never seen his kid brother with a bigger smile.

McCracken announced that Wyoming was casting all its fifteen votes for Jack. And, at least for that fleeting moment, Teddy felt maybe he did belong in the family, after all.

16

AS IN THE PRECONVENTION PERIOD, TEDDY WAS again assigned the western states, but with California, Washington and Oregon now added to his list.

His father apparently felt confident that the arrangement he'd made with Lyndon Johnson assured Jack's victory in Texas, and that the discreet negotiations both he and Jack had carried on with the most influential figures in Chicago guaranteed that Jack would win Illinois. Nonetheless, he considered California, the home state of Republican candidate Richard Nixon, and one with thirty-eight electoral votes, to be potentially crucial.

Teddy would have help in California because it was both too important and too complex to be left entirely in his inexperienced hands, but Jack and the Ambassador— as well as Bobby, who had the title of campaign manager —considered California ultimately to be Teddy's responsibility: the most critical the family had ever given him. And Teddy himself said that, along with New York, it was the one state that was "absolutely vital" if Jack was to win the election.

The more time he was spending in the West—which was also time spent away from Joan and his baby daughter—the more Teddy was coming to feel that his initial instinct about it had been correct: that this was the region where he should make his permanent home.

Unfortunately, it was also a region that proved stubbornly resistant to Jack's charm. Many of its states had been hard-core Republican for years and the voters were not about to be seduced by a brash young Catholic from Massachusetts who spoke with an accent so pronounced as to seem almost a foreign tongue.

The problem was compounded by Teddy's inability to perform at the unrealistic level expected of him. Only a year out of law school, where he'd had to struggle to achieve mediocrity, he was now supposed to direct a presidential campaign in a thirteen-state region that, geographically, comprised almost half the country and with which, until nine months earlier, he'd been totally unfamiliar.

There were so many new faces, so many new names, so many chartered planes in the night. The Pacific Coast, where he'd not worked during the primary season, proved particularly difficult. That he was in far over his head became glaringly obvious during Jack's first campaign trip to the region in late summer.

Even Theodore White, whose veneration of Jack and all around him occasionally bordered on the absurd, was forced to write, "The advance work, particularly in Washington and Oregon, was atrocious and resulted in humiliation for the candidate."

Nonetheless, Jack's campaign quickly gained momentum. On September 12, he made the famous speech to the Protestant ministers in Houston which did so much to lay to rest fears that his Catholicism made him unfit to serve.

Throughout the month, the aura of glamour surrounding him intensified, boosted immeasurably by his association with Frank Sinatra and with other Hollywood stars brought into his orbit by his brother-in-law Peter Lawford.

And then, in late September, in Chicago, he had his first televised debate with Richard Nixon, the single event that almost instantaneously transformed him from youthful political leader into the brightest star in America's heavens.

In 1950, only 11 percent of the country's households possessed television sets. By 1960, that number had jumped to 88 percent. Thus, a national audience estimated at 70 million had its first look at Jack as a presidential candidate during that debate.

Crisp, authoritative, strikingly handsome, Jack projected exactly the image of youthful vigor that America wanted in the man who proposed to lead them across the New Frontier. By contrast, the perspiring, grimacing, pedestrian Nixon seemed the embodiment of all that was most tired and eroded in the national spirit.

From the day after the debate until Election Day, Jack was mobbed by enormous and excited crowds at almost every stop. They tore at his clothes, grabbed for his cuff links, jumped high into the air, shrieking, in order to see him—and in the desperate hope that somehow this new god who had descended into their midst might somehow deign to notice them.

Teddy's mistakes in the West did not arise from lack of effort. As a campaigner—a surrogate Jack—he was tireless, ebullient and effective. But he utterly lacked the vital organizational skills that both Jack and Bobby possessed in such full measure.

By the end, said a California campaign aide, Teddy had been reduced to performing "a public relations role primarily." And his shortcomings were not confined to California. In Colorado, the publisher of the *Denver Post,* which in backing Jack had supported a Democrat for the first time since 1916, blamed the loss of the state entirely on Teddy's "inexperience."

Ten of the thirteen states assigned to him went for Nixon, including California. That was the failure that most embarrassed him, that his father and brothers found inexcusable. "If we had carried California, I could have done no wrong," Teddy said later. But they didn't.

The outcome could not have been closer. Jack won the popular vote by one tenth of a percentage point, 49.7 to

49.6. If only about five thousand Illinois votes had gone the other way—and only about twenty-five thousand in Texas—Nixon would have won.

The Ambassador, of course, did not let that happen. He had never doubted Lyndon Johnson's ability to work magic over the vote-counting process in Texas—it was in part that prowess which had led him to put Johnson on the ticket in the first place—but, as Nixon took a large early lead downstate, he found it necessary to closely monitor developments in Illinois.

Theodore White wrote of these hours, "There was nothing anyone could do in Hyannis Port except hope that Boss Daley of Chicago could do it for them."

But the Ambassador had never been a man content merely to hope. He stayed on the telephone through much of the night. Finally, he was given the assurance he'd been waiting for and he sent word to Jack, who'd already retreated to his bedroom.

"I've brought a message from your father," said the niece whom the Ambassador had dispatched. "He says not to worry, you've got Illinois."

"Who says so?" Jack asked. "Did I miss it on TV?"

"No, your father says so."

Later, the niece reported that Jack's response was a simultaneous curse and grin.

Then Daley called him to confirm it. "With a little bit of luck— and the help of a few close friends," the mayor said carefully, "you're going to carry Illinois." And, despite losing 93 of the state's 102 counties, Jack eventually was declared the winner by 8,858 votes.

Having anticipated at least an impressive victory and possibly even a landslide of historic proportions, Jack was less than jubilant about the outcome. He had won, but in the end, as in the beginning, finishing first had required his father's intervention.

He knew that without Lyndon Johnson, whom he despised, he would have lost. He must also have realized that the family's obligations to Daley and Giancana in Chicago were now as pressing as those they had to J. Edgar Hoover.

And so obviously tainted was the result—Illinois was

only the most flagrant example of many abuses—that for days afterwards both Jack and the Ambassador feared Nixon might challenge the results in court. Casting about for someone to blame, Jack did not have to look far to find Teddy.

He had failed at the most important job ever given him. It was as simple as that. Kennedys finished first, yet in ten of the thirteen states that had constituted Teddy's domain, Jack had lost. The family clown couldn't joke his way out of that.

In Hyannis Port, even before final results were in, Bobby said to Kenny O'Donnell, "I'm worried about Teddy. We've lost almost every state he worked out west. Jack will kid him and that will hurt his feelings."

But there was no way around it. Even the charitable biographer Burton Hersh noted, "As the axiom insists correctly, the Kennedys never shit themselves, and that new gold star beside the kid brother's entry inevitably tarnished a shade overnight."

Thus, quite abruptly, and in a sorely strained atmosphere, Teddy found himself at a significant crossroads. He'd emerged from the campaign with two hard-won pieces of knowledge about himself. First, the intricacies of politics at the presidential level lay beyond his grasp. Second, despite all the difficulties he'd encountered, he felt far more at ease in the West than he ever had in Massachusetts, or Florida, or wherever it was he was supposed to consider home.

In so many ways, over so many years, he had demonstrated to himself and to everyone else within the family that he was simply unable to meet the demands of being a Kennedy. He had neither Jack's cold intellect and wry detachment, nor Bobby's blazing zeal, nor—to any degree—the crude willfulness of his father.

Teddy sensed that as long as he remained a Kennedy first and himself only second, he would never emerge from the shadows cast by those who had come before him. He recognized also that the only way he might break free from the psychic restraints his father imposed upon the male children was through physical separation.

His close friend Claude Hooton, who'd worked with him during the campaign, said later, "He thought his place in the world might be somewhere else. He liked the idea of making it on his own bootstraps."

He had been talking longingly to Joan—this wife of his whom he was just beginning to realize he scarcely knew —of the life he could envision for them in the West. Whatever the specifics turned out to be, there would be no pressure. He would be free in a way he'd never been before. Psychologically and emotionally, Teddy would finally be able to exhale. And possibly, then, to grow up.

"He just about decided to move out there," Joan would say later. "His idea was to practice law for a while and then, in maybe five or six years, run for office. He took me with him to New Mexico and Wyoming so I could see what it was like. His main reason for wanting to move was a feeling that in a new state he would have to succeed or fail on his own."

Then Teddy tried to tell his father what he'd decided and tried also to explain some of the factors that had contributed to the decision.

"Silly" was the mildest adjective the irritated Ambassador used to describe Teddy's plan. At this point in history, having finally achieved his lifelong ambition of putting a son in the White House, Joe Kennedy was simply too goddamned busy to listen to such foolish prattle.

"Why go off someplace and prove yourself for nothing?" he asked impatiently. He did not understand that for Teddy, proving himself would not be for nothing, but for everything.

When Teddy persisted, his father cut him off. This was not a matter for discussion. The next series of decisions had already been made and they most emphatically did not include Teddy's packing up and heading for Wyoming or any other goddamned place full of farmers and cowboys. As for California, the less said about California the better.

He hadn't felt it would be necessary to explain so much so soon, but this harebrained scheme about the West prompted him to disclose to Teddy the details of the futures he was in the process of arranging for his younger sons.

Bobby was going to become attorney general. There is no evidence to suggest that the Ambassador told Teddy at this time just why it was necessary to have a family member in the one executive office with direct control over J. Edgar Hoover and the FBI—and, indeed, he would have had no reason to, nor would he have been likely to entrust Teddy with such potentially devastating knowledge. The simple fact would suffice: Bobby was to be attorney general.

But there remained the matter of the Senate seat from Massachusetts that Jack would vacate when he assumed the Presidency. The governor of Massachusetts would appoint a temporary successor to hold the seat until a special election in 1962 determined who would serve the remaining two years of Jack's term. By 1962, Teddy would be thirty years old, the minimum age at which the Constitution permitted a citizen to serve in the United States Senate.

The Ambassador had already made certain that the outgoing governor would appoint as Jack's temporary successor an old Kennedy family friend—in fact, a former Harvard classmate of Jack's—who had agreed to step down in 1962, clearing the way for Teddy.

So there was no need to waste time talking about pipe dreams such as moving west to prove himself. Teddy was not on his own, he never had been, he never would be. He was not only a member of the Kennedy family but, like all its children, a servant to it. When summoned to family duty, he would respond, just as Jack had done when Joe Junior had been killed.

"I spent a lot of money for that Senate seat," the Ambassador said. "It belongs in the family."

And there was no one but Teddy to fill it, however much of a bungler he might be. For Joe Kennedy had finally run out of sons.

Here, Teddy made his fateful choice. Even after hearing his father's scheme, he could have said no. He could have remained true to his own heart, to his own ambition to prove his worth in his own way.

But Joe Kennedy was not an easy father to defy. Neither Joe Junior nor Jack had ever done it, and even Bobby only once. Kathleen had gone against her mother's admonition and had died. And Rosemary, after becoming inconvenient, had simply been made to disappear.

One suspects that Teddy sensed, deep inside, that the course he had proposed was the better one. Better for him, and, ultimately, better for the family, because, were he once again to succumb to his father's pressure and take on a position for which he was unqualified, he would undoubtedly wind up making the same kind of embarrassing mess he had made so many times before—or worse.

But how could he be sure? How could he be sure of anything? In a sense, his entire life up to this point had been a conspiracy to deprive him of any confidence in his own judgment.

Always, he'd been compared to his brothers and found wanting.

Always, he'd been moved around the country and the world to suit the family's convenience.

Never had he been encouraged, or even permitted, to develop a sense of himself as a unique individual, however imperfect.

And so he could not now sit in this room in Hyannis Port and look his father in the eye—the all-powerful father who had always gotten everything he'd wanted, the father who had never been proven wrong, the father who had bought not only a Senate seat for Jack but the White House!—and tell him no, in this instance his judgment was unsound, that this time he was going too far.

So Teddy said yes, of course the idea of moving west had been only a foolish, childish daydream, and he would be honored to become the second Kennedy son to serve in the United States Senate.

Part of him might even have believed it.

17

THEY WOULD HAVE TO ALLOW A DECENT INTERVAL TO
pass before even permitting speculation about Teddy and
the Senate. The idea seemed so preposterous on the face
of it that premature whisperings could provoke ridicule,
outrage or both. It would be bad enough when Jack announced he'd chosen Bobby—who'd never even practiced law—to be attorney general of the United States.

But that didn't mean preparations should not begin.
In mid-November, the Ambassador told Teddy he'd just
arranged for him to accompany several members of the
Senate Foreign Relations Committee on a sixteen-nation
tour of Africa. In 1962, when it came time to run, Teddy
would need foreign policy credentials. The time to start
acquiring them was now. He was told he would leave for
Africa at the start of December.

Joan, already pregnant again, and living in their recently purchased Boston home, was dismayed both by
Teddy's announcement that he would be leaving for Africa imminently and by his even more unsettling declaration that his father had arranged for him a career that
would begin with a campaign for a seat in the United
States Senate.

The past year, then, had not been an aberration.

Teddy's relentless work on Jack's campaign had not been, as she'd thought and hoped, a final paying of family dues before he and she would move on to a life of their own. Instead, this was the way it would always be: politics, the career, the Kennedy family, would come first. She, Teddy explained, while telling her to start packing his bags for the African trip, would simply have to adjust.

Jack and Bobby were aghast to hear of their father's newest plan. Teddy in the United States Senate? Really, that was ridiculous. And foolhardy, besides.

Were he to win, there would be a national outcry about the Kennedy family establishing a royal dynasty, even staging a constitutional coup. There would be bad jokes, harsh criticism and possibly a public reaction so negative that it would hamper Jack throughout the second half of his term, maybe even make it more difficult for him to win reelection.

Besides, Teddy might lose. And how mortifying that would be for Jack. It would be the end of the myth of Kennedy invincibility, which was one of Jack's strongest assets. It was too much to risk, there was too much potential for damage, too little prospect for gain.

Now that he was President-elect, Jack felt his arguments might prove more persuasive to his father than in the past. But this point had already been decided. Teddy was going to run for the Senate and he would not lose. The Ambassador would not permit it, any more than he had permitted Jack to lose the race for President.

As Bobby later recalled, their father's final words on the subject were that "we had our positions and so Teddy should have the right to his and that it was a mistake to run for any position lower than the Senate."

In only fifteen years, it seemed, the House of Representatives, once so coveted a goal, was no longer worthy of being graced by a Kennedy's presence.

Teddy's African trip served the Ambassador's purposes admirably. In one headline describing the journey, *The New York Times* said, "Brother of President-Elect and Senators Seek Data for New U.S. Policies," adding in the body of the story that Teddy was traveling through Africa "at his brother's request and will report directly to the President-elect."

For the first time, Teddy had received billing equal to United States senators. And the mention that he would "report directly" to Jack on his findings suggested that this youngest brother already enjoyed the full confidence of the incoming President—that his opinions were actually taken seriously by serious men.

Having established that, in mid-December the Ambassador used a favored *Boston Globe* political reporter, Robert Healy, to float the first trial balloon for Teddy's candidacy.

"Ted Kennedy on Senate Trail?" asked the headline. Healy wrote that the possibility that Teddy would run for the Senate in 1962 was "the latest backroom word from the Kennedy camp." He added: "Ted has been looking for a place to settle for the past year. He looked over such states as Colorado and Arizona . . . Now it appears he will settle in Massachusetts, open up a law practice, and, if he follows the Kennedy pattern, he will start campaigning the day he unpacks his bag in Massachusetts."

Healy described Teddy as "certainly the most rugged campaigner of the Kennedy brothers," noting that "he sailed off a ski jump in Wisconsin last winter so that he could say a few words in behalf of his brother to a big crowd gathered for the meet."

The story closed by delicately attempting to defuse what had been Teddy's most public humiliation. "During the past campaign," Healy wrote, "Ted did most of his work in California, where he had the tough assignment of pulling together the many Democratic splinter groups in the state."

That he had failed was not mentioned.

Teddy returned to Boston on December 23. The *Globe* reported that "the younger Kennedy, who toured Africa with three U.S. Senators, consistently refrained from expressing opinions on any of the political controversies of the Dark Continent."

Asked if he did intend to run for the Senate two years

hence, he merely smiled and said, "I have a great many people to talk to in Boston and Washington before deciding on a personal course of action."

Early on the frigid but brilliantly sunny afternoon of January 20, 1961, as Washington lay beneath a gleaming blanket of fresh snow, America's dynamic new President delivered an inaugural address that was instantly acclaimed as not only the finest speech of his life but perhaps the greatest ever delivered by an incoming President.

Never had Sorensen's rhetorical skills been put to more electrifying service. Never had the forty-three-year-old Jack, his face aglow with the remarkable handsomeness of his maturity, delivered an address with more apparent passion and conviction. The speech marked the grand culmination of his articulation of the themes of change, sacrifice and crisis that he had been encapsulating within the phrase "New Frontier."

America was a prosperous nation at peace with the world on the day Jack assumed its highest office, but one could scarcely have guessed that from his remarks. Already, he was driven by the need to cultivate a mythic persona. It was no longer enough that he was President, he would have to be a great President: greater than Roosevelt certainly, perhaps as great as Lincoln.

This was the inevitable extension of the imperative that had guided his father's life: Kennedys always finish first. It was not enough to have beaten Richard Nixon. Jack had already begun his race against the historical reputations of his predecessors as well as against the ghost of his dead older brother. Here, too, it was essential that he win.

That there were no imminent national or international crises was, from Jack's point of view, an inconvenience, but one that, like all previous obstacles, could be overcome by action and rhetoric.

First, he would have to make the world seem to be at a point of near catastrophe: from that perception true crisis would flow soon enough. It was a sense of peril that

Jack needed for his larger purposes and, consciously or unconsciously, it was a sense of peril he would provide.

"Let the word go forth," he proclaimed, "from this time and place, to friend and foe alike, that the torch has been passed to a new generation of Americans, born in this century, tempered by war, disciplined by a hard and bitter peace, proud of our ancient heritage, and unwilling to witness or permit the slow undoing of those human rights to which this nation has always been committed, and to which we are committed today, at home and around the world."

And we felt the stirrings of a national pride which, since the end of World War II, we had not known we possessed.

His early days as President were filled with what critic Morris Dickstein has described as an "imperial buoyancy."

Single-handedly—or with the assistance of his glamorous, elegant wife—Jack would elevate not only our values but our sensibilities. We would be at once more courageous and more refined.

As he ascended to the throne, the *New Republic* said Washington was, "crackling, rocking, jumping . . . a kite zigging in the breeze."

"Brilliant people circulated," one observer noted, "telling each other how brilliant they were."

So, at the start, we asked no troubling questions. It was only much later that we learned how hard Jack had pleaded with Judy Campbell, the mistress he shared with the Mafia leader, to be his guest at the inauguration. And that she, displaying far better taste and judgment than he, had declined, saying, "I just wouldn't be comfortable with your wife and family being there."

And only later that we learned he had sex with three different women—none of them Jacqueline—on the night that followed his inauguration.

And only later of the note he'd written to Frank Sinatra early in the campaign, asking, "Frank—how much can I count on the boys from Vegas for?"

* * *

This time, Teddy returned to Boston filled with images of reflected glory and carrying a cigarette lighter on which Jack had inscribed, "And the last shall be first." The West now seemed a distant, half-forgotten dream. Clearly, Washington was where his future lay.

He could not, of course, admit this publicly. The time was not yet right. Instead he stated, "I have no plans to seek an elective office," and the *Globe* dutifully reported that, contrary to earlier speculation, Teddy "does not plan to seek a U.S. Senate seat from the Bay State."

The Ambassador was pacing this carefully. He obtained for Teddy a job as assistant prosecutor in the Suffolk County district attorney's office, which encompassed Boston. Like so many other men of influence, the district attorney was a family friend and could be counted on to see that Teddy did not embarrass himself.

He performed his minimal duties in the D.A.'s office with no particular signs of enthusiasm, but did give full cooperation to his father's efforts to furnish him with a public image that might make the eventual announcement of his candidacy for the Senate seem less ludicrous.

In an early February interview with the *Globe,* Teddy reiterated that "I have no plans, absolutely no plans now for seeking public office." Indeed, the story said, he had "sought escape from the hurly-burly of Washington for his family by moving into a modest apartment on one of the quietest streets of Beacon Hill."

But the *Globe* also said that despite his youth and apparent paucity of experience, Teddy "has the mature grasp of the large issues which set his brother apart when the President first entered public life as a candidate for Congress in 1946," and that he was especially concerned with "the problems of an awakening Africa, of which he has a first-hand knowledge."

In mid-March, the Ambassador arranged for the *Globe*'s political editor to spend a carefully planned day in Teddy's company, "from morning eggs to midnight snack." The resulting story ran under the headline "Ted Kennedy Wows Bay State Audiences."

Again, Teddy said, regarding running for political office, "I have no plans at all . . . no schedule for that."

The *Globe* said, "His goal is to make his mark as a trial lawyer and practice someday before the state and national supreme courts."

But, most important, his similarities to Jack were stressed. "The tall, handsome assistant D.A. makes a striking figure," the *Globe* reported. "He is very self-possessed . . . [and] has a clear, crisp, distinct voice that carries easily." This voice was so similar to Jack's that "a listener, by closing his eyes, would be uncertain which brother was speaking."

Which was precisely the effect the Ambassador was striving to have Teddy achieve.

18

TEDDY DID NOT PROVE POPULAR WITH HIS COLLEAGUES in the district attorney's office.

"He had no feeling for the job," said one. "None whatsoever. And he didn't try to develop any. He was listless and uninterested. He wouldn't work. He tried cases only when he felt like it, which was seldom. He was one of the worst. He was as bad on his last day as he was on his first. He learned nothing."

Another co-worker said, "He was not only a Kennedy and a Harvard man, but a prep school boy on top of it. Around the courthouse he always acted condescending toward the rest of us, as though we were a bad influence and he'd been advised to stay away from us. No one was unhappy to see him go."

But the Ambassador cared not a whit what Teddy's co-workers thought of him. The Ambassador was already in touch with Tip O'Neill, the congressman who had taken Jack's old seat, informing him of the results of a private poll which indicated that in a Democratic primary for the Senate nomination in 1962, Teddy would easily beat the better-known and more experienced Eddie McCormack, who was then serving as state attorney general and was widely expected to seek the Senate seat.

Eddie's uncle John had just become Speaker of the House of Representatives. The Ambassador said he would hate to see such a fine family suffer humiliation. He suggested that O'Neill persuade the younger McCormack not even to declare his Senate candidacy.

O'Neill forwarded the poll results to John McCormack, who showed them to his nephew. Disdainfully, Eddie brushed them off. He was thirty-eight, an Annapolis graduate, and had been president of the Boston City Council before becoming the state attorney general. He told his uncle that he was going to run for the Senate and that he considered the prospect of Teddy's candidacy an insult to the intelligence of Massachusetts voters.

Stung by the rejection, the Ambassador, operating through intermediaries, offered McCormack a lucrative and influential partnership in a large New York law firm.

The answer was no.

He offered an ambassadorship. Not the Court of St. James's, of course, but something eminently respectable.

No.

He offered to back McCormack's candidacy for governor and pledged full financial support. In case of an unexpected defeat, there would be a fallback position as assistant secretary of the navy, a coveted plum for any Annapolis graduate.

No, said Eddie McCormack. He planned to be the next United States senator from Massachusetts.

Soon enough, Joe Kennedy had bigger problems to contend with. Jack had not yet done anything to oust Castro from Cuba in order to reopen the gambling casinos for the mob.

From the Ambassador's point of view, vacillation on Cuba must have seemed a luxury the Kennedys could not afford. Throughout the primary and general election campaigns, the Ambassador had relied heavily upon his organized crime connections to assure Jack's victories. The FBI had learned that as early as March of 1960, with Frank Sinatra acting as intermediary, such mob bosses as Meyer Lansky and Joseph Fischetti, as well as "other unidentified hoodlums," were "financially supporting and actively endeavoring to secure" Jack's election.

Sam Giancana later bragged openly about how his intervention in Chicago had enabled Jack to carry Illinois. And, through Sinatra, the mob had supplied Jack not only with money and votes but with women. Judy Campbell was far from the only one. Another FBI report from Las Vegas noted that during one of Jack's campaign visits, "show girls from all over the town were running in and out of the Senator's suite."

Now, it was time for debts to be paid. From his winter home in Palm Beach, the Ambassador detected the first stirrings of impatience and even of irritation.

In addition to promising that Jack would move promptly against Castro, the Ambassador had apparently assured the organized crime leaders whose assistance he had sought in Jack's behalf in 1960 that in a Kennedy administration they would have nothing to fear from the Justice Department.

Then he'd made his own son attorney general. He needed Bobby as attorney general in order to assure that J. Edgar Hoover got all he wanted, but he'd failed to take into account just how zealous, how obsessed Bobby was about the Mafia.

Not only did Bobby escalate his pursuit of Jimmy Hoffa into a Justice Department crusade, but he announced in his early weeks as attorney general that his highest priority would be to once and for all end Mafia domination of any segment of American society. He said, "I'd like to be remembered as the guy who broke the Mafia."

Both the Ambassador and Jack well knew that that sort of talk was far more dangerous than Bobby realized. Both must have known that at some point they'd have to bring Bobby under control. In the meantime, quick action against Cuba might be seen as a sign of good faith.

"That syphilitic bastard!" Giancana had once said of Castro to an associate. "Do you have any idea what he's done to me, to my friends?"

There were, of course, other reasons for the United

States government to want a Communist dictator removed from control of a large island only ninety miles from America.

Indeed, as both Jack and his father were well aware, plans for an attempt on Castro's life—to be carried out by members of the very same organized crime syndicate that Bobby had vowed to destroy—had already been formulated.

The CIA had first sought the Mafia's assistance in its plot to kill Castro even before Jack was elected. Using Robert Maheu, aide to reclusive billionaire Howard Hughes as an intermediary, the agency had approached Giancana, John Roselli and Santos Trafficante in September of 1960.

The Mafia bosses knew that an invasion of the island was being arranged and that plans called for Castro to be eliminated before it began. By early March 1961, however, Castro remained alive and in good health.

In the White House, Jack was growing fretful. The murder of Castro was not proving as easy to carry out as he'd apparently been led to expect. He was also worried about the invasion. The idea seemed so palpably crazy and the consequences of failure so potentially severe that Jack could not bring himself to give final authorization.

He feared that if the Soviets learned of American involvement—as he was certain they would—they might respond with a violent and bloody takeover of Berlin.

The situation was further complicated by the fact that Jack's mood was subject to chemically induced alteration, day by day, sometimes hour by hour.

To keep his Addison's disease under control, he had begun to take such high levels of cortisone that his face had grown noticeably puffy. In addition to the cortisone, he was receiving two to three daily injections of procaine, a local anesthetic intended to reduce his back pain.

He had also begun to receive amphetamine injections from a bizarre and mysterious New York physician named Max Jacobson, who numbered among his other clients such pillars of emotional stability as Tennessee Williams and Truman Capote.

Jack had first been introduced to Jacobson by a mutual

friend during the campaign. He received his first amphetamine injection (the drug boosted by a combination of steroids and animal cells) in September, a week after his dramatically successful speech to the Protestant ministers in Houston. Immediately and miraculously, both his chronic pain and his fatigue seemed to vanish.

At least once a week during the campaign and even after his election, Jack continued to receive injections from Dr. Jacobson, who had become, in effect, secret personal physician to the President of the United States, who now was trying to decide whether or not to launch an armed invasion of a foreign country, and was repeatedly proclaiming that each day the world grew nearer to "the hour of maximum danger."

Bobby grew so worried by Jack's new dependence on Dr. Jacobson that he sent the contents of one vial to the Food and Drug Administration for analysis. The report was, as expected, that amphetamines and steroids were the chief active ingredients. When told this and advised by Bobby to stop taking the injections, Jack replied, "I don't care if it's horse piss. It works."

Even at his most euphoric, however, Jack continued to dither over Cuba. Wavering daily, he asked the CIA, on March 11, to scale down the size of the operation. "This is too much like a World War Two invasion," he said of the then current plan.

Four days later, he received a redrawn plan which an aide approvingly described as "unspectacular and quiet and plausibly Cuban in its essentials." Still Jack did not grant approval. Indeed, White House aide Arthur Schlesinger noted in his journal that the President was apparently "growing steadily more skeptical" and that his sentiments were "flowing against the project."

It was at this point that the Ambassador, as he'd done so often in the past, took command.

Jack traveled to his father's house in Palm Beach on Thursday, March 30, for a long Easter weekend.

So many factors were coming into play. There was so much confusion, so much risk. Jack seemed paralyzed by the need to make the first crucial decision of his Presidency. If the Mafia hit men had succeeded in assassinating Castro, Jack could have issued the invasion order instantaneously. In the chaos that would have ensued upon news of Castro's death, United States involvement in a subsequent uprising by the Cuban people might have been effectively masked. But with Castro still alive, well and dangerous, the whole operation became infinitely more treacherous and the likelihood of triggering Soviet retaliation far greater.

It would appear, however, that in Palm Beach, Joe Kennedy swiftly cut through Jack's befuddlement. They had made a deal. It was as simple as that. Giancana and his friends had delivered. Now it was Jack's turn, and Cuba was the gift promised in return.

It was too goddamned bad that they hadn't yet assassinated Castro, but people were getting impatient. People such as Trafficante, Roselli, Lansky, Giancana, and Carlos Marcello, the mob boss who controlled New Orleans. To these men—very serious businessmen—as to the Ambassador himself, time was money.

Jack returned to Washington on Tuesday. His advisors were startled by the change in his attitude regarding Cuba. "He really wanted to do this," said one. "He didn't ask us. He had made up his mind and told us."

This aide added that if he'd known Jack better he would have said, "What the hell happened to you on the weekend?" But he didn't. Instead he said, "Yes, sir."

As Arthur Schlesinger put it somewhat wryly in his diary, "Some of us darkly suspected he had been talking to his father." Jack met with advisors that very night to draw up a final invasion plan.

The disaster that became known as the Bay of Pigs, named for the site at which the CIA-trained exiles went ashore, began on April 17, 1961, and lasted only forty-eight hours.

With the invaders trapped on the beach under ferocious Cuban counterattack, U.S. military leaders implored Jack to authorize American air or naval support.

"I don't want the United States involved with this," he told Admiral Arleigh Burke of the Joint Chiefs of Staff.

"Hell, Mr. President," Burke said scornfully, "we *are* involved!"

But Jack refused to order additional support. One hundred fourteen of the invaders were killed on the beach. The other 1,189 were captured. None escaped. There was no internal uprising, no coup, no assassination of Castro. Just the most egregious American foreign policy blunder within memory.

In Palm Beach, Joe Kennedy, who'd been in unremitting telephone contact with Jack since it first became obvious that the invasion was an utter debacle, said, according to Rose, that he felt like he was "dying."

After less than three months in office, Jack's reputation had suffered perhaps irreparable damage. The Ambassador had to know that his insistence upon the attempt to unseat Castro was the primary cause.

Worse, they had failed. With the mob, as with Joe, trying and failing was not good enough. The mob, like Joe, demanded results.

In the aftermath of the unsuccessful invasion attempt, Jack had Judy Campbell arrange another private meeting between himself and Sam Giancana.

She has reported that the President of the United States and the Mafia chieftain met in the Ambassador East Hotel in Chicago on April 28. Giancana didn't call him "Mr. President." Giancana called him Jack. Giancana was not a happy man. He figured the Kennedy family, having failed to oust Castro and reopen the casinos, owed him a few billion dollars.

Not to mention how much Bobby was pissing him off. Giancana didn't like this talk about Bobby's highest priority as attorney general being the breakup of organized crime. It had to stop. Right away. And Castro still had to go. Fast. Or else there was going to be trouble. Already, Johnny Roselli had advised Giancana to act, saying, "Let them see the other side of you."

Jack did his best to pacify the Mafia boss. Bobby, he said, would be given new responsibilities. For a while he'd considered making Bobby head of CIA, but now thought it would be more useful to have him supervise the assassination of Castro in an unofficial capacity.

There would be a new operation activated. It would have a code name: Operation Mongoose. The goal of Mongoose would be the murder of Castro and the overthrow of his Communist government. With Bobby in charge, the operation would be swift and deadly. And Giancana's men would still be needed.

Giancana was not fully satisfied, but agreed to give Jack more time. As the two talked, Judy Campbell was in the bathroom, sitting on the edge of the tub. They agreed to use her as their private channel of communication. Jack would arrange to see her somewhere, then have her carry useful information to Giancana.

Information, Jack seems to have promised, such as confidential FBI reports that would disclose where and how surveillance of mob activities was taking place.

Campbell herself later said she believed the envelopes she carried also contained money. Perhaps Jack had worked out some sort of installment plan, one in which the payments could be discontinued once Castro was gone and the Havana casinos reopened.

19

In mid-May, Teddy's initiation into Kennedy family rites and political practice continued. He traveled to Italy. His father knew he'd have the Irish Catholic vote in 1962 but wanted to lock in the Italian vote, too.

The trip was described as a "personal, unofficial, good-will mission" to Italy and Sicily. One of Teddy's traveling companions was Boston municipal judge Francis X. Morrissey, the Ambassador's longtime deputy for unpleasant political chores.

And, on the island of Capri, one of the people to whom Teddy and Judge Morrissey spread some personal, unofficial goodwill was a deported mobster named Michael Spinella.

Teddy and Judge Morrissey enjoyed an extremely cordial lunch with Spinella—the sort that would have allowed Teddy to display appropriate respect and to convey the high esteem in which his father held many of Spinella's former associates still residing in America.

While in Italy, Teddy also had an audience with the Pope.

Having thus paid his respects in appropriate quarters, he came home.

* * *

He got back on the day when Jack, in a highly unconventional second State of the Union message to Congress, announced his plan to have an American astronaut walk on the moon before the end of the decade.

It was a grandiose gesture, rich in symbolism, short on meaning and terribly costly. But it would be a heroic undertaking and as its creator and ultimate supervisor, Jack would be hero in chief as well as commander in chief.

"Why, some say, the moon? Why choose this as our goal? They may as well ask, Why climb the highest mountain? Why, thirty-five years ago, fly the Atlantic?

"In a very real sense," he said, "it will not be one man going to the moon, it will be an entire nation. For all of us must work to put him there."

It would also be a race against the Russians. "We have vowed," Jack said, "that we shall not see space governed by a hostile flag of conquest but by a banner of freedom and peace." This was a race we would win.

By beating the Russians to the moon, we Americans would cover ourselves in glory and would be forever the envy of the world.

And Jack finally would have accomplished something on a mythic scale that not even the ghost of his older brother could match.

Back home, Teddy found that being the youngest brother of the President, with no immediate pressing responsibilities of his own, made for a pleasant life.

There was, however, the inconvenience of his wife, who simply was not fitting into the family mold and was growing increasingly disconsolate. She could not sail. She could not ski. She could not even water-ski.

"I'm a flop," she said to one friend after a particularly brutal weekend at Hyannis Port, during which her mother-in-law, her brothers-in-law and, in particular, her sisters-in-law had cruelly mocked her lack of athleticism. "Ted should have married my younger sister, Candy. She plays tennis and golf and rides beautifully, while I'm still allergic to horses. But I guess there's no going back. Ted met me and not my sister."

Still, she said she felt "extra, no good . . . a nobody, nothing, not needed." And Teddy did little to help her, siding, as always, with what he considered the real Kennedy family, which had already passed its harsh judgment upon her.

Joan also continued to display a disturbing tendency toward candor. In one interview, asked about her relationship with Jacqueline, Joan mentioned that "Jackie is trying to talk me into wearing a wig. She has three of them and wears them a lot, especially for traveling, but I tried one on and just felt silly."

Well! Among the minor family secrets that the image-obsessed President and First Lady were determined to keep from the public (along with the fact that Jack, though never photographed while wearing them, needed eyeglasses for reading) was that Jacqueline often wore wigs. But Joan had not even had the common sense to recognize that this was not the sort of personal detail one shared with press and public.

Due to give birth to her second child in September of 1961, Joan spent a thoroughly miserable summer in Hyannis Port, seeing less than ever of Teddy. Even when in Hyannis Port, he would often leave her alone in their house while he attended the frequent and often bawdy parties that sprang up in Jack's house if the President, who was seldom accompanied by his own wife, was spending the weekend there.

One of the bawdiest occurred in late September. The day before, Frank Sinatra had visited the White House, sipping Bloody Marys on the balcony and musing aloud, "All the work I did for Jack—sitting here like this makes it all worthwhile."

The next day, Teddy brought Sinatra and Porfirio Rubirosa, the infamous Latin American playboy, to Hyannis Port. Sinatra brought twelve pieces of luggage and a case each of red wine and champagne. Rubirosa brought his fifth wife. Teddy also invited a contingent of women, who, according to the family chauffeur, "looked like whores to me."

A party ensued to which Joan was not invited. In the

midst of it, she went into labor and was driven by a chauffeur to the Boston hospital where she planned to give birth. Knowing that Teddy, at that point, would be incapable of responding appropriately, she told her attending physician simply that "he's a very heavy sleeper and it may be difficult to reach him."

Indeed, it was not until the next morning that a red-eyed, hungover Teddy even called the hospital. When he did, he was told that Joan had given birth to their first son.

Through that summer and fall, the Ambassador slowly moved Teddy closer to declaring his Senate candidacy.

Judge Frank Morrissey, having escorted Teddy to Italy, now performed the more mundane chore of shepherding the youngest Kennedy brother around Massachusetts, introducing him to those who mattered, instructing him in the art of distinguishing them from those who did not, and making sure the kid committed no gaffe so grievous that it could not be papered over.

Early press coverage was predictably favorable. The *Globe* said Teddy was "covering a wide range of territory in Massachusetts, speaking frequently to crowded gatherings on international problems facing the United States," and adding that "those who saw young Kennedy on the Channel 5 Reports news show . . . must have been impressed by his grasp of the African problem and his ability to communicate the fine points of this delicate issue to the audience."

The story concluded, "The half-hour television show gave viewers a striking picture of the similarities in Ted's mannerisms and those of his famous brother. There were times during the telecast when he sounded exactly like the President delivering one of his articulate speeches. He expressed himself with the same deliberate pauses between important statements that helped build the stature of President Kennedy during the debates with former Vice President Nixon. The same nodding assent to questions, the same penetrating gaze in his eyes . . . ."

At Boston's Faneuil Hall, Teddy warned that "the fall of Berlin could be a prelude to the fall of Boston."

He appeared at the old house in Brookline where Jack had been born, to personally thank those who had volunteered to repaint it. "It was a wonderful idea to repaint the house," he declared, while accepting a commemorative plaque from Brookline officials.

Then, with the Ambassador still keeping potential opponents off balance by planting stories in the *Globe* that Teddy might, after all, choose to run merely for the office of state attorney general ("There are many members of the Democratic Party who claim Asst. Dist. Atty. Kennedy wouldn't dare to run in his first try for public office for one of the top two spots, United States Senator or Governor"), he was off on a whirlwind tour of Latin America, to further strengthen the impression that he possessed a formidable amount of foreign policy expertise.

Upon his return, the *Globe* printed a series of stories under his byline in which he opined that democracy and communism were locked in a life-and-death struggle for the hearts, souls and minds of millions of freedom-loving but impoverished South American peasants.

"Read the EXCLUSIVE reports by the brother of the President—on his Latin American fact-finding trip," exhorted the *Globe*, and hundreds of thousands of potential voters did. First, the Dark Continent. Now the seething masses south of the border. Though only twenty-nine, Teddy, it seemed, had already acquired firsthand mastery over the most complex of global problems. Also, by now, on a clear day he could find Pittsfield without a map.

The trouble was, Eddie McCormack didn't give a damn. He wanted the Senate seat and he planned to fight for it, and he was not lacking in either resources or resourcefulness.

Another difficulty arose from the fact that outside Massachusetts, journalists and political leaders tended to take a far more negative view of Teddy's budding aspirations.

"An insulting comedy reflecting on proud national traditions," grumped the national political columnist of the *New York Daily News*. He went on to write, "Reports that have not been denied are to the effect that former

Ambassador Joseph P. Kennedy favors the Senate try, while the President himself leans to the view that an apprenticeship in public office would be preferable first.''

That was putting it mildly. Jack repeatedly heard from advisors such as O'Brien and O'Donnell—as well as from the hardheaded Bobby—that a run for the Senate by Teddy would bring scorn and contempt down upon the entire family, and the one who would suffer most would be Jack.

It was an added burden he did not need. Besides, he knew that no matter how carefully managed Teddy might be, there was no telling what sticky messes he might get himself into. He could pose as an instant expert on every continent on the globe, but Eddie McCormack was a wily bastard who Jack fully believed could chew Teddy into pieces after breakfast and spit him out before lunch.

Jack and Bobby again protested to their father. This, they reminded him, was no reincarnation of Joe Junior. This was Teddy! Fat Teddy. The butterball. He'd tripped on his cassock as an altar boy, he'd been thrown out of Harvard for cheating, he'd been arrested after a high-speed auto chase, he drank, he womanized flagrantly, and he hadn't even been able to deliver California.

Once, after *Time* reported that Teddy had, on some occasion, smiled "sardonically," Jack responded with a remark that summarized his attitude toward his youngest brother.

"Bobby and I smile sardonically," Jack said. "Ted will learn how to smile sardonically in two or three years. But he doesn't know how to yet." Clearly, such a callow youth was not ready to serve in the Senate.

The Ambassador, however, did not budge. Teddy was going to the Senate. End of discussion. Jack and Bobby should not concern themselves. They had more important matters to deal with—like Fidel Castro. Teddy was the Ambassador's personal project, his final act of alchemy, by which he would turn the dullest of lead into gold.

* * *

Then, on December 19, Joe Kennedy suffered the stroke that would paralyze him and render him speechless for the rest of his life.

While playing golf at the Palm Beach Country Club, he suddenly sat down in the middle of a fairway, complaining that he wasn't feeling well.

With assistance, he managed to stagger to his waiting limousine and was rushed to his home on Ocean Boulevard. There, he collapsed onto his bed, weak, ashen-faced and already having difficulty moving and speaking.

Servants quickly called for Rose. She said there was no point in calling an ambulance or even in summoning a physician. She said she was sure he'd be all right again after his usual afternoon nap, though it was obvious to all that something extremely serious had occurred.

"All he needs is rest," she said, and then—to the amazement of the entire household staff—summoned her chauffeur to take her out for her own previously scheduled round of golf.

And so he lay in his bed, conscious but speechless and paralyzed, for hours. Only when Rose returned did she permit medical assistance to be summoned.

Even then, she did not accompany her husband to the hospital. "There's nothing I can do for him but pray," she said, and went off for her regular afternoon swim.

Teddy rushed down from Boston on a military jet, but by the time he reached the hospital, his father had slipped into a deep coma, from which he would not emerge for three days.

Forever after, the only sound the Ambassador was able to utter was the single word "Noooooooo," which he emitted in a low, wailing moan, much to the discomfort of all.

As he sat at his father's bedside, Teddy had no idea what to do next. He was too far into the Senate race to back out now and he knew how insistent his father had been about it. But without the Ambassador's direction and management he had not the slightest idea of how to go about winning and knew that neither Jack nor Bobby had even wanted him to try.

Two months before his thirtieth birthday, Teddy was forced to confront the fact that for the first time in his life his father would not be able to make all his problems go away.

20

With their father immobilized, Jack and Bobby figured the best thing for them to do was to get Teddy out of the country for a few weeks while they and their advisors determined how best to handle this campaign they'd never wanted.

What he had going for him were his good looks, his energy, his ebullience on the campaign trail, his father's money and the President's name. This might prove enough, but they wanted to ensure that in case it did not, damage to Jack would be minimal.

This meant no direct presidential involvement and as many disclaimers of interest in the outcome as would be plausible. Steve Smith, whose base of operations was New York, not Washington, was given supervision over the campaign. With the utmost discretion, as many presidential advisors as were needed—O'Donnell, O'Brien, Sorensen, Bobby himself—would assume surreptitious control over Teddy's political schooling and the necessary burnishing of his image.

Aside from being both qualified and experienced, Eddie McCormack was tough. He couldn't be bought off and he couldn't be scared off, a phenomenon the Kennedys had seldom encountered before. That meant, at least, that their task was simple: they would just have to grind him into dust, using as much money and muscle as necessary.

But first, while Teddy was abroad "fact-finding," Jack and Bobby had more pressing matters to attend to. Chief among them was the growing impatience of Sam Giancana and his associates about Castro's continued rule over Cuba.

Jack faced a dilemma. Through Judy Campbell, he'd maintained regular contact with the Chicago mob boss and knew the extent of Giancana's irritation. He also knew that some of the very people Bobby seemed most obsessed with putting in prison—Giancana, Roselli, Trafficante, Marcello, Lansky and the rest—were working unofficially as secret United States government agents, essentially under contract to the CIA to carry out the execution of Castro.

Bobby was directing Operation Mongoose, which had grown into the largest clandestine operation America had mounted since World War II, with five hundred CIA case workers directing three thousand Cuban personnel and with a secret budget of $100 million per year.

Back in November, he had informed his Mongoose assistants that an inflexible timetable required the removal of Castro by no later than October of 1962. Whatever was required in terms of manpower, money or technology would be provided. They were simply to get the job done. Bobby didn't want to know details. He only wanted results.

But Bobby seemed to have no notion that the people who were trying hardest to obtain those results—even then the CIA was in the process of supplying Johnny Roselli with a new, improved poison pill for shipment to Mafia assassins inside Cuba—were the very men whom, wearing his public, attorney general-as-crimebuster hat, he was trying to imprison.

As Jack, now deprived of his father's counsel, attempted to extricate himself from what was a decidedly awkward situation, he kept inviting Judy Campbell to the White House and sending her back to Giancana with envelopes, hoping that Castro would be killed before the mob's dwindling store of patience was exhausted, or before J. Edgar Hoover learned that the President was feeding the Mafia secret FBI files.

Teddy left for Europe and the Mideast on February 9, 1962, having not yet formally declared his candidacy but making no secret of his intentions. In Israel, he met with Prime Minister Ben-Gurion. In West Berlin, he celebrated his thirtieth birthday, thus officially becoming eligible to serve in the Senate.

From there, he went to Ireland, where, it was reported, he received "the sort of cheerful welcome that even his brother would have been proud of" and "won enough applause from a couple of whistle-stop speeches to boost his hopes of political success back home."

Returning to Boston late in the month, he announced at an airport press conference, "I've collected a great number of facts and figures from my trip."

Eddie McCormack got back to Boston the same night from his own ten-day trip to Italy and Ireland. But McCormack said his journey had been simply a "family vacation, not a fact finding tour. You can't spend five days in Rome or five days in Israel and say you're an expert."

The day of Teddy's return, February 27, was the day Bobby received one of the worst shocks of his life. It came in the form of a memo from J. Edgar Hoover, informing him that a woman named Judith Campbell, who had been one of Jack's mistresses since 1960, was concurrently having an affair with Chicago Mafia boss Sam Giancana.

For Bobby, the implications were staggering.

From the day he'd been sworn into office, aware of Hoover's unique ability to bring down the entire House of Kennedy through the selected release of unsavory facts regarding the activities of his father and older brother, Bobby had been forced to compromise himself and his principles in what he'd accepted as a necessary effort to appease Hoover.

Hoover hated blacks and thought the civil rights movement was a Communist plot? All right, despite his personal feelings and the plaintive entreaties from so many members of his staff, Bobby would decline to use the full force of federal power to enforce the laws against segregation.

It had been a painful decision, but as much as he respected the rights of the blacks and no matter how he despised the violent racists who continued to trample on them, family interests had to come first.

Right now, that meant Jack's prestige, which Hoover could destroy overnight. His father had driven home the point forcefully when he insisted that Bobby accept appointment as attorney general: at any cost, Hoover's wishes must be granted; his enemies must become Bobby's enemies, while any unsavory or even criminal activities of Hoover's friends must be overlooked. Everything the Ambassador had created was held hostage to the secrets in J. Edgar Hoover's private files.

And now there was more. Now, there was the worst secret yet. A sex triangle that linked the same woman with the President of the United States and one of the most villainous Mafia leaders in the country. If even a whisper of this were ever disclosed, Jack would have to resign. He might even be impeached.

At least twenty times, Hoover's memo informed Bobby, Judith Campbell had visited Jack in the White House. And there were records of more than seventy calls she'd made to Jack's private phone number there. Her contacts with Giancana had been even more frequent. On many occasions she'd traveled directly from one man to the other, as if acting as some sort of messenger.

What was Bobby to do? First, he would have to tell Jack immediately what Hoover knew and insist that his brother have no further contact with Judith Campbell.

But even that offered no protection. He knew that Giancana must already possess more than enough information to blackmail Jack for the rest of his life, information that he could use as a bargaining chip if the Justice Department ever came too close to him.

Bobby saw that Jack's indiscretion—Jack's *craziness!* —had placed him in a trap from which there could be no true escape. For as long as Jack remained President, and even afterwards, he'd be vulnerable to Giancana and other Mafia leaders.

And Bobby would too. The very people he most despised, he now had the most reason to fear. He now knew, beyond any doubt, that they had the power to destroy the Kennedy family.

Entirely unaware of any of this—indeed, in an unusually sunny and confident mood, having been reassured by his brothers that in deference to their stricken father's wishes, they would wholeheartedly support his candidacy—Teddy prepared to make his formal announcement.

There was one final hurdle to clear. It had been decided that in order to minimize the derision that would inevitably greet his declaration, Teddy should test his wings, as it were, on national television.

Arrangements were made for him to appear on *Meet the Press* on Sunday, March 11. If his performance was an unmitigated disaster, there might still be a chance to pull the plug. If not—if he appeared even slightly plausible as a senatorial candidate—then he'd be able to plunge into the formal campaign with the benefit of the momentum provided by a *Meet the Press* appearance.

In the days leading up to the show, Sorensen and others coached him for hours, drilling into him what they considered adequate responses to any conceivable questions.

The stakes were raised on the morning of the broadcast when the Kennedys received a stern reprimand from James Reston in his *New York Times* column for even contemplating a senatorial race for Teddy. This was only the first trickle in what would quickly become a flood of opposition, but it nonetheless took the White House, and Teddy, by surprise.

"This whole exercise," Reston wrote, "might prove to be the first Kennedy political blunder in years. For, any way you look at it, this adventure promises to be an embarrassment to the President. If Teddy wins, it will inevitably be said that the President put him over, even if the President doesn't say a word in his behalf, and if he loses, it will be regarded as a rebuke to the Kennedys for overreaching.''

Reston added that if Teddy "had asked the advice of the President's closest political advisers about running for the Senate they would have given it to him in a single word: 'Don't!' But he is proceeding anyway. . . . Teddy figures: why not go after what you want; everybody else in the family has.''

In conclusion, Reston warned, "One Kennedy is a triumph, two Kennedys at the same time are a miracle, but three could easily be regarded by many voters as an invasion.''

There was not a sentence in Reston's column with which either Jack or Bobby could disagree. But the journalist had failed to consider the one factor that reduced all others to insignificance: this was what their father wanted; this was what their father had told them to do. They had no choice. Nor did Teddy.

On *Meet the Press* he was both bland and evasive. He told at least one outright lie when, in answer to a question from John Chancellor, he flatly said that no polls had been taken in his behalf. When asked the inevitable "dynasty" question, he responded perhaps rather too glibly, "If you are talking about too many Kennedys you should have talked to my mother and father at the time when they were getting started.''

There remained the question of his ultimate goal. Was it, in fact, the Presidency?

He said, "Having seen the problems of my brother, I just wonder whether seeking that job is really worth it.''

Watching from the White House, and aware of how little Teddy truly knew about his problems, Jack had to laugh.

21

THREE DAYS LATER, TEDDY FORMALLY ANNOUNCED his candidacy at a carefully staged press conference held in the living room of his Beacon Street home. As if to reinforce the notion that despite his youth Teddy was a member in good standing of America's first royal—or imperial—family, he required that reporters and photographers sit on the floor while, standing in front of a floor-to-ceiling mirror that surrounded the living room fireplace, he read his announcement from cue cards. One newspaper described the assembled press as being "like persons at a campfire meeting."

In response to a question about his family's attitude toward his candidacy, he said only, "My family is knowledgeable of my plans and there is no indication they disapprove."

In Washington, at a press conference, Jack answered a question about how actively he would support Teddy's candidacy by saying, "I will not take part in that campaign except to vote in the primary in September. My brother is carrying his campaign on his own."

This statement prompted columnist Mary McGrory to write the next day: "This may be true, but it is about as descriptive as saying that Marlene Dietrich is a grand-

266

mother and that the Prince of Wales is a schoolboy." The trick, McGrory said, in discussing Teddy's candidacy, "is to keep an absolutely straight face."

Weeks earlier, the Kennedys had arranged for a sympathetic writer from *Esquire* magazine, Thomas B. Morgan, to spend several pre-campaign days with Teddy, charting his hectic course around the state and—the expectation was—introducing him to a national audience of discerning readers as a man of mental as well as physical substance.

And this, in fact, was what Morgan did. The admiring article was filled with such quotes as, from a civil servant, "The Kennedys say you make allies but not friends in their business, but Teddy's different. I like him."

True, Teddy committed the occasional faux pas, as when he told Morgan, "You have to know your audience. You can't give women too much. They get confused. Besides, if they've seen you on TV they can't think anything bad about you."

And Morgan, during the time he spent reporting the story, heard persistent rumors to the effect that something other than a burst of patriotic fervor had motivated Teddy to leave Harvard for two years and join the army.

"I spent ten days trying to run down the story," he said later. "Finally, I had put together enough of the truth so I felt I had to confront him with it."

But when confronted, Teddy, following what he understood to be standard family practice in such situations, simply lied. And lied very convincingly.

Even years later, Morgan would recall, "His forthright charm convinced me he was telling the truth." And so he wrote it the way Teddy told him it had happened.

His published story said, "At the end of his freshman year at Harvard, Kennedy volunteered for induction into the Army. The Korean War was on and it seemed to him a good time to get his service over."

When he saw an advance copy of the magazine, however, Jack recognized immediately that Teddy had blundered once again. Too many people knew the truth. It was bound to come out. Now Teddy had made it even worse by telling a writer for a national magazine a total falsehood.

Yes, Teddy had followed accepted family practice by lying when asked an embarrassing question, but he still hadn't seemed to grasp the additional principle that when you lied, you did so in such a way as to ensure that you would not get caught. It was like the whole stupid cheating incident in the first place. And like trying to escape from the cop in Virginia by hiding on the floor of the front seat. You just didn't do it if you were going to get caught.

Jack, of course, had always felt himself to be excepted from this rule, but then he'd always managed—and was still hoping to manage—to avoid the consequences of detection. Teddy was not nearly so nimble nor so quick.

Well, the only thing to do was to call Bob Healy of the *Globe*. Jack thought that with Healy and the *Globe* he could work out a deal. If *Esquire* was about to print Teddy's cock-and-bull story about leaving Harvard because of the Korean War, they had better get out in front of it with the contrite confession of a chastened man who realized he'd made a foolish error long ago.

That was the way to handle it. Not as a front-page news story under a six-column headline: "KENNEDY EXPELLED FROM HARVARD FOR CHEATING." No, better to cast it as sort of a feature story if possible. Or maybe as no story at all, if Healy could be persuaded to go along. Maybe as a Kennedy campaign press release. Let Sorensen or somebody draft the thing; then Jack could go over it himself and then they could give it to Healy as an exclusive.

Like *PT 109*, if they put the right spin on it, they might even be able to use it to their advantage. Granted, it was hard to make expulsion for cheating look heroic, but the voters—women, especially—just gobbled up public acts of contrition. Especially from handsome youngest brothers of glamorous Presidents.

Jack felt the difficulty could be resolved if Healy could be persuaded to play ball. And it is likely he believed that Healy, who had seldom in the past seemed reluctant to cover the family favorably, could be persuaded.

As usual, Jack was right. The *Globe* headline was only two columns wide, on the lower half of page 1. It said, innocuously, "Ted Kennedy Tells About Harvard Examination Incident."

Healy's first three paragraphs were crafted exactly as Jack had expected.

"Edward M. Kennedy, candidate for the U.S. Senate, in an interview yesterday, explained the circumstances surrounding his withdrawal from Harvard in 1951 when he was a 19-year-old freshman.

"The story, sometimes distorted, has been making the rounds in the Massachusetts political rumor mill for some time.

"Kennedy said he wanted to set the record straight."

Then Teddy was permitted to explain that he'd made a "mistake" after becoming "apprehensive" about a foreign language course. Once the dean learned of Teddy's mistake, he and his friend had been "asked to withdraw with the understanding that we might reapply for admission after a period of absence, provided that during that time we could demonstrate a record of constructive and responsible citizenship."

He added—falsely—that after his return he had achieved academic "honors," and closed by saying, as Healy dutifully reported, "What I did was wrong. I have regretted it ever since. The unhappiness I caused my family and friends, even though eleven years ago, has been a bitter experience for me, but it has also been a very valuable lesson."

That was the ticket: a valuable lesson. See, this young man wasn't so inexperienced after all. He'd already learned valuable lessons—if not from Harvard, then from the school of hard knocks. Who could not sympathize with, even identify with, such a repentant and sincere young fellow, especially if his name was Kennedy?

Healy and the *Globe* had once again done the family's bidding. Even James MacGregor Burns was to write, "The President summoned Healy to the Oval Office and persuaded him to play down the story. A bargain was reached that the *Globe* would feature not a revelation but a confession by Ted."

The New York Times, however, was less generous. "Harvard Ousted Edward Kennedy" was the *Times* headline, and the accompanying story, while not mentioning his recent lie to Morgan, did say that "rumors that the President's brother had been asked to leave Harvard under a cloud had been gathering since before the formal announcement of his political plans. His statement was issued after he was asked about the incident by a Washington correspondent from Boston who is a long-time friend of the Kennedy family."

But that was as far as the story went. Eddie McCormack, to his personal credit, if not to his political advantage, declined to raise any issues of character, based on either the cheating itself or Teddy's subsequent unsuccessful attempt to cover it up.

Teddy, however, was so fearful that his opponent might spring something on him that at his first joint appearance with McCormack, at a broadcast on a Boston educational television station, one observer commented, "Ted was in a state of shock. Sweating profusely, every bone in his body shaking. He was so nervous he could barely get sound out of his body. And when he was able to speak you saw that it was all memorized questions and answers—often the wrong answer to the wrong question."

And, without even taking the cheating question into consideration, the reaction of the national press to Teddy's candidacy was proving every bit as hostile as James Reston had foreseen.

Liberal columnist Max Lerner called it "a massive error in judgment on the part of the whole Kennedy family . . . a race from which there can be no retreat with grace and in which final victory will carry heavy elements of defeat."

The *Wall Street Journal* commented that "if a third Kennedy acquires high national office the rest of us might as well deed the country to the Kennedys." Which was approximately what the Ambassador had had in mind all along.

But the *Journal,* in a reference that hit closer to home than the writer probably realized, also warned that if

Teddy were to lose, "he might find that at the next family dinner he would have to eat in the kitchen."

Even *The Washington Post* said, "There can be too much of a good thing," and, while acknowledging Teddy's becoming modesty, added, "He has, to use a famous Churchillian phrase, 'much to be modest about.'"

And even Jack, spending a spring weekend at Peter Lawford's house in Malibu and seeing one of Teddy's new campaign posters on the mantelpiece—the one that said: "He Can Do More for Massachusetts"—even Jack, laughing, crossed out the words and scrawled, "Bullshit!"

22

NO DOUBT ABOUT IT, TEDDY HAD PROBLEMS. NOT only did Eddie McCormack command strong respect within the party, but a third candidate, H. Stewart Hughes, a Harvard faculty member and grandson of former Supreme Court justice Charles Evans Hughes, had entered the race as an independent.

Hughes was a "peace" candidate even before there was a war. Far more liberal than either Teddy or McCormack, Hughes advocated a permanent halt to United States nuclear weapons testing regardless of whether the Soviet Union reciprocated, and immediate admission of Communist China to the United Nations. He was supported by such groups as the Women's Strike for Peace and by a legion of long-haired college students, one of the most vocal and active of whom was a young Worcester resident named Abbie Hoffman.

Hughes posed no direct threat, but his very presence in the race was an additional embarrassment to Teddy, who only a few years earlier, it was clear, would not have qualified for one of the Harvard professor's seminars. Even without directly attacking Teddy's fitness to serve, Hughes strengthened the central thrust of McCormack's campaign, which was that Teddy's candidacy was an affront to the integrity of the democratic process.

Later, Hughes offered a vivid recollection of Teddy in the early stages of the campaign. "He would arrive with his bodyguards at these functions and of course they would have nothing to do with the entourages of the other candidates. My attitude toward Ted, whom I regarded as a kid, was, frankly, somewhat supercilious. When we were introduced, he called me 'Mr. Hughes,' and I called him 'Teddy.'

"His performance at this point was, actually, somewhat ragged. His speech seemed to be a sequence of lines he'd learned without getting them together. He leapt from the fishing industry to getting a man on the moon without a real transition.

"It happened that Eddie McCormack was seated next to me at one of the first of these functions and just as Teddy was getting into his text, McCormack leaned over and remarked, you know, a little bit behind his hand, 'Don't you think this kid is a fresh son of a bitch?' "

Publicly, McCormack was somewhat less direct. Throughout the early stages of the campaign, in fact, McCormack resembled nothing so much as the studious and civic-minded high school senior who long ago had had the foresight to obtain a prom date with the prettiest girl in the class, only to see a new rich kid move in and woo her away with promises of a bigger corsage and a ride in his daddy's limousine.

McCormack felt, with considerable justification, that he had earned the right to his party's nomination. He was described by the *Wall Street Journal* as "handsome and poised," though he spoke with a strong South Boston accent and his quite genuine smile often bore a disturbing resemblance to a sneer.

Even when not speaking behind his hand, he tended to talk out of the side of his mouth and did not project well on television. But this was a serious political campaign, he kept insisting, not an audition for the role of leading man in a Broadway musical.

Generationally, he was one step behind the Kennedys in terms of assimilation, being the son of a three-hundred-pound South Boston tavern owner named Knocko McCormack.

On his own, however, he'd done much to close the gap. After his graduation from Annapolis, McCormack had finished first in his class at Boston University law school, had been editor in chief of the *Law Review* there, and had first been elected to the Boston City Council in 1953. After serving three terms, the last as president, he was elected state attorney general, and reelected in 1960 by a plurality of 450,000 votes, the largest margin of victory ever awarded a candidate for that office in Massachusetts.

As attorney general, he had compiled a proud record of accomplishment, displaying a sense of concern for social justice and civil liberties far more advanced than any shown by any member of the Kennedy family.

He'd supported legislation to curb wiretapping, to fight racial discrimination in housing, to establish a code of ethics for public employees, to abolish the death penalty, to strengthen the legal rights of persons arrested and charged with a crime, to ensure that any accused unable to afford private counsel be represented by a public defender of the highest quality.

He was, said the *Wall Street Journal,* "known and respected by old party pros and Harvard professors alike." Now he wanted what he believed was rightfully his.

"I'm a political realist," he said. "I'm fully aware of Ted Kennedy's strength. He has money and the power and prestige of the Kennedy name. But I feel that one of the basic principles of politics is that you should earn what you get. If you want the party nomination, you should be deserving of the party nomination."

Well into April it appeared that with Teddy's candidacy, the family finally had overreached. A Boston radio station poll showed McCormack leading Teddy by a three-to-one margin, and even the *Globe* estimated that among the 1,763 delegates to the party convention in June —whose endorsement, though nonbinding, was considered extremely significant—McCormack held a two-to-one lead.

Moreover, opposition to Teddy from the liberal and academic wings of the party was growing. Harvard Law professor Mark DeWolfe Howe published a letter in which he called Teddy a "bumptious newcomer" and said, "His academic career is mediocre. His professional career is virtually nonexistent. His candidacy is both preposterous and insulting."

Later, joined by historian Samuel Eliot Morison and the theologian Reinhold Niebuhr, Howe charged that Teddy displayed "a reckless desire for self-advancement —an ambition so childishly irresponsible that it pays no regard to the damage which it does to the good name of the President."

For all the private polling they'd done in Teddy's behalf, the Kennedys seemed stunned by the level of animosity his candidacy engendered among the Cambridge intellectuals whose favor the family had so assiduously courted.

Even the faithful Healy had to report that McCormack had "a lock" on support from the Harvard Law School faculty and that additional professors, both at Harvard and at other colleges in the Boston area—except for those who favored Hughes—were overwhelmingly supportive of the state attorney general.

McCormack issued a campaign leaflet which, beneath his picture, listed his many qualifications for the Senate post. On the opposite page, beneath a picture of Teddy, was the single line "Brother of the President."

Teddy himself was berated by a Harvard classmate, who said, "You're an insult to our class, running for this."

"Well," Teddy replied, trying his best to muster his trademark grin, "that certainly is a point of view."

What he wanted to explain, but didn't know how—and of course it would have done no good in any event—was that this wasn't a matter of his reckless desire, or his childish irresponsibility. Left to his own devices, he'd already be living in Reno or Santa Fe or Cheyenne or Phoenix or San Francisco. This was what his father had demanded. And now they were all stuck with the consequences.

By late April, opposition to Teddy had grown so intense that a Boston radio station reported that he was considering withdrawing from the race. Teddy quickly denied the story, but WBZ insisted that Teddy had "conferred with the President this week and may drop out rather than face what appears to be sure defeat at the state Democratic convention in June."

The radio station also mentioned speculation by "veteran observers" that McCormack's convention margin might be as high as four-to-one.

It was at this point that the Kennedys began to show that even with the Ambassador incapacitated, the old blend of big money and raw power still packed a punch.

In the Ambassador's absence, Steve Smith set himself up in a Ritz-Carlton suite and went to work. He stayed almost entirely out of sight. Steve Smith was very much a behind-the-scenes person, in addition to being nasty and smart. It was not an accident that Joe had chosen him to manage the family's financial operations.

From Washington, aides to Jack and Bobby, working even more furtively, made sure that every one of the more than seventeen hundred delegates to the state convention knew that his vote would be public, that the White House and Justice Department would be watching and counting, and that certain consequences—some quite pleasant, some not so—might well ensue.

There were, for example, fifteen vacant postmasterships in Massachusetts in the spring of 1962. As the *New Republic* put it, "For every vacancy, there must be at least six convention delegates who either want the job or have a friend who wants the job. Not one of the vacancies will be filled until after the convention. Not one will go to a delegate who votes for McCormack or to a friend of a delegate who votes for McCormack."

Also available were positions in a soon-to-be-created national park, as well as a variety of posts in the federal judiciary which had been deliberately left open for just this eventuality. Or maybe there was a relative in military service who'd been unfairly passed over for promotion, a situation that could be easily rectified.

On the down side, there were suggestions—never overt threats, but unmistakable implications—that the federal tax returns of certain McCormack supporters might receive especially close scrutiny.

"Teddy has a gloved hand and a mailed fist," one McCormack delegate complained. "If you don't shake the hand, brother, watch out for the fist."

Many prospective delegates, it seemed, were more than willing to shake the hand once the alternatives were explained. One state legislator emerged from a meeting with Teddy saying, "He's completely unqualified and inexperienced. He's an arrogant member of an arrogant family." Then he grinned. "And I'm going to be with him."

A prospective appointee to the federal bench said, "I have no love for the Kennedys. They only use Massachusetts to get elected from. Once they get elected they couldn't care less about the state or the party. But I'm backing Ted with everything I've got. If Eddie McCormack wins, his uncle can't appoint me to that judgeship. But whether Ted wins or not, Jack can. And I want that job."

Another delegate said, "There are plenty who won't decide their vote until they get the sweet smell of money in the convention hall."

Kenny O'Donnell put it even more succinctly. "That convention," he said knowingly, "really is a whore's paradise." And his side had the money to buy whatever exotic favors they might require.

They also had the power to hurt and were not shy about using it. A popular Boston-area politician who declined to accompany Teddy on a campaign swing through his district received this final warning from the young candidate: "Remember, win or lose, I'm handling the patronage in Massachusetts."

As the campaign progressed, McCormack had to admit, "We can't match the offers they are making. But we're sure going to make a fight of it." Suddenly, this did not sound like a man who expected to win the nomination by a four-to-one margin.

The convention, however, guaranteed only the party's official endorsement, something that Tom Wicker in *The New York Times* said "has approximately the value of Confederate money."

Whoever emerged victorious in Springfield in June, the nominee would not be chosen until a primary election in September. Thus, the "family brawl," as Wicker described it, that Teddy had precipitated by announcing he'd seek the party's backing at the convention would not end with the delegates' open balloting.

By secret ballot, ordinary voters, who could be neither so easily bribed nor so thoroughly intimidated as the delegates, would choose the candidate who would oppose George Lodge in November.

Teddy could have bypassed Springfield entirely and still taken on McCormack in September. But the family had all this money and all this power available and their father had trained them to use it as quickly and as efficiently as possible.

"They're cold, they're cold," complained Eddie McCormack's father, Knocko.

And, later, when the inevitable outcome had become more apparent, a resigned McCormack said to an aide of Bobby's, "You're going to win anyhow, so why use all this muscle on me?"

"Because we've got it" was the curt reply.

The mailed fist, of course, was kept carefully shielded from public view by the Kennedys' by-now-perfected public relations extravaganzas.

You want to see Rose, the dear devoted wife of the stricken Ambassador, bravely out on the stump campaigning for her youngest son? You've got her.

You want the alluring young wife, loyally soldiering on despite her innate shyness? You've got her.

You want the sisters, that marvelous traveling troupe of Kennedy gals, able to consume, it seemed, upwards of forty cups of coffee a day, as long as a suitable audience had been assembled? You've got them.

You didn't have Jack or Bobby, of course, because, as they'd promised, they were staying strictly out of the race, but in their stead you had the tireless, gregarious, fun-loving, tender, caring, inspiring, ruggedly handsome and occasionally almost coherent candidate himself, making sixteen, eighteen, twenty campaign stops a day.

But in private—broad grin and hearty hello notwithstanding—the mailed fist was something he was learning how to use effectively.

There was, for example, the day he had his private meeting with Eddie McLaughlin at the men's bar of the Parker House in Boston.

McLaughlin was lieutenant governor of Massachusetts, and, with McCormack and Teddy both vying for the Senate seat, he fully expected to become the next governor. Like McCormack, Eddie McLaughlin had paid his dues for years and it was well understood at the highest levels of the party that 1962 was to be his year.

But that was before Teddy's people began worrying about running against George Lodge in November. Lodge was an Anglo-Saxon Protestant from the most established Brahmin family in the state. McLaughlin, like Teddy, was Irish Catholic.

The Kennedys did not want the Democrats to field what looked like a blatantly ethnic ticket against the Republican WASPs. So a search was conducted and an appropriate Brahmin named Endicott Peabody was found. He had scarcely more political experience than Teddy—and far less aptitude for the game—but he had the right sort of name. Endicott Peabody, III! Nickname: "Chub." Chub Peabody, whose great-grandfather had founded the Groton School. A fine doubles partner at the country club and a fine Anglo-Saxon Protestant to offer Teddy's ticket ethnic balance.

This meant that Eddie McLaughlin had to be unceremoniously dumped in a back alley somewhere, but this was how the Kennedys played the game. Eddie was a big boy. He knew the rules. Kennedys came first and anyone who stood in their way soon wished he hadn't.

But Eddie McLaughlin wanted to be governor every bit as much as Eddie McCormack wanted to be senator.

He announced that he would not go quietly. That no matter what the Kennedys' wishes were, he'd fight Peabody at the Springfield convention.

All spring, he'd been preparing by traveling around the state explaining how he was the only gubernatorial candidate with "experience." Peabody was a novice, an unknown.

This was not a campaign theme Teddy or his handlers were comfortable with. If people were persuaded to value experience in a governor, they might decide they wanted it in a senator, too, which would not work to Teddy's advantage.

So the time had come for a heart-to-heart talk between the two men.

Teddy got right to the point. "Lay off that goddamned 'experience' stuff," he said.

"Teddy," said the genial McLaughlin, "I can't help it. That's all I've got to sell."

"Lay off," Teddy repeated, then stood up and left the room before McLaughlin could even order a drink.

In June, McLaughlin was trounced by Peabody at the convention and, with no funds to carry on a primary campaign, forced from the race. He never did become governor of Massachusetts, instead winding up as a small-town lawyer on Cape Cod.

Even at thirty, Teddy was not someone you wanted to cross. He might not yet be able to grin sardonically, but he was learning.

Still, the attacks against him continued. As Boston University political science professor Murray Levin later wrote in a detailed study of the 1962 campaign, "Nobody could possibly overestimate the hatred of the idea of Kennedy's candidacy by the intellectual community and especially by the professional Irish politicians. They regarded Ted Kennedy as an obscene projection into the political arena."

It was not as if the Kennedys had simply plugged in their brutally efficient machine once again: it was as if they had loosed upon the state a brainless and unruly monster who threatened to level all the secular temples in which Massachusetts political power had resided for decades.

As Burton Hersh has observed, the intellectuals felt Teddy had no intellectual credentials and the pols felt he had no political credentials. It was one of the few times, Hersh said, that "Harvard liberals and downtown pols shared an intense emotion."

The National Committee for an Effective Congress, whose leaders included Archibald MacLeish, issued a statement decrying Teddy's candidacy. It said: "His undistinguished academic career has not been followed by a record of serious personal accomplishment. His candidacy is an affront to the Senate."

But Teddy knew that the party's endorsement would not be determined by a bunch of high-minded intellectuals or Harvard academics. It would be decided by the greedy or frightened or otherwise malleable delegates who would enter the "whore's paradise" in Springfield, only to find that the sole exit was a door marked with Teddy's name. And then the stampede would begin.

He was sure of it because he'd been told so by the people he'd learned to count on most in the months since his father had been silenced. By Jack and Bobby and Steve Smith, and by the hard-eyed, tight-lipped, cold-blooded men who did their bidding.

Teddy also knew how much he could help himself by just showing up in as many places as possible, so as many people as possible could see how closely he resembled, in looks, manner and speech, the beloved President.

During what Steve Smith termed the "comprehensive exposure phase"—a period that lasted from roughly Saint Patrick's Day through the first week of May— Teddy personally met at least a thousand of the prospective delegates to the convention, telling them, time after time, with apparently total sincerity, "You know, Jack was asking about you just the other day." Nobody believed it but they all liked to hear it anyway.

"If you turned your back on him," one said, with considerable awe, "you'd swear to God it was the President himself." Thus, even beyond the muscle and the money, which were of undeniable importance, this—the close identification between himself and Jack in the eyes of the hero-hungry public—seemed the single most valuable asset Teddy possessed.

The comprehensive exposure phase, supported by the expenditure of millions of dollars, proved a smashing success. Joan was admired and beloved by all. At a fashion show designed to showcase the new designs of Oleg Cassini, the *Globe* reported that "among all the lovely Boston models, the blond, slender Mrs. Edward Kennedy won first prize with the women."

Teddy was now the beneficiary of a wave of sheer sentimentality, which, since Jack's election as President, had gathered enormous force. Even the most skeptical of the President's advisors, Kenny O'Donnell chief among them, had to admit they'd utterly underestimated the strength of the blind adulation among Massachusetts voters for any member of the Kennedy family.

If the kid brother sounded and acted so much like Jack himself, so much the better. Seasoned political writer A. A. Michelson noted, "There is a sort of 'princely' effect in the Ted Kennedy campaign. In any dynasty, the king is respected and obeyed, but everyone loves the prince, and Ted Kennedy seems to have that attraction wherever he goes."

As the *Wall Street Journal* reported, "Teddy easily creates more stir than any other candidate as he enters a meeting; children ask for his autograph, ladies sigh happily as he picks up a fallen glove, men recall favors received from his grandfather or brother."

At the start of the year—even at the start of the campaign—it would have been hard to find a professional Democratic politician willing to predict, even privately, that Teddy would totally rout Eddie McCormack at the convention. But in the days leading up to the June 6 balloting in Springfield, it became obvious that this was precisely what was going to happen.

He arrived in Springfield a conquering hero, receiving a carefully arranged tumultuous welcome complete with motorcade and brass band. After making a rousing speech from the steps of the convention hall, he retired to his hotel suite, which, the *Globe* reported, "took on a sort of White House atmosphere, with guards posted at all doors to keep out unwanted guests."

The *Reporter* magazine noted that by this time, Teddy was "looking and acting like a Hollywood casting office's choice of an actor to play his big brother. Bigger and better-looking, he has all the President's mannerisms, from the flat accents of his oratory to the chopping right arm and the downthrust finger. Upon entering a gathering, Teddy makes the same self-conscious motion of sticking his hands in his coat pockets. . . ."

To what degree this was a conscious effort to evoke the omnipotent aura Jack now possessed in Massachusetts, or to what degree it was unconscious hero worship of his older brother has never become clear. Teddy himself, not being a young man possessed of great introspective powers, would probably have been hard-pressed to provide an accurate measurement. The result, however, was unmistakable: this was Jack all over again, only better, because in the person of Teddy we had both Jack-as-President right here among us as well as a younger, sturdier Jack-of-the-future whom we might still have a chance to get close to before the sweeping forces of national renown elevated him forever beyond our reach.

As the *Globe* noted, "There were girls, too—50 of 'em —pretty college co-eds from Mount Holyoke and other colleges in the area. They were dressed in blue-and-white-striped cottons with the Kennedy sailor hat sitting jauntily atop their tresses."

The pretty young girls in sailor hats had been one of Jack's trademarks at the Los Angeles convention in 1960 —a reminder that the universally acclaimed hero of *PT 109* was indeed, as Lyndon Johnson had said, a "fighting sailor who proudly wears the scars of battle."

That Teddy had never gotten closer to the navy than the day he accompanied the rest of his family to the christening of a destroyer named after Joe Junior seemed not to matter. He did, after all, like to sail on weekends and vacations. And he had taken the wondrous Mediterranean cruise with Jack after the 1956 convention, though it was doubtful that any of the pretty girls aboard that craft boasted a Mount Holyoke education.

On the morning of the convention's first day, what the *Globe* referred to as the "pièce de resistance of the Kennedy show" was a picture-taking session involving Teddy, Joan and two professional photographers with oversized Polaroid cameras.

"Those who wanted their picture taken with Ted and Joan," the *Globe* said, "stood in line, waiting their turn to pose with the couple. But the wait wasn't long. The automation took care of that. About ten seconds after each picture was taken the person who posed was handed a print to take home and show to his family and friends."

The effect created was of Teddy as a department store Santa Claus—though admittedly a Santa Claus with a beautiful wife.

The rest was simple arithmetic, a mere formality. "It's pressure, pressure, pressure; post office, post office, post office," said a heavily sweating Knocko McCormack on the floor of the steamy, smelly, non-air-conditioned Springfield Armory. McCormack supporters waved signs saying such things as, "Don't let them twist your arm," and "Mommy, can I run for the Senate?" Loudspeakers outside the arena blared, "Don't be pressured. Stay with Eddie McCormack and we'll win."

But there was never the slightest chance. More than two hundred members of the press, including many writers from national magazines, were present at midnight when, with the balloting more than half over and Teddy leading 691 to 360, McCormack made his way through the smoke-filled, sweat-drenched auditorium, took the stage and said, "I respectfully request my name be withdrawn from further consideration at this convention. I will now take my case to the people."

What did it mean? As Jack had said bitterly in Wisconsin, "It means that we have to do it all over again."

Teddy, however, was far from bitter. He was, in fact, rapidly assuming a regal air. Success agreed with him. It reminded him of the early glory days in London, when dozens of servants stood at the beck and call of "Master Edward."

In his hotel suite, he grandly extended his arms to enable two aides to insert cuff links into the starched folds of his custom-made dress shirt. Then, accompanied by more guards and hangers-on than Jack had Secret Service agents, he proceeded to the convention hall, where, as McCormack conceded defeat, he stood, in the words of one observer, "arms folded, Mussolini-like."

It was even said that he smiled sardonically. In any event, after accepting the party's endorsement, he left the hall immediately, refusing to so much as pose for a picture with his family's handpicked gubernatorial candidate, Endicott Peabody.

Teddy was no longer coequal with anyone in Massachusetts politics. From this point forward, he could be as arrogant, cold and selfish as he pleased. He had the money, the muscle, the royal family connection, and now the unmistakable stamp of a winner.

23

THROUGHOUT THAT SPRING OF 1962, AS TEDDY MOVED toward his endorsement at the Democratic convention, his brothers continued to be preoccupied by larger concerns.

As overseer of Operation Mongoose, Bobby had made the overthrow of Fidel Castro his highest priority. He demanded that the "terrors of the earth" be unleashed against the Cuban leader. One such terror was American military might, and Bobby and Jack both approved extensive Caribbean exercises designed as preparation for an eventual invasion of the island if other means failed.

In alarm, Castro informed the Soviet Union, "We [are] concerned about a direct invasion by the United States and we [are] thinking about how to step up our country's ability to resist an attack."

According to Secretary of Defense Robert McNamara, Bobby had grown "hysterical" about the need to rid Cuba of Castro by October. And McNamara himself seemed none too controlled, as when, at one meeting, he said, "The only way to get rid of Castro is to kill him. And I really mean it."

Bobby did not disagree. This was the atmosphere Jack had fostered, the only atmosphere, it seemed, in which he could thrive. His need to maintain a climate of constant crisis may have been as compulsive as his need for sex. The two, of course, were not unrelated, though just how closely intertwined they were, and just how deadly this linkage would prove, was not yet obvious, even to Bobby.

Others in government, however—older, more experienced men—while not aware of the specific dangers Jack was courting, found themselves disturbed by the mixture of recklessness and detachment that seemed to lie at the core of the President's character.

Dean Acheson, former secretary of state, wrote to ex-President Harry Truman: "I have a curious and apprehensive feeling as I watch JFK that he is a sort of Indian snake charmer. He toots away on his pipe and our problems sway back and forth around him in a trancelike manner, never approaching but never withdrawing; all are in a state of suspended life, including the pipe player, who lives only in his dreams. Someday one of these snakes will wake up, and no one will be able even to run."

For Bobby, the snake woke up on May 7. That was the day he received a visit from the CIA's general counsel, Lawrence Houston, who had come to discuss privately a matter of the utmost sensitivity.

It seemed that Robert Maheu, the former FBI agent then serving as personal aide to Howard Hughes, as well as performing a variety of free-lance jobs for various organizations, had been indicted on federal wiretapping charges.

He'd been caught placing an eavesdropping device inside the Las Vegas home of comedian Dan Rowan. This, it seemed, had been done at the request of Sam Giancana, who suspected Rowan of conducting a clandestine affair with another of his mistresses, the singer Phyllis McGuire.

The Justice Department had filed charges against Maheu. Houston now said the CIA wanted Bobby, as attorney general, to order that the charges be dropped.

Bobby asked why the CIA would want him to do that.

Houston said it was because Maheu was working for

the CIA in its effort to overthrow or assassinate Castro. An operation called Mongoose, Houston said, of which he understood Bobby to be the director.

Bobby said that was correct, but he would do nothing for Maheu. He would not permit Mongoose to interfere with his duties as attorney general. If Maheu had violated federal law, Maheu would have to stand trial. He added that in the future, the CIA might want to be a bit more prudent in its recruiting practices.

So Houston had to go farther. He had to tell Bobby that if the charges against Maheu were pressed, it was likely that the public would eventually learn the identities of some of those whom Maheu had enlisted in the effort to kill Castro.

And who, Bobby asked, might those people be?

Sam Giancana and Johnny Roselli, Houston replied. For starters.

He then informed the Attorney General that both Mafia leaders had been playing key roles in the various plots to assassinate Castro ever since the President took office, and that the President had been aware of their involvement from the start.

"What surely shocked the Attorney General," Harris Wofford, then a Kennedy aide and currently a U.S. senator from Pennsylvania, wrote, "was the recognition . . . that his brother and the government of the United States were entangled with the most evil forces he could imagine, and that Sam Giancana, John Roselli and their like held an enormous power to blackmail . . . John Kennedy and his family [and that] . . . the Mafia leaders were privy to what may have been the worst national secret in the history of the United States, and the most embarrassing personal secret about John Kennedy.

"Nothing could damage the reputation of the United States government and of the Kennedy administration more than disclosure that it had conspired with organized crime to murder the head of a foreign government.

"Nothing could damage the personal reputation of John Kennedy more than detailed and public allegations of a sexual liaison, while in the White House, with a woman who at the same time was having an affair with a notorious Mafia chieftain.''

As Wofford, who knew both Jack and Bobby well, reported, "During the late spring and early summer of 1962, I would see the Attorney General and the President huddled in the Oval Office or walking together in the Rose Garden. Now I know one of the hardest subjects they had to discuss."

It was not Teddy's race against Eddie McCormack.

Bobby recognized that he had no choice but to order the charges against Maheu dropped. And so they were. But he made it clear that he would bend no farther. He would not have his brother, or the office of the Presidency, or the government of the United States, held hostage to organized crime.

He instructed his aides to continue their efforts to prosecute Giancana and all other Mafia leaders. Had Bobby's father been able to speak, he might have cautioned against this approach. But the old man had been silenced and Jack himself did not seem to care.

As Wofford remarked in understated fashion, "It was a bold course" that Bobby chose to follow.

Just how bold did not become fully apparent until November 22, 1963.

24

BLITHELY UNAWARE OF THE OMINOUS FORCES CLOS-
ing in on his brothers, Teddy spent the summer of 1962
campaigning for the September primary in which he
would dispose of Eddie McCormack once and for all.

He hopped happily on barroom tabletops throughout
Boston, belting out rousing choruses of "Southie Is
My Home Town," or his grandfather's favorite, "Sweet
Adeline."

His campaign advertising now included not only the
slogan "He can do more for Massachusetts" but "From
a great American family which has dedicated itself to
public service for three generations."

By this time he was loudly proclaiming that his storied
grandfather had "never lost an election," and the press,
now sure that he was a winner, was so mesmerized by
this newest, loudest and seemingly most congenial of the
Kennedys that no one pointed out that old John Fitzgerald had had a string of defeats stretching over three
decades, not to mention a career riddled with corruption.

It was that kind of summer for Teddy, and in that spirit
(and with his brothers otherwise occupied) he foolishly
agreed to debate Eddie McCormack.

Having already trounced his more experienced rival at

290

the convention, and having far more money, an inestimably superior organization and swelling self-confidence, Teddy had no need to ever again permit the name McCormack to pass his lips.

But after witnessing Teddy's strong-arm tactics at the convention, the liberal intellectuals had intensified their assault. The irrepressible professor Mark DeWolfe Howe called Teddy "an impudent young man." The respected theologian Reinhold Niebuhr termed his candidacy "an affront to political decency." And a retired Harvard professor took out an advertisement in *The New York Times* asking all who "share our indignation" at Teddy's presumptuousness to contribute to the McCormack campaign.

To best McCormack—or at least hold his own—in a face-to-face debate might silence these critics. Besides, hadn't he won the moot-court competition in law school? And hadn't Jack outclassed Richard Nixon in their debate?

But the decisive factor came one hot August afternoon, when he was campaigning in South Boston and passed by a small home whose massive owner was perspiring heavily as he hammered together a series of McCormack campaign signs.

"Hi," Teddy said. "I'm Ted Kennedy."

Without looking up, the bulky man continued hammering. "I know who you are," he grumbled.

"You must get tired," Teddy persisted, "doing all this work."

Finally, the big man looked up. "No," he said, looking Teddy squarely in the eye. "I don't get tired at all."

By then Teddy had recognized him, but it was too late to break off the encounter.

"You see," Knocko McCormack told Teddy, gesturing with the heavy hammer, "every time I drive a nail, I just imagine I'm driving one right into your ass."

The first—and, as it would turn out, decisive—debate was held on Monday, August 27, in the auditorium of South Boston High School, very much Eddie McCormack's home turf. It was televised and broadcast across the state.

Despite his other problems, Jack agreed to spare Ted Sorensen for a few days of pre-debate preparation. Teddy was not only to be schooled on the issues but—more important, given the lingering apprehensiveness about his youth and inexperience—to be taught that no matter what circumstances arose, he was to maintain his dignity and poise.

McCormack knew Teddy had a notoriously quick temper and was especially prone to erupt if anyone attacked his family in any way. Sorensen's chief task was to be sure Teddy recognized the supreme importance of conducting himself with the aplomb for which Jack was so esteemed.

The debate would last from 8:00 to 9:00 P.M. By toss of a coin, Teddy had won the right to make his five-minute opening statement first. Then, after McCormack's remarks, there would be thirty-six minutes of questions from the media, with each candidate answering and rebutting in turn. The debate was to close with two-minute prepared statements from each, Teddy's to be made before McCormack's.

More than eleven hundred people, the vast majority McCormack supporters, packed the South Boston auditorium—harshly illuminated by bank after bank of television lights—an hour before the 8:00 P.M. starting time.

For days, media throughout the state—and even nationally—had been billing the confrontation as potentially one of the most dramatic and significant in the history of Massachusetts politics. That day's *Globe* reported, under the headline "Nation Tunes In on Ed and Ted," that "syndicated columnists and reporters from media in distant cities began descending on Boston, giving the debate an aura of importance akin to the Kennedy-Nixon TV debates."

Just six weeks earlier, Teddy had swept through Springfield like Alexander the Great. Now, taking the rostrum in his dark blue suit, he looked again like the scared little boy who'd been made to cross the portals of so many unfamiliar and forbidding boarding schools during his childhood.

McCormack, on the contrary, seemed eminently at ease in front of so many enthusiastic followers, who so clearly were not intimidated by either Teddy's money or his family's power to bestow favors and inflict pain.

Unsure of himself and obviously ill at ease, Teddy delivered an uninspired opening statement in a flat voice. It was obvious that despite Sorensen, he would not this evening be crossing a new rhetorical frontier.

In startling contrast, McCormack sprang immediately to the attack. "I say that I am the qualified candidate," he began. "I point to three years in city government, three terms, with one term as president of that body. I point to three terms as attorney general of this commonwealth, the second most important office in this state. And I ask my opponent"—and here his voice suddenly grew harsh and shrill—"What are your qualifications? You graduated from law school three years ago. You never worked for a living. You have never run for or held an elective office."

He gazed scornfully across the stage at Teddy. "You are not running on qualifications. You are running on a slogan: You can do more for Massachusetts. And I say, Do more, how? Because of experience? Because of maturity of judgment? Because of qualifications? I say no!"

All the anger that had been building inside McCormack for all these months since Teddy had come along in his rich kid's limousine with his *PT 109* tie clip and his corrupt father and his bland arrogance and his limitless wealth and his brothers' vindictive band of henchmen —since he'd come along out of nowhere to seize from McCormack's hand the brass ring that he'd spent more than a decade preparing to grasp, that he'd earned, goddamnit, that he'd earned!—that anger was boiling over now, on the stage of this South Boston high school auditorium.

"Yours is the most insulting slogan I have ever seen in Massachusetts politics, because this slogan means: Vote for this man because he has influence, he has connections, he has relations. And I say no. I say that we do not vote on influence or favoritism or connections.

"We vote for people who will serve. Yours is a slogan that insults the President of the United States. 'He can do more.' That means that the President is not now doing enough? Or that the President will discriminate against someone other than his brother if he is the senator from this state?

"And again, I say no! I say that the people of Massachusetts will not buy a slogan. And suddenly my opponent . . . I listened to him the other night and he said, 'I want to serve because I care.' "

Again, McCormack shot Teddy a withering look. "Well, he didn't care very much in 1960 when he thought of living out west. Massachusetts is not my second choice!"

He now glared at Teddy with such ferocity it seemed he might leave his lectern and walk across the stage to continue the assault at closer range.

"You didn't care very much, Ted, when you could have voted between 1953 and 1960 on sixteen occasions and you only voted three times." He paused. "Three out of sixteen." He paused again. "And on those three occasions your brother was a candidate.

"You don't care very much about aid to education. While I was serving on the City Council, trying to bring good schools here in Boston for our public school children, not once between the period of 1953 to 1960 did you vote for our school committee.

"And you don't care very much about the hundred and eighty-six thousand youngsters who attend parochial schools either, because while I want to raise the educational standards of all our children, you have said that you will not extend and expand federal aid to parochial schools.

"These are important issues. These, and issues like civil rights. Do you really care about civil rights? I have been a champion of civil rights! And while I was fighting to eliminate the ghettos, you were attending a school that is almost totally segregated—the University of Virginia.

"I say that we don't need slogans. I say that power and

money are not the keys to getting elected to public office. I say we need a senator with experience, not arrogance. We need men in the Senate with consciences, not connections. And I say that the office of United States senator should be merited—not inherited!''

The sweltering crowd, which had at first been taken aback by the vehemence of McCormack's attack upon the junior member of the nation's most illustrious and powerful family, gathered itself and emitted a roar of approval that, coming from so deep within the throats of so many of these distinctly unprivileged, unconnected, noninfluential working people of South Boston, seemed to be something quite close to a primal scream.

Certainly, it was a tribal war whoop, and it was hard to tell which shook Teddy more—McCormack's unexpected vitriol or the crowd's tumultuous endorsement of it.

As the media's questions began, Teddy fought to maintain his composure but there seemed to be only a loose connection between the answers he was reciting and whatever was going on in his mind. A charitable interpreter later wrote that the overall impression during the early phase of the question-and-answer portion was of "his syntax not quite joining at the corners."

Whatever the question, he blurted out a disordered series of preprogrammed responses, often in the same answer veering from sweeping international difficulties to the most parochial of intrastate problems with no connective tissue detectable. Clearly, to the extent that he was able to focus his mind at all, he was preoccupied with the formulation of some sort of response to McCormack's attack.

He prattled on impulsively about the Congo, factory workers in Lowell, dairy farmers in Wisconsin, the Upper Volta project in Ghana, the Sékou Touré regime in Guinea, domestic tax reform proposals and the oil depletion allowance. Whatever the unifying principle may have been, it escaped not only the questioners and the audience, but Eddie McCormack.

Teddy's opponent was impressed, however, by the sheer blizzard of detail that blew through the microphone, across the auditorium and out across the state, replete with repeated references to Teddy's firsthand encounters with heads of state on virtually every continent.

To assure that viewers did not confuse ceremonial introductions with expertise, McCormack went back on the attack. "The thing that fascinates me," he said, "is Teddy's constant reference to his trips, and the fact that he grew up in an atmosphere where they dealt at the international level."

His voice laden with sarcasm, McCormack pressed on. "He did make some trips around the world. He made two European trips and he visited eleven countries in twenty-four days. In Africa, he spent fifteen days visiting nine countries. Well, certainly spending one or two nights might not make you or I experts, but he picks things up more quickly than perhaps I would.

"But the Irish, typical of the Irish, I think characteristically, saw Teddy's trip for just what it was. This is a quote from the *Sunday Independent* of Dublin, the twenty-fifth of February, 1962. 'Arriving in Ireland today is Mr. Edward "Ted" Kennedy, age thirty, a younger brother of President John Fitzgerald Kennedy. Why is he coming to Ireland? He's coming because later this year he is due to be involved in a political fight back home in Massachusetts. He is playing the game political in what has now come to be known as the Kennedy method. You do not spend your time campaigning in your own little patch. You go out into the world, far far afield, hit the headlines. I think the trips are more political than fact-finding.' "

Setting down the newspaper clipping, McCormack again glared at his younger opponent, pointing a finger at him contemptuously. There—even the Irish saw him for what he was.

In the wake of this newest assault, perspiration was now dripping visibly down Teddy's forehead. He was later described as "livid and shaking" with the effort to maintain some semblance of self-control. It was not the derisive references to the overseas jaunts that had upset him, nearly as much as the single, passing reference to his growing up "in an atmosphere where they dealt at the international level."

That, to Teddy, came perilously close to insulting his family. Still, he poured forth his torrent of statistics and not-very-well-assimilated random facts: the percentage of capacity at which the steel industry in the United States was functioning, the exact number of farms in Poland that were operated free of government control, and —out of nowhere—a stirring defense of America's commitment to support democracy in Yugoslavia.

Then it was time for closing statements. Still obviously shaken, he said quietly, "The great problems of this election are the questions of peace, and whether Massachusetts will move forward."

He looked up from his prepared remarks and faced the audience, which had fallen totally silent, eager to see whether he would respond in any way to McCormack's assault and battery.

"We should not have any talk about personalities or families," he said. "I feel we should be talking about the people's destiny in Massachusetts."

For the first time all night, he received more than perfunctory applause. The crowd seemed to admire this obviously sincere effort to retain the ethical high ground. But Teddy was beginning to lose his long struggle for control over his emotions.

He completed his two-minute closing statement with a reference to Oliver Wendell Holmes—a bold stroke in that his most persistent and sarcastic academic critic, Mark DeWolfe Howe, was best known as Holmes's biographer.

But as he spoke, Teddy's voice began to crack and waver noticeably. "In 1860," he said, "Oliver Wendell Holmes said no city had played a greater part in free speech than the city of Boston. I just hope that this program here this evening has provided in this great tradition a fine opportunity for the hundreds and thousands of viewers to help make their determination on whom they feel would be the best senator from Massachusetts. Thank you and good night."

By the end, it was apparent to those seated close to the

stage that Teddy's eyes had become misty, and it even seemed that at least a few of the last drops that ran down his cheeks were not perspiration but tears. Certainly, there was no doubt that his struggle to maintain dignity, poise and a grip on his fiery temper had been monumental. But also no doubt that he had won.

The audience responded with a spontaneous and mighty burst of applause. This might have been an Eddie McCormack crowd, but its members could recognize guts and class whatever their source.

But now it was McCormack's turn. Teddy had faced his own moment of truth: battered by an attack far more personal and painful than he or his advisors had anticipated, he had stood his ground, held his temper, showed through his tone of voice and the brief appearance of tears how severe the emotional hurt had been, but he had emerged with his dignity intact; even, perhaps, enhanced.

For the first time in his life, he had demonstrated that he might be, after all, not merely the spoiled youngest member of America's most powerful and celebrated family, but a man of some substance in his own right.

And so McCormack, like a prizefighter in the final round, aware that for all the blows he'd struck, his opponent might still eke out a decision from the judges, swung from the floor and went for the knockout.

"It's all right," he said, "for my opponent to say that we keep families out of this and we stand on our own two feet. I favor this. I stand on my own two feet. I stand on a record, a record of almost a decade in elective office. I've worked my way *up* the political ladder. I'm not starting at the top."

Now, at the very end, his voice grated as it rose to a new pitch of anger, and his body seemed literally to shiver with barely restrained rage.

"I ask," he said, "since the question of names and families has been interjected—if his name was Edward Moore, with his qualifications . . ." Then he turned to face Teddy directly and began pointing his finger in a furiously accusatory fashion.

"With your qualifications, Teddy, if it was Edward

Moore, your candidacy would be a joke." He turned again to face the cameras, now almost shouting into the microphone. "But nobody's laughing, because his name is not Edward Moore! It's Edward Moore Kennedy!

"And I say it makes no difference what your name is. In a democracy you stand on your own two feet and you say to the people, 'You have the right to vote. You go behind that curtain and you vote without fear, without favor, and you vote for the candidate whom you feel is the qualified candidate, and I place my case in your hands.' "

For a moment, upon the completion of McCormack's remarks, neither Teddy nor the huge crowd reacted. All present were stunned by the fury of the final assault. Teddy's partisans in the auditorium, as suggested by political scientist Murray Levin, may have recognized that McCormack had come "too close to a truth that Kennedy supporters sensed but repressed because it was too painful."

Teddy himself was simply in shock. Within seconds his face turned from bright red to a degree of paleness so alarming that to some it appeared he might faint. Later, Teddy told a friend that at that precise moment, "he had everything he could do to keep himself from punching McCormack in the mouth."

To have insulted Eddie Moore! To have dragged through the mud the name of this faithful family retainer who had served the Ambassador in so many capacities over so many years, whose abilities and loyalty were so treasured that Joe Kennedy had named his own last son after him—this, Teddy perceived as an insult so personal and so vile as to go beyond the bounds of even the most robust political debate.

That the insult was directed not at Moore but quite obviously at Teddy himself was lost in the blur of rage that swept across the youngest Kennedy. Eddie McCormack had gone after family. For that, he would never be forgiven.

For the moment, however, as the crowd belatedly erupted into wild applause and gave McCormack—their own South Boston street-fighter—a standing ovation, Teddy's chief task was to get himself off the stage, out of the auditorium and safely out of sight before he had a public breakdown.

With the crowd whistling, jeering, and many stamping their feet as the moderator, a decorous columnist from the *Christian Science Monitor,* ineffectually tried to restore order by saying, "You are not adding to the dignity of Massachusetts and the cause of this debate by these demonstrations," Teddy stood rigid at his lectern, his face still ashen, the corners of his mouth trembling with rage.

So wild had been the outburst, and so savage McCormack's final attack that the moderator even asked Teddy if he would like additional time for a rejoinder.

"No," he said somberly. "We agreed on the ground rules and I'm satisfied."

As a smiling and waving McCormack stepped down from the stage to be greeted by a surge of exultant admirers ("You wiped up the floor with him, Eddie—you murdered him"), Teddy's aides moved as quickly and unobtrusively as possible to surround their battered candidate, lead him from the stage and shield him from any further onslaught.

Stiffly and silently, his gaze fixed on the middle distance, his blue shirt darkly stained by perspiration, Teddy was ushered from the auditorium and into the sticky August night. He had no comment for the press other than to say, when asked if he thought he'd received fair treatment, "By the panel."

He had little more to say to his advisors, and they were reluctant to risk comment to him while he was still so obviously unnerved. He seemed already to be thinking not only of how he had probably just allowed near-certain victory to crumble into humiliating defeat, but of the jeers and taunts to which both Jack and Bobby would subject him.

Not to mention what his father must be thinking, watching silent and paralyzed from Hyannis Port.

* * *

In the immediate aftermath of the debate, McCormack and his supporters were jubilant. As described by Murray Levin, "McCormack's colleagues were convinced that he had brilliantly and effectively argued his case. They were sure he had scored a magnificent triumph and possibly even eliminated Kennedy as a serious contender."

A Kennedy aide said there were many at headquarters who felt "McCormack's attack was just so shattering that our candidate might not be able to bounce back." And McCormack himself reported gleefully that "Kennedy's lieutenants feel their candidate has been slaughtered."

Mary McGrory wrote in her nationally syndicated column that McCormack had "all but pushed his rival off the stage of the South Boston High School and down the hill into Dorchester Bay." She added, however, that "Teddy kept his head . . . and Eddie hit him so hard and so often that Teddy, who has been running way out front, now qualifies for a sympathy vote. . . . The question remains whether it is smart to push a Kennedy around in Massachusetts."

The answer became clear over the next forty-eight hours, and it was not what either candidate had expected.

Again, as with Jack's first 1960 debate with Richard Nixon, the power of television to transform an event into an entirely different sort of spectacle—the colossal disparity between what had actually occurred and what television viewers had perceived (the perception then, of course, becoming its own, and the only, reality)—had been grossly underestimated, in fact not understood in the slightest, by Teddy, by Eddie McCormack, or by the handlers of either.

Wearing heavy makeup which began to streak as his inner fires burned hotter, McCormack had appeared on television to resemble a character from an old Lon Chaney horror film. The corner-of-the-mouth smile that always seemed so close to a sneer, the reedy voice and the heavy South Boston accent—so extreme as to seem to many in other parts of the state almost noxious, or at least representative of all the worst stereotypes they'd developed about corrupt, old-line, inner-city pols—played very poorly on television.

And the lusty vigor with which the crowd had cheered his every insult seemed on television to be only a mindless racket produced by disorderly rabble.

By contrast, Teddy's grim, stiff determination not to be cowed by McCormack's escalating aggressiveness seemed the stuff from which future greatness might be formed. At the very least, Teddy had proven himself to be a well-bred young gentleman, while Eddie McCormack, on the television screen, had come across as the kind of belligerent Red Sox or Boston Bruins fan who would be quick to pick a fistfight in a neighborhood tavern.

And overriding all else—in the minds of viewers all across the state—was the fact that McCormack had been insulting the President's brother! In Massachusetts, as McGrory had suggested, this remained tantamount to insulting the President himself, and that, in heavily Catholic Massachusetts in the late summer of 1962 and for many years afterwards, was the equivalent of insulting the Pope—or even worse, because the Pope was not a local boy with a glamorous and elegant wife.

Polls taken by both candidates and widespread press questioning of those who'd seen the debate on television —as well as thousands of spontaneous calls from viewers to news organizations—made it clear that Teddy, through his decorum and restraint, had projected leadership qualities as well as a sense of personal decency, while the sneering, jeering McCormack had disgusted many voters who, until then, had been preparing to cast their ballots for him.

Nothing he said had been wrong—he was, in fact, absolutely correct in his implication that had Teddy's full name been Edward Moore he would have been lucky to land a job as a campaign staff aide, never mind being a senatorial candidate himself—but the rude, insulting manner in which he delivered his remarks had, it seemed, alienated all but the most rabid Kennedy-haters around the state.

Women, in particular, were outraged by McCormack's virtual mugging of such a decent, honorable and square-jawed young man from a family that had brought so much glory to Massachusetts.

By the time temperatures cooled and blood pressures returned to normal, it became obvious that as a result of the debate, Teddy's already comfortable lead had become insurmountable. Issues such as his youth, money, arrogance and inexperience had vanished overnight from political radar screens.

Now it was Teddy's steadiness under fire—the sort of profile in courage Massachusetts expected from a Kennedy—that dominated public perceptions. He had been tested, in a most harsh and compassionless way, and he had proven himself to be worthy of his name: Kennedy.

A second debate, before which McCormack rushed across the stage to obsequiously shake Teddy's hand, and during which he referred to him as "Mr. Kennedy," did nothing to alter the images that were already fixed in the public mind.

For good measure, during the final week before the primary, Rose delivered a televised endorsement of her son, and even the Ambassador was wheeled onto his yacht, where he was photographed in the presence of Cardinal Cushing.

Steve Smith also opened the financial valves as wide as they would go, and hundreds of thousands of additional Kennedy dollars came pouring forth, converted almost instantly into the most massive radio and television advertising blitz ever witnessed in Massachusetts politics.

By primary day on September 18, it was no longer a question of who, but only of by how much.

The answer was stunning, even to Teddy's most ardent supporters. He received 69 percent of the vote, trouncing McCormack 559,303 to 257,403.

Politically, Eddie McCormack was finished. Four

years later, he'd win the Democratic primary for governor but lose the general election and retire to private life, the career that had been so bursting with promise utterly pulverized by Kennedy money, Kennedy muscle and Kennedy magic—and by his own need, for one night at least, to rub the rich kid's nose in the dirt.

25

"LIQUIDATION" OF FIDEL CASTRO WAS NOW THE term used at meetings Bobby chaired. He was fully aware of who the liquidators would likely be and to whom their ultimate loyalty lay, but, like so much else in recent months, the Castro assassination plot seemed to have moved beyond his ability to contain it.

Castro's removal from power, either by assassination or through armed U.S. invasion of Cuba, had now become the highest priority of both the President and the Attorney General. Piece by piece, the layers of insulation that had protected them from the full wrath of the mob had been stripped away.

The only place Castro could turn for help against such a powerful and desperate enemy was the Soviet Union. To protect himself against what he feared was an imminent U.S. invasion, Castro persuaded Khrushchev to ship him, secretly, not only thousands of Russian combat troops but the components necessary to build nuclear missiles and the technicians able to put those components together.

With even a limited nuclear shield in place, Castro felt, he might be able to deter the United States. At worst, the dream to which he had devoted his adult life would not

305

die before he managed to inflict at least some damage upon America.

CIA director John McCone, using intuition and logic as well as the fruits of aerial surveillance, had suggested to Jack in late August that the Soviets might be in the process of installing nuclear weapons in Cuba.

Jack dismissed the notion as ridiculous. Just because he was driven to sustain an atmosphere of almost constant global crisis didn't mean Khrushchev was, too. Such a move by the Soviets would be so provocative that Jack considered it an impossibility. Cuba simply didn't, couldn't, mean as much to Khrushchev as it did to him.

So distracted by the chaos of his personal life, by his fears of Mafia retaliation, by his concern that if he showed any sign of support for the civil rights movement J. Edgar Hoover would destroy his career, Jack failed utterly to foresee that the Soviet leader might actually come to the aid of his beleaguered ally, and that he might do so by dispatching nuclear missiles to the island.

Thus, it was not until the first missile components had already arrived in Cuba and the shipment of others was already under way that Jack, in September, issued a stern warning that any such action by the Soviet Union would cause the "gravest issues" to arise.

By then, of course, the time for dire warnings had passed. As Michael Beschloss, one of the most perceptive scholars of this era, has written, "Kennedy . . . issued a warning that was too late to stop Khrushchev's Cuba operation and so precise that it caused him to forfeit the option of responding to the discovery of missiles in Cuba with anything less than full-fledged confrontation with the Soviet Union."

On October 16, Jack learned how badly he had miscalculated. Aerial intelligence photographs revealed the unmistakable presence of Soviet missiles already under construction within Cuba.

There followed almost two weeks during which the world came closer than it ever had before or ever has since to full-scale thermonuclear war.

The confrontation was not only avoidable but pointless. For military intelligence made clear that the missiles the Soviets had shipped, while they would strengthen Castro's defenses against the impending U.S. attack, were not of the type to pose any threat to any significant population center within the United States. Indeed, for defensive purposes years earlier the United States had installed an almost identical type of missile in Turkey, almost squarely on the Soviet border.

Thus, as Beschloss has observed, a "Kafkaesque nightmare . . . now faced the President—risking nuclear war to eliminate missiles that, in his own opinion and that of his Secretary of Defense, did little to harm American security."

Even worse, having conducted the clandestine campaign against Castro entirely through the back-alley channel of Operation Mongoose—a secret enterprise which he could not now reveal to the American people without admitting that his own continuing crusade against Castro (Mafia assassins and all) had been the primary cause of this horrendous crisis—Jack was forced into taking the public position that the shipment of the missiles was an act of naked, unprovoked Soviet aggression.

That the entire planet could have been threatened by a series of events precipitated, at least in part, by Joe Kennedy's promise to mobsters that in return for their help in electing his son President he would guarantee that they'd be able to reopen their lucrative gambling casinos in Havana seems almost too ludicrous to contemplate.

But so intertwined had the Kennedy family's destiny and the fate of the American people become that this was exactly the pass to which matters had come by Monday, October 22, 1962, when Jack went on television to announce to a terrified nation that a nuclear confrontation with the Soviets might be imminent.

By 10:00 A.M. the next day, some twenty Soviet ships, escorted by submarines, approached the quarantine zone the United States had established five hundred miles off the Cuban coast.

"This was the moment we had prepared for," Bobby wrote later, "which we hoped would never come."

But Khrushchev didn't want it either. Some of the Soviet ships bound for Cuba carried such sensitive technology that the Russian military felt it could not risk permitting the vessels to be searched by the United States. Castro already had forty missiles and twenty nuclear warheads in Cuba. For the time being, he would just have to make do with those.

By 10:30 A.M. Wednesday, the Soviet fleet had slowly begun to turn for home. The crisis, however, was far from over. Soviet technicians in Cuba were continuing to assemble the missiles and warheads that had already arrived. Jack insisted that this, too, must stop, and that he would hold off military action "for no more than one or two days."

And on Friday, a Panamanian freighter under Soviet charter steamed across the quarantine line. A U.S. Navy destroyer—it was, as the gods would have it, the *Joseph P. Kennedy, Jr.*—halted the freighter and permitted it to continue toward Cuba only after a boarding party had determined that it carried no weapons.

In Moscow, under considerable internal pressure to hold fast, Khrushchev was displaying far more prudence and sense of proportion than Jack.

He demanded that his military advisors assure him, first, that "holding fast would not result in the death of five hundred million human beings."

Later, Khrushchev would recall that "they looked at me as though I was out of my mind, or, what was worse, a traitor. The biggest tragedy, as they saw it, was not that our country might be devastated and everything lost but that the Chinese or the Albanians would accuse us of weakness. But what good would it have done me in the last hour of my life to know that though our great nation and the United States were in complete ruin, the national honor of the Soviet Union was intact?"

In Washington, by contrast, on Friday night, October 26, Jack was lustfully eyeing a fresh young secretary brought in from the Commerce Department to help with the burgeoning paperwork.

308

"Get her name," he told McNamara, his secretary of defense. "And we may at least avert nuclear war tonight."

It almost seems, in retrospect, that to at least a part of him it didn't matter which way it went. The world might well be incinerated within a matter of days, but finally— to Khrushchev, to himself, to his immobilized father, to the ghost of his dead brother—Jack would have proven himself tough.

Nor is there anything to suggest that he was bothered by his awareness that through the unholy alliances he and his father had forged with organized crime, he'd backed himself into a position where, at the moment of utmost peril, he found it necessary to lie to his fellow citizens about the origins of the crisis while Fidel Castro was free to speak truthfully about America's hostile intentions.

When military leaders were informed that as part of resolving the crisis, Jack had agreed never to permit a U.S. invasion of Cuba (he had also secretly promised Khrushchev that he would promptly remove the U.S. missiles from the Turkish border), the chief of the air force, Curtis LeMay, pounded his fist on the cabinet room table and shouted, "This is the greatest defeat in our history, Mr. President! We should invade today!"

The chief of the navy seconded LeMay's opinion, shouting, "We have been had!"

But the outrage of the military leaders was nothing compared to the level of anger and vows of vengeance that swept through the highest levels of Mafia leadership in America when the crime bosses eventually learned that in order to get the missiles out of Cuba Jack had, in effect —and in violation of his father's explicit promise to the contrary—agreed to the permanent shutdown of the immensely valuable Havana casinos.

No invasion meant that even if Castro were assassinated, there was no guarantee that the government that succeeded his would prove any more hospitable to the Mafia.

The sense of betrayal felt by the men with whom Joe Kennedy had conducted his 1960 negotiations at the Cal-Neva Lodge and elsewhere was profound.

As far as they were concerned, Jack had just burned his last bridge behind him.

26

THE DEFUSING OF THE CRISIS, HOWEVER, CAUSED Jack's popularity to soar to its highest point ever. A Gallup poll showed that 74 percent of the American people approved of the way he was doing his job.

In Massachusetts, of course, the figure would have been even higher. That the senatorial election would be held only nine days after the resolution of the crisis, at a time when Jack was riding such a crest of public acclaim, assured that what might have been a close race between Teddy and George Lodge would be a clear-cut Kennedy victory.

"All I ask," Teddy said with a straight face during another *Meet the Press* appearance, "is that I be judged upon my own ability."

Lodge, handsome, tall, scholarly, and a moderate Republican with not only the family credentials to rival Teddy's but solid experience as an assistant secretary of labor under Eisenhower, had proven an extremely capable and appealing candidate.

But being too much of a gentleman to pummel Teddy in the bare-knuckle fashion of Eddie McCormack—not that as McCormack practiced it this tactic had been successful—Lodge never seemed to know quite how to cope with the magnitude of his opponent's celebrity.

"Teddy is a Hollywood star," said one Lodge campaign aide helplessly. Which, of course, was exactly the effect the Ambassador had been striving to produce for his sons ever since his own early exposure to Hollywood. Through stardom the bonds that restricted the reach toward power of lesser men could be transcended. With enough expenditure of money and the proper attention given to the careful cultivation of image, the Kennedy brothers—even Teddy—could be made bigger than life. As stars, not mere politicians, they would receive an entirely different sort of adulation, blinding in its intensity.

On Tuesday, November 6, as the *Boston Herald* said, Massachusetts "voted its heart rather than its mind."

Teddy received 1,162,611 votes, to Lodge's 877,669. In the wake of national exultation over Jack's Cuban crisis management, H. Stewart Hughes, the "peace" candidate, polled only 50,000.

Absent the sudden and emotional surge in Jack's popularity produced by the impression that, as Secretary of State Dean Rusk had said, "we were eyeball to eyeball and the other fellow blinked," Teddy might have had a more difficult time with Lodge.

As it was, his margin of victory, while solid, was nothing like the two-to-one trouncing of McCormack. And it came in the context of what was, nationally, the best midterm election result achieved by any party in control of the White House since 1934. In the swelling Democratic tide, Richard Nixon even lost his race for governor of California, blaming his defeat not so much on the hostile press as on "the Cuban thing."

Beyond the borders of Massachusetts, hostility toward Teddy continued unabated. "The Kennedys," scolded James Reston, "have applied the principle of the best man available for the job to almost everyone but themselves. Teddy's victorious headlines are resented here [in Washington], because he is demanding too much too soon on the basis of too little."

* * *

it would light every darkened, empty corne

thirty-one, as he gazed at the future from hi
elevated vantage point, Teddy could see nothin
en years ahead, stretching in an unbroken strin
a shimmering, far distant horizon.

While such as Reston fretted over the impact of having yet another Kennedy come to Washington, elsewhere in the country men far less genteel had begun discussions of how and when to remove from power those Kennedys who were already there.

In Miami, Santos Trafficante, who of all the Mafia leaders stood to lose the most from Jack's failure to reopen the Havana casinos, said, "Mark my word, this man Kennedy is in trouble and he will get what is coming to him."

When Trafficante's conversational partner expressed doubt, saying he thought Jack would be reelected in 1964, Trafficante said, "You don't understand me. Kennedy's not going to make it to the election. He is going to be hit."

The man to whom Trafficante made this statement was actually an FBI informant, who immediately reported the threat to the Miami field office, from which, presumably, it was relayed to J. Edgar Hoover. The FBI director chose not to relay the comment to the President.

In Philadelphia, an FBI wiretap picked up a conversation between Mafia leader Angelo Bruno and an associate named Willie Weisburg.

"With Kennedy," Weisburg said, referring to Jack, "a guy should take a knife and stab and kill the fucker. Somebody should kill the fucker, I mean it. This is true. Honest to God. It's about time to go. But I tell you something. I'll kill. Right in the fuckin' White House. Somebody's got to get rid of this fucker."

Angelo Bruno did not disagree.

A New York City wiretap picked up an unidentified member of the Genovese Mafia family saying, "I'd like to hit Kennedy. I'd gladly go to the penitentiary for the rest of my life, believe me."

In Buffalo, an FBI wiretap recorded a Mafia boss named Peter Maggadino saying of the Kennedys, "They should kill the whole family. The mother and father, too."

J. Edgar Hoover, well aware of the reasons for the Mafia's anger toward the Kennedy family and quite possibly less fearful of the Kennedys than he was that the

Mafia might make public evidence of his own homosexuality, chose not to inform either the attorney general or the President of the existence of any of these tapes.

Meanwhile, in Detroit, Jimmy Hoffa conducted a telephone conversation with a New Orleans Teamsters leader named E. G. Partin. Another of the double, triple and quadruple agents who seemed to be swarming across the American and global landscape during the early 1960s, Partin had contacted an aide of Bobby's in advance of his talk with Hoffa, thus enabling federal investigators to eavesdrop electronically on the chat.

What they heard was not pleasant. Hoffa discussed plans to smuggle a bomb containing plastic explosives inside Bobby's Hickory Hill home in order to blow up the attorney general "and all his damned kids."

Even more chilling, Hoffa discussed an alternate method of ridding himself of the man he considered his chief nemesis. This involved the assassination of Bobby by "a lone gunman" with no ties to the Teamsters Union, but equipped with a rifle and telescopic sight. Hoffa suggested that the hit could occur while Bobby was traveling in an open convertible, preferably somewhere in the South, so it would be blamed on "segregation people."

Hoffa said he had the perfect rifle for such a job in his office, a fact verified by many who had met with him there. Often, when Bobby's name came up in conversation, Hoffa would pick up the rifle, sight down the barrel and say, "I've got to do something about that son of a bitch. He's got to go."

The New Orleans Teamsters leader, besides being an FBI informant, had close ties to the Louisiana Mafia, headed by Carlos Marcello, whom Bobby had unceremoniously and illegally deported in 1961, having him dumped deep in a Guatemalan jungle.

Not long after Hoffa's conversation with Partin, Marcello, now returned to power in New Orleans, was repeatedly overheard uttering a Sicilian oath of vengeance which could be loosely translated as, "Take the stone out of my shoe."

Lapsing into American vernacular, his language grew even more colorful and his sentiment less ambiguous.

"Don't worry about that litt[le] goin' to be taken care of."

Cautioned by an associ[ate] of a lot of trouble" if he tr[ied] Marcello impatiently replied, You know what they say in Sic[ily] dog, you don't cut off the tail, you

He then explained the meaning of Bobby was the dog's tail, but Jack wa[s] dog will keep biting you," he said, "if y[ou] its tail. But if the dog's head is cut off, the d[og] tail and all."

If Bobby were killed, he said, Jack would undoub[tedly] retaliate with an even more relentless crackdown on o[r-] ganized crime. But if Jack were to die, Bobby, who was openly despised by Vice President Lyndon Johnson, would be rendered suddenly powerless.

Marcello told his associates that the President would have to be murdered, but that he would arrange it "the way they do in Sicily," whereby "a nut" would be employed to do the job and, in the aftermath, to "take all the heat."

Not coincidentally, perhaps, a Marcello associate in New Orleans had living with him at the time a nephew, recently returned from the Soviet Union, named Lee Harvey Oswald.

Still unaware of this growing menace, on Janu[ary] 1963, Teddy walked down the aisle of the Unite[d] Senate on the arm of his state's senior sena[tor] Saltonstall, to be sworn in as a member most august deliberative body.

The long, painful stretches of loneliness, of helpless ineffectua[lity] longing, of never being able t[o] standard, of constantly fall[ing] his brothers' expectations

Teddy was finally a me[mber] most powerful and celebrate[d] cal history—poised, like his br[others]

Robert F. "Bobby" Kennedy, 12, and Edward M. "Teddy" Kennedy, 6, during their first day at Gibbs School, London, 1938 (UPI/BETTMANN)

Teddy climbing a palm tree on the grounds of the Kennedy family home, Palm Beach, Florida, 1941 (THE BETTMANN ARCHIVE)

Ted playing football for Harvard University, 1955 (AP/WIDE WORLD PHOTOS)

Ted with John F. Kennedy at the Harvard University Commencement when Ted graduated and his brother, then a senator, received an honorary degree, 1956 (AP/WIDE WORLD PHOTOS)

Ted and Joan Bennett Kennedy after their wedding, Bronxville, New York, 1958 (UPI/BETTMANN NEWSPHOTOS)

(*L to R, standing*) Ted, Ethel Kennedy, Robert F. Kennedy, Steven Smith, (*L to R, seated*) Jacqueline Kennedy, Senator John F. Kennedy, Joseph P. Kennedy, Eunice Kennedy Shriver, and Jean Kennedy Smith at a family gathering, 1959 (FRED WARD/BLACK STAR)

(*L to R*) Robert F. Kennedy, Edward M. Kennedy, and John F. Kennedy during a Senate Rackets Committee hearing, Washington, D.C., 1959 (AP/WIDE WORLD PHOTOS)

Kennedy family members and friends with President John F. Kennedy, Vice President Lyndon Johnson, and their wives at an inaugural ball, Washington, D.C., 1961 (BILL RAY/BLACK STAR)

Ted addressing a crowd during his campaign for
the U.S. Senate, Springfield, Massachusetts, 1962
(UPI/BETTMANN)

Ted and
his wife,
Joan, after
winning the
Massachusetts
Democratic
primary in his
senatorial
campaign,
Boston, 1962
(UPI/BETTMANN)

Ted Kennedy and family, 1963
(M.S./BLACK STAR)

(*Front row, L to R*) Mrs. Joseph P. Kennedy, Ted Kennedy, Joan Kennedy, and Jacqueline Kennedy at a requiem mass for the late President, John F. Kennedy, Boston, 1964 (AP/WIDE WORLD PHOTOS)

Ted Kennedy with his father, Joseph P. Kennedy, at New England Baptist Hospital, where the senator was recuperating from a broken back, Boston, 1964 (AP/WIDE WORLD PHOTOS)

Senator Edward M. Kennedy on a tour of the war zone, South Vietnam, 1965 (UPI/BETTMANN)

Senator Edward M. Kennedy, wearing an orthopedic collar, returning with his wife, Joan, from Mary Jo Kopechne's funeral, Hyannis, 1969 (UPI/BETTMANN NEWSPHOTOS)

Senator Edward M. Kennedy speaking in front of a statue of his brother, John F. Kennedy, on the anniversary of the late President's 73rd birthday, Boston, 1990 (UPI/BETTMANN)

27

As soon as he was elected, they had all told Teddy—his sisters and his mother as well as his brothers —that the most important thing was not to say or do anything that would reflect poorly on Jack. This meant saying and doing almost nothing. They wanted Teddy to be an invisible man.

As the Senate's youngest member, not to mention as the youngest brother of the President and the newest member of the illustrious Kennedy family to take the nation by storm, Teddy was a natural for newspaper and magazine feature stories and for television.

But there was to be none of that. The dynasty issue troubled them. For much of the country beyond Massachusetts, Teddy was one Kennedy too many and his presence in Washington, as columnists like Reston had suggested, posed potential problems for Jack. Compared to Jack's real problems, of course, these were not serious, but the public and press knew nothing of Jack's real problems.

And so, from the start, Teddy's presence in Washington was viewed more as an embarrassment than as a personal triumph.

Stewart Alsop wrote in the *Saturday Evening Post* that

his victory "has hurt the President where it hurts most—
politically. Those close to the President stoutly maintain
that the damage has not been deep or lasting. But no one
seriously disputes that the damage, for the moment, is
real. Nowadays the phrase 'Too many Kennedys' comes
more readily to the lips of the voters than any other single
criticism of the President."

So even by doing right for once—by doing exactly
what his father had told him to do and doing it well—
Teddy had caused another problem. It didn't seem fair,
but as Jack took such pleasure in pointing out, life itself
was unfair.

Thus, the most visible and sought-after newcomer to
Washington since Jack himself was told that for the foreseeable future his single most important task—his only
important task—was to stay out of sight, out of hearing
and, as much as was possible, out of mind.

"In his unique situation," Alsop observed, "Ted Kennedy is rather like the poor little rich boy, hedged and
circumscribed by the very wealth of his inheritance."

Alsop also noted that others had accused the Kennedy
family of hubris by pushing Teddy so far forward so fast,
by seizing so much so suddenly for themselves. "According to the rules of classical drama," Alsop wrote,
"hubris is followed by 'ara'—pride by the fall. But this
is not a classical drama, and although the Kennedys have
plenty of pride, they are not accustomed to fall."

But suppose it were classical drama, after all? Suppose
Teddy's role would grow into one of significance? And
suppose that, unlike Jack or Bobby, he would not, in the
end, be able to perform it satisfactorily? Suppose he were
to fail his father, and his mother, and his sisters, and
the ghosts of his older brothers—all of them—and, even
worse, to fail himself, or what he would by then have
come to imagine himself to be?

What would become of him then?

Questions of ultimate destiny, however, did not loom
large in early 1963. Rather, there were minor incidents,
such as occurred while Teddy was celebrating his thirty-
first birthday at a ski lodge in Stowe, Vermont.

He got into a scuffle with a newspaper photographer who'd taken a picture of him in the company of the winner of a local beauty contest. Outside the bar where the photo was taken, Teddy lunged at the photographer, grabbed the camera from him, took it inside, tore it open, snatched the film from it and then threw the exposed film into a wastebasket. Both the camera and its leather carrying case were damaged. The film, of course, was destroyed.

At first, he denied that the incident had occurred. Through a spokesman he said, "The story is ridiculous."

But the photographer was employed by a newspaper owned by William Loeb, a right-wing Republican notably hostile to the Kennedys.

"Being a U.S. Senator has apparently gone to Teddy Kennedy's thirty-one-year-old head," Loeb said, announcing that he'd retained the former governor of Vermont to represent the photographer in a legal action against Teddy.

The ex-governor demanded both an admission that the incident had occurred and an apology from Teddy. This was exactly the kind of thing his brothers had warned him against. Women, booze, his temper: a dangerous combination, one destined to do neither Teddy's career nor—far more important—Jack's image any good.

Faced with the prospect of a lawsuit and the embarrassing publicity it would entail, Teddy signed a letter in which he said he was "truly sorry about last month's misunderstanding" and hoped "that this will serve as a sincere apology for any difficulty it may have caused."

Within the family the incident heightened fear that Teddy could do the Kennedys more harm than good. To those few members of the press or public who paid attention at all, it seemed no more than an early warning sign that an immediate denial from Teddy or his office about a matter of personal misconduct would not necessarily be the last word on the subject.

Back in Washington, Teddy kept his vow of silence. He might have been, as one paper said, "the most talked about man at the Capitol," but, as the same article noted,

"Caution has marked his every step." At least during working hours. "So far as the *Congressional Record* is concerned," one story noted, "he hasn't let out a peep yet."

At night, however, he was letting out more than peeps. As John Tunney had noted in law school, "He turns into quite a different person when he isn't working." Harvard friend and now staff member John Culver, who like Tunney would also later become a senator, was a frequent companion during these nights on the town. One acquaintance recalled the off-hours Teddy of 1963 as "not much more than a happy-go-lucky, arrogant, brash kid, always out for a good time, lots of parties, laughs . . ."

He was not concerned that any of his nighttime activities might become public knowledge. If journalists were not going to report on the even less discreet sexual practices of the President, they were certainly not going to expose the kid brother's private life.

For all the family's worry, it would have been hard for Teddy, in early 1963, to do anything that would embarrass Jack. For years, after all, Jack had been so publicly doing so much more and had not yet managed to embarrass himself.

"They can't touch me while I'm alive," Jack said of the press and his women. "And once I'm dead it won't matter."

This was another of the lessons Teddy learned imperfectly from his brother.

He and Joan had bought a traditional red-brick home in Georgetown, but Teddy spent far less time inside it than did his wife. "I don't know anybody down here," she'd said soon after her arrival, a condition Teddy did little to alleviate.

Most nights, she stayed home alone. She would watch television. She would play the piano. Then she would put her two children to bed and wonder whether or not she'd be seeing her husband that night. Eventually, she found that pouring herself a drink or two while wondering took a bit of the edge off the loneliness.

Pregnant again, she suffered a miscarriage in May.

* * *

In other branches of the family, more lethal pressures continued to build. In June, Bobby was forced to make a humiliating but, from his point of view, necessary public capitulation to Sam Giancana.

Frustrated that circumstances prevented him from taking stronger action, Bobby had ordered the FBI to follow Giancana everywhere, interfering as much as possible with his attempts to lead what for him passed as a normal life.

The constant harassment—FBI agents would even follow him onto golf courses and snicker openly when he missed a putt—prompted Giancana to file a lawsuit against the federal government, charging that the FBI was depriving him of his constitutional right to privacy.

The concept of one of the country's most villainous citizens suing federal law enforcement authorities proved amusing to those unaware of the hidden subtext.

On June 1, Giancana appeared in federal court in Chicago, seeking an injunction against the FBI. The law required that in order to obtain such an injunction, the petitioner had to state under oath, in open court, that he was a "law-abiding citizen," never found guilty of breaking any state or federal laws and thereby justifying such close surveillance. Obviously, the petitioner would be subject to cross-examination by government lawyers seeking to have the request denied.

Nonetheless, Giancana calmly took the stand, was sworn in, and testified that he had never committed any act or spoken any words that could possibly give any law enforcement agency reason to suspect that he might ever have been possessed of criminal intent.

This created the opportunity the Justice Department had been waiting for ever since the first days of the McClellan Committee hearings. They had a Mafia leader on the witness stand, under oath! They could ask him anything. They could use him as a lever to pry open the entire sordid, subterranean treasure chest that held organized crime's most highly prized secrets. If he answered untruthfully, he could be prosecuted for perjury and sent to prison.

And the Justice Department had many hundreds of

cubic feet of business records, prior testimony and other documents which could prove beyond any doubt that Sam Giancana had not only contemplated unlawful activity but had been engaging in it all his adult life and directing much of it for the past two decades.

But Bobby knew all too well the nature of some of Giancana's activities. And he knew, too, that by testifying in open court, under oath—testifying truthfully— Sam Giancana could destroy both Jack's career and the reputation of the entire Kennedy family.

Bobby, therefore, had to intervene. He was forced to by his father's and brother's corruption and by his own more recent complicity. His primary loyalty would always be to the family. His own oath of office, his own sense of integrity, his own passionate hatred of organized crime—all these had to be sacrificed in order to preserve the family's image and power.

He personally issued an order to the U.S. Attorney's Office in Chicago that Giancana not be cross-examined. Thus, in a development that stunned everyone in court except the plaintiff, the Justice Department attorney said he had no questions whatsoever for Mr. Giancana.

With a smile on his face, Sam Giancana left the Chicago courtroom, having been granted the injunction he sought.

By June, it came to seem that Teddy had overdone the invisible man act a bit. Old family friends, such as former postmaster general Jim Farley, loyally sang his praises: "Sooner or later," Farley said, "Teddy Kennedy is going to wind up President. He's got more moxie than Jack. More personality and charm."

But after six months of near-total silence and public inactivity, criticism was mounting. A Republican leader in Massachusetts, reminding an audience of Teddy's promise to "do more" for the state, asked, "What has he done? The answer is nothing. He hasn't accumulated one decent thing to benefit Massachusetts since he got in there."

Even the friendly *Globe* was forced to note that Teddy "has yet to introduce a single piece of legislation," and "the most talkative lawmaking body in the world still awaits his maiden speech."

The *Globe* said, "He is sensitive about his silence," and quoted Teddy as responding testily to a question about it. "We don't have any timetable on this," he said. "If something really struck me, I wouldn't feel inhibited."

In June, something did strike him, hard: the issue of racial discrimination.

After more than two years of stalling and compromising for fear of offending J. Edgar Hoover, Jack as President and Bobby as Attorney General had finally begun to push for legislation that would grant blacks the rights to which they were clearly entitled under the Constitution but which, in practice, especially in the South, they were denied.

The fear of Hoover had not abated, but such black leaders as Martin Luther King, Jr., had awakened the conscience of much of white America. Televised scenes of police brutality inflicted upon peaceful black demonstrators angered and sickened many who witnessed them. A racist gunman's murder, in June, of Medgar Evers, director of the Mississippi chapter of the National Association for the Advancement of Colored People, served as the final catalyst.

Jack and Bobby decided that, the potential cost of Hoover's retaliation notwithstanding, they had to act, or else forfeit all claim to moral and political leadership of the nation.

Their decision to press forward with a civil rights bill finally gave Teddy the freedom to begin speaking out on his own. And he did so with passion and eloquence and persistence.

In Boston, on June 17, he said segregation "is not limited to the South. Here in Boston ninety percent of the Negroes live in an area of three square miles. There are almost no Negroes in many trades and professions here in Massachusetts. Negroes are the last hired, the first fired, and have double the unemployment of white workers.''

He called for new civil rights laws and for stronger enforcement of existing ones. ''The old way,'' he said, ''the easy way, in which Negroes had their place in society and sought no more, must change. Not because what goes on here hurts us abroad or because discrimination is a burden on our economy, but because it is the right and decent and moral thing to do.''

The speech marked the start of what would become one of Teddy's lifelong professional preoccupations. Since his army service, he had recognized that blacks really were treated unfairly. And, at some level of his psyche, this insight began to resonate. The blacks were an underprivileged people, denied access to the full bounty of American society. It was not a comparison he would ever make himself, but the plight of racial minorities in America was something to which he could respond strongly, having lived his whole life at the bottom of the only society that really mattered to him psychologically —his own family.

Emotionally, Teddy was as underprivileged as were the blacks economically. As the last of the Kennedy children—one who'd grown to manhood only after all the psychologically significant events had taken place, only after all the important roles had been filled by older brothers—he had faced barriers of indifference, of inattention and of neglect. Thus, in the plight of the American black, Teddy discovered a social and political issue of overriding importance about which he genuinely cared.

Jack and Bobby were coming to care too. It had been slow to start, but now it was happening and it was real. Once they began to listen, they'd come to recognize the legitimacy of the black complaints. And they'd come to respect and admire the intensity, the honor, the moral and physical courage of men such as Martin Luther King.

Like Teddy—perhaps in even more profound, substantial ways—they were growing. Ever so slowly, both Jack and Bobby were moving farther out from under their crippled father's shadow. In the aftermath of his stroke, his grip on their psyches was lessening. Jack and Bobby, in early middle age and already at the pinnacle of power in America, were finally starting to define themselves.

They would always be their father's sons, but given enough time and the proper circumstances they might become more than simply the instruments by which the mute old man attempted to exercise his will.

Unless, of course, the past in which so many dark secrets lurked, the past which had known so many whispered promises, so many discreet handshakes and transfers of funds, the past which had so compromised them even as it permitted their ascent, were to suddenly reach out to claim its due.

28

"**T**HE DOER MUST SUFFER," PHILIP VELLACOTT HAS written in his introduction to Aeschylus' *Oresteia*, "and by suffering, man learns, though it may take several generations of suffering to drive the lesson home. And the lesson which suffering teaches is not merely how to avoid suffering: it is how to do right.

"The sin of Atreus has to be expiated by his son; but the son too commits sin . . . and thus doubly justifies the fate which is prepared for him."

In Berlin, on June 26, Jack enjoyed the most magnificent public triumph of his life. Warned that he might be risking his life by traveling to such an unsettled region, where adequate security could not possibly be provided, he had nonetheless insisted on the trip.

Arriving on the fifteenth anniversary of the start of the Berlin airlift, Jack—the hero at his apex—received a welcome unlike any ever before accorded a visiting political leader anywhere in the world.

Even before Berlin, upon his arrival in Germany, Jack "waving and smiling" had seemed to the wife of the American ambassador to the Soviet Union "like a Greek god.'' In Berlin, it was as if he personified the entire pantheon of ancient deities.

More than a million citizens of West Berlin massed in the plaza in front of the city hall. Ascending a platform draped with flags, Jack turned to face what William Manchester later described as an ''enormous, swelling, heaving, delirious multitude.''

As the first roar of welcome finally subsided, Jack began to speak. He had not personally written the words, but it was his delivery of them—as Michael Beschloss has said, the ''rhythmic, precisely delineated phrases that turned his words into a kind of angry poetry''—that would echo so powerfully through all the years that followed.

''Two thousand years ago . . .'' he began. His unmistakable accent, such a peculiar cross between pseudo-Brahmin Boston and the vaguely British aristocratic, seemed somehow just right for these words, for this occasion.

''Two thousand years ago,'' he repeated, ''the proudest boast was 'Civis Romanus sum.'

''Today, in the world of freedom, the proudest boast is 'Ich . . . bin . . . ein . . . Berliner!' ''

The response was frenzied, primal, uncontainable.

And that was only the beginning. Never before had Jack held sway over anything like this tumultuous crowd, and never again would he. Indeed, over the next thirty years, no political leader anywhere would enjoy even a fraction of the adulation that washed over Jack and resounded throughout the plaza, feeding on itself and carrying him to a pitch of feeling he'd never before attained.

Flying out of the city in late afternoon, he said to an aide, ''We'll never have another day like this one as long as we live.''

After Berlin, Jack felt invulnerable. Partly, of course, because of the unprecedented acclaim he'd received, but there may have been other reasons, too. Maybe it was from having survived so many childhood illnesses, the sinking of *PT 109,* his Addison's disease, so many compromising situations and potentially deadly scandals.

Whatever the reasons, after Berlin, Jack began to act as if he couldn't be touched. Not physically, not emotionally, not politically. He'd flown too high. He was out of reach. The forces of gravity—and the rules of logic—no longer applied.

After her 1956 miscarriage, Jacqueline had given birth to a daughter in 1957 and a son in 1960. In early August of 1963, she gave birth prematurely to a second son. The baby, delivered by emergency cesarean section, weighed only four pounds, ten ounces, and died within two days.

Standing at the grave site in Brookline on the hot, humid morning of August 10, after attending a funeral mass conducted by Cardinal Cushing, Teddy, who had no sense of the private pressures then facing his older brothers, felt sadness at the infant's death and at Jack's acute distress. (The President, weeping and more obviously stricken than anyone had ever before seen him, had been the last to leave the church, at the end even grabbing for the tiny casket until Cardinal Cushing held him back, saying, "Come on, Jack, let's go. God is good.")

Memories of the deaths of Joe Junior and Kathleen were inescapable. Through death or incapacitation, one third of Teddy's own generation of Kennedys was already gone. His father, always to Teddy such a vigorous, commanding, larger-than-life figure, would never speak again and could only occasionally shuffle a few steps with the aid of a cane.

Now, in the heat of Boston in August, death had for the first time claimed a member of the next generation.

In retrospect, the inevitability of the calamity seems so self-evident that we wonder how the masked actors on the stage could have remained unaware. Yet it is the nature of tragedy that the protagonist remains insensible to any intimation of his fate. Only in retrospect does the design of destiny become clear.

And so from the Brookline cemetery they went their separate ways, these three brothers, these three sons of the most Faustian father America had ever produced— "willing to venture whatever he had in exchange for a chance to move closer to the heart of the American dream,'' Garry Wills has written—never to be reunited, unless one considers as a reunion the far more somber spectacle that would take place at a far larger cemetery, before a far larger crowd of mourners, one hundred days hence.

29

IN SEPTEMBER, TEDDY ENJOYED HIS OWN FOREIGN TRI-
umph.

It had been his newly awakened social conscience that
seemed to drive him most strongly during the summer of
1963. Overwhelmed and deeply moved, in late August,
by the sight and sound of 250,000 blacks and whites together converging on Washington, singing and praying
and listening to some of the century's most memorable
rhetoric—in particular, Martin Luther King's "I have a
dream" speech—Teddy found his passion for the cause
of racial justice growing even stronger.

Soon afterwards, he traveled to Belgrade as America's
representative to the largely ceremonial Inter-Parliamen-
tary Union Conference, at which delegates from fifty-
nine nations, including the Soviet Union, were to engage
in vague and generalized debate about world problems.

Teddy, however, seized the occasion to deliver a stirring address on the subject of racial discrimination
around the world.

The President's youngest brother, who was initially
viewed by other convention delegates as a curiosity, took
the podium on September 15 and told his audience that
as citizens of a country in which slavery had been prac-

330

ticed and, in particular, as the grandsons of Irish immigrants who had faced discrimination because of their heritage, both he and his brother, the President, "realize our special responsibilities. We are determined to clean our hands of racial prejudice so we can go before the world with deeds to match our words."

He said, "The gypsies in Central Europe, the colored in South Africa, the Negroes in England and the United States and the minority racial groups in many European nations suffer from discrimination."

Calling racial prejudice "legally wrong, morally wrong and bad for humanity," he asked the conference to support a resolution condemning it.

At the conclusion of his remarks, the United Press reported, Teddy received a "thunderous ovation." Delegates, including those from the Soviet Union, rose and cheered in what was "the longest and loudest tribute afforded any speaker since the conference opened."

The report noted that with the speech, Teddy was "making his debut in international politics."

It had already become clear that when he was personally engaged by an issue, Teddy shared Jack's remarkable ability to arouse the passions of a crowd.

And now he was finding his issues, he was finding his voice. He returned to America brimming with new confidence and with what seemed a fresh awareness that —as himself, not merely as the President's brother—he possessed powers that verged on the magical and whose potential could scarcely be imagined.

In October, Teddy joined Jack in Boston, where an enthusiastic crowd of seven thousand jammed the Commonwealth Armory to hear the President speak at a fundraising dinner.

In high good humor, Jack used Teddy as the foil for many jokes. "My last campaign," he said, "may be coming up very shortly, I suppose. But with Teddy around, these dinners can go on indefinitely."

The crowd loved it. Obviously, Teddy did too.

Smiling, Jack thanked Teddy for "offering me his coat-tail.'' Then he said, grinning broadly, ''Teddy, you know, has been down in Washington. He came to see me the other day and said he was really tired of being referred to as the kid brother and just another Kennedy, so he was going to change his name and go out on his own.

'' 'Change it to what?' I asked him.

''And he said, 'Oh, just to an ordinary, everyday name: Roosevelt.' ''

That got the biggest laugh and loudest cheer of the night.

It was Jack's last visit to Boston, and, as Teddy would later write on a picture he inscribed to one of Jack's closest personal friends, it was ''the night all Irishmen were smiling.''

On Thursday, November 14, Jack spoke to Teddy by telephone, suggesting that Teddy fly down to Palm Beach to join him and his old Harvard friend Torbert Macdonald for the weekend. Teddy said he couldn't. After a Kennedy Foundation benefit in New York on Friday night, he had to travel to Michigan to deliver a speech.

Teddy had by now earned enough confidence from his older brothers that, in anticipation of the 1964 campaign, they were permitting him to make public appearances outside Massachusetts.

''Well, you're going to be missing some nice weather,'' Jack said. ''But we'll get together soon.'' First, he had to get his trip to Texas out of the way.

It was not a trip to which he looked forward. Its purpose was exclusively political. The Democratic party in Texas was splitting along liberal-conservative lines, with the conservative governor, John Connally, a protégé of Lyndon Johnson's, feuding bitterly with Texas's liberal senator, Ralph Yarborough.

Jack knew he needed to paper over the damage as best he could prior to the 1964 campaign. Especially if he dropped Johnson from the ticket, as he wanted to, Texas would prove a difficult state to carry.

But he disliked Texas and disliked Texans, especially the three proud and arrogant men involved in the current feud, and most especially the venal, untrustworthy Lyndon Johnson. He was aware also that Johnson, seething over three years of condescension by the Harvard types who'd taken the positions of power in the White House —and particularly irked by Bobby's chronic rudeness and spite—did not enjoy being in Jack's company and feared, with considerable justification, that Jack was planning to abandon him in 1964.

"We'd taken a poll down in Texas," Bobby would say later, "and Johnson had lost a great deal of his popularity." Throughout the entire South, in fact, they'd found, according to Bobby, that Johnson "was a burden rather than a help." As Arthur Schlesinger would later write, at the time of the Texas trip, "Johnson's stock was never lower—and he knew it."

So, to Jack, the whole thing seemed like an intolerable mess. Even worse, on Saturday, at the end of the trip, Johnson and his wife were planning to entertain Jack and Jacqueline at their vast Texas ranch.

Jack knew what this would entail. Just once, soon after his election in 1960, he'd been forced to endure a night at the LBJ ranch. The exuberant Vice President–elect had rousted Jack from bed before dawn to take him deer hunting, a sport Jack detested and one in which he never engaged.

As practiced by Lyndon Johnson, the "sport" was even more revolting. Johnson's method of hunting deer was to drive at high speed in his white Cadillac, cradling a powerful rifle in his lap. When he spotted one of the many deer that frequently crossed the roads curving through the thousands of acres of Johnson ranchland, he'd stop the car and shoot the deer. Ranch hands would later come to collect the carcasses.

After that single experience, Jack had commented to George Smathers: "That will never be a sport until they give the deer a gun too."

He had already told Kenny O'Donnell and Larry O'Brien, who were making the trip with him, that they'd have to spend the weekend at the ranch too. "You guys aren't running out on me and leaving me stranded with

Jackie at Lyndon's ranch," he said. "If I've got to hang around there all day Saturday, wearing one of those big cowboy hats, you've got to be there too."

The fact that his wife would be accompanying him added further to Jack's distaste for the enterprise. With her along, there would not even be the chance for private frolic.

She scarcely saw him at the White House and almost never traveled with him, finding politics distasteful and also finding it an increasing strain to appear in public as the ever-adoring wife of a husband with whom she had almost no private communication.

So distant had they grown from each other, in fact, that this would be the first time since his election that she would be traveling with him west of the Mississippi River.

The New Frontier gala in New York that Friday night was a stunning success: the premiere of the movie *It's a Mad Mad Mad Mad World,* followed by a grand banquet at the New York Hilton.

Teddy and Joan attended, as did Bobby and Ethel. The Kennedy sisters were present. Even Rose was there. More than fifteen hundred people had paid for the privilege of a few hours' proximity to this white-hot center of American celebrity. The money would go to Kennedy-funded charities, thus further enhancing the Kennedy name.

Huge throngs crowded behind police lines at the Warner Cinerama on Broadway near Forty-seventh Street, cheering wildly as each new glittering personality emerged from a limousine and into the spotlights.

The family had moved far beyond the realm of the political, into that limitless domain the Ambassador had always felt would someday be its rightful home. With Jack in the White House and the rest of them here, basking in the acclaim of the masses—bigger stars now, all of them, than anyone in politics, anyone in sports, anyone in Hollywood, had ever been—the old man, even if he could no longer be present to witness it, had finally achieved everything he'd ever worked for, everything he'd ever wanted.

He'd fought all his life and now he'd won. He had it all. And it seemed that it would last forever.

Jack spent the weekend in Palm Beach with Torbert Macdonald. Had it not been for the Ambassador's insistence that the seat be reserved for Teddy, Macdonald undoubtedly would have been, at that point, the junior senator from Massachusetts.

Jack had known Macdonald more than half his life, and, at one point that afternoon, as they were swimming in the Palm Beach pool, Jack began to muse about the passage of time. Not long before, he said, he'd found himself in a hotel room with two naked and attractive young women. This was not unusual. What had surprised him was his response, or lack thereof.

"Two naked girls in the room," he said, "and I'm sitting there reading the *Wall Street Journal*. Does that mean I'm getting old?"

Later, Jack and Macdonald discussed the fact that both their fathers had suffered debilitating strokes and that neither of them ever wanted to endure the sort of existence their fathers now faced.

"So how would you want to die?" Macdonald asked.

Jack did not hesitate. "Oh, a gun," he said. "That way you never even know what hit you. A gunshot would be the perfect way."

Flying back to Washington on Monday, he said to George Smathers, who was on the plane with him, "God, I wish you could think of some way of getting me out of going to Texas. Look how screwed up it's going to be. You've got Lyndon. You've got Ralph Yarborough, who hates Lyndon. And you've got Connally. They're all prima donnas of the biggest order and they're all insisting that they ride either with me or with Jackie. And the law says the Vice President can't ride with the President.

"I've got to start off my speech by saying what a fine guy Johnson is, then what a fine guy Connally is, and then Yarborough, and they all don't like each other. I just wish to hell I didn't have to go. Can't you think of some emergency we could have?''

Others besides Jack did not want him to make the trip, for different reasons. They were worried about his safety. In October, right-wing extremists had spat upon Adlai Stevenson as he'd tried to deliver a speech in Dallas.

After that experience, Stevenson told White House aides, "I have serious doubts whether the President should go to Dallas."

Arkansas senator William Fulbright had warned Jack directly of the hazards, saying, "Dallas is a very dangerous place. I wouldn't go there. Don't you." But Jack simply laughed off Fulbright's concerns.

He also ignored a warning from syndicated columnist Marquis Childs, who had just returned from a trip through the region. Childs told Jack he'd been "startled" by the degree of hostility toward the President. "I heard hatred," he said. "From smug editorial writers and from filling station attendants."

They felt Jack had gone soft on the blacks, soft on the Commies. "They were excoriating 'that son of a bitch in Washington,' " Childs told the President. He said he'd found it a "deeply disturbing phenomenon."

"I don't believe it," Jack responded. "I just don't believe that's true. I can't believe that."

Wednesday, November 20, was Bobby's thirty-eighth birthday. He celebrated with a dinner at Hickory Hill. Even there, apprehensiveness about the Dallas trip was expressed. One guest, Ann Brinkley, the wife of television commentator David Brinkley, while not wanting to alarm Bobby at his own birthday party, warned Kenny O'Donnell to "keep the President away from Dallas."

O'Donnell laughed off her concerns. Jack would be fine. He always was. Besides, Kenny was making the trip himself. He'd see to it that nobody made any insulting comments.

At noon on Thursday, November 21, Jack and Jacqueline flew to Houston aboard Air Force One. Lyndon

Johnson was already there. Jack summoned the Vice President to his suite at the Rice Hotel. There, in Jacqueline's presence, Jack rebuked him for the rancor he'd been displaying toward Ralph Yarborough and for his unwillingness to insist that Governor John Connally cease his bitter attacks upon the liberal senator.

Johnson said nothing in response, not even good-bye. "What was that all about?" Jacqueline asked. "He seemed mad."

"That's just Lyndon," Jack said. "He's in trouble."

That night, Jack and Jacqueline traveled to Fort Worth, the city closest to Dallas. There, on the morning of November 22, he made a brief speech across the street from his hotel.

Returning to his suite, he saw the full-page advertisement in the *Dallas Morning News*. It said: "WELCOME MR. KENNEDY TO DALLAS." But there was nothing welcoming about its tone. It accused Jack of having permitted "thousands of Cubans" to be jailed by Castro. It accused Jack of selling out to Russia. It accused Jack of not pressing hard enough in Vietnam.

"Why have you scrapped the Monroe Doctrine in favor of the Spirit of Moscow?" the ad asked. "Mr. Kennedy, we DEMAND ANSWERS to these questions and we want them now."

In its tone and its odd use of capitalization for emphasis, the advertisement resembled much of the crank mail sent to the White House every week by right-wing extremists and by the mentally disturbed. Most of that, of course, Jack never saw. But this he could not avoid. It was not simply a crank letter. It was a full-page advertisement in the leading newspaper of the nearby city he would be entering in a matter of hours.

"We're heading into nut country today," Jack said to Jacqueline, who seemed upset by the advertisement.

Trying to lighten the mood, he said, "You know, last night would have been a hell of a night to assassinate a President. There was the rain and the crowd and we were all getting jostled. Suppose a man had a pistol in a brief-case?"

Jacqueline found this fantasy neither amusing nor reassuring.

The flight to Dallas was short. After a motorcade through downtown, Jack was to deliver a speech at the Trade Mart at 1:00 P.M.

At 12:40 P.M. local time, the presidential limousine slowed to a near halt as it made the first of the two ninety-degree turns that were required for its passage through a section of downtown Dallas called Dealey Plaza.

Seconds later, the car slowed even further as it made the second turn—this one, actually, at an angle of more than ninety degrees. This one placing it directly beneath the Texas School Book Depository and not far from an elevated grassy knoll that lay just ahead and to the right.

Beyond the grassy knoll was a tunnel that led beneath a railroad overpass. It was upon that tunnel that Jacqueline's attention was focused as she rode next to her husband in the midday heat. She'd been told not to wear sunglasses, because the crowds always liked to see her eyes.

"It was hot," she said later. "Wild. Like Mexico. The sun was so strong in our faces but I couldn't put on sunglasses. I saw the tunnel ahead and I thought it would be so cool in the tunnel."

Part Three

Part Three

1

ONE OF THE REMARKABLE THINGS ABOUT TEDDY—
and this would hold true for years to come—was that no
matter what he'd been through the day or night before,
he always showed up for work in the morning.

On Tuesday, November 26, the day after Jack was
buried, Teddy was back in the Senate. He didn't stay
long, but he showed up. There was a vote, he said, in
which he wanted to participate. The bill in question was
the proposal to expand federal aid to public school libraries. It had been the bill under debate the previous Friday,
when the press officer had first approached him. Teddy
cast his vote in favor of the bill, which passed by a wide
margin. Then he flew to Hyannis Port for Thanksgiving.

The oddest thing about Thanksgiving, besides the fact
that Jack was dead, was that Bobby did not come to
Hyannis Port. Always, Bobby had been the most family-
oriented of the brothers. Since their father's stroke, it
had been largely Bobby's energy and Bobby's will that
had held the Kennedys so closely together.

As President, Jack had been too preoccupied to become a father figure. Nor was he so disposed. And
Teddy, as the youngest, lacked the necessary authority.

So, since December 1961, all the Kennedys—not just his own wife and seven children—had looked to Bobby as the family's central figure.

That was why it was so strange that he did not come for Thanksgiving. Bobby had said only that he could not yet face the family; that his pain was too strong, his wound too fresh, his grief too profound. In time, Teddy would come to understand that more was involved. In time, Teddy would come to understand that Bobby needed not just to grieve, but to think. Very soon, he would have to make some decisions. Many factors were involved. It would take Bobby time to sort them out. Jack's murder had not been a simple matter. Nor would Bobby's be, if it occurred, which he considered a real possibility. Much of the knowledge he possessed— knowledge Jack had shared—was dangerous.

But ignorance could be dangerous too. He had to think about Jacqueline. He had to think about Teddy. He had to think about how much to tell them, and when.

For Bobby, this was no weekend for touch football.

With Jack dead and Bobby absent, Teddy found himself in a new and uncomfortable role. Having spent his whole life as the family's youngest member, he was suddenly the oldest male present for a holiday.

He did the best he could, but by family standards it was considered not quite good enough. He could not be both Jack and Bobby all at once.

On Friday, he tried to do what he thought Bobby would have done. He planned to take all the children, including Caroline and John-John, ice-skating at the public rink the family had donated to the town of Hyannis Port as a memorial to Joe Junior. It would be the family's first emergence from their solitude and grief: a sign that though Jack was dead, the Kennedy spirit lived on.

But when he woke up Friday morning, he saw that rain had already begun. An even harder rain than had fallen the previous Saturday, as he'd sat alone staring at the television screen.

The rain was harsh, the wind fierce: it was no day to take small children ice-skating. No day to have the dramatic and emotional pictures—big Teddy on the ice, grinning broadly, as both tentative Caroline and tiny John-John clutched his hands—taken by a photographer for *Life* magazine.

Instead, he took the children for a drive. But it was not fun for any of them riding around in the rain, and before long he gave up and brought them home, where most of the family spent most of the afternoon in the large living room of the main house, saying things that none would choose to remember later, as the cold rain poured and the gale howled. Then, as evening fell and the wind subsided, a frosty mist rolled up from the bay, enshrouding them.

It may have occurred to Teddy that it was no accident that vodka had been developed first in Russia, a vast land where the winters were long and the sadness ran even deeper than the snows. He wished that he could be with Bobby. He wished that Jack were still alive.

Next door, in what had been the President's house, Jacqueline continued her mythmaking.

She had summoned the journalist Theodore White up from New York. Even without the pictures of Teddy ice-skating with her children, she wanted him to write a story about Jack. And about her feelings for Jack. Dead, he was so much easier to revere than he had been while alive. In death, he could never betray her again. Only the revelation of his secrets could betray her, and she wanted from the start to create an atmosphere in which such revelations would seem sacrilegious.

She'd told White she would grant him an exclusive interview—her first—if he would come to Hyannis Port immediately. All day, in a chauffeur-driven limousine, White proceeded northeast from New York City, through the driving rain and gusting winds. "I must go comfort the President's widow," he'd announced, rather grandly, to friends.

Jacqueline had told him over the phone that she wanted to "rescue" the memory of her husband from the "bitter people" who would write about him in history books. Others would later come to believe that her primary fear was that Jack's paucity of accomplishment would cause him to be judged a minor figure. That would be more than she could bear. She needed to create a legend that would be forever beyond historians' reach.

"History!" she said angrily to White upon his arrival late Friday afternoon. "It's what those bitter old men write." She told White her husband had been a man of special powers, a man who had lived on a higher plane than historians would be able to understand, and that White should use the pages of *Life* magazine to "make clear to the people how much magic there had been in John F. Kennedy."

She talked to him for three and a half hours, until almost midnight. "I want to say this one thing," she finally told him. "It's been almost an obsession with me. All I keep thinking about is this line from a musical comedy.

"At night, before we'd go to sleep, Jack liked to play some records. His back hurt, the floor was so cold, so I'd get out of bed at night and play it for him, when it was so cold getting out of bed.

"And the song he loved most came at the very end of this record, the last scene of *Camelot*. Sad *Camelot*."

She recited the lines from memory, in her soft, girlish voice, then she said, "There'll never be another Camelot again." And she sent White to a servant's room to write his story. He emerged within forty-five minutes.

He handed her his text. She read it quickly, pencil in hand, making such alterations as she wanted. Then she told him to call his editors in New York and dictate the story over the phone.

But all the while, she stood at his side. And once, when she detected that the editors were attempting to tone down his florid prose, to suggest that the emphasis on Camelot was overstated, grandiose, even a bit ridiculous, she beckoned to him.

He put the phone down for a moment, listened intently to her, then resumed his conversation. He told the editors that, no, that was the way Mrs. Kennedy wanted it, therefore that was the way it would be: Camelot.

In White's story, published the following week, Jack and Jacqueline had not been merely President and First

344

Lady of a republic which chose its leaders through a democratic process of election, but king and queen of a mythical kingdom.

They reigned during "a magic moment in American history, when gallant men danced with beautiful women, when great deeds were done, when artists, writers and poets met at the White House, and the barbarians behind the walls were held back."

Jacqueline was satisfied.

For Teddy, the immediate transformation of Jack from controversial young President into Lancelot, Galahad and King Arthur, with heavy overtones of Achilles, Abraham Lincoln and even Jesus, made a difficult transition almost impossible.

In death, Joe Junior had become the family legend, whose accomplishments, both real and imagined, set a standard to which not even Jack, in life, could measure up. Now the story was repeating itself, played out this time not behind the compound walls but on the national and international stage.

Teddy had been, by and large, an outwardly cheerful though often reckless and inconsiderate young man who'd learned to appear suitably deferential in public and who had been elevated much too soon to a position far beyond his capacities only because of his father's money and determination and his oldest living brother's fame.

Now, instantaneously, he was transformed into an heir to a sacred throne, a living participant in the most powerful myth that had ever mesmerized the nation.

In death, for the foreseeable future, the legend of Jack could only enlarge and amplify. Already conditioned by a generation of exposure to the fairy tales told by Hollywood and purveyed along Madison Avenue, the American people had become extremely susceptible to and even dependent on legend.

Old Joe Kennedy had seen this coming more than a quarter century earlier and had consciously constructed a collective mythic persona for his family; one that bore little resemblance to the truth, but, because it was so much more satisfying emotionally and psychologically, was far more appealing than blemished and often contradictory reality.

Even in life, Jack had been made to seem larger than life. Now, in death, Jack's legend, the Kennedy legend, would expand to fill every corner of the private imagination, to satisfy every secret inner need and yearning.

Take the world's poor, humbled, downtrodden masses. Expose them to the magic of the legend of Jack. In their fantasy lives, let them dwell in Camelot. They'd be transformed. The aura would intensify through the years. There seemed no bounds beyond which the legend could not grow.

But for Teddy, a mere mortal who, within the family, was viewed with condescension and often scorn, the seeds of the myth were the seeds of his own destruction.

For if Jack could never again disappoint, Teddy could never live up to—could never come close to satisfying—these wildly exaggerated, frantic, desperate, passionate expectations. Human accomplishment, even on a large scale, might not be beyond him. But the public demanded that he become a living legend at the age of thirty-one, asking of him more than he could give.

For the rest of his life he would wander the country and circle the globe, bearing the burden of the legend, eventually drained by the unrealistic demands of the myth, eventually crushed by the incessant pressure to be more than he had the capacity to become.

When the sun came out on Saturday, he organized a touch football game on the lawn. That night, he threw a party at his own house, a mile away. He needed the company of others. He needed distraction. He needed to blur his thoughts and dull his pain and quiet his fears. Drinks were served. Served and consumed. Teddy did not abstain. Jokes were told. Laughter grew louder; laughter, which is all that's left when the last of the tears have been shed.

Jack would not have been offended. Jack would have understood. Jack would have seen that this was necessary.

But not everyone took such a benign view. Much of

the Hyannis Port staff was offended that Teddy had insisted upon a boisterous game of touch football, with the President not even buried a week yet.

And his loud, late night party was considered a worse affront. The more that was drunk, the more stories were told, and, at one point, it occurred to Teddy that—like everything else Kennedys did—somehow this must be made into a contest.

The game became to see who could tell the most outrageous true story about Jack. There was no dearth of material, though it was not the sort of data Theodore White was transmitting to America through the pages of *Life* magazine.

The party went on through the night. In the morning, no one seemed to remember who had ultimately won the contest, but Teddy had certainly put himself in the running with a variety of tales which began as merely bawdy but grew progressively more extreme.

So offended was the governess to Teddy's children that she quit her job and left Hyannis Port that afternoon.

Teddy flew to Washington on Sunday. He was at work on Monday morning. "This is where Jack would have expected me to be," he said.

The following week, with Bobby remaining in seclusion, Teddy attended a Senate session that was convened solely for the purpose of paying tribute to Jack.

For six hours, as Teddy sat still and silent, his eyes vacant, his face a somber mask, colleagues rose one after another and read individual eulogies, each trying to utter words of praise for Jack so ardent and so eloquent that history would forever link them with Jack's memory.

Even Winston Prouty of Vermont made an effort. As Teddy recalled the droning voice that had spoken against the aid-to-libraries bill before the nearly empty chamber early on the afternoon of Friday, November 22, the Vermont Republican now said, "Someday, in the quiet of an evening, when his toys are put aside, a little boy will ask: 'What was Daddy really like?' In that fateful moment, when time stands still and all the world descends upon her, may she who bears the burden of the answer tell no

347

tale of office granted, but speak of him who loved the Lord and saw in the least of us traces of His majesty and in this land the glory of His handiwork.''

At the end, Teddy himself rose to speak briefly. "Many of you," he said in a quiet voice, "were my brother's colleagues and his teachers as well. His career bears your imprint.'' Then he spoke of the need to support Lyndon Johnson. "If the country can be united, the sacrifice will not have been in vain.''

He closed by expressing his family's "heartfelt thanks" for all the tributes received, to the tens of thousands who had already filed past the President's grave in Arlington, to the hundreds of thousands who had braved the bitter chill of the November night in order to view the casket in the rotunda. Their "consolations and sympathy," Teddy said, had sustained the family in its darkest hours, and would continue to do so in the months ahead.

Although he had been a member of the Senate since January, these were the first public words he'd uttered in the chamber.

The *Boston Globe* the next day said, "Another member of the Kennedy family gave impressive evidence yesterday of the courage and the dignity that has marked all of the President's relatives since tragedy struck on Nov. 22. . . . One suspects that many another person, ourselves included, could not have borne up so well under the strain. Sen. Kennedy's performance could not have been more brave and dignified, and was fully worthy of the brother whom the Senate was honoring.''

2

THE FIRST PERSON TO ARRIVE AT BOBBY'S HOUSE ON
November 22, after hearing news of the assassination,
was John McCone, director of the CIA.

Bobby asked him, "Did the CIA kill my brother?"

McCone said no.

Bobby did not press the point.

Within an hour, Lyndon Johnson, not yet sworn in as
Jack's successor, called from Dallas. Johnson said he
feared the murder "might be part of a worldwide conspiracy."

Bobby did not disagree.

A half hour later, walking the Hickory Hill grounds
with an aide, Bobby said, "I thought they'd get one of
us, but Jack never worried about it. I always thought it
would be me."

The aide did not ask him what he meant, or who
"they" were.

That very afternoon, J. Edgar Hoover directed the FBI
to conduct an immediate investigation. He wanted, he
told an aide to Lyndon Johnson, "something issued, so
we can convince the public that Oswald is the real assassin."

On Sunday, when Oswald was murdered by Jack Ruby

inside Dallas police headquarters, the cautious and experienced diplomat George Kennan said, "I am not by nature a suspicious person, but I fairly bristle with doubts."

On November 29, the Friday of the week Jack was buried, his deputy attorney general, Nicholas Katzenbach, acting in Bobby's stead because Bobby had withdrawn utterly from public life, persuaded Lyndon Johnson that in light of the many rumors surrounding the events of November 22 and November 24 in Dallas, a high-level commission composed of public figures of impeccable reputation should be deputized to investigate the circumstances surrounding the assassination of the President and the subsequent murder of Lee Harvey Oswald.

Concurring, Johnson delegated to Katzenbach the authority to choose the members of the commission. Katzenbach selected Earl Warren, chief justice of the Supreme Court, to direct it. The other members were senators Richard Russell of Georgia and John Sherman Cooper of Kentucky; congressmen Hale Boggs of Louisiana and Gerald Ford of Michigan; Allen Dulles, former director of the CIA; and John McCloy, an international banker and pillar of the Washington business and political establishment.

According to Katzenbach, "Robert Kennedy never really wanted any investigation."

The commission met for the first time on December 5. Its mandate, according to a memorandum Katzenbach sent to Johnson assistant Bill Moyers, was not to conduct an unfettered quest for the truth but rather to accomplish two purposes:

"1. The public must be satisfied that Oswald was the assassin; that he did not have confederates who are still at large; and that the evidence was such that he would have been convicted at trial.

"2. Speculation about Oswald's motivation ought to be cut off, and we should have some basis for rebutting thought that this was a . . . conspiracy. . . ."

Four days later, only eighteen days after the assassination and sixteen days after the murder of Oswald, the FBI issued the report that Hoover had wanted: Oswald, a pro-Castro fanatic, had acted alone. Jack Ruby had killed him in a misguided act of patriotism. There was no evidence of any conspiracy of any kind, nothing to suggest that Oswald had shared his intentions in advance with anyone or that he'd received any assistance from anyone.

On December 9, the same day he received this report, Katzenbach contacted each member of the Warren Commission, urging that they jointly and immediately issue a press release commending the thoroughness of the FBI report and stressing that it clearly showed that Oswald had acted alone, that there were no indications of conspiracy.

That evening, however, Bobby told Arthur Schlesinger that "there was still argument if [Oswald] had done it by himself or as part of a larger plot, whether organized by Castro or by gangsters." Bobby added that John McCone had told him that at least two people were involved in the actual shooting.

Later, Katzenbach said of Bobby, "I know he never read the FBI report."

Indeed, during these weeks Bobby scarcely functioned at all. The few actions he took, said one aide, were performed in a "haze of pain." Jack's press secretary, Pierre Salinger, described Bobby during this period as being "the most shattered man I had ever seen in my life."

"He was just inconsolable," recalled another aide. "He was in perpetual pain. It was awful to watch."

Part of this agony clearly was a function of his closeness to Jack. To an extraordinary degree, he had linked his own destiny to Jack's, and thus the death of Jack also represented the death of a major part of Bobby's inner self. The thought that the torch had now passed to him, that he would have to forge onward by himself, would alone have been enough to terrify him, especially as he observed with what abandon, with what raw force, the entire country was insisting upon Jack's immediate canonization as a secular saint; his anointment as a god among men.

But the more frenzied the adulation grew, the wider grew the gap between the country's wish-fulfilling perception of Jack and the far more complex and in many ways quite sordid realities of which Bobby was aware.

He took to writing in private notebooks.

He copied in his notebook a quote from Camus: "I feel rather like Augustine did before becoming a Christian when he said, 'I tried to find the source of evil and I got nowhere.' But it is also true that I and few others know what must be done. . . ."

He wrote: "All things are to be examined & called into question—There are no limits set to thought."

But there were limits to what could be revealed.

Jacqueline, who had grown much closer to him emotionally than she'd ever been to Jack, gave him Greek tragedy and history to read. He underlined many passages.

Such as: "All arrogance will reap a rich harvest in tears."

And: "God calls men to a heavy reckoning for overweening pride."

He also began to carry with him an anthology of world literature which included a selection about a French poet who used to walk around his village accompanied by a lobster on a leash. When asked why, the poet would reply, "Because he knows the secrets of the deep."

Bobby, too, knew such secrets. He knew how dark and tangled were the threads that had come together in Dallas and that now reached out from it in so many directions. And, as United States senator Harris Wofford has written, "Since he dared not unravel these things himself, he could only hope that some of the worst possibilities would be disproved by others."

For he must have known that the disclosure of even part of the truth underlying the assassination of Jack would destroy not only his own future in public life but the entire family's good name and, worst of all, any chance that in death Jack would remain a hero of mythic proportions.

And Bobby seemed determined, no matter the cost, to protect his brother's reputation. He was suffering, Wofford has said, "grief beyond ordinary grief." For, in fact, the murder of Jack "was not a tragedy without a reason." Bobby knew far too many reasons, far too many facts. And, as Wofford wrote, he "must have considered the story those facts told to be worse than the most terrible fiction."

He seemed frozen, rendered as mute and as lame as his father by the unbearable irony of his position: he, the chief law enforcement officer of the United States and a man who hated organized crime with a blazing passion, was forced to stifle inquiry into his own brother's murder precisely because he recognized how likely it was that Mafia leaders had been involved.

"Robert Kennedy knew," Wofford has written, "that the prompt killing of Oswald by Jack Ruby, a shady character with ties to both Teamster and Mafia agents, fit the traditional pattern of underworld murders. . . .

"Presumably the Attorney General soon learned, as the FBI did, that Ruby had been friendly years before in Chicago with two professional killers for organized crime, who in 1963 were associated with Sam Giancana. Kennedy must also have learned, as the Warren Commission did, that Ruby had gone to Cuba in 1959 to visit one of his close friends, a gambling casino operator associated with the Mafia chieftain in Cuba, Santos Trafficante. Ruby's Havana friend later visited him in Dallas, and Castro let Trafficante out of jail to return to the United States.

"The Attorney General should also have found out from the FBI about Ruby's long-distance calls in the month before the assassination to various persons associated with Giancana and Hoffa, including a man whom Kennedy had once described as one of Hoffa's most violent lieutenants. According to Ruby's sister, another man he called was one of his old friends who was a professional executioner for Giancana."

And, as Wofford has also written, "adding to his burden was the obligation he felt to keep all the key facts secret from most, if not all, of his family and friends, and to try to withhold them forever from the people of this country, and the world."

But it does not seem possible that he could have with-them any longer from Teddy. For, in his ignorance and naïveté, Teddy might unknowingly make a tragic situation much, much worse. Unless most of the key facts that led up to the assassination were shared with him, Teddy had the potential to destroy the myth simply by pressing too hard for the truth.

If there are any records of exactly when and where and under what conditions Bobby first began to share the worst of the secrets with Teddy, these are sealed within archives that may remain forever closed.

And with Bobby dead now for so many years, only Teddy could still shed light on this darkest part of his family history. There seems little likelihood that he will, but common sense strongly suggests that Bobby would have had to tell Teddy the truth about the family's entanglements with the Mafia as soon as possible. Otherwise, he would quite naturally have insisted that the most intensive and extensive criminal investigation ever conducted in America be launched in an effort to learn the full truth about Jack's murder.

But this was just what Teddy must not say, for exposure of even partial truth might well have led to the disclosure of Jack's employment of Mafia hit men in an attempt to assassinate Castro; of his sharing a mistress with one of the most notorious organized crime figures in America; and of his father's intervention—through his connections with Mafia leaders—in the electoral process itself.

So Teddy must say nothing, except what a great man Jack had been and how important it was that all Americans devote themselves to bringing about the fulfillment of his dreams. Never, for the rest of his life, was he to express dissatisfaction with the way the official inquiry into the assassination had been handled. Continued probing, Teddy would have to learn to say, would simply be too painful for the family. The family wanted the matter laid to rest. The family had suffered enough and would be deeply grateful if its wishes in this most sensitive of matters were respected. The family fully concurred in the conclusions of the Warren Commission and would have no more to say about the subject.

Before he could learn to say this, however, Teddy would have to be told why it was necessary. And only Bobby could have done that.

Later, many would come to feel that what broke Teddy —in a way that could never be fixed—was not so much the death of Jack, shocking and tragic and painful as that was, but the deliberate destruction by Bobby, so soon after, of the illusions Teddy had clung to all his life.

It was not that prior to the assassination Teddy had been utterly naive about the ways in which his family achieved its successes. Teddy may have been callow and inexperienced and in many ways still largely unformed, but he was not an ignoramus when it came to political realities, especially those involving his own family.

Yet what Bobby would have had to tell him must have been devastating beyond his worst imaginings and beyond his capacity to absorb.

It was one thing to lose an older brother, especially if that brother was the President. It was worse to lose the last of what you might have still been struggling to believe in and, at this same time of psychological crisis, perhaps even the very capacity for belief.

3

TEDDY DID NOT REAPPEAR IN PUBLIC UNTIL THE LAST
week of January. If he was shattered internally, he
showed no immediate sign. Indeed, it almost seemed as
if, reflexively, he'd responded to the awful knowledge
Bobby had shared with him by calling forth previously
untapped sources of energy. As if through constant activity he might be able to exorcise these new demons from
his soul, or at least stay one step ahead of them.

He flew to Los Angeles to campaign for his old friend
John Tunney, who was running for Congress. He said
that had it not been for the outpouring of public sympathy
in the days and weeks after the assassination, his family
would not have been able to sustain itself.

"I am sure," he said, "the Kennedy family will continue to do everything possible to carry forward the ideals
of my brother." Many in the crowd began to weep.

He said that no matter how much personal risk it might
entail, the Kennedy family would remain in public life
"as long as there is a job to do." The weeping spread.

He said, "We intend to devote ourselves to the
achievement of the principles and programs for which the
President lived, and to the eradication of the hatred and

extremism that took him away.'' At the end, thousands were openly crying.

So this was the way it would be. Everywhere he went from this point forward, with every word he uttered, every position he espoused, Teddy would no longer be merely the President's kid brother, but the living personification of the legend.

The nation yearned for a mystical communion with its valiant, slain, heroic leader. The feeling that pervaded America in the early months of 1964 was that, like Jesus, he had died for our sins. We wanted to consume him symbolically—his body and his blood—so that we might be one with him, so that he might live again through our belief in what, in fact, he had never been. And so that in death he might enlarge us and ennoble us in a way he had never managed while alive.

His brothers were as close to him as we could get. They were the resurrection and the life. And with Bobby remaining in seclusion, it was only through contact with Teddy that we could be redeemed and reborn.

And so, among its many other effects, Jack's death took from Teddy permanently any hope he might have had of forging, over time, his own identity. From this point forward, he must embody all the courage, brilliance, glamour, wit, charm and moral leadership with which the legend had already endowed Jack.

By itself, this would have been bad enough. What must have made it so much worse was his awareness of how dramatically different was the image he must project from the reality that lay beneath it. He now knew the truth, and he knew also that for the sake of the family, for the sake of the myth, the truth must remain forever hidden.

Still, on the surface, all seemed well. Indeed, it appeared for a time as if Teddy, not Bobby, might be the one to reclaim the throne. Columnist Jack Anderson wrote that Bobby had "confided to intimates that he may pull out of politics and take over his father's place running the family financial empire. He may leave the political field to his younger brother, who seems to have more ballot-box appeal. Just as old Joe Kennedy spared no effort to help his late son with the White House, Bobby would stay behind the scenes and concentrate on making his younger brother the next President Kennedy.''

There was no question about the ballot-box appeal. By late winter, as the *Globe* was reporting that ''in voice and mien,'' Teddy ''reminds Senate colleagues daily more and more of his brother, the late John F. Kennedy,'' Republicans in Massachusetts were considering supporting Teddy's 1964 candidacy rather than opposing him.

It was obvious that he'd be reelected by a lopsided margin. But, beyond that, in Massachusetts, in the early months of 1964, the notion that someone would try to wrest public office from the slain President's brother seemed not only unpatriotic but sacrilegious. Indeed, any criticism whatsoever of Teddy's conduct, public or private, would have seemed indecent at this time.

Within weeks, he became the most popular politician in America, but more than just a politician, and more than simply a celebrity. It was as if he were now imbued with the martyred President's charismatic power. Aching, the nation turned toward him for solace, for hope, for inspiration.

A Massachusetts journalist observed that where ''he used to walk on tiptoes, now he moves right in. He's become a stand-up guy. He's all muscle. He can speak out. The difference between Ted Kennedy now and a year ago is the difference between night and day.''

''A political development fraught with possibilities,'' said *The Washington Post*, ''is taking place today in the transformation of Edward M. 'Ted' Kennedy into a national political figure. By a curious turn of fate,'' the *Post* observed, ''Robert Kennedy does not now have the firm political base that Ted Kennedy has. If the attorney general's political future is uncertain, Sen. Kennedy is on a course that seems destined to carry him over the years to growing power in the Senate and growing influence in the Democratic Party.''

* * *

On April 8, he finally made his first speech on the Senate floor. For nearly a month, the Senate had been debating the civil rights bill that Jack, at Bobby's urging, had introduced the previous summer. Now, Teddy chose to add his voice to the debate. Civil rights remained the issue that engaged him most thoroughly, with which he felt the strongest personal identification.

Clearly nervous, he rose from his seat in the last row to address his colleagues. "It is with some hesitation," he said, "that I rise to speak on the pending legislation," and if you closed your eyes—as many did, at least briefly —you could swear it was Jack himself you were hearing.

"A freshman senator," he said, "should be seen and not heard; should learn and not teach. This is especially true when the Senate is engaged in a truly momentous debate.

"I had planned, about this time in the session, to make my maiden speech on issues affecting industry and employment in my home state. But I could not follow this debate for the past four weeks—I could not see this issue envelop the emotions and the conscience of the nation— without changing my mind. To limit myself to local issues in the face of this great national question would be to demean the seat in which I sit."

As he gathered momentum and confidence, his strong voice began to fill the chamber. The eyes of all—other senators and spectators alike—were riveted upon him.

"It is true, as has been said on this floor, that prejudice exists in the minds and hearts of men. It cannot be eradicated by law. But I firmly believe a sense of fairness and goodwill also exists in the minds and hearts of men, side by side with the prejudice. A sense of fairness and goodwill which shows itself so often in acts of charity and kindness towards others.

"This noble characteristic wants to come out. It wants to, and often does, win out against the prejudice. Law, expressing as it does the moral conscience of the community, can help it come out in every person, so in the end the prejudice will be dissolved.

"The basic problem the American people face in the 1960s in the field of civil rights is one of adjustment. It is

359

the task of adjusting to the fact that Negroes are going to become members of the community of American citizens, with the same rights and responsibilities as every one of us.''

He then pointed out how in 1780 Catholics in Massachusetts were not allowed to vote, and how through the 1840s no Irishman could get a job above that of a common laborer. And he said, with considerable force, ''I believe that if America has been able to make this adjustment for the Irish, the Italians, the Jews, the Poles, the Greeks, the Portuguese—we can make it for the Negroes. And the nation will be strengthened in the process.

''I want to see an America,'' he went on, ''where everybody can make his contribution. Where a man will be measured not by the color of his skin but by the content of his character.''

He then paused and looked off to one side. When he resumed, his voice was less strong, less clear than before. ''I remember,'' he said, ''the words of President Johnson last November twenty-seventh.'' He paused again, clearly faltering. Then he quoted: '' 'No memorial oration or eulogy could more eloquently honor President Kennedy's memory than the earliest possible passage of the civil rights bill for which he fought so long.' ''

And suddenly, he had to stop. His voice had broken. His last sentence had ended in an audible sob. In the family gallery, his wife, Joan, dabbed at her eyes with a handkerchief. In the spectators' gallery, tears began to flow freely as Teddy struggled for the control necessary to continue.

No, he had not spoken at the grave. But he was speaking now, and he would finish.

''My brother,'' he said, ''was the first President of the United States to state publicly that segregation was morally wrong. His heart and soul are in this bill.''

Momentarily, Teddy had to stop again. His own eyes were wet; his pain seemed not only emotional but physical.

''If his life and death had a meaning,'' Teddy said, his voice so low now, so strained, ''it was that we should not hate but love one another. We should use our powers not to create conditions of oppression that lead to violence, but conditions of freedom that lead to peace.

"It is in that spirit," he concluded, "that I hope the Senate will pass this bill."

As Joan wept openly in the gallery and other onlookers continued to cry, he took his seat, his face as pale as it had been during the debate with Eddie McCormack. And then, one by one, other senators—Douglas of Illinois, Wayne Morse, Hubert Humphrey—rose to congratulate him for the magnificence and nobility of his words and feelings.

"For a moment," said the *Globe* the next day, "the remorse of the nation over the assassination of President Kennedy returned to the Senate chamber."

It would not be the last time Teddy would evoke this response.

As spring progressed, he stepped up his national speaking pace: Pennsylvania, Indiana, Maryland, Georgia. Suddenly, the "silent Kennedy," the invisible man of 1963, seemed to be everywhere.

And everywhere the reaction was the same: great swells of enthusiasm, tempered only by the bittersweet sense of what might have been, of who it was they wanted Teddy to become, of who they were pretending he already was.

By the end of April, *The New York Times*, noting the "emotional appeal of the similarity of his style and manner" to that of his late brother, observed that in only three years he would be thirty-five, the minimum age for a vice president, or, for that matter, a president. The *Times* reported one commentator's view that "for a young Senator with class, experience and wealth, the natural place to look is the White House."

Especially if the young senator's name was Kennedy and if, wherever he went, he uttered such lines as "I am here because I felt he would have wanted me to be here."

Wire services reported that "at each place he appeared, cheering throngs nearly mobbed him."

As Jack so long ago had said when first campaigning in Massachusetts, he was doing it only because the older brother, the better brother, the greater hero, had already laid down his life.

The new waves of adulation were not confined to America, as Teddy discovered during a tumultuous European tour in May. His ostensible purpose was to seek foreign contributions to the planned John F. Kennedy Library, which the family wanted to construct on the Harvard campus as yet another form of eternal flame, designed to glorify Jack in perpetuity.

But the underlying reason for making the trip was to find out just how much of the adulation was transferable; what degree of the charismatic power had been passed on to this new bearer of the torch, this new personification of the myth.

The answer, in brief, was: all of it. At times, the reception given to Teddy during his eight-day, seven-country journey approached the frenzied welcome Jack had received less than a year earlier in Berlin.

Paris was his first stop. "Radiating all the typical Kennedy charm and poise," as the *Globe* reported, he said in a nationally televised speech, "I want to thank the people of France and of Paris for the streets, places, squares and memorials named after my brother."

The next day he moved on to Rome and to Vatican City, site of his first press conference twenty-five years before. There, "sitting in the same chair his brother John used a year ago," he had a thirty-minute audience with the Pope.

As he emerged into St. Peter's Square, he was besieged by fervent admirers who shouted "Eduardo!" and crowded about him, as if it were Teddy and not the Pope who now had the power to bestow blessings.

That evening he flew on to Munich, where a crowd of three thousand was waiting for him at the airport. One German woman pressed forward to hand him twenty marks, then worth about five dollars, pleading with him to use the money to buy flowers for Jack's grave.

The crowd surrounding his hotel was so vast that his motorcade was forced to a halt several blocks away. From there, Teddy got out and walked, waving, grinning, shaking hands. The throngs cheered as police stood at attention, saluting this royal personage who had suddenly descended into their midst.

The next day he flew to Bonn for a meeting with Konrad Adenauer, the eighty-seven-year-old former chancellor of West Germany, who gave him an autographed picture of himself, asking Teddy to bring it home to John-John.

Then on to Hamburg, where the crowds were the largest yet. "Each city Ted visits," the *Globe* reported, "seems to be bent on outdoing the others." But, always, there was room for one old woman to push forward to the front and hand Teddy a personal token. In Hamburg, it was a small bouquet of lilacs and a note that read, "The way to Arlington is so far off. I would like to give these little flowers in memory of your brother, who'll never be forgotten by us all."

He spoke to thousands of students at Hamburg University, then went to the heart of the city to dedicate the new John F. Kennedy Bridge. From Hamburg, he flew on to Frankfurt, then to Zurich, then to Brussels. Everywhere it was the same: he was the reincarnation of Jack.

"Ted," wrote the *Globe* reporter accompanying him, "gives both Europeans and Americans a powerful feeling that they are reliving the not so distant past when JFK was so much alive. Ted instinctively tucks in his tie and smooths his jacket pockets before stepping before an audience—so did JFK. He has the same broad A—and the slight quiver in his voice as he hurries to get out more words without taking another breath. Those who hear him speak and watch the familiar mannerisms begin remembering . . .

" 'I closed my eyes and heard that voice,' one American in Paris said, 'and it was just as if JFK were alive.' "

The reporter also noted Teddy's "phobia-like drive to keep moving. He can't stand delays. He wants a crowded schedule, wants to be on the move." Motion blurred the edges of reality, kept him on the crest of the wave.

But it was not until he reached Ireland, his last stop, that it became obvious that the myth had swallowed him whole; that the option of being simply Ted—whoever that might have turned out to be—was no longer open. His own identity had been subsumed by the legend.

He arrived in Dublin on May 29, the day that would have been Jack's forty-seventh birthday. Less than a year had passed since Jack himself had stood on Irish soil.

As reported by the *Globe,* upon Teddy's arrival, "The mist of Irish tears blended with the roar of Irish cheers. 'God bless him—there's no one like the Kennedys,' were the remarks heard from the crowd."

It was in Ireland, finally, that emotion overcame him as it had the day he'd made his civil rights speech in the Senate. "This is a day of joy and sadness for me," he said after attending a memorial mass for Jack in a Dublin cathedral. "Joy because I am in Ireland on a beautiful spring day, and sadness because this is the President's birthday. And because my brother will not be able to come back and enjoy any more spring days here."

Suddenly, he had to stop. He stood silently for a long moment as a hush fell over the crowd. In a choked voice, he could add only, "But it is his birthday and if he were here he'd want you all to laugh and to enjoy yourselves."

Then, in tears, he stopped again and stepped down from the microphone. As he walked, head bowed, to his waiting limousine, the crowd broke through police lines and surged toward him, driven by love, by the need to worship, and by regret.

"They yelled, cheered, and some even cried," the *Globe* reported. "But all wanted to clasp his hand or at least touch him. This scene was repeated over and over again during the day wherever Ted made a public appearance. Crowds were still waiting in the streets at midnight, waiting for just a glimpse of him. 'He's beautiful . . . He's a Kennedy . . . He's younger, but he looks like the President, God bless him.' "

In Limerick, the adulation was so intense that the crowd forced the open convertible in which he was riding to halt. Then, swarming toward him, they almost tipped the car on its side as Teddy scrambled to keep his balance.

"We'll make you President yet," one man yelled, grasping at the cuff of Teddy's shirt.

At the time, it did not seem to occur to anyone that perhaps that was what he feared most.

Yet the inner tension was building. The gap between expectation and reality was too great. The strain began to take a toll. Back in Washington, he was driving faster, drinking more, staying out later more often and growing rapidly less discreet in his pursuit and conquest of women.

He had, by now, drifted so far and so noticeably from his wife that even in Washington, a city accustomed to the practice of maintaining a marriage more for convenience than from desire, the emptiness of their union was widely noted and much discussed.

While Teddy was abroad in May, Joan had suffered another miscarriage. But, like Jack before him, Teddy had declined to cut short his trip to be with her. Service to the myth—and having a good time—took clear precedence over any sense of obligation to one's wife.

Especially when, like Joan, the wife was proving to be more and more of an embarrassment—with her social awkwardness, her own drinking problem and her growing list of physical ailments, which by early 1964 had come to include abdominal pain of unexplained origin but so severe as to necessitate exploratory surgery.

The fact was, Joan had become a burden just at a time when Teddy was, as a result of all the other forces that had converged upon him over the previous several months, less able than ever to offer solace and support.

He moved fast, both publicly and privately, servicing the legend by day and, at night, seeking from both alcohol and sex some relief from his own strain. He was in no mood to hear about the difficulties of his wife.

Growing more desperate weekly, Joan found herself begging for the attention he did not seem able or willing to pay her. When it was not forthcoming—when for days and weeks at a time he was too busy, too overscheduled, too frantic even to have a conversation with her—she began consoling herself to an alarming degree with alcohol. Even if he refused to recognize it, Joan knew she had, as had her mother before her, a serious drinking problem. That she was, in all probability, an alcoholic.

But Teddy had neither the time nor the inclination to talk to her about her drinking. He had too many problems of his own, of which drinking, at that point, seemed not the worst. "I tried to talk about it," Joan said later, "but I was embarrassed, and Ted was embarrassed too."

And so Joan's "problem" became one more of those family secrets that were not discussed, either publicly or privately. And Teddy, more and more, led a life independent of her, while maintaining for press and public the illusion that his devotion to her was unbounded, his pride in her limitless and his happiness as her husband complete.

It was a life which, by mid-1964, those around him came to doubt he could sustain. He could not continue to maintain so many pretenses simultaneously, yet there did not seem any way out.

4

THE MASSACHUSETTS DEMOCRATS WERE HOLDING
their 1964 nominating convention in West Springfield.
Unlike 1962, for Teddy the event was to be not a competition but a coronation—indeed, the climax to one of the
most rewarding days of his public life.

That Friday, June 19, the Senate was finally to vote on
the civil rights bill. The outcome was not in doubt. The
legislation, which even in its final, tempered version was
of historic importance, would be approved by a wide
margin. But the vote held enormous symbolic significance for Teddy. As the brother of the assassinated President who had introduced the bill, he intended to remain
on the Senate floor until its passage.

Then, as soon as the final vote was tallied, he would fly
to Massachusetts by private plane to accept his renomination by acclamation at the convention.

He could not use the family plane, the *Caroline*, because Bobby was flying to Hyannis Port for the weekend
and Bobby, as the older brother, always had first call on
the *Caroline*.

But the family had a friend in Andover named Dan
Hogan, president of a company that manufactured liquid
detergent and owner of a twin-engined Aero Commander

680 that he frequently flew himself for both recreational and business purposes.

In the less than three weeks since Teddy had returned from Europe, Hogan had already flown him to three separate speeches. But, as he explained that Friday morning to Teddy's administrative assistant, Ed Moss, he would not be able to fly Teddy from Washington to Springfield because this was the weekend of his twenty-fifth reunion at Yale.

His plane, of course, remained at Teddy's disposal. In fact, Hogan told Moss, he'd arranged to have Ed Zimny, an experienced professional pilot whom he knew well, fly the aircraft to Washington and then take Teddy to Springfield as soon as the Senate vote was cast.

If the Senate stayed on schedule, Teddy would arrive at the auditorium in early evening. As was so often the case, however, the Senate did not stay on schedule. Throughout the day, as delays mounted, Moss, who had begun to accompany Teddy on almost every trip he made, was on the telephone repeatedly, rearranging travel arrangements and scheduling for the evening.

Teddy, never a patient man when it came to travel schedules, grew more and more irritated as the Senate slogged slowly through the multitude of procedural details that had to be disposed of before the final vote on the civil rights bill was taken.

The pilot, Zimny, had arrived at 4:00 P.M. and was waiting at the private air terminal at Washington's National Airport. He was eager to leave for Springfield as soon as possible because, as he told Moss several times, the weather, while fine in Washington, was quickly deteriorating to the north.

But there was nothing Ed Moss, or Teddy himself, could do to hurry the tedious pace at which the country's most august deliberative body conducted its business.

Not until 7:00 P.M. did it appear that the vote was finally drawing near. Teddy was supposed to have been in West Springfield already. The delegates had long since assembled inside the convention hall.

Knowing he'd be arriving hours later than expected,

Teddy arranged to speak briefly to the delegates through a telephone-and-loudspeaker hookup.

As in 1962, more than seventeen hundred of them, obscured by cigarette smoke and slick with sweat, greed and their own private fears, were packed into the hot, humid auditorium. The evening had already turned loud and raucous. The only contest was between Governor Endicott "Chub" Peabody—whose two-year term had been widely viewed as unsuccessful—and his challenger, Lieutenant Governor Francis X. Bellotti, who was supported by Eddie McCormack.

The Kennedys had chosen Peabody two years earlier because they'd wanted Teddy's ticket to have ethnic balance, and now they were stuck with him. Teddy had put vast personal distance between himself and Peabody, but so great was Teddy's popularity that the mere implication that he still favored the incumbent was enough to doom Bellotti's chances.

By the night of the balloting it had become obvious that the bland and ineffectual Peabody would easily win the convention's endorsement. Thus, the only spark of excitement the delegates could hope for would be the triumphal entrance of Teddy, however delayed he might be.

As it was announced that he was on a phone line from Washington, the hall fell silent. His voice crackled through the auditorium's loudspeaker system. It was now almost 7:30 P.M. and it seemed he might not actually reach the convention hall until almost 11:00.

"I just want everyone to know," he said, "that I am a candidate this year, even though I am hundreds of miles away." Then he added, "We are now fifteen minutes away from the vote for civil rights." The crowd inside the convention hall cheered. This was Jack's bill and, as such, even to those Massachusetts Democrats personally unstirred by the plight of the blacks, it had acquired the status of sacred writ.

Teddy said he would be with them in person as soon as possible, and closed by adding, "And I ask you not to get so impatient that you decide to nominate Joan instead."

The crowd laughed and cheered. But Joan herself, who detested these sorts of events almost as intensely as Jacqueline had, was not even at the convention hall. She was spending the evening with friends at a private home in Springfield. She planned to wait there for Teddy and travel to the hall only when he arrived.

The Senate finally began to vote at 7:40 P.M. The process took only ten minutes. The final tally was 73–27. Gratified but somber, Teddy hurried back to his office from the floor. Birch Bayh, a Democratic senator from Indiana, accompanied him. Bayh had agreed to deliver the keynote speech at the Springfield convention. He and his wife, as well as Ed Moss, would be flying to Massachusetts with Teddy.

Moss called Zimny at the airport, saying they'd be there within half an hour. Again, the pilot urged Moss to hurry. The weather in western Massachusetts was worsening steadily.

Moss was forty-one years old, married and the father of three. Being that much older than Teddy—as well as being highly competent, affable and discreet—he'd come to occupy a special place on the senatorial staff. An administrative aide, yes, but more than that: like Joey Gargan, somebody with whom Teddy could relax. One of the few who still saw him as a man and not a myth; as Teddy rather than as the reincarnation of Jack.

But even Moss occasionally misjudged the temper of the moment. Anticipating that Teddy would be elated by the wide margin by which the bill had passed, he joked that, to cap off the night, "You should make some kind of spectacular entrance at the convention."

"What do you want me to do," Teddy said tartly, "crack up the airplane?" Beset by many conflicting emotions, he was not in a frivolous mood.

Moss, already recognizing his mistake, suggested that Teddy might at least parachute out of the plane as it flew over the convention hall. The Senator was not amused. With no further comment, he hurried to a waiting car, Moss and the Bayhs trailing behind.

As they started for the airport, Moss mentioned for the first time that the pilot had reported the Massachusetts weather to be less than ideal and that he'd seemed in a hurry to get started.

Teddy himself was always in a hurry. Still, tonight there was a stop he had to make. This had been Jack's bill. On this, the night of its passage, he needed to spend a few private moments at Jack's grave.

He told the driver to stop at Arlington. He got out of the car and knelt, alone, head bowed, at the base of the eternal flame.

Meanwhile, in western Massachusetts, the valleys began to fill with fog.

As expected, Peabody had trounced Bellotti, 1,259–377, but no one except for Peabody, Bellotti and maybe Eddie McCormack seemed to care. Teddy was to be the star of this show. Until he arrived, there was no show. It was now after 11:00 P.M. An announcement was made that Teddy's plane had been delayed but was en route and that he would arrive at the hall before midnight.

But midnight came and Teddy didn't. Delegates mingled aimlessly, fatigue and liquor now blurring their sense of anticipation. Suddenly, and somewhat frantically, the chairman of the convention gaveled for silence. He said he had just received word that the plane bearing Senator Kennedy had crashed while trying to land near Springfield but that the Senator was reported to be alive.

In shock and horror, disbelieving delegates pushed toward the press section of the auditorium, desperate for further information. Already, many were in tears. This could not be. This was too much. No God could permit yet another tragedy to befall this star-crossed family.

And Teddy . . . Teddy, who now filled their hearts with pride as Jack had done . . . it could not be that something had happened to Teddy.

Within minutes, the chairman again gaveled the hall to silence. In his other hand, he held up what appeared to be a wire service news bulletin. To the enormous relief of nearly two thousand stricken listeners, he said the first report had apparently been in error. There had been a crash in the vicinity of Springfield, but it had not involved

Teddy's plane. "The Kennedy plane is still aloft," he announced.

The hall erupted with the wildest cheers of the night. Oh, what a triumphant moment it would be when Teddy —after all this unexpected turmoil—finally arrived.

But then, for a third time, the gavel sounded. Again, the chairman stepped to the microphone. For those close enough to see his face, no words were necessary.

"It now appears that the first announcement was correct," he said. "Senator Kennedy is hospitalized but still alive."

He asked for a moment of silent prayer. Then, at 12:20 A.M., he pounded his gavel for the last time, declaring the convention adjourned. Delegates, many crying openly, poured out of the hall in chaos, running through mist and drizzle toward the nearest car radio, the nearest television set.

Jack Crimmins, a former state policeman who lived in South Boston and served as Teddy's primary chauffeur within Massachusetts, had been waiting for the plane at tiny Barnes Municipal Airport in the town of Westfield, seven miles from the West Springfield convention hall.

Bradley Field, the larger commercial airport that served Springfield, was located south of the city, over the state line in Connecticut. Though far better equipped to handle air traffic in bad weather, Bradley was almost a forty-five-minute drive from the convention hall. Teddy was already too late. He decided, despite the weather and the pilot's concerns, that he would fly into Barnes. Ed Moss had told Crimmins to be there, waiting with the car, by 11:00 P.M.

At 11:05, the dispatcher in the Barnes control room told Crimmins he'd just been in radio contact with Teddy's pilot and, due to poor weather, the flight would be slightly delayed.

Crimmins could see the weather for himself: thick fog, light drizzle, seemingly no visibility at all.

Five minutes later, the dispatcher told Crimmins that because of the fog Teddy's pilot must have decided not to try a landing at Barnes after all, that he must have diverted to Bradley. At least, he'd broken off radio contact.

Crimmins called the convention hall to report this to Teddy's chief aide there. If the plane landed at Bradley, no one would be there to meet him and it would be at least another hour before Teddy arrived at the convention. Crimmins left the Barnes airfield to make the short drive to the convention hall, hoping that by the time he got there somebody who knew what the hell was going on might deign to tell him.

Under the best of circumstances, Jack Crimmins was a man with a low irritation threshold, and all these delays and changes of plans had left him fuming. Crimmins liked to take a drink or two in the evening, a pleasure that thus far he'd had to forgo. Now, if he was going to have to drive halfway to Hartford and back again, it would be 2:00 A.M. before he was finally off the road and able to unwind.

As he left Barnes and turned onto the main road, he saw several police cruisers racing past, lights flashing, heading north, which was not the direction he was going.

He turned on his car radio and heard the bulletin immediately. Teddy's plane had crashed while trying to land at Barnes. Teddy, believed to be alive but badly injured, was being rushed by ambulance to a nearby hospital.

"Sonofabitch!" Crimmins said. He turned and headed not toward the convention hall but back to the private home where he knew Joan was waiting.

The plane had left Washington at 8:35. Normally, in the twin-engined, six-seat Aero Commander, the flight would take an hour and twenty minutes.

They'd be on the ground by ten, Teddy said. He had a car waiting. It would take less than half an hour to pick up Joan and get to the convention hall. A 10:30 arrival, then. That wouldn't be too bad.

Birch Bayh joked that it wouldn't be too good, either. That from his limited knowledge of Democratic politics in Massachusetts he doubted there would be a delegate left still standing by 10:30 P.M. and he was certain that even if there were, they'd be in no condition to hear a belated keynote speech delivered by a senator from Indiana.

Teddy assured Bayh that he would give him such an introduction that the crowd would think they were about to hear Lincoln at Gettysburg. Bayh jokingly warned Teddy not to overdo it: he said the speech his staff had prepared was good, but not that good.

Once they were airborne, Teddy had seemed to relax a bit. He was sitting directly behind the pilot, Zimny, facing the rear of the plane. Ed Moss was in the front seat, next to Zimny. Bayh and his wife were sitting side by side at the rear, facing Teddy and able to converse with him.

Teddy turned to ask Zimny about the report of bad weather in Springfield. The pilot said there were numerous pockets of thunderstorms from New York City north, and drizzle spreading across western Massachusetts. By the time they reached the hills around Springfield, visibility could pose a problem, but he assured Teddy that the Aero Commander was equipped for instrument landings. He did warn, however, that the flight would take longer than expected because he'd be detouring around the worst of the turbulence associated with the thunderstorms.

At forty-eight, Zimny was the oldest man aboard the plane. Both Bayh and his wife were in their thirties. Zimny had been flying since the 1930s and had, in fact, been a combat pilot in World War II, just like Joe Junior.

Teddy joked that it was probably a good thing that Dan Hogan had his Yale reunion. He said that as an amateur pilot himself, he always felt better with a professional— especially if the weather was iffy. But then he stressed that he was already hours late and would appreciate it if Zimny could get them to the Barnes airfield as quickly as possible, even if it meant a bit of turbulence.

As the small plane jounced through the darkness, Teddy, with increasing impatience, kept glancing at his watch. His surface affability was wearing thin. Birch Bayh was one of the brightest and nicest members of the Senate and Teddy liked his wife, Marvella, too, but it had been a long week for all of them, finally pushing the civil rights bill through, and they were tired.

Teddy would take pleasure in the hero's welcome he knew he'd receive at the convention. Just two years ago, Eddie McCormack had actually thought he could deny Teddy the delegates' endorsement. He'd failed in embarrassing fashion, just as tonight, Teddy knew, he was failing again as Peabody routed Bellotti.

But this business of being treated as the personification of Jack every waking minute caused internal strains at many levels. To Bayh, who was immensely fond of Teddy and who'd been an ardent admirer of Jack's, it seemed obvious that the demands of the past six months had extracted a high price from the youngest brother. Teddy seemed brittle; stretched taut.

Bayh sensed that Teddy had been comforted by the cloak of invisibility he'd worn throughout his first ten months in the Senate. It had been almost a security blanket. Suddenly and tragically—and having had no time whatever to prepare—he'd become the least invisible man in America, perhaps in the world. The demands and expectations now seemed infinite. As much as he respected Teddy, Bayh sometimes wondered how, in the years ahead, he would ever manage to meet them all.

They were falling farther and farther behind schedule as Zimny wove his way around the thunderstorms. Teddy's mood was turning dark as the night. It would be at least 11:00 P.M., probably later, before the pilot had them on the ground. It might be midnight before Teddy reached the convention. His great day of triumph threatened to turn into one more insufferable marathon.

Then Zimny, who'd been in frequent radio contact with air controllers, turned to report that the weather had worsened beyond his most pessimistic expectations.

Conditions at the tiny Barnes airfield were now marginal even for an instrument landing. By far the more prudent course would be to divert to Bradley Field. Not only was the airport itself much larger and better equipped, but the terrain around it was not nearly so treacherous as the fog-draped hills that surrounded Barnes.

Absolutely not, Teddy said. Goddamnit, they were late enough already. This was an Aero Commander equipped for an instrument landing, Zimny was an experienced pilot licensed to make instrument landings and Teddy expected him to land at Barnes. He had no intention of diverting to Bradley.

Zimny was not a squeamish man. He was also not lacking in confidence. It was annoying to have an amateur pilot with limited experience looking over his shoulder and second-guessing his every move, but this was, after all, Teddy Kennedy, and Zimny knew both how important the occasion of his renomination was and how late they were for it.

If the Senator wanted to try for Barnes in the fog, with only an eight-hundred-foot ceiling and even that falling fast, well, Zimny would try for Barnes in the fog.

He was five miles from the runway at 11:00 P.M., descending at a rate of five hundred feet per minute. He banked sharply and turned for his final approach. The fog was so dense, Bayh said later, "it was like flying through a black void."

Bayh also could sense Teddy's heightened tension as the plane continued its blind descent. Teddy apparently had unfastened his seat belt and was half standing, twisted in his seat, looking closely at the instrument panel.

Bayh suggested that maybe that bigger airport in Connecticut wasn't such a bad idea, after all.

"Let's give the pilot every chance," Teddy replied. He himself had never had a fear of flying, though as a pilot he had often inspired stark terror in his passengers. Reckless and heedless, Teddy flew a plane the way he drove a car: as if no harm could ever come to him, or else as if he simply didn't care whether or not it did.

With the altimeter showing the plane at eleven hundred feet, Zimny lowered his wing flaps and landing gear. The instrument approach called for him to fly to a predesignated point beyond the runway, maintaining an altitude of at least eight hundred feet, and to notify ground control when he was over it.

But Zimny apparently wanted to get lower. He may not have been entirely comfortable with the instrument approach he'd been instructed to use. He may have wanted to get below the fogbank and see the runway himself before finally committing to a landing.

Still half standing, his jaw now clenched, Teddy looked at the altimeter. Zimny was continuing to descend. He did not level off at eight hundred feet as instructed; he went lower. Zimny had apparently chosen to trust his instincts, not the instruments.

They came out of the fog at six hundred feet, still three miles short of the runway. But the ground was not where it was supposed to be. The ground—or at least the tops of trees—had reached up to meet them.

Bayh saw a momentary flash of what appeared to be white clouds just outside the window of the plane. Later, he realized they must have been apple blossoms. For the fog had obscured an apple orchard covering the ridge of a hill that was three hundred feet higher than the landing strip. A hill and an apple orchard that Zimny had not known about, had not expected to be there.

"I could see the trees," Teddy said later. "We seemed to be riding along the tops of them. It was like a toboggan ride. I knew we were going to crash."

Too late, Zimny pulled back on the stick and threw full power to the engines, hoping to regain altitude. But the plane was already in the trees. Nose down, it plunged toward the ground, tree branches shearing off parts of both wings. As the plane struck the earth, its momentum caused it to cartwheel forward, then plow seventy-five yards farther through the orchard as the roof of its cabin was torn off.

The Aero Commander 680 finally came to rest with its crumpled cockpit smashed against one apple tree and its largely intact tail section pressing against another.

Bayh was first to speak. He turned to his wife, asking how she was.

"I'm all right," she said, but in a very weak voice. Then Bayh became aware of the ominous odor of gasoline and realized that the plane might explode at any moment.

He called to Teddy. There was no answer. Teddy, half standing at the moment of impact, had been thrown about the cabin like an oversized rag doll.

Now he was sprawled across the floor of the plane. "He lay there inert and motionless," Bayh said later. "I was sure he was gone."

Bayh could not even see into the crumpled cockpit but he heard no sounds of motion, no sounds of life. His own left side felt numb and his right hip hurt badly but, smelling the gasoline, he knew he had to get himself and his wife out of the plane and away from it before it exploded.

He pushed Marvella out through a shattered rear window. Then, with her help, he managed to pull himself out. The two of them stumbled down the hillside in fog and drizzle.

They were perhaps fifty yards from the plane when Bayh realized he would have to do something about Teddy. Maybe Teddy was not dead but only unconscious. Bayh could see the red taillight of the plane still spinning and blinking in the darkness. He knew this meant that at least a portion of the plane's electrical system was still functioning. Electricity—perhaps sparks— and a smashed and leaking fuel tank were the most dangerous combination imaginable.

The last thing in the world Birch Bayh wanted to do was return to that airplane, which might explode like a keg of dynamite at any moment. But he did not hesitate. Teddy was in there, perhaps still alive. Bayh had to help him. Bayh had to try to save him, even at the risk of his own life.

In pain and considerable shock, leaving Marvella at what he considered a safe distance from the plane, he struggled back up the wet and slippery hillside in the dark.

A quick check of the cockpit showed that, whether dead or alive, both Zimny and Moss, their heads covered with blood, were trapped by the twisted metal all around them. It would not be possible to pull them free.

Slowly, however, and with great difficulty, Bayh managed to extricate Teddy's massive, limp body from the crumpled midsection of the plane. Teddy was alive but barely conscious and obviously in terrible pain. Also, he was not able to walk and had no feeling in his legs.

Barely able to walk himself, but half carrying, half dragging Teddy, Bayh staggered down the hillside, away from the plane, which he still feared might explode at any moment. Both the air and the ground all around them seemed filled with white apple blossoms, their sweet scent mingling with the stink of leaking gasoline.

Marvella came back up the hill to meet them. Bayh laid Teddy on the ground. He was groaning, still barely conscious. Marvella put her raincoat over him to keep him warm. This was something she knew you were supposed to do when a person was going into shock. Then they left him there, pleading for water, saying he thought he was paralyzed, and they stumbled toward the road at the bottom of the hill, hoping to flag down a passing motorist and get help.

Zimny was already dead by the time the first state police and ambulances arrived. Moss died seven hours later, during brain surgery, without ever regaining consciousness.

Teddy was taken ten miles by ambulance to Cooley Dickinson Hospital in Northampton, not arriving there until after midnight. Doctors at first did not expect him to survive. It was difficult even to assess the nature and extent of his injuries, but it was obvious that he was in shock; that his back had been badly damaged, probably broken; that a lung had been punctured and that he was suffering from massive internal bleeding.

He was only semiconscious, his face gray, his pulse erratic, his blood pressure, one doctor said, "almost negligible." In the emergency room, he was immediately given blood transfusions and antishock treatment.

As soon as they could, they took X rays. At least two ribs were clearly broken but, worse, three vertebrae on his lower spine appeared to be fractured, with one, a doctor said, "crushed pretty completely." What they could not yet determine was whether or not the spinal cord itself had been injured. If it had, in all probability Teddy would be a paraplegic for the rest of his life.

In those first hours, however, it did not seem likely that the rest of his life would amount to much. The doctors were still not at all sure he would last through the night. He remained in deep shock, his blood pressure still dangerously low, suggesting some sort of internal hemorrhage. They could not tell if his liver, kidneys or spleen might be ruptured. He was also finding it extremely difficult to breathe.

During his first hour in the emergency room, Teddy received three units of whole blood through transfusion to replace what he was losing internally. Through intravenous injection and nasal tube he was also given saline solution and glucose in an attempt to bring him out of shock. Then a tube was inserted in his chest to ease his breathing. All the while, he was kept inside an oxygen tent.

Aware of how serious the injuries to his back were, the emergency room doctors quickly immobilized Teddy on a stretcherlike orthopedic frame. He was in terrible pain, but until they were sure he was no longer in shock, until his breathing improved, and until they could identify the source of the internal bleeding, doctors could not administer painkillers or sedatives.

Within the hour, the press was storming the emergency room door. Another Kennedy had died, or might die at any moment! Joan arrived in the company of Jack Crimmins, looking dazed, wandering around saying repeatedly, almost chanting, "He's going to be all right. I know that he'll be all right."

A phone call was made to Hyannis Port. Bobby was awakened and given the news. By 2:00 A.M. he was in a state police cruiser, speeding west on the Massachusetts Turnpike. Joan made sure that Cardinal Cushing was informed. Teddy's sisters were told. It was decided not to awaken either the crippled Ambassador or Rose. There was no need for them to be told until morning. This was a drill that seemed much too familiar. The reflexes of November still functioned all too well.

Bobby reached the hospital at 4:00 A.M. and immediately demanded to know whether Teddy would be paralyzed. The doctors explained that at this point possible paralysis remained low on the list of concerns. Even by dawn, it was not clear that Teddy would survive.

The internal bleeding continued and doctors were unable to locate the source. If it was the kidney, liver, spleen or bowel, surgery would be required, but Teddy's condition remained so unstable that it seemed unlikely he could survive an immediate operation.

By midmorning, twenty members of the Kennedy family had gathered at the hospital. Cardinal Cushing was on his way from Boston. Jacqueline would be arriving on Sunday. Teddy remained semiconscious, his overall condition still grave. Later, the director of the Cooley Dickinson emergency room would say, "I worked on him for two and a half days. But it was a week before we were sure he was going to live."

This new emergency did not bring out the most cordial aspects of Bobby's personality. He held a snappish midmorning press conference. When asked if this newest tragedy might finally force the family's withdrawal from politics, he said curtly, "The Kennedys intend to stay in public life. There is good luck and bad luck. Good luck is something you make. Bad luck is something you endure."

Then he said he didn't want to answer any more questions, and returned to Teddy's bedside, pausing to have several photographers ejected from the hospital.

None of the family, of course, had been ready for this, but Bobby, still brooding over the causes and implications of what had happened in November, seemed least prepared of all.

By lunchtime, he'd calmed enough to sip a cup of soup in the company of the columnist Jimmy Breslin. "I was just thinking back in there," he said, gesturing to the room where Teddy lay. "If my mother hadn't had any more children after the first four, she would have nothing now. I guess the only reason we've survived is that there are more of us than there is trouble."

But that afternoon, taking a quick walk outside with an aide, Bobby said, "I just don't see how I can do anything now. I think I should just get out of it all. Somebody up there doesn't like us."

He knew, of course, all too many reasons why that might be so.

By Saturday afternoon, the local doctors had been joined by experts from both Boston and Washington. Bobby instructed them all to downplay the seriousness of Teddy's condition. He did not want any sort of death watch kept outside the hospital. He did not want world-wide attention focused on the question of whether yet another Kennedy brother would die.

Teddy's condition was not worsening, but it was clear that the spinal damage was severe. Permanent paralysis from the waist down seemed likely. But of more pressing concern, the doctors emphasized to Bobby, was the continued internal bleeding.

Until they could find a way to stop it, or until it stopped on its own, they could not assure Teddy's survival.

On Sunday, Teddy was told that both the pilot, Zimny, and Ed Moss had died in the crash but that Birch and Marvella Bayh had escaped serious injury. He was also told in detail about his own condition and prognosis. Like Bobby, he seemed more concerned by the question of whether or not he'd walk again than by the question of whether or not he would live. Somehow, it seemed, it would not do to have the youngest, most physically vigorous Kennedy son confined to a wheelchair, like his father.

One did not pick up a fallen standard, one did not carry a torch, if paralyzed from the waist down.

5

AFTER TEN DAYS, THE INTERNAL BLEEDING STOPPED. There had been "severe contusions" of the kidneys, a doctor said, but no surgery had been required. Teddy would live.

He would also walk again someday, though perhaps not as well as before and perhaps only with the aid of a cane. Certainly, he would not be a paraplegic.

For months to come, however, Teddy would have to remain immobilized to permit the vertebrae to heal. It was "probable," a doctor said, that surgery would eventually prove necessary. The procedure would involve taking chips of bone from his pelvis and fusing them to the fractured lumbar vertebrae. Eventually, cartilage would form, strengthening and stabilizing the fractured section. It would be a delicate operation, though probably not life-threatening.

In the meantime—and no one was yet quite sure how long the meantime would be—Teddy would have to lie in an orthopedic device known as a Foster frame, as if he were the filling of a sandwich. At regular intervals, the top half of the frame would be lowered and clamped tight. Then the entire apparatus, with Teddy in the middle, would be slowly turned, so that, always rigid, he could be made to lie alternately on his stomach and back. This regular rotation was meant to improve circulation and minimize the likelihood of bedsores.

Locked into the frame, Teddy could move only his hands and forearms. Despite medication, the pain from his ribs and back was steady and intense. Visits, even from family members, were limited to five minutes. So vital was the need for total immobility that Teddy was not even permitted to speak.

Letters and telegrams arrived from all over the world —forty thousand letters and seven hundred telegrams in the first week alone. Lyndon Johnson sent flowers. Cardinal Cushing led a service in which thousands of Bostonians of all faiths prayed for Teddy's full recovery. People sent cakes, statues of the Blessed Virgin and of various saints, religious medals, baskets of fruit, cookies, cakes, records, books.

For Jack, they had not been able to do this. But Teddy had lived and so people everywhere could show him how much he—how much the idealized Kennedys—meant to them.

The Republican party had eventually chosen an extremely reluctant candidate named Whitmore to run against Teddy in November. His seemed the least enviable task ever faced by a candidate for national office. He opened his campaign, such as it was, by assuring Massachusetts voters that he would say or do nothing that might in any way impede Teddy's recovery. Whitmore virtually apologized for having to run at all and said he hoped that neither Teddy nor members of the Kennedy family nor the citizens of Massachusetts would harbor any ill will toward him. At times, it seemed Whitmore might actually announce his own intention of voting for Teddy.

After three weeks, Teddy was transferred from Cooley Dickinson to the Lahey Clinic at New England Baptist Hospital in Boston, a hundred miles away.

It was one of the most peculiar journeys ever made by an American political figure: a bizarre cross between a lengthy funeral procession and a parade celebrating the coronation of a new, if disabled, monarch.

On the drizzly, misty morning of July 9—weather much like that the night of the crash—Teddy was placed in the back of an air force ambulance, his orthopedic frame carefully secured. He wore blue pajamas and was covered by a white sheet. His chief orthopedic surgeon rode alongside him.

Most of the journey was made on the Massachusetts Turnpike, with the ambulance at the center of a five-car motorcade, two state police cruisers preceding it and two following. To avoid jostling, the driver of the ambulance was instructed not to let his speed exceed thirty-five miles per hour. Thus, thousands of cars and trucks sped past in the turnpike's left lane, but almost all slowed to the pace of the ambulance once drivers realized who was inside.

As the *Globe* reported, "With wide glass windows on both sides of the ambulance, Sen. Kennedy was within open view of the many motorists who passed him en route to Boston. They honked their horns and were rewarded by the hand wave and the famous Kennedy grin."

The ambulance stopped at a rest area in the suburbs of Boston and an aide went into a Howard Johnson's to buy Teddy a hot dog and coffee milkshake. State police kept onlookers well back from the ambulance, but could not silence the cheers and applause from the crowd that formed spontaneously once motorists became aware of the identity of the passenger in the ambulance.

The entire nation remained enamored of the Camelot myth, clung to it tenaciously, as if it were necessary for psychic survival—as, for many, it may have been. Nowhere was this more evident than in Massachusetts. Here, it was as if Teddy were truly a knight of the Round Table, wounded in battle while fighting to preserve the honor of his king.

Having been informed in advance that the ambulance would be exiting the turnpike at Weston, toll collectors, road crew workers and even executives of the Turnpike Authority had rushed to tell members of their families, who, in turn, had flocked to the toll booth at Weston, where they stood patiently in the rain, waiting for a chance to glimpse the fallen hero and wish him godspeed.

The route from the turnpike to the hospital was cleared by a Boston police detail of eighteen patrolmen and eight detectives. The ambulance proceeded at thirty miles per hour, all cross-traffic having been halted at intersections.

The news media, told that this would be the day of Teddy's journey—for media coverage of the event was something that Teddy and his staff wanted to encourage—had acceded to the request that they not disclose the information in advance, so as to minimize the likelihood of a large crowd forming outside the Boston hospital. Enthusiastic well-wishers might get out of control, and any jostling of the frame on which Teddy lay could prove disastrous.

Even so, hundreds of people were standing in the rain outside the hospital when the ambulance arrived at 1:15 P.M. Thirty Boston policemen had been dispatched; they set up barricades to keep the crowd back from the receiving platform where Teddy's stretcher would be taken from the ambulance.

Inside the hospital, every window overlooking the ambulance entrance was filled with patients, nurses, students and doctors, hoping for just the briefest glimpse of Teddy.

The ambulance driver maneuvered carefully in reverse, backing as close as possible to the receiving platform. Waiting there, in addition to the director of the Lahey Clinic, was Francis X. Morrissey, the Ambassador's retainer, who'd been sent by the family to supervise the Boston aspect of the transfer.

Joan, who had ridden from Northampton in the front seat of the ambulance, was first to get out. Hatless in the rain, she was instantly recognized by the crowd and a great cheer went up.

Then, in what seemed to some a macabre parody of the arrival of Jack's casket at the Capitol rotunda, eight bearers carefully slid the frame on which Teddy lay from the ambulance to the receiving platform. They seemed unprepared for his weight and, for just a moment, there was a sense of struggle, of lack of full control. But the bearers quickly adjusted, and the stretcher was carried through the Lahey Clinic entrance as a loud and enthusiastic roar erupted from the crowd.

Newspaper photographers were permitted past the barricades so they could obtain close-up pictures of Teddy, flat on his back but grinning and trying to wave with his right hand, which was still heavily bandaged to cover a deep gash he'd suffered when the plane crashed.

One reporter asked Teddy how he felt.

"Okay," he replied in a weak voice.

Then he was gone, vanished inside the clinic. Some doctors estimated that he might remain there for almost a year, as the damaged vertebrae slowly mended.

The crowd dispersed quietly. Had the press not kept Teddy's arrival time secret, it would have been a crowd of thousands, not hundreds, and these relatively few citizens of Boston who'd somehow been able to learn of the arrival in advance felt privileged. Not only had they gained a glimpse of the valiant warrior, but through their cheers and applause they'd let both him and his brave and glamorous wife know how much he meant to them, and always would.

Unlike Jack, Teddy lived. But he'd come close enough to death to leave all America badly shaken. There were only two Kennedys left now and Teddy was the one with no enemies. While Bobby was still mistrusted and disliked by certain liberals, black activists, Mafia chieftains, J. Edgar Hoover and white supremacists throughout the South, no one felt anything but affection and profound admiration for Teddy: so brave, so youthful, so innocent, so dedicated, so badly hurt.

6

THROUGHOUT THE SUMMER, TEDDY ROTATED SLOWLY
in his Foster frame. When he was lying on his back, the
upper half of the frame was removed, making it easier for
him to breathe, to move his arms and, eventually, his
legs. When he was turned onto his stomach, what had
been the bottom of the frame but was now the top was
removed, permitting attendants to wash and massage
him. The frame, with both halves clamped in place and
Teddy between them, could also be stopped at any point
during its rotation, permitting the force of gravity to exert
varying pressures on different muscles and tissues while
ensuring that his spine remained immobile at all times.

He was in a private suite on the fifth floor of the Lahey
Pavilion. He had a telephone within arm's reach of his
bed. Three other phone lines had been connected to a
room across the hall in which a secretary and two staff
members worked every day.

He would spend the nights on his back. In early morning, he would be turned onto his stomach. His head was
supported and holes had been cut in the canvas rectangle
on which he lay when facedown, enabling him to reach
through with his arms and turn the pages of a newspaper
or book. Occasionally, he would play checkers with one

of the medical attendants who cared for him. He was also fitted for a pair of eyeglasses that produced a prism effect, permitting him to read or to watch television while on his back without having to lift his head.

To that degree, Teddy was functional during much of the summer and fall of 1964. The American public was starved for news of him and of his courageous comeback from the brink of death. To feed this appetite, a sampling of the letters he'd received from well-wishers around the world was made available to the press.

A highlight was Teddy's notification that he'd been made an honorary member of the Foster Framers of America—a group of children confined to Foster frames at the University of Missouri Medical Center.

"We are writing to you because we, too, are Foster framers," the children said. "We are boys and girls (mostly girls), who have had spinal surgery of some sort. We have pretty young student-teachers and student nurses plus handsome young student doctors and male student teachers. Life isn't so bad!" The children enclosed some pictures of themselves in their frames, as well as a collection of poems they had written for Teddy.

There was a recording of an original get-well song, written and sung by a group of nuns in Omaha, a letter from Peace Corps volunteers in Thailand, touching messages from children in Japan, Israel, Australia, Ceylon and, of course, Ireland.

Two special favorites were the letter from an eleven-year-old girl in Torino, Italy, that said, when translated, "My heart has not yet stopped aching on account of the inhuman tragedy in Dallas; now the accident that has befallen you seems a grave injustice of fate," and the note from the boy in Bakersfield, California, that said, "I hope you get well soon. Your family is my idol. I wrote to your brother. I am nine years old."

It was not until July 25, five weeks after the crash, that Teddy first received an extended visit from his children, Kara, four, and Teddy Junior, two.

They were accompanied not only by their mother but by a reporter and photographer from the *Globe*. The resulting story, even for the *Globe*, was strong stuff.

"Strapped to a rigid hospital frame," the *Globe* said,

Sen. Edward M. Kennedy laughed Saturday. He roared loudly at the antics of a frog in a bottle—and at the love in the eyes of his little girl.

Little Kara Kennedy, a laughing-eyed blonde—visited her Daddy at the New England Baptist Hospital and brought him a gift which could only be the idea of a 4-year-old.

She brought him a frog—a croaking, gulping, hopping frog in a milk bottle.

And she handed it to him with the love that only a 4-year-old can show.

Inside the bottle, the frog stared pop-eyed.

The Senator stared for a moment . . . and then he laughed.

Minutes later, Kara and her 2-year-old brother, Teddy, Jr., were laughing, too.

They shrieked and howled and laughed.

And their father laughed with them.

Kara's present croaked and gulped and hopped in his bottle.

And nurses stood in the doorway and smiled.

That was the kind of summer it was for Teddy, rotating slowly in his frame, his reelection by a huge margin assured. In many ways, in fact, he was both more comfortable and more secure that summer and fall than was his wife.

Already distressed by the deterioration of her marriage, by her awareness that there seemed little she could do to control her drinking and by her knowledge that her husband apparently had lost any interest in her he might ever have had—from now until it finally ended in divorce, the marriage would exist solely for Teddy's political and public relations purposes—Joan found herself taxed beyond her abilities.

No matter how energetically his staff worked at feeding the press tidbits of heartwarming information, there was only a limited amount that Teddy, in his Foster frame, could do to keep the torch burning, to keep the magic alive.

Personal contact between the Kennedys and the public was deemed necessary, by Teddy himself, by his staff and by his cadre of energetic and forceful sisters, who seemed to feel now that they were responsible for his performance, his image and his future success. Bobby was his own man, remote and unreachable, but Teddy, especially now that he was bedridden for months, was again reduced to the role of helpless kid brother, while Eunice, Pat and Jean, always in consultation with their mother and with Steve Smith, determined how best to keep afloat Teddy's image as the reincarnation of Jack.

There seemed no alternative but Joan, however inadequate she might have been, and so she was pressed into public—and family—service in a way she never had been before.

For five months, she was made to campaign as he would have: relentlessly, across the state and back again. From Hyannis Port, she would depart by car each day for the kind of immersion in public life that Teddy had come to enjoy so greatly but that Joan had always dreaded and always would.

Starting in early July and continuing up to the night before the election, Joan forced herself to do what Teddy insisted on, and what she hoped might finally earn her some respect. Statistics kept by the campaign staff indicate that Joan visited 39 cities and 312 towns in Massachusetts, making an average of more than eight appearances per day—each one, for her, an ordeal she did not think she could survive.

Tense and trembling, she would stand before enthusiastic crowds and recite, in her soft voice, the innocuous words that had been printed for her on index cards. She could not presume, of course, to talk about the issues. But the issues were of no interest to Massachusetts voters. Teddy's recovery was the only issue, and concerning that Joan delivered frequent and optimistic reports.

"I just came from the hospital," she would say, "and Ted asked me to give you a message. He wants to thank you for your support. I guess he's just about the busiest patient New England Baptist Hospital has ever had. He's keeping up with his mail, with office work that's sent to him from Washington, and running the campaign."

No matter how warm the reception, no matter how glowing the notices in the press—and, without fail, they were positive—Joan later confided to friends that she could never escape the feeling of being a fraud. It did not get easier, only harder. And the end of each day left her even more desperate for enough drinks to finally dull the tension, to drive away the fear.

She was no politician. She did not belong in this family of overachievers, married to a philanderer who neither respected her nor even seemed to like her anymore, but there didn't seem any way out.

At least not in the summer of 1964. The press and the public, as well as the family, demanded that she play the role necessary to sustain the myth.

And so she did, day after day, week after week, at terrible cost to herself. To careful observers, a bit of the reality began to creep in around the edges, though no reporter would dare to write of it because it was not what the people wanted to hear.

"Her face seemed hard," said one who followed her closely as the weeks wore on, "and she didn't seem to smile as much as at the start. She didn't seem to give a shit anymore. A couple of times I saw her and she looked like she had crawled through a rathole. The old Joan wasn't like that, never in a million years. The old Joan was always so beautifully dressed. Jesus, the old Joan would have charmed a bird out of a tree. But now there was something very wrong about her. She just didn't seem to give a damn."

And she was still only twenty-eight years old.

In the public portrait, embellished day after day by newspaper stories that more than occasionally bordered on the giddy, no signs of stress or strain were evident. On the contrary. Joan, that summer, was elevated to the plane previously occupied only by the queenly Jacqueline and the saintly mother, Rose.

"A man never had a prettier stand-in to open his political campaign as Sen. Edward M. Kennedy had Monday," the *Globe* said on September 15. "Mrs. Joan Kennedy, blonde and beautiful, stood up before 400 persons and asked them to support her husband . . ."

As the campaign, such as it was, progressed against poor Whitmore, whose name Joan could scarcely remember, veneration of her intensified.

"Ted's beautiful blonde wife Joan, displaying keen wit and a delicate sensitivity to social issues which were always the trademark of her husband, reaches deep into her reservoir of energy and courage to take his place on public platforms, her warm charm and keen rapport with audiences linking the absent Senator closely to the people," began a not untypical story in the *Boston Traveler*.

The *Traveler* also reported that Joan had "something real going for her—the magic combination of genuine warmth, an almost naive simplicity and an empathy for the little people. Her heavy schedule would leave most old pros hanging on the ropes. But the plane accident that would have crushed the spirit of a less valiant woman has brought its consolations to Joan Kennedy, who, for all her Dresden-china fragility, is strong as steel."

Among these consolations, the newspaper said, was the opportunity that Joan and Teddy now had to enjoy some of life's simple pleasures, which until the plane crash Teddy's busy schedule had placed beyond their grasp.

"We listen to operas together," Joan said, "following the librettos of *La Bohème, La Traviata* and *Madame Butterfly*—all the popular ones."

And Shakespeare, too. "Ted's mother sent him Shakespeare's complete plays on records and we love to listen to them," she said. "Wasn't that a thoughtful gift? She has a talent for choosing the perfect present."

For Joan, the strain of concocting such fairy tales on an almost daily basis was almost as great as that of campaigning. The combination—wherein she saw herself portrayed as someone unrecognizable to herself; someone who did not, and could not, exist—caused her to become increasingly befuddled and distressed as time passed.

Even Teddy must have occasionally been startled by the ease with which it was possible to create an image that had nothing whatsoever in common with reality. It was not who you were that mattered, his father had preached, but only what people thought you were. But how easy it was, at least during that summer of 1964, to make them think anything you wanted.

In just two years, having done little more than passively endure the grief of Jack's assassination and survive the plane crash that broke his back, Teddy had gone from being an unqualified, arrogant interloper, whose very Senate candidacy was an insult to the democratic process, to becoming a man seemingly better suited for canonization—even while still living—than mere reelection, no matter how wide the margin.

By late summer, doctors determined that he'd need no spinal surgery. The vertebrae were slowly healing on their own. Recurrent rumors that Teddy would be a cripple for the rest of his life were laid to rest by the director of the Lahey Clinic, who said that while Teddy would be confined to his frame until December and would remain at the clinic until at least February, his eventual recovery would be complete.

The *Globe* editorial the next day was headed, quite appropriately, "Good News."

It said: "Among the grim headlines about the world's crises comes the news that Sen. Kennedy can look forward to complete recovery from his back injury without the need of surgery. This is glad tidings—for his family, for all Americans, indeed for people of all lands.

"The warmly human qualities possessed by the Kennedys have evoked wide admiration, here and abroad. Throughout his long ordeal, Ted has displayed that courage which his brother, the late President, quoting Ernest

Hemingway, defined as 'grace under pressure . . .' This is no surprise, knowing the family tradition . . .''

The day after the September primary, although Teddy had been automatically renominated with no opponent, the *Globe* added yet more rhetorical flourishes. A *Globe* reporter had been summoned to Teddy's bedside the night before, as the results of the primary election were broadcast on television.

"The young, vibrant voice, so familiar to his devoted supporters—and so tragically reminiscent of the voice stilled by an assassin's bullet—remained soft," the story began.

The vigorous, rugged body and the quick arms that would ordinarily have moved in triumph were restrained.

The infectious smile of a confident man, a winning smile which would have flashed on Page One and the TV screens was lost in the quiet of a hospital room.

There, strapped to a frame to make him rigidly immobile, lay the leader of the Democratic Party in Massachusetts, Sen. Edward M. Kennedy.

His back broken, his crusade delayed, the youthful political warrior lay restless.

Tragedy had imprisoned him and had deprived him of a politician's glory on the night of a primary victory.

There could be no tours of the precincts, no speeches, no handshakes, no victorious reunion with his brothers and sisters.

He had no opposition, but it was a night of victory because the voters had used their X's to wish him well and speedy recovery.

By fall, a new thrust of the publicity emanating from the private suite in the Lahey Pavilion was that the Teddy who would finally emerge from seclusion would be very different from the man who had entered—culturally enriched, intellectually stimulated and possessing a profound new awareness of the meaning of life and of man's ultimate place in the universe.

He would no longer be merely an effective senator, no longer simply the best available personification of Jack, but, in his own right, something of a philosopher king. It was widely reported that some of the most luminous members of the faculties of Harvard and MIT were brought in on a regular basis to conduct bedside seminars. Without exception, these renowned academics reported to the press that Teddy was a young man of astonishing depth and maturity, who was using his long convalescence to toughen his mind and to commune more deeply with his soul.

Though a nurse imprudently reported that most of his reading time seemed to be devoted to James Bond spy novels, the phone lines that led from the office across the hall from his hospital room hummed with news of a quite different reading list.

It would have made even his mother—or Joey Gargan—proud. No Fox or Burke, but a biography of Franklin D. Roosevelt (one that, presumably, did not go on at undue length about FDR's ultimate assessment of Teddy's father), the collected papers of the Adams family of Massachusetts, after whom the Kennedys were said to be modeling themselves, Winston Churchill's multivolume history of World War II (again, not a series Teddy's father had much enjoyed) and the collected poetry of Robert Frost, who had recited at Jack's inauguration.

The pattern was clear: Teddy would emerge from the hospital as his own man intellectually, no longer beholden to the outmoded ideas of his father, however beloved his father continued to be. Or, if not as his own man, then as an even purer reincarnation of Jack.

Not included on the reading list was the "Report of the Warren Commission on the Assassination of President Kennedy." A press aide said that Teddy had not read the report, which was issued in late September, nor did he ever intend to.

He was, however, like all other members of his family, fully satisfied that the commission's exhaustive investigation had answered any and all pertinent questions about the circumstances surrounding the assassination, and he dearly hoped that the issuance of the report would lay to rest the whole tragic matter, which continued to be such a source of acute pain for the family.

At the time, and under the circumstances, one would have been deemed gauche in the extreme were one to wonder aloud or in print just how and why, if he'd not even bothered to glance at the evidentiary materials upon which the assessment was based, Teddy could have been so easily satisfied that the Warren Commission's conclusion—that Lee Harvey Oswald had acted alone, from obscure motives, unaided by any conspirators—was correct.

Thirty years later, however, one may wonder. For this very conclusion that Teddy accepted so quickly, so eagerly, so gratefully, was the only one the family could live with comfortably; the only one that would not taint, or even destroy, the myth.

Upon learning of Jack's murder, Malcolm X had said, "The chickens have come home to roost." This comment, Harris Wofford has written,

> may have had more meaning and caused more pain to Robert Kennedy than any of us imagined at the time. Not because Malcolm knew anything special about the killer or killers, but because of what the Attorney General knew. It put into words a thought Robert Kennedy must have dreaded. Was he, to some significant extent, directly or indirectly, responsible for his brother's death?
>
> Given the facts known to Robert Kennedy . . . he could not have avoided asking himself some or all of the following questions:
>
> Had he and his brother, by unleashing the forces of counter-insurgency against Castro, started a process that led finally to the President's own assassination?
>
> By pressing the CIA to use any means short of war to destroy the Cuban regime, had they encouraged the unholy alliance with the Mafia? . . .

By pursuing a campaign against the Mafia, including the very Mafia leaders with whom the CIA had contracted for Castro's murder, had he incited them to conspire to kill the President?

Was the President's own relationship with a woman closely connected with the CIA's Mafia conspirators in any way involved in his death at Dallas?

Given his knowledge of all these circumstances—and others, such as his father's secret meeting with Mafia leaders at the Cal-Neva Lodge, Jack's secret meetings with Giancana, Jack's use of Judith Campbell to deliver envelopes to Giancana on a regular basis—Bobby, as Wofford has written, "would not have wanted the Warren Commission or any other public body to pursue these questions."

Nor would Teddy, now that he presumably knew at least a large part of the truth. But the secrets shared with him after the murder of Jack not only must have caused Teddy to lose belief in family and self, but at some unconscious level also may have angered him so deeply that the adverse effects would display themselves for the rest of his life.

The very people he'd loved and trusted most—the only people he'd truly loved and trusted—his father, Jack and Bobby, the people for whose approval he'd labored so hard and so long, had lied to him and had misled him about matters of the most profound significance; had played him for the fool they so clearly thought he was.

One might repress the rage triggered by the discovery of such betrayal but one does not easily or quickly dispel it. He'd always been the family's outsider, pleading for acceptance from the godlike older figures who comprised the inner circle. He'd lived in the cold far shadows while they had gathered, backs to him, close to the source of the flame, not only warmed and illuminated by it but transformed.

All his life, Teddy had yearned for similar transformation. But now, just at the moment when he seemed to have attained it, he'd found that the fire's glow had been only an illusion.

Teddy was finally an insider, but his achievement had turned out to be a nightmare rather than the fulfillment of a childhood dream. Only now that he was fully inside what he had always considered the charmed circle did he find that it was a circle of hell.

7

IN THE MONTHS SINCE JACK'S DEATH, BOBBY HAD BE-
come the Kennedy without a kingdom, wandering in
solitude across the scorched earth, the parched land, afflicted not only by sadness but by guilt.

As he silently reflected upon Jack's fate and the role
he'd played in it, as he struggled against the realization
that the malignancy that had so violently destroyed his
brother emanated from the family's very core, Bobby
had come close to turning away in despair from the still-
unfinished business of family and country.

After Teddy's plane crash, however, Bobby realized
that he could not simply put his burden down. He would
have to trudge onward, especially now that Teddy, at
least temporarily, could not.

"He was being pushed forward by a momentum outside him," said Bobby's friend and eventual successor as
attorney general, Ramsey Clark. "He was carrying on
less because he really wanted to than because people had
told him he had to."

And even more important than those who might actually have told him were those no longer able to tell him
anything, but whose voices still echoed loudest within

his soul: his stricken father and the indelible image of Jack.

"For Bob," Ramsey Clark said, "the important thing was now the memory of the President. He wanted it to be pure and golden."

As with Teddy, it was by continuing in public life—by enlarging and expanding the Kennedy myth through further achievement—that Bobby could best assure that the memory did not tarnish. But there Bobby faced a thorny problem: he could not remain as attorney general, serving under Lyndon Johnson, a man whom he scorned as deeply as Johnson despised him.

In late summer he resolved his problem by choosing to run for a Senate seat from New York. As with Teddy in 1962, however, denunciation was swift and harsh and came from many quarters. Bobby, who owned homes both in Massachusetts, where he was registered to vote, and in Virginia, was called a carpetbagger. Charges of arrogance and ruthlessness, of insolence and greed, of power-madness and dynastic ambition and disrespect for the principles of democracy were quickly raised.

The New York Times said in an editorial that the question of "why he has any special claim on New York to rescue him from non-office is a mystery. The cold fact is that Mr. Kennedy appears to have decided that his ambitions will be best and most immediately served by finding a political launching pad in New York State. If his brother were not already representing Massachusetts in the Senate, Mr. Kennedy undoubtedly would have run in that state. But to run now would mean that he would have to elbow out another Kennedy. Thus, Mr. Kennedy apparently needs New York. But does New York really need Bobby Kennedy?"

He didn't seem sure of the answer himself. "They're for him," he said to one aide after an especially enthusiastic crowd response. "They're for Jack."

"He hated himself," a state party official said later. "He was being purely and simply President Kennedy's brother." This was a feat Teddy had managed without self-loathing. But Bobby was a very different sort of man.

Near the end, an aide finally shouted at him, "Get out

of your daze! God damn, Bob, be yourself. Get hold of yourself. You're real. Your brother's dead."

He never quite succeeded in emerging from the daze but, combining the power of the myth with his limitless fortune, he won anyway, although his margin of victory over incumbent Senator Kenneth Keating was less than one third that of Lyndon Johnson's over Republican presidential candidate Barry Goldwater in New York.

Teddy encountered no such difficulties at the polls. Still strapped to his frame, he won reelection by more than a million votes, more than four times the margin by which he'd defeated George Lodge two years earlier. Whitmore conceded even before the polls closed. It was, and would remain, the most one-sided triumph ever recorded by a candidate for national office in Massachusetts.

Bobby arrived for a visit the next day. Teddy's frame was wheeled onto a sun porch outside his room so the two of them could pose for photographs.

At one point, Bobby's shadow fell over Teddy's face.

"Watch your shadow," a photographer said to Bobby. "It's in the way."

Flat on his back, Teddy said, "It will be the same in Washington."

On the first anniversary of the assassination, Bobby donned Jack's old aviator jacket, adorned with the Presidential seal, and drove to Arlington to kneel before the eternal flame and pray at the grave.

Returning home, he said to a friend, "You know, I had a conversation with him a couple of days before it happened. He had called to wish me a happy birthday. The thing is, I can't remember what he said. I've tried and tried and I can't remember. I've searched my mind over and over."

Jacqueline contributed a short essay to a special commemorative issue of *Look* magazine, published just prior to the anniversary.

She wrote:

It is nearly a year since he has gone.

On so many days—his birthday, an anniversary, watching his children run to the sea—I have thought, "But this day last year was his last to see that." He was so full of love and life on those days. He seems so vulnerable now, when you think that each one was a last time.

Soon the final day will come around again—as inexorably as it did last year. But expected this time.

It will find some of us different people than we were a year ago. Learning to accept what was unthinkable when he was alive changes you.

I don't think there is any consolation. What was lost cannot be replaced . . .

Now I think I should have known that he was magic all along. I did know it—but I should have guessed it could not last. I should have known that it was asking too much to dream that I might have grown old with him and seen our children grow up together.

So now he is a legend, when he would have preferred to be a man. . . .

The same might have been said of Teddy when he finally left the hospital in mid-December, two months earlier than predicted. Teddy, too, was a legend now, even if he might have preferred to be a man, and from this point forward nothing that might affect the public's perception of him could be left to chance.

His departure from the hospital came just after 9:00 A.M. The night staff had remained on duty late in order to bid him good-bye and a crowd numbering in the hundreds had gathered. One woman held up a homemade placard that said, "On your back or on your feet . . . You're the man that can't be beat."

In subfreezing temperatures, he stood before a microphone in front of the hospital and said, "I just happen to have with me a speech that I didn't get a chance to make at the Democratic convention in West Springfield."

Humor. There must always be self-deprecating humor. That enhanced the sense of valor. That showed the human side. It was a concept Jack had elevated to an art form.

From the hospital, accompanied by his wife and by a *Globe* reporter, he proceeded to Boston's Logan Airport. There, too, a crowd was waiting.

As the *Globe* reported, "Admiration for Kennedy welled in the 200 persons who saw him off. He walked erect from the car. His step was slow and halting, but sure-footed as he climbed the ramp stairs into the plane.

"The same feeling flowed among his fellow passengers as he stepped inside the cabin.

" 'Amazing,' said one.

" 'He's got a lot of courage,' said another."

Then the plane took off for Florida. Teddy would continue his convalescence at Palm Beach. The *Globe* reporter stayed, so that in the days that followed, Boston readers could see such headlines as: "Ted's Courage Prevails," "Children Elated to See Ted," "Ted Takes First Swim."

The reporter was close at hand when Teddy, "in blue bathing trunks and a plastic coated steel frame from neck to waist," first approached the swimming pool.

"It looks longer than it used to," Teddy quipped. Then he said, "This is going to be quite a challenge." Then, gesturing toward his four-pound brace, he said, "I'll probably go right to the bottom with this thing on."

He did not, of course. "Taking methodical free-style strokes," the *Globe* reported, "the 31-year-old Senator moved easily through the specially heated ocean water which had been pumped into the pool. With an easy stroke, he swam the full 60-foot distance, and for him a day's work was done."

The swim was followed by "a quiet lunch with his father." The *Globe* reporter was not invited to attend.

8

AT 11:53 A.M. ON JANUARY 4, 1965—A BRIGHT, chilly day, much like the one on which Jack had been buried—Bobby and Teddy, each with one hand thrust into a side pocket of his suit jacket in the manner made so familiar by Jack, walked side by side through the main doorway of the Capitol and onto the Senate floor.

It would be the first time in more than 150 years that two brothers would serve simultaneously in the Senate. In addition, the swearing in of Bobby would mark the first occasion in American history that three brothers had ever served as United States senators.

For Teddy, this moment of reentry into the Senate was also a personal triumph. Having come so close to death and to permanent paralysis, having been told he'd remain hospitalized until at least February, Teddy had made a private vow: to be walking unaided and to be out of the hospital by Christmas.

He had fulfilled that commitment to himself. Now, much to the surprise and delight of his colleagues, many of whom had expected him to return in a wheelchair or with an aluminum walker, or on crutches at the very least, he walked unsupported across the Senate floor—

stiffly because of the back brace he wore, but carrying only a silver-handled cane.

The spectators' gallery was packed. Teddy was not the only one aware of the historic significance of this occasion. The two brothers of the martyred President, together now to carry forward the fallen standard. And one day, no doubt, to reclaim the keys to the mythic kingdom.

All senators elected in November—whether or not they'd already been serving—were required to take the oath of office. Bobby and Teddy were sworn in together. After they had completed the words of the oath, spectators in the galleries burst forth with applause, then loud cheering. For all present, it was another in the series of dramatic moments the Kennedys doled out to America so frequently.

The next day, Teddy's colleagues rose, one by one, to welcome him back and to praise him. Birch Bayh, who'd risked his own life in order to save Teddy's, spoke first.

"The junior senator from Massachusetts will be written in history as one of the great men," Bayh said, comparing Teddy to Winston Churchill.

Teddy's colleague from Massachusetts, the Republican Leverett Saltonstall, said, "I have admired the courage, the morale, the patience and the frustration he has undergone in the hospital."

Daniel Inouye of Hawaii, a man who'd lost an arm during combat in World War II, recalled Jack's book *Profiles in Courage* and said, "A new chapter should be added, titled 'The Courage and Perseverance of Our Beloved Junior Senator from Massachusetts.'"

On and on the words of praise flowed—the session eventually taking on an eerie resemblance to the day when so many of these same men had stood to offer similar tributes to Jack.

As the afternoon progressed, it became apparent to observers that here, in the Senate, Teddy was not an outsider anymore. If it was home and family he'd always yearned for, he'd found it here.

And here, in this family, in this home, he was accepted as an equal: not made to eat at a separate table, not shunted from boarding school to boarding school, not finding that only paid retainers took pride in his accomplishments and shared his sorrow at insults and slights.

He soon made clear, however, that he no longer intended to defer automatically to the wishes of his elders, as he had done when first elected. The period of apprenticeship was behind him. If not yet ready to become a Senate leader, he was at least prepared to take an active role on issues to which he responded emotionally. Chief among these, in early 1965, remained racial discrimination.

Lyndon Johnson, moving beyond the original civil rights bill presented to Congress by Jack, had introduced even more ambitious voting rights legislation which had already won the support of both Mansfield, the majority leader, and Republican minority leader Everett Dirksen.

One provision directed the attorney general to seek a ruling from the Supreme Court on whether poll taxes required by four southern states as a precondition for voting in state and local elections violated the Constitution by discriminating against Negroes. A constitutional amendment had already prohibited the collecting of poll taxes in federal elections, but Alabama, Mississippi, Texas and Virginia still required a voter to pay a fee before voting in state and local elections.

The bill, as written, was fully supported not only by Senate leaders, both Democratic and Republican, but by Nicholas Katzenbach, Bobby's successor as attorney general, and Burke Marshall, former head of the department's civil rights division and a lawyer whose judgment and expertise both Bobby and Teddy had come to respect deeply.

But in a sudden move that startled all who knew him, Teddy, calling the poll tax nothing more than a device used to prevent Negroes from voting, announced he would lead a fight to attach to the bill an amendment that would immediately abolish all poll taxes in every state, without waiting for the Supreme Court to consider the matter.

First, Katzenbach tried to talk him out of it, arguing

407

that such a flat and universal ban might well be ruled unconstitutional. "What principle requires us to gamble in so important a matter," Katzenbach asked him, "when the same result can be more surely, more safely and more swiftly assured in another way?"

Then, using much the same argument, Burke Marshall tried. For Teddy, these men, like Mansfield and Dirksen, had always been authority figures. Older, wiser men to whose judgment he reflexively deferred.

But no more. Now—and one can only speculate as to the degree to which this new independence was fueled by his unconscious anger at having been so badly misled regarding the essential nature of his family—he would strike out on his own, regardless of the wishes and advice of those to whom he normally would have deferred, including his own brother, Bobby.

So it did no good when Mike Mansfield explained to Teddy that the amendment he was advocating, in addition to being of dubious constitutionality, might prompt a filibuster by segregationist southern senators that would kill the bill in its entirety.

Working harder than he'd ever worked before—harder even than when he'd campaigned against Eddie McCormack—Teddy persuaded thirty-eight senators to cosponsor his amendment.

From Selma, Alabama, even Martin Luther King offered his support, saying that for the Senate to pass a voting rights bill that did not include an outright ban on all poll taxes everywhere would be "an insult and blasphemy."

The Washington establishment, so finely attuned to nuance, expressed shock at first, then admiration for Teddy's unanticipated boldness.

In public, as *Time* magazine noted, Teddy had "established himself as a pleasant young man who listens respectfully to his elders." But no more.

"He has been a teacher's pet on Capitol Hill," Mary McGrory wrote, "a most docile and responsive freshman." But no more.

"I never thought Teddy would have the guts to buck

Lyndon," one veteran senator said. "We felt he was too soft to try anything like this."

But they didn't understand either the source of his energy or, perhaps, the force of his rage. In a private meeting with Mansfield, Teddy was said to have "exploded." The *Globe* reported that "Mansfield, who shares in the widespread Senate affection for the younger Kennedy, was taken aback by the surprising burst of ferocity."

The vote on Teddy's amendment came on May 10. Both Mansfield and Dirksen rose to speak against it. "Let's resolve this matter as it ought to be resolved," said Dirksen, perhaps the Senate's most florid orator, "with a proper respect for our states and our federal-state system. If Congress can tell the states by statute that they cannot impose a poll tax," he demanded, "why not tell them they cannot impose a cigarette tax or any other tax?"

Mansfield's objection was more pragmatic than ideological. "The choice," he said, "is between the course of risk and the course of sureness, the course of speed and the course of possible delay." He said the provision already in the bill which instructed the attorney general to seek immediate clarification from the Supreme Court "avoids any constitutional doubts."

But then, said the *Globe,* "In a rare moment of high drama, young Teddy, his once-broken back tightly braced, rose to his feet to argue in that unmistakable accent and with those painfully familiar gestures."

He wore a navy blue suit and a *PT 109* tie clasp. While speaking, he leaned heavily on his silver-headed cane. His remarks were brief and cogent.

"It is a settled constitutional doctrine that where Congress finds an evil to exist, as in the economic burden in this case, it can apply a remedy.

"This has been my first opportunity to assume the responsibility for a major piece of legislation. We are not in disagreement about what we are attempting to accomplish, but about methods. I say that we ought to do the job if we're going to do it, and do it right now."

In the end, the vote against Teddy's amendment was only 49–45, closer than anyone had expected—except perhaps Teddy, who'd been in round-the-clock consultation with his colleagues, trying persistently but gracefully to win their support.

The press was quick to proclaim that despite the outcome the episode had been a significant triumph for Teddy. Saying, "He went down with flying colors," Mary McGrory, in *The Washington Post,* called it his "bar mitzvah," adding that "with his performance on the poll tax amendment, he earned the right not to be called 'The Kid' anymore."

The *New York Herald Tribune,* never an automatic source of praise for any Kennedy, was even more rhapsodic. "In waging perhaps the most thorough parliamentary campaign since Lyndon Johnson left Capitol Hill, the 'new boy,' the once sheltered darling of the Senate, came into his own. At 33, Ted Kennedy won a stunning political victory that reflected both the talent of his late brother John F. Kennedy for organization and brother Bobby's zest for competition. Yet the resulting brew—a dash of charm, an ounce of tact and gallons of 100-proof learning—was strictly Teddy's own making."

Time said Teddy had "handled himself with a skill and a cool political opportunism that bodes well for his future."

And Richard Strout of the *Christian Science Monitor* and *New Republic* wrote that while "John F. Kennedy made the family voice and accent nationally known—he scattered stardust over the family—" Teddy was proving, even more than Bobby, a worthy successor. "Teddy, many here think, is more relaxed and has more political appeal than his brother. He has a sharp, aquiline nose and a toothpaste smile. In the Senate debate he was the very picture of the handsome young hero in a Hollywood script. It seems impossible that Presidential ambitions have not occurred."

Indeed, not long afterwards, the mayor of San Francisco introduced Teddy to the audience at a fund-raising dinner as the "future President of the United States."

And the June 5 issue of the *Saturday Evening Post* had his picture on the cover, under the headline "Teddy Kennedy: Is he running for President?"

By midyear, whatever his private torments, his public star was shining more brightly than ever.

Back in Massachusetts to deliver the commencement address at Northeastern University, Teddy made his strongest statement yet on racial imbalance in public schools, declaring flatly that it was wrong, that local authorities should eliminate it, and that state and federal educational funds should be withheld from any district that failed to achieve full integration.

Given the extent of the de facto segregation that existed within the public schools of Boston, these remarks were not uncontroversial. Nor was his attack upon the Boston School Committee for its recent firing of a twenty-eight-year-old temporary teacher named Jonathan Kozol for having had the temerity to introduce his largely Negro class to the work of Negro poet Langston Hughes.

"It does not serve the cause of goodwill nor the cause of education when teachers are punished for using, in the teaching of Negro students, books and poems that relate directly to the conditions under which the children live.

"We may deplore the noisy demonstrations around our public buildings, but we cannot deny the facts of injustice that brought them about.

"How can we be satisfied with our state when ten thousand Negro children go to racially imbalanced schools? How can we be satisfied when the annual income of Negroes in Massachusetts is forty-three percent less than that of whites? How can we be satisfied when almost every Negro is restricted to an inferior neighborhood as the place to raise his family?"

Teddy's looks may have resembled Jack's, his mannerisms may have resembled Jack's and his voice may have seemed eerily similar to Jack's, but these were words that no Kennedy before Teddy had ever uttered in Massachusetts; words that articulated concepts no Kennedy before Teddy had so plainly considered to involve not only law but morality.

And the next day, when he was bitterly denounced by Boston School Committee Chairman Louise Day Hicks for interfering in matters that were not his proper concern, Teddy reiterated that this was one state issue in which he intended to remain deeply involved, whether or not it seemed politically expedient.

Later in the week, he drove to western Massachusetts. At sunset, on the evening of June 27, still leaning on his silver-handled cane, Teddy walked slowly up the hillside that led to the apple orchard.

The scars the plane had made in the soft earth were overgrown with fresh grass. No traces of debris remained; nothing to indicate that this was the place where Teddy had come so very close to being the third among his brothers and sisters to lose his life in a plane crash, the fourth of the Kennedy children to have died.

Joan was with him. They said little to each other. He walked back and forth across the site for a few minutes, stood still for a few minutes longer, gazing silently at the ground, and then, just as the last rays of the setting sun glinted across the orchard, he walked slowly back down the hill.

So much death. Joe Junior, Kathleen, Jack, Jack's infant son, and, for all intents and purposes, Rosemary too. Then here, in this orchard, Ed Moss and the pilot, Zimny.

There must have been times when Teddy felt oppressed by what seemed the omnipresence of death, the degree to which it had become so inextricably intertwined with his life. Times when he felt he'd knelt before too many coffins, too many graves that held the bodies of family members whose voices, whose laughter, still echoed too clearly in his ears.

Too much death, too many secrets, too many lies.

Throughout the spring, he repeated like a mantra his unvarying response when asked about the Warren Commission report: "I haven't read it and I don't intend to. May I add that I am completely convinced of the circumstances surrounding the events in Dallas, to my own satisfaction and to the satisfaction of my family. We are satisfied that the Warren Commission report accurately speaks as to the circumstances."

Later, a Harvard graduate student named Edward Jay

Epstein published a book called *Inquest,* in which he suggested that the Warren Commission report had been hastily prepared and was inaccurate in many significant respects and that the commission had failed to prove its central contention: that Oswald had acted alone and had not been part of a conspiracy.

Teddy must have known Epstein was right. If, indeed, the last of his illusions had been shattered by Bobby months before, he also would have known much more. He would have realized, for instance, that Epstein had barely scratched the surface. But, for the sake of the legend, for the sake of Dad, for the sake of Jack, for the sake of all that America needed the Kennedys to be, Teddy would have to feign allegiance to the Warren Commission report and denounce anyone who had the temerity to question it.

This created an awkward situation because, at the same time, in order to avoid detailed questions about discrepancies, inadequate investigation and illogical conclusions, he had to continue to maintain that he'd never read the report. It meant vouching sternly for the accuracy of a lengthy document with which he was simultaneously claiming to be totally unfamiliar.

It was not the most comfortable position to adopt, especially when it implied an extraordinary, even appalling lack of curiosity about why or by whom Jack might really have been murdered. It seems apparent that Bobby must have explained to him that any alternative would only involve them more deeply in areas they needed to keep sealed off permanently from public scrutiny.

And so, when Epstein's book was published, the *Globe* printed a story under the headline "Ted Sure That Oswald Was Lone Assassin." Over this, in smaller type, was a line that read: "Backs Warren Report, But Won't Read It."

In the story, Teddy repeated that he'd never even glanced at the report—"and I do not intend to"—but that he concurred fully with each and every one of its findings.

To ward off further questions about such an inconsistent position, Teddy had to drop the phlegmatic mask with which he usually faced the press.

"Senator Kennedy reacted with emotional pain when asked about recent books questioning the validity of the Warren Commission's findings. He winced and covered his face with one hand. After a moment of silence, he lowered his hand and replied firmly:

" 'I never read the Warren Commission report. However, I am satisfied that it represents at least conclusively the results which I believe are accurate.' The tone of Kennedy's voice made clear that was all to be said on the subject."

But, from professing belief in the Warren Commission's findings to publicly proclaiming love for his wife, Teddy's life, more than ever, had become little more than pretense pasted over facade.

"It is an awesome thing," the *Globe* wrote, "to walk behind Ted Kennedy through East Boston and feel the force and the depth of the affection he generates, the storm of clapping and cheers that swirls around him as he strides through the crowds."

But how frightening it must have been to feel that one was unworthy of this. That through no particular display of personal merit, one had been awarded a paramount role in the mythic life of a nation, and that there would never be any escape.

9

EVEN CRIPPLED AND SPEECHLESS, TEDDY'S FATHER still cast a long shadow. And it was by this that Teddy first found his public reputation darkened.

Years earlier, the old man had told Frank Morrissey, his favorite Boston errand boy and fixer, that if Jack was ever elected President he'd see to it that Morrissey was appointed as a federal judge.

That Francis X. Morrissey, despite serving as a Boston municipal judge, was scarcely qualified to be a bailiff seemed not to matter. He'd been loyal to Joe Kennedy for years, even accompanying Teddy to Capri for his luncheon with deported mafioso Michael Spinella. By 1961, the old man felt that Morrissey had earned a reward.

Despite his father's insistence, Jack could not make himself do it. Frank Morrissey as a federal judge? The notion was ludicrous. Jack had done much that his father insisted upon, but putting Frank Morrissey on the federal bench was more than the President could stomach. The notion offended not his ethics so much as his sense of style.

As with so many other things, Jack told Bobby to take care of the details. They both knew how unqualified Morrissey was: what they needed was an objective statement to that effect to show their father.

Bobby asked the American Bar Association to evaluate Morrissey's credentials, such as they were. Morrissey had received his law degree from a mail-order college in Georgia, and even after that it had taken him sixteen years to pass the Massachusetts bar examination.

Seldom had the Bar Association been given an easier task. "Not qualified," said their report. "Judge Morrissey is lacking intellectual capacity, scholarship and legal knowledge. He lacks legal experience, trial practice and general practice of the law."

Bobby forwarded this report to his father in the fall of 1961. The Ambassador said he didn't give a damn. Of course Morrissey was unqualified: Joe Kennedy didn't need the American Bar Association to tell him that. Qualifications were not the point. Loyalty was—as well as the need for a payoff that would assure a lifetime of silence from Morrissey about certain of the Ambassador's business practices.

Had the old man continued to press the point, Jack might have caved in. Perhaps at a moment of exceptionally high personal popularity, such as after the Cuban missile crisis, he might have tried to sneak the nomination through the Senate. But his father's stroke had taken the pressure off.

Not until after the assassination, when Bobby was so stricken by shock and guilt, did Morrissey make any headway. Preparing to resign as attorney general, Bobby wrote Lyndon Johnson a letter and sent Morrissey a copy.

Once, in passing, Bobby had mentioned Morrissey's name to Johnson, so he could tell Morrissey that he'd personally urged the new President to fulfill the pledge his father had made.

Now, Bobby wrote, "Before I leave the Department of Justice, I want to express to you my appreciation for your statement that, at an appropriate time, you would give sympathetic consideration to Frank Morrissey for appointment to the United States District Court. . . ."

On that point at least, Bobby felt his conscience was

clear. He'd written the letter, thereby demonstrating to Morrissey that he'd done all he could to fulfill his father's promise. At the same time, he had saved the family from embarrassment. So deep did the enmity between the two men already run that Bobby knew there was no chance Lyndon Johnson would accede to his request. Nothing could have more thoroughly ensured that Frank Morrissey would never become a federal judge than a letter from Bobby to Lyndon Johnson asking that consideration be given. Or so Bobby thought.

The matter lay dormant until the fall of 1965, when Johnson, whose resentment toward the Kennedys had not abated, and who gleefully seized any chance to embarrass them, realized that Bobby's 1964 letter presented him with a golden opportunity.

Acting in accordance with Bobby's request, he would submit Morrissey's name to the Senate Judiciary Committee, along with the full text of Bobby's letter, which had said in part that Morrissey "bears an excellent reputation as to character and integrity, has judicial temperament, and is, I believe, worthy of appointment."

As Arthur Schlesinger has written, "Johnson's theory was plain enough. The Kennedys would suffer the obloquy for the nomination; further, it would place them under obligation to him while at the same time exposing their pious pretensions."

From years of having heard the name bandied about in the most contemptuous way, Johnson was certain that Morrissey could not survive Senate scrutiny. Leaving nothing to chance, however, he directed J. Edgar Hoover to launch the most thorough investigation ever undertaken into the background of a judicial nominee.

"I don't want him to get that judgeship," Johnson told Hoover, the day after he'd announced he was submitting Morrissey's name.

Bobby was horrified. He called Milton Gwirtzman in Teddy's office to say, "I don't believe it. Johnson's just nominated Frank Morrissey!"

Bobby knew there was no way for the Kennedys to escape embarrassment. But maybe not all the Kennedys need bear the blame. For instance, maybe not Bobby himself. As on so many other occasions, his status as older brother carried with it advantages.

Not unsarcastically, Bobby reminded Teddy of what a splendid job he'd done fighting for his amendment to the voting rights bill. Hadn't Teddy been hailed everywhere as a master parliamentarian, as a young man who'd come of age? Here, Bobby said, was an unexpected but even more splendid opportunity for Teddy to enhance his reputation.

Teddy, not Bobby, could lead the fight for Frank Morrissey's nomination. After all, Morrissey was a resident of Massachusetts and Teddy was a senator from Massachusetts, so it was only appropriate. And Teddy, over the years, had come to know Morrissey much better than Bobby had. Clearly, Teddy was better qualified to vouch for Morrissey's intellectual acumen and impeccable ethical standards.

He wished Teddy the best. He said he was sorry, truly sorry, that he couldn't join in what he was sure would be a lively and spirited exchange of views as the Judiciary Committee began to probe Frank Morrissey's background.

With that, Bobby smiled sardonically—while Teddy hastily summoned Milton Gwirtzman and others, ordering them to prepare for his immediate use the most eloquent statement possible in support of the Morrissey nomination.

Schlesinger has written that "the nomination was greeted with universal disapproval." The *Herald Tribune* called it "nauseous." *The Washington Post* denounced it, saying that "the chief reproach for this nomination must go to the Democratic Senator from Massachusetts. It is an ominous example of an inclination to use a federal judicial office to repay personal and family political debts." Even the *Globe* opposed Morrissey, in an unprecedented display of independence.

In truth, the *Globe* had little choice after Charles Wyzanski, chief judge of the federal court in Boston, took the extraordinary step of issuing a public denunciation in the form of a letter to the Senate Judiciary Committee.

Confirmation of Morrissey, Judge Wyzanski said, "would corroborate the cynical view that judicial place goes not to those who will honor it but to those who by service have bought it."

Acknowledging that "few if any precedents support a chief judge testifying against the appointment to his court of a judge with whom the President has proposed that the chief judge should thereafter sit," Judge Wyzanski said he nevertheless felt compelled to speak out because he "could not overlook the obvious fact that the ONLY discernible ground for the nomination of Judge Morrissey is his service to the Kennedy family—to Ambassador Kennedy, to President Kennedy and to the Senators Kennedy.

"Local and national bar associations have reported him NOT QUALIFIED—their lowest possible rating. Lawyers from Massachusetts and elsewhere in the nation have at considerable personal risk recorded themselves as opposed to Morrissey's nomination. How can I, without awareness of my own cowardice, remain silent?"

Judiciary Committee files did not disclose any previous example of a chief judge speaking out in such a manner, nor of a chief judge of a federal district court using capitalization to emphasize the degree of his disgust with a judicial appointment. The reference to "personal risk" was also duly noted as indicating Judge Wyzanski's awareness of the fact that Kennedys went to great lengths to exact vengeance from those who defied them.

Yes, this would be a tricky one indeed for Teddy.

He took to the Senate floor on September 28 to defend Morrissey and to attack the press that was so united in its opposition. He accused newspapers of printing stories that were "totally in error and extremely derogatory to Judge Morrissey's record and career. If Frank Morrissey was as unqualified a man as these stories have made him appear, I would never have recommended his nomination," Teddy said.

But in this instance—unusual where the Kennedys were concerned—much of the media knew and reported the truth: that Teddy had been stuck with the unenviable task of defending an indefensible nomination solely because a man to whom his crippled father had made a promise was insisting that it be kept.

What was not so apparent at the time was Teddy's awareness of the potential consequences of not keeping such promises. No one was going to assassinate him or Bobby if Frank Morrissey did not become a federal judge. But Morrissey did possess sufficient knowledge of the means by which the Kennedys achieved their ends so that they may well have feared that unless he was fully satisfied that the family had done all it could for him, he might cause even more embarrassment than was entailed in Teddy's trying to pretend that the appointment was anything but a payoff.

The Morrissey hearings began before a judiciary subcommittee on October 12. Teddy opened the proceedings by reading a statement in which he said, "A judge must be absolutely incorruptible. If he is not, we endanger the people's respect for the law and with it our entire judicial system. Judge Morrissey's qualities of character are of the highest order."

Teddy then read into the record a statement from Cardinal Cushing: "As one who has known him for a quarter of a century, let me say that no one can question his sterling character. I am convinced he would wear the robes of this office with dignity and with credit to the bar."

But then Morrissey himself began to testify. Fidgety, obsequious, looking as if he'd applied the same can of wax both to his hair and to his highly polished black leather shoes, he began perspiring heavily and casting his eyes about frantically as soon as Everett Dirksen, whose voice was a slow and deadly rumble, began his questioning.

Dirksen asked Morrissey about his legal education, in particular about the nature of the Southern Law School in Athens, Georgia, from which Morrissey had obtained his degree in September of 1933.

Did the school have a law library?

"Not as such," Morrissey said.

How large was the faculty?

"Perhaps two."

How long had he studied there?

"A long time."

After referring to notes, Dirksen glared at him. "Is six months a long time in your book?"

"Well," Morrissey said, "it seemed like a long time."

Dirksen asked where Morrissey had been living when he'd finally obtained his law degree.

"Massachusetts."

But had not Morrissey, on September 8, 1933, petitioned to practice law in the Northern District Court of Georgia, and had he not on that same day, in that same petition, claimed to be a full-time resident of the state of Georgia?

"Yes, that is so."

And when, following the filing of said petition, had Morrissey returned to Massachusetts?

"The next day."

In the history of the United States Senate, few members had raised the pregnant pause to quite the art form it became when employed by Everett Dirksen.

After one such pause, Dirksen said, as if to himself, "The next day." He paused again, while Morrissey sweated and glanced about like a rabbit in a trap.

Then, very slowly, very gently, Dirksen spoke in his low but mellifluous rumble. "Judge Morrissey," he said, "if you allege that you live in one state for the purpose of being admitted to the state bar, when in fact you are not a resident of that state, there is a rather unpleasant word for that, as you know. I will not use it, but it bothers me a little." He wondered if, perhaps, Cardinal Cushing had been fully aware of this when he'd vouched for Morrissey's "sterling character."

"Senator," Morrissey blurted in response, "perhaps I showed poor judgment at that particular age. Perhaps I did not show proper maturity. But I never placed any weight on that degree. Nor did I try in any way to try and get into the practice of law in Massachusetts on a reciprocal arrangement."

Dirksen continued to look genuinely puzzled. Again,

he asked Morrissey how much time he had actually spent engaged in the study of law in Athens, Georgia.

"About three months," Morrissey replied this time.

Didn't he think that obtaining a law degree from a Georgia diploma mill was rather a poor way to launch a career?

"I think it was perfectly stupid," Morrissey agreed. But he added that the whole Georgia episode had been little more than a young man's lark. His true legal education, he said, had come earlier, when he'd attended "evening law school at Boston College, in 1932 and 1933."

For the moment, Dirksen seemed to have satisfied his curiosity about Frank Morrissey's legal education. His next area of concern was the extent and nature of Morrissey's experience on the bench.

In his opening statement, Teddy had praised Morrissey's performance effusively.

"The municipal court of Boston," he'd said, "on which Judge Morrissey has served for seven years, is misnamed. It is really a county court, serving the most densely populated county in Massachusetts. It handles twenty percent of all the civil and criminal cases heard in the lower courts of the commonwealth. On the criminal side, it holds probable cause hearings for crimes as severe as murder. . . . In his seven years on this court, Judge Morrissey has decided thousands of cases of almost every conceivable variety and as a judge he has never been overruled by a higher tribunal."

Ever so slowly, Dirksen began to peel away the layers of Morrissey's judicial résumé. It was true that he'd never been overruled by a higher tribunal, but it was also true, Morrissey conceded, that his court handled only such matters as parking tickets, charges of shoplifting and alleged violations of motor vehicle laws.

Never once in seven years, in fact, had Frank Morrissey presided over a jury trial. If a case came to trial by jury, it was automatically transferred to a higher court. Thus, it was no wonder that in his seven years, Morrissey had made no rulings to which a "higher tribunal" had taken exception: he'd never made a ruling at a trial.

"My real experience," he finally admitted to Dirksen, "has been very limited."

"Inconsequential?" Dirksen suggested.

"I would say that was a fair statement," the perspiring Morrissey conceded.

For the moment, Dirksen let the matter drop. He'd made his point: the nomination was both preposterous and insulting. But the Republican leader was experienced enough to know that one ought not to use one's most lethal ammunition prematurely; one should prolong to the maximum extent possible the discomfort and embarrassment suffered by one's opponents.

With the Judiciary Committee firmly controlled by Democrats—even if they were, in this case, embarrassed Democrats who wished the Kennedys were not permitting this to happen—Morrissey's nomination was approved by a 6-3 vote and sent on to the full Senate for further consideration.

In most cases, such confirmation was only a formality. And so, the day after the committee vote, the *Globe* was able to proclaim that Teddy had scored another stirring triumph.

"It is all over but the shouting for Senate confirmation of Francis X. Morrissey for a Federal judgeship," the *Globe* said, "and it was increasingly clear today that Ted Kennedy will always be able to say that he won. He turned out the troops for his friend and political mentor when the chips were down. And he didn't get an iota of help, either, from his brother, Robert, senator from New York."

Not only had Bobby not helped, he'd been appalled by what he'd seen and heard. Morrissey's performance during the hearings had been far worse than Bobby, even at his most pessimistic, had feared.

The *Globe* might consider the committee vote a triumph for Teddy and another example of his unswerving loyalty to an old family friend, but Bobby knew better.

The spectacle of Morrissey's slow-motion dissection by Dirksen had made Teddy's enthusiastic words of praise seem ridiculous. His continuing support of Morrissey would not only cheapen him but would diminish the legend, which Bobby, as its chief guardian, could not permit.

No, the Morrissey business had to stop and Bobby knew how to stop it. Bobby's memory bank may not have been as detailed nor as extensive as J. Edgar Hoover's private files, but in the case of Frank Morrissey it contained enough information to accomplish the desired result, which was to get Morrissey off stage as quickly as possible and to close this whole humiliating chapter that Lyndon Johnson had reopened.

All that was required was a discreet leak to the right people in Boston. From there, it would be a short step to Bob Healy of the *Globe*.

The resulting story was utterly devastating to Morrissey in light of his sworn testimony before the committee.

First, no prelaw or law courses had been offered at evening school at Boston College during the years Morrissey claimed to have attended.

Second, it was only after his failed attempt to pass the Massachusetts bar exam—it would be sixteen years before he did pass it and even then there were questions about the legitimacy of his feat—that he'd traveled to Georgia.

Third, the Southern Law School of Athens was essentially a fraudulent institution, one that would award a bogus law degree to anyone who could pay its small fee. But such was the quality of legal ethics in Georgia at the time, that one could, upon presentation of this "diploma"—and without passing any independent examination—be admitted to practice in at least certain jurisdictions within the state.

All one had to do—besides paying the necessary official and unofficial fees in these jurisdictions—was to swear under oath that one was a legal resident of the state.

Which, during a three-day trip to Georgia in 1934, Frank Morrissey did, in three separate locations, on three separate occasions.

But what Bobby knew—and what Bob Healy and the

Globe found out quickly—was that at the time of his Georgia trip Morrissey was a candidate for a seat in the Massachusetts state legislature, running from Ward 2 in Charlestown, where he would eventually finish fourteenth in a field of sixteen in the Democratic primary.

Healy's stories in the *Globe* caused a sensation. It was apparent not only that Morrissey had lied in 1934, gaining the right to practice law in Georgia by falsely claiming to be a full-time resident while simultaneously running for political office in Massachusetts, but that at best he'd been less than forthcoming in his testimony to the committee the previous week.

The renewed attacks upon him were instantaneous and brutal. Bernard Segal of the American Bar Association's judicial selection committee said Morrissey was "the worst nominee" ever put forward for a federal judgeship. Newspapers across the country—including now the *Chicago Tribune*, the *Washington Star*, the *Baltimore Sun*—demanded the immediate withdrawal of his name.

"The Senate," said *The New York Times*, "will shame itself and abdicate its responsibility—as its judiciary committee has already done—if it confirms this incredible appointment."

Bobby had been certain that in the face of such destructive revelations Morrissey would quickly withdraw to spare both himself and Teddy further mortification. In Bobby's view, it was a hard but necessary lesson for his younger brother. An introduction to the real world, or what passed for the real world among the Kennedys.

So Bobby had done the only thing he could: he had swiftly and cleanly cut the man to shreds, leaving no fingerprints. Morrissey would withdraw and Teddy would survive. As always, the Kennedys would cut their losses and move on.

But Bobby had underestimated Morrissey's avid desire to win confirmation, no matter the cost to himself or to the Kennedys. Having had to scramble and connive for anything he'd ever gotten out of life, having curried favor with the powerful for so long, Francis X. Morrissey was far past the point where he feared humiliation.

Even in the wake of the new and devastating disclosures, Morrissey refused to withdraw his name. Thus, trapped as so often before by his family's past, Teddy vowed to "ride right on through" at Morrissey's side.

This announcement both surprised and displeased Everett Dirksen. He had given the Kennedys too much credit. He had assumed that any documents he possessed that were relevant to Frank Morrissey's fitness to serve on the federal bench would also be in the possession of the Kennedys.

Was it possible that Teddy had failed to understand that at the moment of truth Dirksen would use all weapons in his arsenal? And that perhaps Teddy had also failed to recognize that if such a scenario played itself out, the least of the casualties would be the already mangled reputation of Frank Morrissey?

Before this went any further, Dirksen decided to involve Bobby. He met privately with the two Kennedy brothers at 1:30 P.M. on October 21, the day before Morrissey's nomination was to be put before the full Senate.

The white-haired, seemingly avuncular minority leader, who, mien notwithstanding, possessed political instincts equivalent to the physical reflexes of a mongoose, gestured toward his office wall as he spoke to Bobby and Teddy together.

"You see that bust on the mantel?" he asked rhetorically, pointing to a bronzed image of Jack. "That was one of the best friends I ever had."

Then Dirksen turned to Teddy. "You think I'm out to cut your neck—to ax you," he said. "I'm not." Then he allowed his gaze to encompass Bobby, too. "I'm not interested in either of you. But I'm out to get Morrissey."

He reached into a briefcase and produced a brown manila envelope which he placed on the table in front of him. He suggested that Bobby open it and examine the contents.

The envelope contained a photograph and a story that had been clipped from the May 28, 1961, edition of an Italian newspaper, *Il Mattino,* from the city of Naples.

The picture showed three jolly men, of varying ages,

426

luxuriating in a wine-enriched lunch at an outdoor restaurant on the Italian island of Capri. They were all enjoying one another's company, or at least pretending to for purposes of the photograph.

Wordlessly, Bobby handed the photograph and clipping to Teddy. The three men in the picture were Frank Morrissey, Teddy, and deported Mafia chieftain Michael Spinella.

Spinella, who was sixty-seven at the time of his meeting with Teddy and Morrissey, had an American criminal record that dated back to 1941 and included arrests for assault with intent to kill, robbery and murder. A record, frankly, not totally dissimilar to the records of Carlos Marcello, Sam Giancana and Santos Trafficante, among others, except that Spinella had been deported following a 1952 conviction for falsely claiming United States citizenship.

Dirksen next showed Bobby and Teddy a story in the Rome daily *Il Tempo,* reporting the same meeting and portraying the same bibulous and carefree breaking of bread. He did not need to say more.

Bobby thanked Dirksen for his courtesy in showing the materials to him and Teddy privately before releasing them to the press, to whom he'd promised a "bombshell" the next day if the Morrissey nomination was not withdrawn. Bobby said he and Teddy needed to meet privately. He assured Dirksen that a decision on the nomination would be quickly forthcoming.

And so it was. Neither Bobby nor Teddy would ever speak publicly of what transpired between them during the late afternoon and evening of October 21, 1965, but shortly before midnight Teddy placed a call to President Johnson, who was recuperating from gallbladder surgery at the Bethesda Naval Hospital, and informed him that the next morning he would go before the full Senate to withdraw the nomination of Francis X. Morrissey.

The next day, Teddy delivered a tearful speech in behalf of Frank Morrissey on the Senate floor. "His voice breaking with emotion," *The New York Times* reported,

Teddy explained why Morrissey had gone to Georgia to get a ''quickie'' law degree.

''He was young and he was poor,'' Teddy said, ''one of twelve children, his father a dockworker, the family living in a home without gas, electricity or heat in the bedroom; their shoes held together with wooden pegs their father made. As a child of this family, Judge Morrissey could not afford to study law full-time.''

This aria, sung in behalf of such an overt family flunky, raised questions among some of the less informed members of the Senate and the public. Why was Teddy employing such maudlin rhetoric while at the same time withdrawing a nomination that seemed likely to win Senate approval?

Questions were raised even more forcefully when both Majority Leader Mike Mansfield, and the influential southern Democrat Russell Long of Louisiana confirmed that Teddy had mustered enough votes to assure confirmation.

The most industrious and perceptive reporter of the incident as it unfolded—Fred P. Graham of *The New York Times*—wrote in his lead that Teddy, ''in a surprise retreat, had abandoned his fight to win Senate approval'' for Morrissey's nomination.

Given the power and persistence of his earlier rhetoric in Morrissey's behalf, Teddy's ninth-inning forfeit seemed inexplicable. Especially when Teddy himself told his Senate colleagues, ''I have determined that a majority of the members of the Senate are prepared to support Judge Morrissey's confirmation.'' Kennedys knew how to count. So why this startling last-minute retreat?

Only Graham pursued the answer, and only *The New York Times* published his findings, however carefully couched in the language of happenstance.

''A bizarre sidelight developed,'' Graham wrote, ''as reports swept Capitol Hill that some Republicans had threatened to bolster their attack on Judge Morrissey with Italian press reports of his chance meeting with a deported Mafia figure, Michael Spinella, on Capri, in 1961.''

Bobby inadvertently raised even further questions by

hastily issuing a statement insisting that there was "absolutely no link between" Teddy and Spinella. Until then —except for vague and quickly discounted rumors of the Ambassador's possible involvement in the illicit liquor trade of the 1920s—no newspaper or magazine in America had even hinted at a link between any Kennedy, much less Teddy, and a Mafia figure.

Now, Fred Graham was reporting—in *The New York Times,* no less—that "by insisting that they were giving up their bitter fight with victory at hand, Judge Morrissey's supporters raised questions as to the real motives of the sudden retreat.

"This confusion was increased by reports that Senator Dirksen had quietly circulated copies of Italian newspaper articles telling of the meeting between Judge Morrissey and Spinella." Graham mentioned, farther on, that Teddy had been present at this "chance meeting" on May 26, 1961.

Graham had the presence of mind to actually question Teddy about the circumstances that had led to the meeting. "Senator Kennedy," he reported, "said this afternoon that he and Judge Morrissey had chatted with Spinella because he said he had a son in the Marines, and they had allowed him to guide them to a local restaurant.

"Neither of them knew about his record and neither had any contact with him before or since, Senator Kennedy said. . . . Senator Kennedy's office obtained an affidavit from Judge Morrissey stating that he had never met Spinella before the chance meeting in Capri and that he had never acted as attorney for him."

Given the present state of Morrissey's credibility, the affidavit was an odd document to produce, especially since it raised yet another new question—whether or not Frank Morrissey had ever served as Spinella's lawyer.

The *Boston Globe,* of course, did not pursue these lines of inquiry, nor even refer to them in its account of Teddy's withdrawal of Morrissey's nomination.

Instead, the next day, after Teddy had already fled the country for a firsthand look at the deteriorating situation in Vietnam—perhaps the one place in the world where he'd be spared further questions about Morrissey and Spinella and any alliance they might have cemented over lunch in Capri in 1961—the *Globe* printed an editorial praising him.

It said: "Sen. Edward M. Kennedy acted with characteristic courage. Strongly committed to the candidacy of Judge Francis X. Morrissey for a federal judgeship, he also appreciated the fact that in fairness to his Senate colleagues, as well as to the candidate, further study should be made by the Judiciary Committee.

"He in no way retreated from his sponsorship of Judge Morrissey, but recognized that in light of strong opposition, a more detailed inquiry should be made.

"This action does credit to him, to the U.S. Senate and to his own future."

The *Globe* editorial mentioned neither Spinella nor Capri, nor the fact that *The New York Times* had published such a detailed account of the 1961 meeting.

The following spring, Healy and the *Globe* received a Pulitzer Prize for the "investigative series" that was publicly believed to have caused the withdrawal of the Morrissey nomination.

Bobby, whose sense of humor was growing increasingly puckish, attended the dinner at which the awards were presented. As *Globe* representatives stepped to the dais to accept their prize, friends seated close to Bobby glanced covertly at him to see if he would display any reaction.

As Schlesinger reported, "Bobby bowed his head, turned toward his dinner companion and, with a boyish grin, winked broadly."

As for Teddy, despite the *Globe*'s editorial support, his intemperate defense of Morrissey had made him look both venal and parochial, a willing servant to the old-style Massachusetts cronyism from which Jack had so elegantly distanced himself.

That as the youngest brother Teddy had been forced to take on this onerous task, and that, as always, he'd only been doing his father's bidding, was not a point either he or his supporters raised in his defense.

Some chapters in one's life—public or private—were better closed as quickly and as discreetly as possible. Damage control was a concept with which Teddy was growing increasingly familiar.

10

Through 1965, Teddy and Bobby both supported every step Lyndon Johnson took to deepen American military involvement in Vietnam. It seemed to them an integral part of Jack's legacy.

During a 1964 oral history interview for the Kennedy Library, Bobby flatly stated Jack's position: "The President felt that there was a strong, overwhelming reason for being in Vietnam and that we should win the war." Asked if Jack had ever so much as hinted at the possibility of withdrawal should the struggle prove intractable, Bobby answered, "No." Jack had been accused of being soft on Cuba, soft on Laos, soft on Berlin. It was in Vietnam that he had decided to make his stand against communism, and to both Bobby and Teddy it was clear that nothing would have deterred him.

In May of 1965, months before his first visit to the country, Teddy sent a letter to be read at a Vietnam teach-in taking place on the campus of Boston University. Two thousand people attended, hearing dozens of speeches, as well as letters from such philosophers as Bertrand Russell and Jean-Paul Sartre, all opposing America's rapidly escalating military involvement in Vietnam.

432

Teddy's letter, however, was an exception. He expressed the view that to weaken our commitment to the government of South Vietnam "would endanger nations vital to our security such as the Philippines and Burma. It would also undermine our credibility with other nations in the area."

By July, he'd become even more militant, charging that Communist elements within South Vietnam were "deliberately creating refugee movements in order to hamper the government war effort." He said the Viet Cong were using refugees as a "Trojan horse" strategy that would enable them to infiltrate government-controlled regions.

Then, in October, only seven hours after his emotional announcement that he was withdrawing the Morrissey nomination, Teddy took his first trip to Vietnam.

In truth, the jaunt was something of an escapade, and an escape from the Morrissey debacle. Teddy was accompanied by, among others, his two favorite partying companions in public life, John Culver and John Tunney. His primary mission, a member of the traveling party joked privately, seemed to be an in-depth, hands-on study of the reportedly widespread problem of prostitution in Saigon.

"It was pretty much a nonstop party," said one survivor later. "I'd already seen plenty of Teddy in action and had heard a lot more, but on this trip he was truly amazing."

There were, of course, public moments, staged for the press. In all of these, Teddy was as militant and as hawkish as anyone in America, which was what he thought Jack would have wanted.

In a press conference upon his arrival in Saigon, he said it would be "a great mistake" for the world to think that antiwar demonstrations and teach-ins reflected the will of the nation.

"The overwhelming majority of the American people are behind the policies of President Johnson in Vietnam," he said, and were "prepared to see a long and difficult struggle."

Then, donning combat fatigues and jungle boots, he headed north, toward Da Nang, for what was becoming the politician's compulsory "firsthand look" at the situation.

Posing for photographers and American television crews in a village near Da Nang, he kicked a soccer ball toward a small, bewildered Vietnamese boy. The boy stared at the ball, making no move to either kick it back or pick it up; given what he'd been experiencing on a daily and nightly basis, he had no way of knowing it was not some new sort of land mine.

Teddy retrieved the ball himself, then kicked it again, toward another mystified and frightened Vietnamese child. Again, the child merely stared, then stepped back.

His photogenic grin beginning to fade, Teddy picked up the ball and handed it to a little girl, who, as Neil Sheehan reported in *The New York Times,* "for some reason burst into tears."

Abandoning his attempts to communicate with the youth of the village, Teddy entered a refugee hut, but when Vietnamese residents tried to accompany him, a United States official who was supervising the trip shouted, "Let's everyone clear away and give a clear field to the television. Come on now. Don't gang up."

Later, in the city of Qui Nhon, still accompanied by a full media complement, Teddy asked an American official what single change in American policy would make it easier for him to accomplish his mission.

"To be blunt, sir," the official replied, "if we had fewer people coming out here. In the last forty-five days, we've had thirty-five groups. Each demands the twenty-five-cent tour. It takes up my time. It takes up the province chief's time."

United Press reported that Teddy's reply to this unexpected response "was not completely audible to newsmen."

By the end of the month, he'd moved on to Singapore, where he met privately with a group of university students who opposed America's support of the South Vietnamese goverment.

"Although newsmen were not allowed in," the Associated Press reported, "Kennedy's voice was clearly heard raised in anger. 'That's the way people like you argue,' Teddy said loudly at one point. 'You distort facts and use inaccuracies.' Several students could be heard yelling back."

He returned to America during the first week of November and immediately announced plans for a month-long, campaign-style sweep of Massachusetts, during which he would try to muster support for America's war effort in Vietnam and, as he put it, "to determine to what extent the attitude that accompanies draft-card burning has infected the youth of Massachusetts."

It was clear that he also wanted to associate himself in the minds of his constituents with something other than his incomprehensible support of Frank Morrissey.

Four days a week for the next five weeks, he crisscrossed the state, trying to drum up enthusiasm for the war. Often he'd make up to a dozen appearances a day, starting at 7:00 A.M. and continuing until almost midnight.

It was the classic Kennedy approach: moving fast and often through impossibly crowded days and nights, talking and listening constantly so that there was no time to think.

The majority of his appearances were before audiences of high school and college students. The colleges were chosen carefully for their conservatism: mostly branches of the state's public university system, with students from Massachusetts working-class families. He appeared at Lowell Tech, not MIT; at Brockton State, not Boston University; at North Essex Community College, not Harvard.

Everywhere, his message was the same: to stress to the students and their elders the need to prepare for a long, difficult war in South Vietnam and to emphasize that however much time and money and however many lives might be expended, America would stay the course.

North Vietnamese leader Ho Chi Minh, he said, needed to be "convinced that the American people are determined to carry out this country's commitments to South Vietnam regardless of the time and sacrifices." He said that while dissent was protected by the Constitution, and opponents of the war had the right to voice their opinions—"as long as they are constructive and done legally"—he believed that this kind of activity could only give comfort to the enemy, thus likely prolonging the war and making it more difficult for America to achieve its objective. As for "draft card burners who are violative of the law," he said, "I have no sympathy."

At Lowell Tech, he called Vietnam "the fundamental moral question facing the United States." He asked, "Are we concerned at all about people in a far and distant land? Do we want to defend freedom? We do, because this is our commitment, our heritage, our destiny."

He also directed sharp criticism at "those so quick to condemn the United States for military action," saying, "I wish they had raised their voices against Viet Cong terrorism, against Viet Cong murder, kidnapping and political assassination."

For the most part, his remarks were well received, as was to be expected considering how carefully his staff had chosen the audiences. One Lowell Tech student said, "You'll find the radicals elsewhere, at the big liberal arts colleges," the very campuses Teddy had made a point of avoiding.

By the end, the week before Christmas, Teddy was in Springfield, applauding Lyndon Johnson's decision to bomb Haiphong, saying, "Any facilities in North Vietnam strengthening the Viet Cong should be bombed." He stated, "To conduct the war short of full retaliatory efforts against Communist positions in the North places American and South Vietnamese forces at a considerable and dangerous disadvantage."

It was as if William Westmoreland had replaced Milton Gwirtzman as his chief speech writer.

In mid-January 1966, Teddy reiterated his support for Johnson's forcefulness in Vietnam, saying he was "eighty-nine percent in favor of the Johnson administration policies." He did not explain how he had calculated that figure, but stressed, "The fact that we are there I support. I support very strenuously the efforts being made now. I support our fundamental commitment. I don't have reservations."

This put him oddly out of synch with Bobby, who had abandoned his earlier support for the war and, by December of 1965, was defending antiwar demonstrations, saying, "I don't think you can ever discuss these matters enough."

In regard to draft-card burning, Bobby said, "If a person feels that strongly," he could quite understand taking such action.

Even more startling, when asked about the idea of antiwar Americans donating blood to the North Vietnamese, Bobby said, "I think that's a good idea."

His astonished questioner asked, "Isn't that going too far?"

"If we've given all the blood that is needed to the South Vietnamese, I'm in favor of giving it to anybody who needs it. I'm in favor of them having blood."

"Even the North Vietnamese?"

"Yes."

More than any other public comments he'd ever made, this remark brought down upon Bobby the wrath of the right-wing press. The brother of the martyred President who had launched the American effort in Vietnam, the former chief law enforcement officer of the United States, the former aide to arch anti-Communist Joe McCarthy, advocating the donation of blood to the enemy during wartime?

"Why not go the whole hog?" demanded the *New York Daily News*. "Why not light out for the enemy country and join its armed forces?"

The *Chicago Tribune* published an editorial cartoon that showed Bobby standing atop a flag-draped coffin—much like the one in which Jack had been buried—saying, "I am willing to give my blood to the Communist enemy in Vietnam."

Johnson's 1964 opponent, Barry Goldwater, accused him of coming close to treason.

* * *

The split widened in late January of 1966 when Lyndon Johnson ordered a resumption of the bombing of North Vietnam, which he'd briefly suspended just before Christmas.

Johnson's action immediately brought Bobby, but not Teddy, to his feet on the floor of the Senate.

"If we regard bombing as the answer in Vietnam," Bobby said, "we are headed straight for disaster. In the past, bombing has not proved a decisive weapon against a rural economy or against a guerrilla army. And the temptation will now be to argue that if limited bombing does not produce a solution . . . that further bombing, more extended military action, is the answer. The danger is that the decision to resume may become the first in a series of steps on a road from which there is no turning back—a road which leads to catastrophe for all mankind."

Bobby had already traveled quite a distance down that road in October 1962 during the Cuban missile crisis, and he had no wish to see his country do it again.

Teddy's response was strikingly different. While not speaking out directly, he issued a statement that even the *Globe* derided as being "replete with phrases from the [secretary of state] Dean Rusk handbook on Vietnam."

Teddy expressed sympathy for Johnson's "difficult decision," and said, "If the bombing serves to convince Hanoi and Peking of our determination to stay in Vietnam and defend the people there, this in itself could bring about the changed attitude on the other side that must come before they agree to meaningful negotiations."

Globe reporter Martin Nolan wrote that "few senators reacted so differently" to the resumption of the bombing as had Bobby and Teddy. He added, "This divergence might be of little import if it did not reflect a growing separatist trend in the careers of the Senate's two most famous members—Edward's more and more toward caution and Robert's more and more toward boldness. . . . Robert Kennedy has clearly become the voice of dissent."

* * *

Indeed, Bobby seemed to have emerged fully from the pit of grief, guilt, fear and despair into which he'd plunged after Jack's assassination. There was still much to deny, much to suppress, much about which he would silently brood for the rest of his days, but by 1966 Bobby had at least begun the process of atonement through action.

As a senator from New York, he toured the slums of Bedford-Stuyvesant and was stricken by what he saw. As the bearer of the torch of freedom, he traveled to California and became captivated by the selflessness and courage of the migrant workers' leader, Cesar Chavez.

Bobby, so full of ferocity and zeal, so quick with his visceral responses, was embarking upon an extraordinary voyage toward self-knowledge and a discovery of the "other" America, one whose residents were impoverished, powerless and without hope—a discovery that would both give him a fresh reason for living and bring his life to such a sudden, violent, tragic end.

This was a journey that the cautious, deferential, public Teddy—so grateful to finally be a Senate insider, if still on the outermost fringe of his own shrinking family—did not make. The public risk, the existential approach to policy, was not his way. Rebellion and dissent required both energy and discipline: intellectually, emotionally and physically. For Teddy, by 1966, with his personal life in dreadful disarray, these commodities seemed in short supply.

With the possible exception of himself, Joan continued to be his major problem. Unfortunately, he did not know how to be an adequate husband or how to resolve rather than repress domestic problems. That had not been part of his training. He'd not had parents upon whom he could model appropriate behavior, and without aides who could prepare position papers or write uplifting speeches for him to deliver, he had no clue as to how to give Joan the help she so desperately needed.

"The woman was under incredible pressure," one friend of hers said later. "She was cracking under the strain." There seemed no particular source of the pressure other than her own sense—reinforced by both Teddy and her sisters-in-law—that she was simply not resilient enough or spunky enough or smart enough or mean enough to be a true Kennedy.

It was clear to the family that Teddy's marriage had become the most spectacularly unsuccessful among a series of unions in which happiness and stability had not proven the rule. Yet he was a Catholic who hoped someday to be President; or of whom it was expected that he would someday be President. What he might have hoped personally seemed to have ceased long ago to make any difference.

Thus, divorce or even separation was out of the question. But Joan, unlike Jacqueline, had not managed to establish an independent life in the face of her spouse's indifference to her, nor had she, as Jacqueline had, learned to suffer in silence.

Not only was she seeing two different psychiatrists each week, but night after night, as Teddy slipped into and out of cocktail parties, banquets and bedrooms all over the District of Columbia and environs, Joan would make a series of drunken long-distance phone calls, trying to find someone—an old college friend, someone in Bronxville, her sister—who would care about her plight.

However alienated he grew from his wife, however, Teddy remained devoted, in his own limited way, to his children. Kara was six now, and Teddy Junior five, and, despite the many confusions in his life, and a lessening ability to control his own potentially self-destructive impulses, Teddy was determined that his children would not face the same sort of parental indifference and neglect he had endured.

Almost every evening, before he left his office for wherever his social rounds would take him, Teddy tried to make a point of calling home to speak to Kara and little Teddy on the telephone. His son, in particular, seemed to consider the call the high point of his day.

The routine rarely varied. After asking questions about how Teddy Junior's day had been, Teddy explained in rudimentary terms some of what he'd been doing in the Senate and then swung into what was for both of them the favorite part of the conversation.

For months, maybe years, Teddy had been telling his son a wild and woolly story of the jungle, one that got more absurd and outrageous—and entertaining—as it progressed. The best part came when it was time for one of the increasingly preposterous parade of animals to speak and Teddy adopted the voice intended to mimic that of the animal in question. From lions to cheetahs to wild boars to ostriches, Teddy had the animal voices down pat, and his jungle stories never failed to produce waves of delighted giggling from his son.

Otherwise, calling home wasn't much fun. There was no telling whether or not Joan, on any given day, would even be able to make it to the phone to take his call. And there were many days when he wished she hadn't, so slurred were her words, so incoherent her thoughts, so out of control her emotions. Teddy must have dreaded the thought that his children would have to spend yet another night in the mawkish and often pathetic presence of their drunken mother. Yet he did not dread it so much that it caused him to curtail his own social schedule.

He longed to be a good father. The vulnerability of all small children, not only his own, seemed to touch him at an almost primal level. It was something with which he could identify deeply and instinctively because he continued to experience it himself.

But what he could not cope with was the emotional neediness that accompanied such vulnerability. Having never had anyone fulfill his own psychological needs, he found himself overwhelmed when similar demands were made upon him by his own children, and all too often fled, or avoided, the scene rather than caring for them as a responsible father would have.

Adulthood still seemed a phase of life with which Teddy was not yet comfortable. Thus, despite the genuine love, warmth and affection he felt for his children, the requirements of fatherhood remained an impenetrable mystery.

* * *

By spring of 1966, Teddy's spirit and energy had flagged. The multiple roles he had to play, the constant scrutiny, and the plain and simple fact that consistent abuse of alcohol was taking a physical toll on him just as it was on his wife, seemed to have caught up with him, sapping his energies and causing him to fade from the political foreground just as Bobby surged past to replace him as the Kennedy to whom most attention was paid.

"As a member of the Kennedy family," Meg Greenfield noted in the *Reporter* magazine, Teddy was "able to attract national attention in general and press coverage in particular whenever he desires to do so." She added, however, that he "has been slow to press his advantage —unsure and overcautious. . . . Critics on the hill . . . contend that he is a plodder."

The *Globe* noted that while Bobby was "aggressive, relentless, and tough minded," Teddy had "a butterball delivery" and seemed to "lack the persistence of his older brother."

Newsweek pointed out, in a cover story on the two brothers, that Teddy faced "a major problem in competing for status and prestige with his brother Bobby."

And it was Bobby, not Teddy, who was named in a 1966 Gallup poll as the third most admired man in America, behind Lyndon Johnson and Dwight Eisenhower. It was Bobby's Senate office that received eighteen hundred letters a day, more than three times the number sent to Teddy. It was Bobby, not Teddy, who *Newsweek* said "seems to be carrying the torch for his brother," while noting that "Teddy, in Massachusetts, is commonly criticized for doing too little."

The columnist Marianne Means observed that Teddy had become very much "the other Kennedy—handsome, young, wealthy, powerful, the bearer of a name that will never be forgotten, but very much an also-ran behind his highly publicized brother Robert."

She noted that "immediately after the murder of President Kennedy, public curiosity about the future of the two brothers centered upon the question, 'Will it be

Bobby or Teddy in the White House next?' But now the question has become, 'When will Bobby make it?' "

It was as if neither his own life nor the life of the nation any longer engaged Teddy's interest; as if he were finally, terminally exhausted by his twenty-four-month flight from demons.

II

Lyndon Johnson knew that it was Bobby, not Teddy, he had to fear; that it would be Bobby who would invoke the power of the legend in an attempt to reclaim the Presidency to which the family felt it had a rightful claim as long as any one of them remained alive.

Johnson felt, with considerable justification, that his own performance as President was being measured not against the historical record of his predecessor but against a myth.

"It's impossible," one aide to Johnson complained, "to separate the living Kennedys from the Kennedy legend. I think President Kennedy will be regarded for many years as the Pericles of a Golden Age. He wasn't Pericles and the age wasn't golden, but that doesn't matter—it's caught hold."

And by early 1967, as his popularity dropped to the lowest point of his Presidency, Johnson grew almost paranoid about the prospect that Bobby might attempt a restoration of Camelot as early as the following year.

Much later, in a remarkable monologue, he told Doris Kearns Goodwin of the nightmarish vision that had come to obsess him:

"There would be Robert Kennedy, out in front, leading the fight against me, telling everyone that I had betrayed John Kennedy's commitment to South Vietnam. That I had let democracy fall into the hands of the Communists. That I was a coward. An unmanly man. A man without a spine.

"Oh, I could see it coming all right. Every night when I fell asleep I would see myself tied to the ground in the middle of a long, open space. In the distance, I could hear the voices of thousands of people. They were all shouting at me and running toward me: 'Coward! Traitor! Weakling!' "

The bitter irony of Johnson's predicament was that in order to silence those voices, to hold that angry mob at bay, he had done everything he thought Jack would have done in Vietnam. He'd made a commitment to win the war at any cost. But now it was Bobby who was criticizing him most harshly.

In March, Bobby delivered a fiery oration from the Senate floor. His previous criticisms of Johnson's policies notwithstanding, the speech represented a bold break with the past, an audacious step into a future in which he might transfigure and thus strengthen the legacy.

"I can testify," he said, "that if fault is to be found or responsibility assessed" for the policies that have led the country so deeply into Vietnam, "there is enough to go around for all—including myself."

But the time had come to ask not how or why we had arrived there in such force, he said, but how we might best extricate ourselves while at the same time sparing the people of Vietnam the horrors inherent in an ever-widening conflict. At the time of Jack's death, America had had 16,000 soldiers in Vietnam. By March of 1967, as Bobby spoke, there were 400,000 American troops in Vietnam and the military command was asking for more.

"The most powerful country the world has known," he said, "now turns its strength and will upon a small and primitive land." He asked his colleagues and the

445

American people to try to visualize what this abstraction called war truly meant to the people of Vietnam; to imagine "the vacant moment of amazed fear as a mother and child watch death by fire fall from an improbable machine sent by a country they barely comprehend.

"Although the world's imperfections may call forth the act of war," he went on, "righteousness cannot obscure the agony and pain those acts bring to a single child," nor could we let ourselves avert our eyes from "the night of death destroying yesterday's promise of family and land and home," nor close our ears to "the unending crescendo of violence, hatred and savage fury."

These horrors, Bobby said, were the responsibility of all American citizens, not just the administration's policymakers. "It is we," he said, "who live in abundance and send our young men out to die. It is our chemicals that scorch the children and our bombs that level the villages. We are all participants."

Did we not then have an obligation to explore any and every avenue that might halt the carnage? "No one," he said, "is going to defeat us or slaughter our troops, or destroy our prestige because we dare take initiatives for peace."

Calling for an immediate halt to the bombing of the North and an outright statement of willingness to negotiate promptly, he said, "We are not in Vietnam to play the role of an avenging angel pouring death and destruction on the roads and factories and homes of a guilty land. We are there to assure the self-determination of South Vietnam. Can anyone believe this nation, with all its fantastic power and resources, will be endangered by a wise and magnanimous action toward a small and difficult adversary?"

Emerging from his long torpor, Teddy spoke in Boston two nights later. It was clear that his position had shifted. Whatever the strength of his previous views on Vietnam, it was nothing compared to the force exerted by family loyalty. While Bobby alone might be dismissed as merely a controversial politician hungry for the spotlight, if Teddy were to join him in his antiwar protest the effect

would be entirely different, for Teddy had carefully cultivated a public reputation as a defender of the political
establishment and had repeatedly voiced support for
Lyndon Johnson's Vietnam policy.

But by the spring of 1967, Bobby had come to need
Teddy. This alone—the sense of being needed, the
knowledge that he could help his older brother in a meaningful way—was enough to bring him back to political
life and to cause him to break sharply with his own previously articulated point of view on Vietnam.

"In a serious and constructive Senate speech this
week," Teddy said, "the junior senator from New York
called upon us to take new initiatives for peace. . . . I
feel we must make such unusual efforts, for it appears
that our obligations to the people of Vietnam now call for
less war, not more; negotiations soon, not later.

"There is little more to be gained militarily. The basic
limited objective of stopping the armed seizure of the
South by our adversaries seems to have been reached.
What can only follow now is a prolonged war resulting
in continued death and destruction, with little military
advantage. . . . It is time to talk; it is time for peace. . . .

"We have employed almost four hundred thousand
men, equipped for war with the best that our technology
can produce. In this clash both sides are taking casualties, but the civilian population is bleeding too, perhaps
in numbers greater than their enemy.

"How long, we ask ourselves, can Hanoi and the Viet
Cong take the burdens of war we are imposing? How
long, Hanoi wonders, can Americans stand the effort before they tire as did the French? How long, I would ask,
can the people of South Vietnam stand the punishment
that they feel from friend and foe alike, as punishment
inflicted in their name? . . .

"Can we not do more to heed the counsel of men of
peace in the world? 'We cry to them,' said the Pope,
speaking to all involved. 'We cry to them in God's name
to stop.' It is this, the simple humanitarian reason, above
all others, why negotiated solution of the war in that
tragic place is the most important piece of public business
now facing us.

"Can we not consider whether we, as a large power, whose nation has not been invaded or bombed or beleaguered, cannot take a larger step in that direction than we have?"

He concluded by reminding his audience of the price we were paying for the war, despite our insulation from its violence. "We have not moved on poverty," he said, "nor have we truly met the challenges of prejudice. Our elderly and their welfare, our children and their education, the blight of our cities, are problems yet facing us—and these problems will not wait patiently."

In the *Globe*, Martin Nolan noted that while Bobby's speech received far greater national publicity, Teddy's "may have stung more than the already-expected blast from Robert, the acknowledged leader of the Restoration forces. . . ." For Teddy was not "the outlander speaking. This was the party regular, joining the ranks of those who dissented against the administration's policies in Vietnam."

Nolan concluded that "whatever disclaimers may be issued in the future or whatever denials have already been proclaimed, the brothers Kennedy have launched a massive air, sea and land assault on Lyndon B. Johnson." This was a competition now, a race—and if the Kennedys had entered, obviously they expected to win.

But by 1967 it was not so simple a matter as it had been in earlier times. For now there were the secrets of the deep. Secrets that had the power to destroy the myth. To reduce, in an instant, the grandest tragedy in American history to a sordid cops-and-robbers tale, complete with molls.

So Bobby felt both driven and constrained. An entire generation—more than that, whole segments of American society: the young, the black, the working class—seemed to be turning to him for the inspirational leadership his martyred brother had provided.

Yet the closer he moved to the center of the ring and the more publicly he challenged Johnson, the greater the risk that the always ruthless and now emotionally unstable President might lash out in retaliation by ordering J. Edgar Hoover to throw open his Kennedy files. Were their positions reversed, Bobby himself, no stranger to ruthlessness, might well have done the same.

Thus, "an indefinable sense of depression hung over him," Schlesinger wrote in his journal after dining with Bobby in April, "as if he felt cornered by circumstance and did not know how to break out."

In distress, Bobby even turned once toward his father. "Millions of people need help, Dad," Bobby said, gripping the old man's withered hand. "My God, they need help! I'll make changes. Like Jack."

But the old man responded only with his still-savage and anguished cry of "Nooooo!"

As one commentator of the time has pointed out, Bobby craved his father's blessing for the risks he so desperately wanted to take, but had to accept that the old man had long since become a Sphinx, capable of answering only in riddles.

Teddy, on the other hand, was speaking frequently and with unusual clarity. Despite having joined his brother in criticism of the administration's Vietnam policies, he staunchly opposed any suggestion that Bobby attempt to unseat Johnson in 1968. In his mind, three reasons held sway: fear of assassination, fear of disclosure, fear of defeat.

Bobby could not persuade himself that Teddy was wrong on any count. So he simply made gestures. He grew his hair long in the fashion of the antiwar protesters of the time. He sought out the leaders of the dissident young: Tom Hayden, Staughton Lynd, Allard Lowenstein.

He made statements designed to shock, though whether it was himself or his listeners he wanted to disturb was never clear. "I wish I'd been born an Indian," he would say. Or, to a journalist from the Bedford-Stuyvesant section of Brooklyn, "I'm jealous of the fact that you grew up in a ghetto." Then: "If I hadn't been born rich, I'd probably be a revolutionary."

This anti-Castro, anti-Communist fanatic was suddenly sounding as if he longed for a guerrilla band to take into the hills of West Virginia, from where he might launch an armed assault on Washington.

If only he were free of his past, how much might he accomplish with his future? This seemed the essence of Bobby's private anguish. "He was a tortured guy," said one friend, "and he was moved by the torture of others."

James Stevenson, who profiled Bobby in *The New Yorker,* could discern the outlines of his pain from no more than close observation of his face.

"His expression is tough," Stevenson wrote, "but the toughness seems largely directed toward himself, inward —a contempt for self-indulgence, for weakness. The sadness in his face, by the same token, is not sentimental sadness, which would imply self-pity, but rather, at some level, a resident, melancholy bleakness."

There was simply too much that Bobby knew; too much he never would be able to forget. Blocked politically by his fear of how Johnson might retaliate—and his awareness of how mighty an anti-Kennedy arsenal Johnson controlled—Bobby also felt psychologically paralyzed. Knowing himself to be so compromised, how could he pretend to the moral leadership that was now demanded of him? Yet what would be the cost to him personally and to the nation of turning away from his ultimate moment of truth?

"Don't you understand?" he cried out to one college audience in the fall of 1967. "What we are doing to the Vietnamese is not very different than what Hitler did to the Jews."

So how could he not intervene?

"Do we have a right here in the United States," he asked rhetorically one Sunday morning on national television, "to say that we're going to kill tens of thousands, make millions of people, as we have . . . refugees? Kill women and children?

"I very seriously question whether we have that right. Those of us who stay here in the United States, we must feel it when we use napalm, when a village is destroyed and civilians are killed. This is also our responsibility. . . .

"We love our country for what it can be and for the justice it stands for and what we're going to mean to the next generation. It is not just the land, it is not just the mountains, it is what this country stands for. And that is what I think is being seriously undermined in Vietnam."

Those were not words written for him by Ted Sorensen or Richard Goodwin. Those were his own words, from his own heart, delivered extemporaneously in response to an unrehearsed question.

Yet, given the circumstances, could even the most inspiring, the most challenging, the most haunting of words be sufficient?

For it was not only Vietnam. It was America itself that seemed to be disintegrating, from the core outward, that year. The summer of 1967 had witnessed outbreaks of racial violence, of rioting, looting and killing in the urban ghettos, on a scale that would have seemed unimaginable even in the years of Jack's Presidency.

The rioting had begun in the South, but over the course of the summer engulfed almost the whole country. Twenty-six killed in Newark, New Jersey, during five days in July. Violence in dozens of other northern cities, including the Spanish Harlem section of New York. And then, in late July, forty-three killed during four days and nights of unchecked violence in Detroit.

Some reacted with calls for harsher enforcement of the laws. Bobby reacted with unfeigned compassion and empathy for those whose despair had driven them to acts of rage.

"Today in America," he said, "we live in two worlds." His own, he admitted, was not, on the surface, so unpleasant. "But," he said, "if we try to look through the eyes of the young slum-dweller—the Negro, and the Puerto Rican, and the Mexican-American—the world is a dark and hopeless place."

In a statement that would have been unthinkable five years earlier, he called Che Guevara "a revolutionary hero." He yearned for the freedom to act as Castro and Guevara had acted, as Cesar Chavez and Martin Luther King were acting, even—though he did not go so far as to give voice to this—as Ho Chi Minh was acting in Vietnam.

He continued to speak out, to read, to brood, to underline. In Emerson he marked: "When you have chosen your part, abide by it, and do not weakly try to reconcile yourself with the world. . . . Adhere to your own act, and congratulate yourself if you have done something strange and extravagant and broken the monotony of a decorous age."

The mid-sixties were anything but a decorous age, but for all his empathy, all his angst, all his genuine rage, for all the strength of his desire to seek a newer world, not only for himself but for America, Bobby remained unable to choose his part.

Meanwhile, Teddy remained adamant in his insistence that whatever other courses of action he might choose, Bobby not run for President in 1968. To do that, Teddy said repeatedly—and not only to Bobby himself but to many of Bobby's advisors and even to some of Jack's advisors, and to his own sisters—would lead to certain defeat and quite possibly to destruction as well.

But in September, to Teddy's dismay, a Gallup poll showed that Bobby, who had trailed the President by six points in July, had suddenly surged twelve points ahead of Johnson as the Democrats' preferred 1968 presidential candidate.

The antiwar movement was carrying Bobby ever closer to a point of confrontation with Lyndon Johnson from which Teddy feared his brother would not be able to turn back. Nonetheless, Teddy himself, his conscience now fully awakened, became more actively involved in the movement.

A team of six nationally known physicians, headed by John Knowles, general director of the Massachusetts General Hospital, made a three-week visit to Vietnam in September, in order to assess firsthand the impact of the war upon the civilian population in the South.

Upon their return they delivered to President Johnson a hundred-page report that excoriated the sorry performance of the United States Agency for International Development, which had responsibility for health care of the civilian population in South Vietnam.

Teddy immediately announced that as chairman of the little-known Senate subcommittee on refugees, he would conduct public hearings on the issue of America's failure to care for the victims of the war it had escalated to such a degree.

"Of all the commitments we have in South Vietnam," he said, "none should be more important than our obligation to guarantee the physical well-being of those we are there to defend. It is time we examine the priority level being given to the civilian side of our efforts.

"Our only hope," he added, "after giving thirteen thousand American lives [the eventual toll would surpass fifty thousand] is that the Vietnamese people survive and grow in freedom. The time has come when the whole matter has to be aired in public."

Emphasizing that he had no wish to enter into a political squabble with President Johnson on what was essentially a humanitarian issue, he said he was troubled, nonetheless, "over the relative lack of concern within our own government for the injured and uprooted people of South Vietnam."

He said that unless America moved quickly to provide greater medical help to the "innocent elderly, women and children caught in the crossfire of war, we will leave the country with little to show for our presence but destruction."

The hearings opened on October 9. Dr. Knowles was the first witness Teddy called. He said a "modest" estimate of civilian casualties would be 50,000—equivalent to 750,000 relative to the population of the United States. And, he admitted, the true figure might be far greater. Perhaps even as high as 150,000. Precise estimates, he said, were difficult to obtain under wartime conditions.

Within two days, despite his professed intention to keep the hearings nonpolitical, Teddy was blaming Lyndon Johnson directly for the "scandalous mismanagement" of medical and social welfare programs in Vietnam.

He said America's "failure to care for hundreds of thousands of wounded and displaced Vietnamese peasants is jeopardizing the lives of our troops by prolonging the war and turning the Vietnamese people into foes instead of friends."

He drew from witness after witness testimony that the official policy of the Agency for International Development—a policy adopted by White House officials—was to give "low priority" to questions of health and civilian casualties. This, said Teddy, was a "national disgrace, which deeply distresses me and which, I hope, will distress the American people."

On the fifth and last day of the hearings, Teddy accused the Defense Department of withholding figures that showed the Viet Cong were recruiting South Vietnamese peasants to their cause at an even more rapid rate than in 1965, before the huge American military buildup began. He said more than fifty thousand new recruits had joined the Viet Cong in the first six months of 1967, almost double the number estimated for the full year of 1966.

Assistant Secretary of State William Bundy agreed that if Teddy's figures, which he termed "distorted," were correct, it would be "one clear indication that our programs haven't worked well." But, he added, "If you write a letter to the secretary of defense and ask him for this information, these aren't the figures you'll get back."

"Well, that's just where they came from," Teddy replied. "The secretary's office."

By the end of the month, Teddy and Dr. Knowles had formed a public alliance, each speaking out against the war in addresses delivered at the Harvard Medical School.

Dr. Knowles, one of the country's best-known medical administrators, said, "Bullets and bombs will not win the war in Vietnam. It is a war for the minds of people. America's present course may alienate more people than it wins as friends, both in Vietnam and throughout Asia."

He added that "the best way to take care of civilian casualties is to stop producing them," and said the war was "taking thirty billion dollars a year from this country, which could be used to tackle urban problems at home." This, of course, was exactly the point Bobby had been trying to make for months.

"It is my view," Teddy said, "that the bullet will never defeat the Viet Cong or the soldiers of the North. I believe it is time to redefine our position in Vietnam, to question whether these people can be won and a land secured by guns alone. I believe we must rethink our total approach and ask ourselves whether the losses we have suffered and the resources we have expended have resulted in any real gains in affecting the political inclinations of the South Vietnamese." He closed by saying the time had come for "nothing less than a complete change in philosophy toward the conduct of the war."

Teddy had to be aware that the more pointedly he spoke, the more he encouraged Bobby to take the action Teddy most feared: a direct challenge to Lyndon Johnson in 1968. Yet now that he had come to understand the full dimension of the human suffering caused by Johnson's Vietnam policies, he felt morally obligated to continue.

All summer, Allard Lowenstein, a thirty-eight-year-old antiwar and civil rights activist from New York, had been advancing the nearly heretical proposition that an attractive political candidate who made opposition to the Vietnam War his central issue could defeat Lyndon Johnson in a series of primaries the following year and perhaps even drive him from the race before the nominating convention.

It was to Bobby that Lowenstein had first turned. And Bobby did not disagree with the activist's thinking. "I think Al may be right," he said at one Hickory Hill dinner in early October, just as Teddy was preparing to start his hearings. "I think Johnson might quit the night before the convention opens. I think he's a coward."

But when Lowenstein implored Bobby to run against the President, he was rebuffed. So persuasive had Teddy been in presenting his arguments against running—some of which could be discussed with outside advisors, some of which could not—that Bobby had apparently reconciled himself to being no more than the moral leader of the opposition and not an actual candidate.

"I think someone else will have to be first," he said.

In mid-October, Senator Eugene McCarthy of Minnesota decided that he would undertake the task.

He would enter a series of primaries: New Hampshire, Massachusetts, Wisconsin, California, maybe some others. He had nothing to lose. His own Senate seat was safe for two more years, and an antiwar run against Johnson, no matter how unsuccessful, would at least give him national exposure. Besides, Gene McCarthy really did oppose the war and wanted to end American involvement as quickly as possible.

He recognized, as did Lowenstein, that Bobby would be by far a stronger candidate. Two or three times in early fall, in fact, he'd actually urged Bobby, whom he did not know well personally, to make the run. But Bobby had demurred. So McCarthy decided to do it himself, though, even as late as the following February, in the midst of the New Hampshire primary campaign, McCarthy's wife would remark, "If Bobby would only run, we'd get out tomorrow morning."

McCarthy's decision apparently shocked Bobby deeply. George McGovern, the liberal senator from South Dakota, was the first to tell him of it and recalled, "He was just terribly distressed. What became clear is he desperately wanted to keep that option open. I don't think Bob in his wildest imagination ever dreamed that McCarthy would announce. I think he thought, 'My God, I should have done this.' "

But many who did not understand the hidden reasons for Bobby's reluctance had little patience with his agonizing, or with the view publicly proffered by Teddy, which was that Bobby could not run because he had such a slim chance of winning.

Even the loyal *Boston Globe* said, "There is a schizoid quality in the recent Kennedy utterings. They detest Lyndon Johnson's conduct of the Vietnam war (and lots of other things) but they respect his political power. . . .

The Kennedys know a good deal about running in primaries and their judgment that McCarthy will fail must be respected. But it must also be recognized as a very safe way to talk and act.

"If the Kennedys are right in their view of the tragedy of Vietnam, then these are not times for timid politicians with safe ideas. To paraphrase a wiser student of the system, there are times to ask what the country can do for you and times to do what you can for the country."

Having the most memorable words of Jack's inaugural address flung in his face stung Bobby sharply.

As did the words of Jack Newfield, a journalist with whom Bobby had grown friendly. "If Kennedy does not run in 1968," Newfield wrote in the *Village Voice* at year's end, "the best side of his character will die. He will kill it every time he butchers his conscience and makes a speech for Johnson next autumn. It will die every time a kid asks him, if he is so much against the Vietnam war, how come he is putting party above principle? It will die every time a stranger quotes his own words back to him on the value of courage."

But even Newfield had no clue as to the depth of Bobby's dilemma. Party versus principle would have been easy. He'd be in New Hampshire right now. Family versus principle, however; myth and legend versus principle—these were far more complex equations, to which any solution might prove disastrous.

12

A JANUARY GALLUP POLL SHOWED JOHNSON LEAD-
ing McCarthy 71 to 18 percent nationally and, in a hypo-
thetical race against Bobby, leading 52 to 40 percent.
Teddy found this reassuring and convinced himself all
over again that pragmatism would prevail over zeal and
Bobby would stay out of the race.

Later that month, Teddy took a twelve-day trip to Vietnam for a firsthand look at the plight of civilian casualties
and refugees. He returned to announce that on Thursday,
January 25, before the Boston chapter of the World Affairs Council, he would deliver a major address on the
question of America's continued involvement in the war.

Neither Bobby nor Teddy wanted to help McCarthy.
Not only did both dislike him personally and feel he was
too small a man for the task he'd undertaken, but Kennedy support for him would have been almost as offensive to Lyndon Johnson as Bobby's own candidacy. And
why risk exposure of family secrets to help someone
else?

The *Globe*'s Bob Healy, who generally reflected the
prevailing Kennedy view, saw that Teddy was in an awkward spot. "What he is going to say," Healy wrote, "is
a well-kept secret. But it is known that he was deeply

disturbed by some of the things he saw in Vietnam. Concern can turn to criticism. If Kennedy has a tough speech on Vietnam, it can only help McCarthy. Kennedy has no intention of doing this. . . . He has been a critic of the administration's policies in Vietnam; he does not want to support McCarthy and he cannot support the President against McCarthy. Kennedy's position, then, is difficult."

Increasingly isolated behind the White House gates, increasingly suspicious of any advice on Vietnam offered by others, increasingly "paranoid," as described by ex-aide Bill Moyers, Lyndon Johnson called Teddy and said he wanted to meet with him privately before the speech.

At 11:30 A.M. on Wednesday, January 24, Teddy spent an hour with Johnson, assuring him that while his speech would contain some harsh criticisms of the Vietnamese government and would present the view that America could not much longer tolerate the existing situation, he would make no criticisms of the President or of the President's actions in Vietnam.

Johnson seemed both agitated and careworn, and almost frantic for Teddy's assurance that he would not engage in personal attack. Quite rightly, he considered Teddy merely a mouthpiece for Bobby—less radical, less abrasive, less ferocious, but first, last and always, a Kennedy; and therefore always bound to place family interests, which in 1968 were Bobby's interests, before any other consideration.

And Johnson's hatred of Bobby was surpassed only by his fear. "Every day as I opened the paper," Johnson would later say to Doris Kearns Goodwin, "there was something about Bobby Kennedy. Somehow it just didn't seem fair. Bobby . . . acted like he was the custodian of the Kennedy dream, some kind of rightful heir to the throne. It just didn't seem fair. I'd waited for my turn. Bobby should've waited for his."

And so, on January 24, in addition to wanting assurances from Teddy that the Vietnam speech would contain no criticism of him personally, the President also wanted Teddy's pledge that Bobby would wait: that McCarthy's challenge was not merely a prelude to Bobby's entrance into the race.

Based on his own assessment of Bobby's thinking, and also on his knowledge of what lay behind it, Teddy felt no qualms about assuring Johnson that he had nothing to fear from Bobby in 1968.

Teddy's Vietnam speech became an immediate national event. "Many observers," said the *Globe,* "felt it was among the best he had ever given."

In it, he accused the Saigon government of being "infested with corruption," and said, "I am forced to conclude, with great dismay, that continued optimism cannot be justified. I am forced to conclude that the objectives we set forth to justify our initial involvement in the conflict, while still defensible, are now less clear and less attainable than they seemed to be in the past.

"In essence," he said, "I found that the kind of war we are fighting in Vietnam will not gain our long-range objectives; that the pattern of destruction we are creating can only make a workable political future more difficult; and that the government we are supporting has given us no indication that it can win the lasting confidence of its people."

Unless radical reform was undertaken rapidly in Saigon, he concluded, "the American people, with great justification, may well consider their responsibilities fulfilled."

Given the intensity of Bobby's feelings about the war, and given the realities of the situation to which he'd just had twelve days of personal exposure, this seemed tame stuff. But his meeting with Johnson had left Teddy more cautious than ever, more fearful of saying or doing anything that might prompt retaliation.

Thus, as Mary McGrory wrote, Teddy "attacked President Thieu [of South Vietnam], not President Johnson, and that makes all the difference. He could be forgiven for what he said because of what he did not say. He did not, as brother Robert has continually done since the latest overture from Hanoi, call for a halt in the bombing of the North." Indeed, McGrory reported, Teddy's "measured" criticism was "received calmly at the White House."

The following Sunday, on *Face the Nation,* Teddy went even further in his effort to soothe the embattled President. Knowing that Bobby would not be running, Teddy was able to say, "I expect the President to be nominated and I expect to support him." He added that he offered "no apologies" for supporting Johnson despite their differences over the war in Vietnam.

When asked why he would not support McCarthy, with whose Vietnam position both he and Bobby seemed to agree, Teddy said that not even McCarthy himself believed he could actually defeat Johnson. He then retreated behind the sort of incomprehensibility that would increasingly become a trademark of his political rhetoric in future years.

"It is important to have this kind of debate," he said, "and I think it is important to have it taken out of the street. It is useful and hopefully with the reaction from it we can have a modification of the policy we are in sympathy with."

Two days later, Bobby made a public announcement intended to put a halt to continued speculation about his intentions.

However great his private anguish, Bobby, once again, had made his choice. Reason—and Teddy—had prevailed. On January 30, he announced at the National Press Club in Washington, "I have told friends and supporters who are urging me to run that I would not oppose Lyndon Johnson under any conceivable circumstances."

Shortly thereafter a distraught Allard Lowenstein, considerably disillusioned by having spent the past two months in the enigmatic presence of Eugene McCarthy, pleaded with Bobby to reconsider.

When Bobby remained adamant, Lowenstein turned to leave his office. "We're going to do it without you," he insisted. "And that's too bad—because you could have been President."

"I hope you understand," Bobby said, following him.

"I want to do it and I know what you're talking about should be done. But I just can't do it."

Lowenstein recalled looking back and seeing Bobby standing in the doorway "in real pain."

"I . . . just . . . can't . . . do . . . it," he had said. But only he and Teddy knew why.

Bobby's timing could not have been worse. The same day he made his announcement of noncandidacy, the North Vietnamese and Viet Cong launched the single most dramatic military offensive of the war.

In what became known as the Tet (Vietnamese New Year) offensive, Communist troops struck simultaneously at thirty-six provincial capitals throughout South Vietnam. The ancient imperial capital of Hue fell into enemy hands. Even the American embassy in Saigon was overrun. The bold strike, which changed forever the course of the war and American attitudes toward it, came as an utter and shocking surprise to United States military authorities.

The attackers not only killed thousands of Vietnamese and American troops, but, as Schlesinger has said, also destroyed "what remained of Lyndon Johnson's credit with millions of Americans."

Only a month earlier, General William Westmoreland, commander of American forces in Vietnam, had assured Congress, "We should expect our gains of 1967 to be increased manyfold in 1968."

Instead, despite suffering massive casualties, the Communist forces had demonstrated in the most compelling and striking fashion that the years of talk about "progress" in Vietnam had been the result either of monumental self-deception by the administration in Washington or of the deliberate and persistent deception of the American people.

Though Westmoreland would cling for years to his claim that the Tet offensive had been a crushing military defeat for the enemy, it was, in fact, the defining moment of the Vietnam War, and—by extension—of Bobby Kennedy's life.

Suddenly all previous declarations seemed obsolete. America's sense of confidence—in the inevitability of its military victory, in the wisdom and candor of its political leaders—was shattered beyond repair. What could have been, even for Bobby, a quixotic and largely symbolic campaign, intended more to articulate moral principle than to actually win an election, and therefore not the kind of race a Kennedy should run, was transformed overnight into the sort of legitimate and serious resistance movement Bobby so yearned to command.

Westmoreland assured Lyndon Johnson that all was well, but that the President should ship another 206,000 troops to Vietnam as soon as possible. At this prospect, even staunch conservatives balked. Matters in Vietnam seemed to have spun entirely out of control, with the blood flowing faster and no end in sight. The credibility of America's military leaders and of such men as Dean Rusk, Robert McNamara, Clark Clifford, William Bundy, Hubert Humphrey and Lyndon Johnson himself was reduced almost overnight to nothing.

Only days before he'd announced his decision not to challenge Johnson, Bobby had received a private warning from a poll taker close to the family that he was "coming to be regarded as an extremist," and that, "in this country, a reputation for extremism is a one-way ticket to oblivion."

But suddenly, in the wake of the Tet offensive, the directions seemed reversed. Extremism in pursuit of peace was no longer a vice if America was trapped in a war that was not merely unnecessary and immoral but unwinnable.

Within a week, the full impact of the Tet offensive was felt across the land. What domestic peace activists had failed to accomplish over years was wrought in a matter of days by North Vietnamese and Viet Cong troops. America would never feel the same about the war, nor about the political figures—Lyndon Johnson chief among them—who had insisted upon both its necessity and its imminent success.

By mid-February it had become apparent that Johnson

would not recover politically from the aftermath of the Tet offensive. A dwindling majority of Americans still told pollsters they supported the President, but a new spirit of defiance was almost tangible. To stand by passively seemed to be more than Bobby's own spirit was able to bear. Once again, he confided to friends that he was reconsidering his decision not to run.

Teddy, however, remained intransigent. It was remarkably out of character for the malleable youngest brother to take such a strong stand on a family matter of such urgency, but that seems precisely why Teddy did. In his fervor and zeal, Bobby was losing sight of how extreme the risks of a campaign might be. Tet or no Tet, the underlying circumstances that had forced Bobby's original decision had not changed.

But even Robert McNamara, Bobby told Teddy, was now saying privately that he should run.

Teddy didn't give a damn about McNamara. McNamara was just as wrong about this as he had been, for years, about the war. There was so much, far too much, that was known neither to McNamara nor to any others among the horde of advisors, whose numbers seemed to be increasing exponentially by the week.

Eventually, Bobby wearied of Teddy's stubbornness. The same set of facts was known to both of them, if not to anyone else. But it was Bobby's turn now, Bobby's career, Bobby's life. And it would be Bobby's decision to make. At this point, he told Teddy frankly, he did not need any further input from someone whose position he already understood so well.

Frustrated by Teddy's unwillingness to see what he himself clearly felt to be the larger moral dimension, Bobby gave up his efforts at personal persuasion. In mid-February, he sent Richard Goodwin to Boston to try to explain to Teddy why Bobby felt he should run against Johnson in the primaries after all.

Toward the end of their long evening together, having exhausted all his other arguments, Goodwin appealed to a higher authority.

"What would Jack have advised?" he asked.

"I'm not sure," Teddy said, after a pause. Then he

invoked the highest authority of all: "But I know what Dad would have said—Don't do it."

On March 7, with Gene McCarthy having gathered great momentum in New Hampshire, Bobby took to the Senate floor to issue an even bolder, more specific indictment of the war. This was his fight now, in whatever form he eventually chose to wage it.

Throughout the decade, Bobby declared, America's political and military leaders had insisted that ultimate victory in Vietnam was imminent. And, throughout the decade, they'd been wrong.

Victory had not been imminent—or even remotely achievable—he said, "in 1961 or 1962, when I was one of those who predicted that there was a light at the end of the tunnel." Nor had there been hope of victory "in 1963 or 1964 or 1965 or 1966 or 1967." Nor, he said, was there now. To commit yet more troops to such an obviously hopeless cause would be, both tactically and morally, an indefensible blunder.

"Are we," he cried out toward the end, "like the God of the Old Testament, that we can decide in Washington, D.C., what cities, what towns, what hamlets in Vietnam are going to be destroyed?"

Then Bobby flew to California to participate with migrant workers' leader Cesar Chavez in a mass of Thanksgiving that would mark the end of a weeks-long fast Chavez had endured as penance for acts of violence committed by members of the union he had formed.

The reception Bobby received from the largely Latino crowd that greeted him in the dusty central California farm town of Delano was unlike anything he'd ever before experienced. The workers seemed to feel a need for not just emotional but physical contact with him. They swarmed toward him, reaching, grabbing, clutching.

Later Chavez would recall, "His hands were scratched, where people were trying to touch him. You could see the blood." In the context, Chavez did not think it inappropriate that his followers would see Bobby as a Christ figure. Nor was it improbable that at some point Bobby might have felt messianic stirrings within himself.

He shared with Chavez the communion bread with which the union leader broke his fast. Too weak to speak, Chavez had written a few words, which he asked a colleague to read aloud at the conclusion of the mass.

"When we are really honest with ourselves," Chavez had written, "we must admit that our lives are all that really belong to us. So it is how we use our lives that determines what kind of men we are. It is my deepest belief that only by giving our lives do we find life. I am convinced that the truest act of courage, the strongest act of manliness, is to sacrifice ourselves for others in a totally nonviolent struggle for justice. To be a man is to suffer for others. God help us be men."

On the flight back from California, Bobby came to recognize, irrevocably, that there were imperatives that took precedence over even the myth.

To run would be to risk ruination of the family's reputation. To run might also be to risk his own life, for Bobby had no reason to believe that the leaders of organized crime were yet satisfied that the family's debt to them was paid in full.

Yet, having shared communion with Chavez, and having heard the words Chavez had written, Bobby knew now what he must do.

"Only by giving our lives do we find life."

13

THE NEXT DAY, FRIDAY, MARCH 8, FIVE DAYS BEFORE
the New Hampshire primary, Bobby told Teddy that he
probably would enter the race. Moreover, he directed
Teddy to proceed immediately to New Hampshire and
deliver this unwelcome news to Gene McCarthy personally.

Teddy was both angry and alarmed. His alarm
stemmed from his three original fears: of assassination,
of disclosure and of defeat. His anger was sparked by the
awareness that even with Bobby his judgment counted
for nothing. All the hours he'd spent discussing the question of Bobby's candidacy, all the arguments he'd so
carefully marshaled against it and had, he thought, delivered so effectively had come to naught.

Now Bobby wanted him to go to New Hampshire and
deliver the news to McCarthy personally? Well, screw
that. He wouldn't do it. And what's more, he wouldn't
tell Bobby he wouldn't do it. Let Bobby think it had been
done. And let him find out for himself that it hadn't.

It was a rare, even unprecedented act of defiance on
Teddy's part, and the fact that he was capable of it is the
best clue to the strength of his feelings about Bobby's
decision. Convinced that Bobby's choice would prove to

be both a personal and a political blunder of catastrophic proportions, Teddy sulked and fretted through the weekend. Only on Monday did Bobby learn, as he put it later, with a rather deliberate dryness, that Teddy "had decided on his own that he didn't want to tell [McCarthy]."

It was now the day before the New Hampshire primary, the first test of how politically viable the anti-Johnson insurgency might prove to be. To avoid later charges that he was simply cashing in on McCarthy's success, Bobby wanted to let McCarthy know before the results were in that he was giving serious consideration to announcing his own candidacy later in the week.

Eventually, he reached Richard Goodwin in New Hampshire. After Bobby's earlier decision not to run, Goodwin had gone to work for McCarthy, but was viewed with considerable suspicion by many, who surmised, correctly, that his ultimate loyalty lay with the Kennedys.

Bobby explained that Teddy had failed to deliver the message as requested. Now, he said, with time so short, Goodwin would have to bear what McCarthy could only view as unhappy tidings: that, as Goodwin put it, Bobby "hadn't foreclosed the involvement, definitely."

Upon receiving this message, McCarthy expressed considerable resentment. He'd been there first, he'd signed on as leader when the cause had seemed truly quixotic, he'd slogged through the snow and slush of gray New Hampshire and now, on the eve of his first major test, Bobby, who'd been ducking the fight for months, was telling him that he might attempt a 1968 Restoration of the House of Kennedy after all.

McCarthy's feelings were not dissimilar to those of Eddie McCormack toward Teddy in 1962, but stronger, not only because the stakes were much higher but because he had already been working so hard despite odds that seemed insurmountable. Bobby's "message" seemed to him just another example of that insufferable Kennedy arrogance, that sense of entitlement, their feeling that whatever they wanted they could have simply because they were Kennedys.

The next day, defying the odds and shocking almost all

prognosticators, McCarthy won more than 42 percent of the popular vote in New Hampshire and twenty of the state's twenty-four delegates to the Democratic convention.

As had the Tet offensive, the New Hampshire primary shook the very foundations of conventional wisdom. It was clear now that 1968 would be a year in American politics like none before it.

Had McCarthy done poorly in New Hampshire, Bobby's task would have been simpler. He could have stepped forward to say, with some legitimacy, that while the antiwar message must be heard, it seemed that the first messenger had proven inadequate. That now Bobby himself would carry the standard forward.

But after McCarthy's stunning performance, Bobby could hardly expect him to step aside. In Washington, the day after the New Hampshire primary, Bobby said at an airport press conference, "I am actively reassessing the possibility of whether I will run against President Johnson."

The Chavez experience had crystallized matters in Bobby's mind. If, indeed, his own life was all that really belonged to him, then how he used it would determine the kind of man he was. He had essentially made his choice before New Hampshire, and it was to go forward, even if that meant risking defeat, at the very least. But to many, and not without reason, it seemed that Bobby was simply trying to cash in on McCarthy's unexpected success.

He met privately with McCarthy that afternoon and, after offering appropriate congratulations, suggested that McCarthy might still wish to withdraw from the race. After all, Bobby would stand a much better chance of actually wresting the nomination from Lyndon Johnson.

"He just said I could do what I wanted, and he would do what he wanted," Bobby reported later to a friend. "I would say he was cold." In any event, it was clear that McCarthy had no intention of withdrawing in order to clear the path for Bobby. "That Bobby," he said, not admiringly, to a journalist after the meeting. "He's something, isn't he?"

The next day, more than a dozen Kennedy advisors assembled in Steve Smith's New York apartment to make one last assessment of the pros and cons of Bobby's entering the race. Teddy was among them, looking, as Schlesinger reported, "a bit unhappy."

The meeting meandered through the afternoon and early evening, with such people as Pierre Salinger, Ted Sorensen, Burke Marshall and Teddy repeating all the arguments they'd already made to one another.

At 7:00 P.M. they paused to watch the CBS evening news, aware that Bobby had earlier taped an interview with Walter Cronkite about his process of "reassessment."

They were shocked by how close Bobby came to actually announcing his candidacy. It was suddenly clear that even as they haggled in New York, Bobby had already moved beyond them.

With considerable annoyance, Teddy stood up and said, "What the hell's the point of even holding this meeting? He's already made up his mind and we're learning about it on television!"

Later in the week, in Washington, Bobby lunched with a small group of liberal Democrats. One was George McGovern, who, not having seen Bobby since January, was struck by his appearance. "He looked so much older," McGovern said, "so drawn."

Several in the group urged Bobby to defer any final decision about entering the race himself, suggesting that instead he support McCarthy, at least through the next primary, which was to be held in Wisconsin.

But one, Stewart Udall, who'd been secretary of the interior in Jack's administration, formed the distinct impression, as had Teddy earlier in the week, that Bobby had moved past the point of persuasion.

"I could tell he really wasn't listening to what we said because he had heard the same thing from others, and the whole thing was very clear to him. With all the turmoil in the country and with what he felt was a need for definition of the issues and for the championing of the people who were unchampioned, he was determined to follow his own convictions and to do what was true in terms of his own personality. I sensed that if in the end he lost, he would feel he had done the right thing. . . . He was on fire."

Udall added, "I almost got the feeling that it was like a Greek tragedy in the sense that events themselves had been determined by fates setting the stage, and that there was really little choice left."

On Friday, March 15, Bobby again assembled a large group of advisors at Hickory Hill.

He had already announced that he would hold a press conference in the Senate caucus room the next morning. It was the same room Jack had used to declare his presidential candidacy in 1960.

Knowing the strength of Teddy's negative feelings, Bobby did not want him present during the final drafting of the announcement speech. The truth was, he'd lost patience with Teddy. Bobby did not even tell Teddy personally that he would be announcing his candidacy the next morning. Instead, he sent an aide, Fred Dutton, to bear the message. "On fire," in a way that Teddy simply seemed unable to comprehend, Bobby had become suddenly quite dismissive of his younger brother.

Partly, this may have been because Bobby sensed all too acutely Teddy's fear, even dread, that he might lose his last brother through this campaign. By avoiding Teddy, Bobby would also avoid a stark reminder of the peril of running and of the pain he would inflict on the Kennedys left behind if the campaign were to cost him his life.

Teddy apparently did not perceive this aspect of Bobby's motivation for deliberately putting a new distance between them. Instead he seemed to feel that during the long winter of agonizing indecision, Bobby had taken a penetrating look not only into his own soul but into Teddy's as well. And that, within Teddy, he'd found something vital to be lacking.

As Bobby put it later to a journalist, "Ted thinks I'm a little nutty for doing this, but he's an entirely different kind of person." With some confusion and no small amount of pain, Teddy came to recognize what Bobby already had: that he would never be able to be for Bobby what Bobby had always been for Jack.

Receiving the news from Dutton, Teddy had responded grumpily, "Bobby's therapy is going to cost the family eight million dollars."

Later in the day, Bobby did call Teddy, but only to instruct him to fly to Green Bay, Wisconsin, where McCarthy was campaigning. The Hickory Hill brainstormers had come up with a thoroughly impractical and almost insulting proposal that Bobby and McCarthy run some sort of vaguely defined joint campaign against Johnson and only later worry about which of them would become the presidential candidate.

It was a mission doomed to failure—indeed, a fool's errand—but it would keep Teddy and his well-known misgivings out of the way during the crucial hours when the declaration speech was being drafted.

In Wisconsin, Teddy blundered through a comedy of errors that kept him up most of the night. Despite being told that Teddy was traveling all the way from Washington to submit a "joint candidacy" proposal on Bobby's behalf, McCarthy went to bed at his usual early hour, not even informing his wife that Teddy was expected at their suite.

Upon his arrival in Green Bay, Teddy contacted Richard Goodwin and McCarthy's campaign manager, Blair Clark, both of whom knew he was coming. Clark called the McCarthy suite to say that Teddy, who'd checked into a nearby motel, was about to arrive. McCarthy's wife, who took the call, was dumbfounded.

She put down the telephone and went into the bedroom. "I don't want to see Teddy Kennedy," McCarthy told her. "I'm going to sleep."

Informed of this response, Clark and Goodwin left Teddy sitting in his motel room and rushed to the McCarthy suite themselves. Roused from sleep, McCarthy grouchily agreed to meet with Teddy. But before Teddy could even open the briefcase that contained a rough outline of the joint candidacy proposal, McCarthy motioned for him to keep it shut.

"I'm not interested," he said. He told Teddy that this meeting was a waste of everyone's time and that he did not intend to deprive himself of any more sleep by prolonging it. Then he got up and went back into his bedroom, leaving Clark and Goodwin to usher Teddy, unopened briefcase still in hand, out of the suite and out of Green Bay.

It was dawn before Teddy, traveling by chartered aircraft, arrived back at Hickory Hill. There, he glumly reported McCarthy's rebuff.

An hour later, when Bobby got up, Teddy made one last attempt to persuade him to at least postpone an announcement of his candidacy.

"Well, I have to say something in three hours," Bobby replied.

Then Schlesinger, reversing his own position once again, suggested that Bobby endorse McCarthy. His theory was that when the McCarthy campaign faltered, as he felt it inevitably would, Bobby could inherit McCarthy's delegates and add them to a base he would have whether or not he formally entered the race.

For Teddy, this idea had great appeal. At this point, Teddy was grasping at anything that might forestall Bobby's announcement. But Bobby would have none of it. Schlesinger recalls Bobby looking at him "stonily" and saying, "I can't do that. It would be too humiliating. Kennedys don't act that way."

Downstairs, Teddy, suffering from the effects both of a sleepless night and of his humiliation by McCarthy, was growing frantic.

"I just can't believe it!" he shouted, seated at a kitchen table and waving his arms in the air. "It is too incredible. I just can't believe that we are sitting around even discussing anything as incredible as this!"

Behind him, Bobby, still in pajamas, stood in the doorway. Made aware of his presence, Teddy turned in his chair to face his older brother.

"I'm going ahead," Bobby told him quietly. "There is no point in talking about anything else."

Then he went back upstairs to dress for his press conference, while, in the dining room, a young staff aide named Mary Jo Kopechne typed the final version of the speech with which he would announce his presidential candidacy.

Of the campaign itself, much has already been written. Indeed, never before or since in the history of American politics have so many journalists, in newspapers, magazines and books, devoted so many words to chronicling a political effort that ultimately proved as ineffectual as it was brief.

Bobby set the tone that bright cold morning of March 16 when he proclaimed, in making his announcement, "At stake is not simply the leadership of our party or even our country—it is our right to moral leadership on this planet."

Many have subsequently criticized this statement as being indicative of Kennedy grandiosity, but it would seem, upon reflection, that it was only by casting his quest in such apocalyptic terms that Bobby could justify —to himself, to his stricken father, to the memories of Joe Junior and of Jack—his acting in a fashion that was putting them all at such risk.

Reaction to Bobby's announcement was swift and harsh. Nothing the Kennedys had ever done before— not the appointment of Bobby as attorney general, not Teddy's 1962 Senate race, not Bobby's carpetbagging candidacy of 1964—infuriated so many people upon whom Bobby would eventually have to rely for support as did this seemingly ruthless attempt to seize the trophy Gene McCarthy had just won.

"Even those of us who had anticipated an outburst were astonished by its virulence," Schlesinger wrote.

The tone was perhaps best expressed by columnist Murray Kempton, a longtime friend, who now termed Bobby a coward, "down from the hills to shoot the wounded. He has, in the naked display of his rage at Eugene McCarthy for having survived on the lonely road he dared not walk himself, done with a single great gesture something very few public men have ever been able to do: In one day, he managed to confirm the worst things his enemies have ever said about him.''

Particularly in the early days, there seemed a desperation about Bobby's candidacy and an almost total absence of the exuberance and even joy that had been part of Jack's campaign in 1960.

Matters were not helped by the chaos and confusion that reigned everywhere. No one was in charge and everyone was. Three different generations of Kennedy advisors found themselves in almost constant conflict.

Bobby's new breed felt that the old-timers like O'Donnell, Sorensen and O'Brien simply didn't understand the altered landscape. The older men, who had, after all, conducted a winning presidential campaign, thought the younger ones brash, foolhardy and entirely incapable of grasping that idealism must be melded with practicality: that the purpose of a campaign was not to gain a forum for noble speeches, but to win.

Much murkiness lay ahead, along the trail to the Chicago convention, and the older men felt that only they, having already traversed the ground, had proven themselves reliable guides.

Torn between these groups—and a third, composed of members of Teddy's staff, who seemed primarily concerned with protecting Teddy's long-term interests— Bobby campaigned erratically.

His central problem was, as he had both feared and anticipated, that he did not have a Bobby to run things for him. "I wish," he said at one point, "there was somebody who could do for me what I did for Jack." In truth, however, probably only Bobby himself could have brought order to such a frantic, last-minute, helter-skelter effort. But Bobby, as the candidate, could not also serve as campaign manager.

Dutifully, Teddy tried to step into the role, but it was beyond him, as California had been beyond him in 1960.

"He asked all the correct questions," one observer noted, "but as the answers came back he didn't seem to know what to do with them."

Still, Bobby was a Kennedy at a time the nation craved Kennedys. And it was Bobby who could stir the passions and roil the blood in a way that the laconic Gene McCarthy could not approach.

And it was Bobby—and the threat of all that Bobby represented—who finally panicked Lyndon Johnson. Though he undoubtedly had access to information that could have destroyed Bobby's candidacy, Johnson did not use it. At that point, the President had become so psychologically unstable that it is impossible to do more than speculate about his motivation, but he might well have sensed that he was already so unpopular that his exposure of dark Kennedy secrets, whatever it did to Bobby, would cause Johnson himself to be loathed to an even greater degree.

In any event, upon Bobby's entrance into the race the President seemed to come entirely unhinged. His worst paranoid fantasy now loomed before him, flesh and blood, long, unruly hair blowing in the wind, that shrill, nasal voice accusing him of appealing to the "darker impulses of the American people."

Later, he would describe to Doris Kearns Goodwin a recurrent dream from this period: "I felt that I was being chased on all sides by a giant stampede. . . . I was being forced over the edge by rioting blacks, demonstrating students, marching welfare mothers, squawking professors, and hysterical reporters. And then the final straw! The thing I feared from the first day of my Presidency was actually coming true. Robert Kennedy had openly announced his intention to reclaim the throne in the memory of his brother. And the American people, swayed by the magic of the name, were dancing in the streets."

A Gallup poll in late March bore out the worst of Johnson's fears. While the President was preferred to McCarthy by 59 to 29 percent, Bobby, after only one chaotic, disorganized week in the race, had already moved ahead of him in popularity.

One week later, Johnson went on national television to announce that he would not seek reelection.

Four days later, Martin Luther King was killed. J. Edgar Hoover's hatred of King had grown feverish and obsessive. Knowing now that Lyndon Johnson would no longer be there to provide cover for his most distasteful operations—indeed, aware that unless he, too, were somehow stopped, the hated Bobby might well become Johnson's successor—might Hoover have directed or authorized the assassination of King, or at least hinted that such an act might be in the country's best interests?

The answer is unclear. "We were operating an intensive vendetta against Dr. King in an effort to destroy him," an FBI agent would later testify. Another was said to have "jumped for joy" in Atlanta FBI headquarters upon hearing the news that King had been shot. "They got the son of a bitch!" he'd shouted.

Hoover himself had issued a written instruction to "expose, disrupt, misdirect, discredit, or otherwise neutralize" King and his associates in the Southern Christian Leadership Conference.

"It was a tough and dirty business," a secret counterintelligence agent acting under Hoover's direction would later tell a congressional committee. "No holds were barred. Techniques used against Soviet agents were brought home against any organization against which we were targeted."

As Harris Wofford has reported, "Another agent said he knew people in the FBI who might well have been involved in aiding the assassination. 'It could have happened,' he said. 'I hope it didn't.'"

Wofford added that while we must all hope it didn't, "our country must deal with the ugly fact . . . that in a number of cases involving so-called black nationalist groups, FBI campaigns did include deliberate efforts to 'intensify the degree of animosity' toward targeted groups and 'turn violence-prone organizations' against the targeted leaders."

Originally he'd found it "almost impossible to believe" that Hoover or the FBI could have had a role in the King assassination, Wofford wrote, but his position changed over the years, as it had regarding the role of organized crime in the assassination of Jack.

In print, he wondered if the FBI might not have given at least a "nudge" to the King assassination. "The 1979 investigation of the House Committee on Assassinations could not prove any direct connection between the FBI determination that King was 'the most dangerous Negro in the country' and the killing," he wrote. "But its report points to evidence of a conspiracy to kill King that may have involved white hate groups and the underworld, and by 1968 the FBI had an extensive network of paid 'informants' in both the Ku Klux Klan and the Mafia. Robert Kennedy had pressed Hoover to infiltrate both those targeted groups with the vigor and skill the FBI used to penetrate the Communist Party."

Even without firm evidence of a direct link between the FBI and the King assassination, Harris Wofford concluded that "the story of how Hoover and the FBI helped create the climate that invited King's assassination is probably the single most disturbing story of the 1960s, or perhaps of any decade of American history."

And it was a story in which Bobby—so compromised by the actions of his father and of Jack—was deeply implicated. As attorney general, he had reluctantly granted Hoover the authority to tap Martin Luther King's telephone and to conduct other forms of electronic eavesdropping against the civil rights leader. It had not been Bobby's proudest moment.

As a senior FBI official later wrote, "Bobby Kennedy resisted, resisted and resisted tapping King. Finally, we twisted his arm to the point where he had to go. I guess he feared we would let our stuff [on the Kennedy family] go in the press if he said no."

So Bobby, upon hearing the news of King's assassination, had reason to feel—as in the case of Jack's murder —not merely shock, horror and grief, but a certain irreducible level of guilt. He knew how much Hoover had hated King. He knew to what lengths Hoover would go to persecute enemies. He knew how demented Hoover was. And it was Bobby himself who had permitted and even encouraged the use of Mafia gunmen to carry out violent plots on behalf of agencies of the United States government.

It seemed that a large part of what drove him forward in 1968 was not just his genuine horror at the mushrooming catastrophe of Vietnam, but a need to expiate some of the guilt he bore for his complicity in those earlier actions which had produced such tragic results.

To some extent, he had to have felt responsible for his own brother's assassination.

Just as, to some extent, he had to feel responsible for the murder of Martin Luther King. At the very least, he'd done nothing to prevent Hoover and the FBI from creating the climate that had led to King's death.

So it must have been with an alarming mix of emotions that Bobby entered an Indianapolis ghetto that evening to speak to an all-black crowd that was not yet aware of the assassination.

And out of this volatile mix, on a raw and windy night in early April, came one of the finest spontaneous moments the American political process has ever produced.

Urged by local police officials to cancel his appearance, warned that his own safety could not be guaranteed, Bobby insisted on speaking to the crowd, which had been awaiting his appearance for an hour.

Under the gleam of bright spotlights, his face gaunt, his expression anguished, his slight body hunched inside a black overcoat as the wind blew smoke and dust wildly through the night, he climbed atop a flatbed truck.

"I have bad news for you," he said, "and for all of our fellow citizens and people who love peace all over the world. And that is that Martin Luther King was shot and killed tonight."

There had been fears that the crowd might react with violence to this news. Later, in other cities, many people did. But here the shock was too great and Bobby, as the messenger of the awful tidings, seemed the one man to whom the listeners could turn for consolation.

Struggling to control his emotions, Bobby began to speak extemporaneously. No speech writer was involved here. Not even any notes he'd made himself. He spoke, as Schlesinger has written, "out of aching memory . . . out of the depth of heart and hope."

He said softly, "Martin Luther King dedicated his life to love and to justice for his fellow human beings, and he died because of that effort.

"In this difficult day, in this difficult time for the United States, it is perhaps well to ask what kind of a nation we are and what direction we want to move in."

He said that for those who were black—considering that early evidence indicated that whites had been responsible for the murder—"you can be filled with bitterness, with hatred and a desire for revenge. We can move in that direction as a country . . . black people amongst black, white people amongst white, filled with hatred toward one another.

"Or we can make an effort, as Martin Luther King did . . . to replace that violence, that stain of bloodshed that has spread across our land, with an effort to understand with compassion and love.

"For those of you who are black and are tempted to be filled with hatred and distrust at the injustice of such an act, against all white people, I can only say that I feel in my own heart the same kind of feeling. I had a member of my family killed, and he was killed by a white man. But we have to make an effort . . . to understand, to go beyond these rather difficult times.

"My favorite poet was Aeschylus. He wrote: 'In our sleep, pain which cannot forget falls drop by drop upon the heart until, in our own despair, against our will, comes wisdom through the awful grace of God.'

"What we need in the United States is not division; what we need in the United States is not hatred; what we need in the United States is not violence or lawlessness, but love and wisdom, and compassion toward one another, and a feeling of justice towards those who still suffer within our country, whether they be white or they be black. . . .

"Let us dedicate ourselves to what the Greeks wrote so many years ago: to tame the savageness of man and to make gentle the life of this world."

* * *

In the weeks that followed, though the campaign, despite Teddy's best efforts, continued to trip over its own feet, the response to Bobby personally, to his physical presence, grew so feverish that some close to him became alarmed.

Bobby shrugged. "If they want to get me, they'll get me," he said. "They got Jack." Again, no one asked who "they" might be.

He flew briefly to Hyannis Port to see his father. The old man was badly shrunken now, his hands turned to claws, his vision failing, his limbs trembling with palsy.

Bobby bent over his wheelchair. He leaned close to his father's head. "Dad, I'm going out to California. And I'm going to fight hard. I'm going to win."

And he did. He finished first. He defeated Gene McCarthy in the California primary on June 4, 1968, exactly two months after the assassination of Martin Luther King.

And that night, as he was leaving the Los Angeles hotel where he'd just given a brief victory speech, he was shot in the head at close range with a handgun. He lived for twenty-six hours without regaining consciousness.

Part Four

Part Four

I

On the night of the California primary, the night Bobby was shot in Los Angeles, Teddy was hundreds of miles away, attending an unruly victory rally in San Francisco. So raucous was the atmosphere that it made his administrative assistant, David Burke, uneasy.

"A rough affair," Burke called it later, "a lot of unfamiliar faces. There was an awful lot of physical shoving of the Senator, no sense of control. People kept yelling and screaming things that had nothing to do with Robert Kennedy's victory, and I felt uncomfortable."

At about 11:00 P.M., Burke said, "We ought to get out of here." Teddy did not disagree. The two of them returned to the Fairmont Hotel, atop Nob Hill, where Teddy had a fourth-floor suite and where he'd last seen Bobby briefly two days earlier when Bobby had campaigned in San Francisco.

In the suite, Burke turned on the television. An announcer was saying that there had been a shooting at the rally.

"Oh, my God," Burke said. So strong had been his sense that the mood at the San Francisco rally was about

485

to spill over into nastiness that he wasn't surprised to hear there'd been a shooting.

"We were lucky to get out of there," he said to Teddy. "I didn't like that at all. You know, if we're going to keep doing this sort of thing, we're going to have to find a different way to handle security."

Then he noticed that Teddy wasn't really listening to him. Instead, he was staring at the television screen, where, inexplicably, Steve Smith was asking people to be calm, to remain controlled and to please leave the ballroom as quickly as possible.

Burke was momentarily confused. Steve Smith hadn't been at the rally. Steve was down in Los Angeles, with Bobby. Burke fell silent and, along with Teddy, gazed at the screen.

This had nothing to do with San Francisco. But it had everything to do with Teddy. His last living brother had just been shot.

Teddy stood frozen in the center of the room, unable to take his eyes from the screen.

He spoke only once. "We have to get down there," he said. Nothing else. Just: "We have to get down there." He did not even look at Burke as he spoke. He did not move. He stood in the middle of the suite's living room and did not take his eyes from the screen.

Burke rushed to the front desk to seek help in obtaining the quickest possible transportation to Los Angeles. This was a complicated process that required him to make many phone calls from the office of the assistant manager of the Fairmont. But through all the logistical discussions, he kept thinking of Teddy, standing alone in the fourth-floor room, gazing at the television that was now showing, over and over again, Bobby's brief victory talk, his final grin and wave, his departure from the ballroom, and then the pop of the first, close-range shot, and all the chaos that followed.

David Burke was worried about Teddy. "In between calls," he said later, "I raced up to the room three or four times and he was always standing there, in front of the television set, his jacket off, just standing there watching and not saying a word. I don't know why I kept running back and forth because I wasn't getting much response from him.''

No one did, not for the longest time.

They left the hotel at 1:15 A.M. and were driven to an air force base in Marin County, from which a military jet would fly them to Los Angeles.

Arriving at the base, Teddy was told he had a call from Pierre Salinger in Los Angeles. He spoke briefly and privately to Salinger before boarding the plane.

"How are things?" Burke asked.

"It's going to be all right," Teddy said.

Only after arriving in Los Angeles, following a flight during which Teddy did not say a word, did Burke learn that it wasn't going to be all right and that Salinger had never told Teddy that it would be.

Yet even later, from Los Angeles, even knowing the truth, when Teddy called Bobby's oldest son at boarding school in the East, he said, "Don't worry. It isn't as serious as it sounds.''

And not until the oldest son, Joseph P. Kennedy III, arrived at the hospital hours later and saw his father, unconscious inside an oxygen tent, his head swathed in bandages, his face swollen and darkened, his body lying on an ice-filled mattress intended to lower the temperature of his blood and slow its passage through his mangled brain tissue, did the sixteen-year-old boy realize that his Uncle Teddy had not prepared him in any way for what he would find.

By then it had become apparent to all around Teddy that he was not processing this new information: he had shut down. This had been the one shock too many. He stood silently at Bobby's bedside in the intensive care room on the fifth floor of the Good Samaritan Hospital in Los Angeles, gazing off into the middle distance as the last of the life slowly ebbed from the only brother he had left; the brother with whom he'd ridden his bicycle across the cobblestoned yard behind the embassy residence in London in 1938; the one who'd come to see him at the dreadful Boston boarding schools when no one else in the family had the time. The one he had told not to run for

President because, even more than he had feared defeat, even more than he had feared the exposure of family secrets, he had feared this.

On the morning of Thursday, June 6, Teddy, despite his bad back, helped to load Bobby's casket on board the air force plane sent west by Lyndon Johnson to bear the body home.

The casket was secured in a narrow aisle near the front of the plane. All the way east, Teddy sat alone, close enough to touch it. In New York, he rode in the hearse that carried the casket to St. Patrick's Cathedral. And all that night, even after the other shocked, exhausted and grief-stricken family members had left, Teddy sat in a pew near the altar, still close enough to touch the casket. He did not leave the cathedral until dawn. Others could go to Hyannis Port to be with his parents. This time, Teddy was staying with his brother.

And at the funeral mass two days later, Teddy stepped to a lectern and spoke, as he had not been able to do at Arlington.

"We loved him as a brother and as a father and as a son," Teddy said, in a choked, broken, faltering voice. "From his parents and from his older brothers and sisters, Joe and Kathleen and Jack, he received an inspiration which he passed on to all of us. He gave us strength in time of trouble, wisdom in time of uncertainty, and sharing in time of happiness. He will always be by our side."

Teddy, so pale and so close to the edge of nervous collapse, tightly gripped the sides of the lectern to steady himself as he began to read from a speech Bobby had given to the youth of South Africa in 1966. At Arlington, he had not been able to read the words of Jack. At St. Patrick's, he could not fail to read the words of Bobby, because if he proved unable, there would be no one to take his place. He had been the last and the least of them. Now he was only the last.

" 'There is discrimination in this world and slavery and slaughter and starvation,' " Teddy read. " 'Governments repress their people. Millions are trapped in poverty, while the nation grows rich and wealth is lavished on armaments everywhere.

" 'These are different evils, but they are the common works of man. They reflect the imperfection of human justice, the inadequacy of human compassion, our lack of sensibility toward the suffering of our fellows.

" 'But we can remember, even if only for a time, that those who live with us are our brothers, that they share with us the same short moment of life, that they seek as we do nothing but the chance to live out their lives in purpose and happiness, winning what satisfaction and fulfillment they can.

" 'Surely this bond of common faith, this bond of common goals, can begin to teach us something. Surely, we can learn at least to look at those around us as fellow men. And surely we can begin to work a little harder to bind up the wounds among us and to become in our hearts brothers and countrymen once again. . . .

" 'Each time a man stands for an ideal, or acts to improve the lot of others, or strikes out against injustice, he sends forth a tiny ripple of hope. And crossing each other from a million different centers of energy and daring, those ripples build a current that can sweep down the mightiest walls of oppression and resistance.' "

At the end, with millions watching on television as millions had watched the funeral of Jack, he struggled through a final paragraph that Milton Gwirtzman had written for him.

"My brother," he said, "need not be idealized or enlarged in death beyond what he was in life. He should be remembered simply as a good and decent man who saw wrong and tried to right it, saw suffering and tried to heal it, saw war and tried to stop it. Those of us who loved him and who take him to his rest today pray that what he was to us, and what he wished for others, will someday come to pass for all the world. As he said many times, in many parts of the nation, to those he touched and to those who sought to touch him: 'Some men see things as they are and say, Why? I dream things that never were and say, Why not?' "

Trembling, he then returned to the front pew, where

489

he sat next to Bobby's widow, as, in 1963, he and Bobby had sat beside Jacqueline. The service lasted another hour and forty minutes and included Leonard Bernstein conducting the mournful and unforgettable Adagietto from Mahler's Fifth Symphony.

Teddy flew to Hyannis Port the next day. Joan did not accompany him. She had not even managed to attend the burial the night before. On June 15 he appeared on national television, standing next to his mother on the Hyannis Port lawn, thanking the nation for its outpouring of sympathy. His father had been dressed in a suit and wheeled outside for the occasion.

It was as if the past five years had not existed and he was back in 1963, still stuck in the nightmare that would not end. Only now he was alone. There were still speech writers to craft his phrases for him, and advisors—oh, so many advisors—but there was no Bobby to tell him what to do, and for Teddy that made all the difference.

He could not tell what his father felt. The old man had given up almost all attempts at sound or motion. Whatever his agonies, they would be locked inside him until death set him free. And whatever his sins, this punishment seemed sufficiently severe: to be forced, every waking hour, to confront the stark fact that his drive for power, glory and freedom from the laws that governed man had been satisfied only through the spilling of his children's blood.

Would he have made the bargain anyway? The attainment of the greatest glory any American family had ever known in return for the lives of three sons?

This was not a question that Teddy, or anyone else, would ever be able to ask him. Nor would there be any way to tell whether he asked it of himself as he sat, hour after hour, day after day, frozen in his despair. Of one thing, however, Joe Kennedy was certainly aware: that Teddy was all he had left; the one last hope for a return to the golden age for which he had paid such an unimaginable price.

Teddy was no longer simply the last of the Kennedy children; he was the last Kennedy. Never before had he faced anything like the degree of obligation and responsibility that now confronted him. He must be father to all his brothers' children, as well as a symbol of greatness to the nation: the sole and final bearer of the torch of hope and promise that Jack and Bobby had held so high. And he must, one more time, do his father's bidding.

Overwhelmed by these pressures, he turned, reflexively, to women, alcohol and other drugs. He wanted no part of his own wife and children, who looked to him to satisfy their needs while he had no one to satisfy his own. All he wanted, for the moment, was to dull his pain; to get out from under the dead weight of the legacy, from the knowledge that more than ever, he would have to pretend to be someone he knew he could never hope to become.

Dangerously drunk, he raced a power boat through the Martha's Vineyard harbor. He brought a group of Green Berets to Hyannis Port, had them scale the outside of his father's house, then took them to a nearby bar and, in the comfort of their manly company, got blindly, excruciatingly drunk, imitating them as they drained one drink after another and then smashed their glasses against a wall, shouting, "No man shall drink from this glass again."

He would go sailing, sometimes alone, sometimes sober, but more often not. Later, a friend would comment on the "freneticism of booze and sex" through which he tried, that summer, to hide from a destiny he had not sought, did not want and knew he'd never be able to cope with.

"Afterwards," this friend commented, "there were times of great guilt." Which may have been the central point. Even as America and the world yearned to see in him the best of Jack and Bobby, Teddy seemed to need to prove, first to himself and then to the nation, that he was unworthy to carry the torch, unworthy even to bear the family name.

Never had he wished more ardently that he could somehow be only Edward Moore. But never had the nation demanded more fervently that he be not only Edward, but also John and Robert, Kennedy.

The political talk had begun even before the train bearing Bobby's body reached Washington. McCarthy was finished, they all knew that. Bobby's only opponent at the Chicago convention would have been Hubert Humphrey, the Vice President, the shameless cheerleader for the Vietnam War, the once principled liberal who'd sold out to the most regressive and repressive elements within the Democratic party in return for the dubious privilege of being Lyndon Johnson's lap dog.

Now, Humphrey wanted Teddy to join him. The first overtures went out before Bobby's body was laid in its grave. And there were those on Teddy's staff—so eager for power of their own, so tired of standing in the shadows while Jack's team and Bobby's team got the acclaim —who were prepared to urge him to run with Humphrey.

"One of them," Bob Healy wrote in the *Globe,* "pointed out on the train . . . that Sen. Kennedy does not believe that Vice President Humphrey's position on the war is the same as the President's and that he has been trapped by his position as a loyal member of the administration. He also pointed out that Sen. Edward Kennedy has, through his six years in the Senate, been friendly to Humphrey. As he put it: 'Humphrey's been good to Ted.' Beyond that, it was said that Edward Kennedy's position on Vietnam was slightly different from that of his brother, Robert [who] stressed that it was an immoral war. . . ."

Already, some were seeking to emphasize the gap between the apparent centrist steadiness of Teddy and the energizing but impractical radicalism of Bobby, who'd become such an odd mix, in his last days, of Cesar Chavez and Che Guevara—Bobby, who'd died while attempting an unprecedented act of rebellion against the family precepts that pragmatism came before principle, that political moderation was the key to success and that winning was all that mattered. Yet even as they spoke of Teddy's practicality, tens of thousands of ordinary Americans who had never known power, wealth or fame lined the train tracks in a final attempt at communion with Bobby's spirit.

Other aides, of course, felt that any alliance between Teddy and Humphrey would be an abomination; a betrayal not only of those principles for which Bobby had risked and ultimately sacrificed his life, but of Teddy's own better self.

Teddy himself seemed not to know which way to turn. "I have no plans," he said. "I don't know what I am going to do."

He hosted a July 1 meeting of advisors in Hyannis Port. He was now swamped, overloaded, with advisors. Three generations' worth: Jack's, Bobby's and his own. The air was thick with nostalgia and ghosts. These were the people whom author Victor Navasky had first termed "honorary Kennedys." But now there were so many of them, and only one of him. The ratio, which had once made some sense, which had served some purpose, was now skewed to almost comic proportions.

Teddy still seemed at a loss as to which way, if any, to move next. And now he had three separate sets of courtiers, two of which viewed him with open condescension even as they clamored to serve his interests, as well as their own. To them all, in the summer of 1968, Teddy seemed a frail reed on which to construct their dreams of future prominence.

They sat on the open patio of his father's house, the old man abed upstairs. Ten years earlier, he would have chaired such a meeting, with Jack and Bobby serving as executive officers, directing the flow of conversation, neatly organizing the abundant ideas into patterns from which definitive action would quickly flow.

Now, this army of Camelot was leaderless, the boy prince who would be forced to play the role of heir to the kingdom gazing dully at them, lifeless, dispirited and, though he tried to hide it, scared almost out of his mind.

Had Bobby been killed by a crazed Arab, acting alone, as the public was already being instructed to believe? Or was his assassination the well-planned second act of vengeance against the family for betraying men who did not take betrayal lightly?

Either way, the prospect facing Teddy was terrifying. If it was the second act of an ongoing conspiracy—particularly one that J. Edgar Hoover was aware of, if not actively assisting—who was to say there would not be a third act if Teddy tried to assume a position of national leadership?

If, on the other hand, Bobby was killed by a lone crazy person who had somehow penetrated all the layers of security surrounding a presidential candidate and had managed to shoot him in the head at close range with a handgun, who was to say there was not yet another crazy person out there—or thousands of them?—who would think that to kill the last brother would be the greatest feat of all?

So there was this fear, this raw, physical terror, coupled with the dread that arose from his awareness that not only was he not who he had always pretended to be, but that now an entire nation, as well as his own family and all the honorary Kennedys, would demand that he pretend to be so much more.

Drunkenly, he would say, "All I want, if someone's going to blow my head off, is just one swing at him first. I'm not afraid to die." But then, tearfully and even more drunkenly, he would sob, "I'm too young to die."

Ensnared by the psychological web of neurosis, interdependence, repression and the insatiable demand for victory upon victory upon victory which his parents had woven for all their children even before Teddy was born, he was utterly devoid of the inner resources he would need to rebuild a life in the aftermath of so much death.

When not addled by drink, he felt totally alone and could not envision any point in the future when he would not. He had neither the music of Wagner nor the words of the ancient Greeks or the existentialist philosophers with which to console himself. Teddy had never found solace in words or music, both of which sought to elevate consciousness, whereas his overriding desire was to obliterate it.

Other than liquor and women, his only solace came

from the sea. By moving off shore, by putting some physical distance between himself and the edge of this continent on which the tragic drama of his family history was playing itself out, he could lessen, at least slightly, the panic that threatened to overwhelm him as he faced the fact that he was the last actor left on a stage littered with dead bodies and broken dreams.

2

H E FLED TO SPAIN, THEN TO GREECE AND THE FOUR-
hundred-acre island of Skorpios, which the Greek shipping billionaire Aristotle Onassis had purchased five
years earlier. With Bobby dead, the Kennedys' desire to
keep secret Onassis' romance with Jacqueline, for fear
that it would cause political damage, seemed no longer
relevant.

Only five feet five inches tall and already sixty-two
years old, Onassis, boorish, vulgar and crude, seemed in
almost all superficial ways to be the exact antithesis of
Jack. But he possessed a personal fortune that dwarfed
Joe Kennedy's and, beguiled by the thought of marriage
to the most glamorous widow of the century, made it
clear to Jacqueline that he would assure her total independence, financially and emotionally, from the family
she had come to view as so destructive.

In addition to his own island, Onassis owned a yacht,
the *Christina*, considered the most luxurious seagoing
vessel in the world. One nice touch was that the swimming pool could be drained and its floor, which was dec-
orated with mosaic scenes from Greek mythology, could
be electronically raised to provide a large dance floor
on the yacht's main deck. Sitting rooms contained open

fireplaces; there were nine double guest cabins, lavishly appointed (and fully soundproofed), each named after a different Greek island. Where there was not Siena marble, there was antique Japanese lacquer. An artist had been personally commissioned by Onassis to do a series of original oil paintings of the billionaire in various resplendent poses, and these were hung on the four walls of the dining room. The barstools were covered with tanned skin from the testicles of whales.

To boost Teddy's spirits, Onassis suggested a brief cruise off the coast of Skorpios. Teddy willingly agreed. Another guest later recalled the scene: "Teddy comes in. He holds a blonde goddess by the shoulders. He is wearing a light pink shirt and matching scarf. The indications are that the party will be explosive. Teddy drinks ouzo, permanently. Later, the bouzouki music reaches its peak and Teddy gets up and tries to dance." The attempt, however, proved unsuccessful and, the guest recalled, "Teddy returned to his ouzo."

At one point, however, matters turned ugly when Jacqueline observed a "guest," who was really a journalist operating under cover, take a photograph of Teddy which would have indicated clearly both his degree of inebriation and the degree of intimacy he'd so quickly achieved with his "blonde goddess."

In the ensuing scene, the unfortunate photographer was roughed up, and his film was torn from his camera and destroyed.

Drunkenly, Teddy shouted at him, "If you dare to hurt me, I'll see that you never find another job in Greece." Indeed, when the yacht finally docked, Onassis himself saw to it that the journalist was arrested. Even in his grief, and even burdened by his feelings of inadequacy, Teddy retained a considerable degree of raw power and little hesitation about using it to protect his reputation. In years to come, he would devote more and more of his energies to accosting photographers, destroying film, suppressing stories. In the end it would not make any difference.

* * *

In the summer of 1968, however, America expectantly awaited his return from private mourning to public life, having already conferred upon him the mantle of leadership that had been worn with such élan by both Bobby and Jack.

In fact, upon his return to Hyannis Port in mid-July, Teddy found that the pressure for him to join the Humphrey ticket had grown. In addition, a new and even more ominous movement was starting to build. Michael DiSalle, the former governor of Ohio, announced his intention to nominate Teddy at the Chicago convention not for Vice President on a Humphrey ticket but for President.

Ludicrous as the notion seemed in light of Teddy's emotional condition, it attracted quick and broad support, appealing not only to those who had supported Bobby but to those within the party who longed for a Kennedy Restoration but feared that Bobby was too radical, and to those—including the all-powerful mayor of Chicago, Richard Daley—who simply wanted a Democratic victory in November and feared that Humphrey was too tainted and ineffectual to achieve it.

The California Democratic leader, Jesse Unruh, who'd worked feverishly in Bobby's behalf, now said, "Ted Kennedy would have great support among the California delegation. There is dissatisfaction with the two announced candidates [Humphrey and McCarthy] and their stands."

Quickly, from the other coast, Maine's highly respected Senator Edmund Muskie joined in, saying a "Draft Teddy for President" movement was "a very logical suggestion," and "an enviable subject of speculation." He said, "Ted certainly has the qualities and qualifications, there's no question about that," although, being aware of Teddy's true condition—as the public was not—he wondered aloud whether 1968 was the proper year for such an attempt.

The momentum built quickly. Senator Philip Hart of Michigan said he personally thought it a splendid idea, adding that Teddy was "as fine a Kennedy as I've known, including John and Bob." Governor Richard

Hughes of New Jersey said, "His candidacy would bring great strength to our ticket."

And Richard Daley, while knowing privately that an even more exciting possibility loomed, said he strongly favored Teddy's presence as vice presidential candidate on a Humphrey ticket. "I think the convention will draft him," Daley said. "And I hope so." Given the degree to which Daley would be controlling the convention in his home city, this was tantamount to a direct order to the delegates, one they dared not disobey.

In this atmosphere, Teddy met privately with Steve Smith in New York on July 17 and 18 to discuss the possibilities. He truly had no interest in the Vice Presidency, no interest in campaigning with Hubert Humphrey. But the Presidency itself? Full Restoration? A new Camelot with Teddy as king?

By winning the Presidency, he could redeem himself forever in the eyes of his father and mother. By winning the Presidency in 1968, he would accomplish what he'd felt Bobby could not. By becoming President, he'd become the instant equal of the legendary Jack. The last and least of the Kennedys would finally be not just the sole survivor, but first and foremost among the brothers.

There were grave risks—personal as well as political —but Teddy was just unbalanced enough in July of 1968 to find the temptation seductive. The icy Smith, who could count votes as skillfully and unemotionally as he counted Kennedy family money, advised a cautious, low-profile approach, keeping as many options open for as long as possible.

He knew, as well as anyone, that even under normal circumstances Teddy was unfit to be President. He also knew that now, in the wake of Bobby's death, Teddy was not able to function in any capacity. To put forth a man in such condition as a contender for the Presidency would be to gamble with Teddy's life, the sanctity of the myth, the family's reputation and the destiny of the nation. Nonetheless, it was tempting.

Over the weekend, ex-governor DiSalle of Ohio told the press that delegate reaction to his plan to nominate

Teddy for President was "excellent and widespread." He said, "I think Senator Kennedy has more delegate strength than anybody anticipated."

Even as DiSalle spoke, honorary Kennedys again poured into the compound, bringing with them their varying strategies for Restoration. So hungry for power now were so many generations of advisors that the spacious Kennedy house could scarcely contain them.

This was the Kennedy summit to end all Kennedy summits. Steve Smith presided. There was considerable disagreement as to both short-term tactics and long-term strategy. Some present were humane enough to express concern for Teddy's well-being, but these were in the minority. Camelot beckoned. The castle stood plain to see. There seemed little doubt that a Draft Teddy movement, endorsed by Richard Daley, would sweep the convention.

Later, they'd have to face the question of how a man so blatantly incapable of either sobriety or monogamy—and with so little actual desire to be President, a fact that was noted by all—could wage a ten-week campaign against Richard Nixon. But, there would always be problems. The chemistry seemed right. The stars seemed properly aligned. Maybe this was what the fates had intended all along. Surely the gods had exacted more than enough from this family. Surely they would not strike down Teddy, too.

Maybe, the more mystical among them speculated quietly (though this was not, for the most part, a group inclined toward mysticism), all the prior sacrifices—the deaths of Joe Junior, Jack and then Bobby, as well as the old man's disabling stroke—had been part of a grand design intended to bring this moment, this possibility into being.

Though, watching Teddy lurch gloomily from room to room, they had to wonder.

As was typical at a meeting involving so many people with so many differing points of view, nothing definitive was decided about the Presidency. They did agree—in their blind arrogance and avarice—that within days

Teddy should issue a statement disclaiming forcefully any interest in the vice presidential nomination.

The Vice Presidency was a nuisance, a distraction, and allowed for the possibility of a compromise that no one present at Hyannis Port wanted to see. As it had always been for the Kennedys, it would be all or nothing for Teddy in 1968.

And so, on Friday, July 26, Teddy's Washington office issued a brief statement over his name. In it, he said he would not run for the Vice Presidency under any circumstances, not even if drafted by the convention. The statement said, "For me, this year, it is impossible. My reasons are purely personal. My decision is final, firm and not subject for further discussion."

The statement, however, made no mention of how Teddy might respond if offered the presidential nomination.

He went back out on his sailboat, well stocked with liquor and frequently replenished with women. He even began to grow a beard. When he would come ashore, those who saw him were alarmed. Fears for his physical safety began to grow, along with already intense worry about his emotional health.

Bobby, in the worst of the days after Jack's assassination, had been profoundly grief-stricken, guilt-ridden and depressed, but never had he been this reckless, this self-destructive, this out of control. And still, all across America, people were speaking seriously about Teddy as a possible presidential candidate that fall.

Not until late August—with the Chicago convention about to begin and the Draft Teddy talk growing louder hourly—was he well enough to make a public appearance again. Psychologically, he was in no less distress than before, but he'd come ashore, shaved, weathered intermittent periods of sobriety, and was deemed capable of delivering a short address not far from home. The location chosen was the Kimball dining hall at Holy Cross College in Worcester.

There were no traces of self-pity or even of his recent excesses evident in either Teddy's appearance or his words as he spoke to a crowd of more than a thousand at a Worcester Chamber of Commerce luncheon. Nationally, the speech was carried live on network television and reached an audience of millions.

It was, said the *Globe*, no "hesitant step" back into the public arena but "a bold march," which "does not appear to rule out the possibility of his nomination for the presidency if an emotionally-fueled bandwagon should start rolling at the Chicago convention."

He began on a personal, if not entirely accurate note. "For the last ten weeks," he said, "I have not been active in public life. . . . I have spent much of my time with the sea; clearing my mind and spirit; putting the past behind, opening a way to what lies ahead."

He noted that "some of you have suggested that for safety's sake, and for my family's sake, I retire from public life. . . . But there is no safety in hiding. Not for me, not for any of us here today and not for our children who will inherit the world we make for them. For all of us, the only path is to work, in whatever way we can, to end the violence and the hatred and the division that threatens us all.

"So today I resume my public responsibilities. . . . Like my brothers before me, I pick up a fallen standard. Sustained by the memory of our priceless years together, I shall try to carry forward that special commitment to justice, to excellence, to courage that distinguished their lives."

After acknowledging that like many, he'd originally supported American involvement in Vietnam, he then reiterated his call for the quickest possible end to it, proposing an immediate halt to the bombing of the North and prompt beginning of negotiations with Hanoi.

"This war," he said, "is the tragedy of our generation." But then he said, despite the war and despite racial intolerance and the growth of violent crime in the cities, "we remain a people of great and enduring promise: as Lincoln once said, 'the last, best hope of mankind.'

"That hope is in every one of us. If there was one great meaning to Robert Kennedy's campaign, one ideal that fired the conscience of this nation in 1968, it was that voting every four years was not enough to make a citizen —and not enough to satisfy a man.

"Rather, each of us must take a direct and personal part in solving the great problems of this country. Each of us must do his individual part to end the suffering, feed the hungry, heal the sick and strengthen and renew the national spirit.

"It is that profound personal, moral commitment that we seek to reaffirm today. It is a commitment to passion and action, in the service of our fellowman and the nation we love. . . ."

And, he said, in what seemed a pointed reference to the upcoming convention, "it would be tragic now if all the dedicated efforts of those who worked in both parties for change should count for nothing in the final choice of policies presented to the electorate in November."

Lacking in neither passion nor eloquence, Teddy's talk did indeed seem almost an open declaration of his candidacy. As the *Globe* reported the next day, "It may be painful to recall but it is a fact that Ted Kennedy was a more popular figure than his brother Robert in Democratic circles prior to the New York senator's assassination."

The paper also noted that in the most recent Gallup poll, Hubert Humphrey trailed Nixon by sixteen points, that former Ohio governor DiSalle would definitely be placing Teddy's name in nomination and that "the positions Sen. Kennedy enunciated in Worcester are acceptable to a broad spectrum of Democrats and Republicans." In short: "The political wind is full of straws this week and they seem to be blowing Kennedy's way."

3

THE CONVENTION, WHICH WAS TO PROVIDE THE OCCA-sion for perhaps the most consequential decision of Teddy's life, opened in Chicago, in a poisonous atmosphere, during the last week of August. Hundreds of thousands of war protesters, many of them distinctly not of the nonviolent variety, had for weeks been proclaiming their intention to disrupt the proceedings by whatever means necessary. An equally determined Mayor Daley said he would use National Guard troops as well as his city's entire police force to assure order.

The generational and cultural animosity that had been festering in America throughout the 1960s, which included passionate conflict not only over the Vietnam War but also over civil rights and freedom of expression—free speech, free love, rock music, long hair and the use of marijuana and LSD, among other things—was about to erupt.

By 1968, the younger brothers and sisters of the generation pledged to walk with John Kennedy across the New Frontier now felt that they and their ideals had been betrayed by cynical elders who stubbornly resisted all demands for peace, racial equality and social justice.

Nothing seemed to symbolize this institutional resistance to the will of the people, this disdain of the entrenched old for the disenfranchised young, so much as the Democratic party's plan to nominate for President Hubert Humphrey, who still proudly espoused the same Vietnam War policies that had forced Lyndon Johnson to announce he would not seek reelection. It was as if all the energy that had been expended on behalf of both Bobby and Eugene McCarthy had been for naught.

The mood preceding the convention was ominous. Physical violence on a scale seldom if ever before associated with the American political process seemed a distinct possibility. Teddy was the one figure who might be able to prevent all or much of it. Now, as never before, a large segment of America was crying out for Kennedy leadership. Teddy was the only one left. But when the nation turned its hungry eyes to him, he was nowhere to be seen.

Yet he could not yet bring himself to say no. He could not admit, even privately, that he was in no mental or emotional condition to consider accepting the presidential nomination of his party. Thus, on the eve of a convention that seemed almost desperate to give him, at no cost, the nomination for the office whose status Jack had elevated to mythic proportion, the nomination in pursuit of which Bobby had paid with his life, Teddy found himself unable to accept but also unable to confess his inability. Never before had his Kennedy-ness come into such stark conflict with his own inadequate self.

Steve Smith met with Daley in Chicago on Friday, August 23. Despite knowing Teddy's true condition, Smith wanted the most accurate delegate vote possible. Just because some things were impossible didn't mean, in Smith's view, that they couldn't be made to work.

Nominate Teddy first. Worry about him later. That was one approach, and probably the one that would prove the most direct route back to Camelot. There was always the chance that once nominated, Teddy would rise to the occasion. There was also the chance he might kill himself, accidentally or otherwise, but that might happen anyway. Teddy might even be better off in the White House, where he could be more closely supervised.

The story would be almost too perfect, in a way. Teddy, the last brother, running only eight years later, against the same smug and distasteful opponent, for the same office that the heroic Jack had so narrowly won in 1960. Aside from a few intransigent right wingers, there would not be a reporter or editor in America who wouldn't be rooting for Teddy.

Nixon could talk all he wanted about experience in foreign affairs, Teddy's youth, whatever. He could even drop broad hints about Teddy's instability. It wouldn't matter. America, which had been through so much since Jack's inauguration in 1960, would see the election of Teddy as a return to innocence, a second chance. New Frontier II—or III: but this time without the tragic ending.

After his meeting with Daley, Smith told Teddy that the Chicago mayor, convinced that a Draft Teddy movement would succeed, would be calling in the morning.

The convention was due to open Monday. On Saturday, Daley told Teddy that he'd been talking to a lot of people and they all wondered whether Hubert could make it. Frankly, it didn't look good. Hubert was in trouble. The mayor said he thought Teddy should be the candidate.

"Impossible," Teddy said, without saying why. Daley was aware, as were many influential politicians in America, that things had gone seriously awry, at least temporarily, for this last brother. Still, they needed him. Not him, really, but his name. They needed the unlived portions of his brothers' lives. They needed his brothers' unwaged campaigns.

Teddy in '68. He'd be a winner. He owed it to Jack to make the effort. He owed it to Bobby. He owed it, most of all, to his father. What would the old man say if he were awake and alert and aware that Teddy was being offered the presidential nomination and was turning it down?

Daley urged him to come to Chicago, knowing that

once the delegates caught sight of him inside the convention hall, it would be over. Teddy would be nominated by acclamation.

"I can't do that," he said.

Still unable to foreclose the option, however, Teddy said he'd send Steve Smith back and that Steve, as always, would have full authority to speak and act on Teddy's behalf.

For Daley, it was better than nothing. The door was still open. And both Daley and Smith could count votes, as well as deliver them.

Amid great secrecy, Smith returned to Chicago on Sunday afternoon. He immediately detected signs that the Draft Teddy movement was surging. That morning, Daley had eaten breakfast with the California boss, Unruh. The two had decided that Humphrey had no chance to win the election and that his nomination not only would unleash an unprecedented wave of violence throughout the city but could cause wounds within the Democratic party that might not heal for a generation.

"Let's get another candidate," Daley said.

Unruh said his delegates could be most easily persuaded to back Teddy. Daley said Teddy was precisely who he had in mind. The Illinois delegation was supposed to caucus that afternoon to determine who it would support on the convention's first ballot. With Teddy still refusing to agree to accept even a genuine draft, Daley could not yet commit his troops, but he told Smith he could do the next best thing, which was to postpone the caucus. "The boys," he said, "might decide to hold off for forty-eight hours."

That would give Smith until Tuesday morning to persuade Teddy to fly to Chicago and express his willingness to accept a draft. Were he to do so, Daley assured Smith, he would be nominated by a huge margin the following day. The city would be spared any outbreak of physical violence, the party spared a catastrophic division, and the spiritual wounds of the nation could be healed.

The only word Teddy would have to say was "yes."

Smith said it might work, but that Daley would have to

understand two points with absolute clarity. First, the draft must be genuine; there could be no hint that it was something Teddy or his operatives had tried to engineer from behind the scenes.

Second, Smith himself, while he'd make his usual round of phone calls as part of the nose-counting process, would do no direct lobbying in Teddy's behalf. Personally, he remained far from sure that a presidential candidacy was a good idea, particularly considering Teddy's fragile state. On the other hand, if it was a sure thing and if it meant reclaiming the White House for the dynasty, then, good or bad, it must be done. Such were the family imperatives.

After concluding his conversation with Daley, Smith began the series of dozens of phone calls that would tell him whether, in truth, the draft of Teddy would succeed. If there were the slightest chance of failure—even 1 percent—then he would not permit Teddy to come to Chicago. They would have to be absolutely sure in advance, and Smith, despite his respect for Daley's political acumen, wanted his own independent count.

In Hyannis Port, Teddy remained almost as paralyzed as his father. He could not will himself to go to Chicago and make his desire for the nomination known—an act that would have assured it, given the emotional climate of the time—nor could he bring himself to tell Steve Smith to cease, desist and come home.

Even without him, the Draft Teddy drive was quickly gathering momentum in Chicago. DiSalle formally opened a Draft Kennedy office in his Chicago hotel suite. Tens of thousands of unused "Kennedy" buttons, intended for Bobby's supporters, suddenly materialized, and a growing number of delegates were seen wearing them.

Just as mysteriously, the Kennedy political apparatus reassembled, though no one would admit to having issued a formal call to arms. Pierre Salinger toured the convention hall and later reported that to his amazement, "I saw more of the old Kennedy advance men there than I had ever seen in my life. You could see their lips moving and they were all saying, 'Kennedy.' They were all there, primed and willing to go.''

Then Richard Goodwin, still working at McCarthy headquarters, called Steve Smith. He said McCarthy had already raised the possibility of his stepping aside, even before the first ballot, and throwing his support behind Teddy. Such a move would guarantee Teddy's nomination. It was there, available, beckoning. All Smith had to do was reach out and pick it up. But he thought again of what he knew about Teddy that the nation—and even the mass of convention delegates—did not, and he hesitated.

Goodwin, chafing to board a Kennedy bandwagon that would return him to the White House, impatiently asked Smith, "Are you prepared to turn down the Presidency of the United States?"

He wasn't, but neither was he prepared to accept it on the family's behalf unless he could persuade himself that Teddy could psychologically endure the campaign.

In Hyannis Port, Joey Gargan asked Teddy what the hurry was. He suggested waiting. Teddy didn't have to run this summer. He didn't even have to run in 1972, or in 1976 for that matter. He could even wait until 1980, when he'd still be only forty-eight, the same age Jack would have been during the first year of his second term.

"Forget about 1980," Teddy said. "By that time I'll probably be dead."

"You mean . . ." Gargan began. He didn't want to say the word.

Teddy said it. "Shot? Maybe, but more likely an airplane crash or automobile accident."

Through all this time of indecision, Teddy's wife and children remained in Virginia, out of touch and out of mind, while Teddy sat in his own gloomy, empty Hyannis Port home, communing with the ghosts of his brothers and with the spirit of his stricken father, who lay in the big house down the road.

* * *

Early Monday morning, delegates from all states began pouring into DiSalle's Draft Kennedy suite, clamoring for buttons, assuring support, asking what they could do to persuade Teddy that the party and the nation needed him and needed him now.

Smith, still working the phones, was astonished at what he was finding. Potential Kennedy delegates seemed to be everywhere. Even in Pennsylvania, a state deemed rock solid for Humphrey, he learned that at least a third of the delegates would cast first-ballot votes for Teddy. And even in the South—in Alabama, of all places, a state where Bobby had been despised—it became obvious that Teddy would have remarkable support.

By midday, DiSalle had to move his Draft Kennedy headquarters to a larger suite, to accommodate the traffic. More phone lines were installed. From state after state—Nebraska, Missouri, states where Bobby had never campaigned and was known to have had little popularity—delegates trooped in, asking for more Kennedy buttons, pledging first-ballot support for Teddy. It was becoming the rarest of all American political phenomena: a spontaneous, uninstigated, grassroots draft movement.

As certification of the drive's growing power, Allard Lowenstein showed up at the new Teddy headquarters, grinning, shaking hands everywhere and chattering like a squirrel. "We can stop worrying about America," he said. The deal was done. Teddy was in. The war was over. The spirit of Camelot had been reborn. America could sing again, a people united, with gladdened hearts.

By late afternoon, Smith had completed his personal count. New York, California and Illinois would go solidly for Teddy from the start. Even elsewhere, the desire to abandon Humphrey, to embrace Teddy as the savior of the party and the country, was passionate.

At worst—at very worst—Teddy was certain of enough first-ballot votes to ensure that Humphrey could not even come close to winning. And after that, the stampede would start. There might not even be a second ballot. Humphrey might well withdraw and ask that Teddy be chosen by acclamation.

Then Teddy called. He was fretting over having his name placed in nomination by Michael DiSalle, fearing that the ex-governor of Ohio lacked the necessary prestige. Jack and Bobby would never have let their names be placed in nomination by a washed-up nonentity like Mike DiSalle. Teddy said he wanted to be nominated either by Richard Daley himself or, better yet, by Gene McCarthy, who would announce he was stepping aside in Teddy's favor.

If Smith could arrange that, Teddy said, he would prepare to fly to Chicago and accept.

Smith quickly contacted Richard Goodwin, who spoke again to McCarthy.

"Well," McCarthy said, "we might do it." Teddy wasn't really such a bad fellow. It was only Bobby whom McCarthy had despised. And he knew he himself had no chance to win the nomination. This might provide the most graceful exit. As for Teddy's qualifications, McCarthy said, "Experience isn't really important in a President. Of course he's young, but those fellows in the Revolution were young—Jefferson and Hamilton."

Shortly after midnight Monday, Goodwin called Smith again. He suggested that Smith come to McCarthy's hotel to talk to the senator directly. Recalling Teddy's late-night rebuff in Green Bay, Smith, never one to appear overeager, said only, "I'll let you know."

It was not until 4:30 Tuesday afternoon that Smith finally met with McCarthy in person. By then, the impending draft of Teddy had become the biggest story of the convention: were it to happen, it would be the biggest political story since Jack's victory in 1960.

By then, Smith was certain he could make it work. But he still was not certain he wanted to. Teddy, in Hyannis Port, remained shaky, sodden, and uncertain. Smith had persuaded him that the draft was genuine and that it would lead, with certainty, to his nomination. Already, work had begun on nominating, seconding and acceptance speeches.

But the thought of actually running for President in his current debilitated condition provoked in Teddy feelings of deep melancholy. Currents of the grief he still felt for Bobby mingled with his own sense of inadequacy. These, however, were counterbalanced by his equally powerful feeling of dynastic obligation.

His brother had given his life for this nomination. How could Teddy possibly turn it down? And how could he, as a professional politician, turn his back on a party that clamored for him? He knew the time was not right, but he knew also that for him, the time would never be right. Why not just jump in and get it done? Maybe somebody would shoot him and then he, too, could die a hero, like his brothers. Then the family destiny would be complete.

He was thirty-six. He could have been an insurance salesman or an executive with a brokerage company, or a small-town lawyer and newspaper publisher in the West. Even having surrendered his independence to his father in 1960, when he agreed to run for the Senate two years later, he had never expected that in less than a decade he'd be at this point: isolated and exposed, very near the summit of the mountain, with no shelter in sight and no one to turn to for help.

Talking to Joey Gargan, talking to Steve Smith on the telephone, talking out loud to himself, Teddy spun the same wheel over and over in his mind. Wherever he stopped it, he did not like what he saw, but neither could he see any way out.

By midafternoon Tuesday, with an air of resignation and near despair, he told Smith to go to McCarthy and work out the details. He would do it. He had no choice. Neither he nor his brothers had ever really had a choice about anything.

To others, it seemed remarkable that old Joe Kennedy, a man now so weak and frail, who had not uttered a coherent word for seven and a half years, could still exercise such control over his last living son.

To Teddy, it was not amazing in the least. This, like all else in his life, simply seemed inevitable.

The meeting lasted only ten minutes. McCarthy said, referring to the nomination, "I can't make it. What's Teddy going to do?"

Smith said Teddy still didn't know.

"Teddy and I have the same views," McCarthy said. "I'm willing to ask my delegates to vote for him, but I would like to have my name placed in nomination and even have a run on the first ballot." Then he added, "But if that's not possible . . ."

It seemed apparent that short of nominating Teddy himself, McCarthy would do whatever was necessary to clear the way.

Thus, the final obstacle had been removed. Richard Daley could place Teddy's name in nomination and even if McCarthy did not withdraw until after the first ballot, Teddy was assured of enough votes to stop Humphrey cold. The second ballot, were one even necessary after McCarthy's withdrawal in favor of Teddy, would be merely a formality. Humphrey was through. It would be Teddy who would run, with the ghosts of Jack and Bobby at either shoulder, against Richard Nixon in the fall.

Barring total emotional collapse, there seemed little doubt that Teddy would win. By itself, the nation's distaste for a war that Nixon still supported would have guaranteed that. But even this faded into insignificance when measured against the emotional intensity that a Kennedy campaign for the White House would generate. The last Kennedy, stepping courageously forward to complete the work begun by his older brothers, carrying with him the keys that would reopen the gates of Camelot.

The stage was thus set for the last act in the mythic drama. The triumphant climax seemed preordained by the same fates that had administered such cruel punishment to the family in the past. The scales would once again be balanced, the old man's Faustian bargain complete. And, despite the tragic loss of three sons, it would prove to be a success, after all.

Why, then, did Steve Smith have such a knot in his stomach as he called Hyannis Port to give Teddy the news?

They talked, off and on, for three hours. Teddy was clearly a man in torment, a man agonizing over a decision that seemed far too important for him to make alone. All his life, there had been someone to tell him what to do. Now there was no one, not even Smith—who could only advise and inform, not dictate, because he was a member of the family only through marriage, thus not truly a Kennedy.

Teddy knew he had to do it. Accepting the nomination was what his father would have insisted that he do, what Jack would have told him to do, what Bobby would have told him to do. So there should not have been even the slightest indecision. This was his moment of destiny, and arriving at moments of destiny, then seizing them was what being a Kennedy was all about.

But Teddy was frozen with fear. He was truly afraid that he might be assassinated at any moment should he accept the nomination. But he was also afraid that he might not be. That he would have to live, and function, first as presidential candidate, then as President, at a time when he knew himself to be so unready, so incapable, so wanting in every respect.

All his life he'd known he could never measure up to his older brothers, but he'd resigned himself to that. The Senate had been for him a safe harbor. He'd become an insider there, accepted in a way he never had been within the family. Now he would have to give up all that in order to try to climb to a height where he must have known he could not survive.

He knew the country did not want him for himself. He had known, even shaking hands on Bobby's funeral train, that most of those who grasped his hand and looked him in the eye and murmured words of sympathy would never be able to accept him as his brothers' equal; worse, would never forgive him for having lived while they had died.

What did he owe them? What did he owe his stricken

father? What did he owe his dead brothers? What did he owe the honorary Kennedys who swarmed all over him? What did he owe the country? What did he owe himself?

There seemed no way that all debts could be paid. Still, he felt obliged to try. How could he turn away—from family, from the country, from the myth? To do so would be to repudiate all that the Kennedys had ever stood for. To do so would be to repudiate his father, his brothers, and all the aspects of himself that bound him to them.

But early on the morning of Wednesday, August 28, he made three phone calls. He called Steve Smith, Hubert Humphrey and Richard Daley.

He told each that there were no circumstances under which he would accept a draft, no circumstances under which he would accept the presidential nomination.

It was over.

He dictated a statement for his press secretary to release to the wire services. If his name was put in nomination, he would withdraw it. Even if he was to receive the nomination, he would turn it down. It was over. He was done.

Chicago erupted in violence and bloodshed, tear gas, hatred and shattered glass—unleashing the angriest, most destructive passions ever produced by an American political convention and leading to the election of Richard Nixon as President.

Ignoring it all, turning away from his country, from his family, from the legacy, Teddy headed back out to sea. What he would never know—nor will any of us—was whether the terrible price he would pay for his inability to be the man his brothers had been, the man his father would have demanded that he be, was higher than the price he would have paid had he accepted the gift of the nomination, knowing how unworthy he truly was.

4

 IS AIDE AND FRIEND DUN GIFFORD WOULD LATER
say, "He recognized that he had always been pushed
forward too soon and knew that he just wasn't ready to
be leader of the family in any respect."

Much less the country.

Teddy himself would later rephrase the dilemma, saying, "Bob had gotten into the fight for his own good reasons—the disaffected young, the poverty and minority
problems, the war. Those were the things he was interested in, and it seemed they were all going to be lost.
That was the frustrating part of it. So much had gone into
1968 and now it all appeared lost."

But only temporarily. For there would be 1972. And of
course Teddy would run for President then. That much
was accepted by all, within and without the family, Democrat and Republican alike. The legend would simply go
on autopilot for a while, until Teddy regained his
strength, focus and ambition. There would be four years
to plan his 1972 campaign. It would not be some slapdash
fraternity stunt, as Bobby's mad, tragic dash had sometimes seemed.

There seemed no question but that Teddy was, as the
Wall Street Journal put it in a headline, "Looking Ahead

to '72.'' The paper said, "Despite the tragedy that has dogged the Kennedy clan's pursuit of the Presidency and the family burden he now feels so acutely, few who know the man have much doubt that, starting in 1969, he'll begin a carefully calculated, slow-starting, but steadily accelerating campaign for the highest U.S. office.''

In an apparent step toward that goal, Teddy decided over the New Year's weekend of 1969 to challenge Louisiana's Russell Long for the Senate position of assistant majority leader, also referred to as majority whip. In a frenetic burst of telephone activity from Sun Valley, Idaho, where he was on a skiing vacation, he called colleagues all across the country, interrupting their Bowl watching to spring on them his surprise announcement and to ask for their support.

The issue would be decided when the new Congress convened in Washington the following week. There would be fifty-seven Democratic senators. They would choose their leaders by secret ballot. It was clear that Mike Mansfield would continue as majority leader, but Long, fifty, an openly alcoholic, mean-spirited, right-wing reactionary, had compiled a long list of enemies during the years of his rise to bureaucratic power.

Teddy won, of course, for who, that January, could vote against the last brother? "The winds of change that were so evident in 1968 have expressed themselves in the Senate,'' he said at his first press conference after his selection. And the nation wanted to believe that it was true.

"Kennedy's performance this week in the Senate,'' the *Globe* wrote in early January, "seems to mark a turning point in his career. . . . Under the tutelage of his young but experienced staff and as the result of family tragedy, he has become less cautious. He is more willing to risk a rebuff if the cause is right and the gain is worth the gamble.''

And David Broder wrote in *The Washington Post,* "In a single bold stroke, the last of the Kennedy brothers leapfrogged over'' potential rivals for the 1972 presidential nomination. "The Massachusetts senator with the magic family name is, with his victory Friday, now a clear and present danger to Nixon's hopes for a second term."

In the *Globe*, Bob Healy was even more excited, saying that if, as seemed likely, Mansfield surrendered his majority leader's post in 1971, Teddy would be his successor and then, "there will be no stopping Sen. Edward M. Kennedy for the Democratic presidential nomination. Kennedy would be combining the comparative 1960 powers of Lyndon Johnson and John Kennedy. He would have the great force of the Southern leadership and the pull of the Kennedy name in the nation."

He made the cover of *Time* magazine on January 10, 1969, described as "the fourth and last of a legendary band of brothers," and now a focal point for "millions of Americans who are fascinated by the indomitable Kennedy legend and its latest inheritor.

"There was a kind of poetic symbolism in Ted Kennedy's first real foray into national politics," the magazine said. "It was Jack Kennedy's assassination that brought Lyndon Johnson to power. Bobby Kennedy's energetic campaign helped persuade many restive Americans that the old order might, after all, be redeemable. In the dying days of a Democratic Administration [with Nixon's inauguration scheduled for later that month], the last of the clan rekindled a beacon of courage and change —one that should certainly brighten his party and the Senate and may yet achieve the full promise of a haunted dynasty. His already lustrous presidential prospects are clearly enhanced."

From this point forward, *Time* said, Teddy could "overtly exercise the influence that has hitherto been his primarily by virtue of legend, tragedy and guilt."

It seemed clear that there would be no stopping Teddy —unless Teddy stopped himself.

On January 17, he joined scores of Senate colleagues in delivering oral tributes to departing President Lyndon Johnson. Given the nature of Johnson's relationship with the Kennedys through the decade, more than the usual attention was paid to Teddy's statement.

Aware of this, he said, in remarks that had been crafted

with particular care by his staff, "The circumstances which brought President Johnson to the office he has held made it inevitable that there would be speculations about strained relations between him and my family.

"President Johnson was a loyal lieutenant of John F. Kennedy who had chosen him as his constitutional successor. He campaigned hard and effectively for the election of Senator Robert Kennedy and myself to the United States Senate. He was extremely gracious and understanding to all of us after the events of November 1963.

"None of us agrees with all that President Johnson did. On some issues our disagreement ran deep. But the differences that developed came not from personal grievances but from the obligation of men in public life to discharge their responsibilities to the people of the United States as they saw them and from what at the time were fundamental differences over important public policies."

Then the man who most in the chamber thought would soon hold the office himself briefly alluded to the "overwhelming responsibilities" any President faced and added, "The Presidency of the United States is the repository of the support and the criticism, the hopes and frustrations, the advice and prayers of all of us."

Knowing that about the office, and knowing what he knew about himself, Teddy must have been terrified, at some level, by the seeming inevitability of his accession to it.

Five days later, he presided over a dinner organized to pay tribute to Bobby. More than twenty-five hundred attended the event, held at the Washington Hilton. Although Bobby's achievements were supposed to provide the focal point, Teddy was the star of the show.

"It was obvious," Mary McGrory wrote, "that the participants had come as much to cheer Edward as to mourn Robert. There is little quibbling about Teddy's qualities. If he is not as brainy as John, or as committed as Robert, he enjoys the political process more than either of his brothers. If it seems early to be running, to the Kennedys it has never been too early." The plain fact was, McGrory stated, "Nobody can stand for long in Teddy's way."

She quoted one leading Democrat as saying, "Teddy is ready—that's all there is to it." And another as suggesting that "he has none of Bobby's problems with labor. The kids like him because he's young and the blacks like him because of Bobby. The bosses will go for reform if it's the only way to get Teddy."

Summing it up, this party leader said, "Let's face it: Teddy is a Kennedy without problems."

During the first week of February he made one of his typically frenzied three-day dashes through Massachusetts. On day one he spoke in Everett, Marblehead, Beverly, Andover, Lawrence and Lowell. At Merrimack College he stood under a large "Ted in '72" sign and said, in response to a fulsome introduction by the college president, "Thank you, and I, ah, accept the nomination." He grinned. The crowd of students cheered.

The *Globe* wrote that "he reaches the young people, and they, in turn, reach him." He went to Quincy, Taunton, New Bedford, Holyoke and Pittsfield. Students whistled, shrieked and chanted "We're With You in Seventy-two." The *Globe* noted that "everywhere he went it was the same. Middle-aged women squealed and called him 'a cutie.' Barbers, factory workers and secretaries lined the streets, corridors and doorways through which he walked."

In one town, "Crowds mobbed and pushed so, a nun was knocked over a curb onto the street. Kennedy bent down, his face flinching from his own back trouble, and picked her up. Then, like the Pied Piper, he led the children through the streets to their schoolhouse.

"It was the way of the Kennedys," the *Globe* said. "Other senators visit their home states and little attention is given them. But when Ted Kennedy moves, the nation watches."

Back in Washington, he granted an interview to nationally syndicated columnist Stewart Alsop, who found him "sadder than he used to be, and older."

Alsop wrote that a talk with Teddy was "quite unlike a conversation with any other senator. It is an experience which strangely combines a sense of deja vu and a sense of the future—a feeling of living again with what has already happened, and of experiencing in advance what is probably going to happen."

This was a perceptive observation, even if Alsop did not take it one level deeper: that this strange combination of feelings, this singular, unhealthy mix of past and future, was what Teddy was now experiencing during every sober waking moment of his life.

"Everywhere," Alsop wrote, "there are reminders of the past—a photograph of President Kennedy looking grim, a copy of *Profiles in Courage* on the floor, a picture of Robert Kennedy, tousle-haired and grinning his wolfish grin."

Alsop emerged from the meeting with "a powerful, instinctive feeling that what is very probably coming" for Teddy, "—if fate is not cruel a third time—is the Presidency of the United States."

By fate, he meant assassination.

But fate comes in many forms.

As winter progressed, Teddy's personal condition deteriorated. Some nights he would just turn up at Hickory Hill as if searching for his brother. He was not often sober on these occasions.

"Among people who knew Kennedy well," his early biographer Burton Hersh has written, "there was already concern at his volatility that winter: a terrible aggressiveness at times, then—feeling the old hesitations—a tendency to bolt, reverse himself." Teddy was both "enormous and vulnerable, testy, then incomprehensibly meek."

The *Newsweek* magazine correspondent John Lindsay, who interviewed Teddy soon after his triumph over Long, was himself a recovering alcoholic and recognized in his subject many signs of the disease. He feared, and expressed to others the fear, that Teddy might be slipping finally out of any semblance of control, sliding toward the inevitable crack-up at an accelerating rate.

But that was not the story that people wanted to read. The magazine published instead a description of Teddy as having been from the start "the Kennedy who had everything: the family looks, flair and fortune, a gift for politics that even his brother Jack envied—and the luxurious presumption that the Presidency would one day come to him almost by inheritance."

Through the winter, the publicity machine hummed at its fastest pace yet, as if by producing story after story in national magazines and syndicated newspaper columns about how the newly seasoned Teddy was proving himself a worthy successor to his brothers, it could somehow be made to be true. That the gap between perception and reality had widened to a yawning chasm into which Teddy might plunge at any moment passed largely unnoticed.

On the occasion of his thirty-seventh birthday, *The New York Times Magazine* published an extended profile written by William Honan. The title was "Is Teddy, As They Say, Ready?"

Honan wrote that "after the death of Robert Kennedy last spring, Edward, who had always been outdistanced by the performance of his older brothers, suddenly found himself being thrust forward in political life at such a giddy speed he had to fight for control."

But Honan did not suggest that Teddy was losing the fight. He wrote that while there might be "moments of trial in which Edward Kennedy will think he sees the face of Jack when it is only mist, or hears the voice of Bob when it is just the wind in the rigging . . . nevertheless, what he carries with him that the crimes of Dallas and Los Angeles cannot take away is that special Kennedy amalgam of liberalism and sophistication, steadiness and attack, which were both bred and drummed into his sinews."

The central point promulgated most consistently that winter by members of Teddy's staff and by all the honorary Kennedys elbowing one another for position closest to him was summarized succinctly by Honan: "The fact is that Edward Moore Kennedy desperately wants to prove that he is not coasting on his family reputation but has earned his stripes the hard way—that he could make it even if his name were just Edward Moore.''

Yet Teddy's office, like his heart, was inhabited by ghosts and by relics of the past, which even the most casual observer could not help but notice. The flags that had stood in the Oval Office when Jack occupied it as President now stood at either side of Teddy's fireplace. His desk was the same one used by his father as ambassador.

And everywhere there were the photographs: of Teddy with Jack, of Teddy with Bobby and Jack, of just Jack and Bobby, of all three of them with their father, before the stroke. Always, in the photographs, they were laughing, grinning, as if they hadn't a care in the world. It was these images with which Teddy had chosen to associate himself every working day.

The result, Honan wrote, was that "a heaviness hangs about the office," and, observing Teddy, that "there is little spring in his step. He seems a somehow prematurely stooped curator in this museum of bright promises unkept."

And in a *Look* magazine cover story published the same week—an article clearly intended to celebrate the arrival on the national scene of the "new" Teddy—he permitted himself an uncharacteristic lapse into poignancy. Asked why he persisted in public life, he gave a long, rambling reply, replete with all the necessary platitudes about the ideal of public service that had been taught him by his parents, et cetera, but in which he also said, at one point, "I don't know. I don't know. Maybe sometimes I would like to do other things. But what would I do?"

A Gallup poll in early March disclosed that Teddy possessed "assets that would make any presidential aspirant envious." Ninety-four percent of those polled could correctly identify who Teddy was. This was an awareness score, according to Gallup, "usually obtained only by Presidents, presidential nominees, top athletes and entertainers."

His ratio of favorable to unfavorable opinion was six to one among all Americans and seventeen to one among Democrats—statistics unprecedented in Gallup polling history.

"Two Democrats in every three would like to see him become President," the Gallup organization wrote in a story accompanying its findings, and "eight in ten believe he will actually win his party's nomination." No other potential candidate about whom Gallup pollsters had ever sought information had produced numbers anything like these.

The prevailing attitude toward Teddy seemed well summarized by a young secretary in Pennsylvania who told the Gallup organization, "The whole Kennedy family has exhibited a genuine love for their country and a desire to serve as best they can. What I admire most about Teddy Kennedy is his continued devotion to the nation in the face of the tragedies that have plagued his family."

On March 16, Bob Healy wrote that Teddy was "the inevitable candidate."

And majority leader Mike Mansfield said, not without a certain wariness, "It's preordained. With Ted, I'm afraid it's not a question of choice, it's a matter of destiny."

Another Democratic senator, speaking only under anonymity, said, "Kennedy will have to run in 1972. If he doesn't, he'll be branded a coward."

He owed it to all of them: to his father, to Joe Junior, to Jack, to Bobby, to all the ghosts. What he might have owed to his children or to his wife or to himself—one last chance for peace of mind, perhaps—seemed beyond his ability to comprehend.

5

THROUGHOUT THE SPRING, HE SEEMED TO BE MAKING A conscious effort to replicate Bobby's performance of the previous year.

He flew to Memphis on April 4 to speak at a memorial service marking the first anniversary of Martin Luther King's assassination.

A crowd of thousands had assembled under dark skies in front of City Hall Plaza. Ralph Abernathy, King's successor as head of the Southern Christian Leadership Conference, introduced Teddy.

"I know of no family in America," Abernathy said, "that has made the contribution to the life and the ongoing of America that the Kennedy family has. And we love the only surviving son of that family, Senator Edward Kennedy." Then, invoking the heavens, the Reverend Abernathy cried out, "And we want to spare him because one day he will be the President of the United States."

Rain began falling heavily, even before Teddy spoke. But no one left, no one moved, and Teddy did not even bother to put on a raincoat.

With more open passion than he'd ever before displayed in public oratory, he spoke not only of Martin Luther King but of his brothers, all of whom were now linked in the history of the nation, as well as in his own mind.

"Great men," he said, his voice already trembling with emotion, "gave their talents and their lives so the rest of us can carry on their work. Leaders may be lost, but their cause goes marching on."

Drenched but uncaring, he said, "A year ago on a street corner ghetto in Indianapolis, my brother quoted a line from the Greek poet Aeschylus that had meant a great deal to him over the years.

" 'In our sleep, pain which cannot forget falls drop by drop upon the heart, until, in our own despair, against our will, comes wisdom through the awful grace of God.' "

He had to pause momentarily, to regain control of his emotions, before continuing.

"Today," he said, "we meet in the place where the work of Martin Luther King was interrupted. To some, this is a day of sorrow. To some, this is an occasion for fear." Then he cried out, "To me, this is a day of hope!

"We confess today that the promises we made a year ago, to finish up his work, have not been kept. We said we would see that the peace he pursued would be won. We would see that the justice he sought would no longer be denied. We would see that the love he lived would be returned. We would see that the programs he championed would be enacted."

He paused again, the rain dripping from his hair and rolling down his face, along with what might have been tears. He was talking about Martin Luther King, of course, but he seemed also to be talking about Bobby.

"As we pause to pay honor to his memory today," he said, "we must look at our country's actions—and be honest. Men still die in far-off lands; children still go hungry in America; employers still discriminate with taxpayers' money; schools are still segregated against the law; willing hands go idle; men still live in hate and fear of one another and wealth is still lavished on useless and dangerous arms."

Again, his voice broke. This was what Martin Luther King had died to change. This was what Bobby had died to change too. And, in the wake of their martyrdom, this was the struggle from which Teddy, the only man in America who could have seen to it that their ideals prevailed, had turned away by not accepting the 1968 presidential nomination.

But he was back now. He was ready. Or so he wanted, so desperately, to believe.

As did we all.

Gazing up through the rain at armed policemen patrolling nearby rooftops to guard against an assassination attempt, he said, "If there are risks in this life, we will take them."

Looking straight into the crowd, he said, "If there are sacrifices, we will make them."

And then he said, "For my part, I will fight for these goals all my public life. There is no higher good I can do for my country."

The crowd cheered. Teddy seemed to be weeping as he turned away from the microphone and stepped down from the platform in the rain.

Four days later, he flew to Alaska. It was another trip prompted by ghosts; another attempt to fulfill a brother's legacy. As a member of a Senate subcommittee on Indian education, Bobby had pledged to travel to Alaska for a firsthand look at the plight of Native Americans living there, many in conditions of poverty worse than any to be found in the contiguous United States.

The assassination of Martin Luther King had caused Bobby to postpone the trip. His own assassination had forced its cancellation. But now, a year after it had first been scheduled, Teddy had agreed to make the trip in Bobby's stead.

He was to be accompanied by four other subcommittee members. Officially, the tour was billed as an investigation of the educational system that the federal government provided for the more than fifty thousand Eskimos, Indians and Aleuts scattered across an area more than twice the size of Texas; a state that itself had five separate time zones, and whose capital, Juneau, was accessible only by air or water, not by road.

Unofficially, however, as *The Washington Post* reported, it would be "Edward Kennedy's first trial in a role that his brother filled so dramatically—field trips to America's poverty pockets to underscore the conditions there."

He started drinking on the airplane. The flight to Anchorage was long. He seemed occasionally maudlin, but more often veered closer to open hilarity.

He had been gaining weight steadily for six months. It was so noticeable that sometimes, when taking questions from an audience, he'd find himself asked about the sudden change in his appearance, the excess pounds. He'd smile and mutter something about too much ice cream and move on to the next question.

Now, bound for America's last frontier, he laughed jovially when reporters started kidding him about his weight.

"It's the sauce, boys," he said. "It's the sauce."

In Anchorage, the entire entourage assembled. Besides Teddy, there was Democratic senator Walter Mondale of Minnesota and Republicans Henry Bellmon of Oklahoma, George Murphy of California and William Saxbe of Ohio. In addition, one of Alaska's senators, Ted Stevens, had joined the group.

Together with an average of three staff assistants per senator and a press contingent consisting of two dozen reporters, photographers, broadcasters and television cameramen, the mob that would be descending upon the Eskimos would outnumber, in some cases, the population of the villages they'd come to see.

At the start, Teddy seemed in a jaunty mood, though to those who knew him best his high spirits had an unnerving edge, as if somehow the intensity of his recent experience in Memphis, coupled with the sheer weirdness of suddenly being in Alaska—and there to do the job that Bobby had pledged to do—had begun to loose within him feelings that had been dammed up much too long.

The group flew west from Anchorage aboard an air force C-130, to the southwestern Alaska village of Bethel, where they broke up into smaller parties. They continued deeper into the bush country aboard small aircraft equipped with skis instead of wheels and landed on frozen rivers that flowed through the villages.

Teddy had never seen anything like it. He felt as if he'd stepped out of his own life and into the pages of *National Geographic*. With the temperature below zero, he pinned a button that said "Eskimo Power" to his parka and flew to Tuluksak, Nunatitchuk and Pilot Station.

In Tuluksak, population about 150, he entered the home of a woman named Minnie Hawk. The home was a single room formed by nailed-together pieces of driftwood and corrugated metal. There was no electricity. Minnie Hawk lived there with her husband and five children. The children were suffering from middle-ear infections and receiving no treatment. Teddy was told that such conditions had caused deafness in up to 25 percent of the natives of southwestern Alaska.

Nearby, he entered another rancid one-room shack. There, he gazed down at a pile of garments on a bed, beneath which lay a sick infant whose ailment had not been diagnosed because no doctor ever came to the village. On the wall above the bed was a faded colored photograph of Jack and Jacqueline in evening clothes.

Teddy's staff made sure that the television camera crews and the photographers from the newspapers and magazines were able to record the scene to their satisfaction.

They returned to Bethel in early evening to tour the local hospital. This visit quickly degenerated into even more of a mob scene, with Eskimo children swarming around Teddy, and members of his staff literally elbowing the Republican senators out of the way so that only Teddy would be photographed or televised speaking to sick Eskimos.

Saxbe of Ohio became incensed at Teddy and his entourage, "trooping through with muddy boots, bumping into people, going into the maternity ward. It was going on all day, the pushing and shoving by staff people. You can't talk to an Eskimo with a retinue of twenty-five people around."

In a sour, contentious mood, the group reboarded the C-130 for the night flight to Nome, the old gold-rush town on Alaska's even more remote northwestern coast.

The weather, however, had turned bad. Nome was buried deep beneath a bank of fog. This wasn't 1964 with Zimny. This was a C-130 with air force pilots and more than thirty people aboard. Without bothering to consult the Republicans, Teddy ordered the plane to return to Anchorage for the night. In Anchorage, he knew, he'd be able to get a drink.

Soon after their return, however, matters worsened considerably as staff aides to the Republican senators obtained a copy of a "confidential" forty-three-page memorandum that had apparently been prepared before the trip for Teddy's use. The memo stressed ways in which Teddy could obtain maximum political value and public relations exposure from the trip.

He was advised to "focus television coverage on native poverty contrasted with the affluence of Government installations." It was suggested that he use the word "colonialism" when describing the situation in Alaska.

That was enough for Saxbe. He got up early the next morning and flew back to Washington. He did not inform Teddy he was leaving, he said, because "I figured he was asleep." Given Teddy's consumption of alcohol the day and night before, this was not an unreasonable assumption.

Within hours, Teddy found himself deserted by the two remaining Republicans. Having been informed of the memorandum's contents the night before, and aware that Saxbe had already gone home, both Bellmon and Murphy also pulled out, claiming the entire junket was "a Roman circus" and "a stage-managed scenario," designed only to boost Teddy's presidential prospects.

Saxbe's comment was even more cutting. He called the whole trip "a humiliating indignity to the Eskimo." Which had certainly not been Bobby's intention.

Teddy flew north later that morning, exhausted and unnerved by the defections and by the sudden partisan turn matters had taken. His destination was Barrow, the northernmost settlement in Alaska, three hundred miles above the Arctic Circle.

It was another stone-gray, frigid day, as bleak as the tundra was wide. Teddy was now convinced he'd botched the trip. With the three Republicans gone, the public hearing scheduled for Friday night in Fairbanks would have to be canceled. That was to have been the highlight of the venture, when he could have put pointed questions to appropriate federal representatives. Instead, he faced only two more dreary days of trudging in knee-high snow through frozen, squalid villages, most of which had unpronounceable names, and then flying back to Washington—an exhausting, ten-hour trip under the best of circumstances—to face inevitable questions about having tried to exploit human misery in order to gain political capital.

He slogged on, poking his head into filthy, over-crowded huts, dutifully asking all the questions his staff had told him to ask. Eventually, his gloom gave way to a kind of irreverent mania. Toward the end, as the writer Brock Brower, who was traveling with him, put it, what had been intended as a legitimate fact-finding mission "tailed off weirdly into a kind of polar craziness."

One of the last stops was in the tiny Eskimo settlement of Arctic Village. From there, the group would fly on to Fairbanks, where, after midnight Fairbanks time, they would transfer to a commercial airliner for the five-hour flight to Seattle and then transfer again for the five-hour flight to Washington.

In Arctic Village, Teddy was told that the C-130 had developed a mechanical problem. The engines would not start. The trouble could be fixed, but they'd be stuck in Arctic Village for at least three hours. That night, it became apparent to all who were with him that Teddy truly was losing his grip.

At first, he seemed simply giddy from the sudden sense of isolation and remoteness—and freedom!—that came from being stranded in Arctic Village, Alaska, population sixty, location 130 miles above the Arctic Circle, five time zones and five thousand miles removed from Washington, from the pressure, from the myth.

For a decade now, since Jack had announced his candidacy, Teddy had become increasingly roboticized, to the point where, during working hours, he often seemed to be scarcely more than a mechanical, life-sized Kennedy doll: wind him up and he walks and talks, just like Bobby, just like Jack.

Each of his working days began in the same fashion. An aide would hand him two separate stacks of index cards to carry in an inside pocket of his suit. One stack was of Schedule Cards, telling him what individual or group he was supposed to see at each point during the coming day and evening, and even, in general terms, what he was supposed to say. The other stack was of Call Cards, telling him whom he was expected to telephone next, and for what purpose, during those spare moments between appearances.

For almost ten years, his staff had charted his every working moment for him on these cards, with aides hovering constantly at his side with duplicate sets should he misplace or forget them:

> 6:10—reception at Belgian Embassy, no formal remarks required.
>
> 6:35—office meeting with legislative aides on trucking deregulation bill.
>
> 7:20—5-minute telephone interview, WBZ radio news.
> subject: Vietnam.
> position: no shift in basic view that early withdrawal remains preferable course.
>
> 7:45—drop by Sen. Nelson cocktail party. Brief hello only.
>
> 8:05—call home. Remind Mrs. Kennedy of Thursday's dinner for visiting Soviet scholars.
>
> 8:15—Kennedy Foundation board dinner. (10-minute talk. GIFFORD will meet you there with PREPARED TEXT.)

He had endured day after day, night after night, month after month, year after year of this. He knew no other way: he would not otherwise have been able to function.

Recently, along with the escalating pressures, Teddy's schedule and his forced adherence to it had grown even more inflexible due to the scrupulous attentions of his new chief of staff, David Burke, a policeman's son who watched over him with a Jesuitical vigilance that reminded Teddy of his bleak winter days at Cranwell, the last and most dismal of his pre-Milton prep schools.

But Burke hadn't come to Alaska. And the senior staff aide who had—Dick Drayne, his press secretary—did not have Burke's air of authority, or his ability to keep Teddy's more self-destructive impulses in check.

And now even the Republicans were gone. They had deserted him. They were trying to hurt him politically. He would have to deal with them when he returned to Washington. From Arctic Village, however, Washington seemed to be not just in another time zone but on another planet.

Teddy began to drink heavily while still on the ground and continued, at an even faster pace, once airborne. It seemed to many of those who were with him that he was suffering from both profound fear and piercing loneliness.

Not long before, a friend had noted that since Bobby's death, "Ted doesn't have anyone to turn to. Only his sisters, but they're not the same for him. He misses his brother very, very much. He seems so alone now."

The family, remarked another friend, "never does allow any sadness to creep into their daily life. So it all looks the same. Ted mixes in and talks and smiles. But then, the next thing you know, he's suddenly not there anymore, he's out by himself—and this happened so often after Bobby was killed—walking alone on the lawn and along the dunes. Watching him, you get the feeling that he's so terribly alone."

Even his sister Jean said, in an unusual moment of candor about the emotional condition of another family member: "He has nobody to talk to. With Bobby, he had the same thing he did with Dad. Teddy depended on his judgment. It's hard to find a substitute for Bob.''

And it was even harder to be a substitute for Bob—as well as for Jack.

There were no psychologists flying back from Alaska with Teddy, but some of the journalists—in particular, Brock Brower of *Life* and John Lindsay of *Newsweek*—were perceptive enough to recognize that what they were seeing was no longer simply the juvenile behavior of a spoiled rich kid but a desperate cry for help from a deeply troubled man.

At one point, Teddy slumped in a seat next to Brower. Slowly (''an inch at a time,'' Brower wrote), he removed from his briefcase a silver hip flask.

It had been Bobby's. Bobby had not been a heavy or frequent drinker, but whatever he'd done he'd liked to do with style; hence the hip flask.

''First time I've used it,'' Teddy blearily confessed. ''First time.'' He did not offer Brower a drink from the sacred vessel, but seemed to want to be sure that the reporter understood that his own use of it represented some peculiar form of capitulation. Perhaps, finally, a conscious awareness that he was not Bobby and never could be.

The long trip home was a lurid nightmare for all concerned.

There was Teddy, slumped back in his seat, lapsing into some sort of stream of consciousness, or stream of unconsciousness whose logic was apparent only to himself, rambling incoherently about his father, his dead brother Joe, his dead sister Kathleen, about what had really happened to Rosemary, and then, of course, about Jack and about Bobby.

''They'' had shot Jack, he said. And ''they'' had shot Bobby. And then, near tears, Teddy waving the flask about, shouting: ''And they're going to shoot my ass off, the same way they shot Bobby's.''

Nobody asked him who ''they'' might have been.

* * *

534

And then there was Teddy, no more sober but considerably less enigmatic, saying aloud to no one in particular, "I can't figure it out . . . I can't figure it out."

And then, more loudly, and with so much obvious anguish in his slurred voice: "I am so tired of trying to figure everything out!"

But there were other, less poignant aspects to the journey: the sudden, frightening burst of mania after the transfer to the commercial flight in Seattle, as Teddy charged up and down the aisle, past shocked and appalled passengers, chanting, "Ess-kim-o Power! . . . Ess-kim-o Power!" hurling pillows, grabbing flight attendants and female journalists, succeeding, in one case, in forcing one into an open lavatory where only her screams and the intervention of others prevented an assault from becoming a more serious offense.

One member of the press contingent recalled, "He'd had nothing to eat and it was drink drink drink drink drink, no sleep at all. He was all over the place, weaving up the aisle, pelting one of his guys with a pillow, saying, 'C'mon, wake up! You're not supposed to sleep on these goddamned trips!' "

No one aboard had ever seen Teddy—or any other political figure—so out of control in public. To both Brower and Lindsay, the conclusion to be drawn was as inescapable as it was startling: Teddy did not want to be President. And, at some point before 1972, and probably sooner than later, he would do whatever was necessary to ensure that he would not be.

Brower quickly arranged a lunch with his editors at *Life*, at which he said, "You won't believe this, but I don't think Teddy wants to run."

"Does he say so?" an editor asked.

"He doesn't say so, but everything he's doing says so."

"Ted Kennedy," another editor asked incredulously, "does not want to be President?"

"If he can possibly avoid it," Brower said. "The bad thing is the pressure everybody's putting on him. It's making him come up with some pretty hairy avoidances.''

"Well, if you can prove that," Brower was told, "it's a hell of a story."

Brower decided to set about the task. As he later wrote, "I decided it was maybe just possible to attack his character—to examine his insecurities, fatalism, fast living, etc. and show why Ted Kennedy wouldn't want to run . . . to show that character here was not fate but an effort to escape fate." Brower's goal, he said, was "to help along Teddy's own cause before it was too late."

Lindsay delivered much the same report to *Newsweek*. Such was the strength of the Kennedy mystique, however, that no hint of his insight that Teddy was "an accident waiting to happen" was ever printed.

Instead, later that spring, the magazine wrote that "like the candidate for President he will almost assuredly be three years hence . . . the last surviving Kennedy brother [is] finally ready to claim his legacy as a political warrior."

Later that spring, again on an airplane and again late at night and again while drinking from Bobby's flask, Teddy once more gave voice to his desperation.

"The thing about being a Kennedy," he said to an Associated Press reporter, "is that you come to know there's a time for Kennedys. And it's hard to know when that time is, or if it will ever come again. . . ."

It was a monologue, interrupted by very few questions. "I mean, is it really the best thing for me to do? And how much of a contribution could I make, even if . . .

"I'm really very unresolved . . . maybe over the summer . . . maybe some sailing . . . the family . . . I think perhaps by fall, I'll be settled, have some idea . . . But the fun has gone out of it."

Even, he was asked, when he received a reception as tumultuous as those once given to Jack and Bobby?

"Those kinds of things pretty much turn me off now. When I first came into this . . . in 1962"—and the way he said the date made it seem as if it had been a half century earlier—"it was really good, easy. But the kicks aren't . . . I mean, meeting Molly somebody and hearing all about her being Miss something."

Then, suddenly, he allowed himself to ask, rhetorically, the ultimate question: "What's it all for?"

The words hung heavy in the darkened cabin as he took another long pull from the flask.

Sighing, he said, "I used to love it."

There was another long pause.

"But the fun began to go out of it after 1963, and then after the thing with Bobby, well . . ."

Another pause, another drink from the flask.

"So even if the time is right . . . why should I? You talk about the family obligation for public service. Is running for this the best way to meet that? When my father —I mean . . . " He paused again. He knew, all the family knew, that his father was failing fast; that old Joe Kennedy would probably not live out the year. But Teddy could not bring himself to say it directly.

Instead, he said, "I mean, then, I'll really be it, and that's a lot. Just so many responsibilities . . . I worry . . . the kids . . . never feel I'm giving them enough. I mean, I'm just not sure running around the country, taking on the tough issues and waving the Kennedy flag and running on in everywhere and stirring people up—is that helpful?

"Bobby did it, I know. Spoke right on up on what bothered him, raised all that excitement—and then . . . and then they can elect someone like . . ."

And there he stopped. For once again he'd come back to what would forever be for him the starting point and the end point: what Bobby had done in 1968 and what Teddy had not done and must now have known he would never be able to do.

But there was to be no easy way out. Neither the public nor the press would permit it. Jack and Bobby had given us a taste of something that we now thought only Teddy could fully satisfy. We'd grown addicted to the images of glamour, of charm, of the godlike qualities we'd been led to believe—and wanted to believe—all Kennedys possessed.

In the end, it would be hard to say whose Faustian bargain proved the more destructive: that between the crippled Ambassador and the forces necessary to see to it that his sons successfully lived out his dreams; or between the Kennedy family and the popular press.

Long ago, it had been discovered by both the family and the editors of America's most successful newspapers and magazines that the Kennedys—at least the sanitized, glorified, even sanctified image of the Kennedys—had an extraordinary ability to sell.

They, or rather, an expurgated, simplified, mythified version of them, were also what America wanted to buy in the late 1960s. These super-Kennedys, as presented to the public by the press, satisfied a national craving for heroism, for belief that a higher plane of life existed and that if we could not occupy it ourselves we could at least be permitted to gaze upon it and its inhabitants.

It was the culmination of Joe Kennedy's original insight from the 1920s: People wanted fiction, not fact; they wanted the larger-than-life celluloid image; or, later, the even more potent television image. They did not want the Kennedy men (or women) at all; they wanted the myth. And the press, responding to what was nothing short of a bonanza, was all too happy to feed its readership larger and larger doses until it became impossible to believe that any member of the Kennedy family suffered from any human frailty whatsoever.

But it was a trap for all concerned. For the public, because the process of disillusionment is never pleasant; for the press, because attitudes that seemed entirely appropriate at the time came to be viewed, in retrospect, as embarrassing, even ridiculous, and in some cases actually unprincipled, so different was the standard applied to the Kennedys from that applied to any other public figures in America.

Caught most tightly in the trap, through absolutely no fault of his own, for he had only played by the rules that everyone had always assured him were acceptable, was Teddy himself.

THE LAST BROTHER

He was a hollow man, a burnt-out case. But the nation, led by its press, insisted on exalting him as a hero simply because he was the only Kennedy left. By spring of 1969, America's perception of Teddy had become a case of mistaken identity whose consequences would soon prove calamitous.

Part Five

Part Five

I

TEDDY TOOK A LATE MORNING SHUTTLE FLIGHT FROM Washington to Boston on Friday, July 18. He sat next to Tip O'Neill, speaker of the House of Representatives and the Boston politician who had held Jack's old congressional seat ever since Jack had moved up to the Senate.

O'Neill had known Teddy virtually all his life. The two men had an amicable relationship, both personally and professionally. It was O'Neill whom the family had used as an intermediary in 1962 when trying to persuade Eddie McCormack not to run against Teddy for the Senate. He was a man whose political skills were highly respected and whose discretion could be trusted. Like Teddy, he also enjoyed a good laugh and a good drink from time to time.

On the flight to Boston, however, he found it almost impossible to engage Teddy in even the most desultory conversation. This was surprising, because both for Teddy and for the family legend the weekend promised to be memorable.

It was the weekend of the annual Edgartown Regatta at Martha's Vineyard, occasion for some high-spirited sailboat racing in the daytime and even higher-spirited partying through the night. As was his custom, Teddy intended to participate in both.

He'd be racing his own boat, the *Victura*, on both Friday and Saturday afternoons, and at night would attend private parties whose guest lists had been assembled by Joey Gargan. Among those attending the parties would be six young women who had been active in Bobby's 1968 campaign.

But it was also a weekend that promised to be of enormous historical importance, one that would bring to fruition Jack's most extraordinary dream.

In 1960, Jack had pledged to put an American on the moon before the end of the decade. Now, even as Teddy was flying aboard the shuttle to Boston, a spacecraft containing three astronauts, Neil Armstrong, Edwin Aldrin and Michael Collins, was speeding toward the moon, scheduled to land there on Sunday afternoon.

It was astonishing. After millennia throughout which the moon—so cold, so distant, so mysterious and inaccessible—had inspired religious ritual, poetry, song, tidal currents, mad dogs, menstrual cycles and mayhem, man was about to set foot on its surface.

Through television, the whole world would be watching. The landing would mark one of the most spectacular advances in the long evolution of the human species. It was an event that would forever alter humankind's attitude toward all that lay beyond the small and isolated planet they inhabited.

Even to a generation that had witnessed more stunning technological developments in half a century—aviation, electronics, the atomic bomb—than had any before it, the scope and magnitude of what was to happen this weekend remained nearly impossible to comprehend.

And it was all coming about as a result of the vision, vigor and commitment Jack had displayed in 1960. One would have thought that Teddy, as the last Kennedy brother left alive, the only one who would witness the realization of Jack's loftiest dream, would be in a state of high excitement.

Instead, the effect upon him was just the opposite. To Teddy, the gap between himself and his most heroic, leg-

endary, mythic brother Jack must have seemed as vast
as the space that separated his lowly shuttle to Boston
from the three moonbound astronauts.

Later, Tip O'Neill would say only that Teddy had appeared "tired as hell" aboard the flight. But one senses
that the tiredness was more than physical; that it was
metaphysical—an exhaustion, an utter depletion, of the
spirit.

For Teddy, the decade that had begun with such hope
and promise was dwindling down now to its final few
months. His father was dying, he knew that, and with the
death of his father would come the formal end of the
family's private dynastic dream—the end of the Age of
Kennedy—for Teddy knew too, even if the nation did
not, that he would not be able to carry forward the spirit
of Bobby and of Jack.

Every summer for forty-six years, the Edgartown
Yacht Club on Martha's Vineyard had held a regatta. On
the island, the event was the nautical and social highlight
of the season.

For the Kennedys, who summered at Hyannis Port,
just across Nantucket Sound, the Edgartown Regatta offered both a welcome chance to compete and a natural
occasion for merrymaking away from the inquisitive eyes
of the Washington or Boston press.

At least one Kennedy male, and often more (when
there had been more), almost invariably made an appearance in the afternoon races as well as the late night parties that followed.

"Regatta weekend," said one Edgartown motel owner,
"can be wild." For Teddy, in the mid-1960s, it had been.
A 1966 Kennedy regatta party had turned "riotous," according to one guest, and an equally unrestrained baccha-
nal the following summer had left a rented cottage in
shambles, and had proven the occasion for Teddy's initiation of an eighteen-month affair with the young woman
who'd been his weekend "date." These were not parties
to which Teddy's wife, Joan, was invited.

Bobby's assassination had caused the family to miss
the 1968 regatta, but Teddy had made it clear early in the

spring of 1969 that he expected Joey Gargan to plan a regatta weekend that would be the equal of any in the past.

As he had since childhood, Joey worried about Teddy and felt protective of him. Stories about Teddy's behavior at the 1966 and 1967 regatta parties continued to circulate around Martha's Vineyard and Cape Cod. Now Teddy, as the prohibitive favorite for the 1972 presidential nomination, would be the focus of even more attention. Knowing better than most how serious had been Teddy's psychological collapse in the wake of Bobby's death, and aware that his recent behavior had been more erratic than ever before, Joey Gargan opted for prudence in making the arrangements.

He had traveled to Edgartown in May and reserved a number of motel rooms on the island. For the parties, however, he'd chosen a small and weathered cottage on the adjacent island of Chappaquiddick.

The Indian name meant "separate island," and, though separated from Edgartown by a seawater channel only 150 yards wide, Chappaquiddick, five miles long and three miles wide, was a remote and lonely place, possessing none of the tourist-oriented ambience that had come to overwhelm Martha's Vineyard, especially in summer.

There were no stores or gas stations on Chappaquiddick, and only seven families lived on the island year-round. Even at the height of the summer season the population was under five hundred, scattered among about 150 widely separated cottages.

Chappaquiddick was accessible from Edgartown only by a "ferry," which was really a small, flat barge with room for no more than two cars and twenty people at a time. The little boat operated between 7:30 A.M. and midnight and made the crossing in four minutes.

The two-bedroom cottage Gargan rented was three miles from the Chappaquiddick ferry landing, almost at the end of the island's only paved road. It sat fifty feet back from the road, there was not another cottage within a hundred yards of it and, except for the island's unmanned volunteer fire station, nothing of consequence lay beyond it, meaning very little traffic would pass by. It was as private as one could get in the vicinity of the Edgartown Yacht Club on regatta weekend, and, even better, it offered access, via dirt road and narrow bridge, to a thoroughly secluded and private beach.

Arriving on Martha's Vineyard, Teddy was met by his longtime chauffeur, Jack Crimmins, whose mood was even more foul than usual. Crimmins was the former policeman who'd been waiting at Barnes Municipal Airport in 1964 when Teddy's plane crashed.

The years since had done little to increase either Crimmins's charm or his tolerance for the idiosyncrasies—or even proximity—of others. A lifelong bachelor of sixty-three who was most comfortable in the company of male police officers, he seemed especially to resent the presence of women. When told by Gargan that he'd be driving not only Teddy back and forth all weekend, but also a number of female party guests—or "a bunch of douche bags," as Crimmins referred to them—he'd expressed strong displeasure.

He had driven down from Boston in Teddy's 1967 Oldsmobile on Wednesday, bringing what seemed an ample supply of beer, scotch, vodka and rum. Lacking the status that would have earned him a room at the Shiretown Inn, where a reservation had been made for Teddy, he'd been told by Gargan that he would be spending his nights at the Chappaquiddick cottage.

This displeased him further. "What a fucking dump!" he'd complained to Gargan after his first look at the cottage. He was in an even worse mood by Thursday, after having spent his first night there. A raccoon, a skunk— something he was not accustomed to dealing with in South Boston, anyway—had scratched at the cottage door all night long, and despite consuming more rum than he'd intended to, Crimmins had slept only fitfully.

Matters worsened for him when the first batch of Washington women, all of whom had worked for Bobby the previous year, flew to Martha's Vineyard Thursday afternoon. These were Susan Tannenbaum, Esther

Newberg, Rosemary Keogh and Mary Jo Kopechne. Two others, Mary Ellen and Nance Lyons, would arrive the next day.

All of them possessed an acute awareness of hierarchy and recognized that, as invited guests, they ranked considerably higher than did a paid functionary such as Crimmins. From the start, they made it clear that they expected him to act not only as Teddy's chauffeur but as theirs, too. If they wanted to go to the beach, he would drive them. If they wanted to shop in the Edgartown boutiques, he would drive them, help them carry packages and wait patiently until they were done.

As soon as Teddy got into the car, shortly after 1:00 P.M. Friday, Crimmins began complaining not only about the cottage but the women, grousing that their incessant demands to be taken from place to place were spoiling what he referred to as his "vacation."

Impatiently, Teddy reminded Crimmins that he, and not the chauffeur, was on "vacation." He also said he was hungry. He had Crimmins stop at a fast-food restaurant and pick up some fried clams to go. For Teddy, even on a vacation weekend in midsummer, there was barely a moment to spare. He was to race his boat, a boat that once had belonged to Jack, late that afternoon.

But first he wanted to see the girls and grab a quick swim at the private beach on Chappaquiddick. Since boyhood, Teddy and his brothers had made repeated visits to Chappaquiddick; they knew the island well. Teddy was glad Gargan had rented the party cottage there, close to the beach and isolated. If things got rowdy, as they had in both 1966 and 1967, better that it be in as private a location as possible.

Teddy and Crimmins made the quick ferry crossing from Edgartown, and drove the three miles to the cottage, which was empty. Joey Gargan had already driven the girls to the beach.

Teddy changed into his bathing suit. Then Crimmins quickly drove him half a mile back up the paved road, took a hard right, and bumped down onto a washboard dirt-and-gravel strip called Dike Road. This led, after another half mile, over the narrow wooden bridge that crossed a small pond, to the beach beyond.

Crimmins didn't like driving the Oldsmobile down the gravel road, hearing the little stones fly up and click against the undercarriage. He liked even less the precarious, rickety, seventy-five-foot-long bridge over which he had to slowly maneuver the car in order to reach this private beach. The Oldsmobile was wide and the bridge was narrow—only twelve feet from side to side. And there weren't even any guardrails, just foot-high wooden strips on either side.

Teddy stayed at the beach, swimming and laughing with the girls, for an hour. Their high spirits seemed to energize him. For the first time it appeared that he might enjoy the weekend after all.

The afternoon was hot, humid and still. Not good sailing weather. The start of the race was actually delayed half an hour due to lack of wind. "It was lousy," recalled Gargan, who crewed for Teddy during the race. "Awful hot. I worked very hard."

Despite his efforts, and despite having a Kennedy at the helm, the *Victura* finished a well-beaten ninth. Teddy was annoyed at his poor performance, and fatigued. He was also hot and thirsty, despite having downed several cans of beer during the race.

The winning captain was a sailing friend of Teddy's named Ross Richards. It was traditional, when one knew the victorious skipper personally, to join him on his boat for a congratulatory toast. This, despite his mood, Teddy had no qualms about doing. He was eager for another beer.

The day, however, had been so hot and humid, and so much beer had been so eagerly consumed, that by the time Teddy boarded the victorious sailboat, the supply was exhausted. Instead, Teddy began drinking rum and Coke. He downed three in quick succession, then had Gargan drive him to the Shiretown Inn.

When they arrived, Teddy sent Gargan down to the

inn's bar to have six bottles of cold Heineken brought to the Senator's room immediately.

On the porch outside his room, Teddy drank a couple of these. Then, having changed from sailing clothes to cookout clothes, he went downstairs, where Crimmins was waiting with the Oldsmobile to ferry him across the channel to the party.

2

THE FERRY OPERATOR WHO TOOK TEDDY ACROSS THE channel at about 7:00 P.M. was the last person not at the party to positively identify him until 2:25 the next morning, when the manager of the Shiretown Inn, who happened to be standing outside, observed Teddy coming down a staircase that led from the deck outside his second-floor room.

Dressed in suit jacket and slacks, he seemed, to the manager, "distressed." He seemed also to be in the process of leaving the motel unobserved, and to be quite surprised when confronted by the manager at the bottom of the outside staircase.

"Can I help you?" the manager asked.

"No," Teddy said. Then, according to the manager, he said he'd been awakened by noise coming from a party next door, couldn't find his watch and wondered what time it was.

The manager told him it was 2:25 A.M.

Teddy said thank you, turned and climbed back up the stairs to his room.

"He didn't really complain about the noise," the manager said later. "He didn't ask me to do anything about it."

Wherever he might have been heading—perhaps to the unlit, unoccupied Edgartown airfield, where a private plane, quickly summoned by telephone, could have flown him off the island to the safe haven of Hyannis Port—his chance encounter with the manager had apparently caused him to change his plans abruptly.

Less than five hours later, Teddy returned to the lobby of the Shiretown to ask the desk clerk to reserve for him copies of that day's *Boston Globe* and *New York Times*.

He was freshly shaven, dressed in "yachting clothes," according to the clerk, and "appeared normal in every way."

He also asked for a dime to make a phone call, saying, "I seem to have left my wallet upstairs."

The clerk gave him a dime and he walked to an outside porch, where the inn's public phone booth was located. From there, he called a longtime girlfriend of his in Florida. He told her that "something very serious" had happened and he needed a phone number where he could reach Steve Smith, who was vacationing in Spain. He knew she would have the number, because she was about to leave Florida to join Smith and his wife, Teddy's sister Jean.

This was the Kennedy version of the extended family: even if Teddy can't make it until a day or two later, the girlfriend vacations with the brother-in-law and sister in Europe, while the wife stays home, as Joan was doing at that moment, wondering why she had gotten pregnant for a fourth time.

Teddy had made the call collect, which meant he got his dime back. He returned it to the desk clerk. Then he stepped outside, into the alley that separated the Shiretown Inn from an adjacent motel. There he had another chance encounter, with two drinking and sailing friends, Stan Moore and Ross Richards.

It was Richards who'd won the previous day's race. But it was Stan Moore who had the best story to tell. He'd been staying at a motel called the Harborside with a number of friends. During the course of their postrace party a guest had been tossed over the railing of a terrace and had crashed into a security guard standing below. This had led to Moore's being thrown out of the motel in the middle of the night—or at 5:00 A.M., which passed for the middle of the night on regatta weekend.

He'd been wandering around Edgartown ever since and had encountered Richards on the sidewalk outside the Shiretown. Now, joined by Teddy, the men climbed the stairs to Richards's room.

Teddy said he'd like very much to say good morning to Richards's wife, who was an extremely attractive blonde.

Richards stepped into his room and woke up his wife. "Ted's outside," he said. "He wants to see you."

Compliantly, she soon emerged from the room to join the three men on the porch outside. Teddy, she noticed, was "all dressed up," which seemed odd for that hour of the morning.

They sat around chatting good-naturedly for fifteen or twenty minutes, expressing the hope that the breeze would freshen before the afternoon's race, and listening to Stan Moore once again regale them with the tale of his eviction from the Harborside.

Glancing over the porch railing at about 8:00 A.M., Ross Richards's wife saw Joey Gargan standing at the bottom of the stairs. "Joey looked awful," she said. "His clothes were all wrinkled and his hair was sticking out." Gargan was accompanied by a man Mrs. Richards did not recognize. Both men, her husband later told state police, appeared "soaking wet"—something that struck all who saw them as most peculiar, as if they'd just swum across the channel fully dressed.

Usually a most congenial fellow, Gargan seemed badly out of sorts. Ignoring the Richards's and Stan Moore, he said to Teddy, in a voice that sounded surprisingly stern, if not threatening, "I'd like to see you right now. In your room. Get in there."

But Teddy, in addition to having misplaced his watch and his wallet, had locked himself out of his room, leaving the key inside. Gargan's companion, a former United States attorney from Boston named Paul Markham, went to fetch another. While they waited for him to return, with the dripping-wet Gargan seeming increasingly agitated, Richards asked Teddy to join him and his wife for breakfast. Teddy said he could not just yet, but that he might be able to meet up with them a bit later.

When Markham returned with the key, the three men spent about half an hour in Teddy's room. Then they emerged from the inn and walked the few blocks to the ferry landing, where, shortly before 9:00 A.M., the morning operator was about to cast off for Chappaquiddick.

"Hi!" Teddy called out enthusiastically, and he, Gargan and Markham hopped aboard. He appeared to the operator to be "jovial" on this first morning crossing to Chappaquiddick.

Once he reached the other side, accompanied by Gargan and Markham, he proceeded immediately to an enclosed shack about a hundred yards from the dock and, using his credit card, made a series of long-distance calls from the pay phone inside.

The morning was muggy and cloudy, the sky a darkening gray. By 9:30 a light, intermittent drizzle, more like a mist, had begun to fall. In the absence of even the slightest of breezes, it did not appear to be good sailing weather.

Shortly after 9:30 Teddy was standing outside the shack where the pay phone was, when a man, a stranger, approached him. He'd just arrived at the ferry landing by car, coming from the direction of the cottage, from the direction of the bridge.

"Senator," said the man, whose name was Tony Bettencourt and who owned a year-round home on Chappaquiddick, "do you know there's been a girl found dead in your car?"

Teddy simply stared at him. He did not respond.

"Do you need a ride down to the bridge?" Bettencourt asked.

"No," Teddy replied. "I'm going over to town."

Bettencourt was puzzled. The Edgartown police chief had just dispatched him from the bridge to the ferry to await the arrival of the local medical examiner. The chief had been summoned to Chappaquiddick earlier that morning by a phone call from two fishermen who'd reported seeing an overturned car submerged in about eight feet of water near the rickety, narrow wooden bridge that led to the private beach. As soon as the chief had observed a body inside the car, he'd summoned the medical examiner. Then he'd noted the number on the license plate, L78 207, and called the Registry of Motor Vehicles to obtain the name of the owner.

To his astonishment, the chief quickly learned that plate L78 207 had been issued to one Edward M. Kennedy, Room 2400, JFK Building, Government Center, Boston.

But now Teddy was telling Bettencourt he did not wish to go to the scene of the accident. He said he planned to return to Edgartown. But he didn't do that, either. Instead, he went back to the pay phone and continued to make calls. As Bettencourt awaited the arrival of the medical examiner, the ferry made several of its four-minute trips back and forth across the channel. On one trip from Edgartown, the ferry brought over a hearse; on another, a tow truck with winch and chain.

Teddy, Gargan and Markham observed this activity from the immediate vicinity of the pay phone. After one crossing, at about 9:45 A.M., it occurred to the ferry captain that Teddy still might not know the full extent of what had been discovered at the bridge.

He approached the shack, but when Teddy saw him coming he began to edge away, behind several parked cars.

"Senator," the ferry captain called out. "Are you aware of the accident?"

Joey Gargan, not Teddy, responded. "Yes, we just heard about it." The captain returned to the ferry to make another trip to Edgartown. After a brief whispered conversation, Teddy, Gargan and Markham followed and got on board.

"This time," the captain noted, "Kennedy looked worried." Before the ferry even docked, he jumped off and walked quickly away, trying to duck a newspaper photographer who, having heard about the accident, was preparing to cross to Chappaquiddick. Looking "in fine shape," according to the photographer, Teddy, wearing light blue pants, a white polo shirt and canvas deck shoes, hurried up the street away from the ferry landing.

With Markham trailing behind, Teddy went directly to the Edgartown police station. He said nothing about an accident involving his car, but asked the officer on duty if he might use a telephone. Recognizing him and wanting to treat him with appropriate deference and respect, she directed him to the chief's office, from which he could make his calls in privacy.

In the outer office, a jittery, almost frantic Paul Markham also asked for use of a phone. The officer said he could use hers. He asked her to dial the numbers for him. She placed five calls altogether: two to Washington, one to New York, one to Pennsylvania and one within Massachusetts. Each conversation was brief and Markham spoke in such a hushed tone that the officer could not overhear what was said.

From inside the chief's office, however, Teddy's voice was louder and she could hear several snippets of his various conversations.

"Well, we'll have to notify her parents," he said to someone.

Then, a few minutes later, in a very different tone of voice, "I'm afraid I have some sad news to tell you."

Then, brusque and businesslike again, as if speaking to a staff member, he issued explicit instructions about removing a body from the island as quickly as possible.

Meanwhile, from Chappaquiddick, the police chief was trying to call headquarters to tell someone they'd better locate Teddy. For some time, however, he was unable to get through because Teddy and Markham had both police phone lines tied up with their outgoing calls.

Finally, he got through to the officer on duty and told her to send someone down to the ferry to find Teddy.

"He's right here, Chief," she said. "And he wants to talk to you." She handed the telephone to Teddy.

The chief, whose name was Dominick James Arena, said, "I'm afraid, Senator, that I have some bad news. There's been another tragedy. Your car has been involved in an accident over here and a young lady, a girl —well, she's dead."

"I know," Teddy said calmly.

"Well, Senator, do you know, were there any other passengers in the car?" The chief didn't know if other victims might have been washed from the vehicle by the tide.

"Yes, there were," Teddy said.

"Do you think they might still be in the water?"

"No, no," Teddy said. "Say, I'd like to talk to you. I'd like to see you."

"Sure," said the chief, who wanted to be as accommodating as possible to this last Kennedy, whom tragedy had apparently struck again. "Do you want to come over here?" he asked.

"I would prefer," Teddy said, "if you would come here."

"Of course, of course," the chief said. "I'll be right there." And, still wearing the bathing suit and T-shirt he'd worn when he first dived into the Chappaquiddick water to see if there was a body in the car, the Edgartown police chief hurried back to his station, where he found Teddy and Paul Markham in his private office, still using his phone. Teddy, in fact, was seated behind the chief's desk, in his chair.

Arena, a bulky, amiable man, felt it almost rude to interrupt. Certainly he had no intention of asking Senator Edward M. Kennedy to get out of his chair or to come out from behind the desk. And so the first interview between Teddy and the chief began with an almost absurd role reversal.

"I'm sorry about the accident," the chief said. He felt genuinely apologetic at having to be the one to first confront Teddy personally with what was sure to be distressing news.

Teddy stared at him, as if resentful of the interruption. It occurred to the chief that Teddy might have no idea who he was.

"I'm Jim Arena," he said. Though his first name was Dominick, everyone called him Jim.

Teddy was still gazing at him, a bit impatiently the chief thought.

"Senator," he said, "I'm the Edgartown police chief. I just spoke to you on the phone."

Instantly, Teddy's demeanor changed. He switched on his most affable grin, stood immediately, gripped Arena's hand with a firm shake of his own and said, "Hello, Jim, thanks for coming by."

Their roles still seemed strangely out of synch, something that was apparently occurring to Teddy, for he stepped out from behind the desk and, gesturing graciously, motioned for Arena to seat himself behind it.

"He's in clean, dry clothes," Arena said later. "Poised, confident and in control. Using my office and telephone. And I'm standing in a puddle of water and a state of confusion."

The confusion quickly turned to shock when Teddy calmly informed him, "I was the driver of the car." Until then, Arena had assumed that the young woman—Rosemary Keogh of Washington, D.C., according to identification found in a handbag retrieved from the backseat of the submerged car—had been the driver. And, because Teddy had told him there were no other victims in the water, that any other passengers had escaped.

The chief, totally stunned by Teddy's matter-of-fact statement that he had been driving the car, couldn't think what questions he should ask about the accident.

Instead, he said, "Well, I guess we should notify the next of kin. Do you know how we can reach Rosemary Keogh's closest relatives?"

"It wasn't Cricket," Teddy said, using Rosemary Keogh's nickname. "It was Mary Jo Kopechne, and I've already notified her parents."

Still dripping, Arena tried to behave in as professional a manner as possible. He began to wonder if maybe he shouldn't have taken an extra ten or fifteen minutes and changed back into a uniform. But he was going to go by the book. With a Kennedy involved, this very quickly would become a major national incident—moon landing or no moon landing.

He picked up a pencil and pad and asked Teddy how the victim's last name was spelled.

"I don't know," Teddy said. "I only know how to pronounce it."

From the side of the office, Markham impatiently interjected a comment. "Look, Chief," he said, "we can find out how to spell it later."

Arena nodded. For a moment there was silence in the office. He was not sure how to proceed. And there was Teddy, asking him that very question.

"How shall we handle this?" Teddy asked.

"Well," Arena said, "I guess what we have here is a motor vehicle accident. So probably the first thing we'll need is a statement from you, as the driver of the car, about what happened."

After a pause, Teddy said, "I'd prefer to write it out rather than give it orally."

"That's fine," Arena said, still eager to please.

"And I'd like some privacy while I do it," Teddy said. "I'll need some time undisturbed."

"Of course, of course," Arena said, and led Teddy to an empty town office down the hall.

Accompanied by Markham, Teddy entered the office. But then he turned and spoke again to Arena.

"I'd appreciate it," he said, "if you could go back over to Chappaquiddick to make sure my car is handled properly."

Arena assured Teddy he would do so.

"I mean," Teddy said, as if afraid the chief had missed the point, "I don't want the wrecker to tow the car right through the center of town. The people will all be staring at it. They'll make a big thing out of it."

Arena assured Teddy that the car would be discreetly removed to a secure location and that no sightseers would be permitted to gawk. Riding the ferry back to Chappaquiddick, the chief found himself bewildered by many aspects of what he'd just learned. Most confusing was Teddy's physical appearance and demeanor. For a man who'd been the driver of a car involved in an accident in which a young woman had drowned, he was displaying surprisingly few, if any, side effects.

In fact, as Arena would say later, "I found it hard to believe that the Senator had been in a major automobile accident. His face bore no trace of any marks. He never appeared in any kind of physical discomfort, or in shock, or confused.''

An hour later, when Arena returned to headquarters from Chappaquiddick, it seemed as if Teddy was the only person there who was not in shock or confused.

Townspeople, tourists and journalists—aware that Ted Kennedy was inside the police station and that there had been an automobile accident involving his car and that a young woman had died—had begun to gather both outside and inside the station.

Among the journalists was James Reston of *The New York Times*, who not only was an Edgartown summer resident of many years standing, but had purchased a local newspaper, the *Vineyard Gazette*, two years earlier.

The chief asked everyone to please wait outside. Then he walked down the corridor to the private office he'd given Teddy to use. He saw Jack Crimmins standing outside it, as if on guard. As an ex–state trooper once assigned to Logan Airport, Arena knew Crimmins to be Teddy's chauffeur.

Arena entered the office. Teddy was pacing back and forth across the room, obviously dictating a statement which Paul Markham was writing down, revising as he went.

"We're almost finished," Markham said, suggesting that the chief might want to wait in his own office in order that they might complete their work in privacy.

Shortly after noon, Markham, unaccompanied by Teddy, entered the chief's office with a statement in his own handwriting. Glancing at it, with its many cross-outs and rewritten passages, and arrows juxtaposing certain sentences, Arena could see he might have trouble deciphering the meaning properly.

"Maybe I should type this," he said to Markham. "Do you mind?"

Not at all, Markham said graciously. That seemed, in fact, a fine idea.

The statement was brief. It said:

On July 18, 1969, at approximately 11:15 P.M. Chappaquiddick, Martha's Vineyard, Massachusetts, I was driving my car on Main Street on my way to get the ferry back to Edgartown. I was unfamiliar with the road and turned right onto Dike Road, instead of bearing hard left on Main Street. After proceeding for approximately one-half mile on Dike Road I descended a hill and came upon a narrow bridge. There was one passenger with me, one Miss Mary ———, a former secretary of my brother, Sen. Robert Kennedy. The car turned over and sank into the water and landed with the roof resting on the bottom.

I attempted to open the door and the window of the car but have no recollection of how I got out of the car. I came to the surface and then repeatedly dove down to the car in an attempt to see if the passenger was still in the car. I was unsuccessful in the attempt. I was exhausted and in a state of shock.

I recall walking back to where my friends were eating. There was a car parked in front of the cottage and I climbed into the back seat. I then asked for someone to bring me back to Edgartown. I remember walking around for a period of time and then going back to my hotel room. When I fully realized what had happened this morning, I immediately contacted the police.

The chief returned to the private office to give Teddy a copy of the statement. Teddy said it was fine, but he did not want it released to the press or public.

"We're still trying to get hold of Burke Marshall," he said, explaining that Marshall was "the Kennedy family lawyer." Even though the statement had been dictated in privacy to a licensed Massachusetts attorney—and a former federal prosecutor at that—Teddy said he did not want it to become "part of the record" until he'd cleared it with Marshall.

"Could you hold it until I talk to him?" Teddy asked.

Arena, still eager to oblige, agreed. But he said he had a few questions of his own he wanted to ask, especially in regard to why Teddy had waited so long to report the accident.

At that point, Markham intervened. "The Senator," he said, "will answer questions after he has consulted his attorney."

The chief did not press the point. But he asked if he could at least see Teddy's driver's license.

Teddy said he didn't have it. "I can't find my wallet," he said. Now that he had delivered his statement, he seemed eager to leave the police station as quickly as possible, leaving the mopping up of any technical details for another time, and presumably to be handled by underlings.

It was not, however, quite so simple, for two inspectors from the Registry of Motor Vehicles had now arrived. Charged with conducting an investigation into any accident involving a fatality, they had a number of questions for Teddy.

Before they began, one of them read Teddy his Miranda rights from a printed card. Clearly, this was not just a friendly chat with good-natured Jim Arena in his bathing suit.

"You have the right to remain silent. Anything you say can and will be used against you in a court of law. You have the right to talk to a lawyer and have him represent you while you are being questioned. If you cannot afford to hire a lawyer, one will be appointed to represent you before any questioning if you want one."

Teddy said he understood the meaning of what had just been read to him.

Then one of the inspectors asked for his license and for the registration of the Oldsmobile. The registration, Teddy said, was undoubtedly still in the car's glove compartment. As for the license, he didn't have it. This time, however, instead of invoking the misplaced wallet, he said, "Sometimes I leave it in my car in Washington, because I own two cars. Why don't I call down there right away and see if it isn't there."

From Arena's office, with both inspectors present, Teddy called his Senate office. Although it was a Saturday in July, earlier phone calls had alerted his chief of staff, David Burke, to the fact that Teddy had encountered difficulty overnight and it might be advisable to have senior aides manning their posts.

He asked Burke to check his other car for his driver's license and also to obtain the correct spelling of Mary Jo Kopechne's name, as well as her address and date of birth, more bits of information the Registry inspectors seemed eager to have.

Having read Teddy's statement while Teddy spoke on the phone, one of the inspectors said, holding it up, "I would like to know about something."

All traces of cooperativeness vanished immediately.

"I have nothing more to say," Teddy snapped. "I have no comment."

Markham, who was also present in the office, quickly interjected, "The Senator will make a further statement after he has contacted his lawyer."

Then Markham stated that Teddy wished to return as quickly as possible to his Hyannis Port home.

No one objected. One of the Registry inspectors even volunteered to drive him to the Edgartown airfield, assuring him no further questions about the accident would be asked.

Chief Arena wanted to be even more helpful. When Markham asked about air charter services that might fly the Senator to Hyannis, the chief said he had a better idea. The chairman of the Edgartown board of selectmen was a great admirer of the Kennedy family and had already called headquarters to say he'd do anything he could to assist the Senator in this time of need.

The chairman was also a licensed pilot with his own plane. Arena called him and asked him if he'd fly Teddy off the island as quickly as possible. He agreed immediately and said he'd meet Teddy at the airfield in a matter of minutes.

Arena then helped Teddy sneak out of the police station through a rear entrance so as not to have to face questions from the press. The Registry inspector sped him to the airfield.

As agreed, he asked no questions, but he did recall that in the car, unprompted, Teddy repeated over and over,

"Oh, my God, what has happened? What has happened?"

The plane ride to Hyannis took only ten minutes. The sky had lowered, haze had crept in, rain was falling. Other than asking if visibility would permit a landing in Hyannis, Teddy asked his pilot no questions, but did repeat, as he had in the car, "Oh, my God, what has happened?"

He was soaking, not from the rain but from perspiration. As soon as the plane landed and wheeled to a halt, even before it was tied down, Teddy jumped from the passenger's-side door and ran to a car that had been sent to meet him.

The press was informed by his Washington office that the Senator would have no immediate comment either about the accident or about the forthcoming moon landing.

Instead, he disappeared immediately behind the walls of the Hyannis Port compound, soon to be joined by honorary Kennedys of all generations, come to have one last go at crisis management, to see if there was anything left of the legend that might be salvaged.

That evening, he slowly climbed the stairs to his father's bedroom. The old man was weakening quickly now, in these final months of the decade. How much frailer he looked, how much closer to death, than he had been in November of 1963, when Teddy entered this room to try to tell him Jack was dead.

It was no longer clear how much his father understood. He had long since stopped even making his terrible, haunting sound of "Noooooo!" He'd long since stopped knocking food off his tray or gesturing angrily on the rare occasions when Rose came into his line of sight.

His sight, in fact, was failing too. There was some question as to whether he'd go completely blind before he died.

In the spring, there had been a bad moment when Dwight Eisenhower died and the funeral was shown on television. The old man thought it was Teddy inside the coffin. Nothing anyone could say, no newspaper headline, no television broadcast, could rid him of the notion that the last of his sons had just been buried.

Teddy had been forced to make a special trip to Hyannis Port, just so his father could see he was still alive.

Now Teddy was back. On another special trip. He was still alive but the dream was dead. That was what he would have to tell his father, not knowing how much the old man would understand.

It was over. Chappaquiddick, whatever the legal consequences turned out to be, was the end. The moment Teddy walked into the Edgartown police station, all hope of Restoration, all dreams of future glory, all that the old man had fought so hard for—scheming, bribing, conniving, threatening—was finished and gone forever.

It would take some months yet to play out, and it would be years before the public fully accepted the death of the myth, the end of the dream, and recognized that the plunge of Teddy's car off the bridge had symbolized his final dousing of the torch.

But if his father was still capable of understanding anything, he would be capable, instinctively, of understanding that Teddy had failed once again.

The old man had hoped that the momentum created by Jack and Bobby might carry this last and least of his sons to heights of grandeur too. And it had: but to an altitude he could not tolerate, to a summit on which he could not survive.

And so he'd plunged. Off the bridge, into the pond, assuring that never again would he be required to demonstrate greatness when, for him, the brutal struggle every day was simply to endure.

He stood near the head of the bed and looked down. In 1963, he had not been able to make himself speak the truth about Jack. But this time there was no one left to speak for him.

"Dad," he said.

His father opened his eyes in recognition.

"Dad, I'm in some trouble."

He didn't know what to say next.

This was worse, far worse, than talking to the Kopechnes. And Teddy had never been very good with words unless someone else had written them for him.

How much could the old man understand? How much could he bear? How much of the truth should Teddy tell him?

"There's been an accident, Dad." He paused. He knew he had to say more.

"You're going to hear all sorts of things about me from now on. Terrible things . . ."

His father reached out with the one hand he could still move and clasped Teddy's. He placed Teddy's hand upon his chest. He looked briefly at Teddy; then, still clasping the hand, turned his head toward the wall.

Teddy could not tell him any more.

"I'm sorry, Dad. I've done the best I can." Then he squeezed the old man's hand and left the room. It would be months before he returned.

3

In EDGARTOWN, THREE HOURS PASSED. ARENA HAD heard nothing from Teddy. He'd agreed not to release Teddy's statement until "the family lawyer" had been contacted, but this was an agreement he was finding it increasingly difficult to live up to, as a growing press contingent, led by James Reston, demanded access to what was, after all, a matter of public record.

A wire service bulletin had already gone out: "The body of a young woman believed to be a secretary for Senator Edward M. Kennedy was recovered from the waters of Chappaquiddick Island following an auto accident. It was not immediately determined if the woman was alone in the car. Some members of the Kennedy family are on the island for the annual Edgartown Regatta."

Arena knew that to release the statement—in which Teddy himself admitted to being the driver of the car and then to having allowed ten hours to elapse before reporting that he'd driven it off a bridge and left a passenger inside to die—would be to cause an international sensation, even on the eve of the moon landing.

It also occurred to him that some in the press—and some not in the press, as well—might be tempted to put an unpleasant interpretation on the fact that Teddy had not reported the accident at all until after strangers had discovered the car and the body of the woman.

Nonetheless, by midafternoon, Arena felt he had no choice but to make the statement public. For all he knew, it might be days before Teddy located his family attorney. In the meantime, events were moving forward. The assistant medical examiner, who'd gone to the scene, had announced a preliminary finding of death by drowning; the body had been taken to a funeral home; the car had been secreted inside a service station. The world was not going to stand still waiting for Teddy to track down Burke Marshall.

And so, shortly after 3:00 P.M., Arena stepped into the corridor outside his office and said, "Senator Kennedy has given me the following statement." He read it in its entirety from start to finish three times in order that the reporters could note the salient facts.

He told the press that Teddy had been "cooperative." When asked about the long delay in notifying police about the accident, Arena suggested that Teddy "must have been in a state of shock."

At that point, the attorney who served as part-time special prosecutor for Martha's Vineyard whispered in Arena's ear that it would be a good idea to stop talking.

The chief was also informed that he had a phone call from Paul Markham. Telling the press he would have no further comment for the moment, he stepped back inside his office and took the call.

Markham said they still hadn't located Burke Marshall but wanted the chief to know that they were trying, that it shouldn't be much longer.

Marshall, however, had been contacted hours earlier and had, in fact, arrived at the Kennedy compound even before Teddy returned from Edgartown.

Marshall, who had been Bobby's most trusted legal advisor within the Justice Department and who later served as general counsel for IBM, saw a number of potential problems with the statement, but recognized also that having been given, it could not now be made to disappear. What was important was to delay the release as long as possible, as Marshall contacted lawyers better acquainted than he was with Massachusetts criminal law and motor vehicle codes.

In the meantime, he ordered that neither Teddy himself nor anyone on his staff, nor anyone who had been present at the party—a party to which Teddy had omitted any reference in his statement and of which both Chief Arena and the outside world were thus entirely unaware—speak either publicly or privately about any aspect of the accident.

It was also arranged for Teddy to be quickly examined by the Kennedy family physician. A diagnosis of concussion, of some sort of damage to the head, could prove invaluable later to explain the long delay in reporting the accident.

Teddy himself seemed preoccupied with two aspects of the incident that, at first, appeared to others to be peripheral. He emphasized that his car ought not to be subjected to close inspection, and that the body of Mary Jo Kopechne should be removed from Martha's Vineyard as quickly as possible. It was imperative, he insisted, that no autopsy be performed.

In fact, in his first phone call to David Burke from the shack on the Chappaquiddick ferry dock, Teddy had instructed his chief aide to contact Dun Gifford, who was on nearby Nantucket, and to instruct Gifford to fly immediately to Martha's Vineyard. Gifford was given a twofold mission: to get the Kopechne body off the island as quickly as possible and, until then, to stay as close to it as possible, to assure that any postmortem examination would be minimal.

He again emphasized that under no circumstances should an autopsy be permitted. Teddy's near obsession about this struck many as peculiar. But, apparently, neither then nor later did anyone ask him what he was afraid an autopsy might reveal.

Another former aide to Bobby, William vanden Heuvel, was assigned the task of traveling to New Jersey to offer any and all assistance to the dead woman's parents and to help them in their dealings with the press.

Gifford arrived at the Martha's Vineyard funeral home

even before Teddy left the Edgartown police station. By early afternoon, he and Joey Gargan had arranged to have the five surviving women from the party expeditiously and discreetly checked out of their motel and taken to the mainland, under strict instructions to go underground until further notice.

At this early stage, it seemed to Teddy and to many of his advisors that the damage to his reputation might be minimal, even nonexistent. Played properly, the tragic drowning of a Kennedy loyalist at Chappaquiddick might even be woven into the fabric of the legend. No one was quite sure how, but with proper handling by the press Teddy might yet be made to seem a victim of the same deadly fates that had haunted his family for twenty-five years.

Clearly, they had a cooperative police chief. As for the assistant medical examiner who'd examined the body, he assured Gifford that "death by drowning" was the official finding and that the body could be embalmed and flown to Pennsylvania for burial without delay—and without any autopsy being conducted.

What seemed most important now was to hold off the release of Teddy's statement until more thought could be given to the problem of minimizing its negative implications and filling its gaping holes.

Arena, however, told Markham, "I just released it. I couldn't wait any longer. I never heard from you people, and the press here is driving me nuts."

"Oh, Jesus!" Markham said, and hung up.

Still, the early press coverage was not bad. The *Globe*, in particular, rose to the occasion, as it had been doing for so many years. Relegating the moon landing, which would occur later that day, to the bottom of page 1, the Sunday paper published ten separate stories about the accident, all of them sympathetic to Teddy.

"Senator Wanders in Daze for Hours," was the headline over one, in which Teddy was described as "the only surviving brother in a family pursued by tragedy." The story said Teddy had "narrowly escaped death when his car plunged into a pond on a sparsely populated island off the coast of Martha's Vineyard.''

Teddy, it was said, had traveled to Martha's Vineyard for the weekend to "visit with his wife Joan and the family," as well as to participate in the regatta.

The cooperative Arena was quoted as saying that while state law would apparently require him to file a technical complaint against Teddy for leaving the scene of an accident, "I really believe that the accident is strictly accidental. There is no sign of negligence, speed, things like that." Indeed, it seemed to him just another in the series of tragedies that haunted the family. Upon learning that the car belonged to Teddy, Arena said, "I said to myself: 'My God, another Kennedy.' ''

Teddy, the *Globe* was pleased to report, was "resting comfortably" at the family compound, after having been "given a sedative to help relieve the pain." And the family physician was quoted as saying Teddy had suffered "a slight concussion."

"A Battle with Doom" was another headline. The lead paragraph of that story said, "The last surviving son of Joseph and Rose Kennedy, like his three brothers before him, seems in mortal competition with an unlucky star." The story went on to say that Teddy's escape from death marked the second time he had "avoided the twisted fate" that had snuffed out the lives of so many other family members.

It then listed all the other violent deaths and, toward the close, mentioned the "brood of children under the care of the only adult male Kennedy left, Ted." In conclusion, the story cited a comment from Bobby that "the family lives with a sense of tragedy, a sense of imminent doom," and said, with more passion than clarity, that "Ted is the only male offspring of the patriarch Joseph P., who still lives to deny that awful price."

Yet another front-page story the same day was headlined, "Ted First to Call Victim's Father," as if to accentuate his sense of compassion and his grace under pressure.

From an interview with the victim's father, however,

there emerged two elements that would ultimately prove disadvantageous to the artificial reality Teddy and his advisors were attempting to create.

Mary Jo Kopechne's father said, at 4:00 P.M. Saturday, "We still don't have any real details of what happened."

But hadn't Teddy given him a full report when he'd called from the police station that morning? a reporter asked. No, Teddy had said only, "Mary Jo was in an accident—an automobile accident. She was returning to take a ferry back to the mainland when the accident occurred."

Her mother had asked Teddy if she'd been killed.

"Yes," he'd said. Then, after quickly saying how sorry he was and that members of his staff would be in touch soon to provide any assistance they could, he'd hung up.

Teddy hadn't even said that he'd been the driver of the car.

Now, her incredulous father asked the *Globe* reporter, "Was Mary Jo with him?" It seemed impossible that if this had been the case, the Senator would have failed to mention it and would have failed to provide more details about her death.

The reporter said Teddy had given a statement to police and asked Kopechne if he'd like to hear it read.

"Yes, yes, go ahead," Kopechne said.

When the reporter finished, there was a pause. Then Kopechne said, "Now I don't know what to think."

He added that, of course, he and her mother had been aware that Mary Jo and one of her Washington roommates had been planning a weekend trip to Martha's Vineyard, "along with a couple of girls from Ted Kennedy's office."

He said, "We assume they went to the island to see the regatta with the Senator, but we're not certain." Mrs. Kopechne added that while her daughter had never worked for Teddy, "he entertained them up there at Hyannis Port."

However gracefully this information was presented, it cast a new and disquieting light upon events. Clearly, even as he made the manful gesture of calling the parents to inform them of their daughter's death, Teddy had been less than forthcoming. Worse, an additional element had been added to the story. Girls from Washington, from Teddy's office—spending the regatta weekend with the Senator. That could have an unpleasant ring to it. In his statement, Teddy had made no reference to girls up from Washington for the weekend, only of "walking back to where my friends were eating."

Because Teddy had answered no further questions, no one knew who these "friends" were. By late Saturday afternoon, the press saw this as a question in need of an answer.

The *Globe*'s first call to Teddy's press secretary, Dick Drayne, in Washington, elicited only a "no comment." But after hurried consultation with Hyannis Port, Drayne was instructed to acknowledge the existence of a party. He was to stress, however, that it had had far more to do with remembering Bobby a year after his death than it had to do with Teddy.

The story Drayne told the press on Saturday afternoon was that Mary Jo Kopechne was one of *eight* women invited to a reunion of Bobby's campaign workers, the purpose of which had been to honor their supervisor, Dave Hackett.

That Hackett himself, the guest of honor, apparently had not even been present at the party would remain just one among the many peculiar elements of Teddy's account that were to forever resist clarification.

Another such element was the number of guests. Altogether, Drayne said, "at least twenty people" attended the reunion, including other Kennedy friends and "sailing buffs." Drayne regretted that at the moment he was not able to produce a full guest list, but he stressed that Teddy had made only a brief appearance at the reunion.

"Ted came by to thank the girls," Drayne said. "Then this girl had to leave and they were trying to catch a ferry when the accident happened." He added that Joan had hoped to accompany her husband to the reunion and that had the accident not occurred, she would have joined him in Edgartown the next day. This was utterly untrue.

Drayne said he could provide no further details about

573

the victim because neither he nor Senator Kennedy "had known her very well."

The next day, as Dun Gifford flew with the unautopsied but already embalmed body to Pennsylvania, where Mary Jo Kopechne had been born and where she would be buried, and as the other party guests made themselves invisible, Bobby's widow, Ethel, gave a statement to the press.

"Mary Jo was a sweet, wonderful girl," Ethel said. "She worked for Bobby for four years and was in the boiler room (the phone room used for delegate counts) during the campaign. Only the great ones worked there and she was just terrific. She often came out to the house, and she was the one who stayed up all night typing Bobby's speech on Vietnam. She was a wonderful person."

Her own mother described Mary Jo to the press as "a maiden," and said that so great and undying was her devotion to the slain Bobby that even if she'd lived, she probably would have chosen never to marry.

The reality, according to many of her friends, was somewhat different. Mary Jo Kopechne had enjoyed a normal and active social life in Washington; one that did not preclude romance. Just prior to the regatta weekend, in fact, she'd ended a long and intense relationship with a marine officer stationed at Quantico and thus, like Teddy himself, was in rather unsettled emotional condition when she made the trip to Martha's Vineyard.

As for Teddy, the more the press scrutinized his statement, the more pointed their questions to Chief Arena became. But the chief stood firm and resolute.

Asked if there was any possibility that the accident might have been related to consumption of alcohol at the party, Arena said, "I did not ask that question of the Senator. There was no physical evidence at the scene that there might have been drinking involved. I'm not pursuing that line at all. I'm still standing on the fact that there was no negligence involved." He said his own investigation into the accident was "complete."

Privately, however, the chief was growing more mystified, both by the failure of any representative of Teddy's to contact him in regard to further questions he might have and, the more he thought about it, by Teddy's original statement.

For instance, the statement had not mentioned any party. The first word of a party had come from the Kopechne interview with the *Globe*. It was embarrassing for the chief of police heading the investigation into a fatal motor vehicle accident involving a car driven by the most prominent political figure in America not to have even been aware, until reading the newspapers, that the Senator had driven off the bridge after spending several hours at a party.

It was even more embarrassing when he had to admit to the increasingly inquisitive and ever less respectful press that he still had no idea who, besides Teddy and the victim, had been at the party. No, he had not questioned any of the other guests. Six women from Washington, he had learned, had registered at the Katama Shores Motor Inn in Edgartown for the weekend, but they'd all checked out in a hurry on Saturday morning and left the island before he had a chance to talk to them.

Unlike some members of the press, he saw no sinister implication in any of this, but even so amenable and well-intentioned a fellow as Jim Arena could not help but think that for some reason, neither Teddy nor his famous "family attorney" Burke Marshall wanted the full truth about the dead woman in the submerged car to be told.

Why was everybody suddenly in hiding, he wondered, unless there was something to hide?

4

T HE ANSWER WAS THAT THERE WAS SO MUCH TO HIDE
that behind the walls of Hyannis Port, neither the hastily
assembled courtiers nor the fallen prince even knew
where to begin.

They had trooped in from all over the country, from
around the world. Most of them had not been directly
summoned. They had assembled as if by instinct, or, in
Garry Wills's memorable phrase, "as by some magnetiz-
ing of their PT tie pins."

Robert McNamara, now president of the World Bank,
flew to Hyannis. Also arriving quickly were Sorensen,
Goodwin, Le Moyne Billings, Milt Gwirtzman, Sargent
Shriver, Markham and Gargan, Teddy's own man David
Burke as well as his two closest friends in politics, John
Culver and John Tunney, and of course, Steve Smith, the
master fixer, back from Spain.

It was Smith, with his unerring instinct for spotting rot
at the core, who was first to recognize the true scope of
the calamity. He hired nine separate lawyers to advise
and to represent Teddy, including Edward Hanify, senior
partner of the prestigious Boston firm Ropes and Gray.
Outside of Washington, and certainly in Boston, no lawyer had stronger and deeper ties to the highest levels of

the business and political establishment in Massachusetts than did Ed Hanify.

To have Hanify and Burke Marshall working together on a motor vehicle case was considered the equivalent of bringing in the *Queen Elizabeth* and the *Queen Mary* to tow Teddy's car up out of the pond. But Steve Smith was taking no chances.

Smith knew, before any of them—except perhaps Teddy himself—that the political thing was over now. There would be no presidential run in 1972. It might take the well-massaged public a decade or more to recognize it, but Steve Smith knew by the last week of July of 1969 that Teddy's future was already behind him; that the high point of his career had come and gone. That for him to emerge from this with any career at all would be perhaps the greatest, if least publicly celebrated, triumph of his life.

To one who later wondered why the prolonged silence that so badly tarnished Teddy's image had been permitted to continue, Smith bluntly explained the simple fact of life that governed the behavior of all those behind the compound walls during that time:

"Our prime concern," he said, "was whether the guy survived the thing. Whether he rode out the still-possible charge of manslaughter."

By Sunday, having had the opportunity to scrutinize Teddy's brief statement, the press was bombarding Jim Arena with many legitimate questions to which he did not know the answers.

Most of the reporters had already been to Chappaquiddick. They'd driven the road. And they'd all come to the same, unmistakable conclusion: Teddy could not unknowingly have made a wrong turn onto Dike Road.

First, the paved road, which curved sharply left at that point, had a white line down the middle, and an illuminated arrow on the side of the road indicated clearly the upcoming curve. In addition, the road was banked in the direction of the curve, so that, upon leaving it, a driver not only went suddenly from a surface of smooth pavement to a rough washboard of dirt and rock, but dropped about six inches in the process.

No one whose destination was the ferry could possibly have made that mistake. Teddy had known the name of Dike Road well enough to include it in the brief report he and Markham prepared. He also knew that bumpy, narrow Dike Road led not to the Edgartown ferry but to only one place: the bridge that crossed Poucha Pond and brought one to the deserted private beach he'd visited earlier that day. The implication was unmistakable: Teddy had been taking Mary Jo to the beach, not to the ferry.

Moreover, a large house stood at the side of the road just before the road reached the bridge. It was to this house, rented for the summer by a family from Pennsylvania, that the two fishermen had gone on Saturday morning when they'd first noticed the overturned car in the water. It was to this house that Chief Arena had gone to borrow a bathing suit when he'd first arrived at the scene. And it was from this house that he'd called the police station an hour later in an attempt to find Teddy.

The woman whose family occupied the house had told Arena that she'd heard a car go by "faster than usual" at about midnight the night of the accident. But it was not that comment on which the press initially focused. It was the presence of the house itself. The occupants stated with certainty that lights were on until well after midnight. Yet Teddy, seeking help for a girl who was lying, quite possibly still alive, in his submerged automobile, had walked right past this house and had continued, "exhausted and in a state of shock," for another 1.2 miles until he reached the cottage where "friends were eating."

This course of action seemed scarcely more plausible than his statement that he'd turned onto Dike Road by mistake and had not realized his error until the car went off the bridge.

There were, in fact, three other occupied houses Teddy would have had to walk past before reaching the cottage where the party was taking place. His failure to stop at any of these raised serious doubts as to whether seeking help for Mary Jo Kopechne was at the top of his list of priorities.

Then, on Sunday, reporters spoke to a Chappaquiddick resident named Christopher Look. A deputy sheriff and fuel oil salesman, he also worked part-time as a special police officer at private events.

On the night of the accident he'd kept the peace at the Edgartown Yacht Club's regatta dance from 8:00 P.M. until 12:30. A club employee took him across the channel in the club's launch after the dance. Look's car was parked at the dock.

As he drove home, at about 12:40 A.M. Saturday, he saw the headlights of a car coming toward him. As he later said, "Knowing the road, I slowed down, because there's a sharp corner people usually cut too close. I wanted to make sure I didn't get sideswiped."

He slowed, in fact, to almost a complete halt. A dark sedan rushed past him. "There was a man driving," he said, "and a woman in the front seat and either another person or some clothing in the backseat—what appeared to be a shadow of some kind."

As soon as it passed him, the sedan swung off the paved road and onto a narrow dirt track that led nowhere. Locally, it was referred to as Cemetery Road.

As if realizing he'd made a mistake, the driver of the sedan began to back out toward the paved road. Thinking that the occupants might be lost or in need of directions, Look, a friendly, helpful sort of fellow, got out of his car and walked toward the sedan.

He was within ten yards of it, and just starting to ask if he could be of any help, when the car, which had paused, backed up farther. He was close enough to it now so that when in reverse gear the car's taillights clearly illuminated Look. He was still wearing the police officer's uniform he'd used at the dance.

Before he could get any closer, the sedan backed past him at high speed; the driver then switched to forward gear and, "in a cloud of dust," took off down Dike Road, toward the bridge. Look had been close enough to see that the license plate had the letter *L* on it and that both the first and last digits after the *L* were 7s.

He never gave thought to pursuing it. He wasn't looking for trouble. He had only been trying to help. Who the driver was, and where he was going, was none of his business. His night's work was done. He got back in his car and resumed his drive home.

But only about a hundred yards from the intersection he came upon another curious scene. A man and two women were dancing down the middle of the road in what Look described as "sort of a snake dance, or a conga line." Since they were headed in his direction, he stopped to ask if they'd like a ride.

"Shove off, buddy," shouted the taller of the two women. "We're not pickups." Though Christopher Look, of course, did not know it, this blithe young spirit was another of the Kennedy workers who were attending the Chappaquiddick party.

His Good Samaritan instincts thoroughly squelched for the evening, Look drove directly to his house, noting to his wife upon his arrival that it hadn't been too bad for a regatta night since he was already home and it was only 1 A.M.

His phone rang early the next morning. He was told there was a car underwater by the Dike Bridge and it appeared to contain the body of a woman.

Hurrying to the scene, Look was present with Chief Arena when the car was dragged up from the pond.

"That's the same car I saw last night," he remarked.

"Do you know who was driving?" Arena asked him.

"No. All I could see was a man driving and a woman in the front seat and maybe somebody else in the back."

"Well," Arena said, "it was Teddy Kennedy."

As the press pieced it together on Sunday, Look's story created a problem for Teddy. In the statement Markham had written and given to Arena, he said the accident had occurred at "approximately 11:15."

Now, not only had a woman who lived in the house by

the bridge reported the sound of a car speeding toward the bridge at about midnight, but Christopher Look, a trained sheriff's deputy, was recounting in detail his encounter with Teddy's car an hour and a half after Teddy said the accident occurred. And there could be no doubt about the validity of Look's time estimate. He hadn't left the Yacht Club until 12:30 and he'd arrived home at 1:00 A.M.

Look's story put Teddy in a distinctly less favorable light. He had been on a road leading away from, not toward, the ferry, and the last ferry of the night, as anyone who'd spent any time on Chappaquiddick knew well, departed at midnight.

So not only hadn't he been going to the ferry, by that time there wasn't even a ferry to go to, unless Teddy attracted attention by summoning it after hours.

Perhaps the most severe public-relations blow Teddy sustained on Sunday came from the scuba diver who had extricated the body from the car.

"She was in what I would call a very conscious position," the diver told reporters, meaning she'd been alive and functional after the car had entered the water, roof first. "Her head was at the floorboards where the last bit of air would have been. It seems likely she was holding herself into a pocket of air to breathe."

How long might she have lived in that air bubble? the diver was asked.

He couldn't say, although he'd read of cases where people had survived in similar situations for up to five hours. "If I'd been called soon after the accident," he added, "there was a good chance the girl could have been saved."

Confronted with what seemed to be serious discrepancies between Teddy's written statement and other verifiable fact, Arena fell back on his blind faith in the goodness of the man.

"I'm firmly convinced the Senator told me the correct

story," he insisted. "He impresses me as a senator, and as a man who would tell the truth."

If so, he was not about to tell it in any further detail. That Sunday, at 4:18 P.M., as the lunar landing module touched down on a section of the moon's surface known as the Sea of Tranquillity, dozens of reporters clustered outside the Hyannis Port compound where Teddy was huddling with lawyers and other advisors.

Earlier, as part of their moon-landing coverage, all three television networks had taped interviews in which Teddy recalled Jack's commitment to the dream of putting a man on the moon and spoke movingly of what a wonderful tribute this was to Jack's spirit of adventure and determination and of how much Jack would have loved to see this day.

But with the news—and lack of news—coming from Martha's Vineyard and Hyannis Port, both CBS and NBC decided that Teddy's appearance in such a role would not be appropriate under the current murky circumstances.

And so he lost his last chance for even reflected glory.

What a sad parody it had become, one of those present at Hyannis Port during that time later said privately. In 1959, many of the same men had gathered here in the presence of the Ambassador as Jack confidently sketched for them in detail his plan to become the next President of the United States.

A decade had passed and where were they now? Back here, at Hyannis Port, still in the service of the Kennedys. But what a different kind of service it had become. How much had been lost that would never be regained. How far, to be blunt, they had fallen.

Teddy had been a bit player, on the fringes of the 1959 meeting. Now he was reduced to the role of bit player again as political aides and lawyers—many acting largely out of loyalty to the dead brothers they had once served —schemed frantically to save some slight portion of his future.

The girl was dead, which was sad. But there were

many other girls. And only one Teddy, only one last male Kennedy of the glory generation. It was his reputation, however hollow and even rotted the man himself might be, that would have to be salvaged if the legend was to be preserved at all, if the myth was to retain even a fraction of its power.

5

AT 10:56 P.M. SUNDAY, NEIL ARMSTRONG SET FOOT on the surface of the moon.

The next morning, Chief Arena did the bare minimum required by law, filing a complaint at Edgartown District Court, charging Teddy with "leaving the scene of an accident without negligence involved." The complaint emphasized that Teddy had been driving "with extreme caution" at the time of the accident.

It struck some observers that there was slim basis for either of Arena's assertions. As to the driving, measurements taken by Registry inspectors when the car was still in the water showed that it had landed upside down and backwards, having catapulted more than twenty-three feet forward and more than five feet sideways after leaving the right side of the bridge. As the diver who retrieved the body said, "The car must have been going at a pretty good clip to land almost in the middle of the channel."

Approaching "at a pretty good clip" a twelve-foot-wide bridge that veers at an angle of twenty-seven degrees from the road, and is unlit, unmarked and unprotected by guardrails, did not sound like "extreme caution" to many of those who heard Arena's statement.

The bridge, in fact, was such an obvious traffic hazard

584

that no one had ever driven off it before, because "extreme caution" was always used when crossing it. Only someone whose judgment was seriously impaired would have approached the Dike Bridge with such an astonishing *lack* of caution as to catapult over its foot-high side railings and land upside down and backwards in the middle of the pond below.

As to negligence, the question of how and where and with whom Teddy had spent the hours between the accident and the reporting of it was simply not addressed in his statement, which, thus far, was the only public document in the case.

Emerging from the courthouse, Arena found himself facing his most hostile questioning yet. Many reporters thought the fix was already in.

"Look," Arena protested, "I'm treating this case like any other police case. Some people feel I've gone too far while others think I haven't gone far enough. I'm damned if I do and damned if I don't. But I'm firmly convinced there's no negligence involved. There is only, in my eyes, a violation concerning going from the scene, leaving the scene."

Asked again about the possibility that alcohol had been a factor, Arena repeated, "I'm not pursuing that line at all. I did not ask that question of the Senator."

Then, under the pressure of continued skeptical questioning, the chief blurted out a piece of information he'd not intended to share with the press at that time.

"There's been a lot of hearsay, a lot of talk," he said. "As a result, I have requested the assistance of the district attorney's office to talk to Joseph Gargan, who rented the house at which the party was held, in order to ascertain if the Senator was there and also to talk to the twelve or fourteen other persons who attended."

He gave no basis for his estimate of the number of guests, but it was well below that given by Teddy's own press secretary just two days earlier. Still among those said to have been in attendance, however, as reported by the *Globe* the next day, was David Hackett.

Since Drayne had said the party was in Hackett's honor, it did not seem unreasonable to assume that he'd

585

attended, but attempts to locate him proved as fruitless as efforts to learn any further details from anyone involved.

The district attorney, Edmund Dinis, when first approached by reporters that afternoon, acknowledged that Chief Arena had asked his office for assistance, but said he could offer no assurance that his involvement would accomplish anything the chief had not been able to, because, as he said, "those close to it are extremely reluctant to talk."

Also reluctant to talk, but finally responding to increasingly pointed questions as to his competence, was the assistant medical examiner. After looking at the body of Mary Jo Kopechne for less than five minutes, never fully undressing it, never turning it over from front to back, he had pronounced "death by drowning" and had said no autopsy would be required.

"It was an open-and-shut thing," the assistant medical examiner said with some irritation. "A clear case of death by drowning."

When asked how he could have been so sure, he replied, "There were no bruises, no marks, no injuries. No nothing. Death by drowning. Open-and-shut."

Had he determined a time of death? he was asked.

"Nope. I'm no pathologist."

Reporters later ascertained that in his previous fifteen years of service the assistant medical examiner had issued a "death by drowning" ruling only six times, suggesting that this was not a cause of death with which he had intimate familiarity.

While the *Globe* remained sympathetic and other major news outlets at least not openly judgmental, a whiff of what was to come blew down on Monday from the conservative *Manchester* (N.H.) *Union-Leader*.

Calling on Teddy to resign from the Senate immediately, the publisher, William Loeb, wrote that "a married man was driving a young secretary around the countryside at midnight." Then he directed a series of questions at Teddy, which were precisely the questions the rest of the press would have liked to direct to him.

"Had you been drinking, and was that the reason why you drove off the road into the pond?

"How much of a 'daze' could you have been in to be able to find your way back to your cottage but not to think about calling police to see if the girl's life could still be saved?"

And so on.

Loeb concluded by asking, rhetorically, "Senator, do you really think you are fit to sit in the United States Senate? Don't you think you ought to resign immediately?"

By Monday night, more than forty-eight hours after Teddy had secluded himself behind the compound walls, the silence from Hyannis Port was deafening. But very few of the many advisors present knew enough of the facts to offer sensible advice. And that was apparently the way Teddy wanted it. Steve Smith had determined that Edward Hanify, who seemed by temperament, experience and personal connections better suited to the task than even Burke Marshall, would direct the legal defense.

And the legal defense, Smith and Hanify made clear to the others, took precedence over any political priorities.

From the start, Kennedy's people understood that the Kopechne parents would play a crucial role in determining the extent of the legal consequences Teddy would ultimately face.

If they blamed him, if they clamored for vengeance—or even justice—there was no end to the trouble they could cause. Somehow, they had to be made to feel that Teddy was a victim too. They had to be made to feel almost as sorry for him as they felt for themselves. They had to be persuaded that his own grief, suffering and sense of loss were almost as great as their own.

Teddy, in his first phone call to the family, had done nothing to help his own cause. And so, on Sunday, Joan had been told to call them. It didn't really matter what she said. In the face of increasingly suggestive speculation in the press, any call from Joan would reassure them about the essential innocence of Teddy's brief encounter with their daughter.

Then, after Joan, Ethel had called them. Bobby's widow. It was Bobby whom Mary Jo had worshiped. The Kopechnes needed to hear from Bobby's widow. They didn't only need to read her public statement that Mary Jo had been one of the "great ones"—secretarywise—they needed to hear Ethel's own voice assuring them of the high esteem in which her late husband had held their beloved daughter.

Joan was fine. "It was a sympathy call," Mrs. Kopechne said later. "Nothing was explained, but we didn't expect any explanations from her." But Ethel was truly magnificent.

"Ethel tried to help us so much," Mrs. Kopechne said. "She talked about faith and how it could help us. And then she said, 'We will be at the funeral.' "

The impressions created in the early days of deepest shock and grief are often the ones that linger longest, that do the most to shape a future attitude or course of action. The weekend phone calls from the two Kennedy wives were thus of great importance.

Then, on Monday, Teddy called a second time. His first conversation had been so abrupt, so fragmentary, so unsatisfactory, it had actually created a bad taste. All traces of that needed to be washed away fast. He still did not tell them anything about what had happened, how Mary Jo had actually come to die, but he put on a great display of emotion.

"I could see he was trying to tell us about the accident," Joseph Kopechne said later, "but I still couldn't understand him. He was still sobbing, still so broken up he couldn't talk."

And then, on Tuesday, Teddy made the gesture he had to make. In the company of Joan, Ethel, John Tunney, John Culver and Joey Gargan, he attended Mary Jo's funeral in the northeastern Pennsylvania coal town where she'd been born.

He looked wretched. His face was ashen and lifeless. He seemed almost blind with fatigue, as if he'd not slept a minute since going into seclusion at Hyannis Port.

What attracted most attention, however, was the fact that he was wearing an orthopedic neck brace. This came as a surprise since even his own doctor had never mentioned Teddy's having suffered a neck injury in the accident. But it made for effective television and photographs. Mary Jo was not the only victim, the neck brace implied. Teddy was a victim too.

The day was sultry and oppressively gray. The air both inside and outside the church was rank and humid. Before the mass, Teddy, Ethel and Joan, joined by vanden Heuvel, met briefly with the Kopechnes at the rectory adjacent to the church.

Outside the church, Kennedy aides circulated among the press, emphasizing two points: Teddy had insisted on coming, despite doctor's orders to the contrary, and Teddy had repeatedly offered to pay all expenses associated with the funeral. To date, the Kopechnes had not accepted the offer but the Senator was hopeful that they might change their mind. And, oh yes: the neck brace was a medical necessity, though no details as to the function it actually served were provided.

In the rectory, Teddy seemed almost incoherent, making no more sense than he had over the phone. He was obviously a man in great distress, and with less self-control than Mary Jo's father himself. At one point he muttered, "If only it could have been me. If only it could have been me." Joe Kopechne took this to be an expression of Teddy's wish that he, rather than Mary Jo, could have been the one to die.

At the mass, Teddy received holy communion. Dun Gifford, who had not strayed from the body since first flying over from Nantucket, acted as a pallbearer, along with Dave Hackett.

Seven hundred people had crammed into a church whose seating capacity was only five hundred. Among them were the five known female survivors of the party. The heat and humidity were almost unbearable. A woman fainted. Almost everyone present had come simply to get a glimpse of Teddy, for the Kopechnes had moved out of this town more than a quarter century before and few in attendance had even heard of Mary Jo, much less known her.

As Teddy emerged from the church, a buzz swept through hundreds more onlookers gathered outside under the dark gray sky. "There he is!... There he is!" women shouted, and hundreds of inexpensive cameras began to click simultaneously.

It might have seemed crass, and even disrespectful to the young woman whose body lay inside the coffin, but later Joe Kopechne would say, with considerable insight, "I could understand the crowds. This was the hard core of the mining district. These people have never been distracted before. The Kennedys were coming, and that's a big thing. I understand that. Nothing that big has happened around there since thirty-four settlers were killed by the Indians, and that was before the Revolutionary War."

From the church, a twenty-two-car procession wound up a hilly road that led to the mountainside cemetery in the Poconos. Another coffin, another open grave. How many had Teddy seen by now? How often had he stood silently, off to one side, head bowed, hands clasped, eyes moist?

But this one was different. With this one he must have felt more fear than grief. He had not known her all that well. She had not been part of the family. But this was the first death for which he and he alone had been responsible.

After the burial, he and his group traveled to a nearby restaurant for a farewell lunch with the Kopechnes. Teddy knew how important this meeting was. It would be his last chance to win them over, to assure that they'd be wholeheartedly and forever on his side, no matter what revelations were later made.

This is not to imply that Teddy was not also feeling grief and guilt. But, as with all Kennedys, the equations were complex. The public and private, the real and the mythic, the authentic and the spurious, were so intertwined, as they'd been for so long in Teddy's life, that he could no longer even guess at where one began to slide over into the other.

At the lunch, he shifted into a cheerful, charming mode, almost as if he were campaigning. "We had a great time at lunch," Joe Kopechne said later. "I think he really sacrificed a lot the way he was feeling. It was like one big family. I embarrassed him, I think. I called my nephew over and said to Kennedy, 'Here's a good Democrat.' But the Senator took it beautifully. He laughed and said to me, 'You're really something.'

"You know, I'm a salesman, an insurance salesman, but I don't talk much. My wife could tell you that. But at that lunch I talked a lot with Ethel and I thought I was talking with my sister. That's the way she makes you feel. She's just like the lady next door. She was interested in mine safety and what was being done lately about safety in the mines and asked all about the area."

Joan said little and spent most of her time staring straight ahead. Even indoors, even on a day so dark and gray, she covered her eyes with sunglasses. But all in all the mission proved highly successful.

Then they were gone, by private jet, as quickly as they'd come. Vanished into the gray sky that hung heavily over the worn and ragged Pennsylvania hills.

Two dozen newsmen were waiting at the Hyannis airfield when Teddy returned in early afternoon. They all had the same question: When would there be a public statement?

"I will make one at an appropriate time," Teddy said, speaking to the press for the first time since the car went into the water. "And I don't think this is an appropriate time."

He kept walking toward his waiting sedan. Joan, alongside him, was crying.

Liz Trotta, a particularly forceful reporter from NBC, pursued him closely, microphone in hand. "There has been some question," she said, "as to what effect this will have on your political career."

That stopped him cold. He spun toward her, obviously angry. "I have just come from the funeral of a very lovely

girl," he snapped, "and this is not the appropriate time!
I am not going to have any other comment to make."

He was very fragile, very brittle. They had to get him
safely back behind the walls again as soon as possible.
And so they did. Later, aides said that Teddy would be
making no statement "in the foreseeable future, and he
might never make one."

6

WITH EACH PASSING HOUR OF SILENCE FROM THE COMpound, however, media fever spiked higher. By Tuesday, though there was no actual news to report, more than 450 reporters had crowded onto Martha's Vineyard and not many of them were as sympathetic to Teddy as were Chief Arena and those representing the *Globe*.

Newsweek was first to actually go on the attack. Having been informed by John Lindsay of Teddy's true condition months before, the magazine was able to assert, "The Senator's closest associates are known to have been powerfully concerned over his indulgent drinking habits, his daredevil driving, and his ever-ready eye for a pretty face."

Now, the magazine said, "handsome, high-riding Teddy Kennedy, 37, faced criminal charges in the accidental death of a pretty blonde party companion—and quite possibly the end of a political career that could have taken him to the White House." The magazine also stressed that even days after the accident, "no one was saying who was at the party besides Teddy and Mary Jo."

Faced with this sort of publicity, Teddy's advisors decided that a female guest who had attended the party should speak to the press. They chose Esther Newberg, who, in later years, would become a prominent New York literary agent.

From her suburban Washington home, Newberg granted a series of newspaper interviews. She emphasized that the "party" had been scarcely that; more a quiet, reflective, even sad gathering of people who'd shared the unique experience of working closely with Bobby. She also confirmed the few specific facts contained in Teddy's statement.

Her description, however, was contradicted by the nearest neighbor, a hundred yards away from the cottage, who said, "They were damned loud." And they apparently hadn't quit early, either. "By one o'clock," this neighbor said, "I was pretty well damn fed up with the whole thing. It was a damn farce at that hour of the morning. If they had kept it up any longer, I would have called the police."

Another nearby resident added that the gathering was "one of those loud, noisy brawls," with "yelling, music and general sounds of hell-raising."

And a third said the party "was still going on when I went to bed at 2:30 A.M."

What emerged as most newsworthy from the Newberg interviews, however, was her statement that none of the five women remaining at the cottage after Teddy and Mary Jo left realized until the next morning that anything untoward had happened.

"No one was sitting around watching the clock," she said. "At some point, I guess we wondered where Mary Jo was and decided she had been lucky enough to make the ferry. We just assumed the senator was exhausted and had gone back to his hotel in Edgartown. No one expected him to stay. No one was worried or concerned."

Not even when "some time between 10:30 P.M. and 1 A.M." Joey Gargan and Paul Markham also left the party, their purpose and destination unknown.

Newberg said that neither she nor any of the other women found it strange that of the twelve people she said had first gathered, four had vanished into the night, leaving the five women with no access to the ferry back to the mainland, which meant they'd have to spend the night in the cramped, smoky, hot two-bedroom cottage in the company of Jack Crimmins, whom they disliked, and two other Massachusetts political aides to Teddy, Charley Tretter and Ray La Rosa, whom they scarcely knew.

Apparently without curiosity about any circumstances —including why, if she'd been heading back to her motel, Mary Jo had left her pocketbook behind in the cottage— Esther and her friends scrunched together on couches and the floor and settled in for the night.

Even more peculiar was her description of the next morning. Upon awakening, she'd discovered that the cottage was empty, except for herself and the two Lyons sisters. Everyone else had apparently left for the ferry without saying good-bye.

So, at some point—she didn't really know when because her "Mickey Mouse" watch was broken—she and the Lyons sisters began the three-mile walk to the ferry dock. Along the way they were met by Joey Gargan, who told them, " 'Something terrible has happened.' He told us about the accident. He said Senator Kennedy was all right, but that Mary Jo had not been found."

Later, he'd called them at the Katama Shores motel to say that Mary Jo's body had been found. She had drowned. He suggested that the remaining women leave the island "rather quickly," but she saw nothing strange about this, either. After all, with Mary Jo dead and the party over, "What else would you do?"

Somehow, this was not coming out quite the way she or Teddy's aides had hoped. "Nobody's trying to hide anything," she insisted. "Mary Jo is dead and there isn't anything we can do about it, and I know that Senator Kennedy tried to save her." No, she said, he had not told her personally of any rescue attempts, she just knew "inside" that Teddy had tried to save Mary Jo.

As for drinking, there had been "at most, one or two drinks apiece. It was a steak party. There was talk about the weather and other things that friends talk about when they get together. It was fun."

To one reporter, Newberg conceded that "it had been a long day. Everybody was tired." But not so tired that it occurred to any of them—except, apparently, Mary Jo —to request a ride from the cottage to the ferry so that they might spend the night in the motel rooms that had been reserved for them.

"It was an accident," Newberg repeated, speaking, *The Washington Post* reported, "fiercely, almost despairingly." She said, "What can you do about an accident?" She said again, "Nobody's trying to hide anything."

Why had Rosemary Keogh and Susan Tannenbaum awakened early and gotten a ride to the ferry from Joey Gargan while Esther and the Lyons sisters slept on? She didn't know.

Wasn't she annoyed to find herself having to spend an uncomfortable night in tight quarters with men she did not know well, and then even more annoyed to awaken in the morning and find that they, as well as two of her female companions, had abandoned her?

As Esther Newberg described her version of events over four days of newspaper interviews, it sounded like less and less fun each time. It also sounded less and less plausible. So, after the fourth day, she suddenly stopped talking, and the other women never began. And that's the way it has stayed for almost twenty-five years.

By Thursday, July 24, the day the astronauts returned in glory from the moon, even as sympathetic a commentator as Washington columnist Charles Bartlett, the man who had introduced Jack to Jacqueline in 1952, recognized that Teddy was in the direst of straits.

"At the age of 36," Bartlett wrote, "with less than eight years' direct involvement in political life, the Senator heard from every side that he had no choice, that there was no way he could stay in politics and avoid bearing the Democratic standard in 1972. 'Even if you say you have decided not to run,' he was told, 'they won't believe you or accept it.'

"This was an incredible pressure upon a young man who inherited the Kennedy zest for competition but nursed no deep lust for power. Just as family tradition and the powerful figure of his father were more persuasive than personal ambition in bringing him into politics, he was being persuaded to seek the presidency more by his sense of what the world and his family expected of him than by his own appetite.

"His brothers had become legendary figures while he was still consolidating his own philosophy and finding his own pace. They left him a magic and heady legacy but it obliged him to take up where they had stopped, to absorb all the advisers and pressures which had been part of their lives, and to live with the public fascination which they had stirred. It was in fact a two-edged legacy for a young man geared to a less intense way of life.

"Now the legacy has led him into a painful situation which will test his ability to sustain the legend against the erratic tendency of the masses to consume the heroes they create."

Written less than a week after the death of Mary Jo, this was a most perceptive assessment. It was also far less judgmental than most. For, by Thursday, the patience of the press had been exhausted.

Teddy's continued silence not only was baffling but had come to suggest to many that the true story was far worse than his original superficial written statement had implied.

The New York Times printed a story headlined: "Democrats Urge Kennedy to Speak," with a subhead that said, "In Anonymous Interviews, They See Political Peril."

The first paragraph said, "There is a widely held belief among Democratic leaders that unless Senator Edward M. Kennedy answers all questions about the fatal accident in which he was involved last weekend, he will raise ineradicable doubts about his qualifications for the Presidency."

One Democratic senator was quoted as saying, "There must be some disarray up there because those guys [his advisors] are smart. Because everybody knows they are smart, they therefore assume he is not saying anything because it will hurt him. Now it's reached the point where he's hurting himself more by not saying anything.

He's got to do something. He can't let this thing deteriorate. The longer the delay, the worse it looks.''

In an accompanying editorial, the *Times* said that Teddy's locking himself behind the Hyannis Port walls with a larger group of advisors than Jack had used to deal with the Cuban missile crisis "reinforces the suspicions aroused by his failure to report the accident until after he had conferred or tried to confer with a battery of lawyers that his primary interest from the moment of the accident was to avoid assumption of responsibility."

Life magazine, which was preparing for publication the following week Brock Brower's insightful profile of Teddy as a tormented man who for months had been close to the edge of nervous collapse (and which would, for the first time, disclose details of what had really happened on the Alaskan trip), mocked the spectacle of "all the surviving New Frontiersmen scheming to extract their man from the scandal of an accident." Teddy, the magazine said, was trying to pull off "the classic rich kid's stunt—running away from an accident that dad can fix with the judge."

Dad undoubtedly could have fixed it. If Dad had been functional—or even if Steve Smith had not been unreachable for hours in Spain—Teddy would never have delivered his written statement to Chief Arena. Teddy would have been off the island long before the body was discovered, perhaps watching the flight to the moon in the presence of someone like Cardinal Cushing, and certainly with his own wife and children.

That was the way these matters were handled. Dad had done it for a generation. But Dad hadn't uttered a coherent word since December 1961. He had been the central gravitational mass that regulated the carefully calibrated orbits in which his sons had traveled in their endless quest for glory. His stroke had created a black hole where once that central force had been. The effects had not been immediate but by the summer of 1969 they were unmistakable, as Teddy's current plight made painfully apparent to all.

An Evans and Novak column quoted a "pro-Kennedy congressman" as saying, "With every hour that passes, the situation becomes more ominous." The columnists also raised what was, from Teddy's point of view, the most sensitive and potentially dangerous point of all: the lack of autopsy.

"The lack of an autopsy for Miss Kopechne and the apparent lack of a thorough investigation of possible negligence by Kennedy point to favored treatment. Politically, this could be as damaging as the events themselves."

In an editorial, *The Washington Post* referred to "the bitter whispering campaign that has already begun," and said, "The talk will go on, amplified, about the initial timidity of the police and how the Kennedys managed that; about the drinking and the calls to lawyers and the various damaging versions of what actually transpired that night." While noting that his political advisors were undoubtedly urging caution and reticence, the *Post* said Teddy, "would be better advised to get the politics out of it and clear up the record of this tragic affair."

Even the *Boston Globe*, in a Thursday editorial, called on Teddy to make a prompt and complete public statement. While recognizing that "he has suffered so grievously in recent years," and that "there is a limit to the amount of suffering any human being can bear," the editorial argued that the ever growing list of questions could no longer go unanswered.

"One such question is why, if the lights were on in two houses within a few hundred feet of the accident, Sen. Kennedy could not have stopped there to summon help, rather than walking more than a mile back to the cottage and climbing into the back seat of an automobile.

"Why the 9-hour delay before he or any of his companions notified the police?

"Why was there a long delay in releasing his first statement to the press?

"And why were those at the party not questioned immediately?"

Even more ominously, the *Globe*, too, raised the question of autopsy. "It was most unusual," the editorial said, "and in fact against the interest of Sen. Kennedy and others, to fail to insist that an autopsy be performed.

That could have shown both the circumstances of death beyond all doubt, and how long the victim lived after the accident."

But that was precisely the point. Suppose it would not be in "the interest of Sen. Kennedy"—but, in fact, absolutely devastating to him—if "the circumstances of death" were revealed?

It was not the political advisors but Steve Smith and Edward Hanify who were insisting upon not merely reticence but complete and lasting silence. As pressure built for Teddy to make a televised speech in which he would attempt to explain his actions and inactions, the lawyers held firm.

"If I have anything to say about it," said Hanify, who was far more familiar with what had really happened that Friday night and Saturday morning than were the editorial writers of the *Boston Globe,* "he'll never make that speech."

And, if he had his way, no autopsy would ever be performed. But why? Why had Teddy been in such a rush to get Mary Jo's body off the island and why did he seem so panicked by the notion of an autopsy?

What would an autopsy have revealed? That Mary Jo had engaged in sexual intercourse shortly before drowning? Since almost everyone following the case already assumed that Teddy had at least planned to have sex on the beach with Mary Jo, how much worse would it be if an autopsy disclosed that such an act had already been consummated?

It was not the presumption of fornication that was damaging Teddy so severely: it was the implication that he had callously left a young female companion underwater to drown while he sought only to cover up his own involvement with her. Perhaps he feared that an autopsy would have established this as fact.

One thing seems clear. If either Teddy or his legal advisors felt an autopsy would have been to his benefit, they would have insisted that one be performed.

This makes it difficult to avoid the inference that their frantic and persistent attempts to prevent such a procedure must have arisen from their belief that the findings would in some grave way make matters worse for Teddy.

If that was the case, then better to permit rumor and speculation to rage unchecked.

In any event, it had been assumed that with the interment of Mary Jo's body in the rocky soil of northeastern Pennsylvania, the autopsy issue had been disposed of. But on Thursday morning, July 24, the chief medical examiner issued a statement in which he said his assistant had erred by not ordering an autopsy immediately.

The chief medical examiner had not been working the morning the body was found. If he had been, he now made clear, matters would have taken a different course. There was no evidence of death by drowning, he said. "We don't know if that girl died from a heart attack or a stroke."

The point was, an autopsy would have provided answers. "I wouldn't have let that autopsy go," the medical examiner said. "I would have gone to Washington if I'd had to." It troubled him, he said, that there were "so many nasty questions. It would have been a kindness to Senator Kennedy to have had an autopsy. So that all the nasty questions could be answered."

But it was still not too late. It did not matter that the corpse had been embalmed. It did not matter that the corpse had now been buried. Exhumation was a distinct possibility. All that would be required, the medical examiner said, was an order from the district attorney.

The next blow Teddy suffered Thursday came when the assistant medical examiner, still being hounded by the press in regard to his failure to order an autopsy, attempted to mollify reporters by releasing the results of the test of Mary Jo Kopechne's blood alcohol level at time of death.

Given Esther Newberg's repeated claims that there had been little or no consumption of alcohol at the party, and given the Kennedy staff's attempts to portray Mary Jo as a virtual teetotaler, the figure was remarkably high: .09 percent.

The state police chemist who had conducted the test explained what it meant: "In this particular case, the figure means a person weighing 110 pounds or thereabouts has an alcohol intake of about 3.75 to 5 ounces of 80 to 90 proof liquor—that's up to five drinks within one hour prior to death. More if you measure over a longer period of time, since alcohol diminishes in the bloodstream with the passage of time."

In most states, a person was judged to be legally intoxicated and unfit to operate a motor vehicle when the blood alcohol level reached .10 percent. In Canada and in most European countries, the standard was stricter: .08 percent.

Mary Jo Kopechne had had a reputation for being temperate and responsible. She might not have been a "maiden" as her mother believed (indeed, one of Teddy's closest friends, who also knew Mary Jo well, described her privately as by far the most "sensuous" of the women who attended the Chappaquiddick party), but, unlike Teddy, she was not a habitual abuser of alcohol.

Thus, consumption of an unusually large amount of liquor after a full day spent in the sun could well have caused uncharacteristic behavior.

If nothing else, the blood alcohol figure immediately fueled press speculation that Teddy and Mary Jo had been heading for a tryst on the beach when—no doubt drunk himself—he'd driven the car off the bridge.

When this was reported to the Kopechnes on Thursday afternoon, Mary Jo's mother reacted with predictable and natural distress. Mary Jo had been a good girl. She was no tramp. Under no circumstances, no matter what her blood alcohol level, would she have engaged in sexual intercourse with a married man, even if he was a Kennedy. Of this, Mary Jo's mother was absolutely certain.

It also seemed obvious she was growing increasingly troubled by Teddy's silence. "I'm waiting for him to discuss his part publicly," Mrs. Kopechne said. "There are a few things that happened that haven't been cleared up for the public yet."

But so certain was she of her own daughter's virtue, she said to reporters, that if it would take exhumation and an autopsy to clear the name of her daughter, then she and her husband would not only permit it but might well insist upon it even if the district attorney did not.

"I know there are a lot of sick people in the world. If we can't clear up all the little snide remarks and everything, I would have an autopsy performed—if that's the only way I can clear my daughter."

With this shift in the Kopechnes' attitude, Hanify and Smith came to recognize that the risk of saying nothing now outweighed the considerable risk of making a public statement which, because it could not be forthright and truthful, would only raise more questions than it answered.

The situation was quickly spinning out of the control of both the legal and the political advisors.

A quick change of tactics was required. Arrangements were hastily made for Teddy to appear at the Edgartown courthouse the following morning and plead guilty to the single charge Arena had filed: that of leaving the scene of a motor vehicle accident.

An understanding was reached that after this plea, which would be accepted by a judge who would impose only a suspended sentence, Chief Arena would declare the case closed.

Teddy could then go on national television—that very night—and make an emotional apology and plea for understanding that would, it was fervently hoped, fully satisfy the Kopechnes.

From these decisions, it seems even more apparent that—for whatever reason—an autopsy was what they feared most and would do most to prevent.

As to why that was so, no one who knows has ever said.

THE LAST BROTHER

7

ON FRIDAY MORNING THE WEATHER, ONCE AGAIN, was miserable. A chill rain was falling hard, as it had seemed to incessantly throughout the entire week Teddy spent secreted with his advisors.

He came over from Hyannis Port by boat. The crossing took an hour. The sea was uncomfortably choppy, the fog dense. Steve Smith and Joan were with him. Edward Hanify kept well out of sight; a local lawyer would be used for the court appearance. The goal was to keep this proceeding as quick and as low-key as possible.

Hundreds of reporters and dozens of television cameras were massed around the courthouse entrance in driving rain. Some thought had been given to attempting to keep the proceeding secret from the press; to let Teddy make his plea in privacy. But the argument that such an arrangement would only add to the appearance of cover-up proved persuasive.

Entering the courthouse, Teddy had to stop first at the probation office to fill out a standard identity card. In this respect, he was just another criminal defendant.

Preceded by his local lawyer, Teddy, wearing a blue suit and dark tie and looking, as described by *Newsweek*, "like a ruined man," entered the courtroom with head bowed and quickly took a seat at the defendant's table. Elbows on the table, he rested his chin on clasped hands and stared straight down at the floor.

He seemed to flinch at the sound of the gavel as the bailiff entered at 9:00 A.M. and called out, "The district court of the county of Dukes County is now in session. God save the Commonwealth of Massachusetts."

After all the glitter and glory, all the pomp and promise of the early sixties—especially of that magical eleven-month period when Jack and Bobby and Teddy had all been in Washington together, united in their belief that their time had only begun—it had come down to this. A cramped and crowded Martha's Vineyard courtroom on a dreary, rainy morning in July. This was the price he was paying for having finally screamed out to America that he did not want ever to be President.

The judge entered the courtroom and took his seat. The clerk called, "Commonwealth versus Edward M. Kennedy." He then read: "This complaint charges that Edward M. Kennedy of Boston, Massachusetts, on the nineteenth day of July, 1969, at Edgartown, did operate a certain motor vehicle upon a public way in said Edgartown and did go away after knowingly causing injury to Mary Jo Kopechne without stopping and making known his name, residence and the number of his motor vehicle."

The clerk looked at Teddy and asked, "How do you plead? Guilty or not guilty?"

When he first tried to speak, Teddy could not. He moved his lips but no sound came from his mouth. He glanced quickly at the lawyer seated next to him, then tried again.

This time, in an awful, strangled whisper, he said: "Guilty." He swallowed, then said it again: "Guilty."

Then he slumped down in his chair, buried his face in the open palm of one hand and closed his eyes.

In another five minutes it was over. The judge, noting that Teddy "has already been and will continue to be punished far beyond anything this court can impose," said, "the ends of justice would be satisfied by the imposition of the minimum jail sentence and suspension of that sentence—assuming the defendant accepts the suspension."

His lawyer spoke quickly. "The defendant will accept the suspension, Your Honor." He then nudged Teddy, indicating that he should stand.

Slowly and stiffly, Teddy got to his feet and faced the court clerk.

"Edward M. Kennedy," the clerk said, "on the complaint the court has found you guilty and has sentenced you to serve two months in the house of correction in Barnstable. Sentence is suspended."

By the time he left the courthouse, the rain had slowed to a drizzle. The reporters were shouting questions so loudly that a number failed to hear the one statement Teddy made.

"I have made my plea," he said, "and I have requested time on the networks tonight to speak to the people of Massachusetts and the nation."

Then, with Smith at his side and a trembling Joan clutching his sleeve, he followed two state policemen who opened a way through the crowd. A car stood at the curb. He got in. He did not look back. Steve Smith and Joan joined him. The door closed. The car headed for the Martha's Vineyard airport, where, despite the poor visibility, a chartered plane waited to fly him back to Hyannis Port, from where he would, that evening, deliver perhaps the most wretched public address ever given by a prominent political figure.

Moments later, Chief Arena came out the door of the courthouse and said: "We have prosecuted on the facts we have, and there are no additional facts warranting further investigation. I'm satisfied I did my job, and the case is closed."

Arena had not asked Teddy a single question. He had never questioned any of the other party guests. He'd done nothing except type a statement that Paul Markham had written in longhand, a statement, as it turned out, that Teddy had never even signed. And now he said the case was closed.

The outcome was everything Teddy could have hoped for. To much of the press and public, however, it seemed an outrage. Once again, the Kennedys had put in the fix. Kennedys could get away with anything.

During Teddy's week of silence, much of the press and public had made up its mind about what happened: He'd left his pregnant wife behind and gone to a party with a pretty blond secretary of his brother's, they'd both had too much to drink, he'd decided to slip out of the party and take her to the private beach on the eastern shore of Chappaquiddick and do there whatever it was he did with women.

Instead, he'd recklessly, drunkenly, driven his car off a bridge. And then had left the girl behind, quite possibly still alive and fighting for breath and believing that he or others would quickly rescue her.

He'd left her there to die as he spent the rest of the night and early morning both sobering up and plotting ways in which he might escape involvement. He had reported the accident only after the car and body had been discovered and after the lawyers and advisors he consulted had persuaded him that there was too much risk involved in trying to pretend he hadn't been to Chappaquiddick at all.

It was not a pretty picture. And it may not even have been complete. The lengths to which he was going to prevent an autopsy suggested he feared further revelations. So it was with some skepticism that much of the public would tune in to Teddy's speech that night.

Yet he remained a Kennedy: the last link we'd ever have to Jack and Bobby. We did not want to sever that. We wanted to believe the best. We wanted him to tell us a plausible story that would make the ugly speculation go away. He was the last Kennedy we would ever have. The sixties—the ''time for Kennedys''—were almost over. We wanted, in our hearts, to somehow rewind the tape, go back in time, start the decade all over again. Only this time, we'd write a better script. Jack would not go to Dallas. Bobby would not walk through the kitchen in

Los Angeles. And Teddy would not drive his car off the bridge.

He would deliver the speech from the library of his father's house. In his distress, he was so much still a Kennedy child that he had chosen to speak not from his own home but from his parents', from the house that had once echoed with the laughter of Joe Junior, Jack and Bobby, and Teddy himself.

All three networks broadcast the speech live at 7:30 that Friday night. More Americans watched than had seen Neil Armstrong take his first step on the moon.

Teddy's father was not among them. In his upstairs bedroom, the old man was entirely unaware of what was happening: not only speechless, but powerless now to exert any control whatever over this final episode in the destruction of the dynasty he had made it his life's work to create. His nurse reported that his television set had again been disconnected, as at the time of Jack's assassination. This was not a performance that Teddy wanted his father to witness.

"My fellow citizens," he began, "I have requested this opportunity to talk to you . . . about the tragedy which happened last Friday evening."

His clenched hands, trembling slightly, gripped the pages on which the final draft of the speech had been typed. While many of the advisors had contributed concepts and language, the finished work was essentially a Sorensen product and, as such, could be regarded as an ironic parallel to the stirring inaugural address he had written for Jack in those heady days when the myth had been just bursting into bloom.

Teddy's voice was strangely flat, devoid of emotion or even of what might be considered normal intonation. "This morning," he said, "I entered a plea of guilty to the charge of leaving the scene of an accident. Prior to my appearance in court it would have been improper to comment on these matters, but tonight I am free to tell you what happened and to say what it means to me."

Only one paragraph into it, and already he'd blundered, squandering much of the little credibility he had left. It would not have been "improper" in the least for him to say anything he pleased about the death of Mary Jo at any time during the preceding week. Unwise, perhaps; but clearly not "improper." To suggest now that only his sense of propriety, his determination to observe the legal niceties, had caused him to stifle his instinctive impulse to tell all had many viewers snorting in disbelief even before he got into the details of his fabricated tale.

"On the weekend of July eighteenth," he continued, "I was on Martha's Vineyard Island participating with my nephew Joe Kennedy as for thirty years my family has participated in the annual Edgartown Sailing Regatta. Only reasons of health prevented my wife from accompanying me."

Another false note. Even Dick Drayne's hasty explanation afterwards that the Kennedys were pleased to announce that Joan was, once again, pregnant did little to lessen the skepticism that greeted Teddy's explanation of his wife's absence.

"On Chappaquiddick Island off Martha's Vineyard," he said, "I attended on Friday evening, July eighteenth, a cookout I had encouraged and helped sponsor for a devoted group of Kennedy campaign secretaries. When I left the party around eleven-fifteen P.M. I was accompanied by one of these girls, Miss Mary Jo Kopechne. Mary Jo was one of the most devoted members of the staff of Senator Robert Kennedy. She worked for him for four years and was broken up over his death. For this reason and because she was such a gentle, kind and idealistic person, all of us tried to help her feel that she still had a home with the Kennedy family."

A bit too maudlin too soon, perhaps, for general consumption, but Teddy's inclusion of those remarks had been intended exclusively for an audience of two: the parents of Mary Jo Kopechne. If he would not be able to give factual answers that would satisfy their curiosity about their daughter's fate, he could at least try to persuade them that she had been what she'd always dreamed of being—an honorary Kennedy herself, and not just a "secretary" like the others.

"There is no truth whatever," Teddy said, "to the widely circulated suspicions of immoral conduct that have been leveled at my behavior and hers regarding that evening. There has never been a private relationship between us of any kind. I know of nothing in Mary Jo's conduct on that or any other occasion—and the same is true of the other girls at that party—that would lend any substance to such ugly speculation about their character. Nor was I driving under the influence of liquor."

Wisely, he'd omitted any reference to his own character. The assertion that he'd not been driving drunk was in itself enough to provoke disbelief. But unless any of the party guests talked, no one could prove anything to the contrary. One of the advantages to not reporting an accident until ten hours after it occurred is that one has a chance to get one's blood alcohol content back to a level where, even if a local policeman did check belatedly, no damaging findings would result.

"Little over a mile away," he went on, "the car that I was driving on an unlit road went off a narrow bridge which had no guardrails and was built on a left angle to the road. The car overturned into a deep pond and immediately filled with water. I remember thinking as the cold water rushed in around my head that I was for certain drowning. Then water entered my lungs and I actually felt a sensation of drowning. But somehow I struggled to the surface alive."

This was the point. Keep the focus on himself. His heroic survival, which could not help but stir memories of Jack's heroic survival after the sinking of *PT 109*.

"I made immediate and repeated efforts to save Mary Jo by diving into the strong and murky current, but succeeded only in increasing my state of utter exhaustion and alarm."

But now he'd hit the hard part. Even assuming the truth of everything he'd said to that point, what had happened next? During the next hour, and during all the hours that followed before the two fishermen spotted the car?

"My conduct and conversation during the next several hours, to the extent that I can remember them, make no

610

sense to me at all. Although my doctors inform me that I suffered a cerebral concussion as well as shock, I do not seek to escape responsibility for my actions by placing the blame either on the physical and emotional trauma brought on by the accident, or on anyone else.

"I regard as indefensible the fact that I did not report the accident to the police immediately. Instead of looking directly for a telephone, after lying exhausted on the grass for an undetermined time, I walked back to the cottage where the party was being held, requested the help of two friends, Joe Gargan and Paul Markham, and directed them to return immediately to the scene with me—it then being sometime after midnight—in order to undertake a new effort to dive down and locate Miss Kopechne. Their strenuous efforts, undertaken at some risk to their own lives, also proved futile."

This was a paragraph that would come back to cause him many problems. So exhausted that he had to lie on the grass "for an undetermined time," he'd then regained enough strength to walk more than a mile back to the cottage where the party was being held, bypassing four houses, at least two of them with lights on inside, from which he could have called for help.

And, once back at the party, he had somehow removed Gargan and Markham from it without attracting the attention of any of the women. Viewers tried unsuccessfully to imagine the scene as he described it: exhausted, in soaking-wet clothes, in a state of shock, it seemed far more likely that he would have alerted everyone at the party to what had happened and had them all race to the scene, or to the ferry landing from which emergency equipment could have been summoned from Edgartown.

There is a time for stealth and there is a time to sound a general alarm. If saving Mary Jo's life was the highest priority, neither he nor Gargan and Markham went about it in a very effective way.

If, on the other hand, Teddy was operating on the premise that dead women tell no tales (except at autopsy), then his secretive attempts to lure Gargan and Markham from the party unnoticed made more sense.

They were, after all, the two most experienced lawyers

present, and it would not be illogical to assume that even at that early hour Teddy recognized he was faced with a potentially serious legal problem.

Moreover, members of the family living in the house right next to the bridge reported hearing only one car speed by sometime around midnight. They did not hear a second car, the one that would have borne Teddy, Joe Gargan and Paul Markham. Nor did they hear sounds of splashing and raised voices as Gargan and Markham made "strenuous efforts" to save Mary Jo, "at some risk to their own lives."

Already, Teddy was demonstrating why Hanify and Smith were so wise to resist for so long the idea of making any statement at all. With every sentence, he plunged even deeper into the "strong and murky current" of implausibility.

The time had come to invoke the legend, hoping it still retained enough power to distract.

"All kinds of scrambled thoughts—all of them confused, some of them irrational, many of which I cannot recall, and some of which I would not have seriously entertained under normal circumstances—went through my mind during this period. They were reflected in the various inexplicable, inconsistent and inconclusive things I said and did—including such questions as whether the girl might still be alive somewhere out of that immediate area, whether some awful curse actually did hang over all the Kennedys, whether there was some justifiable reason for me to doubt what had happened and to delay my report and whether somehow the awful weight of this incredible incident might in some way pass from my shoulders. I was overcome, I am frank to say, by a jumble of emotions—grief, fear, doubt, exhaustion, panic, confusion and shock."

The invocation of the curse, the awful curse, revealed the entire statement for what it really was and what it had always been intended to be—a fairy tale. Maybe, if he only waited through the night, a good fairy would come to Teddy and lift the curse, would free him from the awful spell under which he'd been placed.

In midnarrative now, Teddy was stuck. He still had

many hurdles of logic to clear. Before digressing into the realm of awful curses, Teddy had been at the pond again, with Gargan and Markham risking their lives repeatedly in their vain attempt to rescue Mary Jo.

"Instructing Gargan and Markham not to alarm Mary Jo's friends that night"—why tell them that one of their best friends was trapped underwater? They might call for help—Teddy said, "I had them take me to the ferry crossing."

This was where he had supposedly been heading in the first place with Mary Jo. It was by now, of course, after midnight and the ferry had stopped its regular runs. But it was available for after-hour service.

(Indeed, even well after midnight, if Teddy's intention had been to take himself and Mary Jo to the ferry and back across the channel to Martha's Vineyard, he could still have done so.)

On that particular night, because of an unusual level of activity associated with the regatta, and because "it was too hot to sleep," the ferry operator was still up at 1:20 A.M.

"We come out for any legitimate reason," he said later. "It doesn't have to be a case of an accident or injury. If someone wants ferry service after midnight, they just call the house. There's a public phone inside the ferry house at Chappaquiddick. A bell is attached to the side of the building. What people do is drive up to the ramp and leave their headlights on and we come across to get them. Or, if you walk down, you ring the bell."

Teddy, however, did not summon the ferry. Instead, despite his exhaustion, he "suddenly jumped into the water and impulsively swam across, nearly drowning once again in the effort." Having safely reached the other side, he said, and "returning to my hotel around two A.M." he had "collapsed in my room. I remember going out at one point and saying something to the room clerk."

In fact, he'd come down the back stairs, wearing dry jacket and slacks, and had apparently been heading out of the Shiretown Inn when he had his encounter with the manager. The time had been 2:25—less than half an hour after he'd "collapsed" in his room, according to Teddy's new story, having nearly drowned for the second time that night while swimming across the 150-yard channel from Edgartown, fully clothed, and also in a state of exhaustion.

But somehow he'd "misplaced" his watch. He knew it was "around two A.M." when he reached his hotel room, having been fortunate enough not to lose or misplace his room key in all the diving and swimming, but less than half an hour later, after being "awakened" by the noise of a party next door, he'd had to ask the manager what time it was.

"In the morning," Teddy continued, "with my mind somewhat more lucid, I made an effort to call a family legal advisor, Burke Marshall, from a public telephone on the Chappaquiddick side of the ferry, and then belatedly reported the accident to the Martha's Vineyard police."

Why from the Chappaquiddick side? He did not say. Nor did he mention his early morning chat with Mr. and Mrs. Ross Richards and Stan Moore, interrupted only by the sudden appearance of a "soaking-wet" Joey Gargan. Nor did he mention his phone call to his girlfriend in Florida whose aid he invoked in a frantic attempt to locate Steve Smith in Spain.

In his original statement to Chief Arena, he had omitted any reference either to a party or to the repeated attempts Gargan and Markham had made to save Mary Jo. He'd also omitted any reference to his heroic and life-threatening swim, having said in his written statement, in fact, that he'd "asked for someone to bring me back to Edgartown," and remembered "walking around for a period" before returning to his hotel.

On the other hand, in this version, he no longer claimed he had been trying to take Mary Jo to the ferry, nor that he'd turned onto Dike Road without realizing it, nor even that he was "unfamiliar" with the road.

But no point in lingering over detail. Teddy wanted to get as quickly as possible to the peroration Sorensen had prepared.

He said, "Today, as I mentioned, I felt morally obligated to plead guilty to the charge of leaving the scene of an accident. No words on my part can possibly express

614

the terrible pain and suffering I feel over this tragic accident. This last week has been an agonizing one for me, and for the members of my family; and the grief we feel over the loss of a wonderful friend will remain with us the rest of our lives.''

That was the point: Teddy was suffering grief, pain, agony. The Kennedy family was suffering. Once again, America could reach out with love and unquestioning support in an attempt to make the family's burden a little lighter. After Jack and Bobby had sacrificed their lives, and after Teddy—as he'd now revealed—had again come so close to losing his, it would have been churlish to respond with anything less than full forgiveness.

Or so he hoped.

He now appeared to have reached the end of his prepared text and gazed directly at the camera. In fact, standing right next to the camera, holding large cue cards on which the closing words were written, was Joey Gargan.

''These events,'' Teddy said, ''and the publicity and innuendo and whispers which have surrounded them, and my admission of guilt this morning, raises the question in my mind of whether my standing among the people of my state has been so impaired that I should resign my seat in the United States Senate.

''If at any time the citizens of Massachusetts should lack confidence in their senator's character or his ability, with or without justification, he could not, in my opinion, adequately perform his duties, and should not continue in office.

''The people of this state—the state which sent John Quincy Adams, Daniel Webster, Charles Sumner, Henry Cabot Lodge and John F. Kennedy to the United States Senate—are entitled to representation in that body by men who inspire their utmost confidence. For this reason, I would understand full well why some might think it best for me to resign.

''This would be a difficult decision to make. It has been seven years since my first election to the Senate. You and I share many memories. Some of them have been glorious, some of them have been very sad. The opportunity to work with you and serve our state has been much of what has made my life worthwhile.

"And so I ask you tonight, the people of Massachusetts, to think this through with me. In facing this decision, I seek your advice and opinion. In making it, I seek your prayers. For this is a decision that I will have finally to make on my own."

Here, at the very end, Sorensen could not resist quoting from *Profiles in Courage,* the book he had ghostwritten for Jack.

"It has been written," Teddy said, " 'A man does what he must—in spite of personal consequences, in spite of obstacles and dangers and pressures—and that is the basis of all human morality. And whatever may be the sacrifices he faces if he follows his conscience—the loss of his friends, his fortune, his contentment, even the esteem of his fellow men—each man must decide for himself the course he must follow. The stories of past courage cannot supply courage itself. For this, each man must look into his own soul.'

"I pray that I can have the courage to make the right decision. Whatever is decided, whatever the future holds for me, I hope I shall be able to put this most recent tragedy behind me and make some future contribution to our state and mankind, whether it be in public or private life. Thank you and good night."

Reaction was immediate and not favorable. In a television commentary following the speech, NBC's John Chancellor compared Teddy's effort to Richard Nixon's infamous "Checkers" speech of 1952, in which, in an attempt to prevent Dwight Eisenhower from dropping him as a running mate after he was charged with financial impropriety, Nixon had invoked the image of his dog, Checkers, in appealing for public sympathy.

Even Richard Goodwin was appalled. "Almost anything he could have said would have been better than what did happen," Goodwin said. "He did the worst thing he could have, he Nixonized the situation."

One of the female reporters whom Teddy had pursued across the Alaskan tundra and, later, down the aisles of the airplane bringing them home said, "He was like a baby, he was just like a baby, kicking his feet and holding his breath until people will say they've forgiven him."

In *Harper's* magazine, David Halberstam, who'd been a great admirer of Bobby's, said the talk was "of such cheapness and bathos as to be a rejection of everything the Kennedys had stood for in candor and style. It was as if these men had forgotten everything which made the Kennedys distinctive in American politics and simply told the youngest brother that he could get away with whatever he wanted because he was a Kennedy in Massachusetts."

Life magazine said, "He was simply hustling heartstrings, cashing in on the family credibility." The magazine was especially critical of the reliance upon the quote from *Profiles in Courage,* saying Teddy had recited the passage "as though oblivious to the way the meaning rebuked him."

Time magazine also singled out this misappropriation of the words with which Jack had become so identified. Teddy had invoked the concept of heroism, the magazine said, yet "there was nothing heroic about fencing with half-truths, falsehoods, omissions, rumors and insinuations of cowardice." Teddy, "asked to shoulder the blame for what happened, at the same time he was obviously begging to be excused."

And, in perhaps the cruelest blow, the *Globe* echoed Chancellor's view that Teddy's talk had been, at best, a poor imitation of Nixon's Checkers speech.

A year earlier, Teddy had declined the chance to face Nixon in a contest for the Presidency.

Now, he was reduced to purveying pathetic facsimiles of Nixon at his worst.

By first causing the death of Mary Jo Kopechne and then so publicly embarrassing himself in such maudlin fashion one week later, Teddy had succeeded, over the course of only seven days and nights, in virtually destroying the myth of greatness that his father had spent tens of millions of dollars to create and in perpetuation of which his three older brothers had given their lives.

As Garry Wills has written, "The whole point of being

a Kennedy was, in the father's scheme of things, to look good. But now being a Kennedy meant looking bad, and making others look bad, even as the Kennedy name won a series of dim little victories over minor officials."

With his speech of July 25, Teddy had squandered the last of the legacy. Even worse, as Joey Gargan would admit years later to author Leo Damore, "it was made up, all of it, including thoughts and emotions."

8

I N NEW JERSEY, THAT NIGHT, MARY JO KOPECHNE'S
mother passed a handwritten note out the door of her
house to the waiting press. It said, "I am satisfied with
the Senator's statement—and do hope he decides to stay
in the Senate."

Her husband, however, seemed less pleased. He said
he felt Teddy's explanation of the circumstances surrounding his daughter's death was "not enough." For the
moment, he said, he did not think an autopsy would be
"necessary" but it was clear he had not yet fully resolved
the issue in his mind.

Teddy must have felt he had to do more. He met privately with Cardinal Cushing at the compound on the
Sunday after his Friday night speech. Normally, a visit
from the Cardinal was a major Kennedy public relations
event. And one would have thought that especially under
these circumstances—at a moment when Teddy's future
was so in doubt, at a time when his veracity, his judgment, his very character were being scrutinized as never
before—he would have been particularly eager for a
highly publicized appearance at the Cardinal's side, followed by a public statement from the Cardinal praising
Teddy for his courage and his unswerving faith.

But the visit was intended to be secret. The Cardinal, the *Globe* said, "slipped in unnoticed but was spotted by newsmen when he left nearby Hyannis Port by car about midafternoon." Kennedy family spokesmen made no announcement concerning the Cardinal's visit and the prelate himself declined to discuss it with newsmen. "I have no comment," he told a reporter who contacted him by telephone.

This was most uncharacteristic. The alliance of the Kennedys and the Cardinal had been, for years, a staple of the legend, the most public of mutual admiration societies. If, however, the Cardinal had been summoned because Teddy needed to ask him to intervene with the Kopechnes on the question of an autopsy, then one can understand the desire for privacy.

For years afterwards, there were reports that Cardinal Cushing had traveled privately to New Jersey to persuade the Kopechnes that it was their Christian duty to see to it that no autopsy was ever performed; that such a procedure would be a desecration of their daughter's body.

In any event, it was only two days after the Cardinal's most uncharacteristic private visit with Teddy that the Kopechnes said they had changed their minds about an autopsy and would oppose in court any attempt to have one authorized.

Neither Kopechne acknowledged receiving a personal visit from the Cardinal, but Mrs. Kopechne did confirm that "two parish priests came to the house. They told us, 'Mary Jo is with God. She is at rest and don't disturb her.'"

It was never determined just who these two men were or who dispatched them on their mission, but apparently they did their job well, for Mrs. Kopechne said, "We're following their advice," and the parents' new position would prove unshakable.

So that crisis—which Teddy, Hanify and Smith seemed to have considered the greatest of all—had passed. What did not pass was the overwhelming wave of skepticism and, in some quarters, revulsion with which Teddy's television performance was being greeted.

Even the *Globe* expressed doubt about his midnight swim across the channel. "Under the best of conditions," the paper said, "it's a good swim from Chappaquiddick to Edgartown. At night, after a violent automobile accident, with a chronic bad back and a concussion, the swim would have to be considered a supreme physical effort." The paper added that Teddy's claim to have swum the channel "amazed island residents who cross by ferry regularly."

The ferry's chief operator, Richard Hewitt, was more blunt. "I don't believe it," he said. "He wouldn't even have attempted to swim this channel. His speech was a lot of baloney." Hewitt, who had voted for Teddy in the past, added, "I wouldn't vote for him for dogcatcher now. How could he leave that girl in the water for nine hours?"

Among the locals, it seemed that only Chief Arena still supported Teddy. "Despite his bad back," the chief said, "he looks healthy to me. I think he could do it." But even Arena admitted that the speech, as a whole, had left him more confused than he'd been before he heard it. "I thought I was going to hear the complete explanation, and that didn't happen. I had his initial statement—now here was a variation."

The New York Times said that Teddy's talk "raises more questions than it answers," and that "his emotion-charged address leaves us less than satisfied with his partial explanation for a gross failure of responsibility, and more than ever convinced that the concerned town, county and state officials of Massachusetts have also failed in their duty to thoroughly investigate this case because of the political personality involved."

Attempting to stem the rising tide of negative publicity, Teddy's office quickly announced that he'd received "tens of thousands" of telegrams from all over America and they were "running a hundred to one in his favor."

In contrast, the *Globe* reported receiving twice as many telegrams urging Teddy to resign as suggesting that he remain in the Senate. In any case, the inclusion in the speech of such a meaningless plea to voters, who, as James Reston pointed out, "have no way of questioning the cast of characters," and thus no way of determining how much of Teddy's story was true, had been intended only as a diversionary tactic and a public-relations gimmick.

Any attention focused on the spurious issue of his possible resignation—for it was not something either he or his advisors had ever considered seriously—would serve, it was hoped, to keep the focus away from the long list of contradictions and unanswered questions.

His office issued a statement on July 30, which said, "Sen. Edward M. Kennedy is returning to Washington to resume his duties as United States Senator and assistant majority leader. He is grateful to the people of Massachusetts for their expressions of confidence and expects to submit his record to them as a candidate for reelection in 1970. If re-elected, he will serve out his entire six-year term."

"At 37," Martin Nolan wrote in the *Globe*, "he enters middle age abruptly, with youth and visions of youth all vanished. He will find oblivion an alien territory. Since 1962, he has not been allowed to live in the present, only in the past and the future."

Oblivion, however, did not come immediately. There were, first, further storms, both of the legal and public relations variety, to be weathered.

On his first day back on the job Teddy learned that the district attorney, Edmund Dinis, planned to reopen the case. Dinis said he would move on three fronts: first, he would impound Teddy's car for further examination by state police technicians; second, he would conduct a formal inquest for the purpose of determining how Mary Jo Kopechne had died; and, third, he would seek a court order permitting exhumation of her body for purposes of autopsy.

Only days later, syndicated columnist Jack Anderson published an account of Chappaquiddick that disputed several key aspects of Teddy's story and suggested that in the first hours after the accident, Teddy had tried to persuade Joey Gargan to say that he had been driving the car.

Anderson wrote that at the party, Teddy "did his share of drinking," and that "he invited pretty, young Mary Jo to join him for a midnight swim and they set out on a nocturnal adventure not uncommon on Martha's Vineyard."

Teddy, he went on, "consciously, purposefully made a hard right onto Dike Road. He knew where he was going. He had been there many times before. His late brother John F. Kennedy had often sunbathed on the secluded beach. As President, Kennedy continued to use the Chappaquiddick beach, frequently accompanied by members of his family, including his kid brother, Teddy."

Driving carelessly after having had too much to drink, Teddy had plunged off the bridge, somehow managing to extricate himself from the car. Mary Jo was not so fortunate. But saving her life was the last thing on Teddy's mind.

He didn't stop at any of the houses closer to the bridge to call for help because he did not want to be seen. He intended to say he'd never been there, according to Anderson.

And that was why, when he finally returned to the cottage, he stayed outside, shielded by the darkness of a car, as he furtively summoned Gargan and Markham to come to him. He could not let Mary Jo's friends see that he was soaking wet.

Anderson claimed Teddy had returned to the bridge not in an attempt to rescue Mary Jo but because he wanted Joey to be familiar with the scene, so Joey could tell a story that made sense. Joey was going to do the dirty work, as he'd been doing for Teddy all his life.

Teddy wanted Markham, the other experienced attorney at the party, to come with them to the scene in order that he might spend the rest of the night working with Joey on the details of his story, making sure it was a story that would stand up under police questioning and, if it came to that, in court.

Much of the public found Anderson's account far more credible than Teddy's own.

Later that summer came another assault. The *Manchester Union-Leader* reported that during the hours between the time Teddy claimed the accident had occurred and his first report of it to police, seventeen different long-distance phone calls were charged to his credit card. Five of them, said the paper, were made "shortly before midnight" from the Chappaquiddick cottage, the other twelve from the Shiretown Inn.

The New England Telephone Company, on whose board of directors Edward Hanify served, said legal restrictions prevented it from confirming or denying the reports or opening its records to outside inspection.

The implication was both obvious and dangerous: if Teddy and his aides had made seventeen calls from shortly before midnight to shortly after dawn, they had to have been trying to develop an acceptable cover story for Teddy, and were possibly even trying to arrange to spirit him off the island by private plane.

Clearly, if he'd made twelve calls from the Shiretown Inn all through the night, he had not been in a state of shock and exhaustion; he had been scrambling to get himself out of the biggest trouble of his life.

The scramble continued for several more months.

In Pennsylvania, court authorities said that in the absence of a request from the parents they would permit exhumation of Mary Jo Kopechne's body only upon receipt of a court order from Massachusetts. The district attorney's request would not suffice.

One of the many advantages to being a Kennedy in Massachusetts—even the last and most luckless of the legendary Kennedy brothers—was that one had access to the sort of influential legal counselors who, more often than not, were able to decrease the likelihood that an unwanted court order would be issued.

As they worked privately, Joe Kopechne, his spine

stiffened considerably as a result of visits by clergymen and supportive members of Teddy's staff such as Dun Gifford, announced, "They're not going to disturb my daughter. There would be no purpose whatever in an autopsy. I will fight it to the end."

Then, on the eve of the exhumation hearing in Pennsylvania, Mary Jo's mother made her most anguished plea yet. "I don't want my little girl's body dug up," she said. "My tiny, lovely baby."

In such a climate it did little good for the Massachusetts district attorney to argue that "an autopsy is part of the investigation. Without an autopsy, this matter will never be closed."

His request was denied. "In the search for the truth," the presiding judge wrote, "the sensitivities of loved ones and friends . . . should not be disregarded. We must be mindful that Joseph A. Kopechne and Gwen L. Kopechne, the parents of Mary Jo Kopechne, have indicated that they are unalterably opposed to exhumation and autopsy. Thus, it is incumbent that this court give weight to their objections. While their disapproval is not an absolute bar to an exhumation and autopsy, in view of the facts presented to this court, their objections are well taken."

Teddy immediately issued a statement. "I know how much this decision means to the Kopechne family," he said. "It increases their peace of mind, and I am grateful for that."

Later, amid rumors that the real sum was much higher, Teddy admitted that in addition to whatever spiritual guidance he might have provided through Cardinal Cushing and others, he had paid the Kopechnes almost $100,000.

Back in Massachusetts, Edward Hanify's request that the press be barred from the upcoming inquest into the death of Mary Jo was granted. The court further ruled that "The transcript of the Inquest, shall be made available to the public only . . . if . . . the district attorney has filed with the Superior Court a written certificate that there will be no prosecution."

Only if Teddy won, in other words, would the report of his victory be made available.

And there was no question but that Teddy would win. Before it even began, the *Globe* said, "The inquest should be a major piece of good fortune for him if all goes well when it is held. If the present chapter ends in this manner, as one must pray it will, then there is no reason at all for the future chapters of the senator's story to be tinged or even greatly troubled by the heavy darkness that he has recently had to live through. . . . Like all strong men whom an unkind fate forces to traverse the valley of the shadow, the senator himself further seems to have gained in strength and in self-knowledge."

With that statement, the *Globe* had traversed the valley of the shadow into the realm of the surreal. But the paper was right about one thing: with Ed Hanify in command, all would go well at the inquest, which was eventually held in January of 1970.

There were no new revelations and, despite a report by the judge who presided over the inquest that "Kennedy and Kopechne did not intend to drive to the ferry slip and his turn onto Dike Road had been intentional," and "that Edward M. Kennedy operated his motor vehicle negligently . . . and that such operation appears to have contributed to the death of Mary Jo Kopechne," there was no recommendation for criminal prosecution.

Under Massachusetts law, the judge, on the basis of his findings, could have immediately issued a warrant for Teddy's arrest. For clearly Teddy was "an individual whose unlawful act or negligence appears to have contributed to the fatality under investigation."

But the law did not require the judge to issue such a warrant and, with no words of explanation to anyone, then or ever, he chose not to. The day after releasing his report, he retired from the bench and never again spoke about Chappaquiddick.

There was no question but that Edward Hanify had earned whatever fee he ultimately charged the Kennedys.

* * *

"The real thing now," said one of the advisors closest to Teddy, in a moment of rare candor, "is whether the story is dead." That he could even have thought it might be is an indication of how totally Teddy and those close to him failed to understand the larger, mythic dimension which the Kennedys had created for themselves. The legend was the sword by which Teddy had lived; it was now the instrument by which, metaphorically, he would die.

His father, and Jack and Bobby, had built the castle; had created the kingdom of Camelot. The assassinations of Jack and of Bobby had only intensified our yearning for what had been taken from us and increased our baseless and erroneous conviction that Teddy somehow possessed the capacity to give us back everything we thought we'd had. Yet at the same time, we begrudged him the adulation that at some level we recognized he had not earned.

The Kennedys had worked their sorcery upon us. We'd been bewitched by their surface glamour and charm, by the indefinable but enchanting attributes that came to be referred to collectively as "charisma."

But it was our doing as much as it was theirs. We created them as mythic figures because we had, in 1960, after the years of drabness that had followed the intensity of World War II, an emotional need for a new form of distinctly American heroism. When Norman Mailer called his 1960 article about Jack's nomination at the Los Angeles convention "Superman Comes to the Supermarket," he touched the essence of the matter. There were two sides to the equation. If we had not created for ourselves in America this "supermarket"—the national arena into which we would flood to make our emotional purchase of this new form of heroism—Jack would have been just another pretty face with a funny accent.

In an article entitled "The Kennedy Fantasy," Ronald Steel wrote in *The New York Review of Books* that "Kennedyism, like the Beatle-mania of the Sixties that was its cultural counterpart, was not a plot foisted on the public, but an audience response—a response that could never have occurred, whatever the public relations effort involved, had there not been a need for it."

It took what psychobiographer Nancy Gager Clinch called "the cold shock of Chappaquiddick" to wash away the "cobwebby mask that had so blinded us."

And now that our magical mystery tour through the supercharged decade of the sixties was at an end, we were faced with the inevitable letdown. It had been a marvelous trip, a great high—assassinations notwithstanding. It had given a whole generation a wild and fierce emotional and psychological adventure.

But it was over now. Over for the Kennedys and over for us. The "time for Kennedys" had passed. The decade was coming to an end. Our needs and appetites were changing. Teddy, as had been his fate throughout life, was caught up in a phenomenon much larger than himself, and, as had also been his fate, he'd arrived too late on the scene. But neither he nor his advisors had the prescience to recognize what the consequences of this latest shifting of our psychological tectonic plates would be.

The most powerful and painful was this: Teddy, for the rest of his career, would be punished by the once adoring public, not only for his failure to be Bobby and Jack, but for that public's belated awareness that it had allowed itself to be seduced by charming sorcerers, to believe in a kingdom that had never existed at all.

Those who've been made fools of, those who've been betrayed in love, can carry with them for a long time a deep and bitter anger, directed both at their deceiver and at what they recognized only too late as their own gullibility.

For every action, an equal and opposite reaction. It was Teddy's fate, having survived the plunge of the car off the bridge, to face this reaction for the rest of his life.

And it can be argued that to whatever extent he brought it on himself, by surviving, and by being locked forever into living an even bigger lie than before, the fate that Teddy would suffer—the slow death, the long, sad slide into irrelevance—was far more cruel than the quick and violent deaths that had taken his brothers while we still believed that their magic was real.

"In his sorrow last summer," *Newsweek* said, referring to the Teddy of 1968, "he seemed larger than anyone had remembered. Forgotten were the early misadventures of the youngest son of a rich and famous family. Like Shakespeare's Prince Hal, he was not what he had seemed to be, and friends and critics alike saw not an immature Senator from Massachusetts but the legend's last guardian."

Now, on his watch, through his actions and inactions, as a result of his vain and desperate words, so inadequate and so blatantly implausible, the legend had collapsed. The standard lay in tatters at his feet. The eternal flame, while it might still burn at Arlington, was extinguished in millions of hearts across the land.

Newsweek wrote that "any serious hope of the Restoration had vanished during those ten hours in which the last Kennedy was put cruelly to a test of nerve, and, by his own confession, flunked."

"This is the fall of the House of Kennedy," said one friend of Lyndon Johnson's, with something less than regret.

Joan soon suffered another miscarriage and did not conceive again. "After that," she told a friend, "there just didn't seem much point in trying again."

Ed Hanify saw to it that Teddy's car was destroyed by a compactor and that the clothing Mary Jo had worn that night—including a blouse that had bloodstains on the back—was burned.

A leading Republican in Washington said, "It's hard to see Teddy any way but as a coward. He's destroyed the Kennedy myth."

But without the myth Teddy seemed to have no further purpose in life, indeed almost nothing left to live for. Without the myth, in a sense, he didn't even have life.

He had only the fear that the full truth of Chappaquiddick might yet be told.

"I think we have finally come to the end of Camelot," said a Senate colleague who was also a close friend. "He'll never be the same. He'll go through life haunted by the ghost of that girl."

She now joined all the other ghosts that haunted him.

9

FOR WEEKS, THE OLD MAN HAD LAIN UPSTAIRS, ABLE TO move only one hand. He moved it in a single gesture: toward his dimming eyes, as if trying to pluck them from his head.

The old man had not uttered a sound since Teddy had told him of the new trouble, the big trouble, he had caused.

First, he'd stopped eating. Then, he'd used the last of his strength to clench his jaws tight against the shaved ice his nurse tried to give him to keep him from becoming dehydrated.

It had been less than ten years since he'd sat in the place of pride at the inaugural parade, witnessing the fulfillment of his lifelong ambition, and nodding discreetly as Jack tipped his hat.

Now it was over. The dream was as dead as all his sons but one, and that one had killed the dream.

Teddy would drift on for decades, always feeling that unlike his brothers, he had only himself to blame for his fate. Never would he be able to accept the fact that all his life—except, perhaps, on the night of July 18, 1969, and in the early, dark, desperate hours of the morning that followed—he'd been less a perpetrator than a victim of his father's hubristic dreams.

It was now the dreamer's turn to die. The sight was not pretty. A grandson later said, "It made me wonder what my grandfather could have done for God to do this to him."

There were answers to that question, but none that the grandson needed to know. And Teddy, the last son, the last brother, already knew too many, while continuing to deny them, even to himself.

On the night of Monday, November 17, 1969—just six weeks before the end of the decade—Teddy was told that the end, for his father, was very near. Jacqueline had flown in from Greece. Ethel and the children had come from Virginia. One last time, the surviving members of the family assembled at the patriarch's bed.

Teddy spent that last night in his father's room. He lay on the floor, in a sleeping bag.

There was no further communication between them. The old man was too far gone to hear anything his last surviving son might want to say. And what could Teddy have said?

Joe Kennedy died at 11:04 the next morning with Teddy and his sisters gathered around him. Only at the very last moment, when all were sure that he was beyond consciousness, did Rose enter the room. She knelt next to him and placed a rosary in his hands.

A rosary: as if that were what Joe Kennedy would have wanted at the moment of death. What he'd wanted in his hands all his life was the universe. And he'd gotten a bigger piece of it than most men, at least for a while. But he'd paid. And it might have been the only time in his life he'd paid too much.

Now, Teddy, in disgrace, was all there was left to show for it, except for the airports and bridges and plazas and boulevards and schools and institutes that bore the family name.

It was a name that for some time had come to mean something very special in America.

"Brethren," cried out the aged Cardinal Cushing at

Joe Kennedy's funeral, "we have become a spectacle to the whole world, to angels as well as to men."

But Teddy, burdened and finally broken by the name, had become—and would remain for years to come—a very different sort of spectacle. Not at all what either his father, or the Cardinal, had envisioned.

Coda

*Once, when I walked home from kindergarten in-
stead of waiting to be picked up by a nurse, I went
into the house saying triumphantly: "I'm home!"
expecting not only surprise but admiration and respect from my parents for the display of self-reli-
ance. But to my keen disappointment I had to
march promptly upstairs and got a good spanking
with a coathanger.*

*After that, I was confined to my sister Jean's
closet for some time.*

—Edward Moore Kennedy

H E TRIED ONCE MORE TO BREAK AWAY, LATER THAT
fall, not long after his father was buried. He told his
mother he'd had enough, he could not go on. He would
not run for reelection in 1970, or ever again. He could not
continue in public life.

But Rose would not hear of it. "Mother put her foot
down—hard," his sister Eunice said later. Rose reminded him of his obligations—to his father, to his dead
brothers, to what was left of the myth. She told him he
had to go on.

And so, in his exhaustion and weakness and despair,
he did. Through the dreary, awkward decade of the sev-

enties, as his staff tried to rebuild the public image while the man behind it fell even more completely apart.

His oldest son lost a leg to cancer. His daughter ran away from home—or from what passed for home. Joan left him and moved to Boston, no longer making a secret of her problem with alcohol or the fact that she was receiving psychiatric help. In 1980, there was, finally, a bungled, humiliating grope for the presidential nomination, but he ran the race so badly and with so little heart that one could not help but feel he was doing it mostly to punish himself. Not long after the dismal campaign, his marriage ended in divorce.

After that, he seemed to cling to his Senate seat as if it were a life raft. It was all he had left. All that got him out of bed in the morning and enabled him to put on a suit and tie and keep pretending. It was what kept him going through the motions of every day without ever pausing to consider how it had come to pass that he'd spent his whole life wandering in emotional solitude across the wasteland his parents had created for him.

By 1988, Teddy had sunk to a point where his name and picture appeared more frequently in supermarket tabloids than in serious journals of opinion. That summer, the Democratic party nominated the governor of Massachusetts, Michael Dukakis, for President. How unthinkable this would have been twenty years earlier: to nominate a Democrat from Massachusetts who was not a Kennedy.

The same year, perhaps just because he did not know any other way of life and felt it was too late to learn one, he ran again for reelection to the Senate.

I was living in western Massachusetts at the time. I saw a small item in the local paper saying that Teddy would be marching the following Saturday in the annual fall foliage parade in the nearby city of North Adams.

North Adams was a dreary New England mill town from which the mills had long since departed, leaving behind, for the most part, only those too old, too tired or too drained of spirit to have gone with them. It was distinctly not a place where anyone who had been aboard

Bobby's funeral train would have expected to find Teddy twenty years later.

But marching in the parade was apparently part of his Senate reelection campaign. All his life, he'd been marching in parades that had no meaning for him. Now the arc of his career seemed unmistakably to be descending toward a blank horizon and North Adams might have been one of the last stops along the way.

Under a too warm sun and before a thin, uneven line of bedraggled, lackadaisical spectators, Teddy, very much alone, walked stiffly down the main street of North Adams, trailing well behind the band and even behind most of the other politicians.

The heir apparent, the sole survivor, the keeper of the flame. The last brother. Now a jowly, gray-haired fat man in his late middle years, sweating profusely as he labored down the street.

Gamely—or reflexively—he waved and smiled, as if the route were lined by thousands of cheering admirers instead of only a few dozen children whose fingers were sticky from cotton candy and to whom Teddy Kennedy was just a name that did not matter anymore.

But there was something in his face, or maybe in his awkward, graceless stride—some hint of imperfectly concealed embarrassment, of melancholy—that suggested he might know, at some level, that he had become largely irrelevant, vaguely pathetic and even slightly ridiculous.

"Who's that guy?" asked a skinny man in a stained undershirt standing next to me as Teddy passed.

"Teddy Kennedy."

"Jesus." The man squinted for a moment through a swirl of cigarette smoke. "He's supposed to be the kid brother. He's not supposed to be an old man."

A couple of weeks later, I drove to Boston to watch from the studio as he debated his young and overmatched Republican opponent. The outcome of the election was not in doubt. Teddy would win by a more than ample margin, as he always had in Massachusetts. The debate could change nothing. It was just one more formality in a life filled with empty ritual.

But Teddy's hands were trembling so badly he could scarcely hold his notes on his lap. When he tried to speak, he stuttered. Extemporaneous coherence had never been his greatest attribute, but on this night, for no apparent reason, he seemed positively shell-shocked.

His young opponent was polite to the point of being deferential. No difficult questions were asked. Yet Teddy emerged perspiring heavily, his face red and blotchy, his eyes bloodshot and his hands still trembling as an aide helped him into an overcoat.

I had written him a letter, telling him I planned to write a book about him. He had not replied. To me, his life seemed less the stuff of traditional biography than the libretto for a tragic and uniquely American opera, with Teddy the only figure left standing at the end.

Now, on this chilly fall night as he waited impatiently for an aide to appear with his car, I approached him, reintroduced myself and said that if he had no objection I'd like to observe the closing days of his campaign.

He seemed vaguely befuddled, but he said that would be fine.

The next two weeks were most peculiar. I had planned to align myself with the press corps that would be covering his campaign. But there was none. What was quite possibly the last political campaign ever to be run by a member of the mythic generation of Kennedys was not even being covered by Boston's newspapers.

Thinking back to Jack, thinking back to Bobby, thinking back even to Teddy himself when I'd accompanied him in 1973, I was amazed. Often, toward the close of his 1988 race, I was the only person not in his employ to witness his campaign events.

For his brothers, it had ended with a bang. For Teddy, it seemed, fate had decreed the slow, painful acting out of a sad charade. The last surviving male of the Kennedy generation that had created the most powerful mythology in our nation's history was now a bulky and bloated old man, the object of neither admiration nor scorn, but of indifference. I was amazed, and not a little saddened.

His final appearance was at a noontime labor rally in downtown Boston. The event, held outdoors on a raw and blustery day, was sparsely attended. Large blue Kennedy campaign posters tore loose from their moorings and sailed across a concrete courtyard. The wind made his words impossible to hear, but that didn't matter: everyone had heard them many times before. This event was merely a way of marking time. In that respect, it seemed to typify what his life had become.

He'd chartered a train to take him from Boston to Hyannis that afternoon. Aboard would be other members of his family, various political allies, former staff members and personal friends dating back to his Harvard days. The press, I was told, would also be permitted aboard the train.

But no press came. No television cameras, no newspaper reporters—only me.

There was an elegiac air about the journey. More than forty years had passed since Jack had won election to Congress for the first time. Now, the last of the Kennedy brothers was heading home to Hyannis Port for what might well be his own last election eve.

The train passed slowly along the south shore, toward Cape Cod. The afternoon's brilliant sunshine gave way to gathering dusk. Outside, the air was frigid and the wind still strong, but on board the mood was mellow.

Fortified by a few trail's end drinks, Teddy walked from car to car, shaking hands and chatting amiably. Every so often, at a crossing in one of the small south shore towns, the train would stop. Teddy would step onto a platform outside and speak briefly to whatever handful of people had assembled. These were not campaign speeches—the campaign was over. This was, it seemed to me, an indirect way of saying good-bye.

The farther we got—and the more fortified Teddy became—the more jollity accompanied each stop. By the time the train neared the bridge that would carry it across the Cape Cod Canal, Teddy was no longer giving brief speeches, but reciting original limericks, which he and friends would compose between stops.

Toward the end of the journey, walking past me, he paused. I stood to shake his hand, as I'd done twenty years earlier, on the train that had carried his brother's body to Washington.

This time, he initiated the conversation. "I'd like to introduce you to my sisters," he said, grinning broadly. "This is Jean, and this is Pat."

I nodded and smiled and we all shook hands.

"And this," Teddy explained to them, "is Mr. McGinniss. He's going to be writing a very, ah, sober assessment of my past twenty-five years in the Senate." Then he laughed, slapped me on the shoulder and moved on.

It was dark when the train reached Hyannis. He made a quick, final talk from the platform, saying how meaningful it was to return home to the Cape to await election returns, as Kennedys had been doing for forty years. Then he disappeared inside a waiting sedan for the ride to the big house in Hyannis Port—the house that had been the closest thing he'd ever had to a home.

In that house, he had spent most of the summers of his youth. In the water behind it, his oldest brother, Joe Junior, had taught him to swim. On the lawn in front of it, he'd played touch football with Jack and with Bobby. It was that house to which he had returned from his western campaigning in 1960, the day after Jack was elected President. And it was in that house he'd tried to tell his crippled father of Jack's death. From that house he'd given the nation his feeble, dismal alibi for Chappaquiddick. And in that house he'd watched his father die.

His mother still lived there, though her state could scarcely be defined as life. Attended by nurses day and night, her mind no longer functioning, she sat shriveled beyond recognition in a wheelchair.

When Teddy was there, as he would be this night, he slept in the room next to hers. The room that had been his father's bedroom. The room in which his father had died.

He'd been haunted for so long, by so many ghosts.

THE LAST BROTHER

Frozen forever in our memories as the kid brother Kennedy with the biggest grin of all, he was now a lonely, divorced man with a drinking problem, older already by ten years than any of his brothers had lived to be, but still seeming not at all sure how he'd failed to become what they had been.

As his car pulled away from the crowd at the station, I did not envy him either his past or the night and the years that lay ahead.

Author's Note

"History is Story," Theodore White has written. I am, by profession, a teller of stories. This book is my story of what I consider to be the most significant aspects of Teddy Kennedy's life: in particular, of his rise and fall as a mythic figure during the 1960s, the tumultuous decade that wrought such changes upon so many of us and upon the national psyche.

Teddy Kennedy is a real person and the story I have told here is one I believe to be true. In preparation for writing it, I conducted many dozens of interviews with people whose lives have intersected his at different points. Their recollections, perceptions and insights have proved invaluable. I have not acknowledged any of them by name because many—knowing that the Kennedy family did not wish to cooperate with me in any way—spoke only on condition of anonymity. (I should add that even under these circumstances no one with whom I had contact spoke of Teddy in a disparaging way. In almost all cases, those who talked to me conveyed a combination of sympathy, admiration and respect.)

In addition, with the aid of two research assistants, I immersed myself in vast amounts of previously published material: newspaper articles going back more than fifty years, magazine stories and books. From this base of existing knowledge and verifiable source I have tried to distill an essence. I have tried to convey to a reader what it might have been like to be Teddy Kennedy.

The facts of his life are not in dispute. The events described herein took place as described, to the best of my knowledge. The quotations attributed to people throughout the book represent in substance what I believe to have been spoken—at the times and under the circumstances described herein.

Moreover, in almost every instance, the quotations and other facts that form the basis of my interpretations have been drawn from published sources that I believe to be reliable. For example (as should be apparent to any attentive reader), in the section of the book that deals with the assassination of John F. Kennedy, I have relied heavily upon the factual account presented in *The Death of a President*, the book written by historian William Manchester, who was chosen by, and received the cooperation of, the Kennedy family in order to produce an account of the circumstances surrounding that event. Likewise, for other sections, *The Fitzgeralds and the Kennedys* by Doris Kearns Goodwin and *Senatorial Privilege* by Leo Damore were especially helpful.

Teddy Kennedy is far more than simply a seasoned United States senator from a prominent family. He is our last living link to the Kennedys of Camelot, the Kennedys of myth. Whatever else he may be, Teddy remains the embodiment of the central secular myth of our age. I do not believe that anyone else in American public life has been forced, for so long, to live with the burdens that have been imposed upon him, both by his family and by a nation so captivated by the myth. It has not been enough for him to be simply Teddy. We have insisted that to a considerable degree he be Jack and Bobby as well; and not merely the real Jack and Bobby but the mythologized Jack and Bobby, who loom so much larger in death, even after the passage of more than a quarter-century, than they did in life.

For Teddy, I believe this has proved an insoluble dilemma, as well as a terrible burden. And there are few among us, I suspect, who could have done much better than he in coping with it on a daily and nightly basis for half his life.

As Garry Wills has written in *The Kennedy Imprisonment: A Meditation on Power*:

> Edward Kennedy has to keep living three lives at once. . . . [He] has no one but ghosts at his side, and they count more against than for him, eclipse him with bright images from the past. . . . Once brother drew on brother for fresh strength; now brother drains brother, all the dead inhibiting the one that has lived on.

How, then, does one approach the task of writing about him in a way that might go beyond the superficial? Different subjects call for different techniques. I would contend that when an individual is as encrusted with fable and lore as is Teddy Kennedy (and his brothers), a writer must attempt an approach that transcends that of traditional journalism or even, perhaps, of conventional biography.

My goal has been to make Teddy come alive for a reader as he never has in any of the previously published works I've read about him. I think it is important to stress here that the Kennedys are different from you and me. They present both unique opportunities and special problems for a writer. For more than half a century, the family has expended considerable time, money and energy in the effort to create a mythic persona for itself. They have been enormously successful, enlisting, along the way, the aid of many otherwise sensible and skeptical journalists, biographers and historians. To say they have co-opted these people may be an overstatement, but consider this passage from *In Search of History*, the memoir written by Theodore White, the man who, at Jacqueline's request, first presented to America the image of the Kennedys as magical figures who had dwelled in the enchanted realm of Camelot.

First, White describes how, while he was ostensibly functioning as an objective reporter during the 1960 Presidential campaign, John Kennedy, "insisted I rewrite the dreary text for a Kennedy pamphlet." White writes: "I protested; I was a reporter, paid my own fare, was not part of his staff . . . but he insisted, so I did my best."

Soon afterward, White describes the point when, "I moved or was drawn across the line of reporting to friendship. . . . Inside myself I wanted to like this man, could find no reason for not liking him, and gave myself over to the loyalty of friendship."

Yet when White published *The Making of the President 1960*—ever since considered the classic work of objective political reportage—he gave no clue to the reader of how devoted he was to the person and to the political interests of John F. Kennedy.

His experience was hardly unique. Never has a political family proven more seductive to more journalists than the Kennedys. The dictum of Joseph P. Kennedy, "It's not what you are that counts, but only what people think you are," has proven, I would suggest, the most enduring and effective lesson he ever taught his children.

A seduction, however, can be successful only if there is at least some degree of receptivity on the part of the seduced. We, the American people, the objects of the Kennedy seduction, have been not only receptive, but almost desperate to be seduced.

As Daniel Boorstin has written in *The Image,* the problem, to the extent it is one, arises "less from the unscrupulousness of our 'deceivers' than from our pleasure in being deceived, less from the desire to seduce than from the desire to be seduced."

He continues: "We have misled ourselves . . . about men . . . and how much greatness can be found among them. . . . We have become so accustomed to our illusions that we mistake them for reality. We demand them. And we demand that there be always more of them, bigger and better and more vivid."

It was in the hope of examining the effect of this phenomenon on the dutiful, resilient, flawed but willing Teddy Kennedy that I undertook to write this book. I never intended that it be viewed as a formal biography and, as the reader will have observed, it has not been constructed in a way that would encourage such response. This is my view, and perhaps mine alone, of what life might have been like for Teddy—especially during the 1960s, when he was forced to be not only man but myth as well.

In my effort to portray this as richly and fully as possible, within the confines of historical fact, I have, as is apparent, written certain scenes and described certain events from what I have inferred to be his point of view.

One respected book editor has expressed the opinion that in so doing I have created a "virtual reality" at the expense of historical truth. I would respond that it is the Kennedys, over half a century, who have created the "virtual reality" that has come to enmesh us all.

Yet this book is not an attempt at debunking, nor at peeling away the layers of myth in order to reveal any sordid truths that might lie behind. Rather, it represents my best effort at trying to engender in a reader not merely sympathy for Teddy Kennedy, but empathy with him.

Toward this end, especially in the first section of the book, when I try to give the reader a sense of how truly awful the assassination of John F. Kennedy must have been, on a personal level, for Teddy, I have quite consciously written portions as if from inside his mind.

This hardly seems unprecedented. In browsing through the shelves of biography that fill my study I've found instance after instance where respected historians and biographers have taken similar liberties in the interest of making their subject come alive for a reader.

Let me cite three instances. I could list more, but repetition would do little to amplify the point I want to make, which is, essentially, that the writer should be permitted to employ any techniques he thinks best serve his purpose, so long as he informs the reader, unambiguously, of what he is doing.

In the foreword to the 1979 edition of her critically acclaimed biography of Mozart, Marcia Davenport refers to her technique of "conscientious reconstruction" of thought and dialogue. An example:

647

Wolfgang waited, gazing dully through the open door at the next room where Caecilia and the little girls were setting the table for supper. Aloysia came in. She was pale, and her eyes were heavy. Wolfgang kissed her hand silently. Holding it tightly, he turned it over and pressed his lips to the palm. He looked uneasily around the room.

Far from decrying this technique as excessively novelistic, *The New York Times* has said, "It brings a great man to life again."

And, regarding the absence of footnotes in her work, Ms. Davenport has written, "I make no apology. . . . Readers for pleasure are not troubled by this, and readers for duty know, like all Mozart students, whence each quotation comes."

A second example: in the preface to *Citizens,* his history of the French Revolution, Simon Schama writes, "Finally, the narrative, as will be obvious, weaves between the private and public lives of the citizens who appear on its pages. This is done . . . in an attempt to understand their motivation more deeply than pure public utterance allows. . . ."

I would add that even private utterance does not necessarily add to one's understanding of the motivation of a public figure. Can anyone really believe that if a politician —be he a Kennedy or not—tells an author or journalist what he was thinking at a given moment, that this automatically becomes an indisputable historical fact? I think few of us are so naive.

Thirdly, W. Jackson Bate, in his biography of Samuel Johnson, writes the following in the chapter titled "Breakdown and Despair":

For as he desperately tried to pull himself above the surface, the strong aggressive instincts that had been so much a part of him—now defensively aroused to their most extreme degree—inevitably turned on himself. With the iron check that he kept on envy . . . and with his tendency to accept self-responsibility, there was nowhere else for his aggressions to turn except against himself.

By what authority does Bate presume to tell us what Johnson was feeling internally? He did not interview Johnson. In his source notes he cites no specific reference for this observation. Yet I accept it without reservation because I accept that Bate, through his years of immersion in the life of Johnson and in previously printed works about Johnson, and through his own indisputable powers of insight, possesses the authority to present as fact what is, by strict analysis, no more than his informed assessment of what Johnson must have been feeling at that time.

So immersed have I been in the lives and times of the Kennedy family—not only since 1988, when I began work on this book, but since 1960, when John F. Kennedy announced his candidacy for President, that I have not hesitated to present certain events as if from Teddy's point of view.

My view is: let the writers write, let the readers read, let books stand or fall on their merits. Either there is an internal logic and an inherent plausibility to the presentation of a real-life figure in a book or there is not. If not, all the footnotes in the world cannot breathe truth and life into a misshapen portrait. If there is, I would suggest that a book then be accepted for what it is: in the case of *The Last Brother*, an author's highly personal and interpretive view of his subject.

"Whoever turns biographer" Freud once wrote, "commits himself to lies, to concealment, to hypocrisy, to embellishments, and even to dissembling his own lack of understanding, for biographical truth is not to be had, and, even if one had it, one could not use it."

This is a rather bleak assessment, with which I do not entirely agree (although I do think it might well apply to much "authorized" biography). The point that biographical "truth" is elusive, however, and not necessarily attainable by conventional methods, such as the piling of fact upon fact, footnote upon footnote, is provocative.

It may be that in some instances (and Teddy Kennedy, as half-man, half-myth, would be a case in point), an author, in seeking first to develop and then to convey the deepest possible understanding of a subject, not only can but must go beyond the traditional and universally accepted approaches; not only can but must take certain risks with technique.

Freud himself attempted biography, as in his paper on Leonardo da Vinci. As one of his own recent biographers, Peter Gay, has written, "He was trying to put together a jigsaw puzzle with most of the pieces missing and some of the surviving ones virtually indecipherable."

Likewise, in the case of Teddy Kennedy, many pieces seem to be either missing or indecipherable. Still, using those that were available, I've tried to put together the puzzle. In the process, I have freely used my own inferences to fill in some of the empty spaces.

What I have attempted in *The Last Brother* may meet some of the criteria by which biography is traditionally defined, yet I would suggest that, as Kennedy aide Milton Gwirtzman has said, this book is at least as much a "rumination" as a biography, and a rumination not only on the life of Teddy Kennedy but on the nexus between myth and reality in our time.

Unmistakably, it presents also a highly personal and subjective view, reflecting what I have come to sense is truth as it relates to both the internal and external life of Teddy Kennedy, whom I consider to be one of the most fascinating and misunderstood public figures of our age.

I've written what I think, feel and believe. I've examined Teddy through the prism of my own attitudes and experience. Others, undoubtedly, will have very different perspectives.

With considerable dignity and grace—despite many highly publicized lapses—Teddy Kennedy has endured thirty years of wrenching agony and relentless scrutiny. It is impossible not to admire him for his sheer ability to survive.

AUTHOR'S NOTE

Yet neither admiration nor fear of consequences ought to prevent anyone from attempting an honest assessment of his life and of the role he and his family have played in ours. That and that alone is all I lay claim to having done.

—Joe McGinniss
July 2, 1993

Bibliography

Aeschylus. *The Oresteian Trilogy: Agamemnon, The Choephori, The Eumenides*. Translated by Philip Vellacott. London: Penguin Books, 1959.

Beschloss, Michael. *The Crisis Years: Kennedy and Khrushchev, 1960–1963*. New York: HarperCollins, 1991.

Blair, Joan and Clay. *The Search for JFK*. New York: Putnam, 1976.

Boorstin, Daniel J. *The Image: A Guide to Pseudo-Events in America*. New York: Atheneum, 1971.

Bowles, Chester. *Promises to Keep: My Years in Public Life, 1941–1969*. New York: Harper & Row, 1971.

Branch, Taylor. *Parting the Waters: America in the King Years, 1954–63*. New York: Simon & Schuster, 1988.

Brown, Thomas. *JFK: History of an Image*. Bloomington: Indiana University Press, 1988.

Burns, James MacGregor. *John Kennedy: A Political Profile*. New York: Harcourt, 1959.

———. *Edward Kennedy and the Camelot Legacy*. New York: Norton, 1976.

Chellis, Marcia. *The Joan Kennedy Story: Living with the Kennedys*. New York: Simon & Schuster, 1985.

BIBLIOGRAPHY

Chester, Lewis, Godfrey Hodgson, and Bruce Page. *An American Melodrama: The Presidential Campaign of 1968*. New York: Viking, 1969.

Clinch, Nancy Gager. *The Kennedy Neurosis: A Psychological Portrait of an American Dynasty*. New York: Grosset & Dunlap, 1973.

Collier, Peter, and David Horowitz. *The Kennedys: An American Drama*. New York: Summit, 1984.

Corry, John. *The Manchester Affair*. New York: Putnam, 1967.

Damore, Leo. *The Cape Cod Years of John Fitzgerald Kennedy*. Englewood Cliffs, N.J.: Prentice-Hall, 1967.

———. *Senatorial Privilege: The Chappaquiddick Coverup*. Washington: Regnery, 1988.

David, Lester. *Ted Kennedy: Triumphs and Tragedies*. New York: Grosset & Dunlap, 1972.

———. *Joan: The Reluctant Kennedy*. New York: Funk & Wagnalls, 1974.

Davis, John H. *The Kennedys: Dynasty and Disaster, 1848–1984*. New York: McGraw-Hill, 1984.

———. *Mafia Kingfish: Carlos Marcello and the Assassination of John F. Kennedy*. New York: McGraw-Hill, 1989.

Dickstein, Morris. *Gates of Eden: American Culture in the Sixties*. New York: Basic Books, 1977.

Dineen, Joseph F. *The Kennedy Family*. Boston: Little, Brown, 1959.

Donovan, Robert J. *PT 109: John F. Kennedy in World War II*. New York: McGraw-Hill, 1961.

Exner, Judith; as told to Ovid Demaris. *My Story*. New York: Grove Press, 1977.

Fairlie, Henry. *The Kennedy Promise: The Politics of Expectation*. New York: Doubleday, 1973.

Gitlin, Todd. *The Sixties: Years of Hope, Days of Rage*. New York: Bantam, 1987.

Goodwin, Doris Kearns. *The Fitzgeralds and the Kennedys*. New York: Simon & Schuster, 1987.

Goodwin, Richard N. *Remembering America: A Voice from the Sixties*. Boston: Little, Brown, 1988.

Halberstam, David. *The Unfinished Odyssey of Robert Kennedy*. New York: Bantam, 1969.

———. *The Best and the Brightest*. New York: Random House, 1972.

Hamilton, Nigel. *JFK: Reckless Youth*. New York: Random House, 1992.

Hersh, Burton. *The Education of Edward Kennedy: A Family Biography*. New York: Morrow, 1972.

Honan, William H. *Ted Kennedy: Profile of a Survivor*. New York: Quadrangle, 1972.

Howard, Gerald (ed.). *The Sixties: Art, Politics and Media of Our Most Explosive Decade*. New York: Washington Square Press, 1982.

Inglis, Fred. *The Cruel Peace: Everyday Life and the Cold War*. New York: Basic Books, 1991.

Kaiser, Robert Blair. *"RFK Must Die": A History of the Robert Kennedy Assassination and Its Aftermath*. New York: Dutton, 1970.

Kelley, Kitty. *His Way: The Unauthorized Biography of Frank Sinatra*. New York: Bantam, 1986.

Kennedy, Robert F. *Thirteen Days: A Memoir of the Cuban Missile Crisis*. New York: Norton, 1969.

———. *To Seek a Newer World*. New York: Bantam, 1969.

Kennedy, Rose; with Robert Coughlan. *Times to Remember*. New York: Doubleday, 1974.

Koskoff, David E. *Joseph P. Kennedy*. Englewood Cliffs, N.J.: Prentice-Hall, 1974.

Krock, Arthur. *Memoirs: Sixty Years on the Firing Line*. New York: Funk & Wagnalls, 1968.

Lerner, Max. *Ted and the Kennedy Legend: A Study in Character and Destiny*. New York: St. Martin's, 1980.

Levin, Murray B. *Kennedy Campaigning: The System and the Style as Practiced by Senator Edward Kennedy*. Boston: Beacon, 1966.

Lippman, Theo, Jr. *Senator Ted Kennedy: The Career Behind the Image*. New York: Norton, 1976.

Mailer, Norman. *The Presidential Papers*. New York: Berkeley, 1970.

BIBLIOGRAPHY

Manchester, William. *The Death of a President*. New York: Harper & Row, 1967.

———. *The Glory and the Dream: A Narrative History of America, 1932–1972*. Boston: Little, Brown, 1974.

Marrs, Jim. *Crossfire: The Plot That Killed Kennedy*. New York: Carroll & Graf, 1989.

Navasky, Victor. *Kennedy Justice*. New York: Harper & Row, 1972.

Newfield, Jack. *Robert Kennedy: A Memoir*. New York: Dutton, 1969.

Olsen, Jack. *The Bridge at Chappaquiddick*. Boston: Little, Brown, 1970.

O'Neill, Thomas "Tip"; with William Novak. *Man of the House: The Life and Political Memoirs of Speaker Tip O'Neill*. New York: Random House, 1987.

Parmet, Herbert S. *JFK: The Presidency of John F. Kennedy*. New York: Penguin, 1983.

Powers, Thomas. *The Man Who Kept the Secrets: Richard Helms and the CIA*. New York: Knopf, 1979.

Reeves, Thomas C. *A Question of Character: A Life of John F. Kennedy*. New York: Free Press, 1991.

Salinger, Pierre. *With Kennedy*. New York: Doubleday, 1966.

Saunders, Frank; with James Southwood. *Torn Lace Curtain*. New York: Holt, Rinehart & Winston, 1982.

Schlesinger, Arthur M., Jr. *A Thousand Days: John F. Kennedy in the White House*. Boston: Houghton Mifflin, 1965.

———. *Robert Kennedy and His Times*. Boston: Houghton Mifflin, 1978.

Searls, Hank. *The Lost Prince: Young Joe, the Forgotten Kennedy*. New York: New American Library, 1969.

Shannon, William V. *The Heir Apparent: Robert Kennedy and the Struggle for Power*. New York: Macmillan, 1967.

Shaw, Maud. *White House Nannie*. New York: New American Library, 1966.

Sorensen, Theodore. *Kennedy*. New York: Harper & Row, 1965.

BIBLIOGRAPHY

Stein, Jean, and George Plimpton. *American Journey: The Times of Robert F. Kennedy.* New York: Harcourt, 1970.

Swanson, Gloria. *Swanson on Swanson.* New York: Random House, 1980.

Whalen, Richard J. *The Founding Father: The Story of Joseph P. Kennedy.* New York: New American Library, 1964.

White, Theodore H. *The Making of the President, 1960.* New York: Atheneum, 1961.

———. *The Making of the President, 1968.* New York: Atheneum, 1969.

———. *In Search of History: A Personal Adventure.* New York: Harper & Row, 1978.

Wicker, Tom. *Kennedy Without Tears.* New York: Morrow, 1964.

Wills, Garry. *The Kennedy Imprisonment: A Meditation on Power.* Boston: Atlantic–Little, Brown, 1982.

Witcover, Jules. *85 Days: The Last Campaign of Robert Kennedy.* New York: Putnam, 1969.

Wofford, Harris. *Of Kennedys and Kings: Making Sense of the Sixties.* New York: Farrar, Straus & Giroux, 1980.